PC MUSIC HOME STUDIO
Secrets, Tips, & Tricks

Roman Petelin
Yury Petelin

A-LIST, LLC
295 East Swedesford Rd.
PMB #285
Wayne, PA 19087
702-977-5377 (FAX)
mail@alistpublishing.com
http://www.alistpublishing.com

This book is printed on acid-free paper.

PC Music Home Studio: Secrets, Tips, & Tricks
By Roman Petelin, Yury Petelin

ISBN: 1-931769-07-9

Printed in the United States of America

02 03 7 6 5 4 3 2 1

A-LIST, LLC titles are distributed by Independent Publishers Group and are available for site license or bulk purchase by institutions, user groups, corporations, etc.

Book Editor: Jessica Mroz

Contents

Introduction _____ **1**

PART I: ACOUSTIC SIGNAL CONVERSION THEORY BASICS _____ **7**

Chapter 1: Acoustic Signals and Their Main Properties _____ **8**

1.1. Tone and Timbre _____ 8
1.2. Audibility Threshold and Loudness Level _____ 10
1.3. The Acoustic Signal as a Random Process _____ 14

Chapter 2: Spectral Representation of Signals _____ **24**

2.1. Fourier Series and Fourier Integral _____ 24
2.2. Current Spectrum _____ 31
2.3. Instantaneous Spectrum _____ 34
2.4. Displaying the Periodogram _____ 36
2.5. Weight Functions _____ 38
2.6. Discrete Signals and Discrete Fourier Transform _____ 43
2.7. Fast Fourier Transform _____ 47
2.8. More on Digital-to-Analog and Analog-to-Digital Conversion _____ 49
2.9. Sampling _____ 55

Chapter 3: Filtering _____ **61**

3.1. Basic Types of Filter Amplitude-Frequency Responses _____ 62
3.2. Equalizers _____ 65
3.3. Digital Filters _____ 71
3.4. Butterworth, Chebyshev, and Bessel Filters _____ 75

Chapter 4: Dynamic Processing of Acoustic Signals _____ **81**

4.1. Strategies of Manual Level Adjustment _____ 81

4.2. Classifying Automatic Level Controls _____ 82

4.3. Structure and Time Characteristics of Dynamic Processing Devices ___ 85

4.4. Compression _____ 88

4.5. Some Recommendations for Using Dynamic Processing _____ 91

PART II: MICROPHONES, MIXERS, AND EFFECTS _____ **99**

Chapter 5: Working with Microphones and Mixers_____ **100**

5.1. Microphones and Their Basic Parameters _____ 101

5.2. The Typical Hardware Mixer Structure _____ 125

5.3. Sound Blaster Live! Virtual Mixer (Live!Ware 3.0 Drivers) _____ 130

Chapter 6: Sound Effects _____ **138**

6.1. Vibrato _____ 138

6.2. Effects Based on Signal Delay _____ 143

6.3. Distortion _____ 154

6.4. Voice Coder _____ 154

6.5. Shifting the Tone Pitch and Harmonizing _____ 155

PART III: COOL EDIT PRO—A MULTITRACK SOUND EDITOR ____ **157**

Chapter 7: Getting Started_____ **163**

Chapter 8: Working with the Main Window in the *Waveform View* Mode __ **177**

Chapter 9: The *File* Menu—Working with Files _____ **193**

Chapter 10: The *Edit* Menu _____ **203**

Chapter 11: The *View* Menu—Display Management _____ **225**

Chapter 12: The *Transform* Menu—Transforming Audio _____ **245**

Chapter 13: The *Generate* Menu—Sound Generation _____ **357**

Chapter 14: The *Analyze* Menu—Analyzing Audio Data_____ **368**

**Chapter 15: The *Favorites* Menu—Creating a List of the Most Often
Used Operations**_____ **376**

Chapter 16: The *Options* Menu _____ 382

Chapter 17: The *Window* Menu—Managing the Main Window Pages _____ 393

Chapter 18: *Multitrack View*—Multitrack Editing Mode _____ 395

PART IV: VIRTUAL TOOLKIT _____ 415

Chapter 19: Nemesys GigaStudio 160 (V.2) _____ 416

19.1. Introduction _____ 416
19.2. Settings _____ 419
19.3. *Port1, Port2, Port3, Port4*—Working with the Sampler _____ 428
19.4. Audio Mixer; Using Effects_____ 437
19.5. Description of Real Time Effects _____ 441
19.6. The QuickSound Browser; Working with Akai CDs; Track
Import from an Audio CD _____ 447
19.7. The Main Menu and Toolbar; Capture the Signal Generated
by GigaStuio into a WAV File _____ 455
19.8. Practice_____ 457

**Chapter 20: Creating Your Own Sampler Libraries
Using GigaStudio Instrument Editor 2.0** _____ 460

20.1. Creating Your Own Sample Using Cool Edit Pro _____ 460
20.2. Importing WAV Files into the Bank_____ 462
20.3. Creating an Instrument_____ 465
20.4. Editing Modulation Parameters _____ 471
20.5. Setting the Sample-Register Connection; Distributing Registers
Along the Values of the *Velocity* Parameter _____ 483
20.6. Registers Revisited _____ 485
20.7. Creating Instruments without the Wizard; Working Effectively
with the Regions Map _____ 489
20.8. Articulation and Macros _____ 492
20.9. The Main Menu of the Program_____ 494

Chapter 21: Reason—a Virtual Audio Studio _____ **499**

21.1. Program Settings _____ 505
21.2. Remix Mixer _____ 513
21.3. ReDrum Machine _____ 516
21.4. Dr. REX Loop Player—Specialized Drum Loop Player _____ 524
21.5. NN-19 Digital Sampler _____ 531
21.6. SubTractor Synthesizer _____ 540
21.7. Matrix Pattern Sequencer _____ 548
21.8. Effect Processors _____ 551
21.9. Transport Panel _____ 558
21.10. Main Sequencer _____ 561
21.11. Commands of the Main Menu _____ 574

PART V: DIGITAL MASTERING _____ **577**

Chapter 22: Theory _____ **578**

22.1. Main Mastering Tools _____ 578
22.2. Analog and Digital Mastering _____ 584
22.3. Compatibility of the Recording with Playback Equipment _____ 601
22.4. Stages of Mastering _____ 604

Chapter 23: Mastering with T-RackS 24 _____ **607**

23.1. Control Panel _____ 609
23.2. Equalizer _____ 612
23.3. Compressor _____ 613
23.4. Multiband Limiter _____ 614
23.5. Input Signal Module _____ 615
23.6. Console _____ 616

Chapter 24: DirectX Plug-Ins Useful for Mastering _____ **619**

24.1. Using Waves MaxxBass to Provide Compatibility
    of the Recording with Low Quality Equipment _____ 619
24.2. Plug-Ins from the Steinberg Mastering Edition Package _____ 622

We dedicate this book to our daughter and granddaughter, Anna.

Introduction

The development of software intended for sound processing and music editing is progressing at a rapid rate, and the functionality of musical software is constantly being improved and enhanced. This is not only due to the fact that the mathematicians and engineers developing this software are mastering the secrets of musical art, but also because they suggest new technical and mathematical methods of solving tasks, both purely musical ones and those that are both musical and acoustic. It thus gradually happens that musical skills and advanced PC user skills are no longer sufficient for someone who wishes to use the PC for creative activity. Currently, if you want to create music on your PC, you'll need to master scientific terminology, understand the ideas behind operations on sound data, and know the algorithms for processing musical material implemented in musical software.

Of course, it is rather difficult to master the scientific basics of all the new technologies implemented in musical software. In these early years of the 21st century, musical software for the PC has managed to employ the results of scientific investigations in the fields of mathematics, technical cybernetics, and signal processing theory. For example:

- Optimum processing, correlation, and spectral analysis of signals exposed to interference with various statistical properties
- Synthesis of sounds with a specified time-frequency distribution in non-traditional orthogonal bases
- Adaptive methods of analog-to-digital conversion
- Polynomial approximation of the amplitude-frequency responses of the filters
- Elimination of distortions using signal interpolation with the maximum likelihood method

Even recent advances in the field of artificial intelligence and psycho-acoustics are now serving the needs of music.

It is neither fair nor realistic to require the musician to master all of the above-listed skills. Such a task is only within the power of those with encyclopedic knowledge. Still, it is impossible to accomplish anything without an understanding of some principally important aspects.

Contemporary books on the theory of signals contain several aspects that are fundamentally important for the sound engineer or sound producer: statistical radio engineering, spectral theory, theory of digital signals, information on analog and digital filters, etc. However, these books are mainly intended for mathematically skilled radio engineers, not musicians. For example, a great number of awkward mathematical expressions mask from the end-users the ideas behind the physical processes under consideration. In addition, even if you do not lose your temper and manage to carefully follow this labyrinth of formulas, it is still very difficult to find the point where mathematics intersects with music. Many of these books never say even a word on music. Naturally, scientific literature and literature on music theory exist in different dimensions.

Actually, this reasoning was partially what led us to the idea of writing a book, where, besides description of specific musical software and techniques of their usage, we could provide the theoretic information necessary to understand the basic idea of sound processing algorithms. On the other hand, we have also given ourselves the general goal of discussing fundamental ideas using the minimum number of mathematical formulas. When selecting the theoretical materials to be included in this book, we decided to limit ourselves to describing only the basic methods, algorithms, and approaches implemented in the software considered in the book.

If we tried to describe this book using one and only one phrase, we'd say that this book is on sound synthesis and sound processing. We intend to cover the following musical software:

❒ A sound editor

❒ A virtual mixer

❒ A virtual studios

❒ A sample editor

❒ Several plug-ins intended for digital mastering

To work efficiently with these programs, you need to properly understand spectral representation of signals, digitization of analog signals, analog and digital filtering, and dynamic processing.

We'd like to emphasize that if we were describing how to use some sound editor other than Cool Edit Pro, then it probably wouldn't be necessary to discuss mathematics and signal theory. However, a detailed investigation of Cool Edit Pro's functionality and capabilities allowed us to draw the following conclusion: Cool Edit Pro is the sound editor that implements the most advanced methods of signal processing. Such technologies are technologies of the future, ones used in space exploration. And this statement is not only figurative. Optimal filtration with an interference background (which was used when performing the radar exploration of Venus) is also used in Cool Edit Pro for suppression of the noise accompanying a sound track recorded directly from a microphone. Or, take for example the interpolation algorithm that performs the miracle of restoring the initial form of a clipped signal. This algorithm is similar to the ones that allow scientists to restore fragments of signals transferred to Earth from a space apparatus when the signals get lost due to ionosphere disturbances. And only a radio amateur who has spent hours (or, perhaps, days) tuning a 4- or 5-stage filter of a selector station can truly value the capability of synthesizing a 30th order Bessel filter with an ideal rectangular amplitude-frequency response with just a couple of mouse-clicks.

The examples provided above represent only a small part of the advanced signal processing methods implemented in Cool Edit Pro. Besides these, Cool Edit Pro also provides the following capabilities:

❒ Automatic matching of sound track fragments at the points where the sound wave intersects the zero level, in order to eliminate clicks

❒ Universal virtual dynamic processing devices

❒ Special effects based on the time delay of the signal

❒ Software filters and equalizers capable of satisfying the most stringent requirements (and practically the same as hardware devices that would likely cost you several thousand dollars)

❒ The ability to influence the listener's psyche by generating oscillations synchronized with brain activity rhythms

Generally speaking, we have not encountered a more sophisticated and advanced sound editor than Cool Edit Pro. It implements such a variety of advanced scientific ideas and efficient signal processing algorithms that the theoretical part of the book could have been limited to explaining just a few of them.

We also decided that discussion of signal theory basics must be complemented by covering several practical aspects, including the following:

❒ Microphone design and usage

❒ Mixer design and usage

❒ The essence of the most popular acoustic effects

❒ Filter classification and properties

❒ Working principles of dynamic processing devices

❒ Theoretical basics and techniques of digital mastering

Naturally, we don't claim to have discovered something new when describing theory basics. Making scientific discoveries nowadays is rather difficult. The theory was formulated long ago, and is currently fully developed. On the other hand, we were not aiming to create just another thesis, either. This book is mainly aimed at providing a popular and easy-to-read description of contemporary scientific knowledge in the field of signal processing, and attempts to demonstrate their relation to the problems of musical computer technologies.

Among other problems that we have encountered, we wanted to overcome the following difficulty. Digitized musical compositions are non-stationary processes, the spectral analysis of which requires using current and instantaneous spectrums. Such spectrums are the kind calculated and displayed by Cool Edit Pro. However, most textbooks never even mention the existence of the spectral-time approach to signal analysis. Usually, only mathematical abstractions—classical Fourier spectrums calculated at an infinite time interval—are considered. Because of this, the chapters of our book dedicated to spectral analysis at finite time intervals might prove to be useful not only for musicians using their PC, but also to anyone who deals with various aspects of processing signals of any type.

Another distinguishing feature of our approach to discussing theory is the attempt to describe quite complex and advanced concepts in easy and understandable language. We'd like to point out, however, that the theoretical aspects covered here are rather complex, and can't be explained using too simplistic of an approach. To get a clear understanding of these topics, it's necessary to do some intellectual work. It's quite a job, both for your mind and your imagination.

All the theoretical materials presented here are coordinated with the elements of the software discussed in the book.

Besides the Cool Edit Pro sound editor that we have already mentioned, we will also cover the virtual toolkits that have swiftly gained popularity among computer musicians. We are speaking here about Nemesys Gigastudio 160 and Reason. These applications (especially Reason) are powerful and rather complex virtual tools intended for sound and music synthesis, and also capable of replacing extremely expensive hardware sound studios.

Even in 1997 we covered virtual synthesizers in one of our publications. At that time, however, they were more like toys. The main problem that prevented virtual synthesizers from being widely accepted was the fact that the time interval separating the instances of the key being pressed and the sound's generation was perceivable by ear. Technology has made significant advances since then, however. Modern PCs have become faster and more powerful, CPU clock speeds have grown by approximately 10 times, and large amounts of RAM (gigabytes) are no longer exotic. Developers of software whose names contain the "Giga" prefix haven't been asleep at the job either. They have managed to find convenient data formats for storing sound information, and thus have optimized playback procedures.

With the release of Reason, the dream of musicians about implementing a full-featured virtual studio has become a reality. Several years ago, the difference between compositions created in home and professional studios was obvious and clearly noticeable. The situation has now radically changed. The virtual toolkits and several hundreds of CDs with sound samples give a chance of success even to amateurs.

Thus, having briefly described the distinguishing features of the book and its concepts, let us consider the book's structure, which comprises this introduction, and 24 chapters split into 5 parts.

❏ *Part I*: Acoustic Signal Conversion Theory Basics

   The first part includes 4 chapters:

   Chapter 1: Acoustic Signals and Their Basic Properties

   Chapter 2: Spectral Representation of Signals

   Chapter 3: Filtering

   Chapter 4: Dynamic Processing of Acoustic Signals

❏ *Part II*: Microphones, Mixers, and Effects

   The second part is comprised of 2 chapters:

   Chapter 5: Working with the Microphones and Mixers

   Chapter 6: Sound Effects

❏ *Part III*: Cool Edit Pro—a Multitrack Sound Editor

   The third part consists of 12 chapters:

   Chapter 7: Getting Started

   Chapter 8: Working with the Main Window Using *Waveform View* Mode

   Chapter 9: The *File* Menu—Working with Files

   Chapter 10: The *Edit* Menu

   Chapter 11: The *View* Menu—Display Management

   Chapter 12: The *Transform* Menu—Transforming Audio

Chapter 13: The *Generate* Menu—Sound Generation

Chapter 14: The *Analyze* Menu—Analyzing Audio Data

Chapter 15: The *Favorites* Menu—Creating a List of the Most Often Used Operations

Chapter 16: The *Options* Menu

Chapter 17: The *Window* Menu—Managing the Main Window Pages

Chapter 18: *Multitrack View*—Multitrack Editing Mode

❑ *Part IV*: Virtual Toolkit

The fourth part is comprised of 3 chapters:

Chapter 19: Nemesys GigaStudio 160 (V.2)

Chapter 20: Creating Your Own Sampler Libraries Using GigaStudio Instrument Editor 2.0

Chapter 21: Reason—a Virtual Sound Studio

❑ *Part V*: Digital Mastering

The fifth part contains 3 chapters:

Chapter 22: Theory

Chapter 23: Mastering with T-RackS 24

Chapter 24: DirectX Plug-Ins Useful for Mastering

We actively use all software covered in this book in our everyday work. For example, it is the multitrack environment of the Cool Edit Pro sound editor that we used when preparing all materials for our radio and TV programs. When writing this book, we also put to use our experience in teaching musical computer technologies.

You can contact us by e-mail: **petelin@musicalpc.com**.

Part I

ACOUSTIC SIGNAL CONVERSION THEORY BASICS

Chapter 1: Acoustic Signals and their Main Properties

Chapter 2: Spectral Representation of Signals

Chapter 3: Filtering

Chapter 4: Dynamic Processing of Acoustic Signals

Chapter 1: Acoustic Signals and Their Main Properties

Sound vibrations affecting the microphone or emitted by the speaker are known as *acoustic signals*, which are characterized by their sound pressure, sound intensity, and acoustic power. Sound waves transmitted via the analog circuitry of recording and processing devices are electric signals that have voltage, current, and electric power.

The simplest type of oscillations—harmonic oscillations—can be represented by the sine curve (Fig. 1.1). Harmonic oscillations are characterized by a frequency f, a period T, and an amplitude. The last of these variables is designated by the letter U when dealing with electric signals, i.e., when the voltage changes with time.

Oscillation *frequency* is the number of cycles or events (in our case specifically, the number of sound waves) per unit of time, with units commonly measured in $\sec^{-1}$ (hertz, Hz).

Period is the time (in seconds) that elapses for one complete oscillation or cycle. The larger the oscillation frequency, the less is its period, i.e., $f = 1/T$.

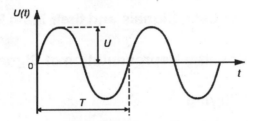

Fig. 1.1. Harmonic oscillation

The human voice is able to produce sound oscillations of a frequency ranging from 80 up to 12,000 Hz, while the human ear can perceive sound oscillations within a range of approximately 20 to 20,000 Hz.

Amplitude is the maximum variation of the oscillating body (represented by a point on the graph) from its initial position (reference point, point of rest) through one cycle. The larger the amplitude, the louder the sound.

1.1. Tone and Timbre

Sounds of music or human speech are complex sound oscillations comprising a large number of simple oscillations differing in their frequency and amplitude. Each sound has an individual combination of oscillations of different frequencies and amplitudes. Because of this, the form of oscillations characteristic for one spoken sound is significantly different from that of another one. Oscillation examples are presented in Fig. 1.2, where Fig. 1.2*a* illustrates the oscillation that corresponds to the monaural sound of human speech, while Fig. 1.2*b* represents musical stereophonic sound.

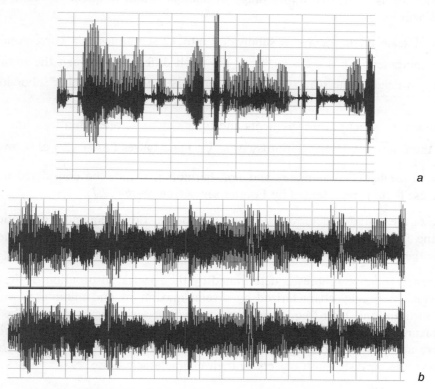

a

b

Fig. 1.2. Examples of monaural (*a*) and stereophonic (*b*) sound

From the perceptional point of view, a harmonic sound oscillation of a specific frequency is characterized by its *tone*. The loudness of a tone of a specific pitch is defined by its oscillation amplitude, while the pitch is determined by the frequency. Oscillations of high frequency are perceived as high-pitched sounds, and low-frequency oscillations are perceived as low-pitched sounds.

The ability of human ear to distinguish adjacent frequencies is not constant within the range of audible frequencies. In the low frequency range (below 500 Hz) it is slightly above 1%, in the high frequency range it is close to 0.5%, and in the medium range it is around 0.3%.

It is a practice in musical acoustics to divide the frequency range by octaves and octave fractions.

An octave is a frequency range interval in which the ratio of the higher frequency to the lower frequency is 2:1. The whole range of audible sound frequencies spans approximately 10 octaves.

The musical scale of the octave is subdivided into 12 semitones that correspond to the frequency increment $\Delta f = \sqrt[12]{2} = 1,054$, or the pitch difference between the sounds produced by two neighboring piano keys. Each semitone, in turn, is further subdivided into 100 cents.

When performing spectral measurements and filter synthesis, one often uses intermediate values of the frequency interval—thirds ($\Delta f = \sqrt[3]{2}$) and halves ($\Delta f = \sqrt{2}$) of octaves.

If the sound oscillation is complex and non-harmonic, it must be considered a sum of harmonic oscillations represented by Fourier series (see *Section 2.1*).

In this case, the sound is determined by a fundamental (low-frequency) oscillation. The ratio of the fundamental tone and overtones (higher harmonics) determines the sound timbre, or the tone color.

The difference in voice timbres is determined by the spectral distribution of the sound's energy, which is usually characterized by several maximums and minimums within the range of medium and high frequencies that lies within a significant part of the audible range. Maximum values are known as *formants*, while minimum values are *anti-formants*. The timbre allows you to distinguish sounds produced by different musical instruments, recognize voices, or distinguish objects by their characteristic noise.

1.2. Audibility Threshold and Loudness Level

The source of sound oscillations emits energy. This energy is transferred to ambient space. The amount of sound energy transmitted per second through an area of one square meter perpendicular to the direction of the sound wave propagation is known as *sound intensity*. Its value I can be calculated using the following formula:

$$I = p^2 / Cp_0 \ [\text{W/m}^2] \tag{1.1}$$

Here p is sound pressure [N/m^2], C is the sound velocity [m/s], and p_0 is the density of the ambience.

From the formula provided above, it is evident that sound intensity increases with sound pressure and, thus, the sound's loudness also increases.

During a normal conversation between people, the energy flux (the energy per unit time per unit area traveling across a surface element perpendicular to the energy flow) or sound power is approximately 10 μW. The power of the loudest violin sound is about 60 μW, while the power of sounds produced by organ can range from 140 to 3200 μW.

The range of sound pressures (intensities) in which human beings are able to hear sounds is quite large. One of the basic reference values in this range is the so-called standard audibility threshold, which is the effective value of the sound pressure created by harmonic sound oscillation at a frequency of 1000 Hz, barely audible to a human being with average hearing sensitivity.

The audibility threshold corresponds to a sound intensity of $I_{s0} = 10^{-12}$ W/m^2 and a sound pressure of $p_{s0} = 2 \times 10^{-5}$ Pa.

The upper boundary of the audible range is defined by a value of $I_{s\ max} = 1$ W/m^2 and a sound pressure of $p_{s\ max} = 20$ Pa. Hearing a sound of such intensity causes discomfort and pain.

Within the range of sound pressures significantly exceeding the standard audibility threshold, the intensity of the sound sensation (L) and the amplitude of sound pressure p_s are related by a dependence known as Fechner's Law of Psychophysics:

$$L = q \log(p_s/p_{s0}),\tag{1.2}$$

where q is a constant factor.

From this expression, it is evident that the L is proportional to the logarithm of the p_s/p_{s0} ratio, rather than to the amplitude of the sound pressure (p_s). Due to this, sound pressure and sound intensity are commonly evaluated in logarithmic units relative to the standard audibility threshold:

$$N_a = 20\lg(p_s/p_{s0}) = 10\lg(I_s/I_{s0}),\tag{1.3}$$

where N_a is known as the *absolute acoustic level*.

The audibility threshold value depends on the frequency. The loudness level (N_l), measured in phones, is the parameter of the curve family. To evaluate this parameter, the sound being tested is often compared to a reference tone having a frequency of 1000 Hz. The sound level in phones coincides with the loudness level (in dB) of the reference sound

$$N_l = 20\lg(p_s/p_{s0})\tag{1.4}$$

provided that both sounds (the one being tested and the reference one) are estimated by the person participating in the experiment as equally loud.

The value of $N_1 = 120$ phones corresponds to the upper limit of the audibility range (the pain threshold). A loudness level of 85—95 phones is preferable for professional listening. The audible range of frequencies narrows significantly with loudness, and this phenomenon is especially noticeable in the area of low frequencies within the audible frequency range.

The variation range of sound pressure at frequencies of 1—3 kHz (from the absolute audibility threshold to the pain threshold) is about 130 dB. This value is significantly lower in the low frequency range. For example, at 100 Hz it equals about 90 dB.

The change of sound sensations (the loudness level, for example) becomes noticeable only when the change in sound level or sound intensity exceeds a specific value (Δp_s or ΔI_s). At the same time, the intensity change detection threshold depends on the loudness level. The average value of this threshold ranges from 0.8 to 1.0 dB. The quantum nature of sound perception is one of the most important properties of human hearing.

Measurements of the frequency resolution threshold are limited to evaluating the minimum perceptible deviation (ΔF_{min}) of the tone frequency (f) modulated by another tone of different frequency. The frequency audibility threshold has a minimum value of $2\Delta F_{min}$, which can be distinguished by ear. The value of this threshold depends on the modulation frequency and on the frequency and acoustic level of the tone being investigated. The ear's sensitivity to the frequency change reaches its maximum at a modulation frequency of 4 Hz. In this case, the minimum perceivable frequency deviation at a sound pressure level of 70 dB fits within a range of 1.5—50 Hz, depending on the selected frequency of the tone being investigated.

If the human ear perceives two or more sounds simultaneously, then the louder sound muffles (absorbs) the fainter ones, and the ear perceives only the loudest sound. This phenomenon is known as "sound masking". Immediately after exposure to loud sounds, the human ear becomes less sensitive to soft sounds. This feature is known as hearing adaptation.

Thus, the audibility threshold depends on the hearing conditions. For example, if the experiment is conducted in silence, the result will be different from the one obtained when measuring the audibility threshold against the background noise. In the latter case, the audibility threshold increases, because the interference masks the legitimate signal. This increase in the audibility threshold of the legitimate signal in the presence of background noise can be expressed by the following formula: $N_{an} - N_a$, where N_{an} is the audibility threshold value measured with background noise, and N_a is the same value measured in silence. When the background noise level increases significantly, it can dominate the legitimate signal and mask it completely. This circumstance must be taken into account when selecting the optimal balance in the course of orchestration. However, in this situation, the sounds of all instruments are at the same time both legitimate signals and interference, which complicates the whole task and makes orchestration an art.

Depending on the ratio between the levels of the legitimate signal and those of the interference, the masking phenomenon manifests itself differently. Here, we'll provide only the most important conclusions formulated based on analysis of this phenomenon:

❒ High-pitched tones of a low level are masked by loud, low-pitched tones

❒ Low-pitched tones of a low level are not masked by loud, high-pitched tones

This partially explains the fact that any mixed chorus always has more female than male singers, and a symphonic orchestra always has more violins than violoncellos. The second, but no less important reason for such a tradition, is the fact that the acoustic power of natural sources of high-frequency sounds is always significantly lower than the power of low-frequency sound sources.

Another important hearing property is the ability to join predefined frequency areas to frequency groups. This concept needs more detailed explanation. If a legitimate signal is concentrated within a relatively narrow frequency band, and the masking noise's spectrum spans this band and gradually expands in both directions, then the audibility threshold of the legitimate signal will stop changing after it reaches ΔF_{fg}. The value of ΔF_{fg} depends on the average frequency of the legitimate signal and determines the width of the frequency group. At frequencies below 500 Hz, the width of frequency groups doesn't depend on the average frequency of the masking noise, and is about 100 Hz. In the frequency range above 500 Hz, the width of frequency groups grows in proportion to F_{avg}, where $\Delta F_{fg} \approx 0.2 \, F_{avg}$. Frequency groups can be generated in any part of the audible range. If you join frequency groups within a single row, then the frequency band from 20 Hz to 16 kHz will comprise 24 frequency groups. If the level of the legitimate signal reaches a specific value as related to the masking noise for that specific band, then the legitimate signal will be heard.

At high loudness levels, so-called *non-linear hearing properties*—when humans hear both the fundamental tone and its high harmonics—start manifesting themselves. Because of this, the dependence between the audibility threshold for the tone masked by the pure tone becomes rather complicated. For example, as the level of the tone being measured increases, the tone of differential frequency becomes audible first, rather than the masking tone itself. Then the measured tone once again becomes audible, along with the differential masking tone. If the frequency of the measured tone is close to the fundamental, doubled, or tripled frequency of the masking tone, you will hear beats in the wide range of the level changes.

The human ear is characterized by a certain inertia. The feeling of sound being produced or stopping doesn't appear immediately. The time period during which the feeling of the loudness level changes by 8—10 phones is known as the *hearing time constant*. This constant depends on the signal parameters, and its average value is about 150—200 msec.

The time necessary for hearing to adapt when evaluating a tone pitch depends on the frequency. At low frequencies it is about 30 msec, while at high frequencies it is somewhat lower.

Perceiving directions and locating sound sources is possible thanks to the *binaural effect*. It can be explained by the influence of the following two factors: binaural time and intensity differences in signals affecting the left and right ears.

Locating sound sources emitting sound at frequencies below 150 Hz is practically impossible. Because of this, it is virtually useless to shift bass and low-frequency percussion instruments from the center of the panoramic view when applying the panoramic technique. Such a shift will have no positive effect on the stereo effect, and, at the same time, the power usage of amplifiers and low-frequency acoustic systems of the right and left channels will not be uniform. Thus it sometimes makes sense to replace two super low frequency acoustic systems (subwoofers) with a single one to which the sum of both the left and right stereo channels is supplied.

Within the frequency range of 150—500 Hz, the direction from which the sound source is coming is mainly determined by the binaural time difference; in medium-range (500—5000 Hz) and high-range (above 5000 Hz) frequencies it is determined by both factors.

The precision of human estimation of where the sound source is located is about 3—4° in a horizontal plane. This allows us to draw the conclusion that placing sound sources too close to one another on a stereo panorama doesn't make any sense when orchestrating a track. If the panoramic view is specified in percentage, then the increment between sound sources (instruments and singers) must not be less than 2—3%. If the panorama is specified in dimensionless units within the limits of −64 to 64 (or from 0 to 127), it makes sense to place the sound sources no less than 3—5 units from one another.

1.3. The Acoustic Signal as a Random Process

An acoustic signal is a random process. Its acoustic or electric characteristics are continuously changing with time. Graphically, an acoustic signal can be represented as a set of random functions.

1.3.1. Acoustic Signal Level

Graphic representations of time functions of the sound pressure $P_s(t)$ or voltage $u(t)$ for a specified time period T_n, are known as graphs of instantaneous values of an acoustic signal, or time diagrams of the signal (Fig. 1.3a)

The acoustic signal level characterizes the signal at a specific instant, and represents the acoustic signal voltage $\overline{u(t_1)}$ (expressed in dB), rectified (Fig. 1.3b) and time-averaged for the time period specified earlier (Fig. 1.3c):

$$N_E(t_1) = 20 \lg [\overline{u(t)} / U_0] \tag{1.5}$$

Here, the overscore signifies the time averaging operation, t_1 stands for the current time, U_0 is some reference value, and $N_E(t_1)$ is the level of electroacoustic signal for time t_1.

Similarly, it is possible to determine the signal level for time t_2, and so on.

Theoretically, using the constant weight factor (Fig. 1.3b) provides the simplest way of time-averaging the instantaneous value of the rectified voltage. Mathematically, this operation can be written as follows:

$$\overline{u(t_1)} = \frac{1}{T} \int_{t_1-T}^{t_1} | u(t) | \, dt \tag{1.6}$$

This expression (1.6) gives the value of the $u(t)$ function averaged by time period T. Here, all rectified values of the $u(t)$ function are assigned a constant relative weight equal to dt/T within the time interval from $(t_1 - T)$ to t_1 (T is the averaging interval here). Outside the averaging interval, the weight factor is equal to zero (dashed line in Fig. 1.3b).

Using a similar technique, it is possible to determine the average value of the rectified voltage for the time instance t_2, and so on. Since an acoustic signal is generally a non-steady, random process, the values of $\overline{u(t_1)}$, $\overline{u(t_2)}$, , $\overline{u(t_n)}$ will be different for different times t_1, t_2, ..., t_n. This will produce the time function for the variation of the averaged rectified voltage (Fig. 1.3c).

The type of this $\overline{u(t)}$ function is determined by specific features of the acoustic signal itself and by the selected averaging interval (T).

Aa $T \to 0$, time functions of the averaged values of the rectified signal don't significantly differ from the time functions of the instantaneous values.

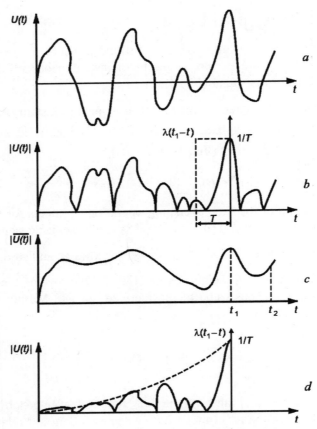

Fig. 1.3. Time diagrams of an acoustic signal

As the averaging interval T increases, the less will the averaged values of the rectified signal change with time. These circumstances must be taken into account by using the sound level meters. The condition $T \to 0$ corresponds to the peak level meter. At small values of T, we are dealing with quasi-peak level meters. A large value of T means that we are dealing with the root-mean-square (RMS) level meter. There is nothing strange in this fact, since calculating the RMS is the same as averaging the function modulus.

If there is a minimum averaging interval of $T = T_0$, after reaching which the averaged value of the rectified signal doesn't depend on the current time t—i.e., if the following condition is true:

$$\overline{u(t_1)} = \overline{u(t_2)} = \overline{u(t_n)}, \tag{1.7}$$

provided that $T \geq T_0$, such a signal is considered a steady signal, and the T_0 value is its steadiness interval.

Both musical and speech signals are non-steady processes by their structure. In rare cases when this condition (1.7) is satisfied, the steadiness interval value (T_0) is very large—about 2—3 minutes. Notice that the value of T_0 for speech signals is normally less than for musical ones. In practice, this means that the human ear can't average the perceived signal for such a long time period. Sound sensation for each specific time moment (for example, t_1) is defined not only by the instantaneous value of the signal, but also by its previous values, the influence of which on the sound's perception is less the earlier they appear in relation to the current time. Because of this, when determining the acoustic signal level, averaging its rectified instantaneous values should be done using a variable weight factor that decreases time elapses. The best approximation of the real properties of human hearing is the exponential weight function:

$$\lambda(t_1 - t) = \frac{1}{T} \exp(-\frac{t_1 - t}{T}) \text{ provided that } t \leq t_1, \quad (1.8)$$

where $\lambda(t_1 - t) = 0$ if $t > t_1$, and T is the time characterizing the inertial properties of the level meter.

When using this averaging method for the time instance t_1, an averaged value or the rectified signal will be expressed by the following formula:

$$\overline{u(t)} = \int_{-\infty}^{t_1} \lambda(t_1 - t) \mid u(t) \mid dt \quad (1.9)$$

Weighing the rectified instantaneous values of the real signal using the weight function (1.8) for time t_1 is shown in Fig. 1.3d.

The time dependence of the rectified voltage averaged for a specific time period using the specified weight factor $\lambda(t_1 - t)$ and expressed in dB is known as the dynamic level of the acoustic signal:

$$N(t) = 20 \lg [\overline{u(t)} / U_0], \quad (1.10)$$

where t is the current time.

The acoustic level is determined not only by instantaneous values of the acoustic signal but also by the time dependence between the weight factor, and by the acoustic inertia of the measuring device. For this reason, when speaking about acoustic levels, it is necessary to take into account the time characteristics of the devices used to perform the measurements.

1.3.2. Statistic Properties of the Acoustic Signal

Statistic properties of acoustic signals are characterized by the following distribution laws:

❏ Time distribution of instantaneous values and sound pressure levels

❏ Pause duration

❏ Continuous existence (lifetime) of specific levels

❏ Frequency distribution of sound pressures

The most complete description of the statistic properties of the random quantity X is provided by the distribution function $p(x)$, which represents the probability of $X < x$, where x is the current threshold value of the random variable.

According to probability theory, the $p(x) = p\{X < x\}$ function is known as the one-dimensional distribution function of a random variable. The derivative—$W(x)$—of this function is known as the probability density of the random variable's distribution. It reflects the probability of the fact that the random value will be in the interval from x to $x + \Delta x$, where $\Delta x \to 0$. The $p(x)$ and $W(x)$ dependencies determine the distribution law of the random variable X. In terms of acoustic signals, instantaneous values of voltage u, sound pressure p_s and levels such as N_a and N_e, are random variables.

The $p(x)$ and $W(x)$ probability distribution laws are stable if the duration of implementation (sampling) exceeds the T_0 steadiness interval. With accuracy sufficient for practical purposes, a spoken acoustic signal can be considered a quasi-stationary process, if the observation interval exceeds 2—3 minutes. For musical signals, the steadiness interval can't be established. If the observation period doesn't exceed several hours, short sampling results differ significantly, and reflect the properties of investigated fragments rather than the properties of the musical signal as a whole.

The results of experimental investigations of the time distributions of instantaneous values of musical signals show that different types of sounds (vocal music, popular music, symphonic music) have similar distribution laws. As a rule, they all have an exponential nature. The distribution of a chorus with an orchestra, popular music, and jazz music has been noted to be close to the Gaussian Law.

In real-world situations, the condition $\Delta x \to 0$ is not satisfied. Therefore, in practice, instead of probability density, one investigates the so-called distribution histogram of the acoustic signal's instantaneous values. The physical concept of this histogram is similar to that of the probability density, with the single exception that Δx is a small value, but it doesn't tend to zero. According to the histogram, one can evaluate the allowable signal amplification and perform an approximate selection of the dynamic processing parameters. The best sound editors provide special sets of tools for observing the histogram of the acoustic signal's instantaneous value distributions. We will give an example illustrating how the information obtained by analyzing the histogram formed by the Cool Edit Pro program can be used in *Section 14.2.2*.

Level distribution of real-world acoustic speech and musical signals depends not only on the characteristics of the sound information and analysis time, but also on the selected weight function of the averaging device. With the increase of T, the distribution laws tend to approximate the Gaussian Law. As $T \rightarrow \infty$, the concept of the distribution law loses its meaning, since only a single value will be produced instead of a set of random values.

Information on the distribution of the lifetimes of signal levels exceeding some specific predefined value (N'_{an}) has a most important practical meaning for selecting manual or automatic level control mode (Fig. 1.4). From the diagram provided in this illustration, one can see that τ_1, τ_3, τ_5, and τ_6 are the intervals where the signal level exceeds the specified N_{an} value.

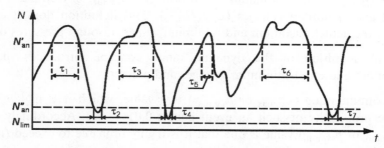

Fig. 1.4. Time diagram illustrating the evaluation of the lifetime of levels exceeding the specified predefined value N'_{an} and not exceeding N''_{an}

Experimental investigations have shown that the range of continuous existence of levels exceeding the specified value is quite large. For example, when analyzing a level that is 5% of the maximum value, the maximum length of peaks for speech signals takes approximately 1 second, while for musical signals it is approximately 4 seconds. The minimum value doesn't exceed a few milliseconds. Most common are peaks lasting 12—17 milliseconds.

Pauses are time intervals that exist on levels below the specific predefined analysis level N_{an}, which exceeds the interference level N_i by a specific predefined value. In Fig. 1.4, the intervals τ_2, τ_4, and τ_7 correspond to pauses.

When determining the pause lifetime distribution law, the N_{an} level is selected as a value less than the nominal by 40 dB. The nominal level is the maximum level at which non-linear distortions introduced by the processing devices don't exceed the maximum acceptable value.

The length of pauses in the acoustic signal has a random nature, and varies within a very wide range. Pauses longer than 2 seconds are highly improbable. The most probable pause length is 50—150 milliseconds. Outside this range, the probability of pauses rapidly decreases.

Data on the distribution of peaks and pauses of an acoustic signal will be useful when selecting time parameters for dynamic processing devices. This data can be used as a starting point, which, of course, will need some correcting in the course of processing a specific acoustic signal.

1.3.3. Dynamic Range and Average Power

An acoustic signal's dynamic range is commonly determined as the ratio of the maximum sound pressure ($p_{s.max}$) to the minimum sound pressure ($p_{s.min}$), or a similar ratio relating the maximum and minimum voltages (U_{max}/U_{min}). This definition doesn't contain any information on the actual maximum and minimum values of sound pressures or voltages.

The theoretical definition of the dynamic range concept introduces the concepts of quasi-maximum and quasi-minimum voltages and pressures.

The quasi-maximum value ($U_{q.max}$ or $p_{s.q.max}$) is a value, which it is highly improbable to exceed (the probability of such an event equals 0.01—0.02). Accordingly, the quasi-minimum ($U_{q.min}$ or $p_{s.q.min}$) value is one that it is highly probable to exceed (in this case, the probability being 0.98—0.99).

The dynamic range of an acoustic signal is calculated according to the following formula:

$$D_a = 20 \lg \frac{p_{s.q.\,max}}{p_{s.q.\,min}} = 20 \lg \frac{p_{s.q.\,max}}{p_{s.0}} - 20 \lg \frac{p_{s.q.\,min}}{p_{s.0}} \qquad (1.11)$$

The dynamic range of an electric signal is calculated according the following formula:

$$D_e = 20 \lg \frac{u_{q.\,max}}{u_{q.\,min}} = 20 \lg \frac{u_{q.\,max}}{U_0} - 20 \lg \frac{u_{q.\,min}}{U_0} \qquad (1.12)$$

Here, $p_{s.0} = 2 \times 10^{-5}$ Pa is the minimum value of the acoustic pressure corresponding to the audibility threshold within the range of the maximum hearing sensitivity of the human ear (1—4 kHz). $U_0 = 0.775$ V is the voltage at a load of 600 ohms, producing a power of 1 mW.

The dynamic range of the signal determined by the expressions in (1.11) and (1.12) is known as the theoretic definition. However, the dynamic range of an acoustic signal can also be defined experimentally using the level diagram as the difference between the maximum (N_{max}) and minimum (N_{min}) levels for a sufficiently long observation interval:

$$D_s = N_{max} - N_{min} \qquad (1.13)$$

This value of the dynamic range depends significantly on the selected time integration period (t_i) of the level meter. The larger the value of t_i, the less the number of short peaks of the acoustic signal, and the less is the value of D_s.

The theoretic value of the dynamic range calculated by analyzing the time distribution of instantaneous voltage or sound pressure values using the expressions in (1.11) and (1.12) will always be greater than the empirical value for the same fragment of the acoustic signal.

Dynamic ranges characteristic for musical and speech acoustic signals of different types, measured using devices set to correspond to the loudness level perceived by ear (at $t_I = 60$ msec), have the following average values:

- 60 dB—symphonic orchestra
- 47 dB—chorus
- 35 dB—popular music or vocalist
- 25 dB—professional orator
- 20 dB—jazz band

When reproducing speech, the maximum acoustic level is approximately 80—86 dB; when reproducing music, it reaches 90—100 dB.

An orchestra creates the maximum possible sound pressure (up to 40 Pa). However, the probability of generating such a pressure is very low, and the length of continuous sound is so small that it can be neglected. The average sound pressure generated by an orchestra at a distance of 12.8 ft is 0.5—0.7 Pa.

The peak value of the sound power depends on the specific musical instrument, and varies within a wide range; for example:

- 0.29 W—bass-saxophone
- 24.6 W—bass drum
- 10—15 W—(most often) symphonic orchestra (the maximum power might reach values of 65 W)

The difference between the quasi-maximum level of an acoustic signal ($N_{q.max}$) and the mean (N_{avg}) level of the signal averaged by a significant time interval is known as the peak factor:

$$\Pi = N_{q.\,max} - N_{avg} \qquad (1.14)$$

The peak factor shows the difference between the average signal level and the quasi-maximum. For musical signals, the peak factor can achieve values of 20 dB or larger (for a symphonic orchestra). For speech signals, the common value of the peak factor is about 12 dB.

Make sure not to mix two different concepts: the dynamic range of an acoustic signal (D_s) and the dynamic range of the processing channel (recording/transmission)—D_{ch}. The dynamic range of the channel depends both on the noise level in the channel and on the nominal voltage:

$$D_{ch} = 20 \lg \frac{U_{nom}}{U_{noise}} - (\Delta N_1 + \Delta N_2) \qquad (1.15)$$

Here, U_{nom} is the nominal voltage, U_{noise} is the noise voltage (notice that these voltages must either both be supplied to the channel input or both to the channel output), ΔN_1 is the noise overlapping level, and ΔN_2 is the overload tolerance (for analog systems, it is about 3—6 dB).

It is obvious that processing and transmitting an acoustic signal without distortion is possible only under the following condition: $D_s < D_{ch}$. For real acoustic signals there may be situations when this condition is not satisfied. Due to this, in such situations it is necessary to pre-process an acoustic signal by limiting its dynamic range. As a general rule, the dynamic range of acoustic signals pre-processed by a sound engineer doesn't exceed a limit of 40 dB.

There are expressions (which will not be provided here because of their awkwardness), that establish the relationship between the average power (P_{avg}) of an acoustic signal and its quasi-maximum power, with the dynamic range of the signal being D_s. From these relationships, it follows that the $P_{avg}/P_{q.max}$ ratio depends on the specified probabilities of exceeding the quasi-maximum ($N_{q.max}$) and quasi-minimum ($N_{q.min}$) levels. The graph illustrating the dependence of the relative average power of the acoustic signal on its dynamic range is shown in Fig. 1.5.

For real values of $D_s = 20$—40 dB, the $P_{avg}/P_{q.max}$ ratio fits within the range of 0.05—0.15 (i.e., it is significantly less than 1). If we require that when transmitting and reproducing such signals their peaks be transmitted without clipping, the subjective loudness will not be particularly high. To increase the average power of an acoustic signal (and, consequently, the perceived loudness), one can employ various devices (or software) intended for dynamic sound processing—compressors and limiters. There are special plug-in modules included with software packages that are specially oriented towards mastering (they will be covered in more detail in *Part 5* of this book). These modules implement complex algorithms of spectral and dynamic processing that provide for optimal compression of the dynamic range.

Thus we have discussed all the basic properties of acoustic signals. In the next chapter, we will proceed with discussing the basics of their spectral representation.

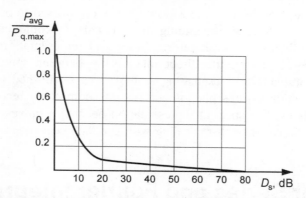

Fig. 1.5. Dependence of the relative average power of an acoustic signal on the dynamic range of the signal

Chapter 2: Spectral Representation of Signals

When Bernoulli, Euler, and later Fourier, first decomposed functions into series, this decomposition was considered a mathematical method of solving the problems of theoretical physics. Fourier himself used the series named after him for integrating the heat conductivity equation. Later on, the Fourier method became the classic technique for solving wave equations such as the string vibration equation and, later on, the telegrapher's equation.

For quite a long time, Fourier decomposition was not considered to be directly related to any physical concepts. However, beginning in the 1920s, in conjunction with the rapid development in the field of radio engineering, spectral representations began to receive wide acceptance. Furthermore, the direct relationship between spectral decomposition and the behavior of real-world oscillating systems was established. Thus, the spectral techniques for describing various phenomena became commonly recognized and widely accepted. The terms used in spectral representation became a universal language understandable for all technical specialists dealing with the technical usage of various types of vibrations.

2.1. Fourier Series and Fourier Integral

The decomposition of a periodic signal to a Fourier series is the best starting point for discussions of spectral representation concepts. The function $s(t)$ is known as a periodic function if the following condition is satisfied:

$$s(t) = s(t + nT) \tag{2.1}$$

Here, T is a constant value denoted as the period, n is any positive or negative integer, and t is the current time. The formula in (2.1) expresses the basic property of periodic functions, namely, the fact that the phenomenon under consideration repeats periodically for $-\infty < t < +\infty$. Obviously, periodic phenomena in the strict sense of the definition (2.1) don't exist in the real world. This formula is an abstraction intended to simplify the description of certain actual processes that take place under real conditions.

Each periodic function (with abstract limitations, which, in our case, are of no practical importance) can be represented as a decomposition to series by trigonometric functions:

$$s(t) = c_0 + \sum_{k=1}^{\infty} c_k \cos(2\pi k \frac{1}{\tau} - \varphi_k) \tag{2.2}$$

Thus, the periodic function $s(t)$ is represented as the sum of expressions of the following type:

$$c_k \cos(2\pi k \frac{t}{T} - \varphi_k)$$ (2.3)

Each of the members of the series is a sinusoidal oscillation with amplitude c_k and initial phase φ_k. To satisfy the equality in (2.2), it is necessary to select appropriate values for c_k and φ_k.

The sets of c_k's and φ_k's factors are known as the amplitude and phase spectrums of the signal, respectively.

The frequencies of all sinusoidal oscillations from which the periodical function $s(t)$ is composed are multiples of the fundamental frequency $F = 1/T$. Specific components are known as harmonics. The oscillation with frequency F is the first harmonic ($k = 1$), one with a frequency of $2F$ is the second harmonic ($k = 2$), and so on.

The c_0 value expresses the average value of the function for a time period. This is the so-called constant component, calculated according to the following formula:

$$c_0 = \frac{1}{T} \int_{-\frac{T}{2}}^{\frac{T}{2}} s(t)dt$$ (2.4)

The expression in (2.2) can be re-written using another commonly used form:

$$s(t) = c_0 + \sum_{k=1}^{\infty} (a_k \cos 2\pi k \frac{t}{T} + b_k \sin 2\pi k \frac{t}{T}),$$ (2.5)

where $a_k = c_k \cos \varphi_k$ and $b_k = c_k \sin \varphi_k$.

The relationship between the expressions in (2.2) and (2.5) is described by the following formulas:

$$c_k = \sqrt{a_k^2 + b_k^2}, \quad tg\varphi_k = \frac{b_k}{a_k}.$$ (2.6)

The factors a_k and b_k can be calculated according to the following formulae:

$$a_k = \frac{2}{T} \int_{-\frac{T}{2}}^{\frac{T}{2}} s(t)\cos(2\pi k \frac{t}{T})dt$$ (2.7)

$$b_k = \frac{2}{T} \int\limits_{-\frac{T}{2}}^{\frac{T}{2}} s(t) \sin{(2\pi k \frac{t}{T})} dt \qquad\qquad (2.8)$$

The most important property of the Fourier series is the fact that if the periodic function is approximated by a finite number of series members, i.e., if the function is represented as a polynomial of the following form:

$$s(t) \cong c_0 + \sum_{k=0}^{N} (a_k \cos{2\pi k \frac{t}{T}} + b_k \sin{2\pi k \frac{t}{T}}), \qquad\qquad (2.9)$$

where the polynomial coefficients are determined by the formulas in (2.4), (2.7), and (2.8), then for any N we will get the minimum root mean square deviation of an approximation of the $s(t)$ function from its exact one.

As the number of decomposition elements (N) grows, approximation accuracy increases, and as $N \to \infty$, the approximate formula tends to the exact one.

An example illustrating the sequence of rectangular pulses with different numbers of harmonic components is represented in Figs. 2.1a–2.1c.

From the example presented in these illustrations, it is evident that when accounting for only one harmonic component, the approximate representation of the signal significantly differs from the original, while the result obtained for $N = 3$ is quite similar to the rectangular pulses.

The Fourier series decomposes periodic functions into trigonometric functions. This method can also be applied to aperiodic functions. Generally, aperiodic functions are considered to be limiting cases of a periodic function, when the period tends to infinity.

It should be pointed out that F is the frequency interval between two neighboring harmonics. If $T \to \infty$, then $F \to df$, and $2\pi k/T \to \omega$. Here the ω parameter is the continuously changing current angular frequency. More detailed information on the mathematical transformations that take place during this limiting process is provided in special literature. Here we will limit ourselves by providing the following formulas:

$$s(t) = \frac{1}{2\pi} \int\limits_{-\infty}^{+\infty} G(\omega) e^{j\omega t} d\omega \qquad\qquad (2.10)$$

$$G(\omega) = \int_{-\infty}^{+\infty} s(t)e^{-j\omega t}\,dt \qquad (2.11)$$

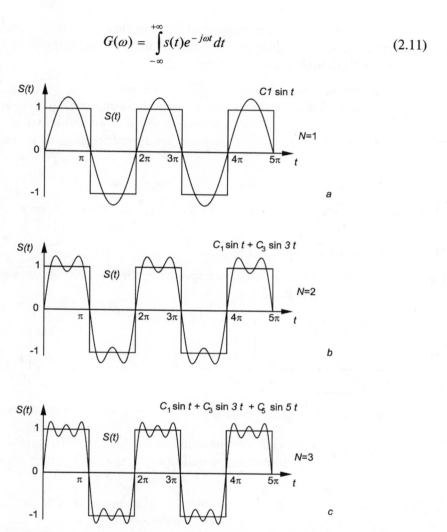

Fig. 2.1. An example illustrating the representation of the periodic signal with different numbers of harmonic components

These formulas are the main relationships of the spectrum theory. They represent a couple of Fourier transforms that establish the relationship between the real time function $s(t)$ and the complex frequency function $G(\omega)$.

Formula (2.10) is known as the complex form of the Fourier integral. The point of the Fourier integral is the representation of the $s(t)$ function by the sum of sinusoidal components. In this case, it is assumed that this function is aperiodic, and therefore can be represented only as the sum of an infinite number of oscillations of infinitely close frequencies with infinitely small amplitudes.

In contrast to the Fourier series, which presents a periodic function as the sum of an infinite number of sinusoidal components with the frequencies taking discrete values, the Fourier integral presents aperiodic function as the sum of sinusoidal components with a continuous sequence of frequencies. Sometimes an aperiodic signal is said to contain all frequencies.

For comparison, let us consider the following two signals:

❏ Periodic sequence of pulses (Fig. 2.2). The duration of each pulse is equal to τ, while the period is T.

❏ A single pulse of duration τ (Fig. 2.3).

Fig. 2.4 shows the amplitude and phase spectra of the periodic signal, while Fig. 2.5 illustrates the same spectra for the aperiodic pulse.

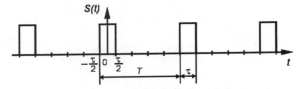

Fig. 2.2. Periodic sequence of pulses

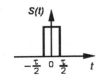

Fig. 2.3. A single pulse of duration τ

The type of pulse sequence spectrum depends on the relative pulse duration, or q—which is equal to the period-to-pulse duration ratio ($q = T/\tau$). The example shown in Fig. 2.4 corresponds to $q = 5$.

From the example shown, it is obvious that the spectrum of a periodic signal is discrete, linear, and harmonic (since it consists of equidistant spectral lines, and harmonic frequencies are simple multiples). With the increase of period T, the fundamental frequency decreases, the spectrum becomes more and more dense, and the amplitudes of harmonic components decrease.

Now let's consider the example of the aperiodic signal. You already know that as a result of the limiting transition from the Fourier series to a Fourier integral, intervals between specific spectrum lines are infinitely decreasing and merging, and the spectrum must be displayed as a continuous line rather than as a set of discrete points. This is a continuous spectrum.

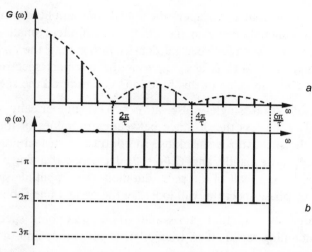

Fig. 2.4. Examples of amplitude (*a*) and phase (*b*) spectra of a periodic signal

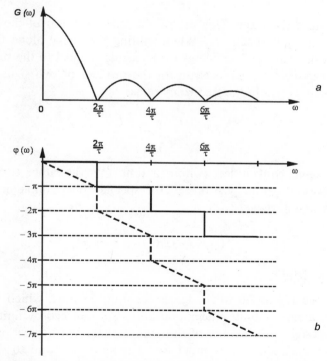

Fig. 2.5. Examples of amplitude (*a*) and phase (*b*) spectra of an aperiodic signal

It should be pointed out that in an aperiodic signal, the amplitudes of specific spectrum components have no significant value, i.e., they are infinitely small. Actually, the $G(\omega)$ parameter represents the so-called spectral density rather than the amplitude. This detail is frequently omitted, and $G(\omega)$ is designated as the complex spectrum of an aperiodic function, while the absolute value of this function is considered the spectrum.

The spectral density of a single pulse at $\omega = 0$ is numerically equal to its area. The longer the pulse, the less the distance between zero values of the spectral function, which means that the spectrum is shrinking. In contrast to this situation, when the pulse gets shorter, its spectrum expands, and $G\ (\omega = 0)$ decreases. If a single pulse shifts in time by an interval equal to, say, half of the pulse duration, the amplitude spectrum will remain unchanged, while the phase spectrum will look like the dashed line shown in Fig. 2.5.

In various literature, one can find ratios and graphs describing spectrums of pulses of different shapes, including rectangular, triangular, exponential, sinusoidal, etc.

There are several theorems related to spectral transformations of signals, briefly described below.

The Fourier transform is linear. This means that the spectrum of the sum of signals is equal to the sum of their spectrums. When shifting the signal along the time axis, the spectrum remains unchanged. The energy of the signal is equal to the sum of the energies of its spectral components. The spectrum of the product of two signals is equal to the convolution of their spectra in the frequency range:

$$G(\omega) = \frac{1}{2\pi} \int_{-\infty}^{+\infty} G_1(v) G_2(\omega - v) dv \qquad (2.12)$$

The concept of signal convolution (within a time interval rather than in a frequency range) will be necessary to analyze one of the special effects implemented in the Cool Edit Pro program (see *Section 12.32*):

$$f(t) = K \int_{-\infty}^{+\infty} s_1(\tau) s_2(t - \tau) d\tau, \qquad (2.13)$$

where K is a normalizing coefficient.

Convolution is especially useful when signals are finite in time, which is always the case in reality. In such a case, infinite integration limits are replaced by finite ones. Convolution is used to investigate the nature of the pulse signal's transformation by means of an electric circuit being supplied to its input, or to model the sound so that it depends on the acoustic properties of the room where the concert is given.

2.2. Current Spectrum

The canonical definition of a spectrum is based on the Fourier transform, provided that the time integration limits are infinite and that the spectrum depends only on frequency. However, the infinite duration of any process is an abstraction that has nothing in common with reality. For example, you can't produce sound for an infinitely long period of time by just pressing a key and holding it. As a matter of fact, music as such exists only when the sounds are continuously changing.

If the function being analyzed reflects some real physical process that can't be predicted exactly just on the basis of theory, then all information on that function can be obtained only on an empirical basis. Thus, when calculating the spectrum, we can only perform integration within limits from $-\infty$ to the current time, t.

Taking real conditions into account, let's introduce the concept of the current spectrum. The current spectrum is defined as the result of a Fourier transform with a variable upper integration limit (the current time). Thus, the modified definition of the spectrum will look as follows:

$$G_t(\omega) = \int_{-\infty}^{t} s(t)e^{-j\omega t}\, dt \tag{2.14}$$

$G_t(\omega)$ is a function of both time and frequency, and is known as the current spectrum.

Under real conditions, the observation of a process (or the process itself) starts at some specific time t_0, different from the current time (t). In this case, provided that t_0 is considered to be the starting time (0), the current spectrum can be determined as follows:

$$G_t(\omega) = \int_{0}^{t} s(t)e^{-j\omega t}\, dt \tag{2.15}$$

When discussing spectrum theory basics, we used the definition of a periodic function (2.1). Actually, this definition also represents a useful mathematical abstraction. This means that in reality, the process that satisfies the conditions determined in (2.1) can't exist. Any real process has starting and ending point and, consequently, is described by the expression in (2.1) only for a finite time interval.

The real cyclic process is considered to be periodic if it lasts for a sufficiently long time. The measure of duration is the number of periods, which must be significantly larger than 1. The periodic nature of the process manifests itself only with time, when its characteristic properties become evident. The current spectrum reflects the process of evolution.

The spectrum of the process (for a short time interval) is uniform, since a short fragment of the process is simply a single short pulse. If the cycle repeats itself with time, maximums at the fundamental frequency and its harmonics will form in the current spectrum. These peaks become sharper and higher with the time, while the spectrum density within the intervals between these maximums gradually decreases. At $t \to \infty$, the continuous current spectrum degenerates into a discrete spectrum of the periodic process.

Certainly, if the duration is significantly large (but not infinite), the peaks become so narrow that they can be treated as lines.

Thus, the periodic process is the limit toward which the real-world repeating process tends with time. Similarly, the spectrum (in the classic sense) of such a process is the limit to which the current spectrum tends, with the increase of the integration time to infinity.

Let us illustrate this concept with an example of the current spectrum of a sinusoidal oscillation.

When integrating within infinite limits, the sinusoid spectrum represents a single line at frequency Ω, where Ω is equal to the sinusoid frequency (Fig. 2.6).

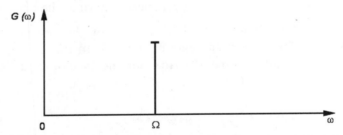

Fig. 2.6. Spectrum of a sinusoidal signal when integrating within infinite limits

Now let's consider how the current spectrum changes with time (using the sinusoid for an example). We turn the spectrum analyzer on, and after some time we turn it off. Thus we are measuring the spectrum of a sinusoidal signal that lasts for some period of time, more or less a long-lasting one, rather than the spectrum of an infinite sinusoidal oscillation. This means that in practice we are investigating the spectrum of a rectangular pulse modulated by a sinusoidal signal. That is, the signal under consideration can be represented as the product of an infinite sinusoid and a finite rectangular pulse. Consequently, the resulting spectrum is the convolution of the spectrums of these two signals.

Obviously, this spectrum convolution is not equal to each of the signals being multiplied. This explains the reason for the fact that, even for a sinusoidal oscillation, as the integration time decreases, the spectral line widens and there appear sidelobes of the spectral function, while its zeros become more and more distant from one another. This reflects exactly the behavior of the rectangular pulse as its duration decreases. Fig. 2.7 shows the spectrum of a rectangular pulse of finite length modulated by a sinusoidal signal.

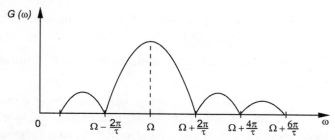

Fig. 2.7. Spectrum of a rectangular pulse of finite length modulated by a sinusoidal signal

If you compare the illustrations provided in Figs. 2.5 and 2.7, you'll notice that the envelopes of the two spectral functions are similar. The main difference is that the spectrum of the pulse modulated by a sinusoidal signal is shifted along the frequency axis by a distance corresponding to the sinusoid frequency. If we consider the spectrum of a single rectangular pulse in more detail and introduce the concepts of negative frequency and complex signal, the graphs provided in these two illustrations would be almost exact copies of one another, except for the fact that the symmetry axis of the first graph would go through the origin of the coordinate system, while the symmetry axis of the second graph would go through the point corresponding to the Ω frequency.

The evolution of the current spectrum of sinusoidal oscillation with changing integration limits is shown by the spectral function relief in Fig. 2.8.

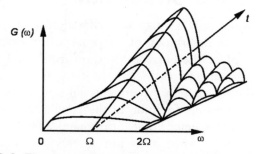

Fig. 2.8. The spectrum relief of the sinusoidal oscillation

Fig. 2.8 clearly shows that when the observation interval is small, the current spectrum is uniform. The peak at frequency Ω forms gradually with the increase of this interval, becoming sharper and sharper. As $t \to \infty$, the graph transforms into a discrete spectral line, corresponding to the spectrum of the periodical sinusoidal oscillation.

Thus, the current spectrum more appropriately reflects the actual signal properties than the spectrum obtained for an infinite time interval.

Notice that the virtual spectrum analyzers calculate the current spectrum (*Section 14.1*), and not the spectrum obtained for an infinite time interval.

An analysis of the results of the current spectrum measurements of a musical composition enables us to:

❏ Evaluate the uniformity of the sound frequency usage and detect certain errors of orchestration and combination of sound tracks with recordings of specific musical instruments (identified on the graph by the valleys of the spectral function)

❏ Detect of undesirable acoustic resonance frequencies that arise in the room where the recording takes place, or in acoustic or electric channels (narrow peaks in the spectral function graph)

❏ Detect and suppress interference from the sources of sinusoidal and pulse electromagnetic radiation (peaks in the spectral function graph)

In order to increase the accuracy of evaluating the statistical spectral characteristics of noise or interference (this evaluation is performed as a part of the first stage of some noise suppression procedure) it is recommended that you increase the analysis time to the maximum allowed (*Section 12.30*). To achieve this, it is recommended that you record the noise for several dozens of seconds at the start of each recording session.

2.3. Instantaneous Spectrum

The current spectrum provides only a rough approximation when performing a transition from the frequency to the time description of the process. For example, imagine a situation where you need to analyze the current spectrum from the beginning of a musical composition to its end, without hearing the music itself. It is possible that the spectral function graph obtained during such an experiment will look relatively broadband. When considering this graph, it is possible to come to the conclusion that the piece is an ensemble played by several instruments. Some instruments have a timbre in which low-frequency components dominate, while other instruments have more medium and high-frequency components in their timbre.

However, when your signal is output to the acoustic system, it proves to be a duet for baritone and soprano, accompanied by the piano. Actually, the sound timbre is continuonsly changing. While the baritone plays, "velvety" low-frequency components dominate, and when the dialog is continued by the soprano, it produces the impression of a small silver bell. However, all these nuances were smoothed and averaged by out the spectrum analysis.

Why then do we need all these spectrum measurements, if they don't provide an adequate pattern of timbre evolution? Certainly, it is hardly possible to develop a detailed strategy for subsequent processing of recorded sound. The problem is that when the process being analyzed is not stationary, both the spectrum calculated at an infinite time interval and the current spectrum are too rough. To approximate the frequency and time representation of the signal, *the instantaneous spectrum*, or *periodogram*, concept was introduced. The periodogram is the spectrum of a process fragment of duration ΔT, which directly precedes the current time t. The mathematical definition of the periodogram is as follows:

$$G_T(\omega, t) = \int_{t-T}^{t} s(\tau)e^{-j\omega\tau}d\tau \tag{2.16}$$

In this definition we are dealing with so-called sliding integration, where the integration interval has a constant length but shifts along the time axis. However, the position of this interval in relation to the current time is constant.

This definition of the spectrum is a long way from the inventions of great mathematicians. However, it is the periodogram that, from the sound engineer's point of view, is the most efficient tool for analyzing the properties of a sound being recorded, or one that was just recorded. The reason for this is that the actual sound signals with which a sound engineer deals are equally far from both mathematical abstractions—a super narrow-band sinusoidal oscillation infinite in time and super broadband white noise infinite in the frequency range.

Music created using a synthesizer is distinguished by its noticeable timbre instability. Perhaps because of this most sound editors use tools for periodogram analysis. One can say that, in this respect, musical software developers have outdone radio engineers. In any case, the concept of the periodogram is not even found in one tenth of signal theory textbooks. As a result, we have met hundreds of students (and even teachers) who were unable to move forward from the idea of the sinusoid spectrum as a single discrete component of the spectrum, independent of the time parameters of the spectrum measurement process. We hope that you now have an idea of the difference between the spectrum, the current spectrum, and the instantaneous spectrum.

2.4. Displaying the Periodogram

From an analytical point of view, a set of instantaneous spectra of a non-stationary process can approximately be written as a matrix, each row of which corresponds to a single instance of a periodogram, while each column corresponds to a single frequency.

Programs intended for analyzing and processing acoustic data provide at least two ways of representing the periodogram. The first method is as a sequence of layers sliding along the time axis. Each layer contains a single implementation of the graph, and previous layers are not erased. As a result, the program forms a relief similar to the one used for representing the spectrum change (see Fig. 2.8).

As an example of this approach, let's look at the Spectrum Analyzer Professional program, intended for analysis of the spectrums formed by any analog source attached to the sound adapter input or saved in WAV files. Fig. 2.9 shows the spectrum analyzer window as it displays the periodogram for a sequence of rectangular pulses, which, by the way, is formed using the functional generator included with the Spectrum Analyzer Professional program. The **Lines** display mode is selected, which displays the spectrum as a continuous line.

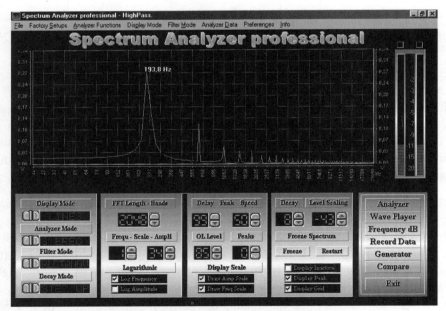

Fig. 2.9. A periodogram displayed with "frequency—spectral density" coordinates

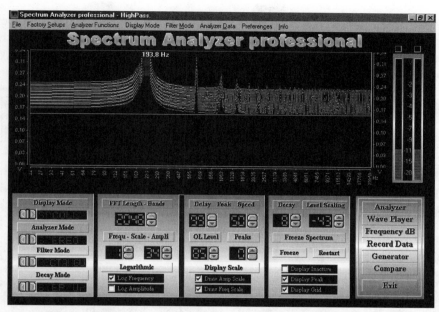

Fig. 2.10. A periodogram displayed with "frequency—spectral density—time" coordinates

Here, the horizontal axis is the frequency axis, while the vertical axis displays the spectral function values. When normal display mode is used, the spectrum display "moves", because the periodogram changes with time. If you are bothered by the screen blinking, you can have just one of the spectrum graph implementations remain on screen by using an instantaneous snapshot. Actually, this capability is of little or no use. After all, we need the periodogram, and not its aged snapshot. Therefore, let the screen blink. However, this mode is inconvenient for a real evaluation of the spectrum's changes, since the display is continuously changing. Because of this, let's select the **Scroll** mode (Fig. 2.10), which allows us to scroll the graphs vertically (top-down).

The horizontal axis still displays the frequency, the vertical axis serves to display the spectral function values, and the third, invisible axis, directed from some remote point towards us and downwards, is the time axis. As a result, the screen displays a quasi-3D figure composed from a set of multiple layers containing displays of the spectral function. This mode is more convenient for observing the change of the current spectrum, since we now have the graphs to compare.

However, this form of representation is also not quite convenient. After the display fills the whole vertical axis of the coordinate area, it will be very difficult to distinguish between specific sections of the spectrum.

The Cool Edit Pro software provides a more illustrative way of representing the periodogram (Fig. 2.11). Here, the horizontal axis is the time axis, the vertical axis is the frequency axis, and the spectral density is indicated by the color—white for the maximum level of the spectral function, black for the minimum level.

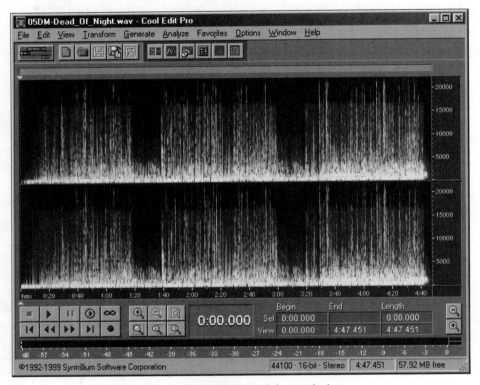

Fig. 2.11. Color display of the periodogram

Intermediate values of the spectrum are designated by other colors. Signal spectrums for the left and right channels are displayed separately.

Using the instantaneous spectrum analyzer of Cool Edit Pro will be covered in detail in *Section 14.1.*

2.5. Weight Functions

Now you are acquainted with the three different approaches to spectrum calculation, as well as their mathematical models. We will now discuss our investigation of spectral transformations. Once again, we'll consider the influence of time on the results of spectral analysis.

How do we calculate a single value on a spectrum graph? (For the moment, whether this is a current spectrum or periodogram is of no importance.) The answer is common knowledge—the calculation is performed using the formulas seen in (2.14) and (2.15). We hope that these formulas don't scare you. It's important to understand their mathematical meaning, so therefore let us explain in simple terms the concepts implied in these mathematical symbols.

First, we must select the frequency f_0. A real or virtual generator will create the sinusoid of this frequency and of the amplitude conditionally equal to the length unit. The signal being investigated is normalized by the amplitude. Starting with time t_0, with an increment of Δt (the smaller Δt, the better the result), at times t_0, t_1, t_2, t_3, ..., t_i, ..., t_N, the following operations are performed over this sinusoid and the signal being investigated:

❏ The sinusoid value is measured

❏ The signal value is measured

❏ The signal and sinusoid values are multiplied

❏ The product is added to the accumulated result

At some specific time, T_m, the process of measuring the spectrum at frequency f_0 ends. The sum is divided by the total number of measurements (N). The calculated result—$G(f_0)$—is recorded and, possibly, displayed as one of the points of the graph.

The process described above is illustrated in Fig. 2.12. Fig. 2.12a shows the signal under investigation, while Fig. 2.12b shows the sinusoid of frequency f_0. Fig. 2.12c shows the product of the signal under investigation and the appropriate values of the sinusoid, and Fig. 2.12d shows the cumulative sum. The last value of the sum is the non-normalized spectrum value G(f_0), which in our case is equal to 2.5. Dividing this value by the number of measurements (in our case 25), we'll get the spectrum function value (-0.1).

Next, the accumulated sum is reset to zero, the frequency value is changed by a value of Δf (and thus the new f_1 frequency value is selected), and the whole sequence of operations is repeated for frequency values f_0, f_1, f_2, ..., f_N, until the whole frequency range is covered.

The above-described procedure for calculating the spectral coefficient is the same thing as calculating a coherence function of the signal under investigation and the sinusoid of the specified frequency. To put it in other words, the calculation process of the spectral component allows us to determine the level of similarity between the signal being investigated and the standard (basic) signal (sinusoid, in our case). The whole process allows us to detect the proportion in which the sinusoid is contained in the signal under study.

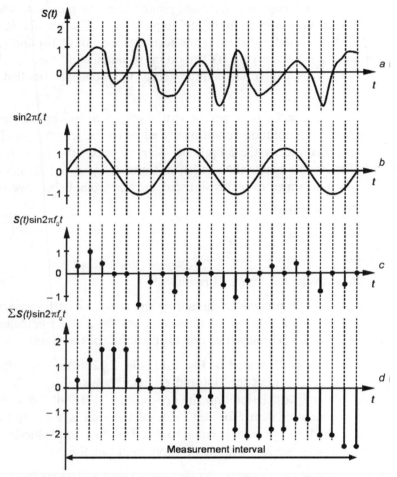

Fig. 2.12. An illustration of the process of spectral component calculation

If the signal being investigated was already recorded, and we have a digital spectrum analyzer capable of storing intermediate results for an indefinite period of time, the measurements of the current spectrum and/or periodogram can then be implemented using the procedure described above.

When the signal is being analyzed in real time, the situation becomes more complicated. Let's say that one spectrum component is already calculated. We must now change the sinusoid frequency and measure the next spectral component. However, the analyzed fragment of the signal is already in the past, and can't be reproduced. Therefore, the second spectral component will be calculated for the second signal fragment, and so on. The result will not represent the current spectrum. Rather, we'll get a set of separate spectral coefficients, not related to each other. Each of these spectral coefficients characterizes totally different signal fragments, which possibly are not interrelated at all. The result of such measurement is comparable to the following: instead of a detailed consideration of one work in a picture gallery, we see one composed from fragments taken from each picture presented in an exhibition.

Actually, spectral analysis can be performed using a different approach, by calculating the set of spectral functions for different frequencies simultaneously. However, this will require very complex devices.

Finally, we need ask only one more question: is the above described mathematical algorithm an adequate representation of the spectral analysis performed by real spectral analyzers and the one performed by the human ears and brain? The answer is predictable: not quite.

The main problem is that the device that analyzes the spectrum and a human being both have a finite memory. This means that past events and details of the process's evolution are gradually erased from memory. The more time that has elapsed since the measurements of the signal under analysis were taken, the less will be their effect on the accumulated sum of the measurement's products, which in turn determines the value of the spectral coefficient.

The actual properties of the analyzer's memory are taken into account using weight functions. A weight function describes the dependence of the contribution of preceding measurements of the studied signal in the calculated spectrum for the time elapsed. An illustrative representation of the weight function is in the form of a so-called spectrum window.

The spectral analysis that we discussed before corresponds to a rectangular spectral window (Fig. 2.13a).

In this case, the weight function is equal to 1 within the limits of the spectrum window. Outside this range, the weight function is equal to 0. When analyzing the current spectrum, the starting point of the spectrum window coincides with the starting point of the time measurement, while the end of this window is equal to the current time. The current time moves forward, and the right boundary of the spectral window shifts rightwards. Thus, the width of the spectral window changes with time.

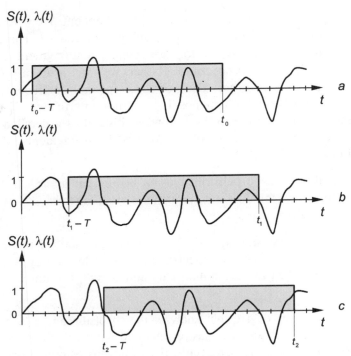

Fig. 2.13. Rectangular spectrum window usage when calculating the current spectrum

When calculating the periodogram, a spectral window of constant width shifts rightwards along the time axis (Fig. 2.13*b*, 2.13*c*).

The exponential weight function reflects the actual nature of spectral analysis more adequately. The spectral window corresponding to this weight function is shown in Fig. 2.14.

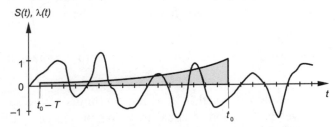

Fig. 2.14. Exponential spectrum window in the course of periodogram calculation

In many respects, the exponential and sinusoid functions can be considered "magic" functions. Most real-world oscillation processes can be described by an exponential function when they arise or fade, and by a sinusoid during the stage of their steady existence. For example, the oscillations in an oscillator used as a basis for real-world spectrum analyzers fade according to exponential law. This means that it is the exponential function that reflects the law used to start the oscillations in that circuit, according to which the oscillator "forgets" the value of the spectral component. The information on past events stored in the human memory is also erased according to exponential law.

Rectangular and exponential spectral windows are the ones most frequently used for calculating the spectrum. The rectangular window is the ideal analyzer with an infinite memory, while the exponential window is more appropriate for reflecting the properties of the human brain and real spectrum analyzers based on resonance filters. On the other hand, there are other weight functions, such as the Hamming function, the Bartelett function, or the Parsen function. By the way, the exponential spectral window is also widely known as the Tukey window.

It is rather difficult to provide specific recommendations on the usage of a specific weight function for spectral analysis of acoustic signals (with the single exception of the exponential function, the usefulness of which can't be underestimated). The only tip that can be provided is as follows: it is necessary to choose a single weight function. If you do so, you can be sure that the difference in the measurement results are due to the difference in the signal properties rather than to the differences in the calculation methods. When you need to solve several problems by analyzing the same signal, it is also advisable to select the same weight function. Spectral analysis and synthesis of filters are examples of such tasks.

2.6. Discrete Signals and Discrete Fourier Transform

Up until now, when discussing the nature of spectral representations, we suggested that the signal has an analog nature, i.e., that the signal can be described by a continuous function.

Actually, the computer is capable of processing only digital signals, which are discrete in time and quantized. For this reason, an analog signal must be processed using the analog-to-digit conversion. After performing the conversion, all the required operations on the signal are performed in digital form (the list of operations includes noise suppression, dynamic processing, filtration, sound effects, mounting, etc). To output a digital recording to the acoustic system and finally to the speaker—which, by its nature, is an analogous element—one must perform a reverse, digit-to-analog conversion.

An analog signal $s(t)$ is transformed to a discrete signal using the amplitude-pulse element that reacts to the discrete values of the input signal separated by equal time intervals at time points set to $t = nT$, where $n = 0, 1, 2, 3, ...$

Upon the output of the element performing the conversion, we'll get a sequence of the following sets: $s(nT) \cong s(t)\,|_{t=nT}$.

In contrast to this, reconstructing the analog signal $s(t)$ by its discrete representation—the sequence of $s(nT)$ sets—is done using various interpolation procedures.

Provided that the conditions formulated by the Nyquist theorem are satisfied, the operations of discretization conversion and analog signal reconstruction are mutually reversible.

In the course of working with analog-to-digital conversion, the signal is quantized and sampled. As a result, a signal that continuously changes with time is replaced by a set of discrete measurements, normally taken using equal time intervals. Intuitively, it is obvious that if the time intervals are too long, the information might be lost in the course of this conversion. For example, important signal changes might be "omitted" by the digitizer, especially if they take place during moments when no measurements are taken. Consequently, the measurement frequency must be the maximum possible. The only limitation is the converter speed. Furthermore, the more measurements are performed per time unit, the larger the memory required to store this information.

The problem of finding a reasonable compromise between the measurement frequency and the resource usage of the information transformation and transmission channels arose long before the arrival of the first sound cards. As a result of investigations, scientists have formulated a rule known as the Nyquist theorem.

If we try to explain these things in simple language, without formulas or scientific terms such as "a system of orthogonal functions", the basic idea behind the Nyquist theorem can be formulated as follows. A signal represented by a sequence of discrete measurements can be transformed back to the source (continuous) form without information loss only if the interval between two adjacent measurements doesn't exceed half of the period of the highest frequency oscillation contained within the signal spectrum.

Consequently, only the signal whose spectrum is limited by a certain frequency—F_{max}—can be restored without distortion. Theoretically, all real signals have infinite spectrums. To avoid signal deviation in the course of digitization, the signal is first supplied to the filter that suppresses all frequencies that exceed the predefined F_{max} value, and only then is the signal digitized. According to the Nyquist theorem, the F_d frequency that must be used for measurements is $F_d = 2F_{max}$.

Now let us proceed with a more strict formulation of the theorem.

If the analog signal $s(t)$ has a finite spectrum $G_a(\omega)$, i.e., one that satisfies the following condition: $G_a(\omega) = 0$ when $\omega > \omega_{max}$ (an approximate representation of the spectrum modulus is shown in Fig. 2.15a), then such a signal can be unambiguously represented by a sequence of samples $s(nT)$, $n = 0, 1, 2, 3$, for $T = 2\pi/\omega_s$, where $\omega_s \geq 2\omega_{max}$.

And:

$$s(t) = \sum_{n=-\infty}^{\infty} s(nT) \frac{\sin \omega_{max}(t - nT)}{\omega_{max}(t - nT)} \qquad (2.17)$$

Consequently, the signal $s(t)$ can be obtained if the sequence $s(nT)$ is transmitted via an ideal analog low-frequency filter (which physically can't be implemented) with the $\omega_c = \pi/T$ cutoff frequency and with the $K(\omega) = T$ amplitude-frequency response within the bandwidth.

The spectrum $G(\omega)$ of the $s(nT)$ sequence is equal (except for the constant multiplier $1/T$) to the sum of the $G_a(\omega)$ spectrums of the respective $s(t)$ signal shifted along the frequency axis by all possible frequency values—multiples of the sampling frequency of $\omega_s = 2\pi/T$,

$$G(\omega) = \frac{1}{T} \sum_{k=-\infty}^{\infty} G_a(\omega + k\omega_s) \qquad (2.18)$$

Figs. 2.15b and 2.15c show the conventional representation of the $G(\omega)$ spectrum modulus of the discrete signal $s(nT)$ for cases when $\omega_s \geq 2\omega_{max}$ and $\omega_s < 2\omega_{max}$, respectively.

In the first case, the spectrum of the discrete signal coincides with the initial signal spectrum within the $\omega < \omega_{max}$ frequency range. In the second case, spectrum overlapping takes place, and here the spectrum of the digitized signal doesn't coincide with the spectrum of the initial analog signal in the $\omega < \omega_{max}$ frequency range. This phenomenon is known as aliasing.

Fig. 2.15d shows an example of a distorted signal restored using a filtration method after its digitization using a frequency lower than the one recommended by the Nyquist theorem. The consequences of spectrum overlapping, due either to an incorrectly selected digitization frequency or to the penetration of the unfiltered high-frequency components of the signal into the channel, as well as from the influence of the interference, will be considered in *Section 22.2.4*.

One particularly interesting problem was posed by one of the discussion forum participants at the site of the *Musical PC* project.

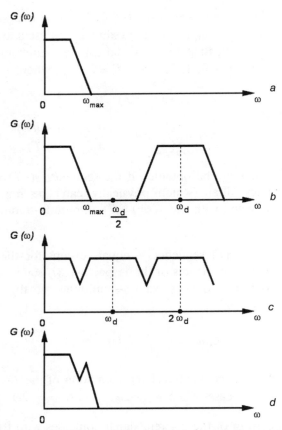

Fig. 2.15. Spectrum of the initial analog signal (*a*), signal spectra after digitization using different frequencies (*b*, *c*), and spectrum of the signal restored after digitization with a lowered frequency (*d*)

This participant provided an example that seemed to be a paradox at first glance. Let's say we select a sampling frequency exactly equal to the doubled upper frequency limit of the spectrum, F_{max}. Each spectrum component, including the one of the F_{max} frequency, is a sinusoid. If measurements are taken exactly at the moments when this sinusoid intersects the zero level, the result of each measurement will be exactly equal to zero. The signal reconstructed using this series of zero-level measurements will also be equal to zero. However, the initial component of the signal that we are trying to reconstruct is a sinusoid. Does this mean that the Nyquist theorem is wrong?

Actually, this example doesn't contain a paradox at all. As a matter of fact, the Nyquist theorem is true only for the signals that are infinite in time and have a limited continuous spectrum. In this case, the oscillation frequency at exactly the upper limit of the frequency represents an infinitely small value (the energy of an infinitely large number of infinitely small components is a finite value).

The signal selected for the above mentioned example can't be considered as such. This signal (sinusoid) has discrete spectrum (with a single spectrum component). The theory states that in such a case, the selection of measurement instances in relation to the oscillation zero points takes on a significant value.

For example, to exclude the particular situation described above, the selected sampling frequency must be somewhat higher than the doubled maximum frequency within the signal spectrum. In this case, even if one of the measurements coincides with the sinusoid zero, other instances will miss zero points. The next coincidence of the measurement and sinusoid zero-crossing will take place after the time period equal to the product of the oscillation periods multiplied by the sampling frequency and the upper boundary frequency of the signal spectrum.

Say we have a periodic sequence—$s(nT)$—with the period NT (i.e., the period contains N measurements). Mathematically, this condition can be written as $s(nT) = s(nT + mNT)$, where m is an integer. The Discrete Fourier Transform (DFT) represents two mutually unambiguous transforms:

$$G(k) = G(k\Omega) = \sum_{n=0}^{N-1} s(nT)e^{-jkn\Omega T}, \quad k = 0, 1, \ldots N-1 \qquad (2.19)$$

$$s(n) = s(nT) = \frac{1}{N}\sum_{k=0}^{N-1} G(k\Omega)e^{jk\Omega T}, \quad n = 0, 1, \ldots N-1, \qquad (2.20)$$

where $\Omega = 2\pi/(NT)$ is the fundamental transform frequency. The formula in (2.19) defines direct DFT, while (2.20) corresponds to the reverse DFT.

Discrete Fourier Transform $G(k)$, similar to the $s(n)$ sequence, is a periodic function of k with period N.

However, DFT can also be used to represent the $s(nT)$ sequence of finite length N, defined for $n = 0, 1, 2, 3, \ldots, N-1$, and equal to zero outside the interval of $[0, N-1]$.

2.7. Fast Fourier Transform

From the formula in (2.19) it is obvious that, in order to calculate the Discrete Fourier Transform of a sequence comprising N elements, it is necessary to complete N^2 operations on complex numbers. If the arrays of the numeric values to be processed have lengths on the order of thousands or more, this algorithm of discrete spectral analysis is quite difficult to use (especially in real-time mode). The Fast Fourier Transform provides a workaround for this situation. It allows a significant reduction in the operations to be completed, thanks to the fact that the processing of the input array is reduced to finding the DFT of arrays with a smaller number of elements. The distinguishing feature of the FFT method is the fact that the number of measurements equals an integer power of two ($N = 2^p$, where p is an integer). This is due to the fact that one of the operations comprising the FFT algorithm is the successive division of the FFT calculation interval by two. Consequently, an accurate calculation of the FFT is possible only for cases when the number of measurements within a signal is equal to 2, 4, 8, 16, 32, 64, 2^p. If this condition is not satisfied, it is necessary to complement the signal with a specific number of non-zero measurements. For example, in order to accomplish the FFT, a signal containing 60 significant measurements must be complemented with four non-zero measurements. Obviously, complementing the signal with additional measurements is equal to changing the signal, which in turn results in introducing additional spectrum calculation error. Normally, however, this error is not very significant and, taking the significant increase of the calculation speed into account, it can be neglected.

Let us divide the input sequence $\{s_n\}$ into two parts, with even and odd index values: $\{s_n\}_{even} = \{s_{2n}\}$ and $\{s_n\}_{odd} = \{s_{2n+1}\}$, where $n = 0, 1, 2, ..., N/2-1$. We will represent the kth index of the FFT as follows:

$$G(k) = \frac{1}{N} \sum_{n=0}^{N/2-1} (s_{2n} e^{-j\frac{4\pi kn}{N}} + s_{2n+1} e^{-j\frac{2\pi k(2n+1)}{N}}) =$$

$$= \frac{1}{N} \left(\sum_{n=0}^{N/2-1} s_{2n} e^{-j\frac{2\pi kn}{N/2}} + e^{-j\frac{2\pi kn}{N}} \sum_{n=0}^{N/2-1} s_{2n} e^{-j\frac{2\pi kn}{N/2}} \right) \qquad (2.21)$$

From the expression in (2.21), it is obvious that the first part of the DFT coefficients of the signal with indexes from 0 to $N/2-1$ can be expressed via the DFT coefficients of the two partial sequences:

$$G(k) = G_{even}(k) + e^{-j\frac{2\pi k}{N}} G_{odd}(k), \qquad (2.22)$$

where $k = 0, 1, 2, ..., N/2-1$.

Considering that the sequences of coefficients related to the even and odd parts of the input array are periodic functions with a period of $N/2$, we'll get:

$$G_{even}(k) = G_{even}(k + N/2), \quad G_{odd}(k) = G_{odd}(k + N/2) \qquad (2.23)$$

The multiplier included into the formula in (2.22), for $n \geq N/2$, can be transformed as follows:

$$e^{-j\frac{2\pi(N/2+k)}{N}} = e^{-j\pi}e^{-j\frac{2\pi k}{N}} = -e^{-j\frac{2\pi k}{N}} \tag{2.24}$$

Using this, we can obtain the expression for the second part of the set of DFT coefficients:

$$G(N/2 + k) = G_{even}(k) + e^{-j\frac{2\pi k}{N}}G_{odd}(k) , \tag{2.25}$$

where $k = 0, 1, 2, ..., N/2-1$.

Formulas (2.22) and (2.25) serve as a basis for the implementation of the FFT algorithm.

Subsequent calculations are performed using an iterative method: even and odd sequences are once again divided into two parts. The process continues until we get a sequence consisting of a single element. The DFT of this element coincides with the element itself.

The number of operations required to calculate the FFT is evaluated as $N\log_2 N$. This algorithm is truly faster than the DFT, requiring N^2 operations to be completed.

Implementation of FFT-based filters included with the Cool Edit Pro software will be covered in detail in *Section 3.4.*

2.8. More on Digital-to-Analog and Analog-to-Digital Conversion

The CD standard specifies the sampling frequency as 44.1 kHz. For digital tape recorders, the standard sampling frequency is 48 kHz. Sound cards are usually are able to function in a wide range of sampling frequencies.

Practically all modern sound cards support 16-bit sound representation with sampling frequencies of 44.1 kHz and 48 kHz. More expensive professional sound cards support 24-bit sound representation with a sampling frequency of 96 kHz.

The more significant digits supported by the digital-to-analog or analog-to-digital converters, the better. As a matter of fact, any continuous (analog) signal is converted to a digital one with some conversion error. The fewer quantization levels (i.e., the larger the interval between valid values of the digitized signal) the larger this error will be. The number of quantization levels, in turn, depends on the number of digits supported by digital-to-analog or analog-to-digital converters. Errors resulting from substituting the analog signal with a sequence of measurements quantized by level can be considered as distortions caused by interference. This interference is known as *quantization noise*.

Usually, the quantization noise is represented as the difference between respective values of the real signal and a signal quantized by level (Fig. 2.16*a*, *b*).

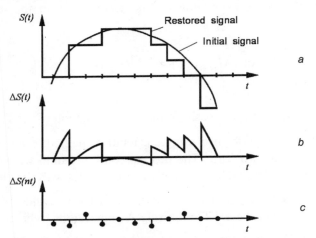

Fig. 2.16. An illustration of the signal quantization process (zero-order interpolation)

Such a representation is not quite correct.

Fig. 2.16*a* doesn't actually represent a digitized signal. The graduated line shown in this illustration actually represents the analog signal restored from the digital one using zero-order interpolation. If we subtract this graduated line from the source signal, a very strange and ugly-looking line will be obtained as a result (Fig. 2.16*b*). Some authors mistakenly state that this line represents the quantization noise. This approach is erroneous. First, why must the digital signal be replaced by continuous steps and not by a tilted section of a straight line or by sections of curves? Furthermore, to perform a correct evaluation, we must compare continuous and discrete signals only at the instances that correspond to the discrete measurements. Therefore, the quantization noise must also be represented as a sequence of discrete measurements (Fig. 2.16*c*).

In theoretical work, it is common to use the delta-function—a pulse of infinitely small duration and infinitely large amplitude—for representing discrete signals. The area of a delta-function is equal to 1. Such a function is assuredly an abstraction that doesn't exist in reality. In practice, measurements are replaced by rectangular pulses of small duration.

If we take a sequence of time-shifted measurement functions and multiply it by the ordinates of the curve corresponding to the analog signal, we'll get a time-sampled signal that can be represented as shown in Fig. 2.16c. In our case, this signal corresponds to the quantization noise represented by discrete measurements.

Ideal filters that allow you to restore the exact analog signal by its discrete values don't exist. However, modern analog-to-digital converters use methods that enable you to minimize conversion errors that result from the non-ideal nature of the conversion.

Fig. 2.17a shows the initial analog signal and the signal restored from the digital one using the interpolation process of the 1st order (the measurements are connected by sections of a straight line).

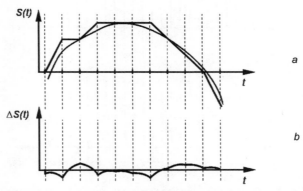

Fig. 2.17. An illustration of the signal digitization process (using 1st order interpolation)

From this illustration, it is obvious that the difference between the initial and the restored signals (Fig. 2.17b) is significantly less than when zero-order interpolation was used (see Fig. 2.16a). Notice that modern digital-to-analog converters use much more advanced algorithms to restore analog signals.

It is obvious that when performing digital-to-analog conversion, digital quantization noise (Fig. 2.16c), is transformed to a particular analog noise. The type of this noise oscillation depends on the specific analog-to-digital converter. However, its level will be significantly lower than the level of the noise process shown in Fig. 2.16b.

A common opinion widely accepted by fans of analog sound claims that "the digitization result is significantly different from the source signal". But this is mainly based on an inadequate representation of the quantization noise (see Fig. 2.16b).

From Fig. 2.18, it is evident that when a signal exceeds the uppermost quantization level ("upper" quantum), and when a signal value drops below the lowermost quantization level ("lower" quantum) (i.e., if the signal is limited) the signal will be distorted. These distortions might be much more significant than the quantization noise.

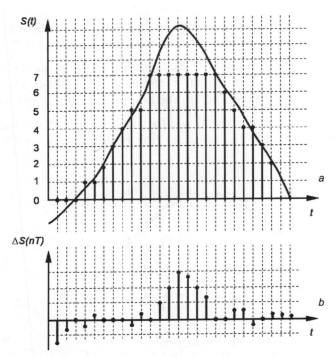

Fig. 2.18. Signal quantization and clipping distortions

To eliminate distortions of this type, the dynamic ranges of the signal and analog-to-digital converter must correspond to each other: signal values must reside between quantization levels corresponding to the lower and upper quantums.

When recording sound from external sound sources, this can be achieved using level regulation. Besides this, dynamic range compression is also implemented, which will be covered in detail later.

Sound editors provide for signal amplitude normalization. After applying this procedure, the lowest level of the signal will become equal to the upper level of the lower quantum, and the maximum value will become equal to the lower level of the upper quantum (in Fig. 2.18, these are represented by the numbers 1 and 6). Thus, the signal will be protected from clipping from below and from above by intervals one quantum wide. Obviously, if the amplitude was already limited during recording, normalization will not prevent the signal from being distorted. It is also not recommended that you use normalization when representing a sound with 16 or less bits.

For a normalized signal, the relative value of the maximum quantization error is equal to $1/N$, where N is the number of quantization levels. The same value, represented in logarithmic units (dB), is used to evaluate the level of the analog-to-digital converter's quantization noise of the sound card. The quantization noise level is determined using the following formula: $\Delta = 20 \lg(1/N)$. For a 3-digit analog-to-digital converter (see Fig. 2.18), $N = 8$, and $D = -18$ dB; for an 8-bit converter, $N = 256$, $\Delta = -48$ dB; for a 16-bit converter, $N = 65,536$, $\Delta = -96$ dB; for an 18-bit converter, $N = 262,144$, $\Delta = -108$ dB; and for a 20-bit converter, $N = 1,648,576$, $\Delta = -120$ dB.

The values provided above show that as the number of digits supported by the analog-to-digital converter grows, the quantization noise decreases. 16-bit signal representation, which at the moment is widely used for sound recording, is considered to be acceptable for digital sound. From the quantization noise elimination point of view, further increase of supported number of bits for the analog-to-digital converters doesn't make sense, since the level of noises of other origin (for example, heat noises, pulse interference generated by the computer circuitry and propagating either by the power circuits or as electromagnetic radiation, etc.) in any case proves to be significantly higher than -96 dB.

However, the increase of the bits supported by analog-to-digital converters is due to another factor—namely, the necessity of increasing its dynamic range. We have already discussed the dynamic range of the sound. The dynamic range of a specific sound processing device can be determined using the following expression: $D = 20 \lg(S_{max}/S_{min})$, where S_{max} and S_{min} are the maximum and minimum values of the level of the signal that can be digitized without distortions or information loss. You have probably already guessed that the minimum value of the signal can't be less than the voltage corresponding to a single quantum, and the maximum level can't exceed the value of the voltage corresponding to N quantums. Because of this, the expression for the dynamic range of the analog-to-digital converter of the sound card will look as follows: $D = 20\lg(N)$, since we can say that $S_{max} = kN$, and $S_{min} = k1$, where k is some constant factor that takes into account the correlation between electric values (such as current or voltage) and quantization level numbers. Comparing the values of Δ and D, we can see that when supporting the same number of bits, these values will differ only in their sign. Because of this, the dynamic range for a 16-bit analog-to-digital converter is 96 dB, for an 18-bit converter—108 dB, and for a 20-bit converter—120 dB. In other words, when recording sounds produced by a sound source with a dynamic range of 120 dB, a 20-bit analog-to-digital converter is required. If a 16-bit converter is used instead, the dynamic range of the sound must be compressed by 24 dB: from 120 to 96 dB.

There are specialized methods and devices for compressing the dynamic range of the sound, and we will discuss them later. However, the operations they perform over the sound (however you soften the wording) still distort the sound. Therefore, it is important to use an analog-to-digital converter that supports the maximum possible number of bits when performing sound quantization. Owners of 16-bit sound cards have no particular reason to be upset, since the dynamic ranges of most sound sources correspond to the dynamic range of such sound cards. Besides which, sound representation with more than 16 bits (24, 32, or even more) is mainly used during the sound processing stage. This data redundancy allows you to minimize errors that accumulate in the course of sound processing. The final products are implemented using 16-bit CD Digital Audio format. According to the most common predictions, more advanced formats are not going to replace CD-DA in the near future.

It is also necessary to mention one common error that even professional sound engineers often make. They claim the following: "The behavior of the restored signal in intervals between measurements is indefinite, and the signal may change randomly". However, when saying so, they forget that the spectrum of the analog signal subject to the digital-to-analog conversion must necessarily be limited. Because of this, when performing analog-to-digital conversion, the signal values between discrete measurements can't be random, and can be restored unambiguously using the measured values.

Quite often, sound card vendors try to prove the advantages of their product by emphasizing such facts as the presence of digital input and/or output. Actually, if the sound card has digital output, where signals are supplied in digital rather than analog form (after digit-to-analog conversion) we can decrease distortions that occur due to additional conversions during subsequent digital processing of the signal outside the sound card.

According to the concept of the virtual sound recording studio, all sound processing must be performed using only one PC. This very PC provides us with the final product—the CD. A digital-to-analog converter of professional quality is required only for monitoring, i.e., to hear the events taking place in the virtual studio. The presence of digital output in the virtual studio is beneficial when it is necessary to make a DAT recording or to use the high-quality acoustic monitors provided with digital input.

The presence of digital input in the virtual studio might be important if you are not satisfied with the quality of the analog-to-digital converter built into the sound card, and you need to use an external analog-to-digital converter of higher quality. Other than this, digital input might be useful when you need to convert a recording from DAT to PC.

There are many interfaces for transferring digital sound. The most common sound cards provide the S/PDIF interface (Sony/Philips Digital Interface Format). However, even within the range of this single format, the interface can be implemented using different physical connectors—electric or optical.

Some other problems of digital-to-analog/analog-to-digital conversion will be covered in more detail in *Chapter 21*, which is entirely dedicated to mastering—the final stage of processing a recording before its release.

2.9. Sampling

Sampling is recording of samples of a specific musical instrument. Sampling is the basis of wave synthesis of musical sounds. Hardware or software that use this method are known as samplers.

In contrast to Frequency Modulation synthesis (FM synthesis), where sounds are derived from processing the simplest standard oscillations in various ways, wave synthesis is based on previously recorded sounds of traditional musical instruments, or the sounds accompanying various processes that take place in nature or are of human invention. You can do anything you like with the samples. For example, you can leave them as they are, and the sampler will give sounds practically indistinguishable from the source sounds. On the other hand, samples can be modulated, filtered, processed by special effects, etc. Doing this, you can produce some fantastic, unearthly sounds.

In general, a sample is no more than a sequence of digital measurements stored in the synthesizer's memory and produced as a result of analog-to-digital conversion of the sounds produced by the musical instrument.

The technology that enables you to bind samples to specific keys or groups of keys on the MIDI keyboard is known as multisampling. The concept of this technology can be illustrated graphically, as shown in Fig. 2.19.

The timbre of real instruments depends on the sound pitch. The spectral characteristic of the sound changes its shape depending on the frequency. For example, the timbre of the sound produced by certain piano keys will be somewhat different even from the sound produced by neighboring keys, to say nothing of more distant keys—the ones located at the leftmost and rightmost ends of the keyboard. If we didn't have to deal with the problem of memory usage, it would be possible to record the sound of the musical instrument for each note, and then bind each of the derived samples to a specific key on the MIDI keyboard. This approach, however, would require quite a large amount of memory to store the sound bank.

Theoretically, the GigaStudio software sampler is capable of implementing such an approach. Actually, the Giga prefix in the name of this software package emphasizes this fact, since the sample banks can consume Gigabytes of storage space. However, this approach is not always justified, and because of this, the memory stores samples for just certain notes rather than for each one. Here, the change of the sound pitch is achieved by changing the speed of the sample reproduction. Groups of keys for which the samples are recorded are selected in such a way as to make the timbre variations of the real instrument's sounds indistinguishable to the naked ear. This provides for a significant reduction in memory consumption, while giving quality approaching live sound.

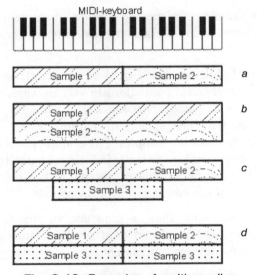

Fig. 2.19. Examples of multisampling

To get various notes, samples are played at different speeds, and in so doing, their length (the sample duration or the period of its cyclic reproduction) varies. The note corresponding to the sound reproduction at the original speed (when the sampling frequency at replay is the same as it was during recording) is known as the principal note.

If you only use a small number of samples distributed by the MIDI keyboard, the effect of the sample duration change will be noticeable. Furthermore, when the sample is replayed at a speed significantly lower than the one at which it was recorded, the high-frequency components that must be present in the timbre of any instrument (even bass ones) will disappear from it.

Let's provide a simple example. Let's say that a sample was written for the C note of the fifth MIDI octave (octave numbering starts from zero) with a digitization frequency of 44.1 kHz. This means that the sound spectrum for this note can potentially span up to 44.1/2=22.05 kHz (according to the Nyquist theorem). To obtain the C note of the fourth octave, the synthesizer must reproduce this sample at a speed two times lower than the one at which the sample was recorded, i.e., with a sampling frequency of 22.05 kHz. According to the Nyquist theorem, 22.05/2=11.025 kHz, which is the maximum frequency of the sound signal. This means that a frequency range area of 11.025 kHz will be missing, i.e., the sound spectrum will be clipped in the high-frequency range by a value of 11.025 kHz.

To minimize these undesirable effects, it is sufficient to distribute two or three samples per octave.

Attempting to use a home studio to create your own quality instrument, such as an acoustic guitar, will probably fail. For such purposes, you'd need a special laboratory equipped with professional instruments. Therefore, it is advisable to use the sound banks created by professionals as the "standard" instruments.

There is another important feature of multisampling. By binding samples of different instruments to specific groups of keys, you can produce the sounds of several instruments on the same MIDI keyboard simultaneously. For example, you can create a double bass for the left hand, and a flute for the right hand. This means that you can use the same MIDI channel for managing several instruments simultaneously. However, in this case the sound ranges of these instruments will be narrowed, since a MIDI keyboard has only 128 keys. Despite this fact, you must make do, especially when considering the fact that to manage computer-based analogues of "live" instruments such as a piano, you by no means need to use all 128 MIDI keys.

Musical instruments (such as the double bass and flute in our example) can be replaced by special effects—for instance, by different phrases articulated by human beings or sounds produced by various phenomena or technical objects.

Another important concept related to samples is multilayering—a technology allowing for simultaneous reproduction, or using various samples to make the sound of a single instrument. As shown in Fig. 2.19b, the "layers" in this case are samples that reside as if they were situated one on top of the other.

Let us discuss the usage of this technology. The first idea to put forth is the capability of creating complex timbres continuously changing with time. Multilayering can be used for creating stereo instruments for samplers that don't support stereophonic samples. Multilayering provides the ability to work around this limitation. If you have WAV files in 16-bit stereo format at your disposal, it is sufficient to divide each file into two 16-bit mono samples and use the resulting samples in a single instrument. Now it only remains to move the samples to different sides of the panorama: move the sample that previously corresponded to the left channel of the stereophonic WAV file to the leftmost position, and the sample corresponding to the right channel to the rightmost position.

Besides this, multilayering is generally used for a more precise reproduction of the particularities of the sounds of the live instruments, depending on the force used to press the keys. When the key is pressed using some force, specific sample is reproduced, and when the key is pressed with a different force, another sample will be heard.

An example of simultaneously using multisampling and multilayering is provided in Fig. 2.19*c*.

The SoundFont 2 and DLS 2 specifications provide "native" support for multisampling and multilayering. As for the GigaStudio sample bank format (*Chapters 20, 21*), it also implements multisampling and multilayering but with some limitations: multisampling dominates multilayering. The MIDI keyboard is divided into zones, and multilayering is supported only within those zones. The boundaries of multisamples and layers always coincide, and correspond to the zone boundaries. However, there is a simple workaround for this limitation: you can use the same samples within different zones. For example, in Fig. 2.19*d*, the second logical layer actually consists of a single sample (Sample 3).

In *Chapter 22*, we'll look at the NN-19 sampler, which is one of the virtual devices of the Reason program. NN-19 supports only multisampling. The samples, however, may be stereophonic.

As was already mentioned, changing the tone pitch of the samples being reproduced is implemented in samplers by changing the speed at which the samples are played. At first glance, everything is clear. However, this is very hard to do in practice. Let's say, for example, that the sampler polyphony comprises 64 voices, which means that 64 samples can be reproduced simultaneously. Each sample can be reproduced at its own speed. However, the sampler output must produce a single data flow with the same fixed sampling frequency. How can we join all samples that must be reproduced at different speeds within a single digital data flow?

Let us consider this problem using an example. Say the speed of data flow at the sampler output corresponds to a sampling frequency of 48 kHz. Assume that we have a sample with a sampling frequency that equals 48 kHz as well, and that this sample is the standard for the sound of the specified note. Suppose it is necessary to decrease the tone of this sample by four half-tones. To achieve this, we'll have to reproduce this sample at a lowered speed, 2/3 of the initial sampling frequency. Fig. 2.20 shows the sound measurements stored in the source sample and reproduced at a lowered speed. The crosses mark the instances on the time axis that correspond to the sound measurements at the sampler output.

Some measurements of the sampler output coincide with measurements of the "slowed" sample, while other measurements don't. To get the values of the sound measurements for the sampler output, it is necessary to create a virtual digital-to-analog/analog-to-digital converter: we must restore the values of the analog signal for any point on the time axis by the available measurements of the sample (in Fig.2.20, this signal is shown by a thin line) and select the values of the analog signal for the time instances that correspond to the measurement of the sampler output. This means that we need to be able to convert the sampling frequency of the source sample arbitrarily, "on the fly". This problem is solved using interpolation methods. Based on the available sound measurements, we can try to calculate the coefficients of the interpolation polynomials of the specified power and, knowing these coefficients, calculate the values of these polynomials in points located between the initial measurements. In practice, however, the power of the polynomials is finite, and the number of sound measurements is quite large. How shall we "weld" the analog signal restored using the calculations to the junction points of the interpolation curves? There are several methods of interpolation that allow us to avoid the junction problem, such as spline interpolation. In any case, virtual Digital-to-Analog/Analog-to-Digital conversions must be performed at the highest possible quality level. For example, one of the most aggressively promoted advantages of the SB Live! Sound card is their "copyright protected, 8-point interpolation". Some people might be surprised: "How can they copyright a well-known interpolation method?" The idea of 8-point interpolation, of course, can't be protected by a copyright. However, a specific implementation certainly can. By the way, most software samplers use interpolation of the first order, i.e., using only two points. Improvement of the interpolation quality of software samplers is for the moment impossible because of the limited capabilities of modern processors and, probably, because of the lack of creative ideas.

Fig. 2.20. An illustration of sample tone conversion

Fans of software samplers may object that some samplers, such as Gigastudio, enable you to store one or even more samples for each note, and therefore interpolation is no longer required, since it is not necessary to change the reproduction speed of these samples. Actually, however, such a necessity almost always exists, if just to provide the capability of implementing such effects as frequency vibrato or Pitch Bend.

As you have seen from all this, the sampler is quite a complex device. Modern samplers are actually a hybrid of a synthesizer and a multichannel digital tape recorder capable of reproducing samples at different speeds. Samples in such a synthesizer are used as oscillators for generating signals of the sound's frequency. A sample reproduced with a specified speed may be subject to various types of real-time processing, such as low-frequency modulation using LFO generators and envelope generators. LFO generators can modulate the oscillator signal both by amplitude (tremolo) and by frequency (vibrato). Envelope generators are used to provide the sample with a shape that changes with time. Envelope generators produce a signal whose level slowly changes with time, starting from the instant that the MIDI key is pressed. During the attack phase, the signal level is usually rapidly growing; then the decay phase starts, after which the signal is supported at the specified level (Sustain) until the MIDI key is released. After that, the release phase starts, during which the signal level of the envelope generator output returns to its initial state. Envelope generator phases are shown in Fig. 2.21.

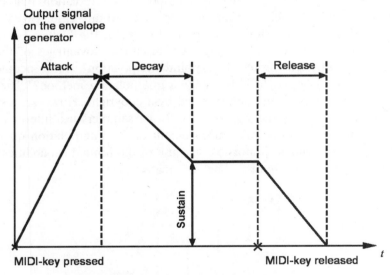

Fig. 2.21. Phases of the envelope generator

Specific implementations of envelope generators can have more phases. The phases listed above and designated by the letters ADSR are present in all generators. Like LFO generators, envelope generators can modulate a signal both by frequency and by amplitude. Besides which, samplers provide filters. These are usually low-frequency filters with a resonance frequency corresponding to the cutoff frequency. All software samplers considered in this book support several types of filters. LFO and envelope generators can manage the main filter parameters (such as cutoff frequency and Q-factor), thus providing the capability of producing various effects of the "wow-wow" type.

Chapter 3: Filtering

If we try to provide a definition for the term "filtering" at these, the earliest stages of discussion, it might look approximately as follows: *filtering*—the procedure of electric signal processing by frequency-selecting devices in order to modify the spectral composition (timbre) of the signal. Such processing might be required to achieve the following purposes:

❏ Amplitude-frequency correction of the signal (amplification or attenuation of specific frequency components)

❏ Total suppression of the signal spectrum or noises within a specific frequency band

For example, if the speaker, the acoustic system, or some other element of the sound channel has an uneven amplitude-frequency response, this non-uniformity can be smoothed using filters. If the results of the spectral analysis show that the interference energy is mainly concentrated within a specific frequency band, and the valid signal energy in that frequency band is rather low, it is possible to suppress all oscillations within that frequency range by filtering.

There are lots of various filtration devices: standalone correction and formant filters, devices for sound separation into several channels according to the frequency (crossovers), double-band and multiple-band regulators (equalizers), presence filters, etc.

Filters are physically implemented either based on oscillatory units consisting of inductors and capacitors, or based on their analogues, also known as gyrators, which are operational amplifiers to which predefined feedback is applied.

Spectral analysis serves as a basis for filters implemented programmatically in sound editors. As was shown in *Chapter 2*, each real signal can be represented as a set of coefficients of series decomposition by harmonic (sinusoidal) functions. Filtering is reduced to multiplication of the spectral coefficients by the corresponding values of the filter transfer function. If the spectrum is represented in complex form, the signal is described by a set of amplitude and phase spectra (AS and PS), while the filters can be described by amplitude-frequency and phase-frequency response. An amplitude-frequency response is the dependence of the filter transfer factor on frequency. The phase-frequency response reflects the frequency dependence of the phase shift of the output signal in relation to the input signal. Here, then, filtering is equivalent to the multiplication of the amplitude response by the amplitude-frequency response and the algebraic addition of the phase response to the phase-frequency response.

Classic spectral analysis consumes a large amount of processor time, and therefore is practically unrealizable under real-time conditions if the number of signal measurements is significant. To decrease the time required for spectral analysis of a discrete signal, special algorithms are implemented that take into account relationships between different signal measurements and try to eliminate repetitive operations. Fast Fourier Transform (FFT), examined in *Section 2.7*, is one such algorithm.

One of the most important components of the sound card synthesizer is the signal processor, which, in turn, contains a digital filter. In general, this filter functions using algorithms similar to FFT. Since some of the operations in this filter are implemented at the hardware level, it can function in real time and is able to process a synthesized signal at the same rate at which this signal is generated. The form of the amplitude-frequency response of the filter is changed programmatically and managed using the drivers supplied with the sound card or with sample editing tools.

3.1. Basic Types of Filter Amplitude-Frequency Responses

Depending on the filter bandwidth's position on the frequency axis, filters can be classified as follows:

❏ Low-pass filters, whose typical amplitude-frequency and phase-frequency responses are shown in Fig. 3.1.

❏ High-pass filters. Typical amplitude-frequency and phase-frequency responses are shown in Fig. 3.2.

❏ Band-pass filters (Fig. 3.3).

❏ Band elimination (band-stop) filters (Fig. 3.4).

You'll need to get acquainted with characteristics of these filters when working with digitized sound.

In the figures shown below, the horizontal axes are frequency axes, while transfer functions $K(f)$ and phase shift values $\varphi(f)$ are plotted on the ordinate.

The section of the amplitude-frequency response where the transfer factor is not equal to zero corresponds to the filter bandwidth. In contrast to this, in the suppression band, the filter transfer factor must have the smallest possible value (or, ideally, be equal to zero).

The responses shown in Figs 3.1—3.4 are the ideal ones: strictly speaking, real filters can provide a zero value for transfer function outside the filter bandwidth. Oscillations within the suppression band are still transferred through the filter, though they are significantly attenuated. In *Section 3.3*, we shall consider the properties of synthesized analytical filters, the frequency responses of which are approximations of the responses of the ideal filters.

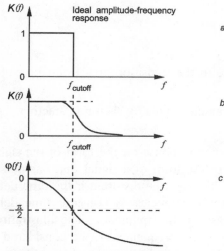

Fig. 3.1. Amplitude-frequency response and phase-frequency response of a low-pass filter

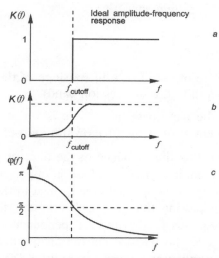

Fig. 3.2. Amplitude-frequency response and phase-frequency response of a high-pass filter

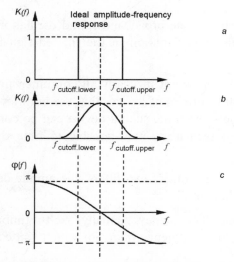

Fig. 3.3. Amplitude-frequency response and phase-frequency response of a band-pass filter

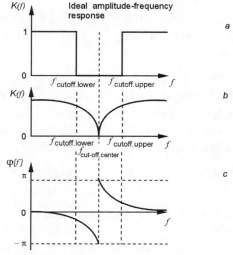

Fig. 3.4. Amplitude-frequency response and phase-frequency response of a band-stop filter

Real low-pass and high-pass filters are characterized by the following main parameters:

- ☐ Cutoff frequency

- ☐ Bandwidth

- ☐ Band-pass variation

- ☐ Rate of cutoff of a filter (slope of the response in the transition area from the bandwidth to the suppression band)

For the band-pass filter there is yet another parameter—Quality factor (Q-factor), i.e., the central frequency/bandwidth ratio of the filter.

Neglecting the influence of the filter phase-frequency response on the form of the signal is a common mistake. Phase is important, because the form of a signal that has passed the filter without amplitude change in the bandwidth might be distorted if the time delay when passing the filter isn't constant for different frequencies. A constant time delay corresponds to the linear dependence of the phase on the frequency. The illustrations provided above show that the phase's dependence on the frequency can be considered as linear only within close proximity of the cutoff frequency, and for the band-pass filter—in the proximity of the resonant (central) frequency. Using the band-stop filter to suppress narrow-band noise results in inversion (multiplication by −1) of the oscillations at frequencies below the rejection frequency.

Thus, you must clearly understand that the filtering of the broadband sound oscillations will always be subject to phase distortions, resulting in variation in the filtered signal's form.

Timbre regulators (both high and low frequency) are present in nearly all consumer amplifiers, receivers, or tape recorders, and represent examples of devices that use both low-frequency filters and high-frequency filters. At the same time, such a device can be considered to be the simplest equalizer. Using such regulators, it is possible to tune the acoustic system to satisfy your preferences.

Regulators of low (bass) and high (treble) frequencies control two filters, the amplitude-frequency responses of which are shown in Figs 3.5a and 3.5b.

The change of the filter gain takes place at the cutoff frequency. Actually, such a timbre regulator consists of a low-frequency filter and a high-frequency filter, for which you can change the gain factors within the bandwidth.

Besides timbre regulators of low and high frequencies, most amplifiers and other systems also contain a timbre regulator for medium frequencies (Fig. 3.6).

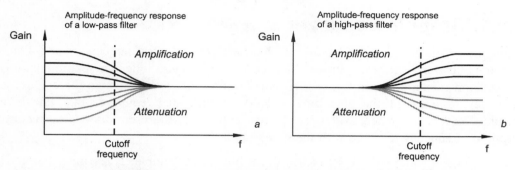

Fig. 3.5. Families of the amplitude-frequency responses of the Bass and treble timbre regulators

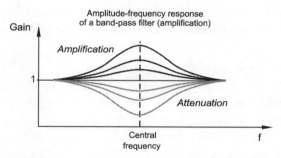

Fig. 3.6. Family of responses of a medium-frequency timbre regulator

Actually, this filter controls the band-pass filter. It is intended for amplification or attenuation of a signal within a relatively narrow bandwidth of the sound spectrum.

3.2. Equalizers

Equalizers are devices that combine several filters in order to change the spectral properties (timbre) of the signal being processed. Initially, the equalizer (EQ) was used to perform the function of the device used to compensate for variations at a specific section of the amplification and sound signal conversion channels.

The presence of equalizer enables you to smooth out an initially uneven amplitude-frequency response. This, by the way, is how the device's name originated. There are several types of equalizers, different in their usage and design:

❑ Graphic equalizer   ❑ Presence filter

❑ Parametric equalizer   ❑ Crossover

3.2.1. Graphic Equalizer

A graphic equalizer is a set of band-pass filters with fixed central frequencies and a variable amplification factor that can be controlled using a slider. Sliders are commonly used as regulators, since the positions of their handles are somewhat similar to the amplitude-frequency response of the equalizer. Because of this, such equalizers are known as "graphic" equalizers. When working with such equalizers, the user "draws" the required amplitude-frequency response with the slider handles.

Thus, a graphic equalizer is a set of band-pass filters that completely separate the predefined frequency bandwidths from one another. To provide the ability to control the frequency response within the whole range of sound frequencies, these filters are connected parallel to each other. The same signal is supplied to the input of all the filters. The aim of each filter is the amplification or attenuation of its respective spectrum range according to the position of the gain regulator (slider).

The frequencies at which graphic equalizers perform regulation are unified, and selected from a series of standard frequencies that span the whole sound range and are separated from each other by some constant interval. This interval may comprise an octave, half of an octave, or one third of an octave. Naturally, equalizers providing the regulation intervals equal to one-third of an octave provide the most powerful capabilities. Because of this, they are the most commonly used.

Each octave corresponds to a power of 2. Therefore, the incrementation of an octave with a central frequency of 100 Hz will look as follows: 200 Hz, 400 Hz, 800 Hz, and so on. For an increment of 1/3 of an octave, the multiplier will be equal to $2^{1/3}$, which corresponds to approximately 1.26. With a first central frequency of 100 Hz, subsequent frequencies will be equal to 126 Hz, 159 Hz, 200 Hz, and so on.

The number of regulated frequency bands varies from 27 (for inexpensive consumer models) to 31 (for professional models).

The lowest-frequency filter of the equalizer need not necessarily be the band-pass filter. It could be the low-pass filter. Similarly, the highest-frequency filter could be the high-pass filter.

Graphic equalizers are most frequently used for processing a composite signal in order to refine the resulting pattern, rather than for processing specific components, which is done using other types of equalizers. Using a graphic equalizer, one can approximately form the required amplitude-frequency response of the sound processing system or acoustic system. For example, it is possible to increase the amplification for specific spectrum ranges and attenuate the same value for the other spectrum areas. However, even a multiple-band graphic equalizer is hardly suitable for fine frequency correction. Because central frequencies of the filters are constant, they might not exactly be the same as the frequencies that need to be emphasized, or might suppress spectral components. Parametric equalizers are the most appropriate ones for such cases.

3.2.2. Parametric Equalizer

A parametric equalizer enables you to control not only the filter gain, but also its central frequency and Q-factor (bandwidth). Having gained some experience, you'll be able to precisely set the values of these parameters in such a way as to emphasize the sound produced by a specific instrument, or to suppress undesirable noise (such as, for example, a 60 Hz background, or unwanted oscillations of the acoustic system) with minimum influence on the other elements of the sound image.

Fig. 3.7 shows several variations of the amplitude-frequency response of a single-band parametric equalizer.

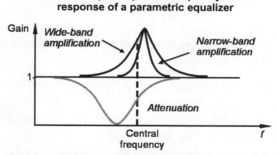

Fig. 3.7. Variations of the amplitude-frequency response of a single-band parametric equalizer

Multiple-band parametric equalizers are used for creating complicated amplitude-frequency responses. The parameters of each of these equalizers can be changed independently. For example, in *Section 12.24*, we will examine the seven-band parametric equalizer implemented in the Cool Edit Pro program.

3.2.3. Presence Filter

A presence filter enables you to produce the impression that a musical instrument (or the voice of the vocalist) is in the same room as the listener. In practice, the presence filter is just a regulated band-pass filter with a central frequency ranging from 2 to 6 kHz.

3.2.4. Crossover

A crossover is a device that separates the input signal into several output signals, ensuring that each output signal contains oscillations that belong only to the specified frequency range. Crossover represents a set of bandpass and threshold filters (according the number of the output channels) with a common input and separate outputs.

Although crossovers are not equalizers in the strict sense of the term, they function based on the same principles.

As a matter of fact, it is practically impossible to create a speaker that would reproduce frequencies of all ranges—high, medium, and low—equally well. If we narrow the range of the frequencies that can be reproduced by the speaker, the development process will be simplified. However, to reproduce the whole sound range we'll require several different speakers. The largest speaker will be used for reproducing low frequencies, and the smallest one for high frequencies. High-quality professional acoustic systems provide a third speaker, intended to reproduce medium frequencies. For the speaker to function normally, only frequencies from within its nominal range must be supplied to the speaker input. Crossovers are used to separate broadband signals into several bandwidths of different frequencies.

Passive crossovers are filters consisting of capacitors, inductors, and resistors. They reside between the amplifier output and speakers. Because the filters work with signals of high power, they also cause high heat loss.

Active electronic crossovers (digital or analog, built on operational amplifiers) process a signal that is usually supplied from the linear output of the mixer, an audio replay device, or a speaker's amplifier. Such signals lack power, and therefore power losses that accompany signal processing by the crossover are negligibly small. Signals from the crossover output channels corresponding to different frequency bands are supplied to the input channels of specific amplifiers, and then to the speakers. Active electronic crossovers provide you with the ability to efficiently use the power consumed by amplifiers and acoustic systems while providing high quality sound amplification.

The typical structural scheme of the crossover is shown in Fig. 3.8.

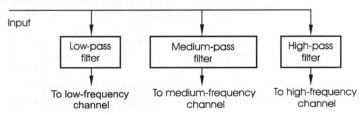

Fig. 3.8. Structural scheme of a crossover

3.2.5. Using Equalizers

An equalizer can be used in practically any stage of any sound processing procedure—from recording a live concert to putting together a multichannel studio recording. Mainly, equalizers are used to correct a sound signal that doesn't meet certain requirements.

It is highly recommended that you observe the following "golden rules" of equalizer usage:

❏ It is highly improbable that you will get high-quality sound by changing the amplitude-frequency response within a wide range. Such a procedure can only spoil the sound.

❏ If one of the instruments within a mix sounds unclear, try to collect specific frequencies in the signals of other tracks.

❏ You can separate tracks that interfere with each other by emphasizing and cutting frequencies belonging to different ranges.

❏ Usually, one has to cut out high and above-average frequencies from high-pitched tracks (guitars or percussion instruments, for example) while adding low frequencies and the frequencies from the lower part of the medium frequency range.

❏ It makes sense to raise medium and high frequencies in bass guitar and bass drum sounds. This is done to make these instruments audible when using systems with cheap speakers of low power (more information on this topic will be provided in *Section 24.1*).

❏ Small drums and guitars will sound "warmer" if you eliminate high frequencies and add some frequencies in the lower part of the medium range.

❏ String instruments and pianos rarely require processing. Cutting out low and medium frequencies from their sound makes sense only if these instruments are performing a background part.

The expediency of using an equalizer to process a voice is determined by the type of the vocal music. It is usually necessary to somewhat raise medium frequencies and the medium part of the high frequency range, while cutting off specific areas of the medium range in the guitar sound (since the voice is "masked" by the guitar sound).

The frequency spectrum of the human voice can be conditionally divided into three ranges according to the character of the sounds—plosive sounds, vowels, and sibilants. Plosive sounds are those from 125 to 250 Hz; they ensure that the speech is intelligible. The main part of the voice energy falls on the vowels, which are in the range of 350 to 2000 Hz. Sibilants reside at 1500 to 4000 Hz, and produce a relatively small amount of energy; however, diction and speech intelligibility strongly depend on these sounds.

The frequency range from 63 to 500 Hz contains about 60% of the total voice energy. However, only 5% of the informational content of speech comes from it. The range from 500 Hz to 1 kHz contains about 35% of information, and the remaining 60% of the informational content comes from the range of 1 to 8 kHz (sibilants), which bears only 5% of the voice energy.

Decreasing the signal level while in the range of the low frequencies and raising it when within a range of 1—5 kHz allows for improving the subjectively perceived articulation and intelligibility of the speech or vocal music. Raising the frequency response to within the range of 100 —250 Hz produces an impression of a resonant chest-voice. Cutting off the range from 150—500 Hz makes the voice sound hollow, similar to sound in a tunnel. Drops at specific sections of the amplitude-frequency response within the range of 500—1000 Hz make the voice sound harder, and rises within the area of 1 and 3 kHz impart a metallic, nasal tint to the voice. Cutting sections within the range of 2—5 kHz makes the voice dull, lifeless, and unintelligible, while amplification of the frequencies from the range of 4—10 kHz introduces additional "color".

An excessive rise in the amplitude-frequency response in specific ranges can also produce undesirable effects, for example:

❐ 315 Hz —1 kHz—an unnatural sound, similar to the voice that you hear when speaking on the telephone.

❐ 2—4 kHz—this might mask sounds such as "M", "B", or "V".

❐ 1—4 kHz—usually produces the impression of hearing fatigue. The simplest way of emphasizing the voice is to raise an area near 3kHz and cut the same area from the sound spectrums of other instruments.

To obtain a good result, it is recommended that you use a parametric equalizer for all voice frequency corrections.

Most instruments generate sounds with complex frequency-space responses, which pretty much can't be implemented if the speakers are positioned too close. Equalizers are ideal for compensating these frequency non-uniformities. The best practice is to record the most natural sound with a microphone, and then to correct all irregularities using equalizers.

The distinctness of the sound produced by most musical instruments is determined by the composition of their harmonics. The human ear is capable of compensating for the sound of poorly audible fundamental frequencies on its own, provided that the perceived signal contains a sufficient number of their harmonics. Taking the human hearing properties into account, we can detect some specific frequency areas of the audible range:

❏ Frequencies belonging to the range of 31—50 Hz impart an impression of power and energy to the music. If these frequencies are over-emphasized, the sound might become unintelligible and dull. Sometimes an excessive rise in this area will also mask high-frequency components of the signal.

❏ An excessive rise in the amplitude-frequency response within a range of 80—125 Hz produces an undesirable buzzing effect.

❏ The most complex part of the audible range is the one from 160 to 250 Hz. Intensive sound within this area will make your mix sound dull. However, cutting off these frequencies will result in lack of warmth and mildness. This is the range where the main components of the bass instruments, such as bass guitar and percussion instruments, reside.

❏ The fundamental frequencies and harmonics of string, keyboard, and percussion instruments lie within the range of 400 Hz—1 kHz. The individual "voices" of practically all instruments lie within the range of medium frequencies. If the amplitude-frequency response is raised excessively in this range, the sound may become unnatural.

❏ Regulation of the amplitude-frequency response near the area of 5 kHz allows you to achieve an effect of "approaching/moving away" and "erosion/aggregation".

❏ The area of 8 kHz—20 kHz is mainly responsible for the subjective perception of the sound quality. Correct tuning of the amplitude-frequency response within this area should impart the composition with a sense of space and deepness. If the sound in this area is too intense, the sound will become unnaturally "thin".

3.3. Digital Filters

Sound processing software usually performs frequency conversions of acoustic signals using digital filters. It is now time to consider the working principles of the digital filter. The $s(nT)$ signal that represents the sequence of numeric values with period T is supplied to the input of the digital filter. When each subsequent number is supplied, the digital filter performs a calculation using the appropriate algorithm, and produces the response—$y(nT)$—supplied to the filter output.

In most cases, the output number is the function of certain previous values of both input and output numbers.

A periodic sequence of numbers with period T is produced at the filter output. Thus, the clock interval is the same for both input and output sequences.

Digital filters are divided into the following two classes: infinite impulse response filters (IIR filters) and finite impulse response filters (FIR filters).

The output signal of an infinite impulse response filter depends not only on the current and the nearest previous values of the input signal, but also on the values of the input signal, which are infinitely distant in time from the current moment.

The IIR filter class includes all analog filters based on reactive elements (capacitors and inductors), which theoretically are capable of storing the energy of the signal supplied from an external source for an infinitely long time. Digital IIR filters can be obtained by transforming prototype analog filters into digital filters by direct calculation methods and methods that implement optimization algorithms.

In any case, all IIR filters share one common drawback: the requirements to the phase-frequency response of the filter can't be specified, and the phase-frequency response is arbitrary.

The filter doesn't introduce phase distortions into the signal being processed if the phase-frequency response of the filter is linear. In the case of IIR filters, this requirement can't be satisfied. The phase-frequency response of an infinite impulse response filter is always non-linear.

The filter has a finite impulse response if the signal on its output depends only on the finite number of measurements supplied as the input signal. A filter with a finite pulse response is a finite memory filter. It processes the input sequence of measurements only within a finite time window that slides along this input sequence. One of the most important advantages of FIR filters is the capability of obtaining a linear phase-frequency response.

IIR filters, in turn, can be further subdivided into the following two classes: non-recursive filters and recursive filters.

For non-recursive filters, the response depends only on the values of the input sequence:

$$y(nT) = F[x(nT), x(nT - T), x(nT - 2T), ...] \tag{3.1}$$

For recursive filters, the response depends both on the values of the input sequence and on the previous values of the output sequence:

$$y(nT) = F[x(nT), x(nT - T), x(nT - 2T), ..., y(nT - T), y(nT - 2T), ...] \tag{3.2}$$

The structural scheme of a non-recursive digital filter is shown in Fig. 3.9. Notice that this is the scheme of the processing algorithm rather than an electrical circuit diagram.

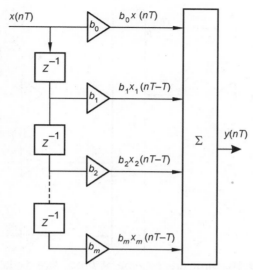

Fig. 3.9. Structural scheme of a non-recursive digital filter

The scheme shown in Fig. 3.9 uses the following notation: z^{-1}—the shift operator (shift register), which delays the sequence by 1 cycle; b_i—the multiplication operator, which multiplies the measurements of the sequence by b_i; and Σ—the summation operator.

A non-recursive digital filter can be implemented provided that the specified pulse response contains a relatively small number of members, which means that it rapidly decreases with the growth of n. This condition must be satisfied, since as n grows, the amount of memory required grows proportionally. In other words, implementing non-recursive digital filters is possible only for relatively small time windows, since filter memory is finite and small.

The structural scheme of a recursive filter is shown in Fig. 3.10.

One of the most important advantages of recursive filters is the reduction in the number of required structural scheme elements (calculations) as compared to non-recursive filters. Owing to this advantage, recursive filters are capable of implementing slowly attenuating pulse responses. However, recursive filters are not free from drawbacks, the most noticeable of which is a relatively large rounding—off error.

The canonical recursive filter (Fig. 3.11) is the result of modifying the structural scheme shown in Fig. 3.10. This structural scheme corresponds to the so-called direct or main form of the digital filter.

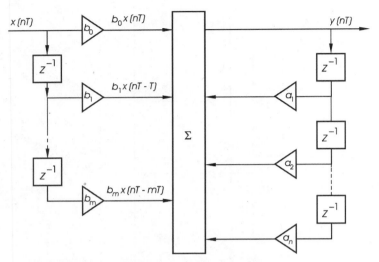

Fig. 3.10. Structural scheme of a recursive digital filter

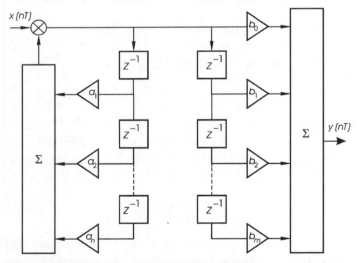

Fig. 3.11. Structural scheme of a canonical recursive filter

A canonical recursive filter can be optimized. As a result of its optimization, we'll get a structural scheme containing the minimum number of units (Fig. 3.12).

Strictly speaking, all algorithms of digital filtering implemented in sound editors are filters with a finite impulse response. However, at the expense of much memory, they can attain properties characteristic for IIR filters.

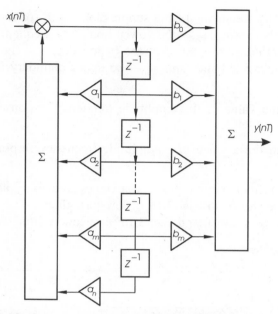

Fig. 3.12. Optimized scheme of the canonical recursive filter

3.4. Butterworth, Chebyshev, and Bessel Filters

You already know that the selective filter serves to separate the frequency components of the input signal that resides within the filter bandwidth and suppresses the frequency components that reside within the suppression band. Filters with ideal amplitude-frequency responses (see Figs 3.1—3.4) can't be implemented physically; such responses can only be approximated.

To solve the approximation problem, it is necessary to define the filter transfer function that would approximate the specified amplitude-frequency response with the required precision. Consequently, we need to specify the initial data for this problem— the tolerances for maximum variation of the amplitude-frequency response within the bandwidth and the maximum deviation from zero within the suppression band.

Thus, to solve the approximation problem, we need to specify the following initial data:

❏ The boundary frequencies of the bandwidth and suppression band (for low-pass filter and high-pass filter these are: ω_{bw}—the boundary frequency of the bandwidth, and ω_s—the boundary frequency of the suppression band; for the band-pass filter and suppression filter these are: ω_{bwl}—the lower boundary frequency of the bandwidth, ω_{bwu}—the upper boundary frequency of the bandwidth, ω_{sl}—the lower boundary frequency of the suppression band, and ω_{su}—the upper boundary frequency of the suppression band)

❏ ΔK_{bw}—the maximum value of the amplitude-frequency response variation within the bandwidth

❏ ΔK_s—the maximum deviation of the amplitude-frequency response from zero within the suppression band

Schemes of amplitude-frequency response tolerances and examples of the amplitude-frequency response are shown in Fig. 3.13 (a low-pass filter), Fig. 3.14 (a high-pass filter), Fig. 3.15 (a band-pass filter), and Fig. 3.16 (a rejection filter).

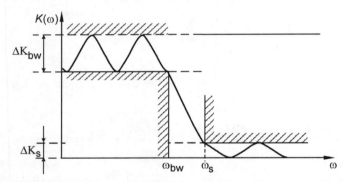

Fig. 3.13. Scheme of the tolerances and example of the amplitude-frequency response (a low-pass filter)

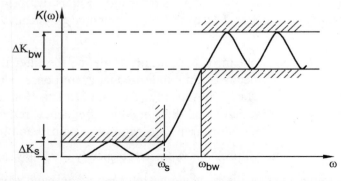

Fig. 3.14. Scheme of the tolerances and example of the amplitude-frequency response (a high-pass filter)

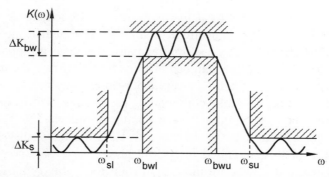

Fig. 3.15. Tolerance scheme and example of the amplitude-frequency response (a band-pass filter)

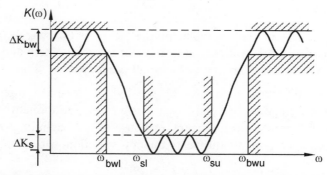

Fig. 3.16. Tolerance scheme and example of the amplitude-frequency response (a rejection filter)

A common method of approximating the ideal prototype of the amplitude-frequency response is by using polynomials. The higher the order of the polynomials used for this purpose, the better the approximation. Polynomial order defines the value of the parameter known as filter order.

Technically, filters are implemented based on first-order units, such as RC-circuit (Fig. 3.17), and second-order units, such as RLC-circuit (Fig. 3.18).

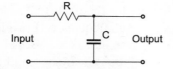

Fig. 3.17. The first-order circuit

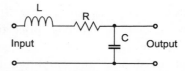

Fig. 3.18. The second-order circuit

Filters are built on such units, after calculating polynomial coefficients, capacity and resistance values, and the appropriate circuit elements. The higher the filter order, the closer its amplitude-frequency response approximates the ideal prototype. On the other hand, as the filter order grows, the number of units and elements increases accordingly. Therefore, tuning higher order filters is a very labor-consuming process. In mass production, the actual parameters of radio components are always slightly different from the nominal values, i.e., there is variation in the parameter values. For example, a resistor marked as "1", might actually have a resistance that fits the range of values from 950 to 1050 ohms. Because of this, mounted filters will always have parameters different from calculated ones. These differences are more significant for higher order filters. As a result, analog filters of higher orders prove to be too expensive to be commonly accepted.

Digital filters are synthesized on the basis of analog prototypes. For digital filters, higher orders can be achieved in practice.

High-pass filters can be obtained by replacing the elements of low-pass filters. Band-pass filters and rejection filters are synthesized as a set of low-pass filters and high-pass filters. In other words, low-pass filters are the basis for all other types of filters.

Let's consider the different methods of specifying low-pass filter characteristics. The most widely used are Bessel filters, Butterworth filters, and Chebyshev filters, differing in the slope of the amplitude-frequency response at the beginning of the suppression band and in the character of amplitude-frequency variation within the bandwidth and suppression band.

The amplitude-frequency response of the Butterworth filter has a relatively long horizontal section, and drops abruptly after the cutoff frequency. The transient response of such filter with a quantized input signal has an oscillatory character. These oscillations become stronger as the filter order increases.

The amplitude-frequency response of the Chebyshev filter drops more rapidly after the cutoff frequency. However, within the bandwidth it is not monotonous, but rather is wave-like, with a constant amplitude. With a given filter order, a more rapid fall of the response after the cutoff frequency corresponds to a larger variance within the bandwidth. Transient process oscillations at the quantized input signal are more intense than with the Butterworth filter.

The Bessel filter has an optimal transient response due to the fact that the phase shift of the output signal is proportional to the input signal frequency. Provided that the filters are of the same order, the amplitude-frequency response of the Bessel filter is more gently-sloping, the amplitude-frequency responses of the Chebyshev and Butterworth filters.

To demonstrate the specific features of various types of filters, let's provide some examples of amplitude-frequency responses.

Fig. 3.19a shows the amplitude-frequency response of a B-type Butterworth filter of the third order.

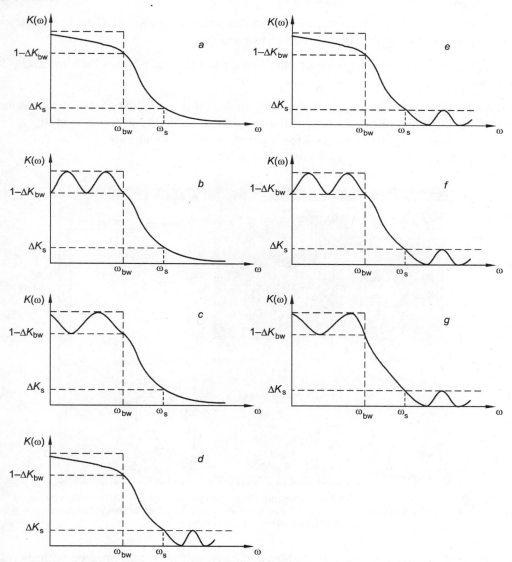

Fig. 3.19. Examples of amplitude-frequency responses for various types of filters

Figs. 3.19*b* and 3.19*c* represent the amplitude-frequency responses of T-type Chebyshev filters of the fourth and third order, respectively.

Figs. 3.19*d* and 3.19*e* show the amplitude-frequency responses of I-type Chebyshev filters of the fourth and third order, respectively.

Figs. 3.19*f* and 3.19*g* illustrate the amplitude-frequency responses of C-type Zolotaryov-Kauer filters of the fourth and third order, respectively.

The amplitude-frequency response of the C-type filter has equal waves both in bandwidth and in suppression band.

Section 12.26 looks at the implementation of analytical filters in the Cool Edit Pro sound editor. The most interesting feature of this program is its ability to implement algorithms that correspond to filters of a very high order. Certain combinations of initial data allow you to produce a filter of the 40th order (Fig. 3.20).

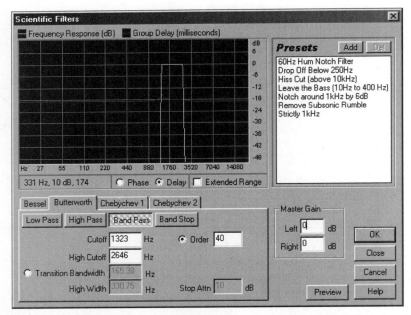

Fig. 3.20. Implementation of a bandpass Butterworth filter of the 40th order. Besides the amplitude-frequency response of the synthesized filter, this screenshot also shows the phase-frequency response

At this point, let us conclude this chapter dedicated to filters, and proceed with discussing aspects related to the dynamic processing of acoustic signals.

Chapter 4: Dynamic Processing of Acoustic Signals

Dynamic processing consists of changing the dynamic range of acoustic signals. It is done using manual and automatic level regulators. In this chapter, we will consider various possible strategies of manual level adjustment, get acquainted with the classification of automatic devices intended for acoustic signal dynamic processing, and describe their typical structure. We'll also provide detailed information on specific features of using the most common devices, such as compressors and gates, when recording vocal music and some acoustic instruments.

4.1. Strategies of Manual Level Adjustment

The necessity of manual level adjustment is explained by the fact that initial (raw) signals often have a very large dynamic range (for example, up to 80 dB for symphonic music). Under home studio conditions, most audio programs are heard at somewhere around 40 dB. Therefore, a sound engineer, in this case, must compress the dynamic range of symphonic music to 40 dB.

There are at least three strategies for manual level adjustment, all of which are illustrated by the diagram shown in Fig. 4.1.

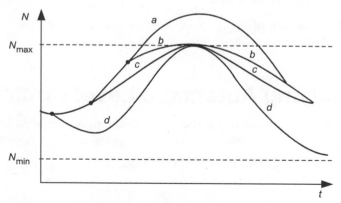

Fig. 4.1. Level diagrams of the signals at each of three manual level adjustment strategies

Graph a corresponds to the level diagram without level adjustment. This example demonstrates that, most of the time, the signal levels exceed the maximum allowed level N_{max}, and therefore level adjustment is required.

When using the first strategy of level adjustment (Fig. 4.1, curve *b*), the sound engineer swiftly introduces the fade directly before an instance where the signal level exceeds the maximum allowed limit. The level won't be exceeded, but this strategy is far from perfect. An audience acquainted with the piece knows that the loudness must grow at a particular point, waits for this to happen, and feels irritated when it doesn't. People who are not acquainted with the piece probably won't notice this distortion. However, they'll get an incorrect impression of the composition.

When using the second strategy of manual level adjustment (Fig. 4.1, curve *c*), the sound engineer starts to introduce the fade well before the moment when the sound level exceeds the N_{max} value. As this takes place, the increase rate of the signal level significantly decreases, and therefore the composition loses expression.

Using the third adjustment strategy (Fig. 4.1, curve *d*), the sound engineer, knowing about the expected increase of the signal level, gradually introduces the fade well before the moment when the level of the source signal starts increasing. Starting from this instant, the sound engineer allows the level to increase at the natural rate. This strategy seems to produce the best impression. The dynamics of the composition will be more natural, since the natural slope of the level increase is preserved.

Manual level adjustment strategies share a common drawback. The sound engineer's reaction is somewhere around 2 seconds, even in cases when he or she knows the score of the composition. As a result, this introduces a maximum level support error of about ± 4 dB in relation to the nominal value.

This results in the necessity of applying devices for automatic processing of signal levels (so-called automatic level controls).

4.2. Classifying Automatic Level Controls

The devices for automatic processing of the signal level can be classified by several criteria, the most important of which are the following two: *response time* and *performed function*.

Automatic level controls can be subdivided into the following groups by their response time criterion:

❐ Non-inertial (instantaneous)

❐ Inertial (with a variant transfer coefficient)

The differences in the working principles of theses types of automatic level controls are illustrated in Fig. 4.2 using an example of a sinusoidal input signal.

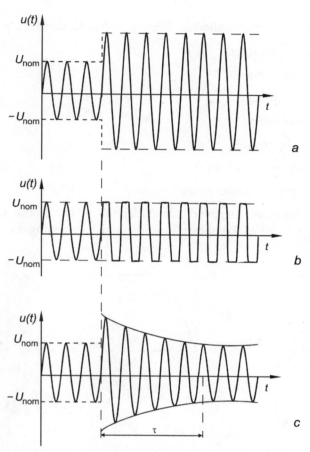

Fig. 4.2. Oscillograms of the input signal (*a*), output signal of inertia-less level control (*b*) and inertial level control (*c*)

When the signal level at the input of the inertia-less level control (Fig. 4.2*a*) exceeds the nominal value, the output signal becomes trapezoidal rather than sinusoidal (Fig. 4.2*b*). Thus, the signal form becomes significantly distorted. Although inertia-less automatic controls are simple, their usage results in significant distortions of the output signal.

Inertial level controls are level controls with automatic adjustment of the transfer coefficient, depending on the input signal amplitude.

When inertial level controls start their operation, they distort the signal form only for a small time interval τ (Fig. 4.2*c*). By selecting the optimal response time, such distortions can be made practically unnoticeable to the ear.

Inertial level controls can be classified as follows, by function:

- Quasi-maximum level limiters
- Automatic level stabilizers
- Dynamic range compressors
- Dynamic range expanders
- Compound noise suppressors
- Threshold noise suppressors (gates)
- Devices with complex dynamic range transform

Fig. 4.3 shows the amplitude responses (dependencies of the output signal amplitude on the input signal amplitude) of the above listed dynamic processing devices.

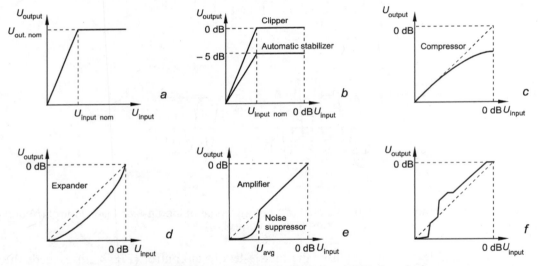

Fig. 4.3. Amplitude responses of dynamic processing devices

Level clipper (limiter) is the automatic control for which the transfer coefficient changes in such a way as to keep the output signal level practically constant, and very close to the nominal value, even when the input signal level exceeds the nominal value (Fig. 4.3). When the input signal doesn't exceed the nominal value, limiter works as a normal linear amplifier.

Limiter must instantaneously react to level changes. In situations where it is necessary to obtain an absolute limitation, a limiter with an instantaneous cut-off circuit is used.

The cut-off circuit can stop peaks too short even for the limiter. Instead of controlling the signal level, the cut-off circuit simply cuts off the top of the signal envelopes which tend to exceed the limiting level. Such limitation periods can be very short. If they don't exceed a value of 1 msec, they won't be noticed by the naked ear.

Automatic level stabilizer is intended for stabilizing the signal level. This might be necessary for balancing the loudness of separate composition fragments. The working principle of the automatic stabilizer is similar to that of the limiter. The difference is that the nominal input voltage of the automatic stabilizer is smaller than the nominal output level $N_{output.\ max}$ by approximately 5 dB, while for the limiter the value of $N_{output.\ nom} = 0$ dB (Fig. 4.3*b*).

Compressor is a device whose transition factor grows as the input signal level decreases (Fig. 4.3*c*).

The compressor increases the average power, and consequently the loudness, of the signal being processed, and compresses its dynamic range.

Expander has an amplitude response (Fig. 4.3*d*) that is the inverse of the amplitude response of the compressor. Expander is used when it is necessary to restore the dynamic range previously reduced by a compressor. A system comprising a compressor and an expander connected sequentially is known as a compounder. Such a system can be used for noise reduction in recording or transmitting sound channels.

Threshold noise suppressor (gate) is an automatic control with the transfer factor changing in such a way that when the input signal is below the threshold level, the output signal amplitude is close to zero (Fig. 4.3*e*). If the input signal level exceeds the threshold value, the threshold noise suppressor works as a simple linear amplifier.

Automatic level controls providing for a complex transform of the dynamic range contain several control channels. For example, the automatic level control, whose amplitude response is shown in Fig 4.3*f*, consists of the limiter, the automatic stabilizer, the expander, and the threshold noise suppressor. This combination enables you to stabilize the loudness of various composition fragments, support maximum signal levels, and suppress noises during pauses.

4.3. Structure and Time Characteristics of Dynamic Processing Devices

Inertial level control is made up of two functional units—the main channel and the control channel. If the signal is supplied to the control channel from the input of the main channel, we are dealing with the direct control regulator (Fig. 4.4*a*). In contrast to this, if the signal is supplied from the output of the main channel, we are dealing with the feedback control regulator (Fig. 4.4*b*).

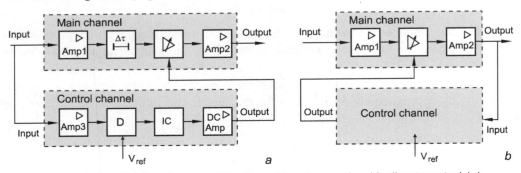

Fig. 4.4. Structural schemas of the sound level controls with direct control (*a*)
and feedback control (*b*)

The main channel in the direct regulation scheme includes sound frequency amplifiers (input amplifier Amp1, output amplifier Amp2), a delay line, and an adjustment unit (AU). The AU, being exposed to the control voltage, is capable of changing its transfer coefficient. The main channel in the feedback control schema contains all the above listed elements except for the delay line.

The control channels in the schemas shown in Figs 4.4*a* and 4.4*b* are identical. The control channel contains an input amplifier of sound frequencies (Amp3), a detector (D), an integrating circuit (IC), and an output direct current amplifier (DC Amp). As long as the voltage supplied to the schema input doesn't exceed the threshold value (reference voltage), the control channel doesn't produce the control signal, and the transfer factor of the adjustment unit doesn't change. When the input voltage exceeds the threshold value, the detector produces a pulse voltage proportional to the difference of the current signal value from the reference voltage. The integrating circuit averages the voltage difference, thus producing a control voltage proportional to the signal level at the control channel input. Thus, the control channel performs operations similar to those illustrated in Fig. 1.3.

The delay line present in the main channel of the direct control schema allows the channel to function with a specified time lead. The signal level spike will be detected before the signal arrives at the regulated unit. Thus the schema provides the capability of eliminating undesirable transitional processes. Level differences can be processed almost ideally. However, the phase-frequency response of the analog delay line is not linear. Different spectral components of the signal will have different phase shifts, which results in the distortion of the broadband signal form passing through the delay line. Digital delay lines are free from this drawback, but require the signal to be digitized. In virtual processing devices, the signal is processed in digital form, and the problems with algorithmic implementation of the functional units shown in the schemas are non-existent.

Most limiters are implemented based on the feedback control schema, since using it simplifies the tasks of ensuring stability and the accuracy of specifying the threshold value. The spike problem in this case is ignored. Unfortunately, transitional processes in the feedback control scheme can be accompanied by self-sustained oscillations, sometimes designated by the term "ringing". These self-sustained oscillations manifest themselves as wave-like variations of the signal level.

Besides the value of the reference (threshold) voltage, the schema usually provides the ability to control the integration time of the integrating circuit. When integration time is small, the channel acts as peak level meter; when this time is large, the channel turns into the root mean square level meter. In high-quality dynamic processing devices (and in all dynamic processing software) you have the ability to change the channel response time in reaction to the following two types of events:

❏ Exceeding the signal level threshold value (the instant of turning the dynamic processing device on)

❏ The signal level drops below the threshold value (the instant of turning the dynamic processing device off)

Thus, the tasks of the control channel consist of detection of the moment the acoustic signal intersects the threshold, measurement of the signal level in relation to the threshold, and production of the control voltage.

The processing type depends on the type of characteristic of the adjustment unit of the main channel. For example, if the transfer factor of the adjustment unit decreases with the growth of the control voltage supplied to the adjustment unit, we'll have a compressor. On the other hand, if the transfer coefficient of the adjustment unit increases with the increase of the control voltage, the processing device functions as an expander. In analog devices, the adjustment unit often represents a circuit consisting of a resistor and a field-effect transistor.

Usually, in the main channel, there is the possibility of changing the gain factors of the amplifiers and the response time of the adjustment unit when turning it on or off.

To implement complex algorithms of dynamic processing, it is necessary to use more than one main channel and control channel.

To assess the dynamic processing time lag, the following two time parameters were introduced: response time and recovery time.

For controlled units of all dynamic processing devices, with the exception of noise suppressors, the response is the reaction of the device upon a signal level increase, and recovery is the reaction to the signal level's decrease. Response time is the time interval between the instant when the source starts supplying the signal with a level exceeding the nominal value by 6 dB, and the instant when the output level drops from 6 to 2 dB in relation to the nominal value.

Recovery time is the time interval between the instant when the level of the signal supplied from the source drops from 6 dB to the nominal value of 0 dB, and the instant when the output level increases from −6 to −2 dB in relation to the nominal value.

For noise suppression, response is a decrease in the amplification factor when the legitimate signal is lost, and restore is the restoration of the amplification when the legitimate signal reappears.

Selection of the time characteristics of dynamic processing devices is mainly determined by the intended function of the specific device type.

Inertial level limiters intended for protecting powerful amplification and acoustic systems from overloading must have a minimal response time that tends to zero. However, taking into account the fact that acoustic signals don't grow instantaneously, this theoretic requirement becomes less stringent in practice. For speech signals, the growth time is about 5—120 msec, while for violins it ranges from 80 to 120 msec. A very small group of sound sources has a grow time of less than 5 msec. Based on these facts, the response time for level limiters is usually selected from within a range of 0.5—1.0 msec, and restore time is usually equal to 1.5 sec.

For speech compressors, the response time must be about 1—2 msec, and the restore time about 300 msec.

For musical compressors, these parameters must be selected according to the dynamic properties of the music. Restore time is especially important.

4.4. Compression

One of the most widely used dynamic processing types is compression of the dynamic range, or simply compression.

The subjective perception of compression manifests itself as an increase in the sound's loudness. The sound becomes more condense, which is not surprising, since compression increases the average power of the undistorted signal. Actually, compression leads to automatic amplification control. When the signal level becomes too high, amplification decreases, and when the signal level returns to normal, amplification is returned to its initial state.

Compression results depend on the correct selection of several parameters, the most important of which are listed below:

❏ Threshold

❏ Compression Ratio

❏ Makeup Gain

❏ Attack Time

❏ Release Time

Let us consider these parameters in more detail.

The threshold determines the level after exceeding which the compressor starts controlling amplification (sometimes it is said that it changes to an active state). While the signal level is below the threshold value, the compressor doesn't influence the signal (this means that the compressor is in a passive state). The threshold value determines whether the compressor will process only individual spikes, or whether the signal will be constantly subject to compression.

The compression ratio determines the measure of compression for the dynamic range of a signal with a level exceeding the threshold value. Numerically, it is equal to the ratio of the signal level at the active compressor output to the level of the signal at its input.

For example, a compression ratio of 2:1 means that a change in the input signal level by 2 dB will result in a change in the output signal level by 1 dB. In practice, this value is the most commonly used, although sometimes it is necessary to set higher values. If the compression ratio is set to, say, 20:1 or higher, this will result in the limitation mode. This means that if a signal exceeding the nominal level is supplied to the input, the output signal won't be amplified.

A compression ratio of ∞:1 corresponds to absolute limitation. In practice, any compression ratio with a value higher than 20:1 produces the same effect.

Fig. 4.5 gives examples of the amplitude response of different compressors. The compressor corresponding to the graph shown in Fig. 4.5a is characterized by a threshold of −40 dB and a compression ratio of 2:1. The compressor corresponding to the graph shown in Fig. 4.5b has a threshold of −20 dB and a compression ratio equal to 4:1.

The attack time determines how quickly the compressor will react to signals with a level exceeding the threshold value.

Fig. 4.6 illustrates the influence of the attack time on the form of the envelope of the output signal. The level of the input signal increases unevenly at the instant where $t_1 = 2.5$ sec, and decreases when $t_2 = 7$ sec (top).

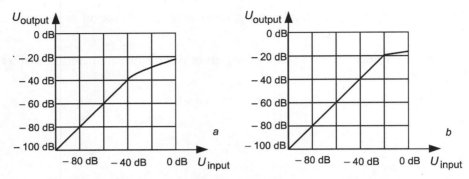

Fig. 4.5. Examples of amplitude responses of different compressors

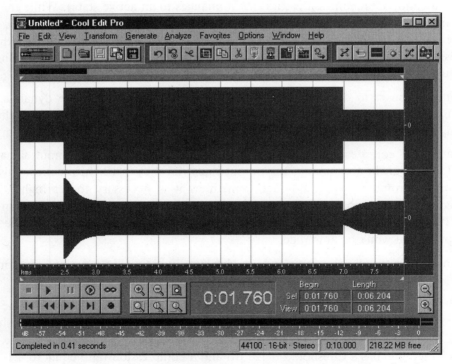

Fig. 4.6. Influence of the attack time and release time on the signal

With large attack time values, the compressor most likely won't be able to react to sharp spikes of the input signal level (Fig. 4.6, bottom). The output signal of the compressor will contain peaks. Spikes (even short ones) can be dangerous for amplifiers and acoustic systems; you therefore need to select these devices in such a way as to either ensure that they can withstand an increase of the signal power for a short time, or can eliminate these peaks by introducing a level limiter into the signal processing channel (before the power amplifier).

If the attack time value is small, you can practically eliminate the output signal peaks resulting from the uneven increase of the input signal level. Notice, however, that this might remove accents from the composition.

Release time is the time required for the compressor to perform transition into a passive state after the signal level drops below the threshold value.

If the release time is too long, the compressor is active for longer time intervals and, consequently, influences the dynamic range even when this is no longer necessary, and is even undesirable (Fig. 4.6, bottom). This produces a sound pulsation effect, noticeable to the human ear, since compression doesn't smooth the signal out.

When the release time is small, smoothing out is more significant. However, when the input signal level is constantly changing in the vicinity of the threshold value, this might produce an undesirable "sobbing" effect.

Selection of the optimal release time is based on a compromise. For instrumental music, it is possible to select a release time of about 500 msec as a rough approximation, and as a starting point for more fine-tuning. This value corresponds to the time interval between two bars with a tempo of 120 fourths per minute. This is the value that was selected for illustration of the compressor's dynamic properties in Fig. 4.6.

For vocal music, it might make sense to increase the release time value to 2 seconds.

4.5. Some Recommendations for Using Dynamic Processing

When recording modern music, the dynamic range of the record is usually subject to significant compression. The dynamic range is nearly always processed by a compressor when recording vocal music and acoustic instruments.

Gates are widely used for suppressing noise and background sounds.

4.5.1. Compressor Usage

Music perception depends on the dynamic range, since the dynamics allow for reproduction of emotional content. If the dynamics are completely smoothed out by producing a constant average level, the music will be dull and uninteresting.

Unskillful vocalists often make significant loudness changes. As a result, some words are masked by the sound of the music while other words are heard too loudly. Therefore, compression is always used when recording vocal music.

If the vocalist has problems with hushing sounds, and changing the speaker type and position doesn't correct the situation, it makes sense to use the compressor in the de-esser mode, which is more sensitive to hushing sounds.

If we suppress all low frequencies supplied to the input of the control channel by using an external equalizer, the compressor will react only to high-pitched sounds. In this case, the signal that controls the compressor is formed only on the basis of those components of the initial acoustic signal that make up the hushing and hissing. This is the basic working principle of the de-esser. The components that need to be controlled by de-esser are selected by ear. The equalizer included into the compressor control channel must amplify frequencies within the range of 4—10 kHz. However, it is important to select the precise amplitude-frequency response. To achieve this result, you should first listen to the acoustic signal without compression, by transmitting it only through the equalizer and adjusting its filters until the hissing tone is maximized. Parametric equalizers are the most suitable for this purpose. It is not recommended that you use a graphic equalizer, since the required frequencies might reside between the central frequencies of the control bands, which will make precise adjustment impossible, and thus de-esser won't be able to perform its work.

The virtual device of dynamic sound processing included with Cool Edit Pro provides a filter that allows you to implement de-esser. Several variations of de-esser are provided in the presets included with the program (*Section 12.7*).

Selecting an equalizer frequency of about 50 Hz allows you to eliminate the "spitting" sounds in the voice part of the recording that are caused by plosive consonants, the most difficult among which is "p". The best thing to do, however, is to eliminate the "spits" during the recording stage (using a microphone with acoustic filters, or using the mesh screen) rather than attempting to correct this drawback by processing.

The optimum values for attack time and release time depend on the musical content. For example, a powerful bass drum within a mix will cause compression of all other sounds. As a result, higher frequencies of softer sounds will sound even softer, which will make the music toneless and hollow. To avoid this effect and impart additional energy to the sound, it is recommended that you increase the attack time, so that the compressor doesn't have time to spring into action. It will thus miss the starting stages of the signals (attack) without decreasing the level, after which compression will take place. The attack phase usually determines the level of high-frequency components in the spectrum of a signal formed by a specific musical instrument.

The above-described method is often used when recording bass drums and bass guitars: the incipient attack mustn't be attenuated. This means that the signal still exceeds the specified level for a short time interval. However, such distortions and overloads are not noticeable to the ear. When working with digital recording devices, and in other cases when it is required to eliminate overloads completely, the limiter is included into the signal processing channel in order to track spikes.

Setting the correct values for the release time is very important. If the release time is too small, the compressor's actuation will be noticeable to the listener. On the other hand, if this time is too small, the compressor might not return to its initial state before the next soft signal appears at the input, and the dynamic range of such a signal will be compressed more than required.

If both the attack and release time values are too small, low-frequency sounds are distorted, since compression takes place at each signal cycle (instead of regulating the amplitude of the whole envelope). To prevent this effect, compressors provide the ability to control the unlocking time: the compressor can't switch to the release state before this time elapses (usually, about 50 msec).

The characteristic compressor sound depends on the reaction of the control channel to changes in the input signal level. The control circuit contains a frequency selection filter for selecting the frequencies to which the compressor must react. A filter is used because the human ear perceives differently-pitched tones as a signals of a different level.

The control channel can be adjusted in such a way so as to react to the signal level spikes, or to control the compression by the average level of the input signal. This difference is noticeable to the human ear.

It is not usually necessary to have a sharp attack for words when recording a vocal. Therefore, the attack time of the compressor should be set to a small value (compression starts immediately). As for the release time, first try to set a value of 0.5 sec. Later you'll probably have to discover on your own whether some other value is more suitable. The sustain time must be very small, or equal to zero. The compression level is selected for each individual performer. For example, for artists performing popular music, this level is set within the limits of 10—15 dB during loud passages.

If the vocal track doesn't contain other signals, it is possible to use the expander/gate built into the compressor in order to clear the pauses between words and phrases. This is done to prevent the compressor from amplifying noises during pauses, sounds of inhaling, etc., especially when a high compression level is required.

It is common to record vocal music with compression; however, insufficient compression is better than surplus compression. You can always add compression when joining all tracks together, which is much easier than eliminating the consequences of excessive compression that happened during recording.

The control channel can be used for managing the compressor from another signal source (the level of the external signal will influence the degree of compression). For example, if the accompaniment is supplied to the compressor input while the vocal part is supplied to the input of the control channel, then the vocal level will influence the accompaniment loudness, and the voice will be clearly audible. When the vocal has pauses, the loudness level of the accompaniment returns to its initial value.

Because the compressor doesn't distinguish a legitimate low-level signal from noises of the same level, it might amplify noises. The compressor changes to maximum amplification mode during soft passages or pauses in the vocal part. Because of this, you must combine the compressor with the gate, which will suppress noises during such intervals. The gate actuation threshold must be selected low enough to ensure that soft music is not suppressed along with the noise.

The compressor can make the sound less clear by attenuating the whole signal when specific instruments produce short spikes. In such a case, soft signals with a high-frequency component are lost. To solve this problem, it is necessary to use a compressor that divides the frequency range into several frequency bands, compresses each band independently, and then combines the compression results (*Section 24.2.1*).

Let us consider in brief specific features of using a compressor to record the most common acoustic instruments.

The sound of an acoustic guitar with metal strings becomes more dense and even after compression. The compressor's settings are generally the same as the ones used for compressing a vocal, with the exception of the attack time. To impart to the guitar sound a clear ringing attack, this parameter must be set somewhere between 10—40 msec. If this is done, the attack of each note or chord will pass through the compressor without changes.

For a bass guitar, just as with the acoustic guitar, the release time must be selected taking into account the playing manner of the particular performer. It is likely that you'll come across a situation where you'll need to increase the compression ratio to 5:1, or even more, in order to get better control over the loud notes. In slow compositions, the release time of the compressor can be no less than 0.5 sec. If you need not emphasize the attack of each note, specify a small attack time.

An electric guitar with a strongly distorted sound (distortion effect) has a smooth dynamic by itself, since the distortion effect works like a compressor. This means that you most likely won't need to apply compression. A rhythm guitar with a clear sound needs nearly the same compression as acoustic guitar. Therefore, the settings will be the same.

In modern music, percussion instruments are recorded with the most significant differences in dynamics. Compression is often used, especially if the performer does not play smoothly enough. This is especially true for the bass drum. In dance music, it is common practice to support the sound level of the tenor drum at the same level. As a starting point, it is recommended that you set the compression factor to be within the limits of 4:1—6:1, and the attack time to 10 ms (to emphasize the percussion). The release time must be set to lower values than the time interval between the beats (approximately 20—100 msec). After that, set the actuation threshold so as to apply smaller compression factors to soft music that are smaller than those for loud sounds.

Cymbals are not ordinarily compressed, or they would sound unnatural.

The advantage of compressing the final mix is that the average loudness level of the composition increases. The music sounds louder, although the peaks remain as they were. If the mix is compressed in order to play it on the radio, it is recommended that you set a short attack time (0—10 msec), the smallest possible value for the release time, and a value of 20—50 msec for the sustain time.

To preserve the balance in the left and right channels, the compressor must operate in stereo mode. Compression in both channels must be the same, otherwise one of the channels will sound louder than the other.

4.5.2. Using Gate and Expander

Noises represent a problem at all stages of recording. They are present in every room, and are generated by the equipment as well. In digital systems, quantization noise is always present. The most common reasons for noises can be poor screening or unreliable grounding circuits. Undesirable sounds, such as the sound produced by turning pages, squeaking of chairs, noise from the audience, etc., can also find their way in.

If the noise is already mixed with the legitimate electric signal, then you have no way of eliminating it completely. If the noises are not significant, there is a chance that they will be audible only in the softest moments of the record. It is very difficult to suppress noise in an already prepared mix, because the periods of silence are distributed unevenly. However, it is possible to correct the noise situation for individual tracks.

In vocals, there are pauses between words and phrases. If you decrease the signal level during the pauses, then the noise level will also decrease. You can't, however, do this for each pause on each track.

The problem of noise suppression during pauses can be solved using an electronic switch that reacts to the level of the input signal. This device is known as the gate, or threshold noise suppressor. Gate switches the signal off when its level drops below a specified threshold value. In doing this, however, you risk losing soft signals. To solve the soft sound loss problem, gates are supplied with a release time control. Instead of immediately switching the signal off when its level drops below the specified threshold value, gate allows the signal to fade during the selected time period. The noise is not turned on or off abruptly (this sounds even worse than constant and steady background noise). Low level signals fade naturally.

The most important gate parameters are attack time and release time. If the gate is opened too abruptly, you will hear a click.

If the gate is opened too slowly, the attack phase might be lost in the sound of the tenor drum.

If the signal supplied to the gate input has a slowly-fading, wave-like form, the signal will produce a "rattle" because of the continuously changing level. To eliminate this rattling sound, you should use a hysteresistic noise suppressor with two values for the threshold level—one for enabling the gate and another for disabling it.

Like the compressor, the gate has a control channel that measures the level of the input signal and compares it with the threshold value. When the signal level exceeds the threshold level, a control signal is generated that enables the gate (with the speed specified by the attack time control). When the signal level drops below the threshold value, the gate is disabled according to the sustain time and release time.

Sometimes, the gate, just as the compressor, can be switched in such a way as to supply control from an external source. In such a case, one signal will cause the disabling of another, for example: a bass drum can lock a bass guitar. If the bass guitar starts to play a little bit earlier than the drum, the sound will not pass the gate until the bass drum starts playing. Later on, the sound of the bass guitar will fade according to the specified values of the sustain and release times. Thus, the gate allows you to make a sound shorter than the original one.

To speed up the gate's reaction to specific frequencies, it is possible to include an equalizer into the control channel. This might be required, for example, when using the tenor drum sound for switching the gate. If the microphone also records the sound of high-hat, the gate will turn on and off in the pauses between the beats of the tenor drum. Using the equalizer, you can filter high-hat frequencies to prevent false switching.

Among all dynamic processing devices, the gate is the only one whose work becomes noticeable if you specify the incorrect settings. For example, an incorrect threshold value or too short of a decay time will result in the spontaneous enabling/disabling of the gate, which is heard as a very significant distortion. Set the actuation threshold as low as possible (this will prevent false switching), after which you should control the sustain and release time in such a way as to prevent the decay phase from being cut-off by the gate. The attack time must be short, but the clicks must not be audible.

Gate and expander are very much alike. Both extend the dynamic range of the signal. However, there are also significant differences. For example, the gate will never open if the signal level is always somewhat lower than the threshold value. On the other hand, expander in such a situation will pass the signal to the output, but increase the signal level. The lower the level of the input signal, the lower the level of the output signal. An expanding factor of 1:2 means that if the signal level at the expander input drops by 1 dB, the output signal level will be decreased by 2 dB. Signals that have passed through an expander sound strange: the peaks are too loud and soft sounds are barely audible. But this only happens to sounds with a level below the threshold value.

When the expansion factor is less than 1:1.5, it is possible to use the combined expander-gate for inconspicuously extending the dynamic range of the signals whose level is below the threshold value. If the threshold value is too high, then the whole signal is processed as a result. This method is applied when it is necessary to restore the natural dynamics of an over-compressed sound.

A signal can be processed using the gate either before or after recording (during the mixing stage). When writing several signals on one track (for example, when recording the sound produced by a percussion set with a large number of drums), it is preferable to use the gate during the recording process.

Don't pass signals containing reverberation through the gate, or part of the reverberation tail will be lost. If you first process the signal using the gate, and then mix reverberation into it, you'll get quite a good result. Fade phases of different sounds will be saved in full measure. Besides this, reverberation will help you to mask the gate's instability.

Most vocal sounds have a sufficiently quick attack and quite a slow fade. The only exceptions are words that end with hard consonants. If the gate is opened too quickly, there is the possibility that words with a soft attack will be accompanied by a clicking sound. The best thing to do is to set the attack time to no longer than 1 ms, which is long enough to eliminate the loss at the attack phase, and slow enough to avoid the click.

The release time must be 0.5 sec, which is sufficient to eliminate the risk of losing word endings with a soft fade. This is also sufficient to cut off all unnecessary noises after words with sharp endings.

For a long-lasting note, if the sound has an unstable level, the gate might be opened or closed, which produces a "rattling" sound. To avoid this rattling, it is necessary to increase the sustain time. Rattling represents a problem only when the release time is small. However, you can't correct the situation by simply increasing the release time, since the signal might end before the gate closes, thus producing noise. A similar problem exists for the threshold level. The smaller the value of the threshold level, the better the result. However, if its value is too small, the gate might be switched by noises rather than by the legitimate signal.

If you compress vocal music while simultaneously passing it through the gate, it is recommended that you place the gate before the compressor. If the gate is placed after the compressor, the dynamic range decreased by the compressor will make it difficult to establish the threshold level correctly.

When processing drum sounds, the gate is used not only to eliminate unnecessary noises, but also to change the sound by creating a quick, clear fade. Bass drums and tom-toms whose sounds contain unnecessary ringing, will close the gate when passing through it. The ringing will be cut off, and the sound will become denser.

For percussion instruments, it is always important to transfer the transitional process; therefore, the attack time must be very short. The release time must be selected by ear.

When recording a percussion set using several microphones, each of which is set close to one of the drums, the gate is often used to improve the channel separation (which is reduced to eliminate the signal from the neighboring drum), and the threshold level must be sufficiently high, since the drums are very close to one another. There is also the very likely danger of losing the soft sounds. To avoid this, use gates with bandpass filters, which can be tuned to the sound of a specific drum while attenuating the sounds of other drums and cymbals tuned for another frequency. Such gates are most frequently used with tenor drums.

The virtual devices for dynamic processing included with the Cool Edit Pro program will be described in *Sections 12.7* and *12.9*.

Part II

MICROPHONES, MIXERS, AND EFFECTS

Chapter 5: Working with Microphones and Mixers

Chapter 6: Sound Effects

Chapter 5: Working with Microphones and Mixers

The recording and playback quality of the sounds produced by actual sources depends on a large variety of factors, the most important of which are listed below:

❑ Analog-to-digital converter

❑ Digital-to-analog converter

❑ Mixing and amplification channel

❑ The room where recording is done

❑ The microphone

In this chapter, we will discuss the last three items on this list.

If necessary, one can find special literature where the requirements for studio rooms intended for sound recording are listed and explained. Such literature also provides examples of studio planning and explains how to decrease the level of electrical and acoustic interference. We won't concentrate on these aspects, since, unfortunately, the implementation of such recommendations is rather expensive and hardly possible under home studio conditions. There is, however, one thing that is clear: to record live sound using a microphone, you should select a room where the noise level is at a minimum (noises from the running computer must also be taken into account). Notice that computer processing of the sound signal enables you to partially eliminate background noises, which gives you some hope of obtaining a recording quality acceptable for demo versions, even in cases when recording is done in a room without special equipment. It is also desirable to minimize the level of sound reflected from the wall or furniture. To achieve this, it is necessary to insulate the room using sound-absorbing materials. If you are going to record sound using a microphone, and then process it using sound editors like Cool Edit Pro, the requirements to the studio room—from the point of view of level distribution and sound wave reflection—become less stringent. You won't need to pay so much attention to the given natural reverberation as you would with analog methods of processing a recorded signal. You'd be better off making sure that the microphone doesn't record reflected signals at all. Sound editors enable you to imitate the acoustic properties of practically any room.

We'll now put all of the other factors that influence the quality of sound recording aside, and concentrate only on the microphone. The microphone can lessen the influence of the room's drawbacks, but it can also emphasize them.

5.1. Microphones and Their Basic Parameters

You can find lots of microphones in attractive packages in any specialized store. How should you choose the right one from such a large variety? Let's consider this problem without diving too deep into the technical side of it.

The working principle of the microphone is based on conversion of sound waves to electric oscillations in such a way as to minimize the changes to the information contained in the sound. To achieve this, the microphone must meet the following requirements:

❏ At working sound levels, the microphone must produce an electric signal sufficiently exceeding the level of its natural electric noises

❏ The electric signal produced by the microphone must not contain significant distortions

❏ It must provide equally good quality when transferring all sound frequencies contained in the signal within the limits of the frequency ranges of the devices into which it is plugged

Microphones convert sound pressure oscillations to electric oscillations using different methods. From this point of view, they can be classified into the following categories: electrodynamic microphones, electromagnetic microphones, electrostatic microphones, piezoelectric microphones, carbon microphones, and semiconductor microphones.

Electrodynamic microphones are further subdivided into moving-coil microphones and ribbon microphones. Electrostatic microphones include capacitor microphones and electret microphones, which are widely used for professional recording. Electromagnetic and piezoelectric microphones are not widely used, due to their narrow frequency range and uneven frequency characteristic. We won't look at carbon and semiconductor microphones, since their working principle doesn't ensure that any of the above-listed requirements are sufficiently satisfied.

The common principle of a microphone of any type is that the membrane (diaphragm) of the microphone receives sound oscillations and transmits them to a unit that converts these oscillations to an electric signal.

The constructions of the microphones most commonly used for high-quality sound recording are presented in the illustrations provided below.

Electrodynamic microphones (Figs. 5.1 and 5.2) work as follows: sound pressure oscillations force the diaphragm to move together with the attached inductor (for moving coil microphones) or ribbon (for ribbon microphones). The movement of these elements in the magnetic field of a permanent magnet generates an electromotive force at the ends of the coil or ribbon. It is the change in this electromotive force that carries the sound information. Permanent magnets are produced using special materials with high values of residual induction and coercitive force. Coil resistance in various models is normally within the range of 20—600 ohms.

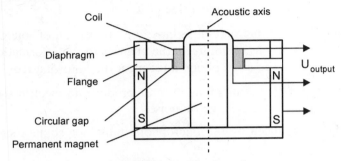

Fig. 5.1. Moving-coil microphone

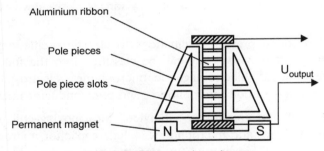

Fig. 5.2. Ribbon microphone

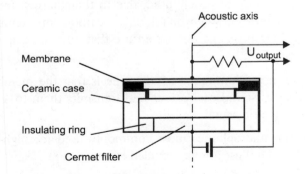

Fig. 5.3. Capacitor microphone

To compensate for electromagnetic interference (alternate current background), moving-coil microphones generally include a background shielding coil connected to the sound coil and usually wrapped around a magnetic system. The coils are connected in such a way as to mutually compensate the noise from the inducted background voltages excited in both coils.

In a ribbon converter (Fig. 5.2), the ribbon, in contrast to the coil, has a very small electric resistance (about 0.1—0.3 ohms). At a pressure of 1 Pa, the signal voltage at its output is only about 20—30 μV, which is comparable to the voltage of electrostatic interference in microphone cables. Because of this, the voltage created by the ribbon is pre-amplified using a shielded step-up transformer placed within the microphone case.

Ribbon microphones are distinguished by their natural softness and transparency when transmitting the timbre of most musical instruments. This is explained by the very small mass of the moving element—the ribbon.

Capacitor microphones require an external power supply. A rigidly strained membrane oscillates under the force of changing sound pressure in relation to the fixed electrode. These two elements are capacitor plates, which thus form the capacitor. As the membrane oscillates, the capacity changes with the frequency of the sound pressure influencing the membrane. Thus, the alternate current in the electric circuit is proportional to the sound pressure.

The unit correlating the resistance value of the microphone converter with that of the amplifying device is an integral part of any capacitor microphone (Fig. 5.3). This electric unit of the capacitor microphone may be of a high-frequency or low-frequency type.

With the high-frequency type of conversion, the plate of the capacitor microphone is connected to the circuit of the high-frequency generator (several MHz). First, the high-frequency signal is modulated by frequency, and after demodulation with the frequency detector, the sound frequency signal is produced. This way of connecting the plate doesn't require a polarizing voltage, and is characterized by a low level of the microphone's intrinsic noises. However, the high-frequency scheme is not widely used, mainly because of the difficulties of frequency stabilization. Most modern models of capacitor microphones are capacitor microphones with a low-frequency unit. In such microphones, the conversion of the sound pressure to an electric signal takes place with the use of external or internal (electret) polarization.

Electret microphones are capacitor microphones according to their working principle. However, they provide a higher efficiency signal conversion, since the voltage at the capacitor plates is provided by the electric charge of the membrane or fixed electrode, and not by a normal external source. The material of these elements has the electret property of being able to keep the charge for a long time.

Capacitor microphones of wide frequency and dynamic range are commonly used under professional studio conditions, often with a switchable directivity pattern (for example, an MC 51 Nevaton or MC 416 Nevaton). Studio capacitor microphones are 5—10 times more sensitive than dynamic microphones, and have practically no audible transitional distortions. Therefore, under studio conditions and in sound amplification systems, recent trends tend toward the increased use of small cardioid capacitor microphones such as 84, 184 (Neumann), and C460B (AKG). Among the drawbacks of capacitor microphones are the necessity of having a constant voltage source (normally a line-operated power supply unit), and the fact that capacitor microphones poorly tolerate high humidity and abrupt temperature changes. Therefore, capacitor microphones are rarely used outdoors or in portable sets.

The main characteristics and parameters that determine the microphone's quality are listed below:

❑ Sensitivity—the ratio of voltage U at the microphone output to the sound pressure that affects the microphone, expressed in millivolts per pascal [mV/Pa]: $E = U/p$.

❑ Sensitivity level—sensitivity expressed in decibels in relation to the $E_{initial} = 1$ V/Pa value, and determined using the following formula $N_m = 20 \lg E - 60$ [Db], where E is the microphone sensitivity [mV/Pa].

❑ Dynamic range—the difference between the sound pressure limit levels and internal noise levels.

❑ Nominal frequency range—the frequency range within which the microphone perceives acoustic oscillations, and within which its parameters are standardized. For professional studio recording, it is common to use microphones of the zero complexity group of the highest quality category, for which a frequency range of 20—20,000 Hz is standard. Microphones of the first complexity group must have a nominal frequency range no less than 31.5—18,000 Hz, and ranges for microphones of the second group should be about 50—15,000 Hz.

❑ Frequency response of the microphone. The variation in the frequency response is determined as the difference between the maximum and minimum sensitivity levels of the microphone within the nominal frequency range, expressed in dB: $\Delta N = N_{max} - N_{min}$.

❑ Directional pattern—dependence of the microphone sensitivity on the angle between its axis and the direction from which the sound is emanating.

❑ Impedance unit (also known as output or internal resistance), whose value is standard at a frequency of 1 kHz. The output resistance of the microphone must match the input resistance of the device to which it is connected.

One of the most important parameters of the microphone is its level of internal noise. Obviously, a high-quality microphone must have a low value of this parameter.

Fig. 5.4 shows the Nevaton family of capacitor microphones. From left to right:

❑ Universal cardioid microphone MC 49

❑ MC 51 microphone with a switchable directivity pattern and double-membrane converter of medium diameter

❑ MC 401 high-directional microphone

❑ MC 47 stereo microphone for XY-mode recording, comprising two double-membrane converters with angle of turn ranging from 0° to 90°, enclosed in a common case

❑ MC 404 stereo microphone with one double-membrane converter of large diameter

In the foreground is the boundary layer microphone, which has an unusual flat form. If you set this microphone on the table (or more precisely, simply lay it on the table surface), it will uniformly perceive the sound from above. Under studio conditions, when performing simultaneous recording of the voices of several persons, such a microphone can replace a number of lapel microphones.

Fig. 5.4. Nevaton capacitor microphones

Generally speaking, it is incorrect to state that a microphone with such and such characteristics is better than another microphone without knowing the conditions under which it will be used and the specific tasks that it must perform. Statements such as "the higher the better" are not suitable for all parameters.

For example, a microphone with high sensitivity is suitable as an interception device for recording sound from a large distance. The same microphone is not good for recording the voice of a soloist accompanied by an orchestra, since it will record not only the voice of the singer, but also the sound of musical instruments that have been distorted in the course of propagation. On the other hand, there is no system of signal conversion and amplification free from internal noise. Since the microphone is the initial unit of such a system, the level of the legitimate signal that it creates determines the "signal/internal noise" ratio of the whole system. Therefore, decreasing the microphone's sensitivity is undesirable.

For correct transmission of the sound produced by bass musical instruments, it is not necessary to use a microphone with a high upper limit of the working frequency range. On the other hand, the wider the working frequency range of the microphone (i.e., the smaller the low frequency limit and the higher the upper frequency limit), the more universal the microphone.

One of the most important parameters influencing microphone selection is its directivity pattern. Graphically, it is represented in polar coordinates as a pattern in a horizontal plane.

Microphones can be subdivided into three groups according to the type of their directivity: omnidirectional microphones, bidirectional microphones, and unidirectional microphones.

As an initial approximation, it is assumed that omnidirectional microphones perceive sound from any direction in the same way. The working zone of an onmidirectional microphone is a sphere, and its directivity pattern is a circle, as shown in Fig. 5.5.

Bidirectional microphones have the same sensitivity for both the front and rear. The directivity diagram is somewhat similar to a figure 8 (Fig. 5.5b).

Unidirectional microphones are sensitive only to sound waves coming from the front. For this type of microphone, the directivity pattern is a curve similar to a cardioid (Fig. 5.5c). Besides unidirectional microphones, there are also high-directional microphones. Fig. 5.5d shows the directivity pattern of such a microphone, which is represented by a curve known as the super-cardioid.

Notice that the directivity patterns shown in these illustrations are idealized. It is important to understand that the actual directivity properties are close to the ideal ones only within a narrow frequency range. The dependence of the directivity pattern on the frequency is especially strong for omnidirectional microphones. The higher the frequency, the smaller the solid angle within the limits of which a unidirectional microphone perceives sound waves.

Besides idealized directivity patterns, Fig. 5.5 represents the actual working areas of these microphones within their respective working frequency ranges.

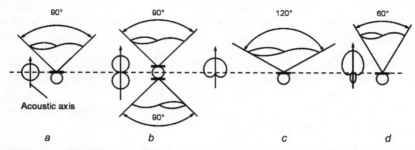

Fig. 5.5. Types of directivity patterns for various types of microphones

Neglecting such facts can result in horrible blunders. For example, if a single omnidirectional microphone is used to record a group of vocalists, then the singers with higher-pitched voices must be placed in such a way as to face the front of the microphone. If this requirement is not fulfilled, the loudness ratio will be violated and certain voices will be subject to amplitude-frequency distortions.

Products from respectable vendors are supplied with certificates that show the graphs of the directivity patterns for several frequencies, similar to the one provided as an example in Fig. 5.6.

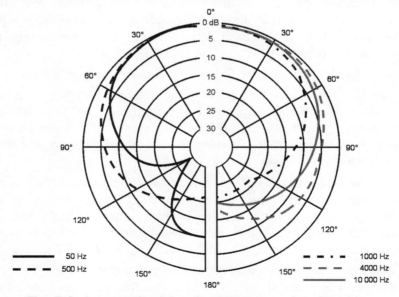

Fig. 5.6. An example of the directivity pattern of a microphone

Unidirectional microphones are used when performers are placed within the limits of a wide angle (when using several microphones during recording) to provide a clear separation of specific groups of musical instruments. This technique is also used when it is necessary to decrease the influence of parasitic noises or lower the value of the reverberation component in the recorded signal.

Bidirectional microphones are used when recording duets, dialogs, a singer and accompanist, when recording small musical ensembles, and when it is necessary to tune out directional noise sources or strong reverberations from the ceiling or floor. In such a case, the microphone must be situated depending on the minimal sensitivity zone, towards sources of noise or reflecting surfaces.

A microphone with a directivity pattern similar to a figure 8 is also used in cases when it is necessary to specially emphasize low frequencies of the soloist's voice or a specific musical instrument. For this, the microphone must be placed very close to the performer.

Omnidirectional microphones are used for rendering the impression of the general acoustic situation of a room when recording with several microphones, or when recording speech, singing, or music in a strongly insulated room.

Sometimes, a special group of microphones is distinguished from the rest—so-called combined microphones, i.e., microphones with a variable (switchable) directivity pattern. In these microphones, practically any directivity pattern can be obtained by combining electric signals from two receivers—omnidirectional and bidirectional, or from two insets of cardioid microphones at a 180° angle, or by changing the value of the polarization voltage at the two halves of the fixed electrodes or at the membranes in double-membrane capacitor microphones.

Microphones can be classified into the following groups by the type of their receiver:

❐ Pressure receivers (omnidirectional). In such receivers, the sound influences the moving elements (membrane, diaphragm) only from one side. Therefore, at low and medium frequencies, where the microphone size is small in comparison to the sound wave length, the microphone's sensitivity practically doesn't change at different angles of incidence of the sound waves.

❐ Gradient receivers or pressure difference receivers (directional). There are two types of such receivers: ones with two, almost symmetric acoustic inputs (in which case the directivity pattern is similar to a figure 8 and is sometimes designated by the term "bidirectional", and ones with two or more asymmetric acoustic inputs (in which case the receivers are unidirectional).

Besides the directivity diagram, another important characteristic of the microphone is its frequency response. The principle requirement of the frequency response of a universal microphone is its flatness. The closer the microphone's frequency response is to a straight horizontal line, the more precisely such microphone renders the timbre of the singer's voice or musical instrument. When using the microphone in the sound amplification system of a concert hall, non-uniformity of a microphone's frequency response might result in the self-excitation of the acoustic system, which is a very unpleasant effect, especially for the public.

As an example, Fig. 5.7 shows frequency responses of the MC 416 capacitor microphone from Nevaton.

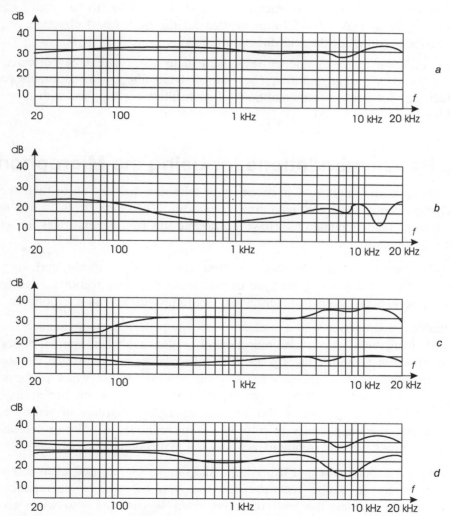

Fig. 5.7. Frequency responses of the MC 416 Nevaton capacitor microphone

Plotted on the abscissas are frequency values (Hz), and plotted on the ordinates is the change in the microphone's sensitivity level in dB. The directivity pattern of the MC 416 Nevaton microphone can be changed using a switch. This pattern can be in the form of a circle, cardioid, figure 8, or wide cardioid. The frequency response, naturally, strongly depends on the selected directivity pattern.

Fig. 5.7a shows the frequency response of the microphone when a circular directivity pattern is selected. Fig. 5.7b corresponds to the cardioid directivity pattern; Fig. 5.7c to the figure 8 directivity characteristic; and Fig. 5.7d to a wide cardioid. The upper graphs in Figs 5.7b—5.7d are plotted for the front (axis) direction (0), while the lower ones are done for the rear direction (180°).

The small variation in the frequency response can to some extent be corrected when processing the signal using multifrequency narrow-band filters with adjustable parameters—equalizers. Software implementantions of such filters are supplied with most sound editors (*Sections 12.21—12.26*).

5.1.1. Recommendations for Using the Microphone

When selecting a microphone, it is necessary to take into account all of their technical characteristics, along with the recording conditions. Therefore, it is rather difficult to provide exact recommendations. However, despite this fact, general rules for selecting microphones still exist.

An omnidirectional microphone can be used for recording music and singing in a strongly muffled room. The same type of microphones is also recommended for rendering the general acoustic environment when recording with several microphones.

A unidirectional microphone with a cardioid directivity pattern is recommended for use in a room with a large number of sound reflections. It is also used when external noises penetrate a room where recording takes place. The microphone rear must face the source of sound interference. Such a microphone is recommended for use when performers are standing in a row, causing a wide source angle. It is also used when performing multi-microphone recording in a home studio for clear separation of groups of performers, and also when a performer is placed very close to the microphone, in order to decrease low-frequency distortions inherent in omnidirectional and bidirectional microphones.

A bidirectional microphone with a figure 8-like diagram should be used when recording in an insulated room. It is also recommended that you use such a microphone when it is necessary to increase the level of reverberated signals, and also when recording the sounds of specific musical instruments and voices of singers for specifically emphasizing low frequencies when performers are placed close to the microphone. This microphone is also used when it is necessary to tune out directed noise sources. To achieve this, the microphone is positioned with its non-sensitivity zone towards the noise source. A bidirectional microphone oriented horizontally proves to be useful for attenuation of the sound waves reflected from the floor, ceiling, and two walls. Such a technique allows you to economize. You needn't buy the notorious carpets, since you only need to perform acoustic processing for the two walls placed behind and in front of the performer.

The most convenient microphones are the ones supplied with a switch enabling you to change the directivity pattern. An example of such a microphone is the Nevaton MC 416 capacitor microphone.

Certainly, the time has come to point out that the graphs of these various properties don't allow for an absolutely correct assessment of the microphone's quality. Does it matter to you what chemical ingredients are in a piece of candy if it tastes bad anyway? The same is true for microphones, since they can have parameters close to the ideal, but at the same time not sound right. Only a group of independent experts can judge whether a specific microphone is suitable for specific conditions. Expertise is a complicated affair, sometimes close to science and sometimes having something of art. It is not accidental that the microphone's sound quality is described by poetic, or at any rate very figurative expressions. For example, the microphone's sound must be warm, voluminous, unsuppressed, flying, etc. Thus, according to specialists' evaluation, the Nevaton MC 416 microphone is preferable when recording male vocalists (the sound is warm and filled) and for mezzo-soprano female vocalists (the sound is natural and even).

In rooms with rigid parallel limiting surfaces (half-empty rooms with walls that are not acoustically processed) so-called standing waves can arise. Standing waves are sound oscillations in the so-called cavity resonator, whose role is played by a room where they slowly fade. The standing wave frequency depends on the room size. Natural acoustic oscillations arise at the frequencies at which some of the room's dimensions (length, width, and height) prove to be multiples of the half wave length. In a rectangular room, the existence of several standing waves of multiple frequencies (oscillation modes) is possible. Sound speed is approximately 1060 ft/sec; therefore, natural acoustic oscillations at frequencies of 55, 110, or 165 Hz will arise along a room's dimension equal to 10 ft. The lowest frequency modes are the most intense. The oscillation amplitudes decrease with the increase of the natural oscillation frequencies. Because of this, if the height, width, and length of the room are larger, the influence of standing waves is weaker, since the frequencies of the most intense modes prove to be outside the lower limit of the microphone's frequency range. Standing waves distort the spectral composition of the signal being recorded. In different points within the room, the amplitudes of the natural resonant frequencies are different, and, therefore, the timbre of the same sound source depends on the microphone's position. The resonant properties of the room and the variation of the microphone's frequency response manifest themselves especially strongly when the sound source generates a broadband signal capable of starting oscillation at practically any of the resonant frequencies. This is especially characteristic for recording the sound of some percussion instruments. When recording speech or singing, hushing and hissing sounds might become unnaturally emphasized.

Naturally, the studio room where recording takes place must be large. Furthermore, it is desirable that the length, width, and height of the room are significantly different from one another, and not multiples of each other. The most unfavorable conditions exist in cubic rooms, where the sound is most distorted during recording.

Sound absorption provides a natural method of suppressing resonance.

For example, an opened window provides complete sound absorption, since it simply allows the sound wave to pass through without reflections. Unfortunately, it also allows street noise to penetrate the room.

Bare walls, floors, and ceilings absorb sound energy at least partially. Therefore, even an echoing room cannot preserve sound energy to infinity. All building materials have some absorption properties. For example, concrete absorbs about 1% of sound energy at a frequency of 500 Hz, stucco walls about 2%, linoleum 3%, and parquet floors 7%. This, of course, is not sufficient. Consider, for example, a soft carpet on the floor that muffles sound by 20—40%.

Sometimes it is sufficient to increase the sound absorption factor of the room (for example, to place a carpet on the floor, hang heavy curtains, bring a bookcase into the room). Furniture, such as sofa, armchairs, chairs, etc., are also excellent sound absorbers. The most efficient are sound absorbers placed in the angles of the room and at the wall joints.

In *Section 6.2.4*, we will discuss reverberation in detail. For the moment, we'll only briefly mention this important phenomenon. Due to multiple reflections of the sound wave from the walls, floor, ceiling, and some furniture items, the sound doesn't fade immediately, but only after a certain period of time. Reverberation is determined by the room's size and the reflecting abilities of the surfaces, such as the walls or the floor. It is generally accepted that a room with good acoustic characteristics has a small reverberation period. For example, a room with a volume of about 1700—3300 ft^3 has a reverberation time approximately equal to 0.1—0.3 sec.

Fig. 5.8 shows a schematic view of the sound source (S) and the microphone (M). The position of the microphone and sound source in relation to one another is determined by the following three parameters:

❏ The angle α between the line connecting the sound source and the microphone and the directivity axis of the microphone

❏ The directional properties of the sound source (the β angle between the SM line and the directivity axis of the sound source)

❏ The distance L between the sound source and the microphone

All musical instruments are conventionally divided into the following three groups according to their directivity properties:

❏ Instruments with clearly marked directivity (for example, brasses)

❏ Instruments without clearly marked directivity (for example, percussion instruments)

❏ Instruments taking an intermediate position between the first two groups (this group is the most numerous)

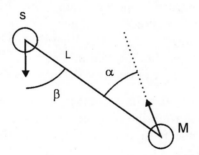

Fig. 5.8. Position of the microphone (M) and sound source (S)

The α, β, and L parameters determine the levels of the signals arriving to the microphone, the timbres of sound sources, and the ratio of the legitimate signal to the interference. When the microphone is turned around on its axis and the α angle increases, the level of the recorded signal changes due to the fact that the directivity pattern is not a circle. Increasing the β angle has a similar effect, because of the change in the direct sound arriving to the microphone. Changing any of these two angles results in high frequency roll-off, which influences the timbre of the recorded signal. This is especially true for muffled rooms or for cases when L is small. This can be explained by the fact that under such conditions, the most important role is played by direct sound, whose energy at point M changes significantly. When L is large, or when the sound is recorded in resonant rooms, where the reflected part of sound waves is large, frequency distortions are less noticeable. For a ribbon microphone whose directivity pattern almost doesn't depend on the frequency at all, changing α doesn't result in frequency distortions. Generally, the best conditions for recording will be provided when $\alpha = 0$ and $\beta = 0$.

When recording using several microphones, it is necessary to pay attention to their phase tuning: signals from the microphones must not be passed out of phase to the recording channel, since this can result in mutual compensation or even total disappearance of the signals.

Without noticeable timbre distortion caused by the interference of the incident and reflected signals, the microphone can be positioned no less than 3—5 ft away from any reflecting surface.

All efforts to improve the recording quality might prove to be useless if you neglect obvious rules. One of the most common errors is holding the microphone. It can be justified only in cases of extreme shortage of money, or when recording the voice of a moving performer. This technique requires significant experience. When you watch TV and see performers running around with a microphone, don't forget that in most cases you are hearing a previously recorded soundtrack rather than live music. Most performers who move around with their microphone don't know how to use it properly. The most common mistakes are the following: using the microphone at a very close distance, swinging it, and moving the fingers holding the microphone. During a live performance this can be tolerated, but there is no excuse for it during a recording session.

The microphone must be securely fixed to a fixed rack equipped with shock absorbers in order to protect the microphone from interference, such as shocks or vibrations from the walls and floor. The signal cable must be shielded, connections must be reliable, and powerful noise sources must not be situated near the cable.

5.1.2. Microphones and Musical Instruments

When complementing compositions recorded using synthesized MIDI instruments with recorded parts of real musical instruments, you should be acquainted with the specific properties of their sounds. This will help you in selecting the appropriate type of microphone, determining the best position for the microphone and the musical instrument, and avoiding distortions of its natural sound.

The frequency range is the most important characteristic of any musical instrument, having a significant influence on the choice of microphone. Fig. 5.9 represents frequency ranges of various musical instruments. The upper row contains the logarithmic scale of frequencies (Hz). To make the diagram more illustrative, these data are provided in comparison to a piano's frequency range, spanning from the *A* of the subcontraoctave (a frequency of 27.5 Hz) up to the *C* of the fifth octave (a frequency of 4,186 Hz). It is important to know that besides the spectrum of the fundamental frequencies, each instrument is characterized by additional frequency components—so-called overtones. Frequency ranges of an instrument's overtones are designated in Fig. 5.9 by grayed strips. The specific sound of each instrument is determined by the distribution of the amplitudes at all frequencies—both fundamental and overtones.

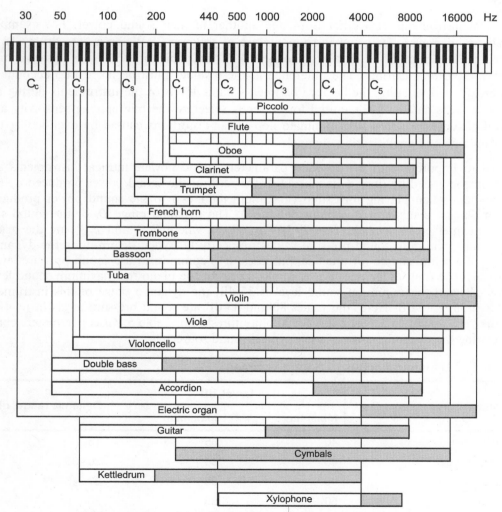

Fig. 5.9. Frequency ranges of some musical instruments

The relative power of sound oscillations emitted by instruments in various areas of the frequency range is different. Most musical instruments amplify the fundamental frequencies of overtones in specific, relatively narrow bands. If this is the case, the frequency spectrum of the instrument has formants. This phenomenon is explained by the resonant properties of the musical instrument's construction. For each instrument, formant areas take specific positions on the frequency axis. For example, formant area frequencies are 250—600 Hz for a trombone, 300—900 Hz for a clarinet, and 350-900 Hz for a saxophone.

Musical instruments also differ from one another in their sound power. For example, peak sound powers for some instruments are as follows: 25 W for a bass drum, 12 W for a tenor drum, 6 W for a trombone, 0.4 W for a piano, 0.3 W for a saxophone, and 0.05 W for a clarinet. The difference in these values must be taken into account in order to avoid violating the balance between volume levels of the instruments during recording. This data is also required for correctly selecting the microphone sensitivity and the distance L, which would eliminate non-linear distortions caused by overloading the microphone and amplification channel.

Equal in importance to the absolute parameter—sound power, musical instruments are also characterized by their dynamic range: the ratio of the sound power produced by the instrument when playing fortissimo (maximum loudness) to the sound power produced when playing pianissimo (minimum loudness). The dynamic range D, or the sound signal, is expressed in decibels: $D = 20 \lg(P_{max}/P_{min})$, where P_{max} and P_{min} are the maximum and minimum sound pressure values, respectively. When determining the dynamic range of a sound source for practical purposes, it is common to use sound pressure levels and calculate their difference. For example, since for the piano the maximum sound level is 80 dB, and the minimum sound level is 35 dB, the dynamic range of this instrument is $80 - 35 = 45$ dB. Here, the values 80 and 35 dB are sound pressure levels in relation to the zero reference acoustic level (audibility threshold). Table 5.1 lists parameters characterizing the dynamic range of some typical sound sources.

Table 5.1. Dynamic Ranges of Sound Sources

Sound source	Level, dB		Dynamic range, dB
	Minimum	Maximum	
Guitar	40	55	15
Female vocal	45	80	20—35
Male vocal	40	85	20—45
Organ	50	85	35

continues

Table 5.1 Continued

Sound source	Level, dB		Dynamic range, dB
	Minimum	Maximum	
Violoncello	35	70	35
Piano	35	80	45
Popular music	45	100	45—55
Symphonic orchestra	35	110	60—75

Musical instruments are commonly joined into groups: strings (bowed or plucked), woodwinds, brasses, and percussion. For the moment, out of all the data on musical instruments, we are only interested in those that influence the successful usage of the microphone. Under home studio conditions, it is highly improbable that you'd need to record the sound of a harp or a real pipe organ. To summarize this section of the book, let us consider only the aspects related to recording the instruments most likely to be used for enlivening the sound of an electronic orchestra.

The bowed strings group includes violins, violas, violoncellos, and double bass. Naturally, MIDI instrument banks contain all of the above listed instruments. However, it is impossible to replace the live sound of a violin or cello, even when using the most perfect synthesizing algorithm.

The violin is the smallest instrument from this group, having the highest-pitched voice. The largest amount of sound energy (especially when playing high-pitched sounds) is radiated from the front side of the violin. Thus, you should aim the microphone towards the soundholes on the upper board of the instrument.

For some sounds of the cello, especially the bass ones, an emphasized resonance is characteristic. This might produce an undesirable effect, especially when the sound frequency coincides with one of the natural frequencies of the studio, the maximums of the frequency characteristic of the microphone, or elements of the amplification channel.

The double bass is the instrument most difficult to record, since the acoustic properties of the room where recording is done have the strongest influence on its sound. Subjectively, this influence is perceived as non-clarity, dullness, and poor distinction of low frequencies. Attempts at correcting this defect by means of raising low frequencies during frequency corrections don't produce any positive results. When recording an ensemble, it is required that you place a separate microphone near the double bass.

The flute and clarinet are the most popular instruments in the woodwind group.

The pecularities of the flute's sound is that even in a muffled room it preserves its airiness and lightness. The presence of registers with a low sound level is characteristic for this instrument, and therefore the microphone must be placed very close to the flute. At the same time, it is necessary to make sure that specific noises, such as hissing sounds produced by air flow at the edges of the mouthpiece, are not audible in the recorded signal.

The clarinet is even more difficult an instrument to record. Here, everything is based on contradiction: if the microphone is placed too close to the instrument, the breathing noise caused by excessive pressure during the attack phase might become audible. In the upper register, the clarinet has a sharp and penetrating sound. Because of these reasons, it is best to increase the distance between the instrument and the microphone. On the other hand, when playing softly in low register, the tender sounds of the clarinet are better recorded by a closely situated microphone.

Perhaps most people will be surprised, but the woodwind group also includes the saxophone. This really seems shocking, especially when you look at this iridescent instrument shining with a clearly metallic brilliance. Despite this impression, it is a woodwind. The inventor of this popular musical instrument, Adolphe Sax, was trying to create a musical instrument somewhere between a woodwind and a brass. To implement this idea, he joined within a single instrument a bell-like outlet with oboe valves and the reed from a clarinet. Since then, there has appeared a large family of saxophones of different sizes and different timbres: sopranino, soprano, alto, tenor, baritone, bass, and double bass. The saxophone has quite a wide frequency range and produces quite a large sound pressure (as compared to other woodwinds). The sounds of a saxophone are characterized by a noticeable vibration. When recording the saxophone, it is necessary to consider the fact that the sound is emitted from the holes on the instrument's body closed by valves, and the sound at the lowest frequencies is emitted mainly from the bell-shaped opening. The microphone should be placed at a distance of 3—5 ft from the instrument.

Brass instruments create intense, high-frequency oscillations in the area of the bell-shaped opening. Thus, when the microphone is placed near the opening, the sound is brighter, and when it is placed at an angle to the opening, the sound is softer. To produce a softer sound, one can use a dynamic microphone.

For woodwinds, most of the sound is emitted from the openings in the instrument body rather than from the larger opening. To produce better quality, place the microphone at a distance of approximately 12 inches from the instrument and direct it to these openings. When recording the flute, place the microphone at approximately 4 inches and direct it towards a point between the mouthpiece and the first openings. Sometimes it might be necessary to use a special screen to decrease the noise from the performer's breathing, or move the microphone further away.

Among the brasses, the most popular instruments are the trumpet and trombone.

The trumpet has the brightest timbre among the brass instruments. When playing loudly in the upper register it is clearly audible, even with a powerful orchestral background. When playing quietly, it can be placed near the microphone, and in general, because of its strong directivity, on one side of the microphone's axis.

The trombone plays in a lower register than the trumpet. Volume is especially high in the range from 2000 to 3000 Hz. Since in this range the ear sensitivity is at maximum, when recording several instruments simultaneously, you might want to place the trombone sideways and at a significant distance from the microphone.

We will consider the only instrument that is not included in any orchestral group—the grand piano. Its most important acoustic part is the soundboard under the strings and the rims glued into the outer case of the instrument.

Sounds from the grand piano are radiated mainly by the upper side of the soundboard, and after being reflected from the cover, are mainly directed parallel to the strings. However, the general directivity of the instrument depends on the sound frequency, and is especially noticeable at large distances from the microphone. The grand piano has several characteristic directivity zones (Fig. 5.10).

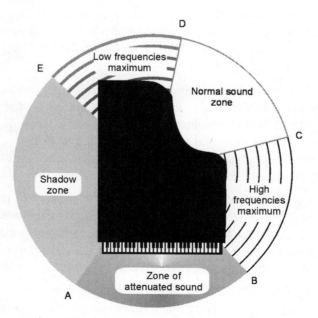

Fig. 5.10. Directivity zones of a grand piano

The AB sector represents a uniform zone of sounds of attenuated intensity. The BC zone in the proximity of the shortest strings is notable for its prevailing high frequencies. The CD sector is distinguished by rich timbre variety, and represents the working zone. Low frequencies are predominant in the DE zone. The DA zone is the so-called shadow zone, characterized by a weak and non-uniform sound.

Usually, the microphone must be set in the working zone during recording. The position of the microphone within the working zone must be selected experimentally, in order to balance the intensity of the sounds of the left-hand and right-hand parts. The microphone is set at a distance of 5—16 ft from the instrument, at a height of 5 ft above the floor, and oriented directly towards the strings. You can minimize the interference caused by interaction between direct sound and the sound reflected from the cover by selecting the microphone's inclination angle. One of the distinguishing features of the piano is that this instrument covers a very wide frequency range. Consequently, to produce a quality sound, it is necessary to use a broadband microphone. Capacitor microphones are the most suitable for this purpose. It should also be noted that microphones with a small membrane perceive sound better.

The microphone's position depends on the sound that you need to record. For popular music, a bright sound is needed, while classical or jazz require a more natural, volumetric sound.

The best method is to use directional microphones (cardioid or supercardioid) to minimize the influence of the acoustic properties of the studio, and omnidirectional microphones for increasing such properties. The microphones must be placed at a height equal to the middle of the opened cover.

On stage, one often uses a closer position of the microphone: inside the piano at a distance of 6—10 inches from the strings, closer to the points where the hammers hit them. In this case, omnidirectional microphones are more suitable. One of the microphones is placed closer to the bass strings, and another one near the strings of the upper register. The distance between microphones must be at least three times greater than the distance between the microphone and the strings (the best ratio is five to one).

The upright piano produces sound that is not as rich (especially in the lower part of the spectrum). You can place a couple of microphones over a piano with an opened cover. It is also possible to place the microphones behind the performer's back and direct them towards the strings (to do this it is necessary to remove the front cover of the piano). If the piano is placed nearer to the wall, this might help to improve the sound of bass voices.

Recording percussion instruments is quite a difficult job. By changing the microphone's position in relation to the drums, you can significantly change the sound of the drum set.

If you need to get more low-frequency components, place the microphone at a distance of 1—2 inches from the plastic. The most marked attack will be received if you direct the microphone towards the place where the stick hits the plastic.

To obtain a more broadband sound for hi-hat cymbals, direct the microphone towards the cymbal edge. If you need to produce a brighter and clearer sound, direct the microphone towards the hat. To emphasize the attack in bass drums, place the microphone within the drum.

The technique of recording with two microphones is employed when it is necessary to obtain a more natural sound for the drum set.

For recording a bass drum, it is recommended that you use dynamic microphones with large membranes. If you are using two microphones, it will make sense to employ microphones that perceive sound differently. By mixing the signals from these microphones, you'll be able to find a balance between drum attack and resonance.

When recording the sounds of a tenor drum, it is recommended that you use dynamic microphones of the vocal type. Usually, the microphone is set directly above the drum, 1.5—2 inches from the plastic, and slightly inclined.

When recording a drum sound using two microphones, try to switch the microphones in antiphase.

When recording tom-toms, it is recommended that you use medium or large dynamic microphones. Having placed the microphones between two neighboring tom-toms, you'll be able to record both of them.

5.1.3. The Microphone and Vocal Music

The pitch range of a singer's voice is determined by the interval between the lowest and the highest-pitched notes that he or she is able to reproduce. By pitch, voices can be classified into male voices (bass, baritone, and tenor) and female voices (contralto, mezzo-soprano, soprano, and coloratura soprano). The ranges of the main groups of singer's voices are distributed as follows. Bass: 82—349 Hz, baritone: 110—392 Hz, tenor: 132—523 Hz, contralto: 165—698 Hz, mezzo-soprano: 220—880 Hz, soprano: 262—1046 Hz, and coloratura soprano: 330—1397 Hz. Such "non-rounded" values are due to the fact that the classification of singers' voices, which originated in the distant past, is not based on frequencies measured in Hz, but rather on specific notes of specific octaves.

A professional singer having a voice in one the above-listed ranges must master it within a range of no less than two octaves. Amateur singers have a narrower range. At first glance, it might seem that for recording vocal parts it would be sufficient to use the low-est-frequency and a narrow-band microphone, but this impression is erroneous. To render the characteristic features of the voice timbre, it is necessary to record a significantly wider frequency range—approximately 80—10,000 Hz.

Each of the ranges contains several distinct registers: low, medium, and high. Each register has a specific timbre. Achieving voice uniformity in all registers is quite a difficult task in a professional signer's education. This task is not always successfully accomplished, and the microphone is especially sensitive to transitions from register to register, emphasizing all non-uniformities and variations of the voice.

Singers' voices, despite all the variety, conform to some common laws: strongly marked high overtones with frequencies of 2,500—3,000 Hz (upper formant) and the presence of a lower formant within the range of 300—600 Hz. The upper format imparts the singer's voice with a "silvery" shade, while the lower makes the voice velvety and concentrated. Even a small roll-off at these frequencies in the sound recording channel distorts the timbre significantly. If these frequencies are insufficient in the singer's voice, it is possible to "correct nature" by the correcting the frequency with appropriate filters.

A good singer must have a command of the vibrato technique: the intensity of the sound emitted when using this technique oscillates with a frequency of 5—7 Hz. This helps to enrich the voice timbre by imparting it with specific coloring, and at the same time masks some characteristic defects, such as small variations in the sound intensity, incorrectness of the intonation, drawbacks of diction, etc. If the singer has insufficient command of vibrato or none at all, the microphone emphasizes all of the above-listed defects.

Singing differs from normal speech by its greater power and loudness. If recording is performed in a muffled room, the singer might get the impression of his or her voice sounding weak and soft. Because of this, the singer will involuntarily try to achieve the loudness to which he or she is accustomed, and thus force the sound. The microphone will inevitably emphasize this unnatural feature.

The dynamic range (maximum difference in the sound power between forte and piano) of a professional singers reaches 20—45 dB. The dynamic range of an amateur singer doesn't normally exceed 10 dB.

We won't concentrate here on the less probable case of recording singing with instrumental accompaniment, since the computerized sound studio provides the capability of first creating the accompanying sound track and reproducing it through headphones.

The main distinguishing feature of microphone usage in sound amplifying systems is the possibility of their self-excitation as a result of a parasitic acoustic loopback arising from the loudspeaker signal (either directly or reflected from the walls, ceiling, or other surfaces) hitting the microphone. This phenomenon usually limits the sound pressure value when making sound tracks of the halls. Increasing the stability of the sound amplification system is achieved both by special electronic sound processing and simple organizational steps:

❑ Place the microphone as close as possible to the source of the initial signal (singer, musical instrument), i.e., use hand-held microphones. In hand-held microphones, which usually are unidirectional, special measures are taken in order to suppress the lower frequencies in order to compensate for their rise when working with a close sound source.

❑ Move the singer and microphone as far away from the loudspeakers or reflecting surfaces as possible (the microphone is mounted on racks at the level of the performer's mouth, or at the level of the musical instrument).

❑ Correctly select the microphone's directivity pattern, and correctly orient its working axis in relation to the source of interference (reflections), and in relation to the working axis of the nearest acoustic systems. In terms of sound amplification system stability, a microphone with a supercardioid directivity pattern is the most universal.

In a concert hall or on stage, there is the risk of significant interference arising due to shocks and vibrations. Because of this, most mounting racks are equipped with a vibration damper, usually placed at the footing. For hand microphones, special vibration protection measures are taken: the inset is damped relative to the microphone case, and special electric filters are used in order to cut off lower frequencies.

Most frequently, vocalists are placed in a separate, acoustically muffled room during recording, and volumetric sound is created artificially by processing the signal with reverberator.

There are no ideal vocal microphones. Each performer and each song require an individual approach. However, there are several common aspects that must be taken into account when selecting the microphone. For example, dynamic microphones are less sensitive to high frequencies, but are more resistant to overloads. Such microphones might prove to be the only acceptable ones for a vocalist with a very powerful voice. However, capacitor microphones with a large membrane are the ones most frequently used when it comes to recording vocal music. Capacitor microphones with small membranes produce less colored sound, which is good for recording background vocals.

One of the most important problems that arises when recording vocal music are plosive consonants and sibilants. This problem is solved by appropriate selection of the microphone's position. The best thing to do is place the microphone slightly above the performer's mouth, approximately at nose level (if the microphone is set from above), or slightly below the mouth (if the microphone is set normally) without orienting it towards the performer's mouth. A mounting rack equipped with special vibration-damping elements protects the microphone from vibration noises that can arise on stage due to stomping, for example. The most widely-known technique of suspending the microphone is the so-called "spider" suspension, when the microphone hangs by bracing wires. Fig. 5.11 shows the Nevaton MC 416 capacitor microphone with a switchable directivity pattern and a double-membrane converter of large diameter fastened in such a suspension.

To produce a high-quality recording, it is necessary to provide comfortable accompaniment. For example, the accompaniment's loudness might influence the singing accuracy, since the softer the sound, the lower-pitched its tone seems. Accompaniment comfort includes both acceptable loudness and a particular balance of the instruments. If a vocal part requires a precise rhythm, make the sound of drums somewhat louder. For more accurate phrasing, it is possible to amplify the sound of instruments determining the song's harmony, for example, bass, keyboard, or guitar. Parts of additional ornamenting instruments can be made softer or can be totally removed. Quite often, vocal music is recorded with the accompaniment of the drums, bass, and/or some harmonic instrument, and the remaining arrangement is created taking the vocals into account.

Fig. 5.11. Nevaton MC 416 capacitor studio microphone fastened in the "spider" suspension

Most vocalists, especially ones who have no studio recording experience, have difficulties when hearing themselves while in earphones, since they are accustomed to controlling their singing in an open acoustic space. Because of this, the best practice is to use open earphones. It is also possible to supply the sound only in one earphone and hold only that earphone to the ear.

Most vocalists have a wider dynamic voice range than the one in the accompaniment, which constantly leads to a loss of balance (the voice is constantly either going to the foreground or becoming masked by the accompaniment). The appropriate technique of working with the microphone (when the vocalist moves farther away at loud notes) allows you to avoid such problems. If the vocalist cannot use this technique, such problems can be solved using a compressor. Typical settings for the voice must be as follows: a ratio of 3:1 and a threshold level 10 dB.

The problem of recording plosive sounds or sibilants can be solved using the de-esser.

5.2. The Typical Hardware Mixer Structure

When it is necessary to record several signals simultaneously or mix signals supplied from several different sources, it is very hard to manage without the mixer (mixer console).

The mixer allows you to solve several tasks, including the following ones:

❑ Mixing signals supplied from different sources in specified proportions

❑ Matching the level of the signal from the source to the sensitivity and dynamic range of the device for recording, processing, and amplification

❑ Measuring the signal level of the output mix (and, in some cases, the level of channel signals as well)

❑ Online tuning of signal levels

❑ Equalization (correction of the frequency properties of a signal)

❑ Supplying signals to external dynamic processing devices and effect processors, and regulating the levels of signals supplied to the processing devices and the levels of signals returned from such devices

❑ Signal switching

❑ Switching the phase of the channel signal

❑ Forming a mix to be subsequently supplied to the control monitors

❑ Muting specific channels and switching them to solo mode

A typical mixer console is shown in Fig. 5.12.

Fig. 5.12. Typical mixer

The typical mixer contains the following elements:

☐ *Channel module section* (sometimes the channel module is designated by the term "mixer input channel"). Each channel module contains switching and tuning controls, using which it is possible to process channel signals separately.

☐ *Buses for parallel connection of effect processors* (aux buses). These buses are used to connect one or more channels to external signal processing devices, and for subsequently returning the processed signal to the common mix.

☐ *Master module.* In this module, channel signals and signals returned from external processing devices are mixed into one or more pairs of stereo signals. The master module also allows you to measure and tune the level of the mixed signal.

☐ *Control signal forming module.* This module forms the mix supplied to the input of the amplifier connected to control monitors or earphones.

The control panel of the channel module contains most mixer controls. The channel module enables you to do the following:

☐ Connect various sound sources (microphone, electric guitar, synthesizer, tape recorder, CD player, and other linear signal sources) to the mixer

☐ Control the sound source volume

☐ Correct frequency properties of the signal using an equalizer

☐ Supply signals (main and monitor) to the system output

☐ Supply signals to the aux buses

Each channel module has controls for selecting various sources (microphone/linear), and allows you to set preliminary amplification factors for each source.

The channel equalizer serves to control the frequency properties of the input signal, both for correction purposes and to achieve a particular artistic effect.

The channel fader allows you to control the gain of a channel.

Some models contain switches that determine the subsequent route of the signal and supply it to different output buses.

Besides the main buses, the mixer also has auxiliary buses (aux buses) enabling you to organize monitoring (create sound track for the entire stage, or supply mixes to individual monitoring systems, such as the earphones of a performer) and connect additional processing devices. Each aux bus is shared by all channels, and the signals are supplied to the same processing device.

Inserts serve to sequentially connect an effect acting on only one channel.

Sequential effects or processings replace the source signal with their own signal. Examples of such effects are: reverberation, chorus, and flanger (see *Chapter 6*). Examples of processings are: equalizer, gate, and compressor. Sequential effects are switched to inserts when it is necessary to process the channels separately. For simultaneous processing of several sources, they can be connected via an aux bus. Unprocessed sound can be obtained by tuning the balance or effect depth on the processing device itself.

Parallel effects mix the source signal with the processed signal in specific proportions, rather than replace the source signal completely.

Most often, parallel effects are switched via an aux bus. The effect is available for all channels, and you are able to set a specific effect depth for each channel.

For parallel effects switched via the aux bus, it is necessary to set the maximum effect depth. Processing depth is adjusted using the feed level control.

If only one channel needs to be processed by the effect, then the effect might be connected to the insert in order to achieve the desired relationship between the processed signal and source signal by regulating the effect balance.

Now let's turn to the switching and controlling elements present in each channel module.

To connect signal sources, there are connector sockets of different types. There must at least be a three-pin XLR connector (for connecting the microphone) and a monojack socket (for connecting linear signal sources). The input selector (the **mic/line** switch) determines which connector socket and which amplification elements will be used by the current channel.

The signal attenuation button allows for attenuating the signal level (by 20—30 dB) before transmitting it to a specific amplification element of the mixer. This helps you to avoid overloading from signals of an excessive level.

Phase switch is used for correcting the consequences of improper switching of the cables or phase changes, when the positioning of a system comprising several microphones requires it. The first position of the switch corresponds to a zero phase shift, the second to a phase shift of 180°. (In other words, the signal is inverted.) This switch usually affects only balanced microphone input, and doesn't influence linear input.

Phantom power is supplied only to a balanced microphone input, and is the power supply for a capacitor microphone. The term *phantom* implies that no additional conductors or power supply are required to supply the voltage. The 48 V supply voltage is sent to the capacitor microphone by signal wires. To separate the direct and alternate current circuits, capacitors are used. Notice that the phantom power switch must be used with extreme care. If the microphone input is switched to a non-balanced signal source, you might burn the device by accidentally turning phantom power on, since this will supply a voltage of 48 V to it.

Balanced signal sources are not subject to negative effects when using phantom power.

Phantom power can also be used for connecting an electric guitar or keyboard. For this purpose, it is required that you observe the following rules:

❐ Make sure that special selector devices are used, attenuating phantom power to the nominal value specified for the device to be connected

❐ Make sure that the phantom power source is not overloaded by a device consuming excessive current

Preliminary amplification control allows you to balance the levels of the signal source and the mixer. This, for example, compensates for volume variance in the voices of different singers and in signal levels supplied from different sources (microphone, guitar, etc.).

Preliminary amplification must be adjusted with the pressed **Solo** button, placed near the channel fader. This button allows you to select the channel signal from the mix, check its level, and evaluate the sound quality independent from the common mix. Amplification at the output must be adjusted so that the peak indications of the level indicator are on the boundary of the red zone (0 VU), but never remain there for long.

A mixer's equalizer usually has three frequency bands: low, medium, and high. Most inexpensive mixers use semi-parametric equalizers that allow you to select the frequency range with which the equalizer will work for all or just for some specific bands. In contrast to a parametric equalizer, the semi-parametric equalizer doesn't allow you to adjust the Q factor of the filter. If the central frequency of the equalizer filter changes, the pass band also changes, and the parametric equalizer is unable to compensate this change.

An expensive professional mixer uses parametric equalizers, for which both the central frequency and the Q factor can be adjusted independently.

If all labels on the knobs are directed upright, the equalizer is in the neutral position. When the knob is turned clockwise, the signal is amplified within the selected frequency range. When the knob is turned counter-clockwise, the signal is attenuated. Signal amplification makes sense when searching the equalization frequency, since amplification will make all sound defects noticeable at this frequency. To achieve tone balance, it is advisable to suppress the frequencies of all the other signals rather than amplify the frequencies of the signal that you want to select (since amplification might result in signal distortion). From the equalizer output, the signal is supplied to the insert and then to the channel fader.

Insert is a socket of the stereojack type with somewhat strangely-wired contact sets. If the response part of the connector is not switched to the socket, the signal from the equalizer output is supplied to the fader input. However, if the jack is inserted into the socket, the circuit is interrupted. Instead of being supplied to the channel fader, the signal from the equalizer output passes through the double-conductor signal cable connected to the response part of the connector, and is then supplied to the input of the external processing device, such as reverberator (this line is known as *feed*), and then returned to the mixer via the line known as *return*. Thanks to the **Insert** socket, feed, and return lines, each channel can process effects independently.

After the **Insert** socket, the signal is sent to the channel fader to adjust the channel signal level on the fly. In most inexpensive mixers, this adjustment is done using a knob. However, the slider fader design is more convenient. Positioning a channel faders in relation to one another creates the general impression of the relationship between channel signal levels.

Fader usually has its optimum position (0 dB) marked. It provides some resources for increasing the level (about 10—15 dB), but is mainly used for decreasing the level. When fader is set to the ∞ position, signal attenuation is at its maximum.

Next to the fader, the console contains pan control, which determines the signal balance between the left and right outputs. Pan control is usually the signal source for the main stereo output.

Pre-fader feeds are used to organize monitoring. The signal is picked up before it passes the channel fader, and therefore the level of the selected signal doesn't depend on the channel fader position. This is convenient, because it allows the monitored mix for artists or for the sound operator and the sound in a concert hall (or at the input of the recording device) to become independent of one another. However, when corrections are required, it is necessary to adjust both the channel fader and pre-fader aux knobs.

Post-fader feed (the signal picked up after it passes the channel fader) is used for applying an effect. The proportions between the signal level supplied to the external sound processing devices and the signal level in the channel are preserved.

Usually, mixers allow you to connect an aux both before and after the fader. This is done using a special jumper.

The master module of the mixer contains level controls for the left and right channels, pan control of the stereo mix, and a level meter of the signal supplied to the mixer output. As a general rule, the mix level control, adjusting the mix level supplied to the mixer output to which control monitors or earphones are connected, can also be found here.

Naturally, from model to model the combination of switching and control elements may vary. Mixers differ in the number of channels (mono and stereo), but all the elements discussed here are usually present in all mixers.

Practically all MIDI audio editors contain virtual mixers that can initiate their hardware analogues more or less successfully. For example, the virtual mixer included with the Cakewalk Pro Audio software enables you to join controls into groups and record the change in status for each of them. Notice that even MS Windows includes a very simple virtual mixer, which, however, is rather limited in functionality and very inconvenient.

Most sound cards have drivers that are actually specialized virtual mixers. In the next section, we will discuss one of these virtual mixers—the one supplied with the popular SB Live! sound card.

5.3. Sound Blaster Live! Virtual Mixer (Live!Ware 3.0 Drivers)

In previous models of the Sound Blaster adapter, the built-in mixer was implemented at the hardware level as a specialized analog chip. The situation has changed with the release of SB Live! Now all signal processing, including mixing, is delegated to the EMU10K1 digital signal processor (DSP). A mixer as such is not present. Its functions are now performed by a set of microprograms loaded into the DSP. As usual, all these operations are transparent to a user who doesn't need to know how the driver functions. The most important thing from the end-user's point of view is how to use the program that provides for interaction with the "microprogram" mixer. The window of this program (the Mixer application) is shown in Fig. 5.13.

Fig. 5.13. Software mixer of the SB Live! sound card

In the left part of the mixer, we see the recording level control (**REC**). If you click the icon above the control corresponding to the signal source type, the menu shown in Fig. 5.14 will appear.

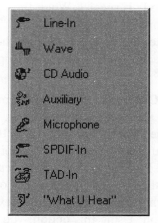

Fig. 5.14. Sound source selection menu

Select the source of the signal to be recorded from this menu (analog signal sources are marked with an asterisk (*)). The signal from this source will be recorded after you click the **Record** button in the musical or sound editor. Possible sound sources are listed below:

❑ **Midi**—SB Live! sampler

❏ **Line-In ***—linear input of the sound card

❏ **Wave**—all sounds reproduced via the virtual audio port (SB Live! Wave Out)

❏ **CD Audio ***—the signal from the analog audio output of the CD ROM drive

❏ **CD Digital** (not in all SB Live! models)—the signal from the digital output of the CD ROM drive

❏ **Auxiliary ***—additional linear input (aux) of the sound card

❏ **Microphone ***—microphone input of the sound card

❏ **SPDIF-In**—SPDIF digital input

❏ **TAD-In ***—voice modem/auto responder output

❏ **I2S In** (not in all SB Live! models)—audio output of the DVD player

If you select any of these sources, only the source signal (not processed by the real-time effects supported by SB Live!) will be recorded. Furthermore, the volume of the recorded signal doesn't depend on the position of the corresponding mixer control. Rather, it is determined only by the **REC** control position. Even if you disable the corresponding input of the mixer completely, it will be possible to record the signal supplied to this input.

The **What U Hear** recording mode is special. When this mode is selected, everything that you hear from the control monitors will be recorded. The only significant restriction is that you'll only be able to use one analog source in the **What U Hear** mode. For example, you won't be able to record a mix of signals supplied through the **Line-In** and **Auxiliary** inputs.

Next, to the right of the **REC** control, there is a group comprising six faders, each of which corresponds to a signal source. Above each fader, there is an icon for each source. If you point to this icon with the mouse, a tip displaying the source name will appear. Actually, there are more sound sources than this. To view other faders, right-click on any of the fader icons with the mouse. Furthermore, any fader can be reassigned to any available signal source. To do so, click the small yellow triangle over the icon of the appropriate fader and select the required signal source from the context menu. Below each fader there is the **Mute/UnMute** radio button. Using this option, you can enable or disable the signal source corresponding to fader positioned above the respective radio button.

Above the microphone input fader there is a red "+" sign. If you click it, the window shown in Fig. 5.15 will open.

This window provides only one option—**Mic Boost (20dB)**, which enables you to boost the microphone signal by 20 dB.

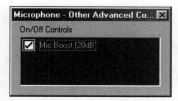

Fig. 5.15. Turning on microphone signal amplification by 20 dB

In the right part of the mixer there are balance controls for the front and rear speakers (**FAD**), the double-band equalizer (**TRE** and **BAS**), general volume (**VOL**), and stereo balance (**L,R**). The **FAD** control is available only if the **4 Speakers** configuration is set in the Surround Mixer program, which will be covered in detail later in this chapter.

To disable the equalizer, set both its controls to the neutral position by clicking the small white triangle next to the appropriate control.

There is a red "+" sign above the volume fader (**VOL**). Clicking this sign with the mouse opens the window shown in Fig. 5.16. Using the **Digital Output Only** option you can disable all analog outputs.

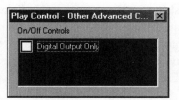

Fig. 5.16. Disabling all analog outputs

Besides the normal mixer, SB Live! software provides another one—Surround Mixer. As is evident from its name, this mixer is intended for managing the placement of the sound sources in virtual acoustic space. From the end user's point of view, this mixer can work as a standalone application. However, of the normal mixer is running at the moment you start the Surround Mixer, both mixers will be united in a single window (Fig. 5.17). The most interesting fact is that you won't find Surround Mixer among the AudioHQ applications. In AudioHQ, this mixer is designated by the name Speaker.

In Fig. 5.17, there is a little button ▣ at the bottom of the normal mixer. Using this button, you can separate/join both mixers. Test it out if you like, but right now we're going to use the next button here—▭—to hide the normal mixer and concentrate more closely on the Surround Mixer.

Fig. 5.17. Combined Surround Mixer and Mixer applications

Fig. 5.18 shows the "pure" Surround Mixer. It is supposed that you start working with this application by selecting your task. This is done by clicking the **Task** button. Example activities include **compose desktop music**, **create mp3**, **listen to CD**, etc. After you select the task, the **Preset** menu opens automatically. This menu contains the names of the presets that will be loaded into the Surround Mixer and the normal Mixer. The entire system is known as Super-Environment Audio (SEA). It is up to you to decide whether or not you are going to use SEA.

Fig. 5.18. Surround Mixer, acoustic system configuration

In the left part of the mixer window, you'll find the following three buttons:

❑ **Effects**—acoustic effects

❑ **Speaker**—acoustic system

❒ **Spectrum**—spectrum indicator

The contents of the mixer window change depending on the button that you click.

Let's start with the **Speaker** button. To select the acoustic system configuration, click this button to open the **speaker selection** list. The following options are available for selection:

❒ **Live! Surround**—the Creative acoustic system, including four speakers and a subwoofer

❒ **Headphones**

❒ **4 Speakers**—two front and two rear

❒ **2 Speakers**

For musical purposes, a configuration with two speakers (or two acoustic monitors) is suitable.

The **test** button is required to test the sound of your acoustic system.

If you select the **Effects** button, the Surround Mixer will look as shown in Fig. 5.19.

Fig. 5.19. Surround Mixer, effects

In the right part of the window, there is an icon displaying a person sitting in an armchair. This is supposed to be you. Icons corresponding to various sound sources are highlighted in yellow. You can position them around the icon displaying the man·in the armchair (Fig. 5.20).

Fig. 5.20. Positioning sound sources in the virtual acoustic space

Select the acoustic environment—the reverberation effect characteristic for the virtual studio—from the **Environment** drop-down list (Fig. 5.21).

By clicking the **Settings** button, you can start the Environmental Audio program. This application enables you to change various effect parameters and create custom settings that will be available for selection from the list shown in Fig. 5.21.

Below the **Environment** group, there is a set of icons symbolizing various sound sources (Fig. 5.22). To position sound sources, drag them with the mouse (Fig. 5.20).

Fig. 5.21. Selecting the reverberation type

Fig. 5.22. Sound source selection

All settings of the Surround Mixer and normal mixer (except for the volume and the **Digital Output Only** option) can be saved. To do so, click the ▣ button in the top right corner of the window. The menu shown in Fig. 5.23 will appear.

To save the settings, select the **Save Preset** command. A dialog containing the **Task** and **Preset** fields will open. By default, these fields are filled with the current task (selected from the **Task** menu) and the preset (selected from the **Preset** submenu), corresponding to this task. You can specify another name for the preset and a new name for the task. By doing this, you'll create a new item in **Task**.

The current settings can be imported and exported to and from special files with the SEA filename extension (SEA stands for Super-Environment Audio). Use the **Export Preset** and **Import Preset** commands from the menu shown in Fig. 5.23 to do this. You can also delete the current settings by selecting the **Delete Preset** command.

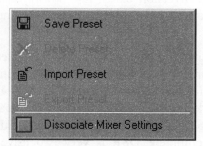

Fig. 5.23. Saving and loading the settings menu

If you select the **Dissociate Mixer Settings** option, parameters of the normal mixer will be ignored when loading the settings. This might sometimes be useful.

Super-Environment Audio provides a flexible mechanism for customizing your acoustic system to perform various tasks. However, if you need full control over your acoustic system, it is recommended that you use custom settings.

Now all that is left is to mention the 24-band spectrum indicator of the signal supplied to the output of the SB Live! mixer (Fig. 5.24). To open this indicator, click the **Spectrum** button. This indicator is not as useless a toy as it might seem at first glance. If you study the displayed spectrum carefully, you'll be able to make a preliminary assumption as to which frequencies are missing from the composition, and which ones are excessive.

Fig. 5.24. Spectrum of the signal supplied to the output of the SBLive! mixer

In this book, we'll look at quite a lot of software mixers. Both in their functionality and in their interface, they are very similar to hardware mixers.

Chapter 6: Sound Effects

Using sound cards, digital conversion cards, and software sound editors provides many ways for a computer musician to use various sound effects and sound processing methods in his or her compositions.

Sound effects may be implemented by hardware and then used in real time, as is done in high quality sound cards, for example. For this purpose, digital signal processors are built into these sound cards. A Digital Signal Processor—DSP—allows you to process sound signals in real time. Its working principle is based on the analog-to-digital conversion of the signal, with further processing based on several algorithms of digital filtering and digital delay. However, a complete DSP is very expensive, and thus it is used only in special professional devices. The sound processors of sound cards are much simpler than professional equipment. They do not usually allow you to use many effects at the same time. Besides which, almost all of the effects are implemented only for all channels at the same time.

MIDI, with the help of controllers, is used to select effects and manage their parameters. Most musical editors have an interface that allows you to manage effect controllers in different ways. Usually this is done by "drawing" the parameter changing chart. The effect controller may also be associated with one of the regulators of the virtual mixer included in the musical editor.

In computer studios, sound effects are often created with software. Sound editors implement and manage effects while only sound signals recorded in digital form are processed. One drawback of the software implementation of some sound effects is that it is impossible to use them in real time. And one of the benefits is that the absence of real time processing allows you to apply the most complicated algorithms, which take a lot of time to complete. Thus the number of various sound effects and variations on each of the effects truly exceeds those available in a hardware implementation. You also have the capability of almost unlimited "nesting" of effects. The limit is not set by the technical (or rather mathematical) abilities, but rather by common sense and aesthetic criteria. We discuss using the sound effects of Cool Edit Pro, one of the most powerful sound editors, in *Part III* of this book. First, though, we will just try to get an initial idea of the essence of the basic sound effects.

6.1. Vibrato

The basic idea of the vibrato effect is the periodical changing of one of the sound oscillation parameters: the amplitude, the frequency, or the phase. The parameter changes (oscillates) at a very low frequency—only a few Hz. You can have an amplitude, frequency, or phase vibrato. In any case, the spectrum of the source oscillation is enriched. Those who are well acquainted with the fundamentals of radio technique realize that what is taking place is the modulation of the sound oscillation by a low-frequency signal. The laws of physics work—the spectrum of the signal is truly widened.

Besides which, there is also the timbre vibrato, which we will discuss later.

As with many other electronic sound effects, vibrato has natural prototypes, originating from folk and classical instrumental and vocal music.

Handling the vibrato effect makes the difference between a very good singer and just a good singer. Tremolo (a particular case of amplitude vibrato) is the basic manner in which a mandolin is played.

Originally, the modulation of any sound oscillation parameter was called "vibrato". But later on, some modifications on this effect got their own names. In many publications on electronic music, only frequency vibrato is said to be vibrato. From our point of view this is not correct, and we shall distinguish among amplitude vibrato, frequency vibrato, and timbre vibrato. Phase vibrato has a special name—*phaser*.

6.1.1. Amplitude Vibrato and Tremolo

Amplitude vibrato includes the amplitude vibrato itself and tremolo.

Amplitude vibrato is the periodical changing of the sound signal amplitude. Its frequency must be very small (from fractions of Hz to 10—12 Hz). If the vibrato frequency is outside of these limits you will not get the desired aesthetic effect. Amplitude vibrato is shown in Fig. 6.1. The source signal is shown in Fig. 6.1*a*, and the same signal with amplitude vibrato is seen in Fig. 6.1*c*.

In order to clearly show the signal with amplitude vibrato, the ratio between the frequencies of the source and modulating signals in Fig. 6.1 is small. This ratio, which depends on the note, can change to anything within a range from tens to hundreds.

The timbre of the signal with amplitude vibrato is wider than the source signal timbre. Different actions may be performed on such a spectrum; for example, the levels of spectral components can be altered by filters.

The vibrato depth characterizes the effect display: $m = \Delta S/S$, where ΔS is the maximum change of the signal with vibrato amplitude, and S is the source signal amplitude. The range of possible vibrato depth values is from 0 to 1. The optimal amplitude vibrato frequency, from a creative point of view, is 6—8 Hz.

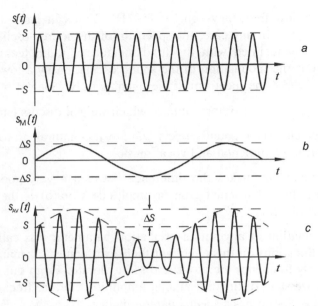

Fig. 6.1. Source signal (*a*), modulating signal (*b*), and signal with amplitude vibrato (*c*)

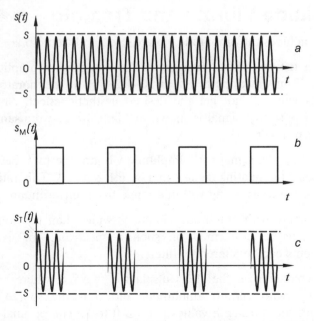

Fig. 6.2. Source signal (*a*), modulating signal (*b*), signal with tremolo (*c*)

Tremolo is a special variety of amplitude vibrato. Its specific features are: a relatively high vibration frequency (10—12 Hz), maximum depth ($m = 1$), and the impulse form of the resulting signal (Fig. 6.2).

The source signals in Figs 6.1 and 6.2 are shown as sinusoidal. In actuality, they are of a more complex form.

In analog devices, amplitude vibrato is implemented by means of signal multipliers. There are many various principal schemes of vibrato devices. The main problem of analog devices is incomplete suppression of the control signal. When the vibrato depth is large, it appears as a clear "knocking" sound with modulation frequency.

Computer musicians will encounter two ways of implementing amplitude vibrato: hardware and software. The hardware implementation assumes the presence of amplifiers with a controlled amplification ratio within the structure of the sound card. The software method multiplies digital measurements of sound oscillations by the function measurement values (normally sinusoidal) that describe the control signal.

Be careful in using amplitude vibrato when processing vocal parts: its depth should not be too large, and tremolo is not allowed.

The peak of popularity of the amplitude vibrato hit decades ago. It is rarely used in modern electronic music, which is quite a shame. The effect is very nice.

6.1.2. Frequency Vibrato

Frequency vibrato is the periodical changing of the sound oscillation frequency.

Frequency vibrato became widespread only after electronic musical instruments were invented. It is a rather difficult to create this effect on adapterized acoustic instruments. However, the construction of the solo guitar does allow for it. The tension of all the strings can be changed at once with a special mechanism: a movable tremolo bar. Here the frequency vibrato is done manually.

Implementing the frequency vibrato in electrical musical instruments and synthesizers is simple and natural. All electronic musical synthesizers, both hardware- and software-implemented, are synchronized by the base generator. If we change its frequency, the frequencies of all synchronized oscillations will also change. This process is called frequency modulation. If the frequency is changed according to the periodical law, frequency vibrato is the result. When the vibrato is partial, the spectrum of the source signal is also widened, and the timbre is no longer constant, but periodically changes with time. The source signal (*a*), the modulating signal (*b*), and the signal with frequency vibrato (*c*) are shown in Fig. 6.3.

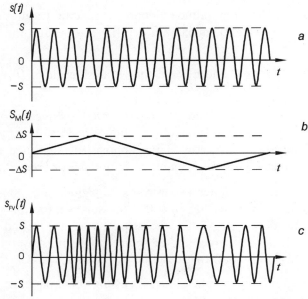

Fig. 6.3. Source signal (*a*), modulating signal (*b*), and signal with frequency vibrato (*c*)

The signal with frequency vibrato in Fig. 6.3 is exaggerated: the frequency changes within limits that are actually too large.

A nice sound can be gotten only if the depth of the frequency vibrato (the relative change of the sound frequency) is not too large. According to the chromatic scale, there is a unit of musical intervals—the cent—that is 1200 times smaller than an octave. The interval between two neighbouring half-tones in the tempered scale is exactly 100 cents. The oscillation of the tone pitch with the frequency vibrato should not exceed a few dozen cents. Otherwise it appears as if the instrument is off key.

The frequency vibrato is used both as a single effect and as a part of more complex effects.

From the point of view of technical implementation, the glissando effect (better described as a performer's trick) is very close to the frequency vibrato. This method is evidenced in one or several of the pianist's fingers sliding along the keys. In electronic music, glissando means modulating the pitch of notes being played. The modulation range may reach an interval exceeding an octave. You can change either the voltage or the digital code, which in turn controls the frequency of the generator. To play the glissando effect in musical synthesizers and MIDI keyboards, there is a special control unit—a wheel or a slider. The MIDI standard includes a special message: the Pitch Bend Change is forwarded when the status of tonal modulation pitch changes. Different from the first electric musical instruments, these means allow you to perform not only glissando, but manual (or finger) frequency vibrato. The law of the sound pitch oscillation depends on the performer, so the effect is no longer mechanic and monotonous.

Since we have spoken about changing the tone pitch, it makes sense to mention that musical editors allow you to accurately change the key of the instruments being synthesized, and modulate to any interval both instruments recorded in separate tracks and the entire composition. Sound editors allow you to perform similar actions not only with musical instruments, but even with recorded voices of singers (*Sections 12.35* and *12.36*).

6.1.3. Timbre Vibrato

The timbre vibrato's effect is also to change the spectrum of sound oscillations. The physical essence of this effect is the following: a source oscillation with a rich timbre goes through a bandpass frequency filter whose frequency settings or bandwidth periodically changes, or it may be that both parameters change using different laws. The filter selects those components that are in its "instant" bandpass from the whole spectrum of source oscillations. Because the bandpass is "breathing" along its width and "travels" along the frequency, the signal timbre periodically changes.

Besides automatic timbre vibrato, manual timbre vibrato (often, "foot" vibrato—pedal controlled) is used. This variant of the effect is known as "wow wow".

An electric guitar sounds unusually beautiful when its signal passes through the timbre vibrato block if the filter modulation cycle is synchronized with the beginning moment of string oscillation. The sound of each chord flows from one side of its timbre area to another.

The timbre vibrato is included in the set of tools provided by sound editors (*Section 12.21*).

If a sound card contains modulated resonance filters, or at least low frequency filters with an adjustable cutoff frequency, this effect may also be implemented by hardware in real time.

6.2. Effects Based on Signal Delay

The following effects are based on signal delay:

- Delay
- Flanger
- Phaser
- Chorus
- Reverberation

In *Chapter 12*, we will discuss how these effects are implemented in the Cool Edit Pro editor. However, it is a good idea to know of their existence before we do so.

6.2.1. Delay

The necessity of the delay effect arose when stereo sound came about. The nature of the human hearing apparatus in most cases assumes that two sound signals arrive into the brain, and that those signals have a different arrival time. If the source of sound is perpendicular to the center of the line crossing the ears, then direct sound from the source reaches both ears at the same time. In all other cases, the distances from the source to the ears are different, so one ear gets the sound first. Let's do some simple calculations. The delay time (the time difference between the reception of the signal by each ear) is maximum when the source is next to one of the ears. The distance between the ears is about 8 inches, so the maximum delay is about 8 msec. These values correspond to a sound oscillation wave with a frequency of about 1.1 kHz. At higher frequency sound oscillations, the wave length becomes smaller than the distance between the ears, and the difference in the time of signal reception by the ears is not perceivable. The maximum frequency of oscillations for which a human can feel the delay depends on the location of the source. It increases as the source of sound is moved from a point right next to one of the ears to a point behind or in front of the listener. Delay is used first of all when a recording of a voice or an acoustic instrument made with a single microphone is "built into" a stereo recording. This effect serves as the basis for stereo recording technology.

However, delay may be applied to get an effect such as the one-time repetition of any sound. In that case, the delay between the direct signal and its delayed copy is greater than the natural delay of 8 msec. Which delay should we select? The answer depends on certain factors. First of all, we should apply aesthetic criteria, creative goals, and common sense. The delay for short and sharp sounds for which the main signal and its delayed copy can be distinguished is smaller than the one for continued sounds. For slow rhythm compositions, the delay may be greater than for faster ones.

In the case of certain relationships between the volume of direct and delayed signals—a psycho-acoustic effect—felt as the changing of the expected source location on the stereo panorama—may be experienced. For example, it is hard to explain, both from an aesthetic point of view and technically, why the piano "jumps" from one place to another while you are listening to a piece. As any other effect, delay should be used wisely, and not throughout the entire composition.

This effect can be implemented using devices that delay acoustic or electric signals. In most cases today, that device is a digital delay line, a chain of elementary cells or delay triggers. For us, it is enough to know the working principle of delay triggers, which is as follows: the binary signal which comes to the trigger input at the start of a clock pulse appears in its output only at the start of the next clock pulse. The more delay triggers are included in the chain, the longer the total delay time in the line. Memory devices can be used as digital delay lines. There are also well-known special algorithms that allows the information to "slide" along the addressing space.

To use the digital delay line, the signal must first be converted into digital form. After the copy of the signal passes the delay line, digital-analog conversion takes place. The source signal and its delayed copy may be directed to separate stereo channels, as well as be mixed in various proportions. The summary signal may be directed to either one of the stereo channels, or to both.

In sound editors, delay is implemented in a programmatic (mathematical) way, by changing the relative numbering of measurements of the source signal and its copy.

There can also be variations of the delay, in which several copies of the signal delayed by different times are formed. We discuss the implementation of the Delay effect of the Cool Edit Pro package in *Section 12.13*, and the implementation of the related Echo effect, which is more complex, in *Section 12.14*.

Virtual delays, like their hardware prototypes, must have regulators for the depth and frequency of the delayed signal modulation, as well as a feedback ratio regulator. From output, the signal once more travels into the delay line. The fading time is set by the feedback regulator. To make the repeat sound like a natural echo, you should increase the feedback ratio. Normally, both real and virtual devices have a regulator that helps select the delay time appropriate for the tempo of the piece.

6.2.2. Flanger and Phaser

Signal delay is the basis for such sound effects as Flanger and Phaser. What is the difference between these effects and delay?

The name flanger is derived from the way this effect is implemented in analog devices—with the help of flange filters that have the same kind of amplitude-frequency response. Flange filters can be built on delay lines. The typical form of an amplitude-frequency response (Fig. 6.4) is that way because of the phase shift when the signal is propagating within the delay line, and because of adding delayed samples of the signal.

By changing the flange filter parameters, we can significantly modify the original sound timbre.

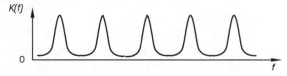

Fig. 6.4. The amplitude-frequency response of the flange filter

The amplitude-frequency response filter is flanged because for some frequencies the delayed copies of the signal have the same phase, and thus get amplified when added, while others are in opposite phases and are mutually annihilated. The periodical structure of the amplitude-frequency response is stipulated by the periodicity of the audio signal components (sinusoids).

It is not just coincidence that there have been attempts to replace reverberation with flanger. Reverberation is caused by multiple reflections of sound waves from the walls, ceiling, and floor of the room (*Section 6.2.4*). Sound oscillations on the way to the listener have delays (phase offsets) of different values. Oscillation interference takes place. If we examine any room with significant reverberation features, we will find that its amplitude-frequency response has a flanged form.

Under certain conditions, digital filters can also have a flanged form of the amplitude-frequency response (*Section 3.3*). It's not surprising, since their work is also based on signal delay and adding its delayed copies.

As we have mentioned, delay imitates the effect of the human brain receiving sound signals at different times. The effect of repeated sound may also be caused by propagating the sound from the source to the receiver in different ways (for example, the sound can arrive directly, or be reflected from an obstacle that stands in the way of the direct path). In both cases, the delay time remains constant. In real life, this corresponds to the improbable situation in which the source of sound, the receiver, and the reflecting objects are motionless. Here, the sound frequency is not changed, no matter which way or to which ear the sound arrives.

If one of the above elements is moving, the frequency of the sound heard cannot stay the same as it was when transmitted. This is just a display of the Doppler effect, which in books is traditionally illustrated by the shifting pitch of the whistle of a moving locomotive.

Real musical sounds are not only forked into several sound waves and different delays (for each of them) while spreading, they also have different frequencies that change for different spectral components.

Both flanger and phaser imitate (each in its own manner) the motion of all of the above elements: the source, the receiver, and the reflector of the sound. Both effects represent the combination of the sound signal delay and the frequency or phase modulation. The difference is just quantitative. Flanger is different from phaser in that the delay time of the copy (or copies) and the change in the signal frequency for the former effect are significantly larger than for the latter. In other words, flanger can be noticed if a singer is approaching a motionless listener at the speed of a car. To feel phaser, there is no need to have a moving source of sound; the listener needs only turn his or her head left and right very frequently. (If you're prone to seasickness, it'd probably be best if you didn't try this.)

The aforementioned quantitative differences of these effects lead also to qualitative differences: first, sounds processed by these effects have different acoustic and musical features; second, the effects are implemented by different technical means.

The delay time values specific for flanger are significantly greater than the period of the sound oscillation, so in order to implement the effect, multibit and multitap digital delay lines are used. A specific signal is taken from each tap that, in turn, is processed by frequency modulation.

Conversely, phaser is characterized by a delay time so small that it seems almost the same as the sound oscillation period. If we have such small relative shifts, we are not talking anymore about the delay of a signal copy within a certain time, but about the difference between their phases. If this difference between the phases is not constant, we are dealing with the phaser effect. So we can thus consider phaser a marginal case of flanger. But if we attentively scan this paragraph again, we'll find out that phaser is actually phase vibrato.

There were quite a few amusing and inventive attempts to obtain these effects before the advent of modern technology.

For example, to get the flanger effect, several acoustic systems were used instead of one, and they were located at different distances from listeners. At certain moments, the source of the signal was attached to acoustic systems in such a way that it gave the impression of the source moving closer or farther away. The sound delay was also implemented with the help of tape recorders with through-traction recording/reproduction. One head was recording while the other was reproducing the sound with a delay equalling the time the tape took to move from one head to the other. Nothing special was invented for frequency modulation. Each analog tape recorder has a specific feature called detonation, which can be compared to the sound "floating". Specially increasing this effect by changing the engine voltage was enough to get frequency modulation.

To hear phaser, chains of electrically controlled phase shifters were used. Sometimes, one could see that in the acoustic system attached to the electric musical instrument or electric guitar, something like a fan started to rotate. The sound was crossed by rotating wings and was reflected from them, and phase modulation was the result. How much effort was made to make the timbre of instruments more lively, and how much it cost!

Modern sound editors allow us to implement such a great number of various effects (for examples, see *Sections 12.12—12.20*), that if we divide the cost of the computer, the sound card, and even of this book by the number of them, the cost of one effect would be very small.

6.2.3. Chorus

Chorus appears as the effect of playing the same sound or the whole part not by a single instrument or a singer but by several. The artificial effect is modeled on the sound of a real choir. We think that a choir singing or the sound of several musical instruments playing at once markedly enriches a musical composition.

On the one hand, the singers' voices and sounds of instruments must sound the same when the same note is played, and both musicians and the conductor will try to attain this. But due to individual differences in the sources, the sound is still different. In space, in the sound amplifying band, and in the human hearing organs, these oscillations interact. The sound spectrum is enriched and, more importantly, it modulates.

We can consider unison to be a marginal case of chorus—a chorus after redundance, so to say. Unison is the simultaneous sound of two sources that have a small difference in frequency.

Unison was known far before synthesizers appeared. This effect is used in the twelve-string guitar and the accordion. In the twelve-string guitar, the difference in frequencies appears naturally, because a sound is produced by two strings simultaneously, and it is impossible to ideally tune the strings with the same frequency.

Just this small difference in frequencies of voices or the sound of instruments is the reason for the pleasant sound of unison (of two voices) and chorus (for more than two voices).

Conversely, in digital musical instruments, the frequencies of secondary generators can be tuned to be absolutely the same. This sound is not life-like because it is too "correct". Chorus is simply used to make the electronic sound more natural.

There are many modifications of chorus algorithms, but they can all be summarized as follows.

The source signal is forked into two or more channels.

In each channel, the signal spectrum is shifted by frequency to a value specified for each channel. Frequency shifts are small, usually fractions of Hz.

The resulting signals are all put together.

Finally, we get a signal in which sound waves "float" with different speeds. Only once during the time proportional to the product of oscillation periods of different frequencies are the signals piled up in the phase, and the "ninth wave" appears—the envelope maximum. And only once during the same time period are signals found in different phases all at once. This results in the "hollow between the waves"—the envelope minimum. As a result, we get a signal whose spectrum is continuously changing, and the period of this change is so long that the repeated signal's spectral features are not heard.

Chorus enriches the sound of instruments; that's why it has become one of the effects that you can find in almost every synthesizer and in many sound cards.

Audio signal processing in sound editors allows you to get multiple modifications of this effect. However, you should apply it carefully, because if you overuse it, the acoustic environment of the composition becomes "dirty" and the voice unrecognizable.

6.2.4. Reverb

Reverberation is one of the most interesting and popular sound effects. Its essence lies in the fact that the source signal is mixed with its copies that are delayed relative to it by various time intervals. This feature makes reverb and delay alike. The difference is that, for reverb, the number of delayed copies of the signal can be significantly larger than in the case of delay. In theory, the number of copies can be infinite. Besides which, the larger the delay time of the signal copy, the less is its amplitude (volume). The effect depends on the time intervals between the signal copies and the speed of decreasing their volume levels. If the time intervals are small, the reverberation effect takes place. It sounds like you are in a large and hollow room. The sound of musical instruments becomes mellow and has an enriched timbre. Singers' voices become more melodious, and their deficiencies are not as noticeable.

If the time intervals between the copies are big (over 100 msec), it is more correct to speak not about reverberation but about the "echo" effect. The intervals between the sounds are now distinguishable. Sounds are no longer joined, and it seems as if they are reflections from distant obstacles.

Let's assume that the primary audio signal emitted by an acoustic system is a short impulse. The acoustic system is located on the stage of an auditorium. The structure of the signal coming to the point where the listener is located is shown in Fig. 6.5.

The vertical axis shows the sound intensity, the horizontal axis shows time.

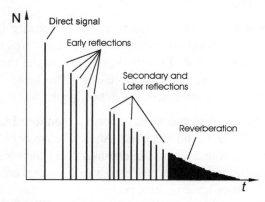

Fig. 6.5. The structure of the audio signal with reverberation

The direct sound reaches the listener first. This signal comes to the listener by the shortest path; that's why its intensity is greater than the intensities of other signals. The direct signal only gives information as to whether the source is located to the right or to the left of the listener.

A short time after the direct signal, the early (primary) reflections come. This component of the sound field is reflected once or twice from the bounding surfaces (walls, ceiling, floor). Interacting with bounding surfaces, the sound wave is not only reflected from them, but also gives them a part of its energy. This energy heats the surfaces, so the intensity of early reflections is less (but not significantly) than the direct signal intensity. Early reflections appear as clearly distinguished echo signals. The time intervals between them are relatively large, due to the fact that the differences in the lengths of the paths by which signals reach the listener are large. The wave can be reflected from the side or rear wall. Some early reflection waves can have several reflections. Early reflections give information not only on the sound source's location, but also on the size of the room. Early reflections make a major contribution to the spatial feeling of the auditorium's acoustics. Early reflections are those that lag behind the direct signal by no more than 60 msec.

Secondary and subsequent (later) reflections are sound waves that are reflected from each of the surfaces more than once. As the number of repeated reflections grows, the intensity of the audio signals notably decreases. Besides which, the spectral content of sound oscillations changes. Because of differences in the configuration of the reflecting surfaces and the features of the materials that these surfaces are made of, different spectral components of the audio signal are not reflected in the same way. Some of them are absorbed more intensively—that's why they fade faster.

As the number of secondary reflections grows, they are diffused, and their number increases. They are eventually not felt to be separate sounds, and are joined into one solid, fading sound. This is reverberation.

In theory, a fading sound is infinite. In practice, by comparing different reverberation processes (and, what is more important, the reverberation features of rooms) the concept of reverberation time was introduced. Reverberation time is the time that it takes for the level of the reverberating signal to decrease by 60 dB. The basic element implementing the reverb effect is the device that produces the echo signal.

The history of the development of such devices is worth a mention. Initially, broadcasting stations and famous concert halls had echo chambers. An echo chamber is a room with reflecting walls where the source of the sound signal (loudspeaker) and the receiver (microphone) are located. This echo chamber is a small-size model of a real concert hall where it is not always possible to provide the necessary acoustic environment. In an echo chamber, it was possible, though quite difficult, to control the distribution of intensities and times of diffusion of repeatedly reflected signals by installing walls that reflected or absorbed the sound. The advantage of an echo chamber is that the sound in it fades naturally, which is really hard to achieve using any other method. As the sound continues to reverberate in three dimensions, the wave is split into multiple reflections that reach the microphone in progressively-decreasing time intervals, long before the sound completely fades. The major disadvantages of echo chambers are connected with their relatively small sizes. It is because of their own resonance that the signal spectrum is distorted for middle frequencies. Another problem is the insulation of the echo chamber itself. But the major problem is that an echo chamber cannot be a popular instrument for attaining natural reverberation because it is too bulky and too expensive.

Besides echo chambers, large steel panels were also used to imitate reverberation. Oscillations were sent to and bounced off them with the help of devices similar to electromagnetic headphones. To reach a satisfactorily even distribution of the amplitude-frequency response, the panel thickness had to be very accurate. This was impossible due to the lack of proper industrial steel rolling technologies. Reverberation was flat, not 3D. The signal had a very specific metal sound.

In the mid-60s, spring reverbers were used to attain the reverb effect. One of the spring ends was connected with an electromagnetic transformer that caused mechanical oscillations of that spring, which reached the other spring end connected to the sensor with a delay. The repeating sound effect was caused by multiple reflections of mechanical oscillation waves from the spring ends.

The sound quality of a spring reverber is quite poor. A spring reacts to any vibrations in the air or of the floor. There is unavoidable feedback between the acoustic system and the spring; the sound has a specific "metal" feel. Also, the reverberation time cannot be controlled.

After some time, these imperfect devices were replaced by tape recorder reverbers. The principle according to which the echo signal is created is as follows: the source signal is recorded on the tape by the recording head, and after the period of time necessary to move the point on the tape to the reproducing head, the signal is read. Through the feedback circuit, the delayed signal—now with a lesser amplitude—is recorded again, which creates an effect of repeated reflection of the sound with a gradual fade. The quality of the sound depends on the tape recorder's parameters. One drawback of tape recorder reverbers is that at acceptable tape-drive speeds, it is possible only to get the echo effect. To get just reverberation, we either have to place the heads much closer to each other (which their construction does not allow) or significantly speed up.

Since the development of digital technologies, we have been able to build high quality digital reverbers. In these devices, the signal can be delayed by any time necessary to get both the reverberation and echo effects. The difference between a reverber and a device implementing the delay effect (that we discussed above) is just that the reverber has the feedback necessary to create fading, repeating copies of the signal. Such reverbers are now widely used not only by musicians and producers, but by radio amateurs as well, who hold that a slight reverb allows voices to be more clearly understood.

The feedback circuit sends a portion of the signal from the output back to the delay line, and thus forms the repeated echo. The feedback ratio has to be less than 1, otherwise each new echo has an increasing volume, when it should be decreasing. This way, we get an effect similar to the self-excitation of an acoustic system.

Some virtual reverbers have a phase modulator. It is present so that if the fading time is small, a barely noticeable tone change will be effected.

Finally, reverberation in sound cards is simply based upon digital delay of signals, so it may not seem necessary to discuss other methods of creating this effect. But the sound editor described in the next part of this book has an amazing feature. It is the built-in echo chamber we discussed when we first spoke about reverberation. Of course, it's just a mathematical model. What do we need it for? The major difference between an echo chamber and other devices is that reverberation in it is natural and 3D. In all other devices it is not reverberation, but its flat, two-dimensional (sometimes one-dimensional) clone. The model of the echo chamber allows us to recreate the acoustics of any room. This is better than a real echo chamber, since it allows us to efficiently change the size of the modelled room and the reflecting features of the walls, the ceiling, and the floor. Besides, there are not one but two echo chambers, where the coordinates of the sources and sound receivers are set separately.

There are some other features as well. Software for synthesizing the voices of new musical instruments can have a simulated reverberation effect to imitate one made with steel panels.

Looking through the history of reverberation tools development, we can expect that some day there will be mathematical models of spring and tape recorder reverberators. It is quite possible that there are people who feel nostalgia for the sound of music that has spring vibration or tape hissing. It does not seem unusual; for instance, for some reason, among the GM standard sounds, there is a sound like the movement of fingers along a guitar's neck while changing chords. It is not an obstacle, but rather an integral part of the guitar's sound.

Modifications of virtual reverbers implemented in the Cool Edit Pro editor are discussed in *Sections 12.15—12.18*.

6.2.5. Specific Features of Applying Effects Based on Delay

Chorus is often used for processing the guitar, bass guitar, and keyboard. To get this effect, the delay time is set to tens of milliseconds, and modulation with a frequency of about 3 Hz is introduced. To get the best results, the direct signal and the reflected signals should be mixed in equal proportions. The modulation depth should be small; otherwise the effect sounds rough.

If we decrease the delay to several milliseconds and remove the unprocessed signal from the mix, we get real pitch (frequency) vibrato that can be used to process the sound of instruments and the voice. If we put the unprocessed signal back, we get an effect similar to phaser; if we introduce feedback, we get flanger.

Flanger sounds better if the frequency modulation is not large (about 1 Hz) and the modulation depth is a little bit larger than for chorus.

Since most effects related to the signal delay are created by mixing the unprocessed and the processed portions of the signal, digital delay on the mixer is linked to sending and returning effects. It can be convenient if you want to apply the same effect to several tracks. You can make the delayed signal panoramic if you want.

Delay and echo are often used to process voices and instruments. In most cases it is necessary to have the delay time correspond to the music tempo (say, to get 1, 2, or 4 echoes in a bar). Then repeats will emphasise the rhythm, not go against it. If we want to create a complex rhythm, we have to select the delay time so that repeats appear in unexpected places.

Echo is often added after separate phrases (usually at the end of a word). To produce this effect, we have to turn on sending to processing before the word is heard, and turn it off just as it is said. Then only this word will be repeated. It is better to control this with a regulator.

Chorus is particularly impressive if the unprocessed signal is panned to one side and the processed one panned to the other.

The result is amazing when we apply two chorus effects. Each of the processed signals is panned to its side. We should select the modulation depth and frequency so that they are a little bit different.

If you connected the effect processor to the mixer through a send point during processing, and want to create an effect somewhere in between the source and the processed signal, set the balance so that the effect processor outputs only the processed signal, and only the source signal comes through the channel. This is the only way to regulate the depth of the effect.

As opposed to chorus, when vibrato is implemented, the unprocessed signal is not mixed, and only the processed signal is used. So to get the vibrato effect, you simply need to attach the effect processor to the mixer through the breakpoint. Since the effect does not contain the unprocessed signal in output, the delay time should always be small (under 10 msec). Be careful with the vibrato depth.

Effects that use phase shift are applied to process those instruments whose spectrum has many higher harmonics.

The quality of the flanger effect depends on an accurate balance between processed and unprocessed signals. The best way is to attach the effect processor at the breakpoint and to search for the balance. After it is found, we can turn on the effect by sending to the aux bus. The processed signal should be made panoramic to one side, the unprocessed signal panoramic to the other side. Music becomes more dynamic, and it seems that the source of sound is moving.

Flanger can be used for processing any instrument or voice. We can get an original effect if the signal itself stays unprocessed and flanger is applied to its reflection.

When we apply the delay effect to a stereo signal, we can set different delay times for different channels. Selecting the delay time allows us to get the effect of the sound "flouncing" about the stereo panorama.

6.3. Distortion

Intentional distortion of the audio signal shape adds a sharp accent to it. Distortion is used mainly as a guitar effect. What we get is the amplifier being pushed to its very limits, and even its self-excitation. Due to this, the source signal becomes almost rectangular, and in it appear a good number of new harmonics that sharply widen the spectrum. This effect can be applied in different variations (fuzz, overdrive, etc.), that differ in:

❑ The signal limiting method (normal or smooth, the entire spectrum or a frequency band, the entire amplitude range or its part)

❑ The ratio of the source and the distorted signal in the output mix

❑ Frequency responses of amplifiers (the presence or absence of filters in output)

6.4. Voice Coder

Voice coder is a speech-synthesizing device based on an arbitrary input signal with a rich spectrum. Speech synthesis is normally implemented by formant conversions: separating the necessary formant set with the necessary ratios from a signal with enough spectrum makes the signal sound like a voice. Initially, voice coders were used for coded speech transmission. By analyzing the source speech signal, we can collect certain information on the changing of the formanta positions when moving from one sound to another. This information is coded and transmitted through the communication line, and at the other end of the line the speech is again synthesized by adjustable filters and amplifiers.

By placing the signal from an electric guitar on a block of speech synthesis and then speaking into the microphone, we can achieve the effect of a "speaking guitar". When the signal comes from a synthesizer, we get a "robot voice". And if we have a signal that has a spectrum close to the oscillations of vocal chords, the voice register changes—from a man's to a woman's or a child's, and vice versa.

The virtual voice coder included in the Cool Edit Pro multitrack editor is discussed in *Section 18.6.2.*

6.5. Shifting the Tone Pitch and Harmonizing

Most real and virtual devices imitate natural effects. But pitch shifters are a special type of processor, because the signal they generate does not have a natural prototype.

The word "harmonizer" was included in the name of the first pitch shifter; it is currently used to describe these types of effects.

Pitch shifter can perform a fantastic conversion: it allows you to get a copy of the input signal whose pitch can be changed by several cents, or by an octave or more.

The operating principle of a pitch shifter is generally similar to that of the digital delay line, but with one specific feature: the signal is recorded into the memory at a fixed speed. It can, however, be read faster or slower, depending on whether the pitch is shifted higher or lower relative to the input signal.

Different speeds of recording and reading cause a serious technical problem. If reading from the memory is done faster than the recording was made, all the data will be used before new data can be input into the memory. If reading is slower, there is not enough time to output all the data. For example, when the pitch is shifted to one octave higher, reading from memory should be performed at double the recording speed.

The problem is solved as follows: the signal enters the memory in very small portions (chunks), and each portion is processed before the next one arrives.

If pitch is increased, the signal read from memory is used before the next portion enters the memory. If it is necessary to preserve time characteristics, we have to fill the short time period that appears between the portions as a result of the higher reading speed with something. In practice, this interval is filled with a repeat of the already processed signal, so part of the signal is heard twice. If the portions are short enough, their repetition does not cause serious changes in the form of the signal's envelope.

If the reading speed decreases, the portions in the output have a length greater than necessary. Such a signal is thus terminated earlier than it really should end, and a part of the information is lost. It does not noticeably affect the quality of the signal if the portions are short enough.

There is another problem. We still need to summarize all the portions of the signal, but they have been pitch shifted, and so the forms of audio signals do not fit each other exactly. During the reproduction, all the breakpoints in the envelope will appear as clicks. Imagine that a recorded tape was taped together 100 times within one second of play!

There are several methods of hiding this sticking effect. Instead of fitting the beginning of one particle to the end of another, the portions are "overlapped", and the signal level at the end of one portion is lowered while the signal level in the other particle is increased by the same amount (crossfade).

Another method is to attach the portions to one another when the voltage crosses zero.

In pitch shifter and in harmonizer, you have the ability to control rough and accurate pitch shifting.

A signal with shifted pitch can be delayed relative to the input signal. This is used for a more natural imitation of artificial unison: two instruments are playing the same thing but there is a small difference in time and pitch.

The mixing regulator allows you to set the balance between processed and unprocessed signals. When the harmonizer is connected through the points sending to the effects, this regulator has to be set so that only the processed signal is included in the output.

The combination of repeated echo and pitch shift allows us to get a number of interesting effects. If the pitch shifting were set to half a tone up, every other echo would be pitch-shifted half a tone up relative to the previous echo, and vice versa—if the pitch shifts down half a tone, it will cause the echo pitch to shift down as well. Such spiral pitch shifting sounds unnatural, but may be useful in certain cases.

Usually, harmonizers have the ability to simultaneously set two different pitch shifts. Thus, if there is one note in the input, the output would be a chord of three notes. Octave duplication (up and down) can also be performed.

We can also trace the input signal pitch. The processor determines which note is ready to be input, and calculates the pitch shift to get the necessary harmony.

The major problem is the unavoidable effect of being out of tune. The greater the shift, the worse the sound quality.

A harmonizer attaches to a mixer in the same way as digital delay—by sending to processing and then through the return point. If you only need to use the harmonizer in one channel, then it makes sense to connect it through the breakpoint of that channel.

Modifications of the Pitch Shifter effect in the Cool Edit Pro sound editor are discussed in *Sections 12.35* and *12.36*. The Music special effect discussed in *Section 12.34* is indeed a virtual harmonizer.

With this, we finish our brief description of the essence of the basic effects included in both sound cards and software musical editors.

Part III

COOL EDIT PRO—A MULTITRACK SOUND EDITOR

Chapter 7: Getting Started

Chapter 8: Working with the Main Window in the *Waveform View* Mode

Chapter 9: The *File* Menu—Working with Files

Chapter 10: The *Edit* Menu

Chapter 11: The *View* Menu—Display Management

Chapter 12: The *Transform* Menu—Transforming Audio

Chapter 13: The *Generate* Menu—Sound Generation

Chapter 14: The *Analyze* Menu—Analyzing Audio Data

Chapter 15: The *Favorites* Menu—Creating a List of the Most Often Used Operations

Chapter 16: The *Options* Menu

Chapter 17: The *Window* Menu—Managing the Main Window Pages

Chapter 18: *Multitrack View*—Multitrack Editing Mode

Part III: Cool Edit Pro—Multitrack Sound Editor

The prototype of the Cool Edit Pro audio editor was developed by just one man—David Jones. The Syntrillium Software Corporation holds the distribution rights. We can also explain the fact that Cool Edit Pro is as popular as it is by the fact that its earlier version (Cool Edit 96) was a *Share Ware* product. Its demo versions are currently available on the Internet at **www.syntrillium.com**.

For a number of years, Jones has been continuously enhancing his product, and has finally made it nearly perfect. The latest version at the moment of writing, Cool Edit Pro 1.2, is a sound editor that provides almost all the abilities of software of that class.

Many specialists give high scores to this product. It says a lot that Cool Edit Pro is included with a number of professional digital conversion sound cards.

To effectively apply Cool Edit Pro to your creative work, you must know some of its principal features, which we discuss here.

The Cool Edit Pro editor is intended for digital sound processing, that is, analog sound waves are preliminarily converted (sampled) into a sequence of binary digital measurements (samples). This conversion is provided by the analog-to-digital converter, ADC. A digital sound image (waveform) is the result of ADC's operation.

Waveforms are stored in various file formats on hard disk. The most frequently used file format is WAV. So when you "assemble" an audio composition (say, a song) in Cool Edit Pro, WAV files are the standard building blocks, similar to the text files used as the standard blocks in text processors to write a book.

In general, there are two methods of sound data editing: *destructive* and *non-destructive*. When we follow the destructive method, editing (cutting, pasting, effect processing, etc.) is applied directly to the original WAV file, so the original sound data is changed. Non-destructive editing assumes that the file on your hard drive is not actually changed. Each editing operation is saved as a separate command instead, and this command is to be executed when running the waveform. For example, changing the sound volume in destructive editing will in fact change the amplitude of the waveform. When we use non-destructive editing, changing the volume is done by a sequence of commands that actually represent instructions to the program on how to vary the sound card amplifier conversion ratio.

Both destructive and non-destructive methods are applied in Cool Edit Pro. However, even destructive editing is not applied directly to the source waveform until you have saved the file. There is also a method used in Cool Edit Pro called *delayed* destructive editing. When you open a WAV file in Cool Edit Pro, the program places a copy of the file into a temporary directory, and this copy is used for editing. The source file is not changed until you save changes to the hard disk (for example, using the **Save** command in the **File** menu). Only when you save the changes made will Cool Edit Pro overwrite the source file with the changes you have made in the copy file.

The current version of Cool Edit Pro has two principally different modes: single waveform editing, and joint multitrack editing of a number of waveforms at once. Each mode has its main menu and main window—**Edit Waveform View** and **Multitrack View**, respectively—two sound editors with different purposes combined into a single functional set. Be aware that editing operations performed in **Edit Waveform View** (cutting, pasting, effect processing) are destructive, and when you save, the changes are made directly to the waveform file. Editing done in **Multitrack View** (cutting, joining waveforms, volume changing) is non-destructive.

You can use the Undo function in Cool Edit Pro in delayed destructive editing. When you apply destructive editing to a WAV file, Cool Edit Pro saves the copy of the file that existed before editing. This is done for each editing action you perform. You can "travel" both forward and backward along your editing history. The Undo function makes you freer when processing waveforms—you don't have to worry about the most interesting results being lost forever. However, freedom costs. In our case, the ability to undo a large number of actions takes disk memory, but all automatically created copies will be automatically removed from the hard disk when you close the file or exit the program. Still, you need to have enough free disk space when working with Cool Edit Pro. You can, however, restrict the maximum number of Undo levels, or just disable this function if you have problems with disk space.

In many musical editors that have tools for audio data processing, two ways to use effects are provided: applying real time effects and recalculating waveforms. The first type is more convenient, since you regulate the effect's parameters and immediately hear the result. However, to apply these types of effects you need a powerful computer. The method of recalculating the waveform allows you to process sound data on a "weak" computer, but processing can take dozens of minutes, or even hours. This can lead to you becoming too impatient to make enhancements and wary of trying something new.

The optimal strategy for using effects, then, might be something like this. First, having turned on the waveform looped play mode in real time, you select the effect parameters that fit your intention best. You then recalculate the waveform after having applied the effect with the selected parameters to it.

In Cool Edit Pro, you can use your own effects as well as effects enabled by DirectX. The basic mode in which you apply them is waveform recalculation. There is no comprehensive real time mode, which causes some inconvenience. But in certain cases there is a substitute for the real-time mode. If the window of any effect has the **Preview** button (real-time probe), you can select the effect's parameters. You change the effect's parameters with regulators in the effect window, and hear the result immediately. But to make sense of preliminary listening attempts, your computer has to provide for high performance.

Unlike an actual real-time mode, preliminary listening allows you to use only one effect.

We have already mentioned that Cool Edit Pro is a multichannel environment that allows you to place any number of waveforms on various tracks, both for synchronous play and to later join all of the tracks into a single one. Mixing consists of joining all the waveforms placed on tracks into two (or more) output channels.

You can edit waveforms and place them in or remove them from tracks, and Cool Edit Pro will be continuously tracing the changes during the multichannel session (waveform moving or removal, changing the volume, etc.). As soon as something has changed, Cool Edit Pro immediately processes this change by adding corrections to the mix going to the program output (for example, the ADC sound card). The program performs changes in the background, or *background mixing*. If your computer is powerful, you can edit your composition non-stop, and background mixing won't disturb you. You simply won't notice it, although the program has a special indicator. This indicator shows the progress, and also allows you to determine which stage of the process you are in. If you are lacking processor and hard disk performance, background mixing will impede your work.

Let us remind you that the stream of played data can be directed to a pair of output devices (a single stereo sound card) or to multiple output devices (several stereo sound cards or a multichannel card). Cool Edit Pro generates mixes for every set of applied output devices. If you use a single stereo sound card, Cool Edit Pro generates only one stereo mix. If a multichannel system is attached to the computer, separate mixes are created for each output device (each stereo pair). Multichannel output requires a lot of processing, and therefore tends to slow down the mixing process. So the audio card and the computer should correspond to each other. It makes no sense to install expensive multichannel sound digital conversion hardware on a cheap computer.

In addition to WAV files, Cool Edit Pro also allows you to use files called *session files* (SES files). We have called WAV files the standard building blocks from which a composition, e.g., a song, is built. If this is true, we can then further assume that a session file is the song itself, although a session file does not actually contain any audio data.

The size of a session file is quite small. It contains only certain detailed instructions to Cool Edit Pro:

❏ Filenames of WAV files and pathnames used

❏ Track names

❏ When to play a particular WAV file and when to stop

❏ The volume level and panorama set before playing each file, and how these parameters change during playing

We can compare a session file to a conductor, and WAV files to band members. The conductor instructs each member when to start and what the particulars of his or her part are. However, the conductor also needs the band. Similarly, a session file makes sense only when both it and the WAV files taking part in the session are in certain directories. You cannot just copy any WAV files used in a session to a floppy disk and then put it on your friend's computer. You also cannot arbitrarily rename or put this file in another directory. If you've done any of the above and then attempt to open a session file and play a composition, nothing happens. The conductor won't find the bandmembers in their places, and the concert will fail. This does not mean that session files and all the WAV files included in them cannot be moved from one directory to another. You can do this, but only by using special features of Cool Edit Pro that save the session to disk.

We must mention that multitrack editing is only one of the new features implemented in Cool Edit Pro. If we compare it to Cool Edit 96 in detail, we can see that many new abilities were introduced, some functions were implemented in a more convenient way, and algorithms and the interface were optimized. The up-to-date version of this popular editor has many more useful features.

Here are the main new elements of the program.

❏ The Full Reverb effect allows you to create a detailed acoustic model of the room, taking into consideration the features of the environment in which the sound will travel: the absorbing and reflecting features of the materials that the ceiling, the floor, and the walls are made of, their amplitude-frequency responses, etc.

❏ The Hard Limiter effect implements hard limiting of the audio signal amplitude, which in many cases allows you to increase the loudness of the composition's sound.

❏ The Pitch Bender effect helps pitch shift the whole part as well as its fragments, and to correct wrong notes from a singer. To do this, you need simply draw a chart.

❏ The DTMF/Notch Filter effect removes not only noises and sounds that accompany using a telephone with tone dialing, but also other narrow-band noises.

❏ The click suppressing filter has become more reliable.

❏ A great number of effects can be used in the preliminary mode (these effects have the **Preview** button).

❏ The ability to automatically detect and remove "silence" between words and separate sounds was introduced. This allows you to clean tracks from noise without touching the foreground sounds.

❏ Functions that allow you to automatically detect and outline the boundaries of phrases in speech recording and beat boundaries in music recording (the Auto-Cue function) were enhanced.

❏ Besides graphic tools for dynamic control, there are tools based on parameters' digital value input that are more familiar to experienced sound engineers.

❏ The implementation algorithms of Chorus, Flanger, Sweeping Phaser, Brainwave Synchronizer, and Clip Restoration effects were enhanced. New presets were added.

❏ You can now record your favorite radio programs automatically, by setting the starting time and the recording duration.

❏ All preliminary settings for sampling frequencies up to 192 kHz are set. The developers state that Cool Edit Pro can operate even with sampling frequencies of about 10 MHz! It just needs hardware that can support such processing.

❏ Different SMPTE formats are supported: Decimal, Samples, Compact Disc 75 fps, SMPTE 30 fps, SMPTE Drop (29.97 fps), SMPTE 29.97 fps, SMPTE 25 fps (EBU), SMPTE 24 fps (Film), Bars and Beats, Custom, SMPTE 29.97 fps.

Before you start learning the Cool Edit Pro sound editor, you have to have some preliminary preparation.

Chapter 7: Getting Started

After the program is started, open the main menu, **Options**. Select the **Settings** command. A dialog box containing eight tabs appears: **Devices**, **General**, **System**, **Colors**, **Spectral**, **Data**, **Multitrack**, and **SMPTE**. We'll open the tabs one by one and select the main parameters.

7.1. The *Devices* Tab—Selecting Recording and Playback Devices

The upper part of the **Devices** tab (Fig. 7.1) contains four lists of device drivers available for MIDI and audio data I/O:

❑ **MIDI In (Sync/Trigger)**—the MIDI data input device

❑ **MIDI Out (Music preview)**—the MIDI data output device

❑ **Waveform Playback**—the sound reproduction device (DAC)

❑ **Waveform Record**—the sound digital conversion device (ADC)

The main addresses of device drivers are put in brackets near their names.

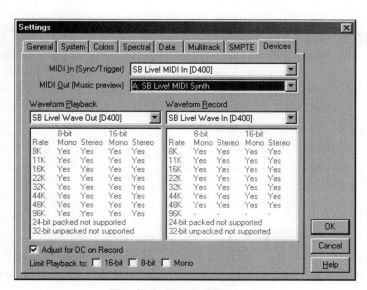

Fig. 7.1. The **Devices** tab

Under the last two above lists there are tables indicating the compatibility of recording and playback devices with different formats of sound signal representation.

The left columns of the table contain sampling frequencies from 8 to 96 kHz. Frequency values are actually approximate (there are no fractional parts; for example, **11K** corresponds to a frequency of 11.025 kHz). All these frequencies have been included in standards, so the sound card will reproduce and record the sound using the standard values of sampling frequencies.

The upper row of the table contains four possible mode combinations: **8/16-bit** (the signal resolution) and **Mono/Stereo**.

This table is as easy to use as the multiplication table. Examine the cell at the crossing of the row and the column that corresponds to the mode you are interested in. If the sound card supports this mode, there is **Yes** in the cross cell.

You also have the **Adjust for DC** checkbox under the table. It is used to enable the correction mode of the direct current component in the recorded signal. Some hardware recording devices may pass the direct current component of the signal voltage to the ADC input, which results in waveform recording with the offset from zero. While such waveforms are being assembled, clicking may occur. If the **Adjust for DC** checkbox is marked, Cool Edit Pro automatically corrects the constant component so that in the main window each waveform on the track is located symmetrically in relation to the zero level.

The options of the **Limit Playback To:** group are used to compensate for limitations of specific hardware devices. For example, if the sound card does not process 32-bit sound and can process only 16-bit data, you can use this option to reproduce low quality 32-bit sound data. To do this, check the **16-bit** checkbox. We hope your sound card supports stereo sound so you won't have to use the **Mono** checkbox.

Besides the standard **OK** and **Cancel** buttons, the **Settings** window (just as most windows in this program) contains a **Help** button. Pressing this button allows you to get information on the current window.

7.2. The *General* Tab—Basic Settings

The **General** tab (Fig. 7.2) contains options that define the main settings of the program.

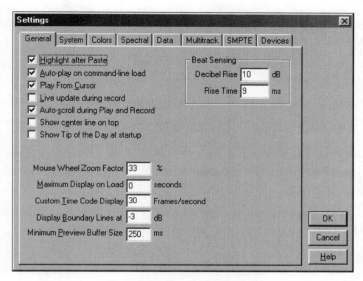

Fig. 7.2. The **General** tab

In the upper left part of this tab there are 7 checkboxes.

Highlight after paste—selects the sound data block pasted into the waveform.

Auto-play on command-line load—enables auto-playing mode when the program is started from the command line and the sound file name is given as a parameter.

Play From Cursor—starts playing from the cursor position.

Live update during record—draws the waveform in the working field of the program during the recording.

Auto-scroll during Play and Record—leaves the current position indicator in its place (the waveform will move in realtion to it).

Your computer's parameters for the last two modes mentioned are critical. If its CPU type is anywhere from a 486 to a Pentium 133, there could be faults during playing and recording.

Show center line on top—defines the red horizontal line of the zero level relative to the waveform image. When the mode is on, this line is in the foreground of the waveform; otherwise, it is in the background.

Show Tip of the Day at startup—shows the "tip of the day" when the program is started.

In the **Beat Settings** group, you can select options that define function's actions when searching for boundaries of phrases, bars, and beats (see the detailed description of the Find Beats function in *Section 10.10*).

Decibel Rise—the amplitude jump (in decibels) the program needs to determine the bar when the Find Beats function is used.

Rise Time—the amount of time (in milliseconds) during which the amplitude should rise to the value set in **Decibel Rise**.

Besides the above interface elements, this tab contains 5 input fields.

Mouse Wheel Zoom Factor—selects the mouse wheel zoom sensitivity.

Maximum Display on Load—the maximum length of sound data (in seconds) displayed in the program window when the program is loaded from disk. If this value is zero, the entire waveform is displayed.

Custom Time Code Display—user format of time coding (hours:minutes:seconds:frames) in which only the number of frames per second can be changed.

Display Boundry Lines at—the number you input here (in decibels) defines the position of horizontal lines that help visualize the signal level. A value of 0 dB corresponds to the maximum possible signal amplitude. Going over this level results in signal limitation, accompanied by notable distortion. If you set the value of **Display Boundry Lines at** equal to −1 dB, and then see that the waveform image is not crossing the horizontal lines, you will most likely be able to avoid distortion.

Minimum Preview Buffer Size—the buffer's minimum size when previewing the audio data processing result. The dialog boxes of many effects have a button that turns on the real-time test preview mode. Different sound cards may require different memory buffer sizes. If during the preview there are playing faults, they may be caused by your computer's lack of performance. Still, you might try to select a larger buffer size, but remember that a larger buffer size requires more memory.

7.3. The *System* Tab—System Settings

The options of the **System** tab (Fig. 7.3) allow you to change the program's system settings.

The first and the most important recommendation is: if you are still not familiar with the purposes of the options in this window, try not to change anything! Use this window only after you have learned the options of the **System** window described below.

Now we'll discuss the **Play/Record Buffer** group.

Total Buffer Size—the total size of buffers containing audio data, measured in seconds. The larger the size of the buffers for containing temporary audio data during playing or recording, the more reliable the program will operate (especially when several Windows applications are running at the same time). However, the more memory the buffers take, the less memory remains for other purposes.

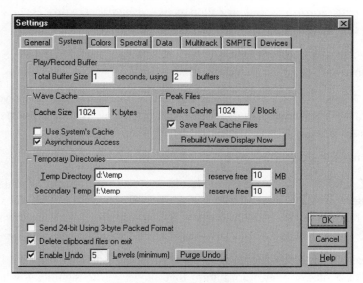

Fig. 7.3. The **System** tab

In the **using ... buffers** field, you indicate the number of buffers. This value can also effect the sound quality. Some sound drivers work incorrectly when there are a lot of buffers, so there could be faults in playing and recording. If this happens, try to decrease the number of buffers, or try to change their total size.

We'll now discuss the **Wave Cache** group. **Cache Size ... K bytes** is the size of the cache memory. The program allows waveforms with durations of up to dozens of minutes and a size of up to hundreds of MB to freely operate. It's not likely that your computer has this much RAM. Therefore, Cool Edit Pro will use the free hard disk space as is necessary. The data exchange rate is less than when using RAM memory, and while processing sound, the program has to address some measurements of the sample many times. If the addressing is only to the hard disk, then creating a reverberation effect for a large waveform could take several hours or even days.

Programmers found an ingenious but simple solution to this in the early days of programming. The data fragment currently being processed is put into RAM memory, and all necessary actions are performed upon it there. Then the processed fragment is written to the disk again, and the next data fragment is put into RAM memory. This process continues until all the data are processed. The more information put into RAM memory, the faster the processing is performed; however, the ratio between these two factors is not linear. The described technology is known as *caching*, and the memory area where the processed data portion is put is called *cache memory*. To process a waveform, it is recommended that you use 1—2 MB of cache memory.

If you want to use the system's cache in Cool Edit Pro, select the **Use System's Cache** option. It is, however, better to avoid it.

Asynchronous Access—you should check this checkbox, since it allows you to perform file reading and writing at the same time. If your operating system supports asynchronous access to the hard drive, file operations will be performed faster.

Now we'll discuss the **Peak Files** group.

In the **Peaks Cache ... /Block** field you should input the number of signal measurements in the data fragment when information is read or written from PEAK files for accelerating WAV file loading and waveform display. When you work with large waveforms (dozens of MB), it is recommended that you increase this value to 1024.

If the **Save Peak Cache Files** checkbox is checked, Cool Edit Pro will save both WAV files and PK files. These files contain information that allows you to significantly accelerate drawing the envelope of sound waves on the screen during repeated loading of the corresponding WAV file. When the amount of memory taken by PEAK files becomes unacceptable, you can delete the oldest files. Remember not to delete a WAV file you really need!

Pressing the **Rebuild Wave Display** button causes the waveform image to be refreshed (redrawn).

We'll now look at the **Temporary Directories** group.

In the **Temp Directory** and **Secondary Temp** fields, you should provide the main and the additional directories for temporary file storage. To increase the program's performance, these directories should be located on different physical disks. For each temporary directory, in the **reserve free ... MB** input fields, you may define the minimum disk memory that will be kept from being filled with service information.

Send 24-bit Using 3-byte Packed Format—if this checkbox is selected, all 32-bit sound data are sent to the sound card in packed 3-byte PCM format. If you don't select it, the data are sent in unpacked 4-byte PCM format. If the sound card does not support the unpacked format, the packed format is selected automatically.

Delete clipboard files on exit—deletes data from clipboard when exiting the program.

Enable Undo—enable and disable the undo mode, with the number of undo levels being defined in the **Levels (minimum)** input field.

Purge Undo—clear the service information needed for undo operations on levels above the maximum defined level. If during the session you performed, for example, 10 operations and then pressed the **Purge Undo** button, and the maximum number of undo levels is 5, you will then only be able to undo not all 10, but only the 5 last actions. Sometimes, if there is not much free disk space, it makes sense to limit the number of times you can Undo.

7.4. The *Colors* Tab—Setting Interface Color Schemes

The **Colors** tab of the **Settings** window is shown in Fig. 7.4. Options of this window allow you to define the colors of the program interface.

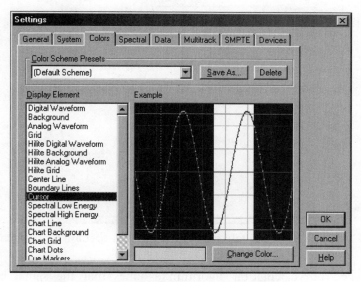

Fig. 7.4. The **Colors** tab; setting the palette

The **Color Scheme Presets** pull-down list contains the names of standard color schemes. Besides the existing palettes, you can create your own. Pressing the **Save As** button allows you to save it under its own name. The **Delete** button deletes the selected palette from the list.

The **Display Element** list contains the names of interface elements, the colors of which are currently available for editing. In the **Example** field there is an example of the program interface's appearance when you press **OK**.

To change the color of the selected element, press the **Change Color** button. The **Color** dialog box standard for all MS Windows applications appears. It allows you to select any color tint you like.

7.5. The *Spectral* Tab—Setting Spectral Representation Parameters

The program allows you to display the sound file in spectral representation. Using the **Spectral** tab options (Fig. 7.5), you can change the parameters of such a display.

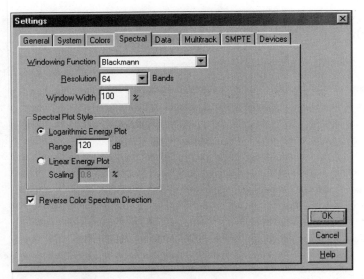

Fig. 7.5. The **Spectral** tab; setting the sound's spectral representation

The classical spectrum calculation algorithm assumes that the signal being analyzed is infinite, and that any changes made to it long ago make the same contribution to the spectrum as current changes do. In reality, any signal has a beginning and an end, the spectrum analyzer is turned on and off at certain moments, and physically implemented spectral analyzers "forget" information about older events.

The **Windowing Function** pull-down list contains the list of conversion algorithms used to display the signal spectrum. Algorithms differ from one another in the nature of the function that uses the analyzed signal's prehistory during the spectrum calculation.

If you aren't in the habit of using a certain spectral analysis algorithm, it does not really matter which line you select from this list. In practice, the difference between the algorithms is not particularly significant.

The **Resolution ... Bands** pull-down list allows you to select the resolution for the signal's spectral representation. The more bands the range of analyzed frequencies consists of, the more accurate is the analysis, but calculations will take more time. Because spectral analysis is based on Fast Fourier Transform (FFT) algorithms, the **Resolution ... Bands** parameter is equal to the FFT size.

In the **Window Width ... %** input field, you can set the spectral window width in percents of the selection size. We recommend that you leave this value at 100%.

The **Spectral Plot Style** group of options defines the plot style when displaying the spectrum. **Logarithmic Energy Plot** is a logarithmic plot. The plot range (**Range ... dB**) is defined in decibels. **Linear Energy Plot** is a linear plot. The scale (**Scaling ... %**) is set in percents.

If the **Reverse Color Spectrum Direction** checkbox is ticked, the palette used for spectrum coloring is inverted.

7.6. The *Data* Tab—Selecting Sound Data Processing Parameters

The **Data** tab options (Fig. 7.6) allow you to control sound data processing parameters.

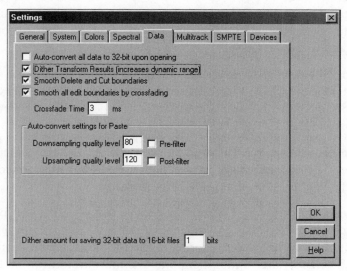

Fig. 7.6. The **Data** tab

If the **Auto-convert all data to 32-bit upon opening** checkbox is checked, all the audio data will be automatically converted into 32-bit format when the file is opened.

If the sound signal is represented by 16-bit counts, we would suppose that to convert it (for example, to make the reverberation effect) 16-bit arithmetics is used. But if this were true, serious distortions would appear after several conversions, because 16 bits is not enough for such conversions. So, for internal sound representations, Cool Edit Pro and many other sound editors use more than 16 bits. Because of widening the dynamics range of the digital signal representation, the error accumulated in audio data processing is decreased. However, after all conversions necessary to create an effect are made, the data are normally converted into 16-bit format. The dynamics range goes down to the standard 96 dB. Of course, a part of the information is lost in sound conversions. To make this loss insignificant, you can compensate it by adding pseudo-random noise with a very small amplitude. It seems that the dynamic range of the signal stays at 105 dB (which corresponds to 24-bit signal representation). This is impossible from the point of view of physics and mathematics, but due to specific features of human auditory perception, when pseudo-random noise is added it seems to the listener that the sound quality is better than with 16-bit sound representation. This approach is also used in the Cool Edit Pro editor.

The effect of widening the dynamic range is enabled and disabled by checking or unchecking the **Dither Transform Results (increases dynamic range)** checkbox.

You should select the **Smooth Delete and Cut boundaries** checkbox to smooth out fragments of waveforms in the places you join them together after performing **Cut** and **Delete** actions, and to avoid clicks.

A ticked **Smooth all edit boundaries by crossfading** checkbox means that smoothing takes place on the boundaries of edited fragments. This action is similar to **Crossfade**. The time taken to smoothly increase and decrease the volume is defined in the **Crossfade Time ... ms** field in milliseconds.

In the **Auto-convert settings for Paste** group, you can set the parameters of automated conversion when pasting. Automated conversion works when the pasted data fragment has a format different from the edited waveform format.

Downsampling quality level and **Upsampling quality level**—define the precision of decreasing and increasing the sampling frequency within the range between 30 and 1000. The **Pre-filter** option enables special filtering of the waveform before decreasing the sampling fequency. The **Post-filter** option option allows the waveform to be filtered after increasing the sampling fequency.

Dither amount for saving 32-bit data to 16-bit files ... bits—in this input field you should give the number defining the pseudo-random signal value that is added to save 32-bit data in 16-bit files (from 0 to 1). A value of 1 enables this mode, while a zero value disables it. To partially add the pseudo-random signal, select a value of 0.5.

7.7.The *Multitrack* Tab—Multitrack Editing Parameters

Unlike earlier versions, Cool Edit Pro is a multitrack editor. After individual waveforms are edited, you can place them on separate tracks and assemble the audio program. Operating in multitrack mode is described in detail in *Chapter 18*. Now we'll describe the **Multitrack** tab's options (Fig. 7.7). This tab defines some parameters of this mode.

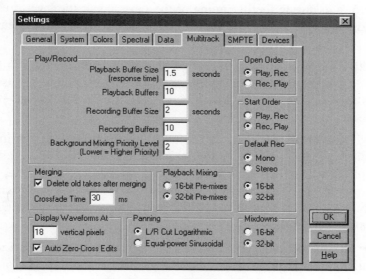

Fig. 7.7. The **Multitrack** tab

In the **Play/Record** group, you can reset the number and the size of memory buffers used in playback and recording modes.

Playback Buffer Size (response time) ... seconds—buffer size for playback.

Playback Buffers—the number of playback buffers.

Recording Buffer Size ... seconds—buffer size for recording.

Recording Buffers—the number of recording buffers.

Background Mixing Priority Level—priority level for mixing in the multitrack session relative to other processes. Lower values indicate a higher priority compared to other system events. You can also input fractional values, for example, 0.8.

In the **Merging** group, you can select options for merging waveforms from different tracks into one mix.

Delete old takes after merging—deletes old takes after merging is complete. This action frees up disk space.

Crossfade Time ... ms—the time crossfade takes to record a new fragment to the existing waveform. Two fragments are not stuck together by rapidly turning one off and then turning the other one on, since a click would then be heard, which is almost unavoidable. It's done like this. At the end of the previous signal, its level is smoothly lowered from nominal to zero, and during the beginning of the next signal, the level rises from zero to nominal. The boundary between the signals is not heard. This is the meaning of cross-fade.

In the **Playback Mixing** group, you can select the number of bits used in mixing: **16-bit Pre-mixes** or **32-bit Pre-mixes**. For all intermediate actions it makes sense to select the maximum possible number of bits. You should only use 16 bits before you record the completely processed soundtrack.

In the **Display Waveforms At** group, we see an input field for the track image height in pixels (**... vertical pixels**), and the **Auto Zero-Cross Edits** checkbox that automatically changes the place where certain editing actions (**Splice**, **Cut**, **Delete**, **Trim**, **Adjust Boundaries**) are performed, to the point where the waveform envelope becomes zero. We recommend that you select this checkbox, since it allows you to avoid clicks on waveform and fragment boundaries.

In the **Panning** group, you can select one of two panning methods: **L/R Cut Logarithmic** (the logarithmic panning normal for older versions of Cool Edit) or **Equal-power Sinusoidal** (panning that preserves the constant sinusoidal power).

Sound cards that support duplex mode can be used for multitrack editing. In the **Open Order** group, you have to select the order of using the sound device driver in a multichannel enviromnent. In the **Start Order** group, you select the order in which to use the sound device drivers with the **Start** Command. Some sound cards require this order to be specific. For example, if you have a Sound Blaster sound card, you have to select the **Rec, Play** option.

In the **Default Rec** group, you should select the audio file recording format by default.

In the **Mixdowns** group, you can select the number of bits applied to the **Mixdown** action (mixing, combining several tracks into one). By default, the **16-bit** value is set.

7.8. The *SMPTE* Tab—Synchronizing Options

The **SMPTE** tab (Fig. 7.8) contains options that define the synchronization of parameters on the SMPTE interface. Most computer musicians are not interested in this tab, as in home studios it is rarely needed to compile audio data recorded by different devices. However, we have to mention that Cool Edit Pro supports the SMPTE interface, and the **SMPTE** tab allows you to optimize these parameters.

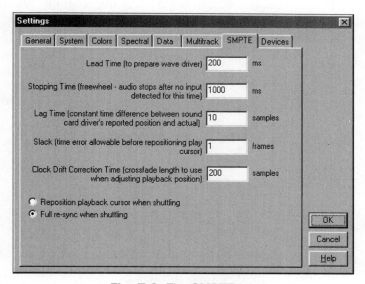

Fig. 7.8. The **SMPTE** tab

The **SMPTE** tab has five input fields.

☐ **Lead Time ... ms**—the time playback will run before the program has to set full synchronizing. It is recommended that you select a value from 500 to 1000 msec.

☐ **Stopping Time ... ms**—the time Cool Edit Pro will operate in autonomous mode after the synchronizing signal disappears.

☐ **Lag Time ... samples**—synchronizing signals offset relative to the time scale (defined in the number of samples). A nonzero value for this parameter must be selected when audio data has a constant offset relative to the time code.

❑ **Slack ... frames**—the maximum allowed number of frames reproduced between a synchronization fault and restoration. It is not recommended that you set this value over 2—3; otherwise, the time difference between the tracks will be noticed.

❑ **Clock Drift Correction Time ... samples**—the number of samples meeting the clock drift correction time when moving from one waveform to another.

Besides the input fields, this tab contains two radio buttons:

❑ **Reposition playback cursor when shuttling**—resets the current position when going into a loop.

❑ **Full re-sync when shuttling**—full synchronization updating when going into a loop.

Having completed the preparation, we can begin using the program. We should certainly start with the most simple and often used actions. That's why we shall first learn the elements of the main window in separate waveform editing mode.

Chapter 8: Working with the Main Window in the *Waveform View* Mode

In the current version of Cool Edit Pro, there are two principally different operating modes:

❑ Editing separate mono or stereo waveforms

❑ Joint multitrack editing of all waveforms

Each of these modes has a main menu and a main window: **Edit Waveform View** and **Multitrack View**, respectively. Indeed, they are two different sound editors with different purposes combined into one functional set.

The specific features of operating in the multitrack environment are discussed in *Chapter 18*. Here we will start a detailed description of the tools available for the user when editing separate mono or stereo waveforms in the **Edit Waveform View** window.

8.1. Basic Elements of the Main Window

After the program is launched, the main window looks like Fig. 8.1.

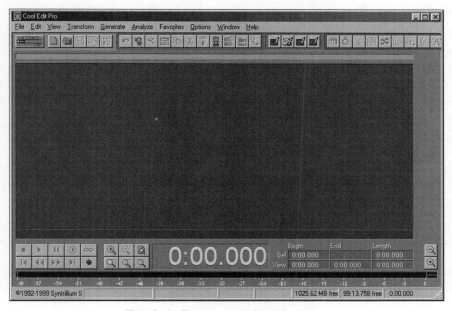

Fig. 8.1. The program's main menu

In the upper part of the window we see the toolbar. You can change its appearance and contents according to your needs by adding or removing elements (buttons corresponding to menu items). Select the tools displayed in the main window with the **Toolbars** sub-menu of the **Options** menu.

To find out the purpose of any of the elements, move the mouse pointer to it and hold it still for a second or so. A tool tip that contains the list of functions will then appear. We won't describe these elements in detail here, since they are not constant, and they are also exactly the same as the items of the main menu that we describe in detail in *Chapters 9—17.*

Please pay attention to the left button of the toolbar. It is used to quickly change from the mode for editing individual waveforms (in this mode, the main window is called **Waveform View**) to the multitrack mode (**Multitrack View**). The appearance of the button changes according to the current mode. In the **Waveform View** mode it looks like this: ▨▨▨, and in **Multitrack View**—like this: ⊪⊪⊳.

In Fig. 8.1, you see a working field that is not yet filled in. It is empty because you have not loaded the sound waveform into the program's memory yet. If you read an audio file from the disk or record a sound from any of the available inputs of the sound card, the waveform is displayed in this field. We will describe this field as soon as we begin dealing with waveforms in general.

Before we continue learning the elements of the main window, we have to agree on two terms: *marker* and *current position indicator.* Both objects are shown as vertical lines, but the marker is dashed and the current position indicator is solid. They are not shown in Fig. 8.1, because the waveform has not yet been created. You will see these lines in other figures, but we need only mention them right now.

The marker points to the place (time) in the waveform from which playback or recording starts. The marker can be seen only in the program's static state—in the Stop mode.

There is also a current position indicator seen only in dynamic states: during playback and recording. In the waveform graphic image, it points to the place currently being played or recorded.

In the lower right part of the window there are some buttons (Fig. 8.2) that look like they belong on a tape recorder. This is the control panel, often called the *transport panel.*

Fig. 8.2. The control panel

These buttons are used to control recording, playback, and display of waveforms. We'll now go into more detail on them.

(Stop)—playback or recording stop button. After this button is pressed, the current position indicator returns to the marker. The next playback or recording session starts from the marker position.

(Play)—button for beginning playback. Only the displayed waveform fragment can be played. After the current position indicator reaches the right margin of the screen, playback stops, and the current position indicator returns to the marker. If there is a waveform fragment selected, only this fragment is played. After playback, the current position indicator returns to the beginning of the selected fragment.

(Pause)—button for temporarily stopping playback or recording. If you press the pause button, the current position indicator stays where it was at the moment this button was pressed. Pressing this button again continues playback (recording).

(Play to End)—another button to start playback. This button causes the entire waveform to be played, not just its displayed or selected part. During playback, the waveform image is scrolled so that the current position indicator is always in the middle of the screen. After playback is over or the **Stop** button is pressed, the waveform fragment around the marker is shown (the waveform area from which playback was started).

(Play Looped)—button for beginning looped playback. Playback starts from the marker position. When the current position indicator reaches the right margin of the waveform fragment displayed on the screen, playback is not stopped, but continues from the left margin. If there is a fragment selected, only this fragment is looped.

(Go to Beginning or Previous Cue)—button that moves the marker to the waveform's beginning or to the previous position of the automatic marker of the phrase and bar borders (*Section 10.11*).

(Rewind)—the "rewind" button. If the program is in the Stop state, pressing this button will move the marker to the beginning of the waveform. If you press this button once, the marker moves one step. If you press the button and do not release it immediately, the marker moves until it reaches the waveform's beginning or until you release the **Rewind** button.

By right-clicking the **Rewind** button, you open a menu (Fig. 8.3) in which you can select the rewind speed. The two upper lines of the menu correspond to variable speed: the more you keep the **Rewind** button pressed the faster rewinding is done. Selecting any of the other menu lines sets a fixed rewinding speed.

If you press the **Rewind** button during playback, the current position indicator—but not the marker—moves backwards. When you release the button, playback is started from the position of the current position indicator.

(Fast Forward)—the fast forward button. It differs from the **Rewind** button only in direction.

(Go to End or Next Cue)—this button moves the marker to the waveform's end, or to the next position of the automatic marker of the phrase and bar borders.

(Record)—button that begins recording.

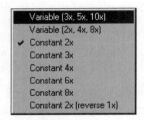

Fig. 8.3. The rewind speed selection menu

The main window contains some other elements and instruments, but now is not the time to discuss them: first we have to put a waveform into the main window. There are several ways to do this. We can load a waveform from a file, paste it from the clipboard, or just record it. Let's start by recording.

8.2. Recording the Waveform

The **Record** button is the only button available after Cool Edit Pro is launched. Other buttons are not active since the waveform is not yet loaded and thus there is nothing to be played or displayed.

Before you press the **Record** button, make sure that the signal from the sound source (CD player, microphone, sound card synthesizer, or any other source) is given to the ADC input. You can do this very simply: just minimize the Cool Edit Pro window for a while and start the sound card mixer. Select the sound source and set the recording level so that there are no non-linear distortions at maximum loudness.

To precisely set the recording level, Cool Edit Pro provides a very convenient tool. In the lower part of the window there are indicators of the signal level and the scale (Fig. 8.4). By default, the scale limits are set to 0 and -60 dB (numbers from 0 to -57).

You can change the range of the levels displayed by right-clicking the scale and selecting the range of the levels displayed (from 30 to 120 dB) in the context menu.

Double-click the scale, or select the menu item **Options>Monitor Record Level**. The scale will then become active. If stereo format is set for the waveform, the levels of the right and the left channels will be indicated. The two horizontal lines will become longer or shorter, depending on the instantaneous values of the signal levels in the right and the left channels. To give you the ability to control the maximum level values, indicators will remember them for a short time. If the format is mono, you will see one and not two lines.

Indeed, double-clicking the recording level indicators (what you just did) is considered "idly" starting the ADC, and sound samples are not accumulated in the computer's memory; only the current signal level is displayed.

Your main task is to not allow the levels to get to 0 dB, and to not make them too small.

To the right of the **0** mark, there are two indicators that will show any overloading of the left and the right channels. They flash when the amplitude reaches or exceeds the maximum allowed value. Zero decibels is the maximum permissible value for the sound signal's digital sample. If this value is exceeded by the recorded signal, the bit scale of the ADC is overfilled. You'll hear this as a serious signal distortion, especially if the number of bits is frequently exceeded or exceeded for a long period of time. This is why the overload indicators are made red: to warn you that the recording session may end up being of bad quality!

Fig. 8.4. Signal level indicator. The signal level is big enough, but not over 0 dB

If the sound source allows you to repeat the recorded material (for example, when you are recording from a CD) it is better to listen to the whole composition first. Any time the overload indicators flash you should:

❏ Stop playback

❏ Lower the signal level by regulating the sound card mixer (using the virtual mixer)

❏ Cancel the overload indicator (turn off the virtual LEDs by clicking them)

❏ Rewind the composition (set the marker before the place in the waveform where you encountered overloading)

❏ Control this fragment of the composition again

Having selected the required level with the mixer, do not forget to stop the idle operation of the ADC: double-click the level indicators or press the **Stop** button ▪ .

Now you have to select one of two possible recording modes. Right-click the **Record** button ⬤ . A menu that allows you to select the recording mode appears. It contains two items: **Instant Record** and **Timed Record**.

If you select the **Instant Record** mode, recording starts at the moment you press the **Record** button.

Selecting the **Timed Record** mode allows you to program the starting time and the duration of the recording session. We'll describe how to do this at the end of this section.

Select the **Instant Record** mode. Now you can press the **Record** button. Recording does not start immediately as you probably will notice; first you have to select the recording format. The **New Waveform** dialog box shown in Fig. 8.5 will appear so that you can do this. (It will also appear when you select the main menu item **File>New...**).

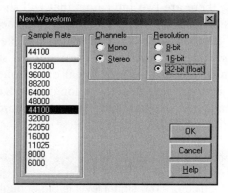

Fig. 8.5. The **New Waveform** dialog window for selecting the waveform format

The **New Waveform** dialog box is used to define the format in which the digitally converted sound is to be stored. You can look at it another way if it makes it any easier: until the required parameters are selected in the dialog box and you close it, the waveform does not exist. Only after you close the **New Waveform** dialog box can we say that there actually is a waveform. The recording session has not started yet, and the existing waveform contains no samples.

Select the sampling frequency from the **Sample Rate** list.

In the **Channels** group, select the following:

❏ **Mode—Mono** or **Stereo**

❏ **Resolution—8-bit**, **16-bit**, or **32-bit** signal representation

As soon as you press the **OK** button or the <Enter> key, the **New Waveform** window is closed and recording starts.

You can control the recording time using the indicator panel in the lower part of the program's window. One of its possible views is shown in Fig. 8.6. During the recording process, the values on the indicator table change.

Fig. 8.6. The recording time indicator panel

In our example, the value shown—**3:31.076**—means that recording started 3 minutes, 31 seconds, and 76 milliseconds ago. In this example, time is presented in decimal format, but you can select another time representation format. We'll explain how to do this in *Section 11.4.*

The working field of the main window is used to display the waveform. The working field is a coordinate plane.

The horizontal axis is used to measure time. Units of measure are user defined, but this we will go into detail about in *Section 11.4.*

If you select the mono waveform format, only one track is displayed in the working field. In stereo format, there would be two tracks placed one behind the other. The track corresponding to the left channel is the upper track, and the one corresponding to the right channel is the lower one.

The values on the vertical axis (separate for each track) correspond to the values of the signal samples. For a 16-bit signal, this range is from $-32,768$ to $32,767$, for an 8-bit signal, it is from 0 to 255. For users' convenience, there are two other variants of the vertical axis layout:

❏ As a percentage of the maximum allowed signal sample, which is 100%

❏ Normalized layout—as proper decimal fractions (the maximum allowed signal measurement is 1)

Now we'll describe the program's main window in the waveform displaying mode. Not only the waveform itself can be displayed, but also its current spectrum as well. In this case, frequency, and not signal level value, is measured on the vertical axis. This form of information representation is discussed in detail in *Section 11.1.*

At the bottom of the main window, we see the status bar (Fig. 8.7). In its fields, the data on the recording already made are shown.

| Stopped | L: -2.2dB @ 0:02.934 | 44100 · 16-bit · Stereo | 692 K | 0:04.028 | 980.64 MB free | 94:52.604 free | 0:02.866 |

Fig. 8.7. The status bar

In the **Data Under Cursor** field, the current mouse cursor coordinates are shown. In the example shown, the information shown in this field means that the cursor arrow is aimed at the point where the waveform level of the left channel is −2.2 dB, and the distance between this point and the beginning of the waveform is 2.934 sec. The most useful way to utilize this field is to estimate the signal level at specific points. To do this, you should aim the mouse cursor at a particular one of them.

The next field (**Waveform Format**) contains a note on the format selected for the waveform created.

After these come the fields where the following information is displayed:

❏ Memory space taken up by the waveform (**File Size**)

❏ Waveform's total duration (**File Size [time]**)

❏ Free memory space on the logical disks where temporary directories are created to store copies of the file with the waveform formed by the program during the current sesion (**Free Space [K]** and **Free Space [time]**)

The **Time Display** field displays the point on the time axis where the marker, the current position indicator, or the beginning of the selected fragment are located.

During recording and playback, the content of these fields changes, providing you with detailed information.

If digits flashing in the status bar divert your attention, you can disable the display of some or all of these fields. Right-click the status bar, and in the context menu that opens, uncheck the fields you don't want to be displayed.

The display format depends on the settings we describe in *Section 11.4.*

We have described the recording waveform in the **Instant Record** mode. Recording then starts immediately after you press the **Record** button ⬤ and define the waveform's parameters.

There is also another recording mode—**Timed Record**. With it, you can program the starting time and the duration of a recording session. This mode can be useful, for example, if you are going to record a radio program and you know exactly when it begins. To program Cool Edit Pro for automated recording, right-click the **Record** button. A menu will open, from which you can select the recording mode. Select **Timed Record**. The **Recording Time** dialog box will open (Fig. 8.8).

Fig. 8.8. The **Recording Time** dialog window

The status of the switches in the **Maximum Recording Time** group defines the recording session's duration. If you select **No Time Limit**, the recording is limited only by the amount of free disk space.

If you select the **Recording Length** option, you also have to set the recording session's duration.

The **Start Recording** group contains options that define the start of the recording mode.

If you selected the **Right Away** option, recording starts immediately after you press the **OK** button in the **Recording Time** window. In this case, the **Timed Record** recording mode differs from the **Instant Record** mode only in that you can define the recording session's duration.

If you select the **At ... on ...** option, recording starts at the defined time on the defined date.

Other window elements are used to select the format of time and date representation:

❑ **24 hr**—the hour is defined by a number from 0 to 23

❑ **12 hr**—the hour is defined by a number from 0 to 11, and with an indication of **AM/PM**

❑ **dd/mm/yyyy**—the date is defined in the day/month/year format

❑ **mm/dd/yyyy**—the date is defined in the month/day/year format

We'll take it for granted that you somehow have turned the recording mode on. If your computer has a high enough performance, recording should go smoothly: no errors should occur, and the values of the time parameters and the amount of memory shown in the information fields should change steadily.

If you decide to temporarily stop recording, use the **Pause** button.

You can only say that there is a waveform after you press the **Stop** button. So press it!

8.3. Waveform Display and Playback

You have now recorded a waveform on your own. After this, the appearance of the main window will change. The waveform graphic image (oscillogram) is shown in the working field. One possible view of a stereo waveform's oscillogram is shown in Fig. 8.9.

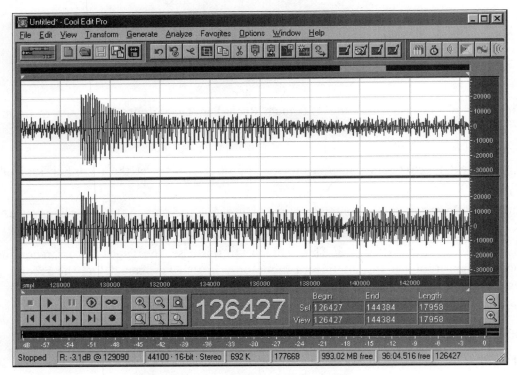

Fig. 8.9. A stereo waveform's oscillogram

Pay attention to the fact that just after recording stops, the recorded fragment is automatically selected.

In Fig. 8.9, the time position is reflected by the sample number, and that's why the numbers on the horizontal axis contain many zeros.

Often, the entire waveform image cannot be shown in the working field of the main window, and only part of it is visible. To help you understand which part it is that is being shown, there is a diagram above the waveform. The lit rectangle in the diagram indicates the viewed area. By moving this rectangle with the mouse, you can "rewind" the waveform. If the entire diagram is lit, the entire waveform is shown in the window.

The relation between the rectangle's size and the entire diagram is the same as between the duration of the fragment shown and the total duration of the waveform. When you double-click the diagram, the **Viewing Range** dialog box appears. This box allows you to precisely define the beginning and the end of the waveform fragment shown (Fig. 8.10).

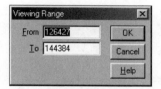

Fig. 8.10. The **Viewing Range** dialog window

The waveform fragment shown starts from the sample number defined in the **From** field, and ends with the sample defined in the **To** field. If you select another time display format in this window, you have to supply units other than sample numbers.

There is also another way to wind the waveform. Aim the mouse at the horizontal ruler with the time marked off above the main window field. The mouse pointer takes the form of a hand. Keep the left mouse button pressed, and rewind or fast forward the waveform by moving to the left or right.

To change the vertical scale of the waveform's image, use the **Zoom Out Vertically** and **Zoom In Vertically** buttons in the lower right-hand part of the main window.

The waveform image's horizontal scale is defined by these buttons:

Zoom Into Center—increases zoom

Zoom Out—decreases zoom

Zoom Out Full—shows the entire waveform

Zoom to Selection—increases zoom to display the entire selected waveform fragment

Zoom to Left of Selection—increases zoom and displays the left margin of the selected fragment

Zoom to Right of Selection—increases zoom and displays the right margin of the selected fragment

Later you won't be able to do without these tools that allow you to select waveform fragments.

Suppose you need to listen to a fragment not from the very beginning, but from a particular point. Position the mouse pointer to it, and click the mouse button. If the waveform is stereo, try to keep the mouse pointer near the line delimiting the tracks of the left and the right channels (you must not position it exactly on this line). In the position you click, the marker will appear, a vertical line "paperclipped" to the main window at is two ends. In the example shown in Fig. 8.11, this vertical line is at 25,000.

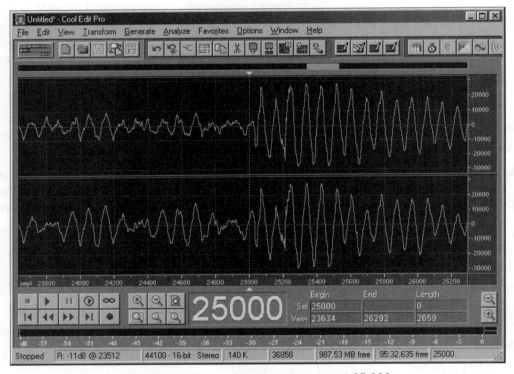

Fig. 8.11. The marker at measurement 25,000

If you press the **Play** button or the spacebar, playback will start from the marker's position.

Try to place the marker exactly in this position. It's not an easy thing to do on your first try. It is especially hard to "aim" when the waveform is long. When visually positioning the marker, the error is always by several samples, or sometimes even by tens of samples. Sometimes precision is critical. If this is the case, use one of the six input fields in the lower part of the window to the right of the time indicator panel.

These input fields are arranged in a table of two rows and three columns.

In the upper row (**Sel**), the temporary parameters of the selected fragment are displayed and edited. The lower row (**View**) allows you to edit the temporary parameters of the displayed waveform.

The left column (**Begin**) corresponds to the first moment of the waveform fragment, and the middle column (**End**) to the last one. The right column (**Length**) contains information on the fragment's length.

To precisely define the marker position, click the input field at the crossing of the **Sel** row and the **Begin** column, thus making this field available for editing. Input the value and press <Enter>. Although we used the tool for waveform fragment selection, we are also able to use it to precisely position the marker.

To precisely define the boundaries of the selected fragment, we have to define them in the input fields where the **Sel** row and the following two columns meet:

❏ **Begin** (left margin of the selected fragment)

❏ **End** (right margin of the selected fragment)

The **Begin** and **End** input fields of the **View** row repeat the options in the **Viewing Range** dialog window (see Fig. 8.10).

To define the boundaries of the selected or displayed fragment, you can define its beginning and end. We have just described this method. We could also do it another way: define the fragment's left margin and its length. For this purpose, we use the fields of the **Length** column. We have to mention that, in any case, only two values that define the waveform fragment's temporary parameters are independent. If you have defined the fragment's right margin, the value in the length field is defined automatically, and vice versa.

The numerical method of margin definition is precise but is not always convenient. It may slow down working with the waveform. It is easier and faster to use the graphic method.

As we have mentioned, to position the marker, you have to click the main window once. If you double-click the waveform, the fragment displayed in the main window is selected. If you want to select just a part of this fragment (an even shorter part of the waveform), do the following.

Put the mouse pointer at the position corresponding to the fragment's beginning (or end) and hold the left mouse button down. Keeping the button pressed, move the mouse pointer to the end (beginning) of the fragment. Release the button. The result is similar to that shown in Fig. 8.12.

If you have to change the boundaries of the selected waveform area, you needn't repeat the above actions. As soon as you click the waveform, all selections previously made are cancelled. To avoid this, use the right mouse button to precisely define the margins of the previously selected area.

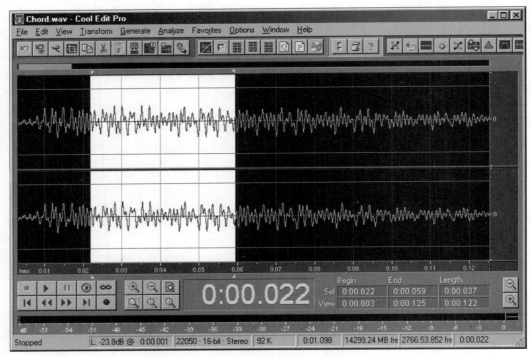

Fig. 8.12. A selected waveform fragment

You have now selected the waveform fragment. If you press the **Play** button, only this selected fragment will be played. But we select the fragment not just to play it back. The program is built so that all actions apply only to the selected fragment.

Cool Edit Pro allows you to work with each of the stereo channels separately. For this, you have to specially select the fragments. This is easily done. Point the mouse pointer not to the line delimiting the tracks, but to either the upper or to lower track (to operate the left or the right channel, respectively). As soon as you put the mouse button at the height you need, it changes its appearance: besides the usual arrow, the letter **L** (left) or **R** (right) appears. Now you can work with the audio information of separate channels the same as with the entire waveform. The selected waveform fragment of the left channel is shown in Fig. 8.13.

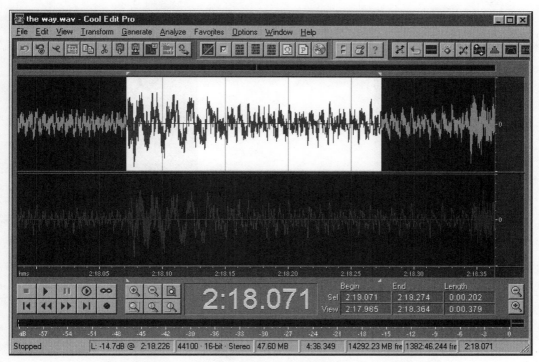

Fig. 8.13. A selected waveform fragment of the left channel

Maybe you have noticed that during playback there is a solid vertical line that crosses the waveform image. This is the current position indicator that points to the fragment being played at the moment. Under certain conditions (when the fragment displayed in the window is significantly less than the entire waveform, and when special playback is on), the current playback position is displayed in another manner. The vertical line stands in the middle of the window, and the waveform image itself moves.

In the main window, you can edit the waveform on the sound measurement level (microlevel). This can be useful for eliminating short impulse noises (clicks). You can manually draw the shape of the sound wave for future use with your own musical instrument with a unique timbre.

Let's use this editing mode in practice. To edit the waveform on a microlevel, you have to set the appropriate zoom. Pressing the **Zoom Into Center** button makes separate measurements not just visible but also available to be used with the mouse cursor (which looks like a hand). In this mode, sound measurements are shown as small squares connected by thin lines (Fig. 8.14).

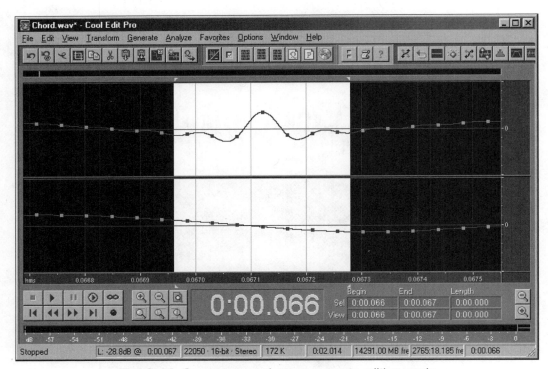

Fig. 8.14. Separate sound measurements editing mode

These lines help you understand what the form of the signal passed through the DAC of the sound card will be. You can move these squares vertically using the mouse. The signal's form is edited on the microlevel in just this manner. However, you can return to a normal zoom (editing on the level of the amplitude envelope, but not on the level of separate measurements) using the **Zoom Out** button as many times as you need, or by pressing the **Zoom Out Full** button once.

Now that we have covered the basic operating modes in the main window, we can continue learning the main menu.

Chapter 9: The *File* Menu—Working with Files

The **File** menu contains the following commands:

- ❒ **New...**—creates a new file
- ❒ **Open...**—opens a file
- ❒ **Open As...**—opens a file having re-defined its attributes
- ❒ **Open Append...**—opens a file without closing the previously opened file, and place new sound data in the existing tracks one by one
- ❒ **Revert to Saved**—reverts to the last-saved file
- ❒ **Close**—closes the active file
- ❒ **Close All Waves and Session**—closes all files of all sessions
- ❒ **Close Only Non-Session Waveforms**—closes any open audio files not used in the current session (not inserted in a multichannel environment)
- ❒ **Save**—saves the file with its name
- ❒ **Save As...**—saves the file with a user-defined name
- ❒ **Save Copy As...**—saves a copy of the file
- ❒ **Save Selection...**—saves only selected waveform fragments
- ❒ **Save All**—saves all currently open waveforms and sessions; if the data does not exist as a file yet, the **Save As** window is opened
- ❒ **Flush Virtual File**—allows to use the open file by another application
- ❒ **Free Hard Drive Space...**—opens the window containing information on the free memory left on the hard disk for purging and reserving disk space
- ❒ **Exit**—exits the Cool Edit Pro application

9.1. *New*—Creating a New File

The first command of the **File** menu is **New**. It is used to create new waveforms. If a file with another waveform is opened, this waveform will not be lost. It will remain in the program and will be placed on another page. You can access any of the opened files using the **Window** menu.

When you select the **File > New** command, the **New Waveform** dialog window appears (see Fig. 8.4). You learned about this box when recording your own waveform (*Section 8.2*).

If you select the **New** command before recording and define the waveform format, after pressing the **Record** button in the main window the program will not call the **New Waveform** window again, but simply start recording.

9.2. File Opening and Closing

The **Open** command opens a sound file. The **Open a Waveform** dialog window appears. It is shown in Fig. 9.1.

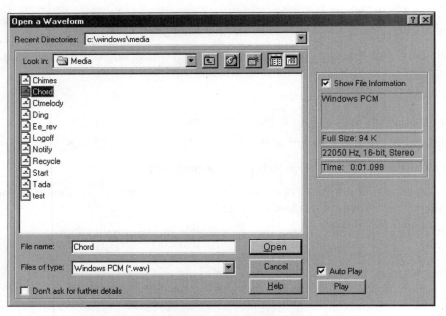

Fig. 9.1. The **Open a Waveform** dialog window

Besides the standard elements for opening files found in any Windows application, this window contains the additional fields we describe below.

The **Recent Directories** pull-down list contains the directories (folders) which you addressed earlier when opening files. To quickly change the directory, you should select the line you need from the list.

If the **Show File Information** checkbox is selected, information on the format of the se-lected sound file, its duration, and the memory space it takes up is displayed in the **Open a Waveform** window.

If the **Auto Play** checkbox is checked, the files you select from the **Recent Directories** pull-down list are played. You can also listen to the selected file by pressing the **Play** button.

If you enable the **Don't ask for further details** checkbox, you won't be asked additional ques-tions on the file format that usually come up after you press the **Open** button. You might be asked for details if you want to load a sound file of a specific format, but not a WAV file. Pos-sible questions relate to the discretion frequency, resolution, methods of sound compression, etc. The reason for this is that sound files stored in certain formats do not contain any infor-mation on certain details. Thus the program attempts to get the missing information from you.

You select the sound file type from the **Files of type** pull-down list (WAV by default). Cool Edit Pro can operate with various sound file formats (about ten), including those used with other platforms (Amiga, Mac computers). But we're working on an IBM PC-compatible platform, so we are not interested in "foreign" formats of audio data. We just wanted to give an example of the most exotic format Cool Edit Pro can process.

Audio data can be stored in a text file with the TXT extension. Each count is represented by a number in decimal format. Data of different sound channels are separated by tab characters. Each sample (a pair of stereo samples) is separated from the next one (pair) by a non-printed carriage return character, i.e., by pressing the <Enter> key. Service information is written in the beginning of the file. Each line consists of a key word, a colon, and a tab character fol-lowed by the parameter value (a digit or a word). The following record is an example of such a file:

```
SAMPLES:            31
BITSPERSAMPLE:      16
CHANNELS:           2
SAMPLERATE:                 44100
NORMALIZED:                 FALSE
246                 246
-242                -242
-725                -725
-1180               -1180
-1617               -1617
-2057               -2057
-2495               -2495
-2901               -2901
...
```

The record in the first line (with the SAMPLES keyword) means that the file contains 31 samples; the second line (BITSPERSAMPLE) contains information on the number of bits per sample; the third line (CHANNELS) contains the number of channels; the fourth line (SAMPLERATE) represents the sampling frequency. The last line contains information about whether or not normalization is applied to data with values ranging from −1.0 to 1.0 (TRUE—yes, FALSE—no).

Here is an example of a text file containing the described file but with normalization enabled.

```
SAMPLES:            31
BITSPERSAMPLE:      16
CHANNELS:           2
SAMPLERATE:         44100
NORMALIZED:         TRUE
 0.00750732          0.00750732
-0.00738525         -0.00738525
-0.0221252          -0.0221252
-0.0360107          -0.0360107
-0.0493469          -0.0493469
-0.0627747          -0.0627747
-0.0761414          -0.0761414
-0.0885315          -0.0885315
-0.0993958          -0.0993958
 . . .
```

As it shows, the values of sound samples are within a range of -1.0 and 1.0. In this case, the normalization option does not effect the quality of the sound, and it is used only for a different representation of audio data.

Remember that the above format of audio data representation is not compact. A text file with audio data takes up 10 times more space than a normal WAV file. So what is this form of audio data intended for? One possible example of using the text format is audio data transfer between the sound editor and programs that do not work with WAV files. So why load sound waveforms in such programs? One reason is to analyze sound using mathematical applications, since most of them read numerical arrays from text files.

We must mention that Cool Edit Pro can load several sound files one after another. To do this, select the filenames of files you are interested in in the **Open File** window and press the **Open** button. The selected files will be loaded into the program. Each of them is placed on a separate page of the program's main window.

Now we would like to describe how to select several files at a time. It's simple. Using the mouse, select a file from the list. Then press the <Ctrl> key and keep it pressed. Using the arrows, move along the list and select the next file you need, and then press the spacebar. Now two files are selected. Move the cursor to the next file and select it too. Do this as many times as you need. Only after you have selected all the required files should you release the <Ctrl> key. You can do it another way as well: while keeping the <Ctrl> key pressed, click on all the required filenames. Then press <Enter> or the **Open** button. All the selected files are now loaded.

The next command of the **File** menu—**Open As** is similar to the previous command. The difference between them is that while loading the waveform you can convert the audio data of the selected file into another format (define a new sampling frequency, a new number of bits and another number of channels). After selecting one or more files in the **Open As** window, a window appears similar to the one shown in Fig. 8.5, but this one is called **Open File(s) As**, not **New Waveform**. Using this window, you can define a new format for the loaded waveform (or waveforms).

The **Open Append** command is used to open files just like the **Open** command. But loading one or more files with the **Open Append** command places waveforms on one track (one pair of tracks) one after another. In other words, this command is used to combine several source waveforms stored in different files into one waveform.

The contents of two pages of the main window after loading the CHORD.WAV and DING.WAV files using the two **Open** commands are shown in Figs. 9.2 and 9.3. Fig. 9.4 illustrates opening the DING.WAV file with the **Open Append** command (the CHORD.WAV file was loaded before).

The **Revert to Saved** command may be useful if you decide to reject at once all the changes you made after the audio data was last saved on the disk, or after you last executed the loading command. In other words, the **Revert to Saved** command loads the file with the filename currently displayed in the main window header. When performing this action, the program asks permission to save the current waveform in the file.

The **Close** command closes the currently edited file. More precisely, it frees the memory used by the waveform being edited. The program then returns to the initial state.

The **Close All Waves and Session** command closes all files of all sessions.

The **Close Only Non-Session Waveforms** command closes any open audio files not used in the current session (files not inserted in the multitrack environment).

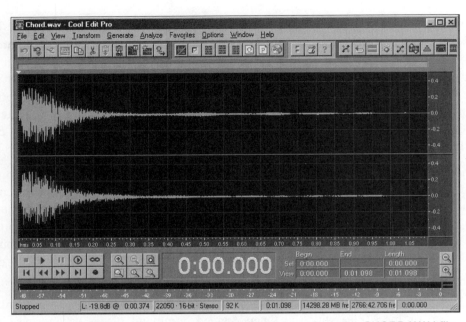

Fig. 9.2. The main window page with the waveform from the CHORD.WAV file

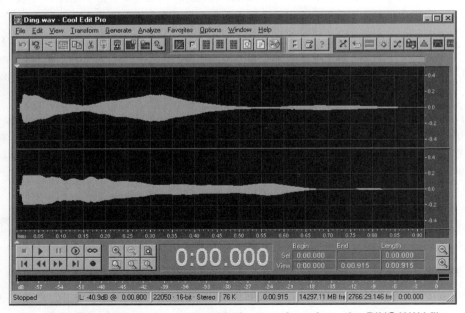

Fig. 9.3. The main window page with the waveform from the DING.WAV file

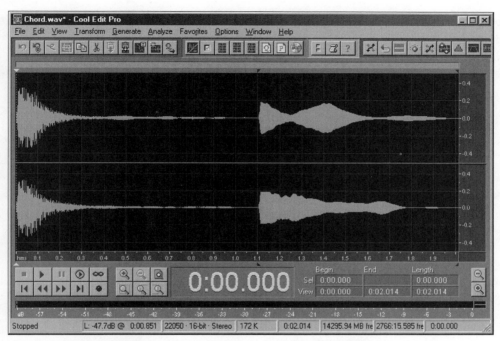

Fig. 9.4. Waveforms combined using the **Open Append...** command

9.3. Saving Files

The **Save** command saves the edited file on the disk with the same name that it was loaded from the disk with. If the file was created using the **New** command instead of the **Save** command, the **Save As** command is executed.

The **Save As** command saves the file with a user defined name. After calling this command, the **Save Waveform As** dialog window appears (Fig. 9.5), which contains the standard controls, but also has two specific features.

The first feature is the **Options** button. When you press this button, a window appears that looks different for different audio file formats. For some formats, the **Options** button is unavailable. The options of the additional window may also differ: for example, those options used to select the compression method for audio data may very. For the text format described above, you can enable or disable normalized representation mode in the options window.

The second feature is the **Save extra non-audio information** checkbox. If it is checked, besides the format specification and the waveform itself, other information—such as the waveform name, copyright, etc.—is written into the audio file. Additional information supplied with audio data is discussed in *Section 11.5*, in the description of the **View>Info** command.

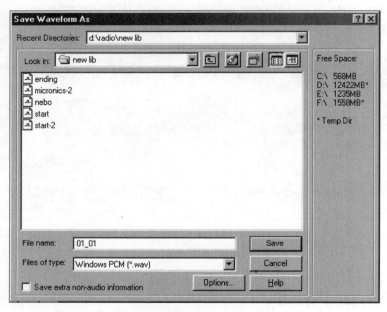

Fig. 9.5. The **Save Waveform As** dialog window

The next command of the **File** menu—**Save Selection**—is similar to the **Save As** command. The difference is that only the selected waveform fragment is saved in the file.

The **Save All** command, intended for file saving, is available in the Waveform View mode only if you have applied the **Open Append** command before. It allows you to save all combined waveforms in one file. Be careful when using this command. The program does not ask for the filename of the file that will contain the combined waveform. The file with the combined waveform is saved under the name of the file that was loaded first (and to which you appended other files). You may lose the source file. You can certainly try to restore the lost file, but to do it you'll have to cut all the appended waveforms.

9.4. *Flush Virtual File*—Releasing the Opened File for Use by Another Application

Working with Windows applications, you have certainly come across a situation where you had to perform a certain action with a file currently opened in another application. However, Windows does not always allow you to do so. For example, you cannot put a file with a document opened in Microsoft Word in another directory using Windows Commander.

The **Flush Virtual File** command releases a file opened in Cool Edit Pro so that it can be used by another Windows application.

9.5. *Free Hard Drive Space*

The **Free Hard Drive Space** command opens the **Free some Hard Drive space** dialog window (Fig. 9.6) intended for flushing and reserving disk space.

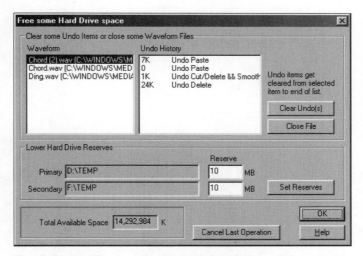

Fig. 9.6. The **Free some Hard Drive Space** dialog window

The **Clear some Undo Items or close some Waveform Files** group contains the following lists:

❐ **Waveform**—the list of opened audio files. Select a file you are not using at the moment and press the **Close File** button.

❐ **Undo History**—the Undo function's history. Select an action you do not need to return to and press the **Clear Undo(s)** button.

In the **Lower Hard Drive Reserves** group you can set the minimum amount of free disk space on the first (**Primary**) and the second (**Secondary**) audio disks. These parameters are input in the corresponding **Reserve** fields in megabytes. By pressing the **Set Reserves** button, you tell the program that new parameters are set for the reserved memory.

In the **Total Available Space** field, the total amount of free disk memory space is displayed.

While the Cool Edit Pro editor is operating, the free disk space decreases. The program thus automatically opens the **Free some Hard Drive space** dialog window so that you can use the **Cancel Last Operation** button to cancel the last action (because there is not enough disk space to complete it). You then have to free some disk space either using this dialog window or using the operating system to continue working with Cool Edit Pro.

We have discussed the **File** menu commands. The next menu is **Edit**, which you will likely use very often in your work.

Chapter 10: The *Edit* Menu

The **Edit** menu contains the following commands and submenus:

- ❏ **Undo (Can't Undo)**—undoes the last editing action
- ❏ **Enable Undo**—enables Undo mode
- ❏ **Repeat Last Command**—repeats last command
- ❏ **Set Current Clipboard**—selects the clipboard
- ❏ **Copy**—copies the selected data to the clipboard
- ❏ **Cut**—cuts the selected data
- ❏ **Paste**—pastes the selected data from the clipboard
- ❏ **Paste to New**—creates a new file and paste the data to it from the clipboard
- ❏ **Mix Paste...**—mixes audio data from the clipboard and audio data on the track
- ❏ **Copy to New**—creates a new file and pastes the selected data to it
- ❏ **Insert in Multitrack**—inserts audio data into the multitrack environment
- ❏ **Insert Play List Multitrack**—inserts files from the **Play List** into the multitrack environment
- ❏ **Select Entire Wave**—selects all audio data
- ❏ **Delete Selection**—deletes the selected fragment
- ❏ **Delete Silence**—deletes silent fragments
- ❏ **Trim**—deletes all data besides the selected fragment
- ❏ **Zero Crossings**—moves the beginning and the end of the selected fragment to the nearest points where the sound wave crosses the zero level (submenu)
- ❏ **Find Beats**—selects the fragment corresponding to the signal level changes (submenu)
- ❏ **Auto-Cue**—defines boundaries of spoken or musical phrases or beats (submenu)
- ❏ **Snapping**—selects options for attaching the boundaries of the selected waveform fragment to the time ruler (submenu)
- ❏ **Adjust Sample Rate...**—changes the sampling frequency
- ❏ **Convert Sample Type...**—converts the sample type
- ❏ **Edit Tempo...**—edits the tempo

Now let's start discussing the abilities the **Edit** menu provides to the user.

10.1. *Undo* and *Redo* Actions

The first command of the **Edit** menu is **Undo**. This command cancels the action performed last. If you keep using this command, you undo each previous editing step until you can't undo any more. If the action cannot be cancelled, you'll see the dimmed **Can't Undo** message instead of **Undo**.

The **Enable Undo** command allows you to enable (or disable) the undo mode. To do this, check (uncheck) the corresponding menu item.

To provide the ability to use the **Undo** command, the results of each step are automatically saved in special temporary files that can hold a lot of memory. If your hard disk does not have enough free space, it might make sense to disable the undo mode, and then these temporary files won't be created. But then you'd obviously have to be more attentive at each step, since you won't be able to cancel an incorrect action. We have already discussed how to limit the maximum number of undo steps (*Section 7.3*).

The **Repeat Last Command** (<F2>) allows you to repeat the last command performed. You have to watch carefully, because the command that Cool Edit Pro has performed is repeated regardless of which waveform you were editing at that time—the current one or another one. If the command opens a dialog box that contains changeable options and parameters, their settings will be the same as they were the last time that you executed the command.

We should mention that not all commands can be repeated. If the last command can be repeated, the **Repeat Last Command** (<F2>) line in the **Edit** menu is available.

10.2. *Set Current Clipboard*

If you select the **Set Current Clipboard** from the **Edit** menu, a submenu is opened (Fig. 10.1).

In this submenu, you can select the current clipboard. The program has 5 internal clipboards and 1 external (system). The clipboard selected in this submenu will be the one used for editing.

The external (system) clipboard allows you to exchange data with other Windows applications.

The advantage of using the internal clipboard is that if you turn off your computer and some time later you continue working with Cool Edit Pro, you'll find that the information put into the internal clipboard has been preserved. You see, the internal clipboard is a file.

When you create a composition of several waveforms in which some of them are used several times, multiple clipboards could be useful. You can copy each waveform into a separate clipboard to paste them when necessary. You'll need to remember which waveform is in which clipboard, and to change the current clipboard on time.

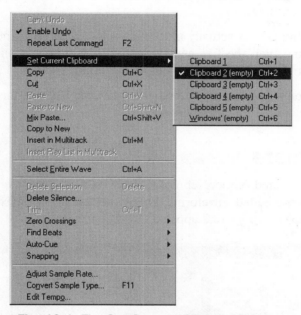

Fig. 10.1. The **Set Current Clipboard** submenu

10.3. *Copy, Cut, Paste*

The following editing commands also use the clipboard:

❒ **Copy** (<Ctrl>+<C>)

❒ **Cut** (<Ctrl>+<X>)

❒ **Paste** (<Ctrl>+<V>)

❒ **Paste to New**—creates a new file and paste clipboard data into it

❒ **Copy to New**—creates a new file and paste the selected data into it

To copy or cut a waveform fragment, you have to select it first. We have discussed how to do this both graphically and numerically in *Section 8.3.*

When using the **Copy** and **Cut** commands, the data are placed in the current clipboard.

The **Paste** and **Paste to New** commands also allow you to paste the data from the current clipboard.

If you execute the **Paste** command, the data are pasted into the waveform on the current page. The pasted fragment starts from the marker position, or from the beginning of the selected waveform fragment.

The **Paste to New** command is actually more than one action: first, the new page is created automatically, and then the fragment is pasted to it from the clipboard. The fragment then becomes a new waveform. You can save it in a file and give it a name.

The **Copy to New** command is also a number of actions. The fragment selected in the current waveform is copied into a newly created file.

10.4. *Mix Paste*

The **Mix Paste...** command is more complex. It is used to paste the audio data stored in the clipboard into the edited waveform. When you execute the **Mix Paste** command, the dialog window shown in Fig. 10.2 appears.

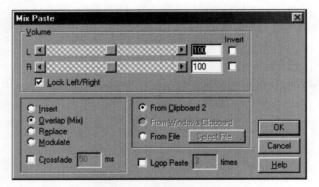

Fig. 10.2. The **Mix Paste** dialog window

In the **Volume** group, there are elements to control the pasted fragment volume for the left (**L**) and right (**R**) channels. The volume level is set in percents (100% by default) either using the sliders or digitally. If you check the **Lock Left/Right** checkbox, the volume of both stereo channels can be changed simultaneously. A checked **Invert** checkbox allows you to invert the waveform before pasting. The term "inversion" has many meanings; in this case, it means multiplying each count by -1.

You can select the paste method in the lower left part of the window.

❑ **Insert**—inserting when the edited waveform is "expanded" to include the contents of the clipboard.

❑ **Overlap (Mix)**—mixed inserting. The contents of the clipboard is "mixed" with the edited waveform.

❑ **Replace**—inserting and overwriting. The contents of the clipboard writes over the audio data in the given waveform area.

❑ **Modulate**—inserting with amplitude modulation. Each sample of the original sound signal is multiplied by the corresponding sample from the clipboard.

The **Crossfade** checkbox is used to set the smoothing mode. When you select an audio data block, the values of the signal counts at the ends of this block are not necessarily zero, which can later cause clicks to be heard when playing back the audio data pasted from the clipboard. You have to eliminate these clicks, and the crossfade mode is intended just for this purpose.

If we examine this mode in detail, we'll find that the program not only pastes the audio block into the waveform, it does so "rationally", by controlling the volume. This means that at the beginning of the block, the volume level grows smoothly from 0 to 100%, and some time before the block's end, the volume level smoothly goes down to 0%. The time of volume change is defined to the right of the checkbox. It is very small (about ten milliseconds), and the crossfade is not heard. Not only the described software, but also professional studio equipment include this ability. Otherwise, we would always hear clicks in audio recordings, and in TV and radio programs.

You define the time interval in which the volume changes from 0 to 100% (or vice versa) in the **Crossfade** field.

Another group of switches allows you to select the source of the pasted block.

❑ **From Clipboard** N—the internal clipboard. The **N** character is replaced by the reference in the text to the current clipboard. The program helps you to not confuse the fragment you are pasting.

❑ **From Windows Clipboard**—the system clipboard.

❑ **From File**—a file.

If you want to paste the data from a file (and you have chosen the appropriate radio button), then you have to select the file you need by pressing the **Select File** button (the file load window opens). If you do not do this, loading is done from the clipboard, regardless of whether the **From File** radio button is set.

The **Loop Paste** option allows you to paste the waveform contained in the clipboard several times. (You define the number of times in the field to the right of the checkbox).

When you have defined all the parameters, press **OK** or <Enter>.

Now you can see that the **Mix Paste** command and the corresponding dialog window represent a powerful tool for creating audio compositions. This tool was of great importance before Cool Edit Pro became a multitrack editor.

10.5. *Insert in Multitrack*—Inserting Audio Data into a Multitrack Session

We are now describing how the Cool Edit Pro editor works in the Waveform View mode. In fact, however, the program combines two editors: one is a waveform editor, which we are now learning to operate, and the second is the multitrack editor (the Multitrack View mode). The main task—assembling a composition containing separate waveforms—is performed in the multitrack editor. We describe this in detail in *Chapter 18*. To assemble waveforms in a multitrack environment, we first have to insert them. For this purpose, the **Insert in Multitrack** command is used.

Getting a little ahead of ourselves, we can say that there are truly many tracks, placed one behind the other, in the multitrack editor window. It also has its own marker. If you are working in the Waveform View mode and select the **Insert in Multitrack** command in the **Edit** menu, the waveform on the active page will be inserted in the track of the multitrack editor, and the beginning of the inserted waveform will be the same as the marker position.

If you use the **Insert in Multitrack** command for the first time, the waveform is inserted into the first track, the second waveform is inserted into the second track, and so on. However, you can change this insertion order: for example, you can insert several waveforms into the same track. You can also skip some tracks. We describe this in detail in *Chapter 18*.

10.6. *Insert Play List Multitrack*—Inserting Files Listed in the *Play List* into a Multitrack Session

The **Insert Play List Multitrack** command allows you to insert waveforms from files listed in the **Play List** into a multitrack session. This command is one of the tools that allow for automated processing of a great number of files. Instead of inserting files into a multitrack environment one by one, you just have to make a list of these files and apply the **Insert Play List Multitrack** command.

Working with the **Play List** is described in detail in *Section 11.8*.

10.7. Selecting and Deleting

The **Select Entire Wave** (<Ctrl>+<A>) command allows you to select the entire waveform. Waveforms loaded into the program but not placed on active pages are not selected. If you insert a selected waveform into a multitrack environment, it remains selected.

The **Delete Selection** (<Del>) command is used to delete the selected audio block.

The **Trim** (<Ctrl>+<T>) command, on the other hand, deletes all the audio data from the current waveform except for the selected fragment. The remaining fragment remains selected.

10.8. *Delete Silence*—Deleting Fragments with Silence

The **Delete Silence** command is intended to delete sound samples from those parts of the waveform that do not contain useful audio data, such as pauses between words and phrases. If the recording was made from a microphone, it contains noises or undesirable sounds recorded between words and phrases. You can select those parts of the waveform manually, but we will now describe a tool that allows you to automate this process.

The **Delete Silence** command opens the dialog window with the same name (see Fig. 10.3). We'll now describe the options of this window.

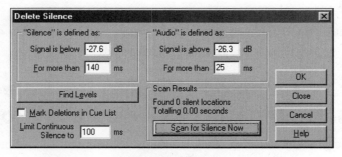

Fig. 10.3. The **Delete Silence** dialog window

In the **"Silence" is defined as:** group, you should define the conditions under which the program classifies the waveform fragment as one that contains only silence.

In the **Signal is below** field, define the maximum signal level value (in decibels) for silence.

In the **For more than** field, input the minimum value of the time interval (in milliseconds) during which the signal cannot exceed the level at which the program considers this signal to be "silence".

In the **"Audio" is defined as:** field, you should define the conditions under which the program classifies the waveform fragment as one that contains useful sound.

In the **Signal is above** field, define the minimum signal level value (in decibels) that corresponds to useful "sound".

In the **For more than** field, input the minimum time interval value (in milliseconds) for which the signal level cannot stay below the indicated level at which the program considers this signal "sound".

If you press the **Find Levels** button, the program automatically defines the criteria for silence and sound for the selected waveform fragment.

If the **Mark Deletions in Cue List** checkbox is checked, all parts of the waveform with deleted silence will be marked.

In the **Limit Continuous Silence to** field, you define the minimum duration of the non-deleted fragment of silence. If the silent area found is shorter than the value in this field, it will not be deleted. If the silent area found is longer than the value in this field, after deleting, only a fragment equal to the value of the **Limit Continuous Silence to** field remains.

The **Scan Results** group contains only one button: **Scan for Silence Now**. By pressing it, you turn on the mode that preliminarily finds fragments containing silence. As a result, the program informs you of the number of silent areas found; however, these silent areas are not deleted. This information is displayed in the field behind the **Scan for Silence Now** button. To delete the silent areas, press **OK**.

You must be aware that, as a result of using this command, the duration of the waveform changes.

10.9. *Zero Crossings*—Moving the Selected Fragment Boundaries to Zero Level Points

The **Zero Crossings** submenu (Fig. 10.4) contains a command that allows you to move the beginning and end of the selected audio block to the positions where the sound wave crosses the zero level. This is 0 for the 16-bit format, and 127 for the 8-bit format. This function, as well as the Crossfade function, haves the same goal: to avoid clicks in the beginning and in the end of the inserted fragment.

Fig. 10.4. The **Zero Crossings** submenu

When you use the **Adjust Selection Inward** (<F4>) command, it means that the boundaries of the selected fragment will be automatically moved to the nearest zero points within the selected interval. In Fig. 10.5, you see an example of an incorrectly selected waveform fragment. You can see that the fragment's boundaries are at points where the samples have non-zero values. If you cut such a fragment and glue it together with another waveform, you will hear clicks.

In Fig. 10.6, you see the same waveform after the **Adjust Selection Inward** (<F4>) command was applied to it. Compare the figures and you'll see that the boundaries of the selected fragment have moved to the nearest zero points and become closer to each other.

If you execute the **Adjust Selection Outward** command, the boundaries of the selected fragment will be automatically moved to zero points outside the selected interval.

The **Adjust Left Side to Left** command moves the left boundary of the selected fragment to the nearest zero point on the left.

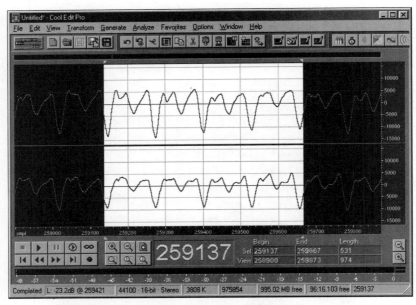

Fig. 10.5. An example of a selected waveform fragment

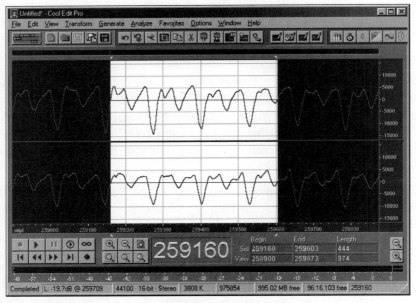

Fig. 10.6. An example of a selected waveform fragment with boundaries moved into the selected interval

The **Adjust Left Side to Right** command moves the left boundary of the selected fragment to the nearest zero point on the right.

The **Adjust Right Side to Left** command moves the right boundary of the selected fragment to the nearest zero point on the left.

The **Adjust Right Side to Right** command moves the right boundary of the selected fragment to the nearest zero point on the right.

If you practise moving the boundaries of the selected fragment several times, it may seem to you that they are not always moved exactly to the nearest zero points: it might seem like Cool Edit Pro is jumping over them. The reason is that if you have selected a fragment of a stereo waveform, the program finds the points where the signals of the right and the left channels are zero at the same time. Sometimes you won't notice what may seem to you as insignificant differences in the waves of the right and the left channels, but they actually are important.

If you select a waveform fragment in only one of the channels, the selection boundary moves to the nearest zero point.

10.10. *Find Beats*—Selecting the Fragment Coinciding with Signal Level Changes

The **Find Beats** command opens the submenu shown in Fig. 10.7.

Using this submenu, you can select the waveform fragment whose boundaries coincide with signal level changes.

Sometimes the **Find Beats** command is called the bar detection function. When working with musical material, this may truly be the case. In music (especially modern music) drum beats are usually on the boundaries of bars, and the program identifies these drum bars as strong changes in the signal level.

Here's an example. Assume you have the waveform shown in Fig. 10.8.

In Fig. 10.8, the marker is on the left boundary of the waveform. To select the fragment, you have to define the positions of its left and right boundaries. We thus apply the **Find Next Beat (Left)** command. Scanning is done from the beginning and towards the end of the waveform. As a result, the marker moves to the nearest level change to the right (Fig. 10.9). This marker position shows the future left boundary of the selected fragment.

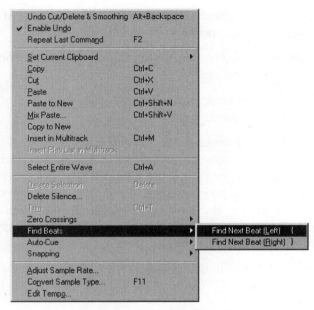

Fig. 10.7. The **Find Beats** submenu

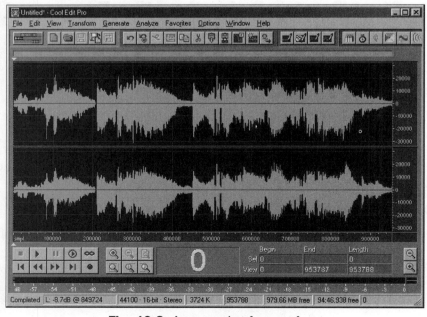

Fig. 10.8. An example of a waveform

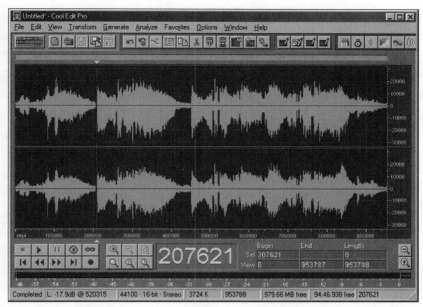

Fig. 10.9. The result of applying the **Find Next Beat (Left)** command

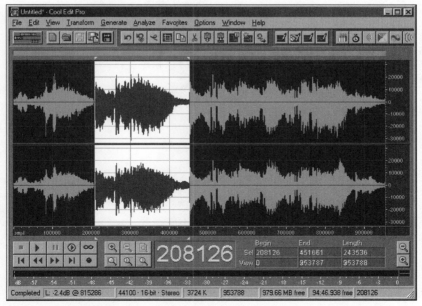

Fig. 10.10. The result of applying the **Find Next Beat (Right)** command

Now we apply the **Find Next Beat (Right)** command. The program finds the right signal level change nearest to the marker. This point will be the right boundary of the selected fragment. After analysis, you'll see a waveform with the selected fragment (Fig. 10.10).

You can see that the boundaries of the selected fragment correspond to the signal level changes. It's very likely that we have found the bar boundaries (or bar beat boundaries).

The function we discuss is very useful. It allows us to find specific parts of the recording faster. In any case, you can at least find the approximate boundaries. You can perform any necessary adjustments by ear or visually (having set a scale along the time axis that allows you to watch the waveform in detail).

The criteria that determine the signal level change are assigned with the **Beat Settings** options of the **General** tab in the **Settings** dialog box (*Section 7.2*).

10.11. *Auto-Cue*—Defining Spoken or Musical Phrases or Beats

The **Auto-Cue** command opens the submenu shown in Fig. 10.11.

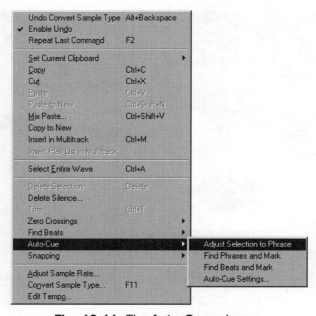

Fig. 10.11. The **Auto-Cue** submenu

The commands of this submenu allow you to determine the boundaries of spoken or musical phrases or beats, as well as to set the criteria according to which the program will look for these boundaries.

The **Adjust Selection to Phrase** command starts the search algorithm within the selected area, and after it is completed the highlighting is corrected.

The boundaries of the selected fragment are moved to the boundaries of the found phrase. Silence is ignored. New elements are not added to the **Cue List**.

The **Find Phrases and Mark** command starts the search algorithm within the selected area of phrase boundaries. The boundaries found are marked on the screen and are given numbers. They are then added to the **Cue List**. This list also contains information on phrases' positions along the time axis.

The **Find Beats and Mark** command starts the search algorithm within the selected area of beat boundaries. The boundaries found are marked on the screen and are given numbers. They are then added to the **Cue List**. This list also contains information on the beats' positions along the time axis. See information on using the **Cue List** in *Section 11.7*.

The **Auto-Cue Settings** command opens a dialog box (Fig. 10.12), and using its options, you can set the search criteria for phrase and beat boundaries.

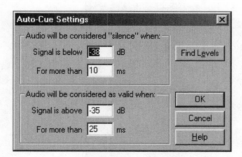

Fig. 10.12. The **Auto-Cue Settings** dialog box

In the **Audio will be considered "silence" when:** group, set the conditions under which the program considers the examined sample silence.

If the signal level is above the limit (set in decibels) in the **Signal is Below** field, and this low level continues longer than the time period specified in the **For more than** field (in milliseconds), the selected waveform fragment is considered silent.

For very quiet, high quality audio, the dB value will be lower (−60 dB). For noisier audio, it may be much higher (about −30 dB).

To keep groups of words together in a phrase, specify higher values for the time in the **For more than** field.

In the **Audio will be considered as valid when:** group, set the conditions under which the program considers that the examined sample contains audio.

If audio is above the threshold specified in the **Signal is above** field (in decibels) for more than the number of milliseconds given, this waveform fragment will be considered audio. Use higher time values to ignore short periods of audio (like clicks, static, or other noise). However, if this value is too high (above 200 milliseconds), short words may be skipped.

Pressing the **Find Levels** button allows you to activate the algorithm for automatically determining phrase borders for the selected waveform fragment.

10.12. *Snapping*—Options for Snapping the Selected Waveform Fragment Boundaries to Ruler Tickmarks

The **Snapping** command opens the submenu shown in Fig. 10.13.

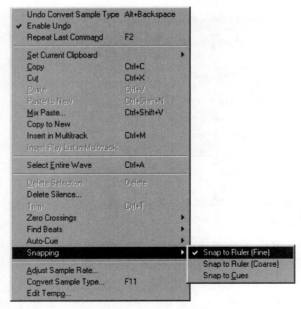

Fig. 10.13. The **Snapping** submenu

The commands of this submenu allow you to simplify manual attachment of the selected waveform boundaries to specific locations, to time ruler tickmarks, or to the phrase/beat boundaries.

Select the **Snap to Ruler (Fine)** command, and start selecting the waveform fragment. Click the mouse's left button and, keeping it pressed, slowly move the cursor to the left, for example. The selection area widens, but the movement of its right boundary does not always correspond to the mouse's movement. As soon as you move the selection boundary to a ruler tickmark, the boundary quickly crosses it. If you move the mouse further, the boundary leaves that division. This algorithm imitates the small "pull" of the selection area boundary towards the ruler tickmarks.

If you select the **Snap to Ruler (Coarse)** command, the process described above becomes more visible: the "pull" of the ruler tickmarks on the selected area's boundary is stronger.

When you select the **Snap to Cues** command, the selected area's boundary is not "pulled" to the ruler numeric divisions, but to the lines that show the boundaries of bars and beats after you have applied the **Auto-Cue** command.

If none of these commands is selected, the selection boundary movement exactly corresponds to the mouse cursor's horizontal movement.

10.13. *Adjust Sample Rate*—Changing the Sampling Frequency

The **Adjust Sample Rate** command allows you to change the sampling frequency. This command opens the **Adjust Sample Rate** window (similar to the **New Waveform** window shown in Fig. 8.5) in which you can specify a new sampling frequency. For example, if the waveform was initially recorded with a sampling frequency of 44,100 Hz, and you change its value to 22,050 Hz, the tone will be one octave lower, and the waveform duration will duplicate during playback, i.e., the waveform is now played at a half of the initial playback speed.

This command does not perform any sample conversions. It simply changes the information on the sampling frequency that is stored in audio files.

You can select sampling frequency values only from those supported by your sound card.

Options that set the number of bits and the format (mono/stereo) of audio data representation are present in the **Adjust Sample Rate** window, but are accessible only for PCM files.

10.14. *Convert Sample Type*

After you select the **Convert Sample Type** command, the dialog window shown in Fig 10.14 appears.

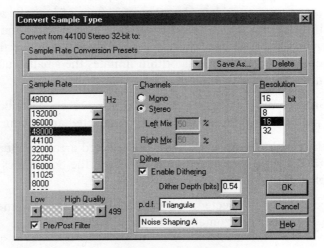

Fig. 10.14. The **Convert Sample Type** dialog window

Unlike the previous command, this command effects neither the waveform playback speed nor its pitch. The only parameter that can change (though it does't always) is the recording quality, which may become worse.

In the **Sample Rate** group, you can specify the new sampling frequency for audio data.

If the new frequency value is greater than the frequency used for recording, it does not effect the quality of the waveform sound. The quality is determined by the frequency of the initial sampling. There is no additional information in the waveform on the sound wave's behavior.

If you specify a new frequency value less than the previous one, the frequency range of the sound signal becomes narrower (high frequencies disappear).

When the sampling frequency changes, the sample values are recalculated in some manner. You can set the precision of these calculations using the lever below the frequencies list (precision can be **Low** or **High**). The greater the precision, the more time it takes to convert the waveform.

The status of the **Pre/Post Filter** checkbox determines whether to perform special sound filtering before decreasing the sampling frequency (**Pre**), or after increasing it (**Post**). This filtering allows you to avoid side effects when changing the sampling frequency. The checkbox is available if you select a new sampling frequency value (different from the sampling frequency at which the waveform was recorded).

In the **Channels** group, you can select the number of channels. If the converted waveform is in stereo format, and you need mono, the program mixes the signals of the left and right channels. The proportions of this mixture are defined in the **Left Mix** and **Right Mix** fields. By default, mixing is done "fifty-fifty".

If you want to leave only one channel (for example, the right one), set the following values: **Left Mix** 0%, **Right Mix** 100%.

Be careful when setting the proportions (volume levels) in which channels are to be mixed. A newly created mono waveform can be much louder than its stereo "parent", which results in non-linear distortions. This situation can be caused by such settings as **Left Mix** 100%, **Right Mix** 100%. The amplitude may overcome the upper boundary of the dynamic range of the sound card.

In the **Resolution** group, select the resolution: 8 bits, 16 bits, or 32 bits. When changing from a higher resolution to a lower resolution (for example, from a 16-bit format to an 8-bit format), the **Dither** group becomes available (an additional pseudo-random signal for reducing unwanted effects of the process).

When the digital sound resolution is low (meaning the 8-bit format) and the signal level is low (the sound measurements change to some quantum from the level 127), an unpleasant crunching effect appears. This happens because the signal level is close to the quantization noise level, which you cannot remove, neither in theory nor in practice. However, certain features of the human ear allow you to hide this effect. Before changing from a 16-bit representation to an 8-bit representation, you should add a low-level random noise to the signal. Then, a lower order byte is removed from each sample of the 16-bit signal (this is exactly what it means to switch from a 16-bit representation to an 8-bit representation). Because of the added noise, the crunching effect disappears, and the noise itself is not as annoying to the listener. He or she gets used to the permanent, even noise, and stops paying attention to it.

Mixing a noise signal while lowering the number of sound representation bits is called *dithering*.

The level of random noise (or its intensity) is defined in the **Dither Depth (bits)** field. Here we are only talking about bits of a future, 8-bit digital audio signal. The exact value of the noise level is selected by listening to the specific waveform: you select a value, and if you don't like the sound, just undo the action, etc. According to our own experience, the optimal noise level is found within a range of 0.01 to 0.5. This noise is low, and it won't annoy the listener.

Below the **Dither Depth (bits)** field, you'll see the **p.d.f.** (Probability Distribution Function) drop-down list, from which you can select several noise models. Which of them fits best is up to you. The only criterion is your estimation of the sound quality of the waveform you get after conversion.

The developer recommends that you apply the **Triangular** probability distribution function to reach a compromise between two objective statistics: the worsening of the signal/noise ratio (SNR Loss) by 4.8 dB, and noise modulation.

Another method of noise reduction, called *noise-shaping,* means applying special algorithms rounding-off samples when lowering the number of bits. After applying this method, most of the energy of the quantized noise is concentrated in high-frequency areas, which are the areas least perceptible to the human ear. Usually, noise-shaping is applied together with dithering.

In the lower part of the window, in the **Dither** group, there is another untitled drop-down list. From this list, you can select the noise-shaping type that corresponds to one of the variants of noise spectrum distribution within the sound frequencies band. Having selected a good one, you can hide the quantization noise and the noise added when dithering is applied. The developer recommends that you select the following variants:

❒ **Noise Shaping A** and **B** for sampling frequencies not over 32 kHz

❒ **Noise Shaping C1**, **C2**, and **C3** for sampling frequencies no less than 44.1 kHz

❒ **Noise Shaping D** for a sampling frequency of 48 kHz

The number of options for creating the noise spectrum is increased in every new version of the program, so use **Help** to find out more. But, more important than this is that you experiment. You can save all the settings made in the **Convert Sample Type** window in a file. In the **Sample Rate Conversion Presets** group, there is a list of presets (in Fig. 10.14, it is empty). To the right of the list, you'll see the **Save As** button that allows you to save all the settings with a given name, which is then added to the presets list. The **Delete** button allows you to delete elements from this list.

The abilities of the described window may be useful if you have several waveforms with different sampling frequencies and different numbers of bits, and you have to combine them into one waveform. You'd then have to adjust their formats, sometimes by decreasing the sound quality, since you cannot work with waveforms of different formats at the same time.

10.15. *Edit Tempo*

The **Edit Tempo...** command opens the window with the same name (Fig. 10.15) that is intended for calculating and editing the tempo of the musical composition within the waveform. The unit of measure is *Beats per Minute, BPM*. The tempo is measured by the signal level pulsation frequency in the selected fragment of the waveform. The tempo measurement results are used, for example, to show the waveform in the **Bars and Beats** time representation format (*Section 11.4*); bars and beats are placed along the time ruler.

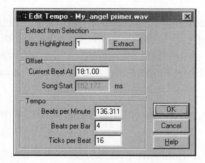

Fig. 10.15. The **Edit Tempo** dialog window

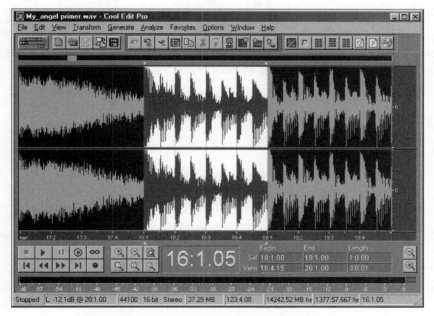

Fig. 10.16. A waveform with one bar selected

In the **Bars Highlighted** field of the **Extract from Selection** group, specify the number of bars per selected fragment. By default, the program allows you to analyze the tempo, assuming the selected waveform fragment corresponds to one bar. Judging from just listening to the composition, we have selected exactly one bar (Fig. 10.16).

In the **Beats per Bar** field of the **Tempo** group, you should input the number of beats in a bar (4 by default), and the number of ticks in a bar set in the **Ticks per Beat** field. You then press the **Extract** button, and the program automatically measures the duration of the selected fragment and performs all the necessary calculations.

In the **Beats per Minute** field of the **Tempo** group, the calculated tempo value appears. The **Current Beat At** field of the **Offset** group contains the distance from the waveform's beginning to the marker, or to the left boundary of the selected fragment in the following format: Bar:Beat:Tick. The **Song Start** field contains the same distance, but measured in milliseconds.

By pressing the **OK** button, you correct the time ruler of the main window according to the calculated tempo.

You can see that some input fields in that window are available for changing the indicated parameters. All calculations are made assuming that the interval that corresponds to the number of bars given in the **Bars Highlighted** field is selected. However, not every composition has its drums accented as shown in Fig. 10.16. That's why mistakes are possible in selecting the bar visually and by ear, which may cause calculation errors and lead to unexpected results (say, the calculated tempo could be thousands of beats per minute). Manual calculation correction is used in such cases.

Chapter 11: The *View* Menu—Display Management

The **View** menu includes commands and submenus that allow you to control the display of the program interface elements:

❑ **Multitrack View**—enables the multitrack view mode

❑ **Waveform View**—enables the stereo tracks pair (mono track) view mode

❑ **Spectral View**—enables spectrum view mode for an instantaneous signal

❑ **Show Grid**—shows a grid

❑ **Show Boundaries**—shows the maximum allowed waveform amplitude

❑ **Show Cue Bars**—shows the lines indicating phrases or bars

❑ **Show Status Bar**—shows the status bar

❑ **Show Level Meters**—shows the signal level meter

❑ **Show CD Player**—shows the CD player control panel

❑ **Viewing Range...**—opens the window for selecting the time boundaries of the displayed waveform fragment

❑ **Display Time Format**—submenu for selecting the time display format

❑ **Vertical Scale Format**—submenu for selecting the vertical scale format

❑ **Info...**—opens the window with the information on the audio data being edited

❑ **Sampler Info...**—opens the window for audio preparation for the sampler

❑ **Cue List**—opens the **Cue List/Ranges** dialog window

❑ **Play List**—opens the **Play List** dialog window

❑ **Time Window**—shows the current time display window

11.1. *Spectral View*—Displaying the Instantaneous Signal Spectrum

The **Multitrack View**, **Waveform View**, and **Spectral View** commands switch between audio information display modes. The first mode is described in *Chapter 18*. You have already learned the second mode, since we've been working in it. In these modes, audio is represented as waveforms.

In the third mode, the signal's instantaneous spectrum (Fig. 11.1) is displayed as gradations of brightness and color. We covered the concept of *the instantaneous spectrum (periodogram)* and this form of its display in *Section 2.4*.

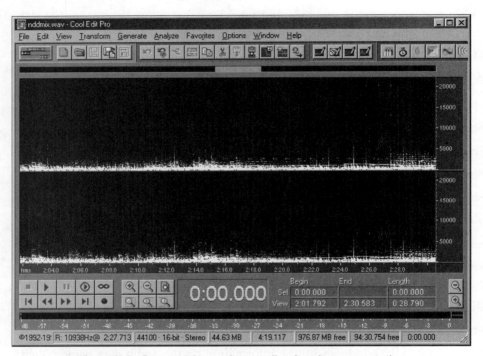

Fig. 11.1. Spectral form of an audio signal representation

What does the picture we see in the **Spectral View** mode tell us? How can we use the information we get from watching the instantaneous spectrum?

The X-axis represents time, and the Y-axis represents frequency. The color and brightness of the picture depend on the level of the spectral component in the analyzed waveform at a certain frequency (the brighter the picture, the higher the level).

Watching the spectral chart allows us to form an opinion on the frequency concentration area of the signal's energy at different points of the waveform. This information is useful when putting several tracks into a mix. It is desirable that the signal spectrums of these tracks don't overlap frequencies too much. You can avoid this by filtering. While signals are processed by filters, you can see and compare the resulting signal spectrum to the initial signal spectrum with spectral diagrams, and thus estimate whether processing is being done correctly.

It is very important that Cool Edit Pro in the **Spectral View** mode allows you not only to watch the signal spectrum, but also to edit the waveform. You can select and edit a fragment you do not like, or simply delete it.

As an example, in Fig. 11.2 we show the instantaneous spectrum for a small waveform fragment. To see all the details, the zoom was increased using the button 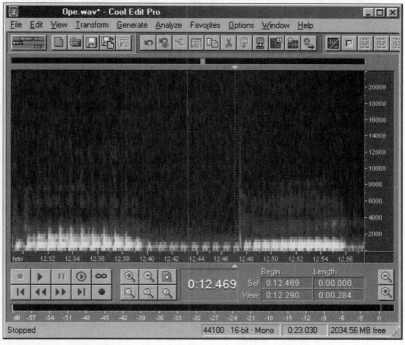 that you know well.

Fig. 11.2. An example of the instantaneous spectrum containing anomalies

This is the instantaneous spectrum of a signal representing a radio announcer's speech. Areas with a relatively wide spectrum correspond to words; areas with a narrow spectrum correspond to pauses between them. You can see that at the beginning of the second word (to the right of the marker) the instantaneous spectrum is wider than the average spectrum of the entire word. Here, you see an abnormal peak of the spectral function. A wide spectrum always corresponds to a quick change in the signal values, or to a short impulse. There's probably a click here. If we wanted, we could select the area with this peak in the middle, adjust this selected area to the signal zero levels, and press the <Delete> button. The click would be deleted. When you become experienced, you can do it like this. But for now, we will watch the peak. We select the **Waveform View** command from the **View** menu. In the main window, we see the image of the waveform (Fig. 11.3). The same waveform fragment is shown that we saw in Fig. 11.2, and notice that the marker position has not changed.

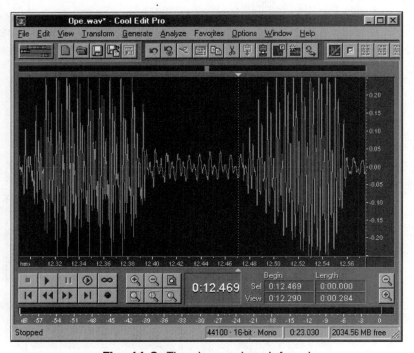

Fig. 11.3. The abnormal peak found

Here we've found our troublemaker: the small to the peak right of the marker. It's not so hard to find if you know what you're looking for, but what would be the result if we were searching within the entire sound wave? Even if we had enough time and were accurate, it very well might remain unnoticed.

Was it really so important to find this anomaly? To answer this question, we can just listen to the fragment. It sounds pretty bad: kind of like the sound made by two lips opening after pausing between words.

By looking at the spectral representation, we can find any abnormally fast changes of the signal level. Some of them can be caused by clicks, noises, anomalies in speech, etc. Sometimes jumps in the sample values appear in the recording as a result of the recording's inaccurate assembly. For example, it might be that fragments of different signals are assembled, and even just one of them has a constant offset or a super-low frequency component. It might also be that, while making cuts of fragments, the sound engineer wasn't paying attention to the fact that the cutting points should have corresponded to zero points of the sound wave.

11.2. Enabling Display of Basic Elements of the Main Window

The next six commands of the **View** menu are intended to enable the display of basic elements of the main window:

❏ **Show Grid**—grid; allows you to position sound samples or waveform fragments along the time ruler, and to estimate the signal level at certain points

❏ **Show Boundaries**—lines limiting the maximum allowed waveform amplitude (we describe in detail how to position this line in *Section 7.2*)

❏ **Show Cue Bars**—lines limiting phrase or bar boundaries (we describe in detail how to define phrase and bar boundaries in *Section 10.11*)

❏ **Show Status Bar**—status bar (see Fig. 8.7)

❏ **Show Level Meters**—signal level meter (see Fig. 8.4)

❏ **Show CD Player**—CD player control panel

The last command of the **View** menu—**Show CD Player**—shows the CD player control panel. If you check this command, all the usual elements of CD player controls appear in the lower part of the Cool Edit Pro main window (Fig. 11.4).

In the lower part of the CD player control panel, there are playback control buttons. From left to right, they are as follows:

▪—stop

▶—playback

◀◀—previous track

▶▶—next track

⟳—go to remembered position

⟳—remember position (during playback)

⏏—input/eject disk

To the right of the control buttons, there is an information field in which total playback time is shown.

In the upper part of the player, there are digits corresponding to tracks on a CD. For example, to turn to track 7, simply click 7. The number of the track being currently played is darkened.

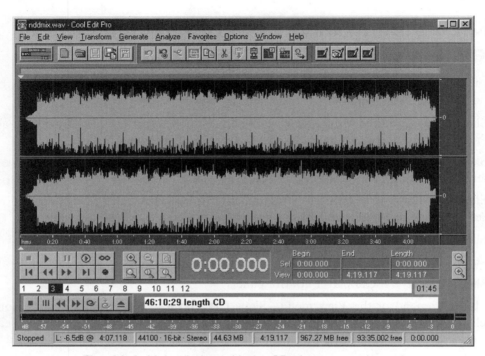

Fig. 11.4. Main window with the CD player control panel

In the right part of the player, there is a field in which the time that has passed since the current track's playback started is displayed.

You've probably already guessed why Cool Edit Pro has a built-in CD player. That's right—to make recording from CDs that much easier. You can use any other player program you like, but then you'll have to switch between applications.

11.3. *Viewing Range*—Calling the Window for Selecting Temporary Boundaries of the Displayed Waveform Fragment

The **Viewing Range** command calls a dialog window we already described in *Section 8.3* (see Fig. 8.10).

In this window, you can specify exactly the region of the signal displayed on the screen. Define the number of the first sample in the **From** field and the number of the final sample in the **To** field. Press **OK** or <Enter>.

We have to mention here that in some cases, Cool Edit Pro provides the user with several ways to implement certain operations. You can select a command in the main menu, use the corresponding tool of the toolbar in the main window, or use shortcut keys. Certain commands can be selected from context menus by right-clicking any interface element.

Some dialog windows (for example, the **Viewing Range** window) can be also accessed by double-clicking the corresponding element of the graphic interface.

11.4. *Display Time Format*—Selecting the Time Display Format

In the **Display Time Format** submenu (Fig. 11.5), you can select time display formats used when displaying waveforms.

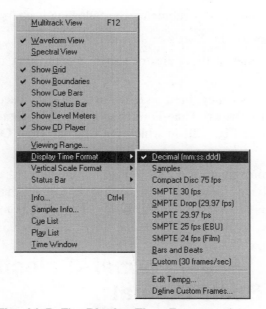

Fig. 11.5. The **Display Time Format** submenu

The following time display formats are available:

❏ **Decimal (mm:ss:ddd)**—usual format (minutes:seconds:milliseconds)

❏ **Compact Disc 75 fps**—in the CD Audio standard with a frequency of 75 frames per second

❏ **SMPTE 30 fps**—in the SMPTE standard (hours:minutes:seconds:frames) with a frequency of 30 frames per second

❏ **SMPTE Drop (29.97 fps)**—in the SMPTE standard with a frequency of 29.97 frames per second

❏ **SMPTE 25 fps (EBU)**—in the SMPTE standard with a frequency of 25 frames per second

❏ **SMPTE 24 fps (Film)**—in the SMPTE standard with a frequency of 24 frames per second

❏ **Samples**—using the numbers of digital sound samples (from the waveform's beginning)

❏ **Bars and Beats**—in bars and beats

❏ **Custom**—in the user-defined SMPTE format for which you can define custom frame frequency

When you select a new line in this submenu, the following is changed:

❏ Digital representation of the X-axis of the main window field

❏ The time display format in the indicator panel, and in input fields of the main window and dialog windows

To define the frame frequency in a user-defined format, select the **Define Custom Frames** command in the **Display Time Format** submenu. The **General** tab of the **Settings** dialog window opens (see Fig. 7.2), in which the **Custom Time Code Display** input field is prepared for editing.

Now let's say a few words about the **Edit Tempo** command of the **Display Time Format** submenu. We have already described this command and its dialog window while describing the **Edit** menu (*Section 10.15*, Fig. 10.15). The **Edit Tempo** command is placed in both menus to make it convenient for users.

11.5. *Vertical Scale Format*—Selecting the Vertical Scale Format

The next command of the **View** menu is **Vertical Scale Format** (vertical zoom of the waveform display). It calls a submenu that contains four commands:

❏ **Sample Values**—the vertical axis represents the digital values of sound samples

❏ **Normalized Values**—the vertical axis represents normalized values of sound samples (within a range from −1 to 1)

❑ **Percentage**—values along the vertical axis are measured as percentage

❑ **Hz**—values along the vertical axis are measured in Hz (in the spectral representation of the sound signal)

The last command is available only if the **Spectral View** (*Section 11.1*) mode is set in the main window.

11.6. *Info*—Saving and Displaying Information on the Edited Waveform

The **Info** command calls the **Wave Information** dialog window, which allows you to get and change information on the waveform being edited. The meaning of the information displayed in the fields of this window depends on the status of the **Standard RIFF** and **Radio Industry** radio buttons. In Fig. 11.6, the **Wave Information** window is shown for a case when the **Standard RIFF** radio button is selected.

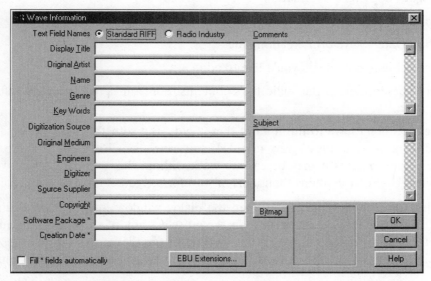

Fig. 11.6. The **Wave Information** dialog window (Standard RIFF radio button selected)

Now we describe the fields of this window and the information they contain.

❑ **Display Title**—for example, when audio is displayed as an OLE object. This field allows you to input the entire filename, even if there is a limitation on the filename length in the operating system.

❏ **Original Artist**—artist name.

❏ **Name**—waveform name.

❏ **Genre**—kind of music.

❏ **Key Words**—key words used, for example, to search for waveforms in the audio database.

❏ **Digitization Source**—sound source (CD, tape recorder, radio, vinyl record, microphone, etc.).

❏ **Original Medium**—sound type (noise of rain, flute, organ, etc.).

❏ **Engineers**—sound engineers (names of waveform editor(s)).

❏ **Digitizer**—name(s) of sound digitizer(s).

❏ **Source Supplier**—name(s) of person(s) or organization that provided the source sound data.

❏ **Copyright**—copyright information.

❏ **Software Package**—software used to digitize and edit the audio data.

❏ **Creation Date**—waveform creation date.

❏ **Comments**—any comments you'd like to add.

❏ **Subject**—description of the audio file's contents. Sometimes the copyright information is put here.

Of course, you don't have to fill in all of these fields. But sometimes the information you input and store in audio files is very useful. If you have a small number of audio files and remember their contents it may be easy to work without this info. But if you work with an audio database that contains thousands of waveforms, you cannot do without it.

By pressing the **Bitmap** button, you open the dialog window intended for loading BMP files that contain graphic images. As soon as you select any of these files, the image appears in the field near the button. By loading the image file you get an icon (size 32×32 and 16-bit color), which is then used to indicate the associated waveform in multimedia viewers.

If the **Fill* fields automatically** checkbox is selected, the fields marked with the "*" character (**Software Package** and **Creation Date**) are filled in by the program automatically when a new waveform is created.

If the **Radio Industry** radio button is checked in the **Wave Information** dialog window, it takes on a different appearance (Fig. 11.7).

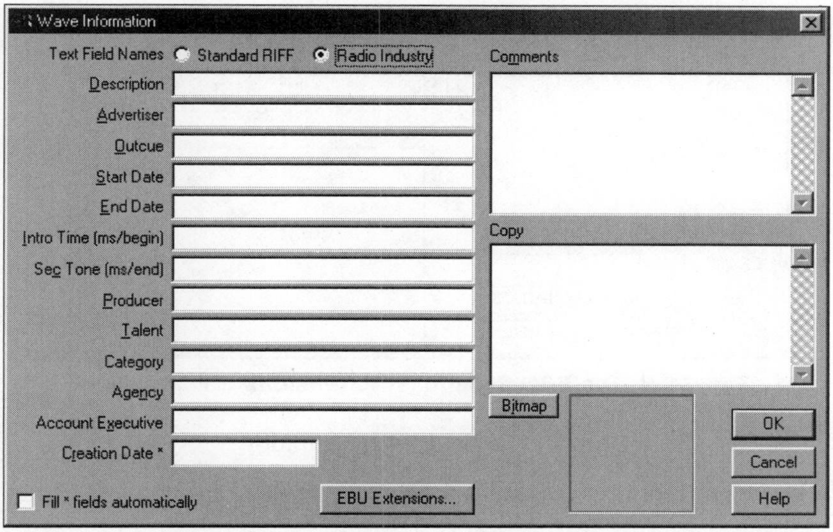

Fig. 11.7. The **Wave Information** dialog window (**Radio Industry** radio button shown)

This version of the **Wave Information** dialog window differs from the one shown in Fig. 11.6 in the contents of most of its fields:

❏ **Description**—description of the audio data

❏ **Advertiser**—information on the advertiser

❏ **Start Date (MM/DD/YY)**—date of the first broadcast

❏ **End Date (MM/DD/YY)**—date of the last broadcast

❏ **Intro Time (ms/begin)**—audio beginning time

❏ **Sec Tone (ms/end)**—audio ending time

❏ **Producer**—producer

❏ **Category**—category

❏ **Agency**—agency

You should supply this information with audio data if you are preparing it for a radio station.

Pressing the **EBU Extensions...** button opens the **EBU Broadcast Extensions** dialog window (Fig. 11.8), in which you should supply additional information on the audio file recommended by the EBU (European Broadcasting Union).

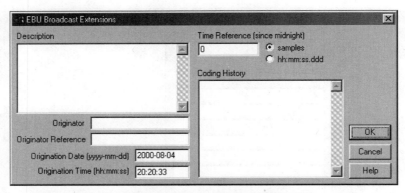

Fig. 11.8. The **EBU Broadcast Extensions** dialog window

Here we'll describe the meaning of the fields in this window:

❏ **Description**—description of the audio data

❏ **Originator**—audio data author (producer)

❏ **Originator Reference**—author of the audio data description

❏ **Origination Date**—audio creation date

❏ **Origination Time**—audio creation time

❏ **Time Reference (since midnight)**—audio description creation time

❏ **Coding History**—code of any changes you made to the existing audio. (You can find more on these codes by doing an Internet search for "European Broadcasting Union".)

11.7. *Sampler Info*—Audio Preparation for Sampler Processing

The **Sampler Info** command calls the dialog window shown in Fig. 11.9. Using the options of this window allows you to prepare the sample for processing in a sampler.

When preparing samples for processing in a sampler, you should use certain special tools of Cool Edit Pro. We must mention that in real life you won't use all the abilities provided in this dialog window, but some of them may be very useful.

We'll now describe the options of the **Sampler Information** dialog window.

The **Target Manufacture ID** and **Target Product Code** input fields are reserved for future versions of the program.

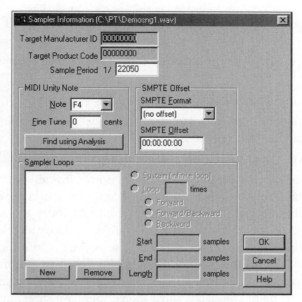

Fig. 11.9. The **Sampler Information** dialog window

Sample Period 1/ is the value inverse to the sampling frequency, i.e., the discretization step. By default, the value in the **Sample Period** field corresponds to the sampling frequency, but it can be changed to "deceive" the sampler. It will not get the real sampling frequency at which audio data was digitized, but rather a frequency you define.

In the **MIDI Unity Note** group, you can define to which note the sample sound corresponds (**Note**). Normally, this is not enough, and you have to adjust the sample sound using cent precision, just like you tune guitar strings. Adjustment is made in the **Fine Tune** field. However, the process of tuning the sampler is not so complicated. You simply press the **Find using Analysis** button, and the program figures out to which note the sample corresponds and finds its tuning parameter, in order to make the adjustment ideal.

In the **SMPTE Offset** group, you can select the **SMPTE format** and the offset according to this format (**SMPTE Offset**). The latter parameter can be used in some samplers, but we most likely won't need it. Using the elements of the **Sampler Loops** group may be useful. Here we mean "looping" samples. The sample playback starts from the beginning to the mark of the loop's end, and then playback repeats until the MIDI key is released. In other words, while the MIDI key is pressed, the sampler reproduces an infinite sound. The memory of the sampler is limited, so you cannot load samples of any length you want. The most reasonable decision is to playback in a loop. It is important to define the loop parameters so that the sound played in the loop doesn't sound like a scratched vinyl record.

After you release the MIDI key, playback of the sample can happen in three different ways:

❏ The sound stops immediately after the sample ends

❏ The sound is looped until the sampler processes the fade phase (the volume is smoothly lowered after you release the MIDI key)

❏ The sampler leaves the current loop and immediately turns to another loop

The third method of sample playback is not supported by all samplers. On the other hand, we did say that after you release the MIDI key, the sound moves to another loop, but that is not literally correct. In theory, there could be more than two of these loops. To make the sampler move to the third loop, would we have to release the key again? But wouldn't that mean that we'd have to press it sometime before that? The thing is that in different samplers, going through loops is implemented in different ways, but Cool Edit Pro provides you with universal abilities. For example, if the user needs to have two loops, there are two; if he or she needs three loops, there are three, and so on.

To prepare the sample for further processing in the sampler, we start by selecting the sample region we want to go through the loop during playback. It is important that the sound wave at the beginning of this region seems to be a natural continuation of the wave at the end of the loop.

Let's look at the process of sample preparation. Select the sample region intended for looped playback. Then call the **Sampler Information** dialog window and press the **Find using Analysis** button. In the **Note** input field appears an indication of the note that the sample sound is most similar to. In the **Fine Tune** input field, you'll find a value that allows you to get an exact correspondence between the sample's tune and the given note.

The next step (if you intend to loop the sample) is to press the **New** button in the **Sampler Loops** group. The first loop is created. Its **Start**, **End**, and **Length** parameters correspond to the waveform region you have selected in the main window. If you enable the **Sustain (infinite loop)** option, you are telling the program that the selected sample fragment is to be infinitely played in the loop (until playback of the entire sample stops for any reason). After you perform all the above actions, the **Sampler Information** dialog window will look similar to the one shown in Fig. 11.10.

For some samplers, you cannot define an infinite loop, but you can set playback of the selected waveform fragment for a number of times (**Loop** n **times**, where n is the number of times).

There are three methods of going through a loop.

❑ **Forward**—going through the loop from the beginning to the end, then immediately returning to the beginning, going through the loop again, and so on. This method is set by default.

❑ **Forward/Backward**—from the beginning to the end, then immediately changing direction and "reversing" playback (from the end to the beginning). As soon as the program reaches the beginning of the loop, the direction is altered again, and so on.

❑ **Backward**—loop "reverse" playback (always from the end to the beginning).

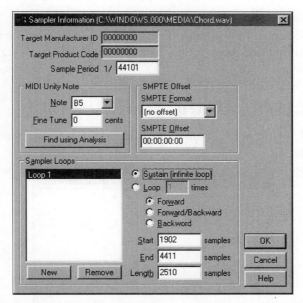

Fig. 11.10. An example of waveform preparation for loading into a sampler

You can select any of these playback methods using the corresponding radio buttons, but note that not all samplers support all of these methods.

For example, the EMU8000 chip, on which the WT AWE sound card synthesizer is based, reproduces waveforms using only the first method. It often becomes necessary to use the second method of going through the loop. This method (sometimes called "ping-pong") allows you to easily put a waveform into a loop without side effects. Even if the sampler does not support the **Forward/Backward** method of looping, you can simulate it manually in Cool Edit Pro. Select the area to be looped, copy it to the clipboard, and then paste the audio data block from the clipboard at the end of the original material. As a result, you get two identical fragments, one following the other. Now you have to reverse the second fragment using the **Transform>Reverse** command. The loop is now ready (both audio fragments are within the loop); just define its beginning and its end and select **Forward** playback. Now, even if you are using the EMU8000 synthesizer, the **Forward/Backward** playback method can be implemented. However, this approach requires memory enough to store the additional data.

Be patient and accurate while implementing the above actions. Making even one mistake in a sample when defining the waveform position leads to clicks. When you become more experienced, however, you will get much pleasure from creating your own waveforms and music.

To finish with the **Sample Information** dialog window, we must mention that you can create an arbitrary number of loops in this manner. You can always delete them using the **Remove** button.

11.8. *Cue List*—Editing the Cue List

The next command of the **View** menu—**Cue List**—calls a dialog window with the same name, shown in Fig. 11.11.

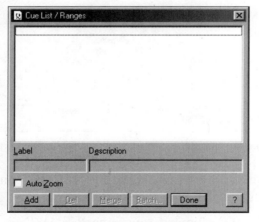

Fig. 11.11. The **Cue List** dialog window

Cue List is a list of time cues, or locations defined within an audio file or session. Examples of such cues are: the beginning and the end of the loop, the beginning and the end of the selected region, or just the cursor position. Using the cue list and double-clicking the desired position, you can quickly move to the corresponding position in the waveform. The maximum number of cues in the list is 96.

The cue list shown in Fig. 11.11 is empty. But if you create a loop, it is automatically put into the list. To save the marker position or the selected region in the list, press the **Add** button. In Fig. 11.12 we show four temporary cues.

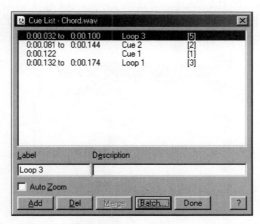

Fig. 11.12. An example of the cue list

As you see from the picture, cues are sorted by time. Each offset has its own number, assigned in brackets. By default, cues are defined by name: **Cue** or **Loop** (for a loop), and their consequent numbers. However, for each cue, you can define a name in the **Label** field. You can put any comments you like in the **Description** field.

Pressing the **Del** button allows you to delete the current cue from the list. The **Merge** button allows you to combine several cues into one cue. To do this, you should first select these cues from the list. Pressing the **Done** button closes the window.

It is convenient, but not particularly evident, that each time period from the cue list can be associated with a particular key. To do so, write **KEY** and the key name (a capital letter) in the **Label** field, **A** for example. If, while working in the main window, you then press the <A> key, playback of the corresponding waveform fragment starts.

When the **Auto Zoom** checkbox is selected, the auto zoom mode is enabled, and the displayed waveform fragment is maximized to full screen.

All time cues are displayed in the main window as colored triangles along the sides of the work area.

11.9. *Play List*—Editing the Sequence of Waveform Fragment Playback

The **Play List** command calls the dialog window shown in Fig. 11.13. It allows you to make a list of waveform fragments and playback the fragments included in this list. There will be no pauses between fragments during playback. They will sound like one continuous waveform.

Fig. 11.13. The **Play List** dialog window

In the example, you can see that the list contains no elements. However, the **Open Cue List** button is available, which allows you to open the time cues list. In Fig. 11.14, you see one possible view of the **Play List** and **Cue list** windows after pressing this button.

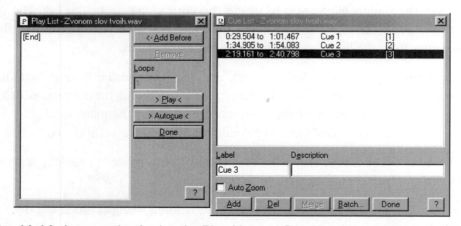

Fig. 11.14. An example of using the **Play List** and **Cue List** dialog windows together

Select the element you are interested in from the list and double-click it (by doing this, you go to the corresponding region of the waveform). The **Open Cue List** button in the **Play List** window changes its name to **<-Add Before**. By pressing this button, you put the current element of the **Cue List** before the current element of the **Play List**. In our example, it is the fictitious element **[End]**, which indicates the end of playback. The **Play List** window looks like Fig. 11.15 after performing these actions.

Now the **Remove** button is available. It allows you to delete elements from the list. In the **Loops** input field, you can specify the number of playback loops for each audio fragment. Pressing the **>Play<** button starts playback of fragments from the list.

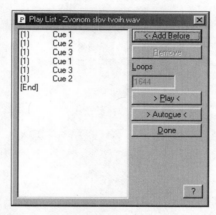

Fig. 11.15. Example of the fragment list for playback

The **>Autocue<** button plays the current element of the **Play List** (or its first element, if no element is selected) the number of times defined in the **Loop** field. Playback stops at the next element.

Pressing the **Done** button closes the window.

All time cues and the list of fragments for playback are saved in a WAV file.

11.10. *Time Window*—Creating an Additional Current Time Display Indicator

If you select the **Time Window** command from the **View** menu, another current time display indicator appears in the main window field. (More precisely, this indicator displays the time corresponding to either the current position marker or to the left boundary of the selected fragment).

By default, the indicator is a small rectangle, but you can make it as large as the main window field using the mouse (Fig. 11.16).

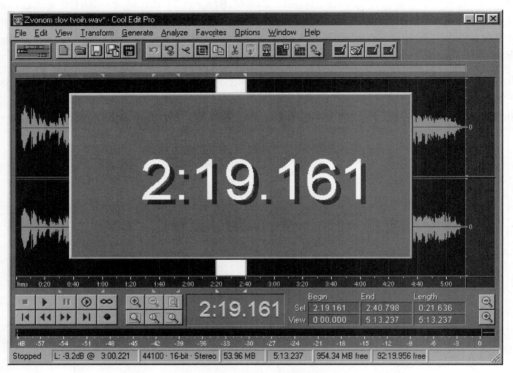

Fig. 11.16. Additional time display indicator

Now you can see the current recording or playback time from far away.

The elements we described above form the basis of the user-friendly Cool Edit Pro interface. No program offers such features to users as Cool Edit Pro, which you now know.

Chapter 12: The *Transform* Menu— Transforming Audio

We can call the **Transform** menu the basic menu of the Cool Edit Pro editor. This menu alone contains all the commands that allow you to get fantastic sound processing results. Other menus generally provide actions that are important, but nonetheless auxiliary. All sound transformations are made and all effects are created using the **Transform** menu.

❏ **Invert**— inverts the sound signal

❏ **Reverse**— reverses the sound signal

❏ **Silence**—sets absolute silence for the selected waveform fragment

❏ **DirectX**—opens the window of the audio effect plugged in using DirectX

❏ **Amplitude**—amplitude transformations. This submenu contains the following commands:

- **Amplify**—transforms the level of the sound signal

- **Channel Mixer**

- **Dynamic Processing**

- **Envelope**—controls the amplitude envelope shape

- **Hard Limter**

- **Normalize**

- **Pan/Expand**—transforms the stereo image of the sound source

❏ **Delay Effects**—effects based on delay. This menu contains the following commands:

- **Chorus**

- **Delay**

- **Echo**

- **Echo Chamber**—imitates a room's acoustics

- **Flanger**

- **Full Reverb**—universal reverberation processor

- **Multitap Delay**

- **Reverb**

- **Sweeping Phaser**

❏ **Filters**—audio signal filtering. This submenu contains commands that open windows for the following effects:

- **FFT Filter**—filter based on the Fast Fourier Transform
- **Graphic Equalizer**—universal graphic equalizer
- **Notch Filter**—five-band rejecting filter
- **Parametric Equalizer**—seven-band parametric equalizer
- **Quick Filter**—eight-band graphic equalizer
- **Scientific Filters**—Bessel, Butterworth, and Chebyshev filters

❏ **Noise Reduction**—this submenu contains the following commands:

- **Click/Pop Eliminator**—finding and correcting clicks and/or lost samples
- **Clip Restoration**—restoring the signal after clipping
- **Hiss Reduction**—spectral hiss reduction
- **Noise Reduction**—noise reduction based on analysis of the noise features

❏ **Special**—a submenu of special effects. It includes:

- **Brainwave Synchronizer**—synchronizing with cerebration
- **Convolution**
- **Distortion**—amplitude limiting
- **Music**—playing the melody

❏ **Time/Pitch**—converting the waveform's duration and pitch. This submenu contains the following commands:

- **Pitch Bender**—pitch shifting a waveform
- **Stretch**—changing the duration of a waveform

Most operations related to sound transformation in any menu item are applied to the selected waveform fragment. If a waveform fragment is not specified, the entire waveform is automatically selected before the action is performed.

The three first commands perform simple but amazing transformations of the sound signal.

12.1. *Invert*—Inverting Audio Signals

Invert inverts the sound signal. Each sound sample measurement is multiplied by −1.

First, of course, you have to select the waveform fragment in which you need to invert the sound waves.

Compare these two pictures: the source signal shown in Fig. 12.1, and the inversion result shown in Fig. 12.2.

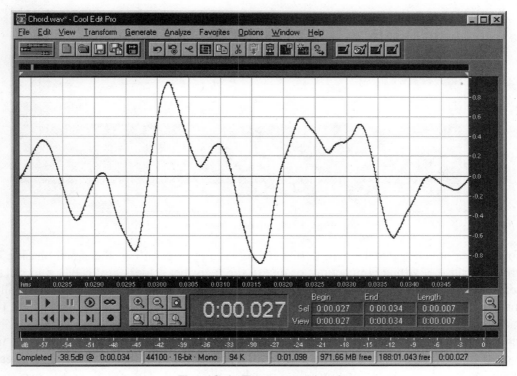

Fig. 12.1. The source signal

You can see that positive halves of sound waves become negative, and vice versa. This is the effect of inversion.

The **Invert** operation is identical to the function of the **Invert** button provided in the channel connection tools of advanced mixers.

When is inversion useful?

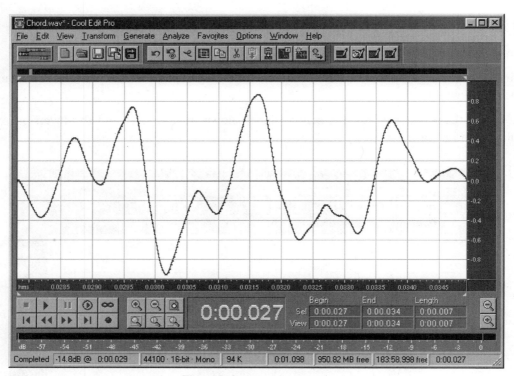

Fig. 12.2. Inversion result

You need to invert a signal when, during stereo waveform recording, the signal phasing is wrong because of wrong connection, or due to the incorrect soldering of cables and jacks. Left and right channel signals are then recorded in opposite phases. This fundamentally changes the stereo image, and leads to the mono-incompatibility of the recording. In other words, if you were to make a recording in, say, a concert hall with monophonic acoustic equipment, or have a stereophonic recording played over the radio, but listen to it on a monophonic receiver, then in a worst case scenario, you won't be able to hear much more than the occasional grinding or wheezing sound. The signals of the two stereo channels in opposite phases (for basic spectral components), when added to a mono signal, almost cancel each other out. To avoid this, you have to accurately control things so that the phase transformation remains identical in mixer stereo channels and in switching and processing devices. If you weren't able to avoid mistakes, you can apply the **Invert** command to any of the stereo signals.

The second thing you can do using signal inversion is expand the stereo base. Signals of the right and left channels are inverted and filtered. Then, the processed signals are cross-mixed in some proportion with the source signals. The stereo image is distorted, but gives the impression that the stereo base has expanded. Some tape recorders have a button for expanding the stereo base. This button activates the circuit that implements the above transformations. An extreme case of such processing is the transformation of a monophonic signal into a pseudo-stereo signal.

12.2. *Reverse*—Reversing Audio Signals

Reverse is the next command of the **Transform** menu. After this action is performed, the sound is recorded in reverse order. The beginning and the end of the waveform are exchanged. This command applies to the selected waveform fragment.

An example of the source signal is shown in Fig. 12.3, and the signal processed using the **Reverse** command is shown in Fig. 12.4.

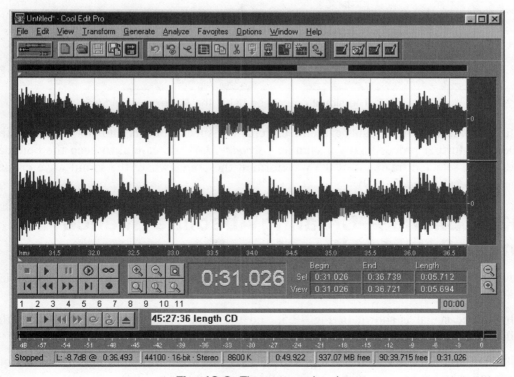

Fig. 12.3. The source signal

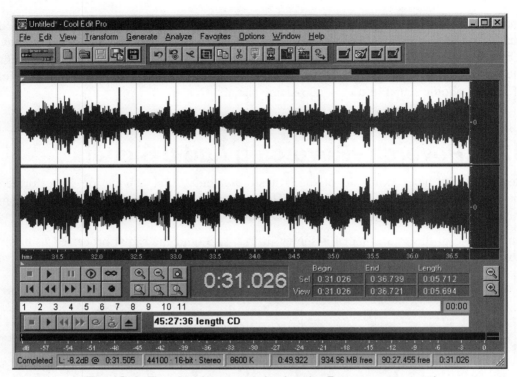

Fig. 12.4. The signal processed using the **Reverse** command

The **Reverse** command can be useful for creating special effects and for preparing the audio for further processing by a sampler (*Section 11.6*). Be careful to keep the boundaries of the selected fragment of the waveform at the points where the sound wave crosses the zero level (*Section 10.9*).

12.3. *Silence*—Creating Absolute Silence in the Selected Waveform Fragment

After the **Silence** command is applied, absolute silence is created within the specified waveform fragment. Values of all sound samples within this fragment will become zero.

The source signal is shown in Fig. 12.5, and the same signal after processing with the **Silence** command is shown in Fig. 12.6.

This function may be useful when parts of a signal (a word, a phrase) are separated from each other by long pauses that contain nothing but noise (Fig. 12.5).

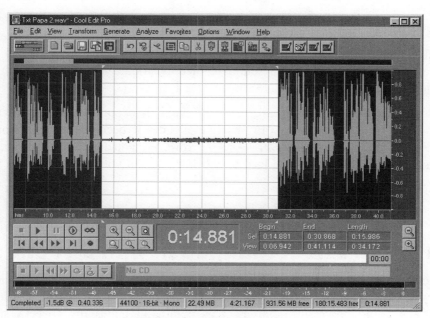

Fig. 12.5. The source signal

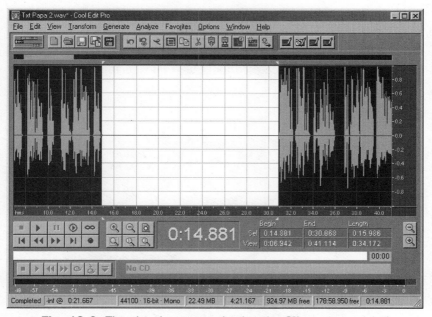

Fig. 12.6. The signal processed using the **Silence** command

If it is permissible to offset fragments of useful sound over time, you can then simply cut pauses from the recording, or do it automatically with Cool Edit Pro (the **Delete Silence** command of the **Edit** menu is described in *Section 10.8*). However, when you need to preserve all the fragments of useful sound in their positions, and you can't cut pauses, you should replace noise with absolute silence (see Fig. 12.6).

If the pauses are short and there are many of them, it becomes difficult to cut them manually and later replace them with absolute silence. It becomes more reasonable to apply noise reduction (*Sections 12.27—12.30*). However, you have to realize that using noise reduction algorithms does not lead to absolute silence; you only reduce the noise to some lower level.

12.4. *DirectX*—Opening the Window of an Audio Effect Plugged in with DirectX

The **DirectX** command of the **Transform** menu allows you to use plug-in module effects together with Cool Edit Pro. These modules are plugged in using DirectX, which considerably widens sound processing abilities. This command opens the **DirectX** submenu. Further actions depend on which DirectX plug-in modules are installed on your PC, and how they are organized.

On the PC used to prepare graphics for this book, all Cakewalk FX packages of modules and a few separate plug-in modules were installed. That's why the system of submenus through which these modules are accessed looks as it does in Fig. 12.7.

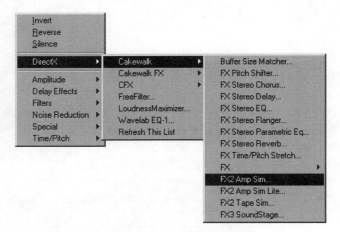

Fig. 12.7. The system of **DirectX** submenus

On your PC, other DirectX plug-in modules may be installed, so this menu will look different.

Before you start to work with the plug-in module, you should select the data for processing (the entire waveform or part of it). Then you should find the required effect in the submenu system and open the corresponding window by clicking it. As an example, we opened the **Wavelab EQ-1** plug-in module (Fig. 12.8)—the three-band parametric equalizer from Steinberg.

Fig. 12.8. The **Wavelab EQ-1** parametric equalizer window

This example is not the best one. In real life, you probably won't need to use this effect, since among the effects provided by Cool Edit Pro there are various types of equalizers, including a five-band parametric equalizer (*Section 12.24*).

We should again mention that Cool Edit Pro does not support a real-time mode for DirectX plug-in modules. To select the effect's parameters, you may use the preview button if it is provided in the effect window. In Fig. 12.8, this button is called **Purchase**. After you have heard the sound and are sure that you defined the effect parameters you need in order to achieve the desired result, press **OK** in the effect window. The data within the selected waveform fragment is then recalculated.

The next item of the **Transform** menu is not a separate command, but rather the **Amplitude** submenu. It contains a group of commands that affect the sound amplitude:

Amplify, **Channel Mixer**, **Dynamic Processing**, **Envelope**, **Hard Limter**, **Normalize**, and **Pan/Expand**.

Now we'll describe each of these commands in detail.

12.5. *Amplify*—Transforming the Audio Signal Level

Although this command is called **Amplify**, it actually affects not only sound signal amplification, but the sound signal amplitude as well, whether it increases or decreases. This command calls the **Amplify** dialog window, which contains two tabs: **Constant Amplification** (Fig. 12.9) and **Fade** (Fig. 12.10).

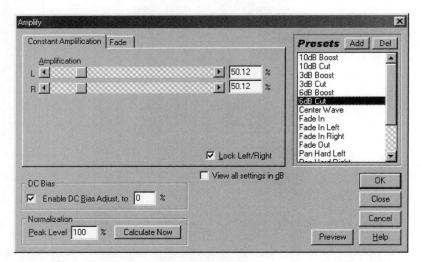

Fig. 12.9. The **Constant Amplification** tab of the **Amplify** window

Using the **Constant Amplification** and **Fade** tabs, you can select the method you wish to use to affect the amplitude: a *fixed* or *variable* change within the specified fragment.

When you use fixed amplitude change, the amplification ratio is specified by the **Amplification** regulators (**L** and **R**), or by inputting values in the corresponding fields. For example, if you input 50 into both fields, signal amplitudes for the right and left channels for the entire selected fragment decrease by half.

Using the **Lock Left/Right** checkbox, you can "attach" amplification regulators of the right and left channels to each other. If this checkbox is ticked, changing the position of either one of them causes the position of the other to change as well.

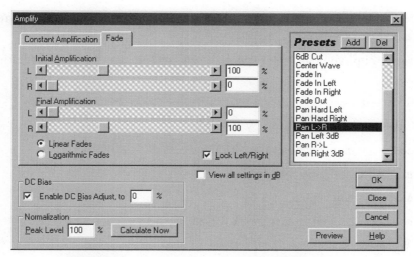

Fig. 12.10. The **Fade** tab of the **Amplify** window

When you use variable amplitude change, you can specify the amplifier ratio change within a range from **Amplification Initial** to **Amplification Final**. You can use either sliders or input fields. When you select the **Linear Fades** switch, the ratio is changed linearly, and with **Logarithmic Fades**, the ratio is changed logarithmically.

Depending on the status of **View all settings in dB**, the values of amplification ratios are defined as a percentage or in decibels.

In the **DC Bias** group, you can adjust the sound signal offset relative to a specified level. To do so, enable the **Enable DC Bias Adjust** option and define the offset as a percentage. Signal offset adjustment could be very useful. A sound could have been recorded with a certain offset, or a particular offset might appear after processing the signal with some other sound editor (other than Cool Edit Pro, which performs all transformations correctly), or the signal could contain a large constant component or low-frequency components with large amplitudes. In all of these cases, before you continue with further transformations, you have to get rid of this offset. Centering the signal relative to the defined level allows you to eliminate unwanted low-frequency components in further processing. These components normally appear as clicks when you assemble the recording.

The **Normalization** group contains elements allowing you to control signal normalization. The signal peak level is defined in the **Peak Level** field. For example, a value of 100% means that the signal occupies the entire dynamic range.

By pressing the **Calculate Now** button, you tell the program to calculate the amplification ratio that allows the signal to have the specified dynamic range after performing the

Amplify operation. Amplification sliders are then automatically set to the corresponding position.

In the **Presets** group, you can select standard settings (presets) for controls in the **Amplify** dialog box:

- ❒ **10 dB Boost**—increase signal level by 10 dB
- ❒ **10 dB Cut**—decrease signal level by 10 dB
- ❒ **3 dB Boost**—increase signal level by 3 dB
- ❒ **3 dB Cut**—decrease signal level by 3 dB
- ❒ **6 dB Boost**—increase signal level by 6 dB
- ❒ **6 dB Cut**—decrease signal level by 6 dB (see Fig. 12.9)
- ❒ **Center Wave**—center sound signal relative to zero
- ❒ **Fade In**—volume gradually increases from 0% (−240 dB) to 100% (0 dB)
- ❒ **Fade In Left**—volume gradually increases in the left channel from 0% (−240 dB) to 100% (0 dB); volume in the right channel is not changed
- ❒ **Fade In Right**—volume gradually increases in the right channel from 0% (−240 dB) to 100% (0 dB); volume in the left channel is not changed
- ❒ **Fade Out**—volume gradually decreases from 100% (0 dB) to 0% (−240 dB)
- ❒ **Pan Hard Left**—full panning of the audio to the left channel
- ❒ **Pan Hard Right**—full panning of the audio to the right channel
- ❒ **Pan L->R**—audio panning from left to right (see Fig. 12.10)
- ❒ **Pan Left 3dB**—audio panning to the left channel (with a level difference of 3 dB)
- ❒ **Pan R->L**—audio panning from right to left
- ❒ **Pan Right 3dB**—audio panning to the right channel (with a level difference of 3 dB)

Using the **Add** and **Del** buttons, you can add your own adjustment scheme or delete existing ones from the list. Above these buttons, there is a field in which you should supply the name of the new adjustment pattern, and only then press the **Add** button.

If you have selected mono format for waveform creation or transformation, the tabs look simpler: there are less sliders, fields, and variants of standard adjustment patterns. In Fig. 12.11, the **Constant Amplification** tab is shown for a mono waveform, and the **Fade** tab, also for a mono waveform, is shown in Fig. 12.12.

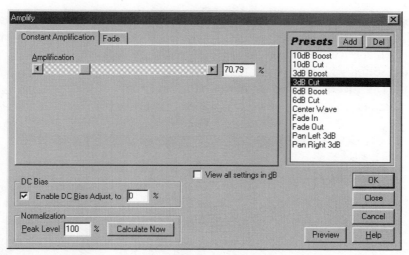

Fig. 12.11. The **Constant Amplification** tab for the mono waveform format

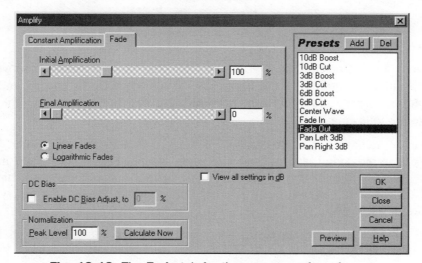

Fig. 12.12. The **Fade** tab for the mono waveform format

12.6. *Channel Mixer*

Channel Mixer (the next command of the **Amplitude** submenu) calls the dialog window for the channel mixer (Fig. 12.13).

The channel mixer allows you to mix signals of stereo waveform signals in any way you like. The **New Left Channel** and **New Right Channel** groups contain regulators for the mixing proportions of the newly created (as a result of mixing) left and right channels. With the **L** and **R** regulators, you set the sound levels of the left and the right channels. Adjustment is made within a range from −100 to 100. A negative value of the ratio indicates that the sound will be inverted relative to the zero level (as if the signal was multiplied by −1). The **Invert** checkboxes allow you to invert any of the resulting signals of the new stereo channels.

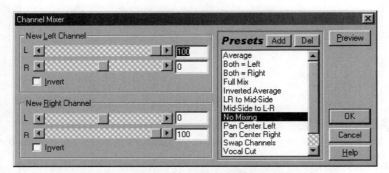

Fig. 12.13. The **Channel mixer** dialog window

As with most of the other functions of the program, the channel mixer allows you to use standard adjustment patterns. In the **Presets** field, you see a list of settings and the **Add** and **Del** buttons, which allow you to add or remove elements from the list. The standard settings are the following:

❑ **Average**—averaging, mutual penetration of stereo channels into each other. With this operation, stereo sound is converted into monophonic. Signals are mixed in proportions of 50% to 50%. If the amplitude of one of the source signals goes higher than half of the maximum allowed value, even if only at several points, there may be some distortion after mixing.

❑ **Both = Left**—puts the signal of the left channel of the source waveform into both channels of the new waveform.

❑ **Both = Right**—puts the signal of the right channel of the source waveform into both channels of the new waveform.

❑ **Full Mix**—this action is similar to **Average**: a stereo sound is converted to monophonic; however, the signals are mixed in a proportion of 100% to 100%. This can be applied only at low signal levels; otherwise, distortions appear after mixing.

❑ **Inverted Average**—a stereo sound is converted to monophonic. The signals in the left and right channels are equal, but are in opposite phases. The difference between inverted average and simple average is that inverted average makes it feel as if the source of sound is inside the listener's head.

☐ **LR to Mid Side**—the sum of signals of the left and the right channels is put into the new left channel, and their difference is put into the new right channel. The mixing poportion is 50% to 50%. This has the audible effect of widening the stereo base, with its center moved to a new location.

☐ **Mid Side to LR**—this preset is similar to the previous one. The mixing poportion is 100% to 100%.

☐ **No Mixing**—the signals of the channels are unchanged.

☐ **Pan Center Left**—the stereo base center moves left.

☐ **Pan Center Right**—the stereo base center moves right.

☐ **Swap Channels**—switches the left and the right channels.

☐ **Vocal Cut**—cuts the sound source from the center of the stereo panorama (Fig. 12.14).

☐ **Wide Stereo Field**—widens the stereo panorama (two options).

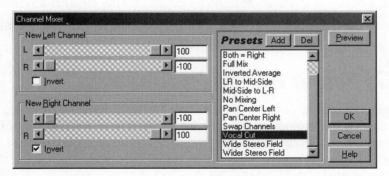

Fig. 12.14. Setting the sliders of the channel mixer for **Vocal Cut**

We didn't show you the standard settings for **Vocal Cut** for nothing. With the settings shown in Fig. 12.14, **Channel Mixer** turns into a robbery weapon. The sound source located in the center of the panorama is cut out. And what, you may ask, is usually located at the center of the panorama?—the soloist's voice. So to start, grab your favorite song from a CD (somebody else's, of course) and load it into Cool Edit Pro. Process it with **Channel Mixer** using the standard **Vocal Cut** settings. The musical instruments and back vocals are practically unchanged, but the voice of the lead vocalist has disappeared. You now have a negative waveform with a beautiful arrangement to do as you like with.

You can sing the words yourself, if you're so inclined. In time, you'll build up your repertoire and start performing yourself.

Fortunately, we can't delete the vocals from just any waveform. In popular songs, everything is usually done perfectly: the melody, the vocal, the arrangement, the mixing, etc. This means, though, that the singer's voice was almost certainly processed with special effects like reverb or delay. The singer's voice is not formed from only one point of the stereo image. What we hear to the left of the center is different from what we hear at a symmetric point. So, to remove the voice, you have to apply a more accurate and precise processing than simply adding the right and the left channels in opposite phases, and then further inverting one of the newly created signals.

It is hard to describe the result of applying any of the presets of the channel mixer. We can say one thing, though: the stereo image of the recording greatly changes, and in some cases, the timbre changes as well.

It is better to do it like this. Load any short and clear waveform into Cool Edit Pro. Make a copy of this waveform and process it using the channel mixer, selecting one preset after another. You can listen to the results separately, but to notice the difference, combine the resulting waveforms and to listen to them in one loop. Thus you get a clear understanding of the real results of sound processing by the channel mixer.

It makes sense to test other processing methods and effects provided by the program in the same manner.

12.7. *Dynamic Range Processing*

The **Dynamic Processing** command opens the **Dynamic Range Processing** dialog window. The universal virtual device for dynamic processing is implemented in this window. Depending on the parameter values selected, it can be a gate, a compressor, an expander, a limiter, or a de-esser. You can specify the type of processing and parameter values both graphically and digitally.

The **Dynamic Range Processing** dialog window contains four tabs:

❑ **Graphic**—this tab is used to graphically change the features and the parameters of dynamic processing

❑ **Traditional**—the purpose of this tab is the same as for the **Graphic** tab, but parameters are controlled numerically

❑ **Attack/Release**—this tab is intended for selecting the parameters that effect the enabling and disabling of dynamic processing

❑ **Band Limiting**—this tab allows you to select the processed frequency range

12.7.1. The *Graphic* Tab of the Dynamic Range Processing Dialog Window

The **Graphic** tab is shown in Fig. 12.15.

The coordinate plane takes up a significant part of this tab. The values of the source signal in decibels are put along the horizontal axis, and the values of the output signal in decibels are put along the vertical axis. Thus the graph shows what level of output (processed) signal corresponds to a certain level of input (non-processed) signal. This graph therefore represents the amplitude response of the dynamic processing device.

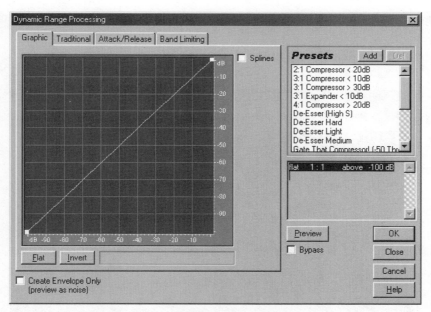

Fig. 12.15. Graphic tab of the **Dynamic Range Processing** dialog window

If the graph is a straight line from the lower left corner to the upper right corner of the working area (see Fig. 12.15), this means that there is no dynamic processing done to the signal. The level of the input signal matches the level of the output signal exactly.

By clicking the left mouse button on the graph, you create a point where you can bend the line. To move a point on the graph, click and hold on the point and drag it to a new location. The coordinates of the point are displayed under the grid. By releasing the mouse button, you fix the location of the point, and the dynamic processing parameters corresponding to the graph you create are displayed in the information field to the right of the grid. Each point is described by two lines. At the beginning of the line, the dynamic processing type is shown: **cmp** (compressing) or **exp** (expanding), followed by the dynamic range transformation ratio. At the end of the line, the range of the input signal level within which processing takes place is shown. For example, the following

exp   2 : 1   above   −30 dB

means widening the dynamic range by a ratio of 2:1 for values of the input signal above −30 dB. And this

cmp   1.75 : 1   below   −30 dB

means that for values of the input signal below −30 dB, compression is done using a ratio of 1.75:1.

The graph for these parameters is shown in Fig. 12.16.

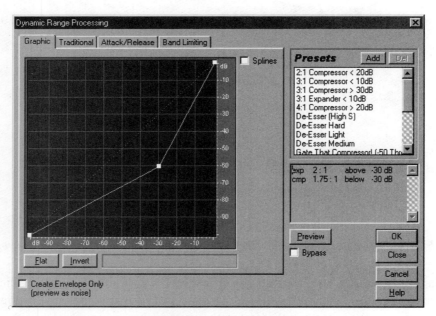

Fig. 12.16. Example of a graph

By double-clicking the left mouse button (or by right-clicking) on a certain point in the graph, you open the **Edit Point** dialog box (Fig. 12.17), in which you can exactly specify the point's coordinates numerically.

Fig. 12.17. The **Edit Point** dialog box

To do so, give a value for the input signal level (the point's horizontal coordinate) in the **Input Signal Level** field, and a value for the output signal level (the point's vertical coordinate) in the **Output Signal Level** field. The permitted range of values is below zero. If you make a mistake and input, for example, 40 instead of −40, the program replaces the invalid value with zero. To remove a point from the graph, input nothing in these fields.

The **Invert** button allows you to invert the graph, i.e., to replace the graph with one entirely opposite to the initial graph: compression would be replaced by expansion, and vice versa. In Fig. 12.18, you see the graph after using the **Invert** button (the initial graph is shown in Fig. 12.16).

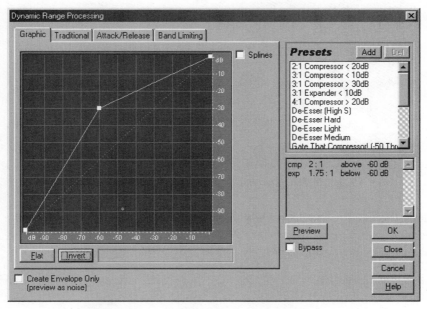

Fig. 12.18. The result of using the **Invert** button

You can invert the graph only when it crosses the two corner points (−100,−100 and 0,0) and each point is above its rightmost neighbor.

If you tick the **Splines** checkbox, the "angled" graph is replaced with its spline approximation (it is smoothed out). The graph shown in Fig. 12.18, after replacing the real function with its spline approximation, looks like Fig. 12.19.

It is important to understand that after you apply this function, not only the graph changes, but the actual relationship between the input and the output signals changes too.

Using the **Flat** button, you return the graph to its initial default state (the graph turns into a straight line and all the nodes are removed).

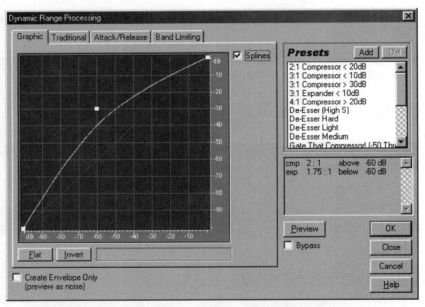

Fig. 12.19. The result of using the **Splines** button

If you check the **Create Envelope Only** checkbox and press **OK**, you create the envelope of the waveform amplitude. To get an idea of what the amplitude envelope is, compare Fig. 12.20 (source signal) and Fig. 12.21 (waveform amplitude envelope).

You can see that the resulting signal does not have the tonal carrier that is characteristic of the source waveform. All periodical oscillations have disappeared. There is only the function, and its graph describes the law according to which the amplitude of the source waveform changes over time. You can compare not only the graphs, but also the sound of the initial and resulting waveforms. You probably won't be satisfied with the result: you'll hear nothing but cracklings and rustling. But the purpose of the envelope

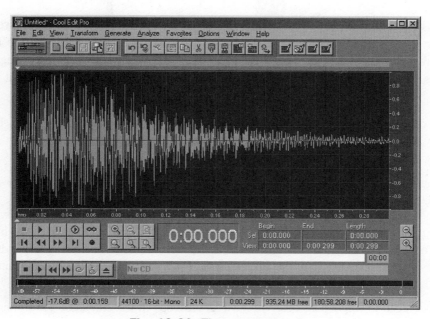

Fig. 12.20. The source signal

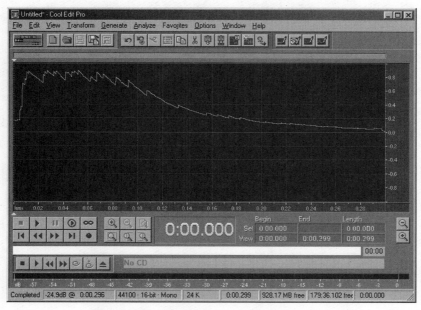

Fig. 12.21. Waveform amplitude envelope

is not to be listened to separately from the tonal carrier. Notice the words **preview as noise** near the **Create Envelope Only** checkbox. This explains that when you are listening to the waveform using the **Preview** button, noise is used as the envelope carrier. This is good because it allows you to get a "pure" impression of the envelope, without it being "masked" by the tonal carrier.

You can copy the envelope or save it in a file. Either way it is a waveform, but with a specific sound. One reasonable question might then arise: what is the purpose of this "skin peeled from the waveform"?

Later, when processing further, you can use the envelope to synthesize brand new sounds by modulating the amplitude of another sound with the envelope. For example, you can a play a note on the piano, record it, create the envelope, and then modulate a waveform containing a vocalist's voice (singing a note or even speaking a phrase) with this envelope. As a result, you get a fantastic sound that most likely cannot be reproduced by a human. All sound phases, such as attack, fade, etc., are characteristic to the piano. Just think of the eerieness of hitting a piano key and hearing: "Don't touch me!".

Now we just need to implement this. We have an envelope in the clipboard. Load the file containing the waveform being processed (Fig. 12.22). The contents of this waveform is a pure *A*.

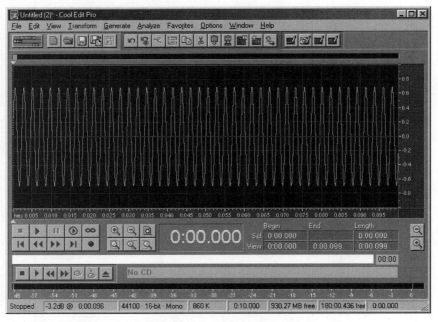

Fig. 12.22. The processed waveform

Then, using the **Edit>Mix Paste** command, open the **Mix Paste** window (*Section 10.4*). In this window, you should select the **Modulate** and **From Clipboard** options, specify the modulation depth, and press **OK**. Assume that the clipboard contains the waveform with the envelope shown in Fig. 12.21. The result will thus look as shown in Fig. 12.23.

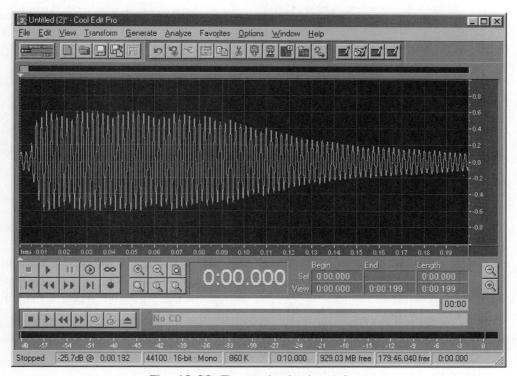

Fig. 12.23. The synthesized waveform

Note that you can use the **Create Envelope Only** option regardless of whether dynamic processing is applied or not.

12.7.2. The *Traditional* Tab of the *Dynamic Range Processing* Dialog Window

The **Traditional** tab (Fig. 12.24) contains the same information as the **Graphic** tab, but the information is represented numerically and not graphically.

Switches 2 through 6 correspond to the control points of the graph. There cannot be more than six points.

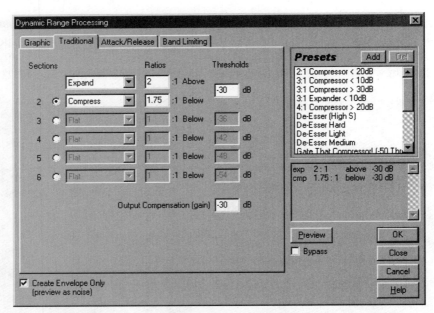

Fig. 12.24. The **Traditional** tab of the **Dynamic Range Processing** dialog window

To the right of each of the switches, there is a drop-down list in which the dynamic processing type that applies to the graph part above the corresponding point is displayed. You can edit the contents of this list by selecting one of three possible types of dynamic range processing: **Expand**, **Compress,** or **Flat** (unchanged).

In the **Ratios** input columns, the values of ratios of the dynamic range processing are displayed. They can be changed not only by editing the input fields, but also by adjusting the angles of the straight parts of the graph.

In the **Thresholds** input columns, you can edit the values of thresholds (the levels to which the points of the graph correspond).

In the **Output Compensation (gain)** field, you can change the amplification ratio of the output signal to compensate the signal level change caused by the applied effect.

12.7.3. The *Attack/Release* Tab of the Dynamic Range Processing Dialog Window

In the **Attack/Release** tab (Fig. 12.25), you can edit the parameters of the amplifying and detector channels (*Chapter 4*) of the virtual dynamic processing device.

The **Gain Processor** group contains the **Joint Channels** option (joint processing of both channels) and the following input fields:

❑ **Output Gain**—amplification ratio at output

❑ **Attack Time (Out)**—attack time for the output signal

❑ **Release Time (Out)**—release time for the output signal

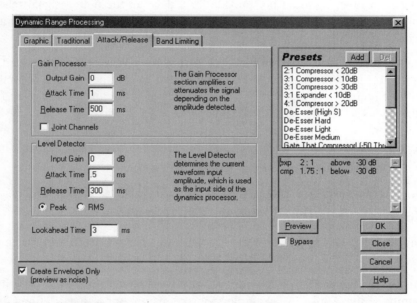

Fig. 12.25. The **Attack/Release** tab of the **Dynamic Range Processing** dialog window

The **Level Detector** group contains the following input fields:

❑ **Input Gain**—amplification ratio at the level detector input

❑ **Attack Time (In)**—attack time for the input signal

❑ **Release Time (In)**—release time for the input signal

Using the **Peak** or **RMS** switches, you can select the type of amplitude detector: peak or root-mean-square.

In the **Lookahead Time** field, you should specify the time by which the dynamic processing device should anticipate the sharp change of the signal level. Let's go into a little more detail on this parameter.

Cool Edit Pro does not allow you to process audio data in real time. Sometimes this is considered a disadvantage, but some processing algorithms just can't be implemented in real time. What would be the reaction of a real-time dynamic processing program that, say, tried to suppress sharp signal level changes from the signal? The sharp level change would be detected and the command would be given to recalculate the values of the signal amplitude. This would take some time, and thus the amplitude would be changed not at the moment of the level change, but some time later. This means that an impulse could get to the output of the virtual processing device, and the duration of this impulse would be determined by the program's reaction time. If we do not provide for a delay of the output signal relative to the input signal, we cannot avoid signal distortions when the processing is turned on and off. In real time, such delays are impossible since time cannot flow backward.

If the processing doesn't take place in real time, the above problem can be avoided. The program analyzes and transforms the audio data contained in the file, making several attempts. During the first attempt, the signal measurements matching the given criteria are found. For example, the points where the signal value sharply changes are marked. Then, the processing starts exactly from where the points were found, or even some time ahead. You can thus achieve a result characteristic of ideal, non-inert processing devices that don't exist in real life.

12.7.4. The *Band Limiting* Tab of the *Dynamic Range Processing* Dialog Window

In the **Band Limiting** tab, you should specify the lower (**Low Cutoff**) and the upper (**High Cutoff**) frequencies of the processed range.

The options of this tab allow you to process not an entire waveform, but only its separate spectral components. Thus, for example, for the parameter values defined in the tab shown in Fig. 12.26, dynamic processing is provided within the frequencies range specific for human whistling sounds. The virtual de-esser is implemented in this manner.

In the list of standard settings of the **Dynamic Range Processing** dialog window, all plausible methods of dynamic processing are implemented. Their brief characteristics are as follows:

❒ **2:1 Compressor < 20 dB**—compression of signals with levels below −20 dB (the compression ratio is 2:1).

❒ **3:1 Compressor < 10 dB**—compression of signals with levels below −10 dB (the compression ratio is 3:1).

❒ **3:1 Compressor > 30 dB**—compression of signals with levels above −30 dB (the compression ratio is 3:1).

❒ **3:1 Expander < 10 dB**—expands the dynamic range of signals with levels below −10 dB (the expanding ratio is 3:1).

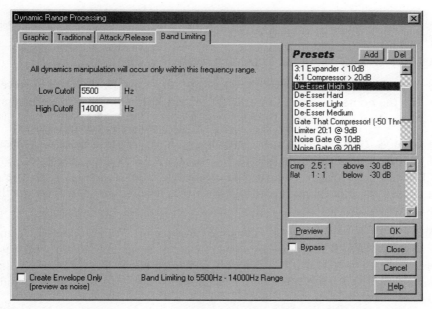

Fig. 12.26. The **Band Limiting** tab of the **Dynamic Range Processing** dialog window

☐ **4:1 Compressor>20 dB**—compresses signals with levels above −20 dB (the compression ratio is 4:1).

☐ **De-Esser (High S)**—suppresses whistling sounds; compresses signals with levels above −30 dB (the compression ratio is 3:1) within a frequency range of 5.5 to 14 kHz.

☐ **De-Esser Hard**—suppresses whistling sounds; compresses signals with levels above −35 dB (the compression ratio is 2.99:1) within a frequency range of 4 to 12 kHz.

☐ **De-Esser Light**—suppresses whistling sounds; compresses signals with levels above −24 dB (the compression ratio is 1.5:1) within a frequency range of 4 to 12 kHz.

☐ **De-Esser Medium**—suppresses whistling sounds within a frequency range of 4 to 12 kHz.

☐ **Gate That Compressor! (−50 thr)**—complex dynamic processing combining the gate, the expander, and the compressor. Fully suppresses signals with levels below −50 dB; expands the dynamic range of signals with levels from −50 to −45.7 dB (the expanding ratio is 14.38:1); expands the dynamic range of signals with levels from −45.7 through −24 dB (the expanding ratio is 1.62:1); and compresses signals with levels above −24 dB (the compression ratio is 5.45:1). During this processing, noises are removed, the level of quiet sounds is raised, and the level of loud sounds is lowered.

This type of processing may be useful for improving the quality of recordings made on a magnetic tape.

❏ **Limiter 20:1 @ 9 dB**—limit the signal at a level of −9 dB.

❏ **Noise Gate @ 10 dB**—"noise gate" processing. Compresses signals with levels below −19.6 dB (the compression ratio is 18.7:1); expands the dynamic range of signals with levels from −19.6 through −10 dB (the expansion ratio is 8.93:1).

❏ **Noise Gate @ 20 dB**—"noise gate" processing. Compresses signals with levels below −30.8 dB (the compression ratio is 18.7:1); expands the dynamic range of signals with levels from −30.8 through −20 dB (the expansion ratio is 7.06:1). This type of processing is used for processing records with a noise level lower than those in the previous example.

❏ **RealAudio® Compander**—special dynamic processing. Fully suppresses signals with levels below −71.9 dB; compresses signals with levels from −40 through −9 dB (the compression ratio is 1.14:1). This type of processing allows you to improve the quality of signals recorded from a microphone when the sound insulation of the studio is inadequate.

❏ **Vocal Compressor (great!)**—expands the dynamic range of signals with levels from −100 through −24 dB (the expansion ratio is 1.26:1); compresses signals with levels above −24 dB (the compression ratio is 5.45:1). This type of processing is used for processing records made in a good studio, with a low noise level. It allows you to improve recorded vocals and to smooth out occasional level changes that occur with loud signing.

❏ **Vocal Compressor II**—a modification of vocal dynamic processing. Compresses signals with levels from −100 through −67.4 dB (the compression ratio is 1.69:1); expands the dynamic range of signals with levels from −67.4 through −24 dB (the expansion ratio is 1.76:1); compresses signals with levels above −24 dB (the compression ratio is 5.45:1). This type of processing lowers the level of noises caused by inadequate sound insulation of the studio. It makes quiet sounds clearer, and smooths out the unevenness of relatively loud noises caused by changing the distance between the microphone and the singer's mouth.

❏ **Vocal Limiter**—expands the dynamic range of signals with a level from −100 through −24 dB (the expansion ratio is 1.26:1); signals with levels over −24 dB are limited at the −4 dB level. This type of processing is used for processing recordings made in a good studio, with a low noise level. The voice expressiveness is improved, and details can be clearly understood in quiet parts of the recording. The difference in levels in loud parts of the composition is entirely removed.

So as not to complicate understanding the processing types, we have not provided the timing parameters of the virtual amplifier and the signal level detector. You can find these parameters in the **Attack/Release** tab.

12.8. *Envelope*—the Amplitude Envelope Shape Control

The **Envelope** command of the **Amplitude** menu calls the **Create Envelope** dialog window (Fig. 12.27). Using this command, you can give the waveform amplitude envelope the selected shape.

Now we'll again deal with a graph. The time values are put along the horizontal axis, and the signal level values are put along the vertical axis. Pay attention to the fact that the envelope length is equal to the duration of the waveform fragment selected in the working field of the main window.

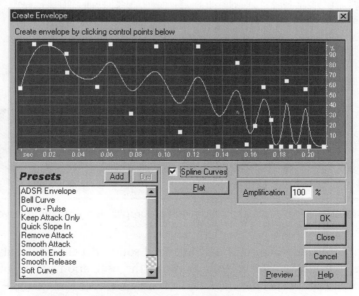

Fig. 12.27. The **Create Envelope** dialog window

Here you can "draw" an envelope of any shape, for example, like the one shown in Fig. 12.27. You create points by double-clicking the line. Moving the nodes, you can get the desired shape of the envelope.

The envelope shape greatly effects the spectral contents of the signal and, accordingly, the sound timbre. A pure A tone is a sinusoid oscillation with a frequency of 440 Hz (see Fig. 12.22). It sounds nasal, tedious, and not like music at all. But if we replace the straight envelope of the waveform shown in Fig. 12.22 with the envelope shown in Fig. 12.27, the sound timbre significantly changes. The sound becomes musical and live, and the waveform looks something like Fig. 12.28.

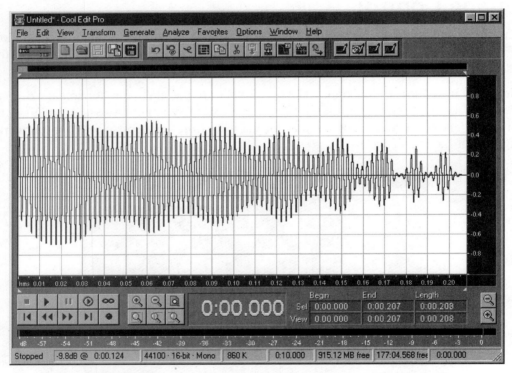

Fig. 12.28. Wide-band oscillation with a complicated amplitude envelope

We must mention that the timbre of a synthesized sound depends not only on the shape of the envelope, but also on the relation between the oscillation period of the tonal flavoring and the duration of specific fragments of the envelope. For example, in Fig. 12.28, you can see that each "lobe" of the waveform contains only a few periods of the carrier oscillation. According to the classification used in modern radio engineering, this signal is wide-band, even super-wide-band. Its timbre is very rich. When it is reproduced, the envelope oscillations won't appear as volume changes. They are so fast that separate oscillations cannot be heard. If we give the same envelope shape to a longer waveform (see Fig. 12.27), then each of its "lobes" will contain tens or even hundreds of oscillations of the tonal carrier signal. In Fig. 12.29, you cannot see separate oscillations of the tonal carrier. The timbre of such a sound is richer than the timbre of an ideal sinusoid. Here, the envelope oscillations appear as clear changes in the sound's volume.

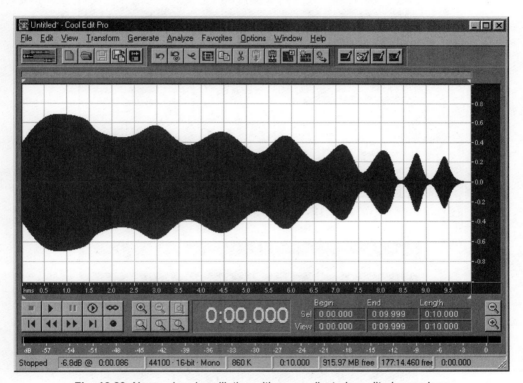

Fig. 12.29. Narrow-band oscillation with a complicated amplitude envelope

We have already described the **Spline Curves** checkbox. When it is checked, the angled graph replaced with its spline approximation. The envelope change becomes smooth.

In the **Amplification** input field, you can specify the value of the highest point of the envelope.

If you press the **Flat** button, all nodes are removed from the curve, and it becomes a straight line.

To save a well-selected envelope, press the **Add** button, and in the dialog box that opens, supply the preset name.

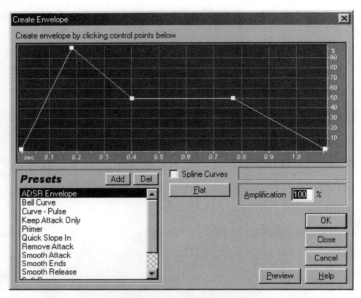

Fig. 12.30. The **ADSR** envelope

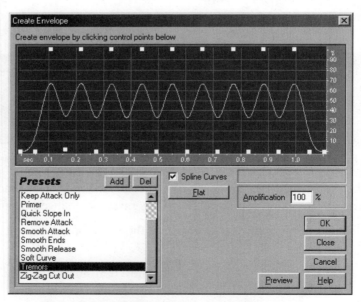

Fig. 12.31. The **Tremors** envelope, modified

You can use the built-in presets until you have more experience with this software.

We won't describe all of the presets, because the corresponding curves are rather complex. We must mention, however, two important elements of the list.

☐ **ADSR Envelope**—the envelope on which is based the operation of many musical synthesizers (Fig. 12.30). The sound process and the envelope are conventionally divided into four phases: Attack, Decay, Sustain, and Release (*ADSR*). The duration and the level of each phase determine the timbre of the synthesized sound.

☐ **Tremors**—the envelope that helps implement amplitude vibrato or tremolo. It makes sense to modify this envelope as shown in Fig. 12.31, i.e., to move the initial and final points to the zero level. This allows you to definitely avoid clicks in the places where the waveform fragments are glued together.

12.9. *Hard Limiter*

The **Hard Limiter...** command opens the **Hard Limiter** dialog window (Fig. 12.32). Using it, you can lower the amplitude of sound oscillations to the assigned threshold if it passes some limit, and leave the amplitude of all sound fragments below this threshold unchanged.

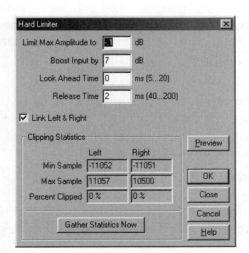

Fig. 12.32. The **Hard Limiter** dialog window

This can be very convenient if you have combined all tracks into a single (32-bit) audio file, and there are only a few fragments with clipping. You could also normalize the entire waveform (*Section 12.10*). However, this approach is not that useful: because of the large peaks present in the signal, its average level is low. **Hard Limiter** effects only the parts that were clipped.

Now we'll describe the options of the **Hard Limiter** dialog window.

Limit Max Amplitude to—the maximum allowed amplitude of the waveform. To avoid clipping of a 16-bit waveform, input a value between −0.1 and −0.5 dB in this field. This gives you a small reserve on the amplitude. You will need it for any further editing actions.

Before you limit, you can first amplify the sound. To make the selected waveform louder, and to ensure that clipping will not occur, you may use the **Boost Input by** field. Specify the amplification value in this field (in dB).

In the **Look Ahead Time** field, you should input the amount of time that it will take to attenuate the audio before the loudest peak will be hit. If this parameter value is small, it can result in audible distortions. Values anywhere from 4—10 milliseconds are recommended (the default value is 7 milliseconds).

In the **Release Time** field, you should input the time it takes for the attenuation to rebound back 12 dB (or roughly, the time it would take for the audio to resume normal volume if an extremely loud peak was encountered). To preserve very low bass frequencies, it is recommended that you define a **Release Time** parameter value equal to 100 milliseconds. If this value is too long, the audio may stay abnormally quiet for a long time. A value of 2000 milliseconds, for example, would give you an Automatic Gain Control effect.

If the **Link Left & Right** checkbox is checked, the signal levels of both channels will change together (according to the same function), which preserves the stereo image of the source sound. You can allow the independent processing of the left and right channels by not selecting this checkbox.

After you press the **Gather Statistics Now** button in the **Clipping Statistics** field, the current clipping statistics are displayed. For each channel, the maximum and minimum waveform values and the percentage of signal values that would be clipped if limiting was not performed are shown. You should use the **Gather Statistics Now** button each time you alter any of the parameters of this window.

12.10. *Normalize*

The next command of the **Amplitude** menu is **Normalize**. It calls the small **Normalize** dialog box shown in Fig. 12.33.

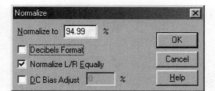

Fig. 12.33. The **Normalize** dialog box

In the **Normalize to** field, you specify the level to which the waveform should be amplified in decibels or as a percentage (depending on the **Decibels Format** checkbox status).

After you press **OK**, the program analyzes the selected fragment and finds the digitized audio measurement that has the greatest absolute value. As a rule, there is only one, but there could be several (which in fact does not matter).

The ratio is calculated automatically. After multiplying by this ratio, the maximum value becomes equal to the level you specified.

Each measurement of the selected waveform fragment is then multiplied by this ratio.

Finally, the maximum value takes the value you specified, and the values of the rest of the measurements are increased or decreased proportionally.

Normalization is usually applied when you want the waveform's loudness to be at its maximum, but without being clipped. You can amplify the signal using the options of the **Amplify** window, but in this case, it is not guaranteed that you have avoided clipping. Therefore, normalizing is basically optimal signal amplification: the signal is amplified to get the maximum loudness, and clipping is avoided. We'll now describe an example that illustrates such normalizing.

In Fig. 12.34, there is an example of a waveform in which the maximum value is reached between 39 and 40 seconds (this region is highlighted in the picture).

We select the entire waveform, open the **Normalize** dialog box, input 100% (or 0 dB) in the **Normalize to** field, press **OK**, and examine the result (Fig. 12.35).

From Fig. 12.35, you can see that now:

❑ The waveform graph at its maximum point touches the line for the 100% level (this area is highlighted in the picture)

❑ The values of all the rest of the measurements have increased

Sometimes, it may become necessary to normalize over 100%. The question then arises, though: will this lead to clipping and audio non-linear distortions? Of course it will. However, in some cases, we can allow this. Here is an example.

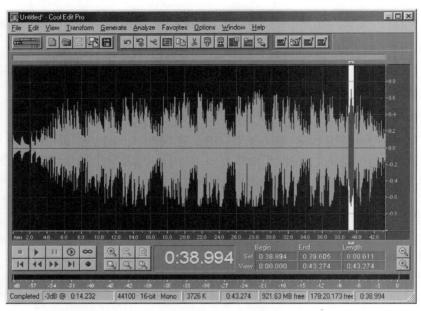

Fig. 12.34. Example of the waveform before normalizing

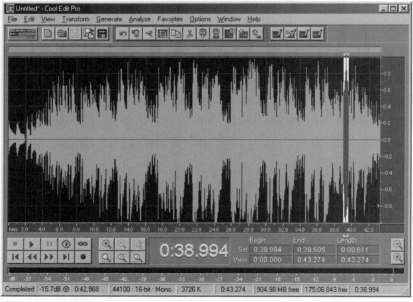

Fig. 12.35. Example of the waveform after normalizing

Assume there are one or more impulse interferences within a waveform, and that their amplitude values are significantly more than the audio signal value. After 200% normalizing, the audio signal becomes significantly louder, but the clicks cannot become louder due to the defined limit. However, additional, non-linear distortions of these impulse interferences arise. How to eliminate them is another topic entirely. We have achieved our main aim—the audio signal has gotten louder.

The **Normalize** dialog box contains two other checkboxes. If the **Normalize L/R Equally** checkbox is ticked, normalizing is performed as follows:

❑ From two stereo channels, the channel that has the signal with the maximum amplitude is selected

❑ On the basis of this information, both channels are normalized simultaneously

As a result, the signal in one of the channels is potentially below the maximum allowed level. This is not a problem, because in stereo sound, signals in different channels need not be equal.

Sometimes it becomes necessary to normalize stereo channels separately. For example, say the left and the right channels contain different signals from different sources. In such a case, it would not make sense to select the **Normalize L/R Equally** checkbox.

We have already described the **DC Bias Adjust** checkbox (*Section 12.5*). Using this checkbox, you center the signal relative to the zero level, and suppress the low-frequency component.

Normalizing is not as simple as it seems. Without a good reason, you should not apply it to the same signal several times. This is because any computations with numbers represented by a fixed number of bits lead to errors. In multiple computations, these errors accumulate. Errors are heard as signal distortions, and when errors have accumulated, these distortions become more noticeable.

12.11. *Pan/Expand*—Expanding the Stereo Panorama; Shifting the Center Channel

The **Pan/Expand** effect is used to pan, or shift, the so-called *center channel* of a stereo waveform. It also allows you to expand or narrow the stereo separation of the left and right channels.

The stereo panorama is expanded by adding a signal from one channel into another. The phase relationship in the added signals are corrected. The center channel is created as the sum of the signals of the left and right channels. You can expand the stereo panorama and change the position of the center channel dynamically. To do so, define the graphs that illustrate the dependence of these parameters on the time. This gives the effect of a stereo recording having four channels.

Changing the position of the center channel is heard as moving sources of sound, which before processing were in the center, along the panorama. Other sources are heard as stationary. The window of the **Pan/Expand** effect is shown in Fig. 12.36.

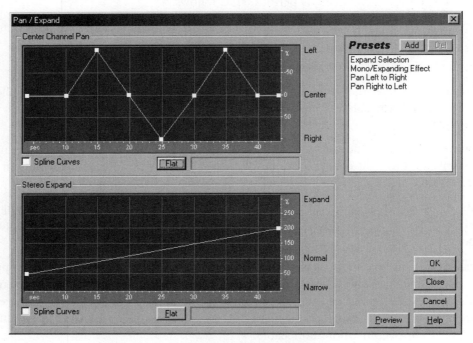

Fig. 12.36. The **Pan/Expand** effect window

The effect applies to the selected waveform fragment.

In the **Center Channel Pan** field, you draw the graph that represents the pan position of the center channel of a stereo waveform over time using the mouse. You can use the graph to position the center channel anywhere from extreme left (−100%) to extreme right (100%), or to make the center channel move from right to left, or vice versa.

You can change the graph's shape by moving its nodes vertically and horizontally. To add a node to the graph, click in the grid on the location where you want to place the point. To remove a node, drag it off the graph area. When the mouse cursor is located over a point, you will see it change from an arrow to a hand. To enter time and panning for a control point numerically, right-click on the point to open a dialog box similar to the one shown in Fig. 12.17.

Similarly, you can draw a graph of the expansion level over time in the **Stereo Expand** field. Values over 100% correspond to expanding the panorama width. By changing the expansion level, you can create various effects, for example the effect of converting a monophonic signal into a signal with a very wide stereo panorama.

Spline Curves enables the mode of smoothing "broken-line" graphs with splines. The curve that best fits is generated, instead of just a straight line between the nodes of the graph. When you use spline curves, the line will not ordinarily go directly through the nodes; rather, using the nodes, you control the shape of this curve. When you want to have smooth curves that better reflect the details of the original graph, create many nodes close to each other.

The **Flat** button is used to reset the graph to its default state. All the nodes are removed and the graph changes to a straight line.

The following changes of the waveform stereo image correspond to the graphs shown in Fig. 12.36:

❐ The center channel is first in the center; then it moves left, then right, and then returns to the center.

❐ The stereo base at the beginning of the waveform is narrowed to 50% of the initial one. Its width then continuously grows and reaches 200% of the initial one at the end of the waveform.

In this window, like in many others, a tool is provided to save the presets you create, and to use built-in presets. There are only four built-in presets.

❐ **Expand Selection**—expands the stereo base of the selected waveform fragment. The position of the center channel is unchanged, and the stereo base is smoothly widened to the max during a short period of time. It remains wide for a long time, and then smoothly and quickly is narrowed to its initial state. Sometimes, it makes sense to process the entire composition. Changes in the stereo base will be at the beginning and at the end of the composition, i.e., those parts of the recording where the loudness increase stops (**Fade In**) and where it begins to decrease (**Fade Out**). Some panoramic defects may be present at the beginning and at the end of the composition, which will become more noticeable if the stereo base is expanded.

❐ **Mono/Expanding Effect**—a stereo imitation of an initially monophonic waveform. The stereo base width is periodically changed relative to a value a little bit over 100%.

❐ **Pan Left to Right**—left to right paning. The center channel is gradually moved from the leftmost point of the panorama to the rightmost.

❐ **Pan Right to Left**—right to left paning. The center channel is gradually moved from the rightmost point of the panorama to the leftmost.

If you decide to experiment with the **Pan/Expand** effect, you will find that the results do not always match the results expected in theory. For example, not only is the center channel expanded, but the sources of sound offset from the panorama center are as well. This is not surprising. First, the processing result is significantly affected by the stereophonic features of the initial waveform. Second, this effect is based not on spectral or psycho-acoustic transformations, but simply on inverting, adding, or subtracting the values of the right and left channels. In other words, the **Pan/Expand** effect transforms audio the same way as the channel mixer does (*Section 12.6*). The basic difference is that the **Pan/Expand** effect provides the user with a tool for stereo panorama transformation control, and the channel mixer does not.

With this, we finish with the abilities provided by the **Amplitude** submenu, and will start describing the **Delay Effects** submenu. It deals with effects for adding copies of the audio signal that have been processed and delayed over time to the signal itself.

Cool Edit Pro provides powerful tools for creating delay effects. You can potentially create countless effects in this manner.

The **Delay Effects** submenu contains the following commands:

❐ **Chorus...**

❐ **Delay...**

❐ **Echo...**

❐ **Echo Chamber...**—imitation of a room's acoustics

❐ **Flanger...**

❐ **Full Reverb...**—universal reverberation processor

❐ **Multitap Delay...**

❐ **Reverb...**

❐ **Sweeping Phaser...**

These commands open windows for effects based on signal delay.

12.12. *Chorus*

The **Chorus** command opens the **Chorus** window (Fig. 12.37). Chorus enriches the sound of the composition by imitating its being played by several voices or instruments. *Chorus* is one of the methods for creating the presence effect, i.e., separating the singer's voice or the leading instrument from the accompaniment. You can also use chorus to create a pseudo-stereo effect for a monophonic waveform, or to enrich the harmony of the vocal part.

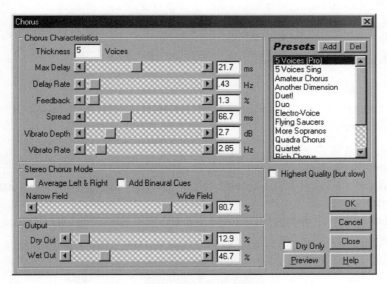

Fig. 12.37. The **Chorus** window

In Cool Edit Pro, the direct modeling method of the Chorus effect is used: new voices are created from each of the initial voices, and they all sound different from the original, due to shallow frequency modulation and time shift, and pseudo-random intonation. The usage of feedback in the processing algorithm makes the effect continuous.

The options of the **Chorus** window, shown in Fig. 12.37, are as follows:

The **Chorus Characteristics** group defines the effect parameters.

In the **Thickness ... Voices** field, you specify the number of voices used to create the Chorus effect.

To control the Chorus parameters, the following sliders and input fields are used.

❐ **Max Delay**—maximum voice delay. It is recommended that you set this value somewhere within a range of 15 to 35 milliseconds. If the setting is very small, all the voices will start merging into the original, and an unnatural flanging effect may be noticed. If the value is set too high, everything will start to sound as if a tape is being eaten by a cassette deck.

❐ **Delay Rate**—delay modulation frequency.

❐ **Feedback**—feedback depth.

❐ **Spread**—additional delay to each of the voices (up to 200 milliseconds). Highly spread values will cause separate voices to start at different times. With low values, the effect is of all the voices singing in unison.

❐ **Vibrato Depth**.

❐ **Vibrato Rate**.

The **Stereo Chorus Mode** group contains the options that influence the stereophonic features of the effect.

If the **Average Left & Right** checkbox is not selected, the source signals of the left and the right channels are processed separately by the effect. The stereo image gets minimal distortions. When you check this checkbox, an average stereo image is formed, since a mix of channel signals is processed. Actually, the program first creates a monophonic signal, and then makes it stereo by distributing separate voices along the panorama.

If you process a monophonic signal, you should untick this checkbox to avoid wasting time transforming a mono signal into a mono signal.

When the **Add Binaural Cues** checkbox is ticked, different delays for the left and the right channels are added to the created signal. Voices from different points of the panorama then appear at different moments. If you are going to listen to the recording through headphones, it is recommended that you tick the checkbox, and then disable it when you listen to it through speakers.

The slider and the input field below the described checkboxes are intended for selecting the effect width in the stereo panorama. If the slider is in the **Narrow Field** position (0 is input), all voices are put in the center of the stereo panorama. When you set the slider in the 50% position, all voices are placed along the panorama from left to right. For example, if a choir of 5 voices is being imitated, the voices are placed as follows:

❐ The first voice—in the leftmost point of the panorama

❐ The second voice—in the middle of the left part of the panorama

❏ The third voice—in the middle of the panorama

❏ The fourth voice—in the middle of the right part of the panorama

❏ The fifth voice—in the leftmost point of the panorama

If you select a value for the parameter over 50%, then while moving the slider to the right, the voices begin to move to extreme points of the panorama: the left voices move to the left and the right voices move to the right.

If you operate with an odd number of voices, one voice is always in the center of the panorama.

When the number of voices is even, there are no voices in the center. Half of the voices are concentrated in the right part, and the other half are in the left part.

If the slider is in the **Wide Field** position (the parameter value is 100%), all the left voices are in the leftmost point, while all the right voices are in the rightmost point.

The **Output** group contains sliders and input fields that allow you to select the mixing proportion of the processed (**Wet Out**) and initial (**Dry Out**) signals.

If you tick the **Dry Only** checkbox, regardless of the status of the sliders in the **Output** group, only the unprocessed signal is put into the effect output.

If you check the **Highest Quality (but slow)** checkbox, an algorithm that provides a higher quality (a lower level of distortions) is used to implement this effect, but the time taken for computations increases.

As we usually do, let's briefly describe the settings of the standard delivery set:

❏ **5 Voices (Pro)**, **5 Voices Sing**, **Another Dimension**—variants of a choir of 5 voices

❏ **Amateur Chorus**, **Thick Chorus**—variants of a choir of 12 voices

❏ **Duet!**, **Duo**—duet variants

❏ **Electro Voice**—imitation of an electronic-sounding voice

❏ **Flying Saucers**—according to the developers, this is what flying saucers sound like

❏ **More Sopranos**, **Soprano Chorus**—variants of a choir of sopranos

❏ **Quadra Chorus**, **Quartet**—variants of a quartet

❏ **Rich Chorus**, **Rich Chorus In Unison**—variants of a choir with enriched sound

12.13. *Delay*

The next command of the **Delay Effects** submenu is the command that implements delay—the **Delay** command. This command opens the **Delay** window (Fig. 12.38).

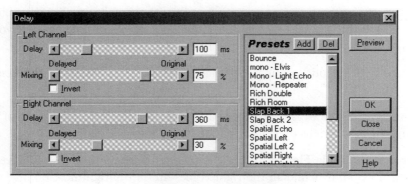

Fig. 12.38. The **Delay** window

The **Left Channel** and **Right Channel** groups contain the elements for setting delays for each of the stereo channels.

Using the **Delay** slider, or the input field to the right of it, you can define the delay time in milliseconds.

Similar interface elements, under **Mixing,** allow you to specify the level of the delayed signal added to the initial signal (as a percentage). The **Invert** switch defines whether the phase of the mixed signal is to be inverted.

Traditionally in Cool Edit Pro, the window of this effect contains a list of presets **(Presets)**, but we won't give any more commentary on that here. We cannot describe completely all the ways of mixing the signals of the left and the right channels with delayed signals. It would be better if you try and figure out the abilities of the presets provided with the **Delay** effect yourself.

12.14. *Echo*

The next effect—**Echo**—is more complex. The basic difference between this effect and delay is that delayed copies undergo additional processing: their spectrum is changed. The sound processed by the **Echo** effect is more natural than the sound processed by the **Delay** effect. A natural echo is created as a result of multiple reflections of sound waves from obstacles (houses, walls of a room, mountains, etc.). Different spectral components of the sound are reflected from obstacles in different ways. The lower the frequency (the greater the wave length), the easier the wave gets by obstacles. A high-frequency wave cannot easily get past an obstacle, and is thus partially reflected from it and partially absorbed by it, finally turning into heat energy. But we cannot forget that high-frequency sound waves, while propagating in the air, fade faster than low-frequency waves.

To sum up here, we can state that the echo contains the initial signal offset over time, with reduced low and high frequencies. How they change exactly depends on the particular conditions of sound propagation (the distance to the obstacle, what it is made of, etc.). Using the **Echo** effect (Fig. 12.39), we can imitate these conditions. The window for this is opened by the **Echo** command of the **Delay Effects** submenu.

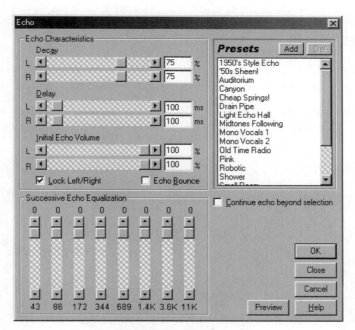

Fig. 12.39. The **Echo** window

The **Decay** sliders define the level of the delayed signal relative to the initial signal (as a percentage)—the echo level. **Delay** represents the time (in milliseconds) by which the signal is delayed.

Initial Echo Volume—the level at which the echo is added to the initial signal.

The **Successive Echo Equalization** group is the equalizer that allows you to change the spectrum of the delayed signal.

You should tick the **Continue echo beyond selection** checkbox if you want to allow the echo to fade beyond the selected waveform fragment.

When the **Lock Left/Right** checkbox is selected, the sliders of the left and the right channels are combined.

If you check the **Echo Bounce** checkbox, the echo sound is accented.

The **Presets** group contains the list of presets for different types of echos.

12.15. *Echo Chamber*—Imitating Room Acoustics

The **Echo Chamber** command allows you to model sound propagation in a room. A similar effect is implemented in the Cakewalk Pro Audio software as a plug-in.

The dialog window opened by the **Echo Chamber** command is shown in Fig. 12.40. It is called **3-D Echo Chamber**.

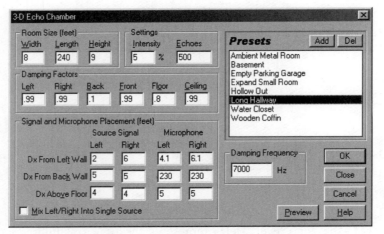

Fig. 12.40. Modeling sound propagation in a 3-D room

This window has several options. In **Room Size**, you specify the room's size (in feet): **Width**, **Length**, and **Height**.

In the **Settings** group, specify the **Intensity** and the number of reflections (**Echoes**).

In the **Damping Factors** group, you define the absorption ratios of the materials of which the ceiling, the walls, and the floor are made:

❐ **Left**—for the left wall

❐ **Right**—for the right wall

❐ **Back**—for the back wall

❐ **Front**—for the front wall

❐ **Floor**—for the floor

❐ **Ceiling**—for the ceiling

In the **Damping Frequency** field, define the upper frequency of the processed signal. Frequencies above this value are suppressed.

In the **Signal and Microphone Placement** group, specify the location of the **Source Signal** and the listener or microphone (**Microphone**) in the virtual room. It would be correct to say that there are two source signals—from the left and right source channels. The number of microphones (like listener's ears) is also two, and the location of each of them can be determined by three coordinates:

Dx From Left Wall—distance from the left wall

Dx From Back Wall—distance from the back wall

Dx Above Floor—height above the floor

The **Mix Left/Right Into Single Source** option allows you to combine the left and right source channels into a single point of the source sound.

12.16. *Flanger*

The flanger effect is based on the sound of an old-fashioned bobbin tape recorder. The bobbins rotate faster or slower, and the sound "floats". Maybe some readers do not know what we are talking about, because problems with CD recorders are of a different nature. However, if we look at a ruined tape recorder from scientific point of view, we get the pleasant effect called **Flanger**. The **Flanger** effect dialog window (Fig. 12.41) is opened by the **Flanger** command of the **Delay Effects** submenu.

The options of this window are as follows. Using the **Original-Expanded** slider (or **Original-Delayed** slider, depending on the mode selected in the **Mode** group), you set the relationship between the mixed signals of the source sound and the distorted (floating) sound. **Initial Mix Delay** and **Final Mix Delay** are the initial and the final delay for a half-period of the "floating" sound. The sounds of the left and the right channels can be delayed differently. Using the **Stereo Phasing** slider, you can set the phase difference for stereo channels. The position of the **Feedback** slider determines the feedback depth.

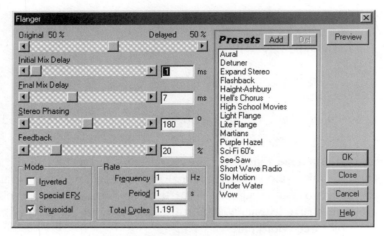

Fig. 12.41. The **Flanger** window

In the **Mode** group, you can define different combinations of the three modes: **Invert**— inversion of the processed signal; **Special EFX**—signal mixing (special mode); **Sinusoidal**—delay of the processed signal from the initial signal according to the sinusoidal law. If this mode is not specified, the delay changes from the initial value to the final (and back) linearly.

In the **Rate** group, you define the parameters of the processed signal: the **Frequency** or **Period** of the entire cycle "initial-final-initial delay", and **Total Cycles**—the total number of such periods.

As usual, there is an expandable list of **Presets**.

12.17. *Full Reverb*—Universal Reverberation

To create a detailed model of an acoustic room, universal reverberation (**Full Reverb**) is used. This effect provides some unique features:

❏ Realistic modeling of signals of early reflections

❏ Changing the sizes and acoustic features of the imitated room

❏ Modeling any material of the reflecting surfaces

❏ Changing the absorption features within the room

❏ Correction of the signal frequency spectrum using a three-band parametric equalizer

The **Full Reverb** command opens an effect window with the same name. It contains three tabs: **General Reverb** (Fig. 12.42), **Early Reflections** (Fig. 12.43), and **Coloration** (Fig. 12.44).

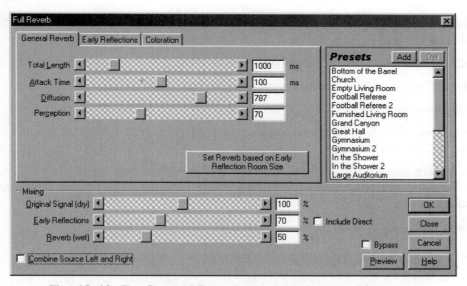

Fig. 12.42. The **General Reverb** tab of the **Full Reverb** window

First we'll describe the elements of this window general to all tabs.

In the **Mixing Section** group, there are elements that regulate the following parameters:

❏ **Original Signal (dry)**—the level of the unprocessed signal

❏ **Early Reflections**—the level of early reflections

❏ **Reverb (wet)**—the level of the signal processed by the effect

The **Include Direct** option represents the phase shift of the sound in the left and the right channels in order to coordinate the directions of the early reflections of the signal and the location of the sound sources on the stereo panorama.

The **Combine Source Left and Right** checkbox effects the combination of the left and the right channels of the sound source before the effect is applied, to reduce the computation time. The stereo image of the sound source is destroyed.

The **Bypass** checkbox disables the effect (the signal bypasses the effect).

The **Preset** list contains the names under which the effect templates you create (presets) are saved. By pressing the **Add** button, you open the dialog box in which you should give the new preset a name. To delete the selected preset name from the list, press the **Del** button.

The effect window also contains three tabs: **General Reverb**, **Early Reflections**, and **Coloration**.

The **General Reverb** tab (Fig. 12.42) contains elements for adjusting general reverberation parameters:

☐ **Total Length**—total reverberation time

☐ **Attack Time**—time to reach the maximum level of the effect

☐ **Diffusion**—absorption features of the sound diffusion environment

☐ **Perception**—reverberation perception: from a slurred sound due to many close obstacles, to a distinct echoing

☐ **Set Reverb based on Early Reflection Room Size**—automated coordination of general reverberation with the parameters of early reflections, the room, and the diffusion environment

The **Early Reflections** tab is shown in Fig. 12.43.

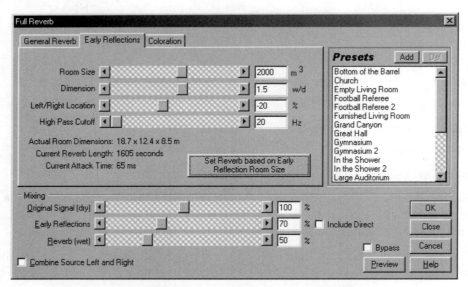

Fig. 12.43. The **Early Reflections** tab of the **Full Reverb** window

The parameters defined in the **Early Reflections** tab are as follows:

❑ **Room Size**—the room size in cubic meters

❑ **Dimension**—the ratio of width to length

❑ **Left/Right Location**—location of the sound source on the stereo panorama

❑ **High Pass Cutoff**—cutoff frequency of the filter passing high frequencies

The **Coloration** tab is shown in Fig. 12.44.

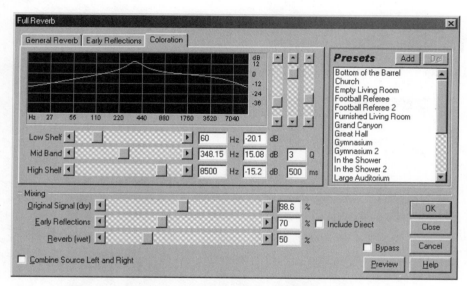

Fig. 12.44. The **Coloration** tab of the **Full Reverb** window

The graph in the **Coloration** tab is the amplitude-frequency response of the filter through which the reverberation signal is passed. The X-axis represents the frequency values, and the Y-axis represents the values of the amplitude-frequency response in decibels. The filter is actually a three-band parametric equalizer. You can use the following options to edit the shape of the graph:

❑ **Low Shelf**—cutoff frequency of the filter that controls passing the low-frequency spectral components

❑ **Mid Band**—central frequency (resonance frequency) of the band filter

❑ **High Shelf**—cutoff frequency of the filter that controls passing the high-frequency spectral components

❑ The three vertical sliders to the right of the graph regulate the signal's amplification/lowering level with each of the three parametric equalizers

❑ **Q**—this value describes how wide the mid band's affective area is frequency-wise. The greater this value, the sharper the peak of the band filter (the narrower its passing band)

❑ **ms**—reverberation time of the high-frequency signal components (the greater this value is compared to the total reverberation time, the faster the high-frequency components fade in the processed signal)

12.18. *Multitap Delay*

The **Multitap Delay** command opens the **Multitap Delay** window (Fig. 12.45).

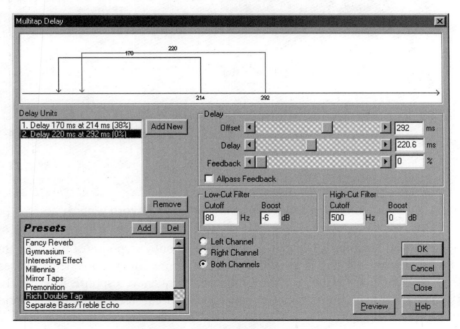

Fig. 12.45. The **Multitap Delay** window

The **Multitap Delay** effect represents the combination of delay, echo, filter, and reverberation.

In the diagram in the upper part of the **Multitap Delay** window, we can clearly see the algorithm used for processing sounds with effects. The algorithm consists of a number of loops. Each loop corresponds to a line with an arrow at the end. The numbers shown at the beginning of the lines indicate the placement of the echo in relation to the source sound. The numbers on top of the lines indicate how long the signal waits in the return circuit.

The algorithm of the effect shown in Fig. 12.45 consists of two cycles. In the first cycle, a single delay of 214 milliseconds is created, and the reverberation is created by sending the delayed signal to the feedback chain, whose delay time, in turn, is 170 milliseconds.

Not clear? Well, that's not surprising since the effect itself is rather complicated. Comparing it to a classic tape recorder reverber might help us understand it a little better. If there are two magnetic heads in the reverber—one for recording and one for playback—then we can get a simple delay effect, as well as reverberation. Let's say that the speed at which the tape moves and the distance between the heads is such that we get the heads to delay for 214 msec. We get simple delay if we send the unprocessed (input) signal and the signal taken from the playback head to the output of the device. Reverb (or repeating echo, depending on the size of the delay) happens when we turn the delayed signal—that now has a lower level—back to the recording head. Thus we'll get a repeating echo, but the delay between each repeat will also be 214 msec. Now imagine that we add another recording head to our imaginary tape recorder. The tape takes 170 msec to get from this head to the playback head (the delayed sound signal). We thus have a situation similar to the scheme presented in Fig. 12.45: a one-time delay of 214 msec, and an echo repeating every 170 msec.

In other words, one loop of the effect is analogous to a tape recorder with two recording heads and one playback. The algorithm in Fig. 12.45 consists of two loops—that's already five heads (with one shared recording head).

There can be up to ten delay units created, each with its own delay, feedback, and filtering settings. To get this result using a tape recorder, it would have to have 29 heads.

Select the effect pattern from the **Presets** list. After this, the parameters of each of the delay units are displayed in the **Delay Units** list. Using the sliders of the **Delay** group or the corresponding input fields, you can adjust the following parameters of each unit:

❐ **Offset**—offset relative to the source sound

❐ **Delay**—delay in the feedback chain

❐ **Feedback**—feedback depth

Changing the positions of the first two sliders influences the graphs of the loops. Note that all the sliders, input fields, and options control only the parameters of the current loop—the one selected in the **Display Units** list.

You can add another item to this list by clicking the **Add New** button. If at least one loop already exists, the newly created loop will take the same parameters. If there are no existing groups, you'll have to click on a **Delay** group element after clicking the **Add New** button to display the graph of the loop.

To delete a loop, select it in the **Delay Units** list and press the **Remove** button.

You should tick the **Allpass Feedback** checkbox to avoid the constant component appearing in the processed signal.

The **Low-Cut Filters** and **High-Cut Filters** groups contain fields for entering the **Cutoff** frequency and the **Boost** for the **Low-Cut Filter** and the **High-Cut Filter**, respectively. However, if you assign a value greater than 0 in the **Boost** fields, its frequency won't be cut off, just strengthened. But we don't recommend that you do this since something akin to the self-excitation of the acoustical system might occur; the level of each subsequent signal will be higher than the previous one. You might actually want to give a positive value to the **Boost** parameter if you're trying to get the effect of an echo with a unique timbre that doesn't fade, or even one that grows stronger. But you also have the option of giving the **Feedback** parameter a value over 100% if you want to simulate the self-excitation of the acoustical system.

Using **Left Channel**, **Right Channel**, and **Both Channels**, you select the channels to be processed.

It is hard to describe the processing algorithms contained in the **Presets** list. It's easier to just find a waveform and apply these algorithms to it to understand them.

12.19. *Reverb*

The next effect is reverberation. Parameters are set using the options of the **Reverb** effect window shown in Fig. 12.46. You can open this window from the **Delay Effects** submenu with the **Reverb** command.

In the left part of the window, the following sliders and input fields are placed:

❑ **Total Reverb Length**—reverberation time in milliseconds

❑ **Attack Time**—reverberation increase time

❑ **High Frequency Absorption Time**—the fading time of the sound spectrum's high-frequency components due to absorption by the environment and reflecting surfaces

❑ **Perception**—the type of reverberation: **Smooth**—a soft sound reflected from many surfaces; **Echoey**—a reflected sound reminding one of an echo

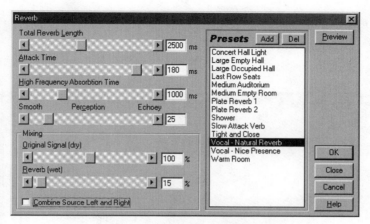

Fig. 12.46. The **Reverb** window

In the **Mixing** group, you define the parameters for mixing the source signal (**Original Signal (Dry)**) with the signal processed by reverberation (**Reverb (Wet)**).

A ticked **Combine Source Left and Right** checkbox allows you to combine signals of the stereo channels into one signal, and then to calculate reverberation and to further mix the processed and source (stereo) signals. The calculation is twice as fast, but the source stereo image of the sound is destroyed.

In the **Presets** list, we see the traditional set of reverberation variants: imitation of the acoustic features of different rooms, and popular algorithms of artificial reverberation.

12.20. *Sweeping Phaser*

The last command of the **Delay Effects** submenu—**Sweeping Phaser**—opens the **Sweeping Phaser Effects** window (Fig. 12.47).

The new sound of the waveform is mainly due to changing phase relations either between the signals of the right and left channels, or between separate components of these signals. Among the effects implemented in this window are flanger, phaser, and a great number of untitled types of processing based on sound phase transformations.

The **Filter Characteristics** group contains sliders and input fields that change the parameters of the filter used to implement the effect:

❑ **Sweep Gain**—amplification

❑ **Center Frequency**

☐ **Depth**—depth of the effect

☐ **Resonance**—resonance filter quality

☐ **Sweeping Rate**

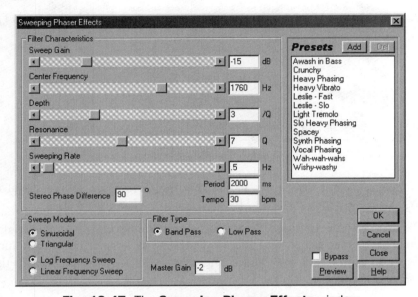

Fig. 12.47. The **Sweeping Phaser Effects** window

In the **Stereo Phase Difference** field, the phase difference of signals in stereo channels (in degrees) is input.

In the **Sweep Modes** group, you can select the sweep mode (the law for phase changing):

☐ **Sinusoidal**

☐ **Triangular**

☐ **Log Frequency Sweep**—logarithmic

☐ **Linear Frequency Sweep**—linear

In the **Filter Type** group, you select the filter type:

☐ **Band Pass**—the filter passing the band

☐ **Low Pass**—the filter passing low frequencies

In the **Master Gain** field, you can correct the total amplification by compensating the signal change when processed by the effect.

If the **Bypass** checkbox is ticked, the source signal is not processed by the effect, neither when it is previewed nor when the waveform data is recalculated. Windows of many effects provide such a checkbox or a button with similar functionality. It is convenient to use this to the source with the processed waveforms contrast.

In the **Presets** list, there are a number of original preliminary schemes of the effect:

❏ **Awash in Bass**, **Crunchy**—variants of flanger

❏ **Heavy Phasing**, **Slo Heavy Phasing**, **Synth Phasing**, **Vocal Phasing**—variants of phaser

❏ **Heavy Vibrato**

❏ **Leslie-Fast**, **Leslie-Slo**, **Spacey**—variants of the Leslie effect

❏ **Light Tremolo**

❏ **Wah-Wah-Wahs**, **Wishy-Washy**—variants of wow-wow

The next item of the **Transform** menu is the **Filters** submenu. It contains the following commands:

❏ **FFT Filter**—filter based on Fast Fourier Transform (FFT)

❏ **Graphic Equalizer**—universal graphic equalizer

❏ **Notch Filter**—multiband notch filter

❏ **Parametric Equalizer**—seven-band parametric equalizer

❏ **Quick Filter**—eight-band graphic equalizer

❏ **Scientific Filters**—Bessel, Butterworth, Chebyshev filters

12.21. *FFT Filter*—Filter Based on the Fast Fourier Transform

The **FFT Filter** command opens a dialog window with the same name (Fig. 12.48).

From the name of this window, we can conclude that a filter based on the Fast Fourier Transform is implemented here. The same dialog window and filter were also found in Cool Edit 96. That version of the software had only two filters: the **FFT filter** and **Quick Filter**. Using **Quick Filter**, you were able to quickly (and roughly) filter the signal.

Actually, the algorithms for any filter in Cool Edit Pro are all based on the Fast Fourier Transform (FFT) to some extent.

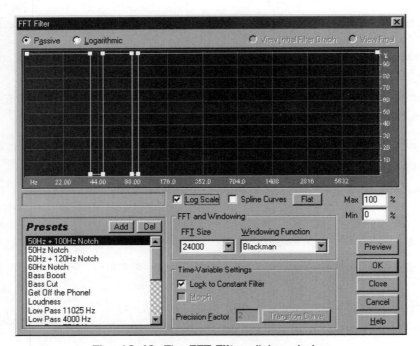

Fig. 12.48. The **FFT Filter** dialog window

We can basically say that the volume of calculations using the FFT is proportional to the product of $N \times \log_2 N$, where N is the number of sample measurements. If we want to calculate the spectrum right away, without using the fast transform algorithms, the volume of calculations will be relatively proportional to the product of $N \times N$. If it weren't for the FFT, even the most modern computer wouldn't be able to handle performing spectral analysis and signal synthesis. Hard to believe? Let's just think for a minute. Soon you'll find out that in the sample parameter configuration given in Fig. 12.48, the signal has 4096 measurements. Thus for the FFT we have $4096 \times \log_2 4096 = 4096 \times 12 = 49{,}152$, and for the "slow" algorithm—$4096 \times 4096 = 16{,}777{,}216$. The ratio is $16{,}777{,}216/49{,}152 = 341.(3)$, which is approximately equal to the time saved by using the FFT.

What do these numbers mean? Let's say that on your computer, a filter using the FFT algorithm takes 1 minute to perform its calculations. Using the regular algorithm, a spectral analysis would take almost 6 hours to do the same thing. Or you could say that for the regular algorithm to complete its calculations in a minute, you'd need a computer 341 times as powerful as yours. So you have an Intel Pentium 4 with a frequency of 1400 MHz? And soon you'll probably be able to buy an even faster processor? Even if so, a processor frequency of almost 500 GHz is not very probable.

And so, all filters in the **Filters** submenu are based on FFT. Then why is the name given only to the filter that we're looking at here? Most likely because its window (**FFT Filter**) recalls the interface of programs for implementing the Fast Fourier Transform. It even includes the special **FFT and Windowing** group, where you can assign the parameters that influence the result of filtering.

The drop-down **FFT Size** list contains the FFT sizes. The bigger the size, the clearer the sound, but the longer the computations take.

In the **Windowing Function** drop-down list, we see a list of functions that determine what the temporary window will look like, as well as how to take into account the history of the analyzed signal. We won't give you any recommendations on setting this parameter. Try working with different functions, and if you don't like the result, there's always the **Undo** button.

The element of the FFT Filter window that stands out the most is the coordinate plane that contains the graph of the filter's amplitude-frequency response. The horizontal axis measures the frequency, and on the vertical axis we find the filter transfer ratio for each frequency value.

Select **Passive** mode to have the vertical axis be expressed in percents, where a setting of 100% represents no change. 200% means that the amplitude of the particular spectrum component is doubled, and a value of 50% means that it is halved.

Select **Logarithmic** mode when you want to express changes in terms of dB, where 0 dB represents no change.

If you tick the **Log Scale** checkbox, you'll see the frequency axis using a logarithmic scale, which allows you to see the amplitude-frequency response of the filter in detail in the low-frequency areas. For example, in Fig. 12.48, the most informative area of the amplitude-frequency response is within the range from 50 to 100 Hz, and it can be seen clearly. If you haven't enabled the Log Scale box, you see a linear scale on the horizontal axis. This allows you to see the amplitude-frequency response in a more natural form with all the proportions maintained, but it will be hard to see anything in the low-frequency areas, since all the details of the graph are bunched together (Fig. 12.49).

Neither mode is particularly convenient for precisely controlling the form of the amplitude-frequency response graphically. The information field in the left part of the window under the amplitude-frequency response graph makes it easier. The current coordinates are displayed in this window, and thus this is a method that allows you to precisely define the node coordinates and the amplitude-frequency response's entire form.

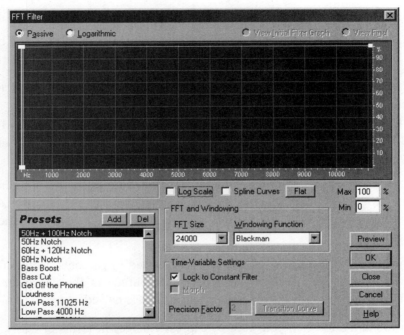

Fig. 12.49. Amplitude-frequency response of the filter when the linear scale is selected on the frequency axis

The **Spline Curves** checkbox allows you to enable the spline approximation of the graph. The amplitude-frequency response of the filter from Fig. 12.48 will then look like it is shown in Fig. 12.50. Note that not only the graph's appearance changes, but the actual amplitude-frequency response of the filter changes as well.

When the **Lock to Constant Filter** checkbox (in the **Time-Variable Settings** group) is unchecked, the amplitude-frequency response of the filter may vary within the processed fragment according to your preferences. You need only perform a few operations. Select the **View Initial Filter Graph** option and, using the mouse, place the nodes in the filter response graph. We can get an amplitude-frequency response, for example, like the one shown in Fig. 12.51. This response is the initial one.

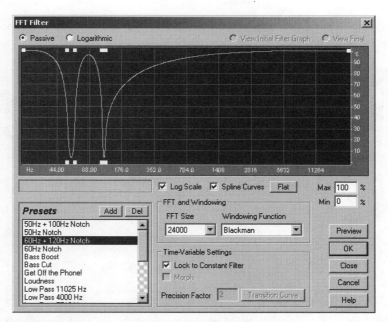

Fig. 12.50. Spline approximation of the filter amplitude-frequency response

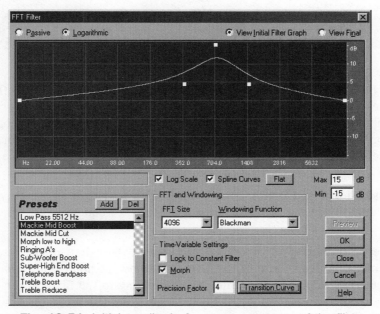

Fig. 12.51. Initial amplitude-frequency response of the filter

After enabling the **View Final** mode, you should define the final filter response (for example, as shown in Fig. 12.52).

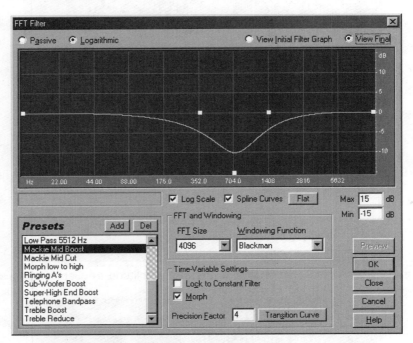

Fig. 12.52. Final amplitude-frequency response of the filter

Using the options of the **Time-Variable Settings** group, you define the mode in which the shape of the initial amplitude-frequency response of the filter gradually turns into the final response during waveform fragment processing. This is done using the **Morph** option. In the **Precision Factor** field, you should specify the waveform processing precision (the extent of smooth transition from the initial response value to the final value).

When the **Transition Curve** button is pressed, a window appears in which you can draw a graph that determines the character of the amplitude-frequency response transformation.

The X-axis represents time, and the Y-axis represents the extent of the response's similarity to its **Initial** or **Final** form. If the **Graph response at point** option is enabled, the amplitude-frequency response of the filter corresponding to the node of the graph is displayed in the lower part of the screen. You can always reset the graph to a straight line by pressing the **Flat** button.

In Fig. 12.53, the **Transition Curve** dialog window is shown, which is called by clicking the left control point of the amplitude-frequency response transformation graph. The initial response is displayed in the lower part of the screen.

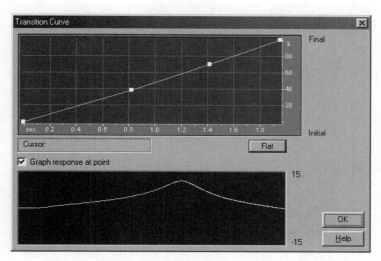

Fig. 12.53. The **Transition Curve** dialog window

If you click on the graph control point second to the left, the filter response in an intermediate moment of time is displayed (Fig. 12.54).

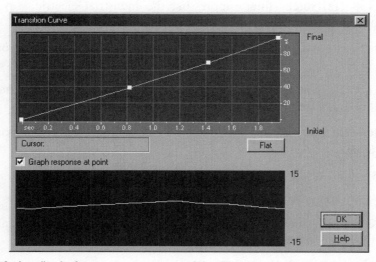

Fig. 12.54. Amplitude-frequency response of the filter at an intermediate moment of time

Clicking on the rightmost control point results in the display of the final amplitude-frequency response of the filter (Fig. 12.55).

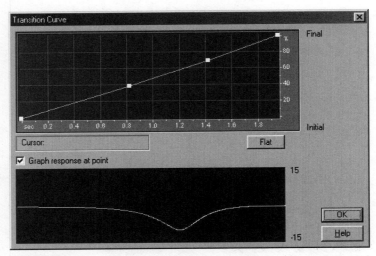

Fig. 12.55. Final amplitude-frequency response of the filter

Now we return to the **FFT Filter** dialog box. The **Presets** list contains a good number of original presets:

- ❏ **50 Hz + 100 Hz Notch**—filter suppressing the industrial electricity network background at a frequency of 50 Hz, and its second harmonic

- ❏ **50 Hz Notch**—filter suppressing the industrial electricity network background at a frequency of 50 Hz

- ❏ **60 Hz + 120 Hz Notch**—filter suppressing the industrial electricity network background at a frequency of 60 Hz and its second harmonic

- ❏ **60 Hz Notch**—filter suppressing the industrial electricity network background at a frequency of 60 Hz

- ❏ **Bass Boost**—filter raising low frequencies

- ❏ **Bass Cut**—filter suppressing low frequencies

- ❏ **Get Off the Phone!**—filter highlighting the frequency spectrum of the standard phone signal band, to ban noises of lower and higher frequencies

- ❏ **Loudness**—filter raising the bass and high frequencies

❐ **Low Pass 11025 Hz**—filter suppressing frequencies above 11025 Hz (should be used for processing signals before lowering the sampling frequency from 44.1 to 22.05 kHz)

❐ **Low Pass 4000 Hz**—filter suppressing frequencies above 4000 Hz (should be used for processing singals before lowering the sampling frequency to 8 kHz)

❐ **Low Pass 5512 Hz**—filter suppressing frequencies above 5512 Hz (should be used for processing singals before lowering the sampling frequency to 11.025 kHz)

❐ **Mackie Mid Boost**—filter raising the middle frequencies

❐ **Mackie Mid Cut**—filter lowering the middle frequencies

❐ **Morph low to high**—filter with an adjustable amplitude-frequency response: at the starting moment low frequencies are raised, and at the final moment high frequencies are raised

❐ **Ringing A's**—a line of narrow-band octave filters tuned to the frequencies of the *A* tone of several neighboring octaves

❐ **Sub-Woofer Boost**—filter raising super-low frequencies

❐ **Super-High End Boost**—filter significantly raising the highest frequencies

❐ **Telephone Band Pass**—filter suppressing all the spectral components off the standard band of a telephone signal

❐ **Treble Boost**—filter raising high frequencies

❐ **Treble Reduce**—filter lowering high frequencies

12.22. *Graphic Equalizer*

The **Graphic Equalizer** command opens the window of the multiband **Graphic Equalizer** (Figs. 12.56—12.58).

The multi-band graphic equalizer is has three main variants:

❐ 10-band equalizer consisting of octave filters; the **10 Bands (1 octave)** tab, Fig. 12.56

❐ 20-band equalizer (half-octave filters); the **20 Bands (1/2 octave)** tab, Fig. 12.57

❐ 30-band equalizer (third-octave filters); the **30 Bands (1/3 octave)** tab, Fig. 12.58

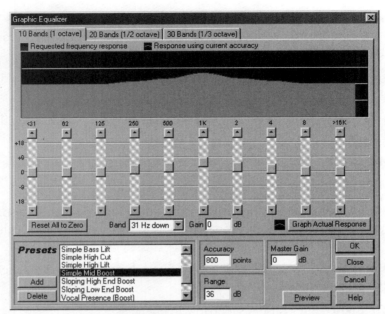

Fig. 12.56. The **10 Bands (1 octave)** tab of the **Graphic Equalizer** window

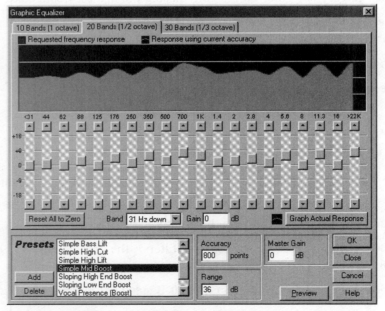

Fig. 12.57. The **20 Bands (1/2 octave)** tab of the **Graphic Equalizer** window

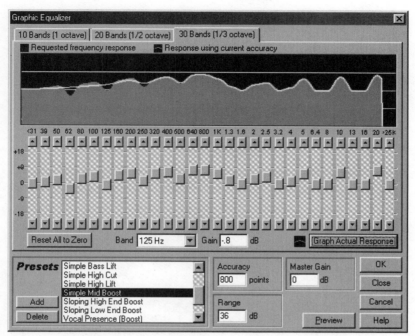

Fig. 12.58. The **30 Bands (1/3 octave)** tab of the **Graphic Equalizer** window

The purpose of the main elements of this window is clear. Using sliders, you can change the signal level at any frequency. The approximate value of the center frequency for setting the particular elementary filter is indicated above the slider. For the rightmost and the leftmost sliders, these values are not the values of the resonance frequency, but the values of the cutoff frequency. For convenience, this window contains a special field in which the amplitude-frequency response is displayed.

This window is organized rather sensibly: the upper frequency limit available for amplitude-frequency response adjustment depends on the waveform sampling frequency. In Fig. 12.58, the **Graphic Equalizer** window is shown opened for editing a waveform with a sampling frequency of 44.1 kHz. That's why all 30 sliders are available. In Fig. 12.59, you see the same tab opened for a waveform with a sampling frequency of 22.05 kHz.

You can see that three right regulators are not available. At a sampling frequency of 22.05 kHz, the upper limit of the band reproduced without distortions is not above 11 kHz. It is useless to increase the level signal at frequencies of about 16—25 kHz, because you have no useful signal, only noises and distortions.

The slider that you click on is selected. You can also move it up and down using the mouse.

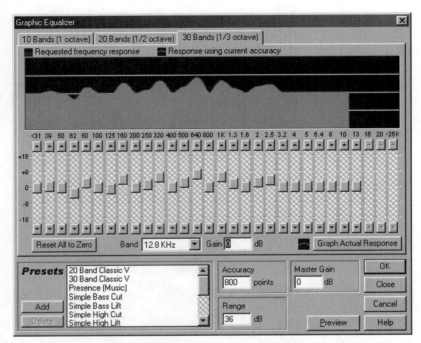

Fig. 12.59. The **30 Bands (1/3 octave)** tab of the **Graphic Equalizer** window
at a sampling frequency of 22.05 kHz

Besides amplification sliders for each of the bands, the window contains the following elements:

☐ The **Reset All to Zero** button—sets all sliders to the neutral position

☐ The **Band** drop-down list—the exact value of the center frequency (cutoff frequency) of the selected filter

☐ The **Gain** field—input the exact value of the signal's amplification ratio at the center (cutoff) frequency of the selected filter

☐ The **Graph Actual Response** button—gets the actual graph of the amplitude-frequency response of the equalizer

☐ The **Accuracy** input field—here you define the processing accuracy (recommended parameter values are 500 through 5000; the less the lower limiting frequency in the signal spectrum, the greater this value must be)

☐ The **Range** input field—select the range within which the parameter can be changed by the slider (standard equalizers have a range from 30 to 48 dB)

☐ The **Master Gain** input field—input the signal's general amplification

The purpose of the **Graph Actual Response** button is as follows. Using the sliders, you set the desired shape of the amplitude-frequency response; but to implement each of the elementary filters, numeric algorithms based on the Fast Fourier Transform (FFT) are used. When modeling any process, a numeric algorithm always gives an approximate result. The margin of error depends on many factors, especially on the digital format and the number of sample measurements. When modeling an equalizer, precision also depends on the quality level of each of the filters and the law selected for changing the given parameter, increasing the central frequency. In Cool Edit Pro, the relationship between these factors allows you to get an acceptable result in an acceptable period of time. The real amplitude-frequency response, especially in the region of low frequencies, differs from the one you define. Such errors are always present in any program of spectral analysis/synthesis, which many developers are reluctant to speak about. The developers of Cool Edit Pro not only attract users' attention to the difference between the desired and the real amplitude-frequency response, but provide them with a measuring tool activated by the **Graph Actual Response** button. By pressing it and waiting while the program makes all the necessary computations, you get the actual graph of the equalizer's amplitude-frequency response (Fig. 12.60).

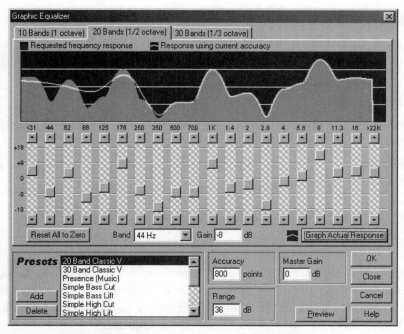

Fig. 12.60. The **30 Bands (1/3 octave)** tab of the **Graphic Equalizer** window after calculating the actual amplitude-frequency response

Requested frequency response and **Response using current accuracy** help you to remember that the desired amplitude-frequency response is marked blue on black, and that the actual amplitude-frequency response is in green. For the amplitude-frequency response shown as an example in Fig. 12.60, we see significant differences between the desired and the actual values in the low frequencies region. As the frequency increases, the difference disappears.

Regardless of the frequency area, the actual response will always match the desired one if it changes smoothly and in short intervals. Experts recommend applying significant frequency corrections very accurately.

The **Presets** list contains the following ready-to-use presets:

- ❒ **20 Band Classic V** and **30 Band Classic V**—20- and 30-band V-shape response (raising lower and upper frequencies)

- ❒ **Presence (Music)**—presence filter for selecting the musical accompaniment

- ❒ **Simple Bass Cut**—simple filter for lowering the bass level

- ❒ **Simple Bass Lift**—simple filter for raising the bass level

- ❒ **Simple Mid Boost**—simple filter for raising the middle frequencies' level

- ❒ **Sloping High End Boost**—filter for raising the upper frequencies with a slope rising with frequency increase

- ❒ **Sloping Low End Boost**—filter for raising the lower frequencies with a slope rising with frequency decrease

- ❒ **Vocal Presence (Boost)**—presence filter for selecting the vocal (raising the signal level at frequencies specific for vocal)

- ❒ **Vocal Presence (Cut)**—presence filter for selecting the vocal (lowering the signal level at frequencies specific for vocal)

12.23. *Notch Filter*—MultiBand Rejecting Filter

The filter opened by the **Notch Filter** command is used for suppressing unwanted low-frequency components in the signal spectrum. It is useful when suppressing background components at the frequency of the industrial electricity network (50 Hz) and harmonics of this frequency that appear as a result of non-linear transformations.

The **Notch Filter** dialog window is shown in Fig. 12.61.

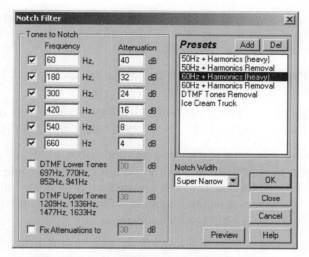

Fig. 12.61. The **Notch Filter** dialog window

In the **Tones to Notch** group, you can select the **Frequency** value and **Attenuation** for each of the attenuated spectral components.

The **DTMF Lower Tones** and **DTMF Upper Tones** checkboxes enable/disable the mode for attenuating spectral components at frequencies specific for dual-tone multifrequency modes. You can specify attenuation separately for each group of low-frequency and high-frequency tones.

If the **Fix Attenuations to** checkbox is ticked for all frequencies, the lowering level is the same (it is input in the corresponding field). If the checkbox is unticked, you can select individual lowering levels for each frequency.

In the **Notch Width** drop-down list, you can select the filter order (*Section 3.5*), and in doing this, select its passband: **Narrow**, **Very Narrow**, or **Super Narrow**. The recommended values for lowering are:

❑ **Narrow**—not above 30 dB

❑ **Very Narrow**—not above 60 dB

❑ **Super Narrow**—not above 90 dB

The **Presets** list contains the following ready-to-use settings:

❑ **50 Hz + Harmonics (heavy)**, **50 Hz + Harmonics Removal**—variants of filters suppressing background components at the industrial electricity network frequency of 50 Hz and 5 harmonics of this frequency

- ❑ **60 Hz + Harmonics (heavy)**, **60 Hz + Harmonics Removal**—variants of filters suppressing background components at the industrial electricity network frequency of 60 Hz and 5 harmonics of this frequency

- ❑ **DTMF Tones Removal**—filter attenuating spectral components at frequencies specific for the dual-tone multi-frequency mode

- ❑ **Ice Cream Truck**—filter significantly raising (by 25 dB) the level of spectral components with frequencies of 1000, 1333, 1500, 2000, 2666, and 3000 Hz

The last of these filters is particularly interesting, and needs some additional explanation. Each of the elements of this filter recalls the contour of percussion excitement with a high quality. When a short impulse (or even an oscillation with a small amplitude) whose frequency coincides with the resonance frequency of the contour meets the contour itself, a slow-to-fade oscillation with a large amplitude arises in it.

A signal with a rich spectrum (for example, human speech) after processing by this effect becomes melodic: an additional sound appears that recalls the sound of the *C major* chord. This is not surprising, since the tuning frequencies of the elements of the filter called **Ice Cream Truck** in the presets list have approximately the same relationship as the frequencies of the *C, E,* and *G* tones.

As the filter is called the **Notch Filter**, we can sort of guess that its purpose is to suppress certain frequencies. But the **Ice Cream Truck** preset is quite different. It does not suppress frequencies, but rather emphasizes certain ones. We think that the **Notch Filter** has some features not described in the user manual. After a short period of experimentation, it became clear that the filter's behavior (lowering or raising spectral components of the signal) depends on the sign of the parameter input in the **Attenuation** fields. For example, if you input 25 dB, the program understands that it should raise the frequency component by 25 dB. If you input −25 dB, this is understood as lowering the component by −25 dB, which is equal to raising the frequency component by 25 dB.

If you have doubts about the abilities of the **Notch Filter** to raise some spectral components, try the following experiment. Load any waveform recorded from a mirophone. In the presets list, select **60 Hz + Harmonics (heavy)**, and in the **Attenuation** fields, change the signs (use minuses) and process the waveform. After listening to the result, you will see that the level of the background signal has become unacceptably high.

If we take a recording of noise as the sample to be processed (producing noise is covered in *Section 13.3*), we can use the **Notch Filter** to synthesize a sound that has the five spectral components positioned in any manner. As noise is a wide-band process, its spectrum includes components at any frequency (or at least from a few hertz to tens of kilohertz), we can always find a frequency to select with the **Notch Filter**.

12.24. *Parametric Equalizer*—Seven-Band Parametric Equalizer

The **Parametric Equalizer** command opens the **Parametric Equalizer** window (Fig. 12.62)—the seven-band parametric equalizer that allows you to set almost any shape of amplitude-frequency response of the filter with high precision.

Traditionally, the amplitude-frequency response graph is displayed in the upper part of the window.

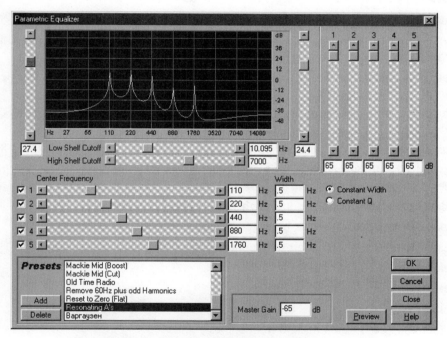

Fig. 12.62. The **Parametric Equalizer** dialog window

Sliders and the **Low Shelf Cutoff** and **High Shelf Cutoff** input fields are used to control the cutoff frequencies of the low- and high-frequency shelf filters. The sliders to the left and to the right of the graph are used to regulate the levels of raising/lowering the signal with these filters.

The **Center Frequency** group contains 5 checkboxes for setting the filters, and 5 sliders for the center frequencies. The exact value of the center frequency is displayed in the field to the right of the slider.

The **Width** column contains fields in which you can input a new quality value for the corresponding filter, thus changing the width of its passing band.

The level of raising/lowering the signal with each of these filters is regulated by the corresponding slider. These sliders are in the upper right part of the window.

If the **Constant Width** option is selected, then while the filter frequency changes, its passing band remains unchanged. If the **Constant Q** option is selected, its quality is preserved, i.e., when the tuning frequency increases, the passing band is extended proportionally.

The **Master Gain** field is used to change the general level of increase.

The **Presets** list contains the following elements:

- ❑ **250 Hz Cut with Low End Shelf**—attenuates the signal at a frequency of 250 Hz and decreases the level of low-frequency components
- ❑ **Added Dimension**—emphases frequencies around 1 kHz and simultaneously decreases the level of low- and high-frequency components of the signal spectrum
- ❑ **High Boost with 16k notch**—sharply boosts high frequencies and supresses 16 kHz frequencies
- ❑ **Highs Softener**—slightly decreases the level of components around 1 kHz and 8 kHz
- ❑ **Hum and Hiss Removal**—suppresses the component at a frequency of 60 Hz, lowering the level of components above 16 kHz
- ❑ **Loudness**—slightly boosts low and high frequencies
- ❑ **Mackie High (Boost)**—boosts high frequencies
- ❑ **Mackie High (Cut)**—cuts high frequencies
- ❑ **Mackie Low (Boost)**—boosts low frequencies
- ❑ **Mackie Low (Cut)**—cuts low frequencies
- ❑ **Mackie Mid (Boost)**—boosts middle frequencies
- ❑ **Mackie Mid (Cut)**—cuts middle frequencies
- ❑ **Old Time Radio**—imitates the sound of an old-fashioned radio
- ❑ **Remove 60 Hz plus odd harmonics**—attenuates the component with a frequency of 60 Hz and its 5th, 7th, and 9th harmonics
- ❑ **Reset to Zero (Flat)**—resets the amplitude-frequency response to a neutral state
- ❑ **Resonant A's**—selects the *A* of the major, minor, 1st, 2nd, and 3rd octaves

The regulators and other interface elements are easy to operate, since any changes in the equalizer's parameters are immediately displayed in the graph of the amplitude-frequency response.

12.25. *Quick Filter*—Eight-Band Graphic Equalizer

The Quick Filter actually works faster than any of the filters described above. However, you don't have the ability to fine tune its amplitude-frequency response, since the quick filter in Cool Edit Pro is an 8-band graphic equalizer (Fig. 12.63).

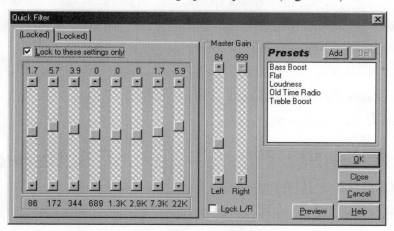

Fig. 12.63. The **Quick Filter** window

The advantages of this filter are its simple interface and the absence of "unnecessary" regulators. As with all the other processing methods and effects of this software, this filter adjusts to changing parameters (when moving to a waveform with another sampling frequency, the resonance frequencies of all elementary filters change, and the cutoff frequencies change for the upper and lower regulators).

The setting frequency is shown under the corresponding regulator, and the boosting/attenuation level is shown above the regulators.

In the current version of Cool Edit Pro, there is a more adequate graphic equalizer, which you read about in *Section 12.22.* **Quick Filter** was the only graphic equalizer in Cool Edit 96. Nevertheless, although it is simple and has an old-fashioned interface, it has certain advantages over **Graphic Equalizer**: for the **Quick Filter** as well as for the **FFT Filter** (*Section 12.21*), you can make the amplitude-frequency response change over time. To do so, you should specify the shape of the initial and the final amplitude-frequency response (initial and final positions of the equalizer regulators). The **Lock to this settings only** checkbox should not be checked. The initial amplitude-frequency response is specified by selecting the **Initial Settings** tab, and the final amplitude-frequency response is specified by selecting the **Final Settings** tab.

When the **Lock to this settings only** checkbox is ticked, the shape of the amplitude-frequency response is not time-dependent.

Using the **Master Gain** regulators, you can set the total amplification level after filtering. Traditionally, by enabling the **Lock L/R** checkbox, you can interconnect the level regulators of the left and the right channels.

You can select presets from the **Presets** groups, though there are only five of them:

❑ **Bass Boost**—boosts low frequencies

❑ **Flat**—sets the equalizer regulators to neutral position

❑ **Loudness**—boosts low and high frequencies, cutting super-low frequencies

❑ **Old Time Radio**—imitates the sound of an old-fashioned radio

❑ **Treble Boost**—boosts high frequencies

12.26. *Scientific Filters*—Bessel, Butterworth, Chebyshev Filters

The **Scientific Filters** command opens the **Scientific Filters** window (Figs. 12.64—12.66).

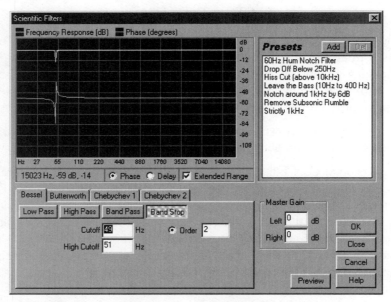

Fig. 12.64. The **Bessel** tab of the **Scientific Filters** window

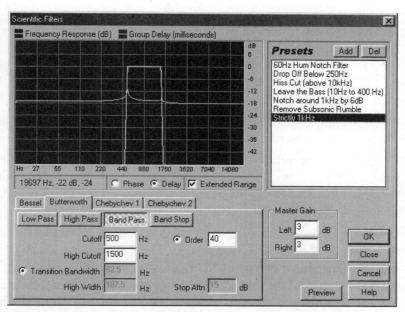

Fig. 12.65. The **Butterworth** tab of the **Scientific Filters** window

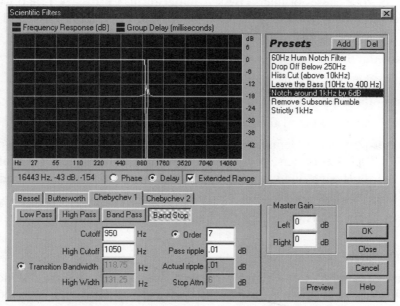

Fig. 12.66. The **Chebychev 1** tab of the **Scientific Filters** window

In the **Scientific Filters** window, "theoretical" filters of the following classes are found:

❏ **Bessel** (Fig. 12.64)

❏ **Butterworth** (Fig. 12.65)

❏ **Chebychev 1** (Fig. 12.66) and **Chebychev 2** (actually, the correct spelling is Chebyshev, but if the tab says Chebychev...)

You can learn about the features of these filters in *Section 3.5*. Here we'll describe the interface elements in the **Scientific Filters** window.

You can see two graphs: the yellow graph is the amplitude-frequency response of the filter, and the red graph is the phase-frequency response (if the **Phase** radio buttons is selected), or the dependence of the signal delay in the filter on the frequency (if the **Delay** radio buttons is selected).

Under the coordinate grid, you can see the field in which the cursor's coordinates—frequency, the value of the amplitude-frequency response, and the value of the phase-frequency response—are displayed. The **Extended Range** checkbox is used to switch the displayed range of values of the amplitude-frequency response. When the checkbox is unticked, the limits of the displayed values are within a range from −54 dB to 12 dB; when you select the checkbox, the range of the displayed values is from −120 dB to 12 dB.

For each of the four classes of filters (**Bessel**, **Butterworth**, **Chebychev 1**, and **Chebychev 2**) you can select the filter type using the **Low Pass**, **High Pass**, **Band Pass**, and **Band Stop** buttons:

❏ **Low Pass**—the filter passing low frequencies

❏ **High Pass**—the filter passing high frequencies

❏ **Band Pass**—the bandpass filter

❏ **Band Stop**—the band cutoff filter (the rejecting filter)

The number of parameters defined is determined by the filter's class and type. For the **Low Pass** and **High Pass** filters, you can only set the cutoff frequency (**Cutoff**). For the **Band Pass** and **Band Stop** filters, this parameter indicates the lower cutoff frequency. For bandpass filters, the **High Cutoff** parameter is the upper cutoff frequency.

For all classes of the filters except for the **Bessel** filter, you should specify four additional parameters.

❏ **Order**—the filter order.

❏ **Transition Bandwidth**—(for example, for the bandpass filter, it is the distance from the suppressing region to the passing region). When this parameter is selected, the filter order is set automatically (and vice versa).

❏ **High Width**—the width of the frequency band of the upper transition (for example, for the bandpass filter, it is from the passing region to the suppressing region). This parameter is specified only for bandpass filters.

❏ **Stop Attn**—stop the attenuation of spectral components in the stopband.

For the **Chebychev 1** and **Chebychev 2** filters, you can select the maximum allowed value for the amplitude-frequency response's overshots in the passing or suppressing regions: **Pass Ripple** or **Actual Ripple**.

In the **Master Gain** group, you can set the general amplification (for the left and the right channels independently).

The **Preset** list contains 7 very useful presets.

❏ **60 Hz Hum Notch Filter**—Bessel filter of the 2nd order intended to reduce noise with a frequency of 60 Hz. It is different from the previously described similar filters, in that it has almost no effect on the neighboring frequency components.

❏ **Drop Off Bellow 250 Hz**—Butterworth filter of the 6th order, which provides for a reduction of spectral components below 250 Hz.

❏ **Hiss Cut (above 10 kHz)**—Chebyshev filter of the 6th order, which provides for a reduction of spectral components above 10 kHz.

❏ **Leave the Bass (10 Hz to 400 Hz)**—Chebyshev filter of the 2nd order, which provides for reduction of all frequencies except those within the range from 10 Hz to 400 Hz, specific to the bass.

❏ **Notch around 1 kHz by 6 dB**—Chebyshev filter of the 7th order, which provides for cutting components around a frequency of 1 kHz.

❏ **Remove Subsonic Rumble**—Butterworth filter of the 18th order, which provides for reduction of infrasonic spectral components (below 27 Hz).

❏ **Strictly 1 kHz**—Butterworth filter of the 40th order that has a pass band precisely equal to 1 kHz.

Using a Butterworth filter of the 40th order as an example, it becomes clear that its phase-frequency response is uneven and complicated. By making the filter more complicated, it becomes possible to implement an almost ideal rectangular amplitude-frequency response, and in the pass band of such a filter there would be no amplitude distortions of the signal. However, the phases of the spectral components of the signal that get into the pass band of such a filter are unpredictable. This certainly affects the timbre of even a mono waveform, not to mention a stereo waveform.

We have now finished describing the frequency filtering tools of the program. We'll now move on to the **Noise Reduction** submenu, which contains the following commands:

☐ **Click/Pop Eliminator**—discovers and repairs clicks and/or individual measurement pops

☐ **Clip Restoration**—restores clipped areas

☐ **Hiss Reduction**—reduces spectral hiss

☐ **Noise Reduction**—reduces noise based on an analysis of the noise sample properties

12.27. *Click/Pop Eliminator*—Discovering and Repairing Clicks and Pops

There are various types of noise in the waveforms you record. Here are some of them:

☐ Even wideband noise (almost white; the noise in the circuits of the sound card, the noise of the magnetic tape, quantization noise, etc.)

☐ Various background sounds that get into the microphone during recording, which, after mixing, becomes "colored" noise

☐ Noises caused by non-linear distortions during an overload of the analog-digital converter

☐ Clicks caused by incorrect assembly of waveform fragments

☐ Clicks and individual measurement pops mainly caused by errors of reading data from the disk

☐ Clicks caused by scratches on the disk surface

Cool Edit Pro contains tools to eliminate the above noises, but now we will describe one tool in particular that will automatically search for and repair clicks and individual measurement pops: **Click/Pop Eliminator**.

We can say that a individual measurement pop is a "reverse click". Clicks and pops sound almost the same as clicks. Large differences in the values of neighboring individual measurements (sharp changes of the level) are characteristic of clicks and pops. Sharp changes are not natural, especially in wave processes. You can hear sharp changes in the level, and even see them when you examine a waveform with high resolution or when you analyze its current spectrum (*Section 11.1*). However, the appearance of intense clicks and pops is not very likely. Many formats of audio data storage use special codes that detect and correct a defined number of errors. The structure of these codes removes the probability of significant errors while reading the data. A margin of error comparable to the maximum value of the digitized audio occur rarely, but there are many small errors.

They are hard to detect and remove manually. You also cannot manually detect and re-move all the clicks caused by scratches on the surface of the disk. You should apply **Click/Pop/Crackle Eliminator** for these purposes.

The **Click/Pop/Crackle Eliminator** window (Fig. 12.67) is opened using the the **Click/Pop Eliminator** command.

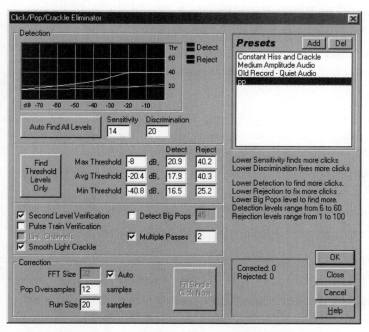

Fig. 12.67. The **Click/Pop/Crackle Eliminator** window

This window contains many elements; here we'll describe them all.

In the **Detection** field, the graphs distributing the number of found (**Detect**) and rejected (**Reject**) clicks, depending on their level, are drawn. Using the **Auto Find All Levels** button, you enable an automated search for clicks of all levels according to the settings of following parameters: **Sensitivity** and **Discrimination**.

With the **Find Threshold Levels Only** button, an automated search for clicks at thresh-hold levels is done: maximum (**Max Threshold**), average (**Avg Threshold**), and minimum (**Min Threshold**).

The **Second Level Verification** checkbox enables the second verification level, which allows you to avoid mistakes when some "useful" changes in the signal level are considered clicks.

You should tick the **Pulse Train Verification** checkbox when incorrect click detection takes place too often.

If the **Link Channels** checkbox is selected, clicks are searched for in both stereo channels. This increases the probability of correct click detection.

A checked **Smooth Light Crackle** checkbox allows you to decrease the number of errors of the same type. The **Detect Big Pops** checkbox and the input field allow you to organize the search for and rejection of long pops.

If the **Multiple Pass** checkbox is ticked, the multiple processing mode is enabled. You should specify the number of passes in the field.

The **Correction** group contains the following input fields and options:

❒ **FFT Size**—the number of waveform measurements for the Fast Fourier Transform algorithm. This value should be equal to a whole power of two. When the **Auto** checkbox is ticked, the size is set by the program automatically.

❒ **Pop Oversamples**—widens the time span for processing a click found.

❒ **Run Size**—processes several clicks—the distance between which is less than the value in this input field—as a single click.

❒ **Fill Single Click Now**—restores removed single clicks.

In the untitled field in the lower part of the window, the results of preliminary processing—the number of corrected (**Corrected**) and rejected (**Rejected**) clicks—are displayed.

The **Presets** list contains presets for the above parameters that differ in value. They allow you to clear samples with different concentrations of clicks and pops.

12.28. *Clip Restoration*—Restoring Clipped Areas

The **Clip Restoration** command opens a window of the same name (Fig. 12. 68).

Let's look at an example. Fig. 12.69 shows the left waveform, which was recorded with normal quality. The recording level was selected so that no measurements go over the maximum allowed value. In other words, this waveform was not clipped. But it is not always possible to set the recording level correctly, and thus many measurements might get clipped.

In Fig. 12.69, the right waveform is one in which most of the measurements have been clipped. The right waveform is the same as the one on the left, but so amplified that it exceeds the recording level, hence the distortions. Now we'll compare the sound of both waveforms. When the first waveform plays, we hear a pleasant female voice, and when the second waveform plays we just hear a grinding sound.

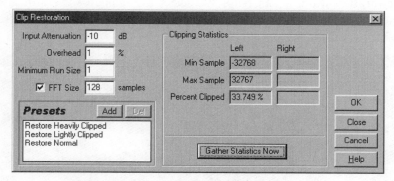

Fig. 12. 68. The **Clip Restoration** window

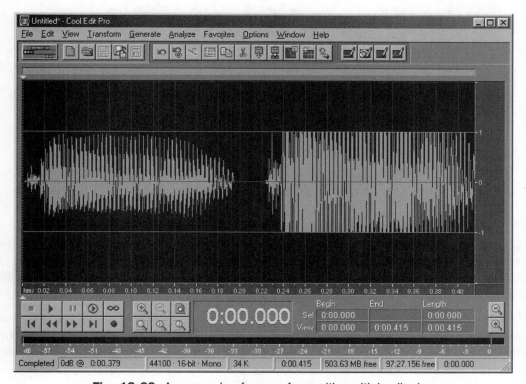

Fig. 12.69. An example of a waveform with multiple clipping

We could try to reduce the level of the distorted signal, but it won't work. The sound becomes quieter, but the distortions persist.

The **Clip Restoration** window can help. We select the clipped waveform and apply this restoration tool. As a result, we get the waveform shown in Fig. 12.70 (the distorted source waveform is on the left).

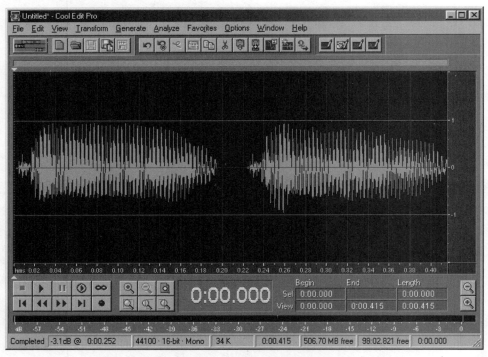

Fig. 12.70. The result of applying Clip Restoration

Most of the envelope of the clipped waveform can be represented by a straight line (Fig. 12.69), and the envelope of the processed waveform has curves, and looks like the envelope of the source waveform. Of course, when we compare the left and the right waveforms shown in Fig. 12.70, we notice the difference. The sound of these waveforms is also different and yet has a certain resemblance.

How does Cool Edit Pro know the form of the waveform envelope? From interpolation based on statistical hypotheses. First, the values of all measurements of the waveform are divided by some constant value, say 4. This gives us space to reconstruct the initial waveform within flat areas caused by clipping, since now the signal maximum value becomes 25% of the dynamic range instead of 100%.

The program then analyzes the series of measurements whose value is equal to the maximum. Assume that three such neighboring measurements are detected. The following hypothesis is then posited: the values of the right and the left measurements were probably 25% during recording, and, if there were no clipping, the value of the middle measurement would likely be over 25%.

The speed of changing the values to the left and to the right of the analyzed clipped fragment is then estimated. The value of the middle measurement is calculated using one of the interpolation algorithms.

This procedure is applied to each detected series of clipped measurements. At the final stage, the waveform is normalized.

It is just such a procedure allows you to recover clipping. But it is clear that the restored waveform cannot be an exact copy of the waveform that would have resulted if the correct recording level were set.

Here, at least three sources of errors are considered.

❐ The hypothesis does not necessarily reflect the real situation. In our example, the middle measurement could not be more than the clipping level, but could be equal to it.

❐ The speed of changing the measurements' values is not constant.

❐ In a case with a long series of clipped measurements, the values that overcome the clipping level can be changed in any manner. The envelope can monotonously rise and then monotonously fall, but its change can also be oscillatory.

Now we'll describe the options of the **Clip Restoration** window. We start with the input fields, as follows:

❐ **Input Attenuation**—signal amplification before processing. The total volume of the waveform after processing depends on this parameter. This parameter contains the information on the level to which normalization of the waveform measurement values is made. To better understand this, recall that in the example shown in Fig. 12.70 the value of the **Input Attenuation** parameter is equal to -10 dB.

❐ **Overhead %**—the limit value. After it is passed, the signal is considered clipped. For example, if this parameter is 0, only those measurements that reach a level of 100% are clipped. If the value of the **Overhead %** parameter is 1%, all the measurements that have reached a level 99% of the maximum possible level are clipped.

❐ **Minimum Run Size**—the minimum number of neighboring measurements that have reached the assigned limit necessary to consider the current fragment of the signal clipped.

❏ **FFT Size**—the sizes for the Fast Fourier Transform. The greater the size, the more precise the calculation; however, a precise calculation takes time.

In the **Clipping Statistics** group, statistics are provided for each of the stereo channels: the value of the minimum measurement (**Min Sample**), the value of the maximum measurement (**Max Sample**), and the percentage of clipped measurements (**Percent Clipped**). To get these statistics, press the **Gather Statistics Now** button.

The **Presets** list that appears contains the following options:

❏ **Restore Heavily Clipped**—restores heavily clipped waveforms

❏ **Restore Lightly Clipped**—restores lightly clipped waveforms

❏ **Restore Normal**—processes waveforms whose clipping is not seen. You may apply this processing to any waveform. If the waveform does not contain clipped measurements, the processing lowers the normalization level by 1%.

12.29. *Hiss Reduction*—Noise Reduction Using Spectral Limitation

The **Noise Reduction** submenu contains several commands that allow you to use various noise reduction tools. Some of them are universal, while others are specific. **Hiss Reduction** is a special noise reduction tool. As soon as you have learned to work with this window, you'll have a powerful tool for reducing magnetic tape noise.

The **Hiss Reduction** window (Fig. 12.71) is opened by the **Hiss Reduction** command.

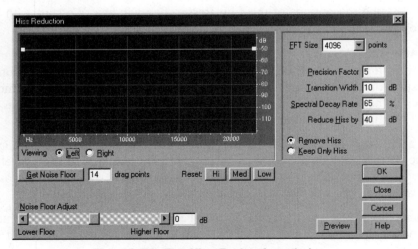

Fig. 12.71. The **Hiss Reduction** window

The greater part of the window is occupied by the coordinate grid in which you can create the graph of the amplitude-frequency response of the noise reducer. This amplitude-frequency response is not typical. We can say that it is "reversed": the higher any point in the graph, the greater the reduction of the spectral component corresponding to this point.

If you select the **Viewing Left** option, the amplitude-frequency response of the left channel is displayed; if the **Viewing Right** option is selected, the amplitude-frequency response of the right channel is displayed. In the **drag points** input field, you specify the number of graph nodes. By moving these nodes, you can edit the graph of the amplitude-frequency response.

In the **Reset** group, there are three buttons that allow you to turn the graph of the amplitude-frequency response back to its initial state (it becomes a straight line). In doing this, the same noise reduction level is set for all frequencies:

❏ **Hi**—the reduction level is −50 dB (applied when the noise level is very high)

❏ **Mid**—the reduction level is −70 dB (for middle level noise)

❏ **Low**—the reduction level is −90 dB (for weak noise)

Dragging the ending nodes of the straight-line graph with the mouse, you can change the vertical location of the graph, setting another reduction level. By giving the **Hiss Reduction** such an amplitude-frequency response, you directly reduce the noise in all parts of the sound spectrum, regardless of the presence of noise.

You can, of course, make the line diagonal or manually give it the form that, in your opinion, best fits the noise spectrum: at those frequencies where the noise is more intensive than the amplitude-frequency response, the suppression filter should go higher, and where it is less intense, lower. But your idea of the noise's spectrum might not be a good representation of the real situation. If this is the case, the noise won't be optimum: certain areas of its spectrum will seem as if they weren't suppressed enough, and in those areas where the actual spectral density is not high, the legitimate signal will suffer unnecessarily.

In the **Hiss Reduction** window, there is a very effective tool—the **Get Noise Floor** button, which starts a spectral analysis of the noise sample.

At any tape's beginning, there is always a region containing only noise. Select this region, and remember that the longer the region, the more precise the analysis results. Press the **Get Noise Floor** button. The progress indicator appears. After some time, the graph of the amplitude-frequency response of the filter appears. It corresponds to the envelope of the noise spectrum (Fig. 12.72).

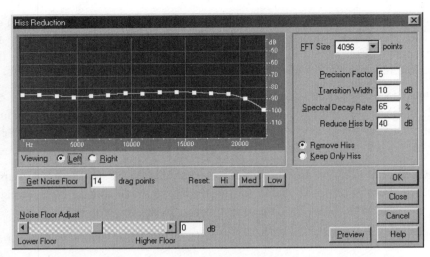

Fig. 12.72. An example of an actual envelope of magnetic tape noise

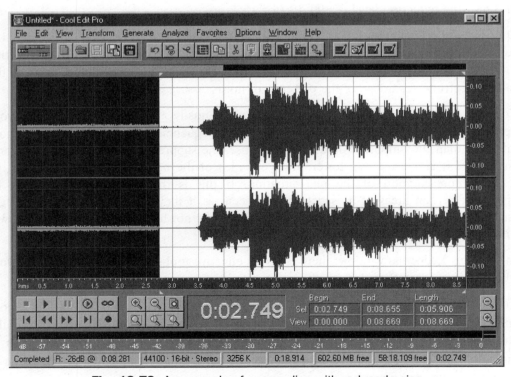

Fig. 12.73. An example of a recording with reduced noise

If after that you select the entire waveform, including the regions containing only noise and the regions containing a mix of the legitimate signal and noise, and then apply **Hiss Reduction**, the noise reduction will be optimal.

Having selected the detailed view of the waveform, you'll notice that the intensity of the noise has decreased. If this decrease is not adequate, use the **Noise Floor Adjust** regulator or the corresponding input field. These elements provide for approximate and fine adjustment of the noise reduction level, respectively, within a range from −40 dB to 40 dB. To increase the noise reduction level, specify positive values for this parameter. When you have applied all the above listed actions, the result should look like Fig. 12.73.

To make it more convincing, on the left there is a fragment of the waveform with unreduced noise. To the right there is what was the noise, and then follows the audio signal cleared from noise.

To ensure that the noise was really reduced, and to control the noise reduction, you can reopen the waveform fragment that previously contained the noise: open the **Hiss Reduction** window and press the **Get Noise Floor** button again. You get the graph of the envelope of the reduced noise spectrum (Fig. 12.74).

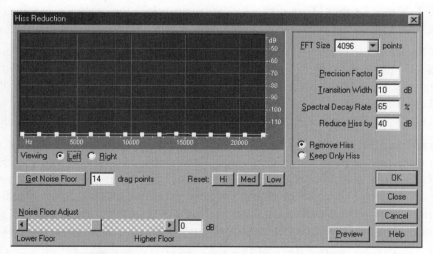

Fig. 12.74. Envelope of the reduced noise spectrum

Let's compare the resulting spectrum to the source spectrum of the noise (see Fig. 12.72). In the unprocessed waveform, the measured level of noise is within a range from −80 dB to −90 dB. After the processing, it doesn't go over −120 dB. We cannot say that these values are measured absolutely precisely. We took the noise on the tape of the unprocessed fragment to be higher than the measurement showed (see Fig. 12.72). The measured absolute value of the noise level significantly depends on the measurement method, and in part on the value to which the measurement results are normalized. But the estimation of the relative increase in quality can be considered reliable, since both graphs (see Figs. 12.72 and 12.74) were created using the same method. Thus, the noise reduction in the given example is from 30 dB to 40 dB.

The example above is taken from processing an actual waveform from one of the participants in our "Musical Computer" radio show. One of the technical requirements we have for submissions is that we only accept WAV or CD Audio files; no cassettes. However, in this case, the author wasn't able to record his work on a CD, but the composition itself was very interesting. So we thought we'd try to restore it ourselves. We were able to get rid of most of the noise, as you can see. But we eventually decided not to play it on the air due to the high detonation and the non-uniformity of its level due to the loose connection of the tape to the magnetic head. You can try to get around this, of course, but it takes a lot of time. Sometimes it's just not worth it.

The **Hiss Reduction** window also has some other options that can significantly affect the quality of your work.

In the **FFT Size ... points** drop-down list, you can select the sizes for the Fast Fourier transform.

Precision Factor is the coefficient that affects the precision of the calculation while reducing the noise. This parameter affects the external noise's fading time. Larger values give the best results, but they increase the processing time. Small values might give you a few milliseconds of noise before and after a loud fragment. Preferred values for this parameter are anywhere from 7 to 14. When the precision factor is over 20, there is almost no increase in quality.

In the **Transition Width** field, the "transition range" parameter is input. Instead of reducing the noise at once, the program gradually goes from a noisy state to a noiseless state. This allows you to avoid audible changes in the noise level. The human ear negatively reacts to the complete absence of noise in pauses, because it is not natural. Some signal systems transmitting words and phrases with pauses include comfortable noise generators to fill the pauses. Moreover, the parameters of comfortable noise are translated by radiowaves.

In the **Spectral Decay Rate** field, you input the spectral decay speed. In a waveform, the fragments in which the sound prevails are always near the fragments containing the noise, and the sound level in the decay phase can often be compared to the noise level. Correctly choosing a value for the **Spectral Decay Rate** parameter (within a range of 40%—75%) allows you to avoid cutting part of the legitimate signal, prevents the music from sounding "artificial", and staves off unnaturally long reverberations.

In the **Reduce Hiss By** field, you should specify the reduction value of those noise components that do not go over the noise reduction level set in the **Reset** group. When the value of this parameter is about 3 dB, some noise components can remain unreduced. When the levels are higher (especially over 20 dB), significant noise reduction can be implemented, but the sound might get distorted.

If the **Remove Hiss** option is selected, the noise is removed; if the **Keep Only Hiss** option is selected, only the noise remains, and the legitimate signal is removed. When selecting the parameters of the noise reducer, you usually control the noise reduction. You can almost remove the noise, but the useful signal is also affected seriously. Listening to the processed recording, you notice the absence of the noise, but it is more difficult to assess whether the signal has been spoiled or not. It is in this case that the **Keep Only Hiss** option comes in handy. Enable this option, process a waveform or its fragment (it must contain not only noise but a legitimate signal as well) and listen to it. If you hear nothing but the noise you have selected the parameters of the noise reducer correctly. Cancel this operation, enable the **Remove Hiss** option, and perform final noise reduction without changing any parameters.

If you failed to find the best combination of parameters, then after you apply noise reduction with the **Keep Only Hiss** option enabled, you will certainly hear sounds coming through the noise. This means that with the selected parameters, some elements of the legitimate signal were added to the noise. Cancel the action (for example, you can turn the **Noise Floor Adjust** regulator to the left) and try again. When finally there are no traces of the useful signal to be heard, you can stop your experiments and work with noise reduction.

We should note that the noise reduction tools we described are relatively specialized. Its main purpose is reduction of quasi-white noise, similar to the noise of a magnetic tape. In the next section, we describe another noise reduction tool that is universal.

12.30. *Noise Reduction*—Noise Reduction Based on the Analysis of Noise Features

The **Noise Reduction** command of the **Transform** menu performs one of the most useful operations. When you become experienced in using this simple but powerful tool, you will know how to reduce noise. No matter what the noise level is, Cool Edit Pro can reduce it. It may seem that noise reduction is performed without somewhat sacrificing the quality of the signal and without distorting its spectrum. Certainly this is not the case. The developer of Cool Edit Pro is not only a programmer but also a talented sound engineering specialist. He has managed to create an effective noise reduction technology that assumes the psycho-acoustic features of the human ear. Distortions are present after noise reduction, but are not audible.

The **Noise Reduction** dialog window is shown in Fig. 12.75.

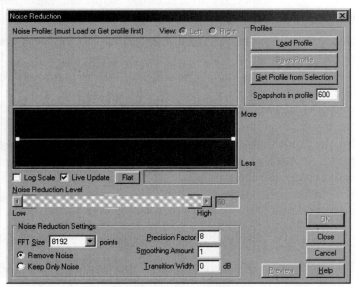

Fig. 12.75. The **Noise Reduction** dialog window

To perform noise reduction, you have to get some information on the noise. The more statistics on the noise you have, the more effective is noise reduction. How can we get this information? The **Noice Reduction** function, in a way, is like a police dog: it needs to snuff a criminal's shoe to find the criminal. Before you call the noise reduction window, go back to the program's main window and select a fragment containing nothing but noise. It would be best if this fragment is long enough to get more information about the noise. The program now considers this fragment as one containing only noise. Now call the **Noise Reduction** window. Press the **Get Noise Profile from Selection** button. The information about the noise is collected and displayed in the upper coordinate grid (Fig. 12.76).

Here, an amplitude-frequency response of suppression is given that is the same as the spectrum of the analyzed waveform fragment. The horizontal axis is the frequency, and the vertical axis is the value of spectral components. During processing, the noise reduction level directly depends on the value of the amplitude-frequency response. In the grid, you can see three noise reduction graphs: the upper graph (red) is the amplitude-frequency response of the filter for the maximum noise reduction threshhold, the lower graph (green) is the amplitude-frequency response of the filter for the minimum noise reduction level (the program creates these graphs automatically, and you cannot change them), and the middle graph (yellow) is the amplitude-frequency response of the filter for the level of noise reduction that is acually set. The value of the last parameter is regulated by the **Noise Reduction Level** slider or input (as a percentage) in the field near the slider. If you experiment with this slider, you'll see that when it is in a position on the left, the yellow graph runs into the green one, and when on the right, it runs into the red one. If the slider is in the middle, the yellow graph has its own form.

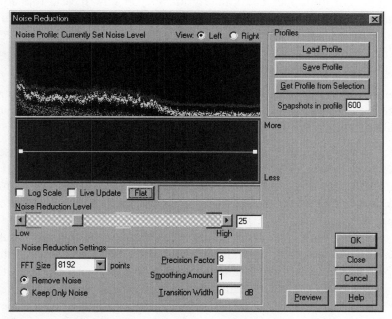

Fig. 12.76. The **Noise Reduction** window after collecting information on the noise

When the value of the **Noise Reduction Level** parameter is small, almost no changes are made to the spectrum of the legitimate signal. However, sometimes you may need deeper noise reduction. But then the signal spectrum will probably become distorted and painful for ears. We use this noise reducer to process vocals in our compositions that were not recorded under particularly favorable circumstances. We also use it to process recordings of interviews and the spoken part of our *Musical Computer* show. As a rule, at a value of 60% for the **Noise Reduction Level** parameter, external recorded noise is decreased to a level at which it is not heard in pauses at average volume. If you select a higher noise reduction level, an increase in the sense of silence in pauses does not appear, but the legitimate signal gets metallic-sounding distortions.

The yellow graph represents the dependence of the noise reduction level on the frequency. You can affect not only its total level (using the **Noise Reduction Level** slider), but also correct this level for separate frequency regions. For this purpose, the lower coordinate plane is used. To correct the dependence of the reduction level on the frequency, you can use the graph. As usual, using the mouse, you can create nodes on this graph. By moving the nodes in the coordinate grid, you can make any shape for the graph that you desire. All the actions you perform on this graph immediately change the shape of the graph in the upper coordinate grid. So you now have a tool for correcting the amplitude-frequency response that was created by the program automatically. This can be useful in cases where you cannot apply deep automated noise reduction to the entire frequency band, and must preserve the high quality of the legitimate signal. This could be an acceptable compromise.

You can save the noise characteristics in the file by using the **Save Profile** button. Then, if you want to clear the noise from a sample recorded in the same noise environment as the current file, just press the **Load Profile** button and load the file.

However, we do not recommend that you use this feature often, because the noise characteristics of the room in which the recording is made can be considered stable only when the sound insulation is good. This is not often the case with home studios, in which some sudden and non-stable components of the noise can appear. No matter what you hang on your walls and furniture, you still won't be able to get true sound insulation. Once while recording there was a car warming up throughout the whole session under our window. Another time, our upstairs neighbor decided to drill holes into his walls. One of the best features of **Noise Reduction** is that this tool, if compared to the noise reducer described in *Section 12.29*, can remove not only noise but also regular noisy signals that accompany the recording (for example, if the sound of a running car engine can be heard during the entire recording time of the sample, it can be almost entirely removed. But this noise profile is of course not helpful when removing, for example, the sounding of an electric drill).

For the files with the noise data, you can set the **Number of Statistical Snapshots in Profile**.

We have just described the most important elements of the **Noise Reduction** window. It contains some other useful options as well.

If the **Log Scale** checkbox is ticked, a logarithmic scale is selected for the vertical axis. You have already learned that this allows you to watch the low-frequency region of the spectrum in detail. When this checkbox is not selected, the scale is linear, which is more convenient for analyzing the high-frequency region of the spectrum.

A ticked **Live Update** checkbox enables the mode of amplitude-frequency response modification in real time. This means only that the graph of the amplitude-frequency response changes continuously, while the nodes of the reduction graph are moving. Otherwise, changes in the graph that is located in the upper coordinate field are made only after you have moved the node of the graph in the lower coordinate grid and have released the mouse button.

By pressing the **Flat** button, the graph of the reduction level returns to its initial state: a straight line.

To the right of the **Flat** button, there is a region in which the coordinates of the mouse cursor are displayed (the frequency and the level as a percentage) if the cursor is within the lower coordinate grid.

The **Noise Reduction Settings** group contains the settings of the noise reduction procedure itself. You have already learned about the **FTT Size** list. This list contains the sizes for implementation of the Fast Fourier Transform algorithm used for noise reduction. The higher this parameter, the better the sound processing, and the more time it takes.

You have already learned about the **Remove Noise** and **Keep Only Noise** radio buttons in *Section 12.29*. We described in detail how to use them to find out whether or not you cut some of the useful signal along with the noise.

In the **Precision Factor** field, you input the coefficient that affects the precision of the calculation. The higher the value is, the better. However, when this value is over 10, no significant improvement of the sound occurs, but the calculation time increases significantly.

We already described the **Transition Width** input field in *Section 12.29*.

The extent of smoothing done to the amplitude-frequency response is based on the **Smoothing Amount** parameter. For noise with greater dispersion (similar to white noise) you can leave the value of this parameter equal to 1—the default value. For noise with a regular structure (similar to background noise with a frequency of 50 Hz) you should try to increase the value of the **Smoothing Amount** parameter. You may be able to more completely suppress the regular noise by somewhat increasing the noise level. We cannot give any more details as to how to apply this parameter. You should experiment if you are not satisfied with the noise reduction results.

With this we finish with the **Noise Reduction** submenu, and turn to the next item of the **Transform** menu—the **Special** submenu in which special effects are combined:

❑ **Brainwave Synchronizer**—synchronizes the pulsation of the waveform sound with the brain's rhythm

❏ **Convolution**—makes convolution of two audio signals

❏ **Distortion**—enriches the timbre by limiting the amplitude

❏ **Music**—plays the melody (changing the pitch of any preliminarily recorded sample)

12.31. *Brainwave Synchronizer*— Synchronizing the Waveform Sound Pulsation with the Brain's Rhythm

The dialog window intended to control the **Brainwave Synchronizer** special effect is shown in Fig. 12.77. As the developers of the program claim, you can affect the human subconscious with this function and lead him or her into a state similar to meditation. For this to happen, the listener would probably have to listen to the processed stereo sound through headphones for a long time. The developers claim that the effect is stronger if the processed waveform contains wide-band noise with an even spectrum, but not a melody that's easy to remember. Well, a wide-band noise "affects" the brain even without the special effects. For example, sounds of the rain or breaking waves are able to inspire beautifil music or verses!

We've tried meditating while listening to this sound synchronized to the brain's rhythm more than once, but we have to confess that it didn't quite work for us. Who knows, though? Maybe it will for you.

Using the graph, you can change the features of the modulation signal during the wave-form playback. But first you should define the lower (**Low Settings**) and the upper (**High Settings**) limits of these changes.

Using the **Frequency** sliders, you can set the frequencies of the brain waves' activity. The lower frequencies—**Delta** (1—3 Hz)—correspond to deep sleep, and the highest—**Beta** (above 13 Hz)—correspond to stress. **Gamma** frequencies are higher, but no one knows what consequences the use of these frequencies might lead to.

Using the **Intensity** sliders, you regulate the modulation intensity (depth). The position of the **Centering** sliders defines the apparent location of the source of super-low-frequency pulsation of the stereo panorama. It is suggested that it is thus possible to affect the left or right cerebral hemispheres responsible for different components of the human identity. One of them controls the emotional sphere, and the other is responsible for the rational sphere. So set these sliders first all the way to one side and record the best computer music of all time, and then set it to the other side and try to convince people to buy it.

So here it is: all you need to start conducting experiments on your psyche right now.

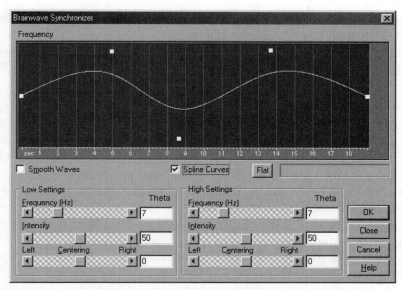

Fig. 12.77. The **Brainwave Synchronizer** window

12.32. *Convolution*—Convolution of Two Signals

The **Convolution** command opens the **Digital Convolution** window (Fig. 12.78).

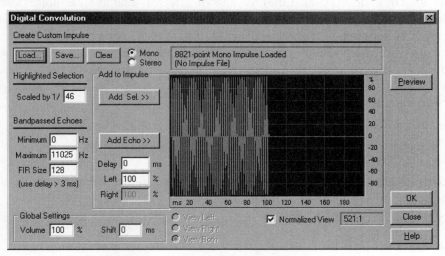

Fig. 12.78. The **Digital Convolution** window

This special effect is called **Digital Convolution** by the developers of this software, and is implemented in this window. Convolution is well known among mathematicians, radio engineers, and sound engineers. It's probably high time for musicians to understand this term and (which is more important) to learn how to apply it.

Convolution is an action taken upon a pair of signals. It can be explained like this: simultaneous measurements of two waveforms are multiplied by each other and then all the products are added up. The resulting sum is called the convolution value at zero time shift. Now, take the products not of simultaneous measurements but ones at the distance of one sampling step (as if one of the waveforms were delayed). The resulting sum will be the convolution value calculated at the unit time shift. Thus we may "move" one waveform along the other and get the convolution values depending on the time shift. In a sense, this feature uses one waveform to "model" the sound of another waveform. The result can be that of filtering, echoing, phase shifting, or any combination of these effects. That is, any filtered version of a waveform can be echoed at any delay, any number of times. For example, "convoluting" someone saying "Hey" with a drum track (short full spectrum sounds such as snares work best) will result in the drums saying "Hey" each time they are hit. You can build impulses from scratch by specifying how to filter the audio and the delay at which it should be echoed, or by copying audio directly from a waveform.

The result of convolution mainly depends on the extent of the convoluted signals' *correlation*, or how much the convoluted signals are alike or different. In general, you cannot guess what the convolution of two different signals will look like. However, for signals from some sources, their auto-correlation function (the convolution of the signal itself and its copy offset over time) is known. If, for example, a noise sample is convoluted with its copy, the convolution will look pretty much like one peak—large in size and short in duration. If a sinusoidal signal (a pure tone) is convoluted with its copy, you'll end up with a sinusoidal signal. If a rectangular impulse is convoluted with its copy, you get a triangular form. And if you convolute the end section of a sinusoidal signal (a radio impulse) with its copy, it will result in a signal with a sinusoidal carrier frequency and an envelope with a triangular form.

These statements are scientific, and we should mention that the window described in this section can not only help you get specific audio effects, but can also be a useful tool for discovering the correlation features of signals.

To demonstrate **Digital Convolution**, we will convolute a sinusoid radio impulse with its copy. The source signal is shown in Fig 12.79, top.

In Fig. 12.79 at the bottom, you see the signal resulting from the convolution. It is clear that:

❏ The convoluted signal has a sinusoidal carrier with the same frequency as the source signal

❏ The shape of the convolution envelope is triangular

❏ The duration of the resulting impulse is twice the duration of the source signal

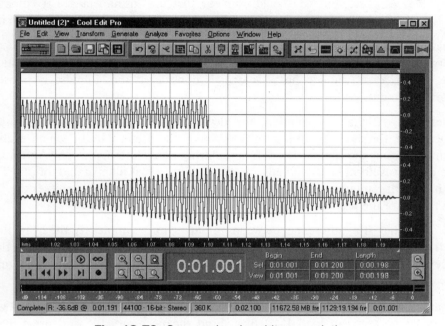

Fig. 12.79. Source signal and its convolution

This illustration also proves that Cool Edit Pro performs convolution correctly, since the result you get is equal to the expected result. Of course, the timbres of the source and processed signals are different.

Once, while preparing for our show, one of us had the chance to attend a most curious gathering of musicians. It seemed that most of them were big fans of stochasticism in music, which lead to an interesting paradox: while mercilessly exploiting randomness, these people thought that they were looking for "their own" style. They had some very curious approaches to generating random music. One of them creates the height and duration of sounds according to growth of the branches of a houseplant. Another one asks his students to pull papers with numbers written on then from a hat, one by one. Yet another uses the computer keyboard instead of the MIDI keyboard, the keys of which he has configured notes unknown to him. The most mathematical of the musicians used a program that generated pseudo-random number sequences. But now to go back to the **Digital Convolution** effect, we should probably note that, since it's generally impossible to guess the form of a signal gotten as a result of convolution, you also can't know beforehand how the sound of the sample processed with the effect will change. So the musical stochasticism apologists have something to rejoice over—they now have one more instrument they can use. And you could even say that this instrument is not empirical but scientific, based on strict mathematics. So it's now probably time to start learning how to use it.

We should emphasize that the convolution operation is a mathematical expression to calculate a waveform's changes due to passing through a filter or propagating in an acoustic environment. In this case, the second waveform is considered the "impulse response" of a filter or environment.

When describing **Digital Convolution**, the developers use the term *impulse* instead of *impulse response*, for short. By this term, they mean the preset data by which each signal measurement within the sample is multiplied during convolution. Yet only in a relatively rare case can a waveform be the impulse response of an actual filter or auditorium. Thus, in Cool Edit Pro, the impulse is, in the end, just a sample. In a particular case, the impulse could be a copy of the processed sample.

We can state that the difference between impulses and samples is the way they are treated: the former are stored in IMP files. Some of these files are supplied with the program (they are stored in the COOLPRO/IMPS directory). By convoluting the signal with impulses stored in these files, you can get different variants on the sound.

To load an impulse into the effect, press the **Load** button. The standard file load window appears, in which you can load IMP files. Find the necessary file and press the **Open** button. The impulse image appears in the field of the **Digital Convolution** window (Fig. 12.80).

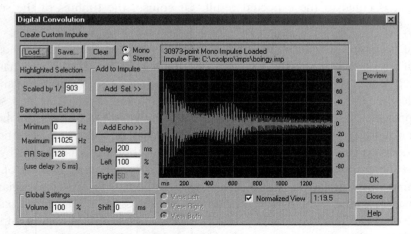

Fig. 12.80. The **Digital Convolution** window with the impulse loaded

As we have already mentioned, some files containing impulses are supplied with the program. These files can be useful for illustrating the abilities of **Digital Convolution** and for learning how to work with impulses. To achieve really original results, you should collect different impulses by finding them among your own waveforms or by recording them from a microphone.

If you have the appropriate impulses, you can model the acoustic features of any real room. For example, say you have an impulse recorded in your favorite concert hall, and you convolute this impulse with any mono waveform (the signals of the left and right channels should be formed in the same manner). As a result, you get the impression that the audio was played in this concert hall.

The technology of getting the "concert hall impulse" is rather complex. You should put the source of sound (the acoustic system) on some point on the stage, and a non-directed stereo microphone should be located somewhere in the hall. The microphone should be raised to the height at which the listener's ears are normally located. The sound generated by the source should not have tonal specifics. It would be better if it were a really short impulse (click). You should record the sound received by the microphone. Use the resulting waveform as the impulse when you perform convolution. The convolution of a mono waveform with this impulse sounds as if the listener is located in the same place as the recording devices, and that the sound is coming from some point on the stage. The reverberation features of the hall are taken into account automatically.

How can you create an impulse yourself? First, select a part of the waveform in the main window. The waveform can be either monophonic or stereophonic. The processing that we will now go through is done in the **Digital Convolution** window. Press the **Add Sel** button. It is available only when a short part of the waveform is selected that, if compared to the entire waveform, could be considered an impulse. The image of the selected fragment appears in the coordinate grid. The waveform has now become a draft of the impulse.

Pay attention to the **Mono** and **Stereo** options. If the source waveform is monophonic and the **Mono** option is selected, the impulse is monophonic. A stereo impulse results from a stereo waveform when the **Stereo** option is selected. This is rather obvious. Other cases are more complex. If for a mono waveform you select the **Stereo** option, the result is two impulses (for the left and the right channels), and the actual format of such an impulse is two-channel mono.

If you select the **Mono** option for a stereo waveform, a monophonic impulse is the result. Reverse conversion of the impulse is impossible.

The **View Left**, **View Right**, and **View Both** options are available only if the **Stereo** format is selected. They control the impulse display format:

❑ **View Left**—display impulse of the left channel (blue)

❑ **View Right**—display impulse of the right channel (red)

❑ **View Both**—display impulse of both channels

By pressing the **Save** button, you open the standard file save window. The file has the IMP extension. Name the file and save it.

The **Clear** button is used to remove the impulse from the **Digital Convolution** window. The coordinate plane is cleared.

You can load an impulse from an IMP file, or you can get it by selecting waveform fragment, but you can also combine those methods. You can add a waveform to an impulse loaded from a file. In the **Scaled By** field, the denominator of the weight ratio is shown. With this ratio, a waveform is added to the impulse. By default, the optimal value of this parameter is set, which is automatically calculated by the program. If it becomes necessary, you can input another value yourself.

By pressing the **Add Echo** button, you switch the coordinate plane to the echo structure display mode.

The operation for creating delayed copies of the right and left channel signals is added to the convolution algorithm. In the **Delay** field, you should input the delay value (in milliseconds), and in the **Left ... (%)** and **Right ... (%)** fields, you should specify the levels of the delayed signals of the left and right channels, respectively (as a percentage). The graph shown in Fig. 12.81 corresponds to a delay of 200 milliseconds.

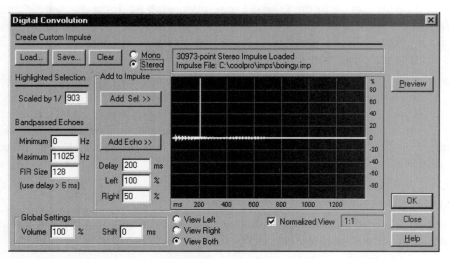

Fig. 12.81. The **Digital Convolution** effect window. The echo structure display mode

To create several copies of signals with different parameters—for example, delayed by different times—you should enter them several times in the **Delay**, **Left ... (%)**, and **Right ... (%)** fields. You should finish inputting the parameters into the processing algorithm by pressing the **Add Echo** button.

You can form a delay structure only if you have loaded the impulse first.

The **Bandpassed Echoes** group contains the input fields that determine the parameters of the filter forming the frequency properties of the delayed signal:

❐ **Minimum ... Hz**—the lower cutoff limit

❐ **Maximum ... Hz**—the upper cutoff limit

❐ **FIR Size**—filter time window size

Below the **FIR Size** field, the allowed delay values calculated by the program are displayed.

The **Global Settings** group contains the following input fields:

❐ **Volume ... %**—the amplification ratio that determines the total loudness level of the resulting signal (convolution)

❐ **Shift**—initial offset of the beginning of the impulse relative to the beginning of the selected waveform fragment

If the **Normalized View** checkbox is ticked, the vertical size is normalized so that the maximum allowed coordinate plane is used: the entire impulse image is displayed, and the details can be seen.

12.33. *Distortion*—Limiting Amplitude

The next effect is **Distortion**. It comes from the intentionally adding significant distortions to a signal. This effect is most often used to process a guitar's sound. The window of this effect is shown in Fig. 12.82.

You define distortions using the graph. The instantaneous values of the source signal are put along the X-axis level in decibels. The new signal level values (new values of the measurements) are put along the Y-axis. This operation is similar to compression, but with distortion you can also define different methods of distortion for positive and negative values of the signal separately.

By default, distortion is defined symmetrically for sound measurements of different polarity: the **Symmetric** option is enabled. If this option is disabled, using the **Positive** and **Negative** tabs, you can select and edit the two graphs: one for positive and one for negative values of the signal.

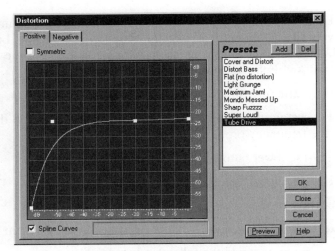

Fig. 12.82. The **Distortion** window

The **Presets** list contains several original patterns. You can listen to them and compare your impressions with the graphic representation of the processing algorithm, and this will help you select the presets you need. In Fig. 12.82, a graph is shown that corresponds to the **Tube Drive** preset. This effect imitates softly limiting the signal amplitude that is specific for electronic valve amplifiers.

12.34. *Music*—Playing the Melody

What would you say about the ability to make almost any sound musical? Assume you cannot sing at all: you have neither an ear for music, nor a voice, but you know the melody (the notes). Try to sing as best as you can, record your voice with the sound card, and, using a special processing program, listen to the result: some singer is singing the song. He or she sings better than you do, but he or she sings in your voice and does it well! This is not fantastic. This is advanced computer technology.

Music is this special function provided by Cool Edit Pro. The **Making Music** dialog box (Fig. 12.83) allows you to make a melody based on the selected waveform fragment.

This is done rather simply. Using the mouse, drag a note or pause from the bar above and drop them in the staves.

Before you start writing the melody using notes, you should select the key (the **Key** drop-down list). The key signatures corresponding to it appear at the beginning of the staves.

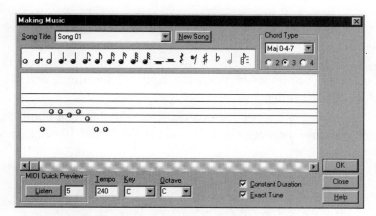

Fig. 12.83. Making a melody based on a waveform

You can transpose the recorded melody by a whole number of octaves up or down (the transposition range is +/– 3 octaves). The **Octave** drop-down list is used for this purpose. Selecting **C** indicates no transposition.

If you have to record a chord, you should first select its type from the drop-down list of the **Chord Type** group, and, using the switches, specify the number of notes in the chord (**2**—interval, **3**—triad, **4**—chord of four notes with a duplicated base tone). You can form the following intervals and chords (Fig. 12.84):

☐ **maj 0-4-7**—the *major third* interval for two notes; the *major chord* for three notes (C if created from *C*)

☐ **maj 0-3-8**—the *minor third* interval for two notes; *minor chord with a fifth semitone up* for three notes ($C_{m\#5}$ if created from *C*)

☐ **maj 0-5-9**—the *pure fourth* interval for two notes; the major chord of the 4th step (F if created from *C*)

☐ **min 0-3-7**—the *minor third* interval for two notes; the *minor chord* for three notes (C_m if created from *C*)

☐ **min 0-4-9**—the *major third* interval for two notes; the C_{69} chord for three notes if created from *C*

☐ **min 0-5-8**—the *pure fourth* interval for two notes; the F_m chord for three notes if created from *C*

☐ **3rd 0-3-9**—the *minor third* interval for two notes; the C_{m6} chord for three notes if created from *C*

☐ **3rd 0-6-9**—the *diminished fifth* interval for two notes; the A_{m6} chord for three notes if created from *C*

❑ **3rd 0-3-6**—the *minor third* interval for two notes; the E_{bm6} chord for three notes if created from *C*

❑ **?? 0-4-8**—the *major third* interval for two notes, a non-classified chord for three notes. It contains 4 semitones between the first and the third, and 8 semitones between the first and the fifth

❑ **?? 0-7-10**—the *pure fifth* interval for two notes, a non-classified chord for three notes. It contains 7 semitones between the first and the third, and 10 semitones between the first and the fifth

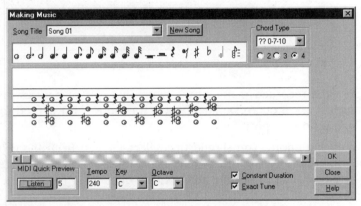

Fig. 12.84. Chords that can be created in the **Making Music** window

A chord is recorded in two stages. First, place the note on the staff from which the chord is formed, and only then should you place the chord signature.

You can vertically move notes or chord signatures using the mouse and thus shift the pitch of a separate sound or sounds of the chord. The necessary alteration signs are formed by the program automatically, according to the intervals within the chord. These intervals are defined by the chord type selected from the **Chord Type** list.

To delete a note, a pause, or a chord from the staff, drag the deleted sign and move it away from the working field.

You can select the **Tempo** according to your taste.

Before you press **OK**, which will cause your PC to be solving arithmetic tasks for a long time, you can listen to the music being made, played by any of the MIDI instruments. To do so, specify the preset GM number (the instrument number) in the **MIDI Quick Preview** field, and press the **Listen** button. If you hear nothing, the reason is probably that you have incorrectly selected the driver for the MIDI output. To correct this mistake, in the **Options>Settings** command, open the **Settings** window, and then open the **Devices** tab (see Fig. 7.1). In the **MIDI Out (Music preview)** drop-down list, select the driver.

Automatic tuning is enabled using the **Exact Tune** option. (If the waveform contains a wrong note, the program will replace it with a correct one).

When you enable the **Constant Duration** option, computations will take more time, but the duration of all the notes will be "right". Otherwise, the duration of notes might be shorter than they should be. To discover the reason for this, you should know (or at least have an idea) how the **Make Music** function works. It is based on the sampler principle: sounds of notes are played at different speeds, which results in a different pitch. The faster the waveform is played, the faster it finishes, and the note stops earlier than it should. The **Constant Duration** option does not allow the waveform to finish before the specified time.

Thus we finish describing the editing tools of the **Special** submenu.

The last item of the **Transform** menu is the **Time/Pitch** submenu, which contains the following commands:

❏ **Pitch Bender**—pitch of the waveform offset

❏ **Stretch**—transform the waveform's duration and pitch

12.35. *Pitch Bender*

Both the changing the duration and pitch shifting can be done with the **Stretch** command that we describe next. Earlier versions of the program did not provide the **Pitch Bender** command. From our point of view, the basic advantage of the **Pitch Bender** window opened by this command (Fig. 12.85) is the visible representation, and the convenience of entering the dependence of the pitch shift (or tempo changes) on the time. This dependence is defined graphically in the coordinate plane. The Y-axis represents the values of pitch shift (measured in semitones) or the tempo change value (measured in beats per second), and the X-axis represents time (in seconds). The graph corresponds to the waveform fragment you have selected in the main window.

You can control the shape of the graph by creating and moving nodes using the mouse. If the **Spline** checkbox is checked, the graph is a smooth curve. If it is unchecked, the graph is an angled line.

With the **Flat** button, you can reset all the changes made to the source graph: it turns back to a part of a horizontal straight line.

Using the **Zero Ends** button, you place the rightmost point of the graph to the zero level. This function may be useful when you need to process several sequential waveform fragments. If there is a zero pitch offset or the same tempo is at the end of each of the fragments, it becomes easier to combine them.

To the right of the **Zero Ends** button, there is a field in which the cursor coordinates are displayed (if you aim it at one of the points in the plane). The pitch shifting value is measured with cent precision (one hundredth of a semitone). The tempo is measured with a precision of one hundredth of a beat per second. Time is measured with a precision of one millisecond.

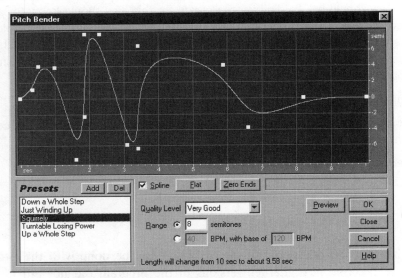

Fig. 12.85. The **Pitch Bender** dialog window

In the **Quality Level** drop-down list, you can select the quality of transformations. There are 6 quality grades, from **Low (fastest)** to **Perfect (slowest)**.

Note that when you edit audio data in the described window, the pitch of the waveform is shifted and its duration changes. If the pitch is shifted up after the transformation, the duration of the waveform decreases, and it increases if the pitch is shifted down.

Using the options of the **Range** group, you set the range for displaying the parameter put along the Y-axis of the grid. The range may be defined in one of the following formats.

❐ In the semitone format if the **Range ... semitones** option is selected. The pitch shifting up and down is connected with the scale tickmarks logarithmically. In the field, you should specify the maximum limit for pitch shifting. If you have to remove small mistakes from a vocal or instrumental part, select a limit of 1—2 semitones. This will allow you to draw the graph precisely. If processing is performed to get a large pitch shift (glissando), the limits, accordingly, have to be higher.

❐ In the format of beats per minute if the **BPM, with base of ... BPM** option is selected. The pitch shifting is connected with the scale divisions of the Y-axis linearly.

Each way of labeling the Y-axis is useful for a certain purpose. If you are adjusting the pitch of a vocal part (and as we all know, some "singers" aren't always able to get the tone quite right), select the semitone as the unit of measure. Listen to the recording and find the incorrect notes, and then correct the pitch for each of these fragments.

When you correct the tempo of a composition, it is convenient to use the number of beats per minute as the unit of measure. In the left **... BPM, with base of ... BPM** input field, you should specify the amount of the maximum displayed deviation of the tempo. In the right field, specify the value of the composition base tempo to which you are going to bring the incorrect tempo.

In the lower part of the window, you see **Length will change from ... sec to about ... sec**. This line contains the following information:

❏ The duration of the source (selected) waveform fragment

❏ How the waveform duration changes after transformations determined by the graph are implemented

You can save the graph you create and the set parameters in the **Presets** list. The developers offer you several ready-to-use presets that illustrate the abilities of this window:

❏ **Down a Whole Step**—fast pitch shift by one tone down at the beginning of the waveform, and return to the initial pitch at the end of the waveform

❏ **Just Winding Up**—sharp pitch shift by two octaves down at the beginning of the waveform, and gradual (exponential) return to the initial pitch

❏ **Squirrelly**—glissando according to a complicated undulating wave law within 8 to −6 semitones, with gradual (exponential) return to the initial pitch

❏ **Turntable Losing Power**—pitch shifting down exponentially by 48 semitones (4 octaves) of the nominal value

❏ **Up a Whole Step**—fast pitch shift up by one tone at the beginning of the waveform, and return to the initial pitch at the end of the waveform

Now you have learned how to operate yet another convenient window. However, pitch shifting has a significant disadvantage: it causes the duration of the waveform to change, just as changing the waveform causes pitch shifting. It also does not allow you to make certain pitch corrections.

In the next section, we'll describe a tool that allows you to pitch shift and change the waveform duration separately.

12.36. *Stretch*—Transforming the Waveform Duration and Pitch

Using the **Stretch** function, you can perform fantastic transformations of the duration and pitch of the selected waveform. More precisely, you can:

☐ Change the waveform playback speed without affecting its pitch

☐ Change the pitch of the waveform without affecting its duration

☐ Simultaneously and independently change the pitch and the playback speed of the selected waveform

What is the purpose of this tool? Let's return to the previously discussed example of recording a song. The stretching function would be very useful in correcting both the duration of words or whole phrases of the song, as well as wrong notes. Maybe you want to change the range of your voice, or make it very low like a monster's? The **Stretch** command is just an instrument; the result of applying it depends on your imagination.

The stretching method is based on the preliminary division of the audio fragment into small portions—chunks. Then (if necessary) each of these portions is processed. The resulting signal is combined from these chunks, and each of them can be repeated. This increases the duration of the waveform, and the pitch can remain unchanged. But this is theory, so now let's turn to practice.

The **Stretch** dialog window is shown in Fig. 12.86. Some control elements are in the **Constant Stretch** and **Gliding Stretch** tab, and some are placed directly in the **Stretch** window. These tabs correspond to two different modes of the pitch and duration transformation.

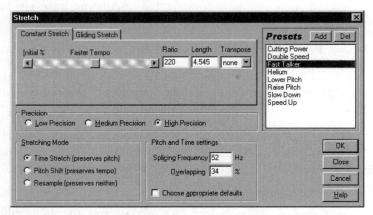

Fig. 12.86. The window for changing the pitch and/or the duration of the waveform (the **Constant Stretch** tab)

Using the options of the **Constant Stretch** tab, you can only process all fragments of the selected waveform in the same way (you can transform them over time, or pitch-shift them with the same ratio).

Using the slider, or directly in the **Ratio** numeric input field, you allow for the pitch shifting of the waveform. When the value of this parameter is 100, no pitch shifting is performed. When the value is below 100, the pitch is shifted up; when the value is above 100, the pitch is shifted down. In the **Transpose** list, you can select the number of semitones by which the pitch is shifted up or down. The contents of the **Ratio** field changes automatically.

In the **Length** input field, you specify the ratio for changing the duration of the waveform (or the tempo of the composition). You can change this value using the **Lower Pitch** slider. However, this parameter may be not available (this depends on the mode set in the **Stretching Mode** group).

You can gradually change the pitch and the tempo within the selected waveform fragment. To do so, select the **Gliding Stretch** tab (Fig. 12.87) and define the **Initial %** and **Final %** values of the above parameters.

In the **Precision** group, the precision of calculations is defined: **Low Precision**, **Medium Precision**, or **High Precision**.

In the **Stretching Mode** group, you can select one of these operating modes:

❑ **Time Stretch (preserves pitch)**—stretching (or compressing) the waveform with a fixed pitch

❑ **Pitch Shift (preserves tempo)**—pitch shifting with a fixed waveform duration

❑ **Resample (preserves neither)**—simultaneously changing the pitch and the duration of the waveform

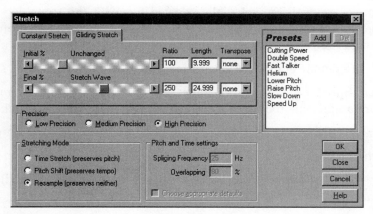

Fig. 12.87. The window for changing the pitch and/or the duration of the waveform (the **Gliding Stretch** tab)

In the **Pitch and Time Settings** group, parameters whose values should be selected experimentally for each particular waveform are defined.

❑ **Splicing Frequency**—The splicing frequency determines the size of the chunk of audio data used when preserving the pitch or the tempo while expanding or stretching a waveform. The higher the value, the more precise the placement of stretched audio over time. At a higher precision, lower splicing frequencies may add a stutter or echo; if the frequency is too high, it may sound tinny, or like talking through a tunnel. For noisy or atonal waveforms with a wide spectrum, the value of this parameter is not that important, and it won't hurt to keep the default value. If you transform a waveform containing a pure tone, choose an interval rate that's evenly divisible into the frequency of the sample with the **Frequency Analysis** dialog window (*Section 14.1*). Then, divide the measured value by a whole number to get the best value for the **Splicing Frequency** parameter. For example, if the tone was reported to be 438 Hz, dividing by 20 gives us 21.9 Hz. Thus, using 21.9 Hz as the interval rate will greatly improve the quality by reducing phase distortions.

❑ **Overlapping**—the extent of chunk overlapping. When stretching or compressing, chunks of audio are overlapped with previously transformed chunks. This setting determines how much the current chunk will overlap with the previous and next ones. If you find you are getting a chorus effect when stretching, you can lower the overlapping percentage; however, doing so may produce a "choppy" sound. If it does, adjust the overlapping to strike a balance between the side effects.

❑ **Choose appropriate defaults**—set the values of the above parameters by default.

If it is hard for you to understand these settings, experiment with **Presets**.

❑ **Cutting Power**—gradually stretches the selected fragment (no stretching at the beginning of the waveform, and at the end it is multiplied by 5). For monotonic waveforms, it sounds like a gunshot or a flying missile.

❑ **Double Speed**—doubly compresses over time, with a simultaneous pitch shift up.

❑ **Fast Talker**, **Speed Up**—variants of increasing the tempo (if the entire waveform is selected) or compressing the waveform fragment over time with the pitch preserved.

❑ **Helium**, **Raise Pitch**—variants of shifting the pitch up, with the duration preserved.

❑ **Lower Pitch**—lowering the pitch of the selected waveform, with the duration preserved.

❑ **Slow Down**—slowing down the tempo (if the entire waveform is selected) or stretching the fragment over time 1.5 times, with the pitch preserved.

With this, we finish describing the abilities of Cool Edit Pro to transform an existing sound (the **Transform** menu), and will now start describing the next menu—**Generate**.

Chapter 13: The *Generate* Menu— Sound Generation

Up until now, we have been discussing only digitized sound editing. However, you can initially synthesize the sound in digital format and calculate its parameters using mathematical methods. We'll now describe how to do this using the tools in Cool Edit Pro.

The **Generate** menu contains the following commands:

❑ **Silence**—generates silence

❑ **DTMF Signals**—generates dual-tone multi-frequency signals

❑ **Noise**—generates noise

❑ **Tones**—generates tone

Before we start describing these functions, we have to mention that the beginning of the generated signal will be placed at the current marker position in the waveform.

13.1. *Silence*—Generating Silence

Sometimes it becomes necessary to put silence (a waveform fragment that does not contain sound) into a waveform, for example, to lengthen a pause between two phrases. You can do this using the dialog box shown in Fig. 13.1.

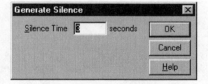

Fig. 13.1. Dialog box for pause duration input

Before you select the **Generate>Silence** command, put the marker at the position in the waveform where you want to insert the pause (Fig. 13.2).

Generating silence is very easy: in the **Generate Silence** dialog box, specify the pause duration (in seconds) and click **OK** or press <Enter>. As a result, the samples of the initial waveform are moved to the left and to the right from the position where the marker was in the initial waveform (Fig. 13.3).

Cool Edit Pro provides another method of inserting silence as well—the **Transform> Silence** command (*Section 12.3*). It somewhat differs from the **Generate>Silence** command. The latter command allows you to specify the duration of the pause between existing samples of the waveform, while the **Transform>Silence** command replaces samples contained within the selected waveform fragment with silence.

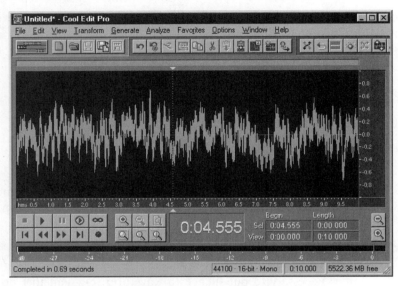

Fig. 13.2. Select the pause's starting position

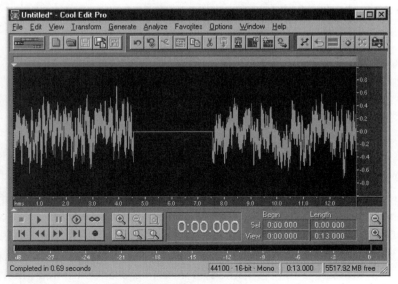

Fig. 13.3. Silence inserted into a waveform

13.2. *DTMF Signals*—Generating Dual Tone Multifrequency (DTMF) Signals

The **DTMF Signals** function does not seem to be very useful, but we'll describe how to use it anyway. Dual-tone multifrequency signals are generated using the dialog window shown in Fig. 13.4.

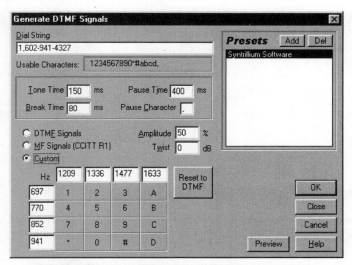

Fig. 13.4. Generating dual-tone multifrequency signals

To generate dual-tone signals, input the combination of digits and special characters in the **Dial String** window. In the **Usable Characters** field, the permitted characters are listed: **1, 2, 3, 4, 5, 6, 7, 8, 9, *, #, a, b, c, d**.

The **Tone Time** field is used to define the tone's duration. In the **Break Time** field, you should specify the duration of the pause formed automatically between tones.

In the **Pause Time** field, specify the duration of the pause formed within the sequence of characters at the position pointed to by the pause character. Using a pause may become necessary, for example, when you dial a long distance number. If you do not insert the pause character between the character indicating a long distance call and the number, the telephone station may not have enough time to make the necessary connection. You can insert the pause character in the **Pause Character** field. By default, a comma is used as a pause character.

If the **DTMF Signals** option is selected, Cool Edit Pro will generate DTMF signals, in which frequency combinations of 697, 770, 852, 941, 1209, 1336, 1477, and 1633 Hz are used.

When you select the **MF Signals (CCITT R1)** option, the program will generate MF signals specific for internal telephone networks that use frequency combinations of 700, 900, 1100, 1300, 1500, and 1700 Hz.

You can map a pair of arbitrary frequencies to each of the allowed characters. To do this, select the **Custom** option. Fields where you can input values of these frequencies become available. Characters are organized into a table. A pair of frequencies (one of them is a column, the other is a row) corresponds to each character.

The **Amplitude** field is used to input the amplitude of the generated signal. The value is defined as percentage of the maximum allowed value.

Using the **Reset to DTMF** button, you cancel custom frequencies and return to the initial frequencies for DTMF signals.

13.3. *Noise*—Generating Noise

Sometimes it becomes necessary to generate noise. Cool Edit Pro provides this ability. The **Generate Noise** dialog window is shown in Fig. 13.5.

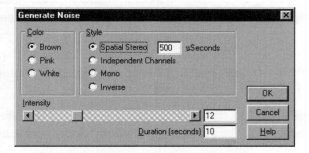

Fig. 13.5. Noise generation dialog window

In the **Color** group, you specify the parameter describing the spectral composition of noise. Each color: **Brown**, **Pink**, or **White**—has its own characteristics. To better understand, we'll use an analogy between light and sound waves. The minimum frequency of the optical spectrum visible to humans is red (that is, about 20 Hz for sound), the maximum frequency is violet (that is, about 20 kHz for sound).

"Brown" noise has a spectral frequency of $1/f^2$; "pink"—$1/f$, where f represents the spectral components' frequency. This means that "brown" noise has many more low-frequency (red) components. "Pink" noise also contains many red components, but the rest of its spectral components have more energy than those in "brown" noise. The noise containing all the accepted sound frequencies in equal proportions is called *white*. Indeed, white sound (as well as white light) cannot be generated. Even sunlight is not really white.

In the **Style** group, you specify the method of noise generation.

Spatial Stereo. Here, sound is generated by mixing three noise components from one noise generator. The output signal is delayed by the time period the user specifies in the **... μSeconds** input field. One of the noise sources is put on the left, the second on the right, and the third in the middle. This makes the impression of the sound coming from all around. The minimum delay value is zero, and the noise is mono (signals from all of the three sources are equal).

Another way to generate noise is by using **Independent Channels**. Two independent noise generators are used for each stereo channel. **Mono** is mono noise (one noise generator for stereo channels). And **Inverse** is when one noise generator is used but signals in the right and the left channels have different signs (they are inverted relative to each other). The listener gets the impression that the noise source is in his or her head.

Define the noise intensity using the slider or the **Intensity** input field (as a percentage of the maximum sample value in the generated noise signal). This parameter corresponds to the dispersion of the randomly formed process. The upper limit of the intensity level is 40%, because even when intensity is from 10% to 20%, many samples in the generated noise are clipped.

In the **Duration (seconds)** field, you define the duration of the generated noise waveform.

A waveform containing white noise might look something like Fig. 12.6.

White noise generated by the program can be considered a wide band signal whose spectrum is evenly spread within the area of sound frequencies. In other words, such noise contains oscillations of all sound frequencies. Any of these frequencies or frequency regions can be singled out using a filter. This means that you are using the *subtractive method of sound synthesis*.

If you want to synthesize a sound based on a noise process (for example, the wind blowing, the sound of a space shuttle starting), you may do as follows. Generate a waveform containing noise (see Fig. 13.6). Using the **Transform>Filters>FFT Filter** command, open the window of the filter based on the Fast Fourier Transform (FFT) (*Section 12.21*). Build the chart of the filter's initial amplitude-frequency response (Fig. 13.7).

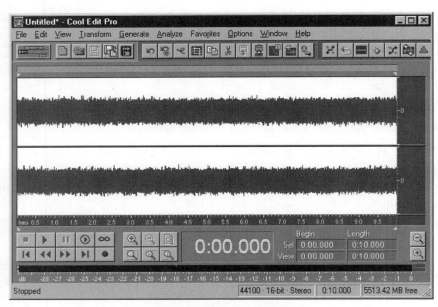

Fig. 13.6. Generated white noise

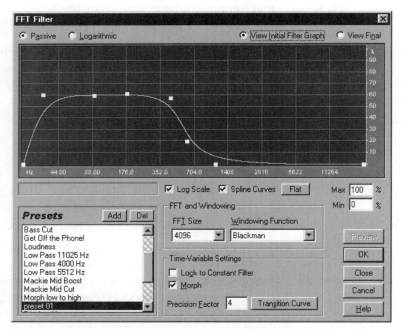

Fig. 13.7. Chart of the filter's initial amplitude-frequency response

When the amplitude-frequency response looks like this, low frequency components are emphasized at the beginning of the noise waveform.

Then, create the final amplitude-frequency response (Fig. 13.8).

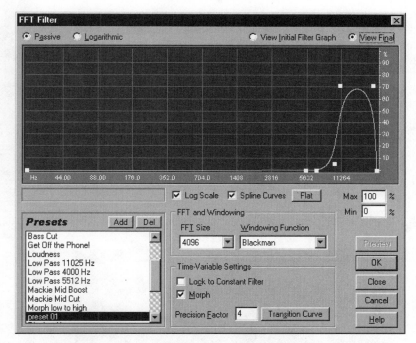

Fig. 13.8. Graph of the filter's final amplitude-frequency response

At the end of the waveform, high frequency components of the signal spectrum are emphasized.

At intermediate points of the waveform, the amplitude-frequency response maximum is "sliding" along the frequency axis.

Finally, we get a waveform (Fig. 13.9) whose sound really recalls a space shuttle starting up.

You can apply the described method not only for generating noise. For example, if you select the **Ringing A's** preset in the **FFT Filter** window (Fig. 13.10) and process the noise with a filter with such an amplitude-frequency response, you will hear melodic sounds created from the *A* notes of seven octaves instead of noise.

In the next section, we'll discuss another tool of musical sound synthesis, in which another classical synthesis method—the *additive method*—is used.

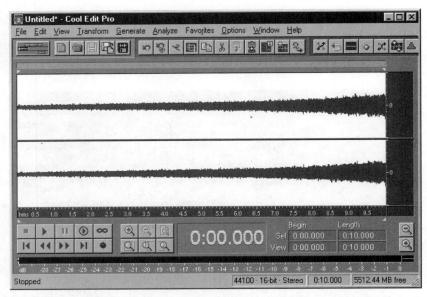

Fig. 13.9. A waveform with the synthesized sound of a space shuttle starting

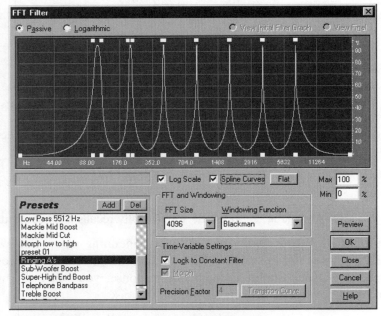

Fig. 13.10. An example of a filter's amplitude-frequency response for selecting musical sounds from noise

13.4. *Tones*—Generating Tone

This function may be useful when creating musical waveforms of your own that you intend to later process in a sampler. You can generate sound with a relatively complex timbre. Open the **Generate Tones** dialog window (Fig. 13.11).

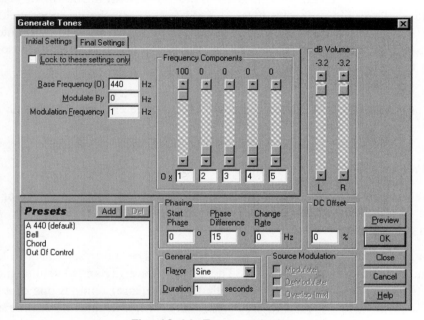

Fig. 13.11. Tone generation

As is traditional for Cool Edit Pro, you can alter the generation parameters during waveform generation. To define the initial parameter values, select the **Initial Settings** tab (see Fig. 13.11). The final parameters are defined using the options of the **Final Settings** tab. If you want generation parameters to remain fixed for all generated audio data, check the **Lock to these settings only** checkbox.

Now we'll describe the options of the **Generate Tones** window.

Base Frequency (0) is the base signal frequency. **Modulate By** is the frequency of the signal that modulates the base signal. **Modulation Frequency** sets the modulation frequency.

In the **Frequency Components** group, the levels and frequencies of five spectral components (harmonics) of the generated signal are defined. The frequency of each harmonic is defined indirectly, relative to the base frequency. For example, if the base frequency is 220 Hz, and a coefficient of 4 (for the fourth harmonic) is defined, the frequency of this harmonic is $220 \times 4 = 880$ Hz.

You can also set the coefficients in the **O x** input fields, found under the amplitude regulators for the harmonic components of the signal generated. This means that the signal—for example, one based on sinusoids—is not necessarily made up of just the first 5 harmonics. If you input, for example, 1, 3, 5, 7, and 9 in the described fields, the sinusoid signal is created from the base tone sinusoid and its four odd harmonics. If you input values of 1, 2, 4, 6, and 8, the signal is created from the base tone sinusoid and its four even harmonics. The timbres of these signals are quite different.

For synthesis, you can select any sequence of harmonics, for example 1, 4, 7, 12, 23. If you don't want the synthesized sounds to be completely unreal, remember that in natural physical processes, when sound is generated, the amplitude of spectral components as a rule decreases with the frequency's (harmonic number) increase.

The **dB Volume** group is used to regulate the level of the generated signal.

In the **General** group, you can define the form of the flavoring signal (**Flavor**) and the signal duration in seconds (**Duration**). By "flavoring", we mean the form of the wave used for sound generation.

The form of the wave significantly affects the timbre. The most "soft" and "cold" sounds correspond to a sinusoidal (**Sine**) wave. The triangle wave (**Triangle**) sounds more rough and "electronic". The sound of the rectangular wave (**Square**) reminds one of a computer speaker. The **Sawtooth** wave has the roughest sound. More complex flavors are also available, such as sinusoid to the second power (**Sine^2**), "inverted" sinusoid (**Inv Sine**), **Inv Sine^2**, sinusoid to the third power (**Sine^3**), and **Inv Sine^3**.

Generate the sound using different flavors, and examine the form of the signal. Use the zoom button in the main window. An example of Inv Sine^3 is shown in Fig. 13.12.

In the **Phasing** group, the parameters of stereo channel phase control are defined. The phases of signals of the right and left channels are different, and thus the impression of stereo sound is produced. **Start Phase** is the initial phase of sound oscillations with the assigned form of the wave. **Phase Difference** is the phase difference (phase shift) between the left and right channels. **Change Rate** is the phase shift frequency (the number of 360° full turns of the phase shift per second).

There is yet another way to generate tones. It does not generate a sound, but rather modulates (**Modulate**) or demodulates (**DeModulate**) the selected waveform fragment by the generated signal with the assigned parameters. It can lead to fantastic results.

We must mention that if you have selected a waveform fragment, but have not selected any of the options from the **Source Modulation** group, the generated signal will replace the selected waveform fragment.

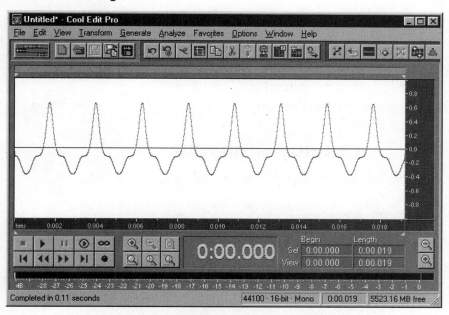

Fig. 13.12. Inv Sine^3 type flavoring

Now you can experiment with combining sound generation methods and various parameters. The number of values for options in the window for all kinds of sound generation (and thus the number of timbres) is infinite. You might even create a new timbre destined to become wildly popular among musicians.

Chapter 14: The *Analyze* Menu— Analyzing Audio Data

The Cool Edit Pro editor is a powerful tool that allows you to record, edit, process, and generate sounds, but it also provides analytical abilities to users. The **Analyze** menu contains two commands:

❑ **Frequency Analysis**—does a frequency (spectral) analysis

❑ **Statistics**—gets statistics on the waveform and the histogram of sample values

14.1. The Frequency Analysis

The frequency (spectral) analysis dialog window **Analysis** is shown in Fig. 14.1.

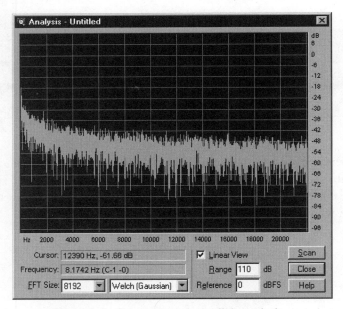

Fig. 14.1. Spectral analysis dialog window

When you open the **Analysis** window, the spectrum of a short waveform fragment is calculated (the marker position corresponds to the fragment's beginning). If the waveform fragment (or even the entire waveform) is selected, the extract of the signal in the middle of the selected fragment is analyzed. It is obvious that based just on an extract, you cannot get the full picture of the signal's spectrum.

To start a spectral analysis of the entire selected fragment (or the entire waveform), press the **Scan** button. Some time after the spectrum calculation is completed, the image changes.

Calculation is done separately for the right and left channels. On the chart, spectrogram curves for different channels have different colors.

If you have some experience in operating an analyzer and have some professional knowledge, you can find even a tiny area where interference energy is concentrated in a chart using the signal spectrum. Then, using a filter, you can remove this part and considerably improve the sound/noise ratio.

If the window with the spectrum chart seems small to you, you can enlarge it traditionally, using the mouse.

Now let's look at the chart. The horizontal axis represents the frequency (in Hz), and the vertical axis represents the level of the signal's components at this frequency.

When the **Linear View** checkbox is checked, the horizontal axis is marked in linear scale. The linear scale is more convenient for viewing the entire spectrum, including its high-frequency region. If you do not select this checkbox, the horizontal axis is marked in logarithmic scale. The logarithmic scale allows you to observe the low-frequency area of the spectrum in detail. For comparison, in Fig. 14.2, the logarithmic scale is shown along the frequency axis, and in Fig. 14.1 we see the spectrum of the same noise signal using a linear scale.

In the **Range ... dB** input field, you specify the range of values of the spectral function shown along the vertical axis. If you want to analyze the chart of the spectrum throughout the entire range of its change, specify a bigger value for this parameter. The maximum allowed range is 240 dB. If you specify a value greater than 240, the program automatically sets a range of 240 dB. Practice shows that it is not reasonable to set a range over 120 dB. When you need to watch the chart in more detail, set a smaller range of displayed values.

You might need to move the chart vertically in order to observe the spectral function in detail in a specific region. In the **Reference ... dBFS** field, you can specify the offset value from zero for the chart. Don't forget to set a value of zero for this parameter before you start to measure absolute values of the spectral function for any frequencies. Otherwise, a systematic error in measurement will occur equal to the offset you have specified.

Pay attention to the fact that the numbers displayed in the **Cursor** field are not the mouse cursor coordinates. The values you see in this field are the mouse cursor coordinates on the frequency axis and the corresponding value of the spectrum.

This simplifies calculation of the spectrum values. You need not find the exact point. All you need is the required frequency value in the **Cursor** field, and the program will automatically calculate and display the spectrum value for it.

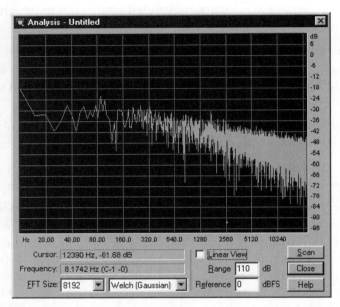

Fig. 14.2. The noise spectrum when the frequency axis is scaled logarithmically

In the **Frequency** field, the frequencies of spectral components where the maximum amount of energy is concentrated (the frequencies of the highest peaks on the chart) are shown for the signals in the right and left channels.

In the **FFT Size** drop-down list, there are several standard values for the size of the FFT (Fast Fourier Transform). The drop-down list to the right contains variations of this conversion, and each of them has its own plusses and minuses (*Sections 2.3—2.5*).

The spectral analyzer window is not modal, i.e., it exists as if it was independent from the program's main window. In other words, the **Analysis** window may remain open while you are working with the main window (select waveform fragments, move the marker, etc.). All changes made to a waveform immediately affect the spectrum. This is done for the user's convenience: while working with a waveform, you immediately see the results of spectral analysis. Also, if the Fast Fourier Transform size is set equal to 1024 or less, you can reproduce the sound and watch how the dynamics of its spectrum change at the same time.

14.2. *Statistics*—Getting Statistics on the Waveform

The **Waveform Statistics** dialog window consists of two tabs: **General**—statistics on the waveform parameters, and **Histogram**—a histogram of the waveform sample values.

14.2.1. The *General* Tab

The **General** tab that contains the statistics information on the selected audio fragment (or the entire waveform) is shown in Fig. 14.3.

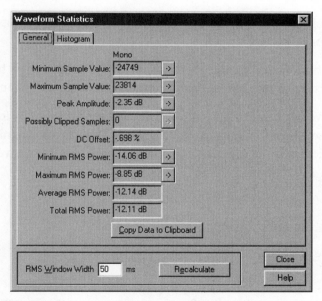

Fig. 14.3. The **General** tab of the Waveform Statistics dialog window

In columns for the left and the right channels, the following information is provided:

- **Minimum Sample Value**—minimum value of the sound measurements
- **Maximum Sample Value**—maximum value of the sound measurements
- **Peak Amplitude**—signal peak amplitude
- **Possibly Clipped Samples**—number of measurements that have the same level as the maximum or minimum quantized value

❏ **DC Offset**—the average value of the samples (the level of the constant component in the selected waveform fragment)

❏ **Minimum/Maximum RMS Power**—the maximum and minimum root-mean-square (RMS) values of the signal (the fragment length is defined in the **RMS Window Width** field)

❏ **Average RMS Power**, **Total RMS Power**—variants of the root-mean-square values of the signal

In the **RMS Window Width ... ms** field, you can change the size of the window in which the program displays the RMS while searching for minimum and maximum values.

If you decide to change the fragment length, the RMS deviation is recalculated after the **Recalculate** button is pressed.

Most fields have buttons having the **->** character. By pressing such a button, the marker in the waveform is set to the sample that corresponds to a certain parameter.

If you want to save parameter values in a file for further printing or, for example, inserting into a Microsoft Word document, use the **Copy Data to Clipboard** button. The tab's contents are copied into the clipboard. Below, we show a text received this way in the window shown in Fig. 14.3.

```
            Mono

Min Sample Value:          -24749

Max Sample Value:           23814

Peak Amplitude:            -2.36 dB

Possibly Clipped:              0

DC Offset:                 -.699

Minimum RMS Power:        -14.07 dB

Maximum RMS Power:         -8.86 dB

Average RMS Power:        -12.15 dB

Total RMS Power:          -12.12 dB

Using RMS Window of 50 ms
```

14.2.2. The *Histogram* Tab

The **Histogram** tab, containing the histogram of the sample values of the selected waveform fragment, is shown in Fig. 14.4.

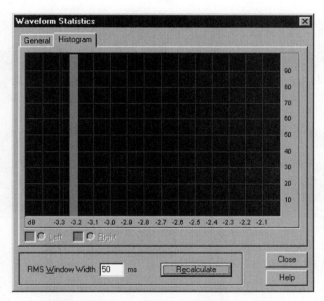

Fig. 14.4. The **Histogram** tab of the **Waveform Statistics** dialog window

A *histogram* is a common form of representing information on any process. In our case, a histogram is a chart in which the number of samples whose RMS value is within the given interval depends on the sample value in dB. To make this more clear, in Fig. 14.4 there is a histogram of a mono waveform that contains a sinusoid signal created using the **Generate>Tones** command. In this case, we know that when the signal was created, its amplitude was set equal to −3.2 dB. The histogram shows this fact correctly. 100% of the samples are within the interval from −3.25 to −3.20 dB. The analyzed signal does not contain samples with large values. If you want to convert the amplitude of such a signal (amplify it), you can set any amplification coefficient not greater than 3.2 dB (*Section 12.5*). There will then be no distortions.

In the same way, you can analyze signals whose features are unknown. The analysis results can be useful when making decisions on any amplitude conversions, for example on amplifying a signal or compressing its dynamic range. Let's look at another example. In Fig. 14.5, you see an example of an actual spoken waveform.

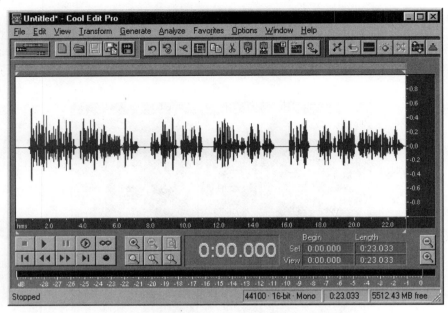

Fig. 14.5. Waveform of a spoken signal

The statistics on this signal are as follows.

```
        Mono

Min Sample Value:          -15467

Max Sample Value:           18242

Peak Amplitude:            -5.09 dB

Possibly Clipped:              0

DC Offset:                     0

Minimum RMS Power:        -64.48 dB

Maximum RMS Power:        -11.63 dB

Total RMS Power:          -22.45 dB

Using RMS Window of 100 ms
```

The value of the `Total RMS Power` parameter is low (−24.63 dB). The speech will sound very quiet compared to the sound of music recorded from a CD over the speaker.

We will now analyze the histogram of this signal (Fig. 14.6) and make a decision on how to process it in the best way possible. It would be good to maximally increase the signal's average energy (and thus its subjectively perceived volume) with minimal distortions, as well as decrease the noise level.

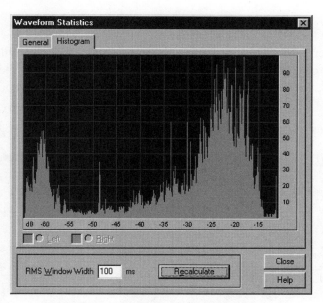

Fig. 14.6. Histogram of a spoken signal

First of all, the signal level decreases non-monotonously (the histogram elements have large values within the range from −55 to −65 dB). This waveform was probably recorded in an unfavorable environment with much noise, or the recording device had a high level of its own noise. Samples whose value is less than −55 dB we will consider to be noise. Thus, one of the processing steps will be limited noise reduction, and the limit is to be set to −55 dB.

Second, analysis of the histogram shows that there are very few samples whose level is above −12 dB. So we should get a good result if we limit the signal to a level of −12 dB with further amplification by 12 dB.

After completion of each dynamic processing procedure, you should check the result (listen to it) and ensure that you are on the right path.

Chapter 15: The *Favorites* Menu—Creating a List of the Most Often Used Operations

We have not yet looked at the **Edit Favorites** command, and it is the only command in the **Favorites** menu left. This menu might soon contain a large number of commands: you create these on your own by giving them names and defining their contents. Using these commands, you can apply the actions you use in audio data processing most frequently.

The **Edit Favorites** command opens the **Favorites** dialog window (Fig. 15.1).

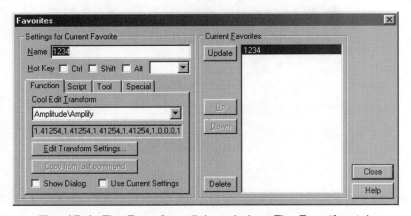

Fig. 15.1. The **Favorites** dialog window. The **Function** tab

Favorites are the most frequently used audio data editing or Windows applications actions. The **Favorites** dialog window is intended to simplify, accelerate, and to some extent automate using the favorites. The tools of this window allow you to create, delete, edit and organize the menu items of the **Favorites** menu. Each menu item corresponds to a separate operation or number of operations, or to a command calling an external program (an MS Windows application).

Creating the favorites list starts in the **Name** field. The field is in the upper part of the **Settings for Current Favorite** group. You should create a hierarchic menu using the slash character. For example, if you input the **Effects\Hall Reverb** name, the **Hall Reverb** item appears in the submenu **Effects**.

Using the **Hot Key** options, you can select hot keys for actions that correspond to the current favorite. In the untitled drop-down list, select one of the functional keys (from <F1> to <F12>). This does not mean that the keyboard limits you to only twelve hot keys, of course; you can use combinations of keys using the <Ctrl>, <Shift>, and <Alt> keys as well. This way, you can call up to 36 favorites with hot keys.

Below the **Hot Key** line, there are tabs that allow you to define the sequence of actions performed after calling a favorite.

The **Function** tab is for selecting one of Cool Edit Pro's built-in operations as a favorite. The operations available are listed in the **Cool Edit Transform** drop-down list. This list contains all types of processing and effects accessed through the **Transform** menu by the **Amplitude**, **Delay Effects**, **Filters**, **Noise Reduction**, **Special**, and **Time/Pitch** commands. The first line of the list corresponds to the **Amplitude>Amplify** command, and the last one to the **Time/Pitch>Stretch** command.

Under the drop-down list, there is a field in which comma-separated parameter values for the corresponding type of processing or effect are listed. For example, the values in this field shown in Fig. 15.1, according to the selected processing type (**Amplify**), indicate the following.

❏ **1, 41254**—signal amplification is 3 dB (the **Amplification** parameter is 3 dB), signal amplification at the starting point of the selected waveform fragment is 3 dB (the **Initial Amplification** parameter is 3 dB), signal amplification at the ending point of the selected waveform fragment is 3 dB (the **Final Amplification** parameter is 3 dB).

❏ **1, 0, 0, 0, 1**—status of the **Linear Fades**, **Logarithmic Fades**, **View all Settings in dB**, **DC Bias**, and **Normalization** checkboxes and options (**1** corresponds to a selected option or checked checkbox, **0** corresponds to an unselected option or unchecked checkbox).

To efficiently change the processing parameters, use the **Edit Transform Settings** button. In the above example, the **Amplify** window in which you can change the necessary parameters opens. Then, to update the parameter values of the favorite command, press the **Update** button in the **Favorites** window. It replaces the **Add** button when a name that is already present in the favorites list is input in the **Name** field.

After a favorite is created, the **Copy from last command** button becomes available. If you press it, all setting parameters will be copied from the last successfully completed processing.

When the **Show Dialog** checkbox is ticked, a processing or effect dialog window opens after you select one of the favorites from the **Favorites** menu. This allows you to correct parameters of that dialog window. Otherwise, the window does not open, and the program immediately starts processing.

If the **Use Current Settings** checkbox is selected, the current setting parameters are used in processing.

The **Script** tab (Fig. 15.2) is intended for organizing *scripts* (a group of actions performed one after another). Scripts are created using the **Scripts & Batch Processing...** command of the **Options** menu (*Section 16.1*).

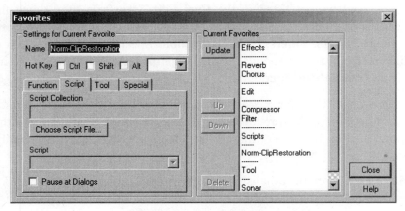

Fig. 15.2. The **Script** tab

To load a script (stored in a SCP file), press the **Choose Script File** button. The standard file loading window appears. Using this box, find and load the file containing the desired script. In the **Script Collection** field, the full pathname to the loaded file appears, and the script name is shown in the **Script** field.

A script can contain a long sequence of commands. Each command corresponds to a certain audio data editing action. If you want the script to implement itself, don't check the **Pause at Dialogs** checkbox. If it is checked, a dialog window will be opened before each action is performed. This may be convenient when you need to correct parameter values, but you have to be at your PC during script implementation. To proceed to the next step, you'd at least have to press **OK** in the next dialog window.

The **Tool** tab (Fig. 15.3) allows you to add to favorites those commands that open any Windows applications. These applications don't necessarily have to be for audio data processing. You can program the items of the **Favorites** menu or hot keys, for example, to start MS Word.

The **Tool** tab makes the **Favorites** menu a convenient tool not only for working with favorite sound processing commands in Cool Edit Pro, but also programs on your PC that you use frequently. To use this tab, specify the application-favorite. Then in the

Command Line field, specify the path to the executed file that runs this application. If you do not remember the path, press the **Browse** button. In the dialog window that opens, find the required file and press **OK**. The path to the file appears in the **Command Line** field.

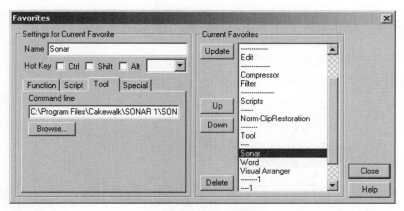

Fig. 15.3. The **Tool** tab

And so you have selected:

❏ An operation from Cool Edit Pro

❏ A script

❏ An external processing tool (Windows application)

The selected object was given a name. Then, in the **Current** group, press the **Add** button. The object name is displayed in the Favorites List of the **Current Favorites** group. After closing the **Favorites** window, the command with this name also appears on the **Favorites** menu. Now you can apply it to start the processing sequence you need. Using the **Favorites** window, fill the **Favorites** menu with all the commands you need. To implement them, you won't need to use other menus. The most frequently used commands will be associated with hot keys. It makes working more convenient and increases performance, especially when you have to implement similar actions frequently.

To move a command up the list, use the **Up** button; to move a command down the list, use the **Down** button. The **Delete** button allows you to delete a command from the Favorites List and, accordingly, from the **Favorites** menu.

The **Special** tab contains no options. It only contains information on how to use separator characters for structuring the menus.

In this example, we are given the option of separating one functional group of menu commands from another using lines containing a different number of dashes. Indeed, in the **Name** field you can specify any name to be used as a header in the list of **Favorites** menu commands. This header will also be a command—an empty one—since calling this command does not result in the program or the system performing any actions. An example of a **Favorites** menu is shown in Fig. 15.5.

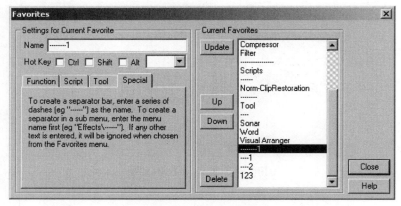

Fig. 15.4. The **Special** tab

Fig. 15.5. An example of a filled **Favorites** menu

Horizontal lines are created when you insert at least three "-" characters as a separator. The line length does not depend on the number of these characters. Therefore, you needn't insert a long string containing lots of "-" characters—just insert three of them followed by the separator line number, for example:

---01

---02

---03

Each of these records creates a horizontal separator line in the **Favorites** menu, and the program ignores the line number.

Pay attention to the fact that you cannot specify two favorite names that are the same, or two of the same separators. For example, you cannot specify a separator that contains the same number of "-" characters. If in the **Name** field you input a sequence of characters that is already used in the favorites list, the **Add** button is replaced with the **Update** button. This is a hint that you need to choose a different favorite name or separator.

Chapter 16: The *Options* Menu

The **Options** menu contains the following commands and submenus:

❏ **Loop Mode**—this command does not work.

❏ **Timed Record**—recording starts according to a timer (*Section 8.2*).

❏ **Monitor Record Level**—enables the signal level meter. You can double-click the signal level meter in the program's main window instead of selecting this option.

❏ **Show Levels on Play and Record**—displays the signal level not only in recording mode, but also in playback mode.

❏ **MIDI Trigger Enable**—enables program control through the MIDI interface. The parameters of this mode are defined using the **Shortcuts (Keyboard & MIDI Triggers)** command.

❏ **Synchronize Cursor Across Windows**—enables the mode in which the cursor position or the position of the waveform's selected fragment is saved when switching from one open file to another (useful for assembling recordings). Consider the following example. You have selected this option and you are working with the 1.wav file. You select the fragment between 0:01:00 and 0:02:00. If you then switch to the main window to view the 2.wav file, the fragment from 0:01:00 to 0:02:00 is selected in this waveform as well.

❏ **Scripts & Batch Processing...**—edits the list of signal processing actions (the script).

❏ **Settings...**—sets parameters and modes of the program. Getting started is described in *Chapter 7.*

❏ **Shortcuts (Keyboard & MIDI Triggers)**—selects shortcuts (using the PC and MIDI keyboards).

❏ **Toolbars**—selects the displayed toolbars.

In earlier versions of the program, using the **Loop Mode** command turned on or off the mode in which the selected fragment or the entire waveform is played within the loop. If this option is selected, the **Play** button in the program's main window changes its title to **Loop**.

Starting with Cool Edit Pro version 1.2, there appeared a special button on the control panel to turn on the looped playback mode (*Section 8.1*). You also have the **Loop Mode** command in the **Options** menu, but it does not work.

16.1. *Scripts & Batch Processing—*
Editing the List of Signal Processing Actions

The **Scripts & Batch Processing** command calls the **Scripts and Batch Processing** dialog window (Fig. 16.1) that is used to create and copy records of sequences of actions (scripts), and then execute them.

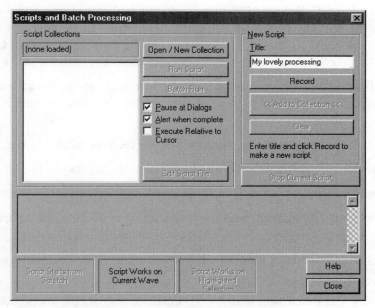

Fig. 16.1. The **Scripts & Batch Processing** dialog window

The word "record" in this case is synonymous with "macro". Macros can be useful when you have to perform the same sequence of actions many times. This sequence may be dynamic processing, filtering, applying effects to a signal, etc. You just need to write the sequence of actions (the macro) once to perform it in the future using only one command. You can write macros into a file to store them on your hard disk. The term "script" is also used in place of "macro".

Before you write the processing script (using the **Record** button) you have to assign it a name in the **Title** input field. If a script doesn't yet have a name, the **Record** button is inactive.

As you write the audio data processing script, you implement a certain sequence of actions in the main menu. You can use commands of the main menu, open different windows, or define parameter values. The program saves this information. After you complete the actions you need to perform, you have to return to the **Scripts and Batch Processing** dialog window and press the **Stop Current Script** button. This stops writing the given script. If for some reason you decide to delete the entire script, press the **Clear** button.

In the text editor field in the lower part of the screen, you can add comments to the script.

Using the **<<Add to Collection<<** button, you can add the script to the list of scripts. This list is saved to your hard disk using the **Open/New Collection** button. Using the same button, you can also load a previously saved file containing script. Cool Edit Pro includes five files (collections) of scripts that demonstrate the abilities of the program.

Besides simplifying, routine processing scripts allow users to exchange not only waveforms but technologies of their own creation over the Internet, or simply using floppy disks.

Three fields in the lower part of the window indicate the type of the current script:

❏ **Script Starts from Scratch**—the script starts before the waveform is created

❏ **Script Works on Current Wave**—the script applies to the current waveform

❏ **Script Works on Highlighted Selection**—the script applies to the selected waveform fragment

The name of the current script type is in black, while the other two names are dimmed.

There is also a special type of script that allows you to process a sequence of several audio files (using the **Batch Run** button). To create such a script, you shouldn't associate it with a specific waveform: before you press the **Record** button there shouldn't be a waveform loaded in Cool Edit Pro (use the **File>New** command).

In the future, using the programming language built into Cool Edit Pro, you can edit a macro stored as a sequence of commands. To do so, press the **Edit Script File** button. The Notepad text editor window opens (Fig. 16.2).

The script text is not that hard to understand. It contains a sequence of the following elements:

❏ Boundaries of the selected waveform fragment

❏ Name of the next processing procedure

❏ Notes

❏ Parameter values for processing or effects

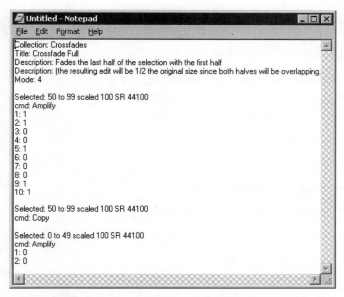

Fig. 16.2. Notepad window containing the script text

To execute a script, select it from the list and press the **Run Script** button.

If the **Pause at Dialogs** checkbox is checked, while the script is running, the executed program stops before any processing step starts. A dialog box opens in which you can alter the necessary parameters. If this checkbox is not checked, the processing is executed without pauses.

When the **Alert when complete** checkbox is checked, the program beeps to indicate that the script execution has completed.

If the **Execute Relative to Cursor** checkbox is checked, the program defines the position from which script processing should start according to the current marker position. Consider the following example. There is a script according to which the processing starts from the marker position of 0:10:00. If the **Execute Relative to Cursor** checkbox is checked, the waveform processing starts from the point to the right of the current marker position by 10 seconds. For example, if the marker is in the position at 0:05:00, processing starts at 0:15:00. If the **Execute Relative to Cursor** checkbox is not checked in our example, the processing starts at 0:10:00.

So that you don't get confused, and to ensure that you start processing from the current marker position, put the marker at 0:00:00 before recording any script, and check the **Execute Relative to Cursor** checkbox before processing starts.

16.2. *Shortcuts (Keyboard & MIDI Triggers)—* Selecting Shortcuts

Cool Edit Pro provides many ways of controlling the program using shortcut keys. Many users are of the opinion that using shortcuts is more effective than using the mouse. Here we describe the shortcut keys for some basic actions.

File management shortcuts:

❑ <Ctrl>+<N>—create a new file (**New**)

❑ <Ctrl>+<O>—open an existing file (**Open**)

❑ <Ctrl>+<W>—close the current file (**Close**)

❑ <Ctrl>+<S>—save the current file to disk (**Save**)

❑ <Ctrl>+<Q>—exit Cool Edit Pro (**Exit**)

Waveform fragment selection shortcuts:

❑ <Ctrl>+<A>—select the current waveform

❑ <Ctrl>+<B>—enable editing of both channels

❑ <Ctrl>+<L>—enable editing of the left channel

❑ <Ctrl>+<R>—enable editing of the right channel

❑ <←>—move the left boundary of the selected waveform one sample left

❑ <→>—move the left boundary of the selected waveform one sample right

❑ <Shift>+<←>—move the right boundary of the selected waveform one sample left

❑ <Shift>+<→>—move the right boundary of the selected waveform one sample right

❑ <Ctrl>+<Shift>+<A>—select all open waveforms

❑ <Escape>—undo selection and return marker to zero

Shortcuts for editing:

❑ <Ctrl>+<Z>—undo the previous action (**Undo**)

❑ <F2>—redo the last action (dialog box opens)

❑ <F3>—repeat the last action (dialog box opens)

❑ <Ctrl>+<C>—copy the selected fragment into the internal clipboard

❏ <Ctrl>+<X>—cut the selected fragment and paste it into the internal clipboard

❏ <Ctrl>+<V>—paste data from the internal clipboard (or from the system clipboard if the internal clipboard is empty)

❏ <Ctrl>+<Shift>+<N>—open a new file and paste data from the internal clipboard into it

❏ <Ctrl>+<Shift>+<V>—execute the **Mix paste** command

❏ <Ctrl>+<M>—insert the selected waveform fragment into a multitrack session

❏ <Delete>—delete the selected fragment

❏ <Shift>+<Delete>—cut the selected fragment

❏ <Ctrl>+<T>—delete the entire waveform except for the selected fragment

❏ <F11>—open the **Convert Sample Type** dialog window

❏ <Ctrl>+<1> <Ctrl>+<5>—select one of five internal clipboards

Shortcuts for playback and recording:

❏ <Space>—switch between **Play/Stop** modes

❏ <Ctrl>+<Space>—switch between **Record/Pause** modes

❏ <Shift>+<Space>—play the waveform starting from the marker position

❏ <Ctrl>+<Shift>+<Space>—play the waveform starting from zero

❏ <Alt>+<P>—enable the **Play** mode

❏ <Alt>+<S>—enable the **Stop** mode

Shortcuts for display and zoom:

❏ <F12>—switch the main window between the **Waveform View/Multitrack View** modes

❏ <Home>—move the displayed fragment to the waveform's beginning

❏ <End>—move the displayed fragment to the waveform's end

❏ <Ctrl>+<End>—change display zoom for the area to the right of the selected fragment or marker position

❏ <Ctrl>+<Home>—change display zoom for the area to the left of the selected fragment or marker position

❏ <Ctrl>+<↑>—increase vertical zoom

❏ <Ctrl>+<↓>—decrease vertical zoom

❏ <Ctrl>+<→>—increase horizontal zoom

❏ <Ctrl>+<←>—decrease horizontal zoom

❏ <Page Down>—scroll waveform forward (if there is just a waveform fragment displayed on the screen)

❏ <Page Up>—scroll waveform back (if there is just a waveform fragment displayed on the screen)

Special shortcuts:

❏ <F1>—call help

❏ <F4>—call the **Settings** dialog box

❏ <F6>—enable program control through MIDI

❏ <F7>—enable slave mode for the program through SMPTE mode

❏ <F8>—add cursor position or boundaries of the selected fragment to **Cue List**

❏ <F9>—call the **Waveforms List** window

❏ <F10>—enable signal level meter

❏ <Ctrl>+<I>—call the **Wave Information** window

❏ <Alt>+<Z>—call the spectrum analyzer window

❏ <Ctrl>+<Tab>—turn to the next page that contains an open waveform

❏ <Ctrl>+<Shift>+<Tab>—turn to the preceding page that contains an open waveform

These are just the keys set by default. But you can change this, and/or widen the list of functions controlled by shortcut keys. You can also use not only your PC's keyboard but the MIDI keyboard for creating shortcut keys.

The **Shortcuts (Keyboard&MIDI Triggers)** command opens the dialog window (Fig. 16.3) used to select the shortcut keys.

The **Function** field lists the functions you can control using shortcuts. Setting PC keyboard shortcuts to the function selected in the **Function** field is done using the options of the **Shortcut key** group. In the drop-down list, all the keys of the PC keyboard are listed. Select one of them. By checking the **Ctrl**, **Shift**, and **Alt** checkboxes, you can set not just one shortcut key, but a combination of two or three keys for a function.

If you select a function for which a shortcut is set by default, it is displayed in the **Shortcut key** group. If there are no default shortcuts for the function, **none** is displayed in the list.

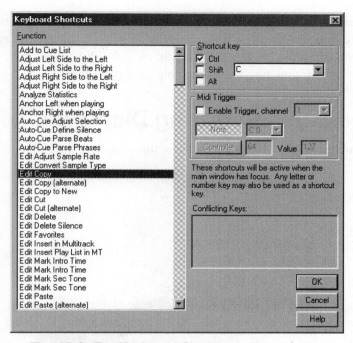

Fig. 16.3. The **Keyboard Shortcuts** dialog window

If you have a MIDI keyboard and you want to use it while operating in Cool Edit Pro, you can define MIDI shortcuts instead of PC keyboard shortcuts. You can even define "shortcut elements of MIDI controllers" such as wheels, buttons, sliders, and levers on the MIDI keyboard, or its pedals. These are assigned in the **Midi Trigger** group. To make the options of this group available, check the **Enable Trigger** checkbox. In the **channel** drop-down list, you should select one of 16 MIDI channels. If you intend to use the keys of a MIDI keyboard, press the **Note** button and select the key definition (from **C0** to **E9**) from the drop-down list. If you prefer to use a controller, press the **Controller** button and input the controller number in the field to the right of this field. In the **Value** field, you should specify which controller value corresponds to the "Shortcut key pressed" command. Actually, the latter option allows you to select the most convenient controller sensitivity. For example, if 127 is input into the **Value** field, and you use a pedal, you should press the pedal "to the max" to execute the command. It is best to specify a number more than 64 (for example, 70, 80). You can then send a command to the program by lightly pressing the pedal.

If you try to assign shortcut keys already used to control a certain function to some other function, a message appears in **Conflicting Keys:** with information as to what function you are trying to assign the given combination of keys to and what function it is already used for. In this situation, you can do as you like, but it is probably better not to change the default shortcut settings. If you do, it might be difficult to work with other instances of the program, and no one but you will be able to operate your PC.

16.3. *Toolbars*—Selecting Displayed Toolbars

The **Toolbars** submenu (Fig. 16.4) is used for setting the user interface.

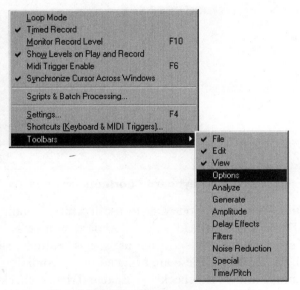

Fig. 16.4. The **Toolbars** submenu

By checking one or several lines in the submenu, you make the corresponding toolbars visible in the main window.

Unlike many other Windows applications, Cool Edit Pro toolbars are in one line only, in the upper part of the main window. You cannot drag a docked toolbar from the main window to another place on the screen. The tools in the toolbars duplicate the basic commands of the main menu. You can learn their purpose by reading the tip that appears when you position the mouse pointer over the tool you are interested in.

The **File** toolbar is shown in Fig. 16.5. It contains tools for working with files (working with files is described in *Chapter 9*) and the button for switching the main window between the multitrack mode and the waveform editing mode.

The **Edit** toolbar (Fig. 16.6) contains all the tools used for the basic editing actions described in *Chapter 10*.

Fig. 16.5. The **File** toolbar   **Fig. 16.6.** The **Edit** toolbar

The **View** toolbar (Fig. 16.7), described in *Chapter 11*, is used for controlling the display of the waveform.

The **Options** toolbar (Fig. 16.8) contains tools that duplicate the **Settings...** (*Chapter 7*), and **Scripts and Batch Processing...** commands (*Section 16.1*) of the **Options** menu, and a button that gives information on the interface elements of the program.

Fig. 16.7. The **View** toolbar   **Fig. 16.8.** The **Options** toolbar

The tools of the **Analyze** toolbar (Fig. 16.9) duplicate the commands of the menu of the same name described in *Chapter 14*.

The **Generate** toolbar (Fig. 16.10) duplicates all the commands of the menu of the same name described in *Chapter 13*.

Fig. 16.9. The **Analyze** toolbar   **Fig. 16.10.** The **Generate** toolbar

The tools of the **Amplitude** toolbar (Fig. 16.11) duplicate the **Invert**, **Reverse**, and **Silence** commands of the **Transform** menu, as well as the **Amplify**, **Channel Mixer**, **Dynamics Processing**, **Envelope**, **Hard Limiter**, **Normalize**, and **Pan/Expand** commands of the **Amplitude** submenu (*Sections 12.1—12.3 and 12.5—12.11*).

The **Delay Effects** toolbar (Fig. 16.12) duplicates the commands of the **Transform>Delay Effects** submenu (*Sections 12.12—12.20*).

Fig. 16.11. The **Amplitude** toolbar   **Fig. 16.12.** The **Delay Effects** toolbar

The **Filters** toolbar (Fig. 16.13) duplicates the commands of the **Transform>Filters** submenu (*Sections 12.21—12.26*).

The **Noise Reduction** toolbar (Fig. 16.14) duplicates the commands of the **Transform> Noise Reduction** submenu (*Sections 12.27—12.30*).

Fig. 16.13. The **Filters** toolbar   **Fig. 16.14.** The **Noise Reduction** toolbar

The **Special** toolbar (Fig. 16.15) duplicates the commands of the **Transform>Special** submenu (*Sections 12.31—12.34*).

The **Time/Pitch** toolbar (Fig. 16.16) duplicates the **Pitch Bender** and **Stretch** commands of the **Transform > Time/Pitch** submenu (*Sections 12.35—12.36*).

Fig. 16.15. The **Special** toolbar   **Fig. 16.16.** The **Time/Pitch** toolbar

It makes sense not to display more than three toolbars at the same time. For the most part, you will be using the **File** and **Edit** toolbars, and one of the toolbars that duplicates the commands of the **Transform** menu.

Chapter 17: The *Window* Menu—Managing the Main Window Pages

If there are no open audio files, the **Window** menu contains only one command—**Waveforms List**. When you open files with audio data, items that contain paths to these files and their filenames appear in the menu. Each of these items represents a command that opens a new page and switches the main window to display the corresponding waveform. Thus, to access and edit previously opened files, you can change pages directly from the **Window** menu. If you have to perform more complex actions on the opened files, use the **Waveforms List** command. A dialog box with the same name will appear (Fig. 17.1).

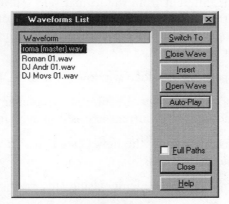

Fig. 17.1. The **Waveforms List** dialog window

The **Waveform** list contains all open files. If you check the **Full Paths** checkbox, the full path to the file is also displayed in the **Waveform** list (Fig. 17.2).

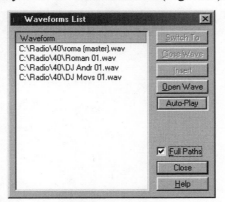

Fig. 17.2. The **Waveforms List** dialog window. Full path to each open file is displayed

Take note of one specific feature of the **Waveforms List** window: it can be open even when you are working with other windows or menus.

Some buttons of this window are available only if the list of open files has a file selected.

If you select any line from the list and press the **Switch To** button, the selected file becomes current and is displayed in the main window.

When you press the **Close Wave** button, you close the selected file. Its name disappears from the **Waveforms List** window and from the **Window** menu.

The **Insert** button is used to insert the selected file into a multitrack session. If the format of the file being inserted is different from the format selected for a multitrack session (in other words, if the multitrack already contains the file in another format), the **Convert Sample Type** dialog box opens after you press the **Insert** button (*Section 10.14*), and you have to change the format of the inserted file.

The **Open Wave** button opens the file load window (*Section 9.2*).

The **Auto-Play** button is used to play the file whose filename is selected in the list. You will hear it even if another file is current and is displayed in the main window.

And thus with this we finish describing the how Cool Edit Pro works in the editing mode for separate stereo or mono waveforms.

The program also contains the **Help** menu. Using this menu is the same as with any Windows application.

The next chapter describes using a multitrack environment to assemble complex audio recordings and musical compositions from waveforms edited using the tools described in *Chapters 7—17*.

Chapter 18: *Multitrack View*—Multitrack Editing Mode

We have already described working with Cool Edit Pro in the waveform editing mode (**Waveform View**). In older versions of this sound editor, the audio composition was compiled from separate files to one (the only) pair of stereo tracks (or the only mono track). To do this, we were only able to apply the standard operations, such as cutting, pasting, copying, and mixing. Assembling a recording was similar to sticking together the fragments of a magnetic tape. This procedure required a lot of time to adjust the fragments and to reach a balance in the mixes.

The version of Cool Edit Pro that we are dealing with provides computer musicians and audio engineers with a brand new assembling tool—the multitrack environment—which can be considered an editor within an editor. Unfortunately, most audio editors that were previously considered to be rivals to Cool Edit Pro still do not provide such abilities.

18.1. The Program's Main Menu in the *Multitrack View* Mode

To switch to the multitrack environment (the **Multitrack View** mode), either select the **Multitrack View** command in the **View** menu, or press the  button in the main window. The program's main menu is shown in Fig. 18.1.

In Fig. 18.1, you'll see elements you are familiar with: the transport bar, the time indicator panel, zoom control elements, input fields for the boundaries of the displayed and selected waveform fragments, the signal level meter, and the status bar. If you like, you can open the control panel for the CD player. The main menu is displayed in the upper part of the window.

However, these are the only things that are similar to the main window that we saw in the **Waveform View** mode. One difference is that in the multitrack environment, the main menu contains seven, and not ten items. The main difference is that the main window contains not just one pair of stereo tracks, but a number of such pairs. If you set the minimum vertical zoom, you can count the number of tracks—21.

Generally, we can assume that operating in a multitrack environment comes down to placing the waveforms into certain time positions in a certain track. You have to preliminarily prepare the waveform: cut all the unnecessary fragments, perform noise reduction and dynamics processing, apply filtering, process using effects, and normalize. We have already gone over these actions. In the multitrack environment, you can move the waveform over time and along the tracks, as well as cut it into several parts and mix them (to one stereo or mono track). In this chapter, you will learn how to control the loudness and the panorama of each waveform in each separate track. However, these parameters are changed not by recalculating the values of the digitized audio samples, but by adjusting the settings of the virtual audio reproduction devices. The waveforms themselves are not transformed, and the values of their samples remain unchanged.

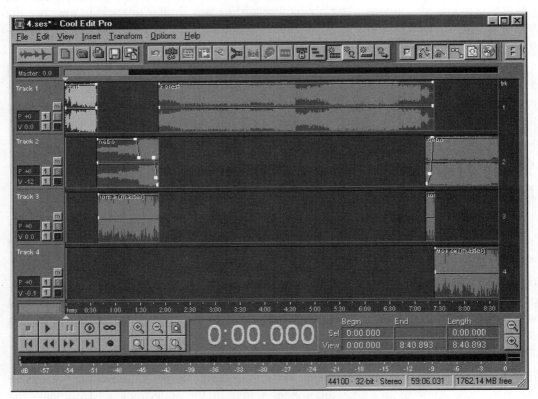

Fig. 18.1. The program's main window in the **Multitrack View** mode

There are at least two ways to put a waveform into a multitrack session: insert the waveform opened in the current page in the **Waveform View** mode into the multitrack environment (using the **Edit>Insert in Multitrack** command), or load the waveform (waveforms) to a **Session** in the **Multitrack View** mode. In the latter case, all the files containing waveforms within a session are opened in the pages of the main window in the **Waveform View** mode (and, accordingly, their names are listed in the **Window** menu).

You can read about the third method of inserting a waveform into the multitrack environment in *Section 18.5*.

Now it's time to explain what a session is. A *session* is actually a SES file containing the following data:

❑ Paths to files with waveforms placed in the tracks (within the given session)

❑ The relation of waveforms to specific tracks

❑ Starting times of each waveform playback

❑ Laws according to which levels and panoramas of each track change with time

A session file takes up a small amount of memory space, since the digitized audio samples themselves are not stored in it. This file contains information on where to find these samples and how and when they should be played, and all of this does not require much memory. We can say that (forgetting for a moment about files and disks), from the user's point of view, a session is a number of waveform images placed in tracks of the multitrack editor.

It's easy to change the position of the waveform. First, select it by clicking the left mouse button. Then, holding the right mouse button down, drag it along the track or to another track. To select several waveforms, keep the <Ctrl> button pressed.

In certain cases, you will need to select not the entire waveform but only a fragment of it. Position the mouse pointer on any of the horizontal lines that separate the tracks at the point where the selected fragment begins. Press the left mouse button, and holding it, move the pointer to the ending point of the selected fragment. After you release the button, you will see a gray vertical line. This is not a selection, but rather a temporary selection model. Press <Ctrl> and click the left mouse button on the waveform whose fragment you are going to select in the area where the waveform crosses the gray line. The entire waveform is highlighted, and the fragment you are interested in is selected.

If you have to select the fragments of several waveforms overlapping in time, the order is the same. The only difference is that at the final step, while holding the <Ctrl> key, you have to click all the fragments you are interested in.

To select arbitrarily placed waveforms, click each of them holding the <Ctrl> key.

You can delete the selected waveform by pressing the <Delete> key.

In Fig. 18.1, you see a fragment of the *Musical Computer* radio show. The introduction is in the first track, the announcer's voice is in the second track, and the music is in the third track, all at the same time. Then (again in the first track) the audio composition is played, etc. All the fragments' amplitudes are processed and normalized. You might ask yourself, why does the music not drown out the announcer's voice?

The reason for this is that for each separate track, you can set not only the initial values of the level and the panorama, but also the graphs of the change in these parameters over time. To learn more about the balance and panorama adjustment tools, we'll increase the tracks' vertical display zoom and examine Fig. 18.2.

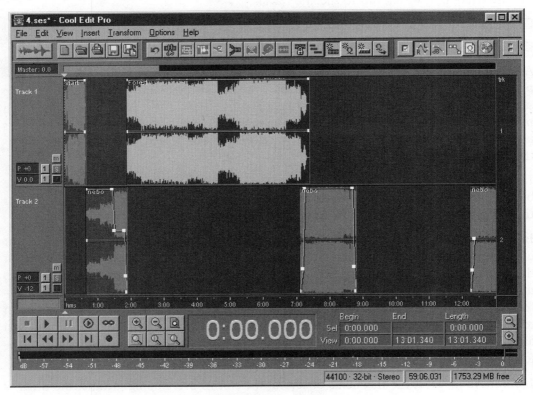

Fig. 18.2. Tracks in larger scale

Note that the zoom is adjusted so that the maximum number of tracks displayed in the window is 21 (2 is the minimum). There's no sense in increasing the zoom to display only one track, and so the program does not provide this ability.

Each track begins with a field containing several elements:

❑ Track number

❑ Two input fields

❑ Two numeric buttons

❑ Two letter buttons

The field with the letter **p** is used to input the initial value of the panorama of the given track. You can input the value using one of two methods, as follows.

Click the left mouse button on the field, and holding it, move the cursor up (decrease the parameter value, and in doing this move the sound source to the left) or down (increase the parameter value, and in doing this move the sound source to the right). The zero value corresponds to the center of the panorama, negative values to the left part, and positive values to the right part of the panorama.

Or, click the right mouse button on the field and open the dialog box shown in Fig. 18.3. Then adjust the panorama using the slider.

Fig. 18.3. Dialog box for adjusting the panorama's initial value

The field with the letter **v** is used to input the initial value of the track's volume. You can input this value using one of two methods.

Click the left mouse button on the field, and holding it, move the cursor up (increase the level value) or down (decrease the level value).

Or, click the right mouse button on the field, and open the dialog box shown in Fig. 18.4. Then adjust the level using the slider.

Fig. 18.4. Dialog box for adjusting the volume level's initial value

Buttons marked by numbers (the number 1 in Fig. 18.2) allow you to open dialog windows for selecting device drivers for audio data output (Fig. 18.5) and input (Fig. 18.6).

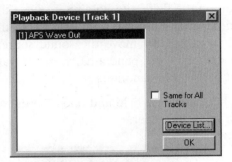

Fig. 18.5. Dialog window for selecting the device driver for audio data output

If the **Same for All Tracks** checkbox is checked, the given driver is selected for all the other tracks.

The number **1** under the track name indicates that the data is output to the first of the system devices.

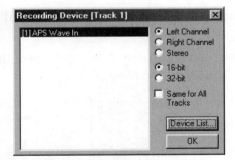

Fig. 18.6. Dialog window for selecting the device driver for audio data input

In this dialog window, you can select the number of bits of audio data (16 bits or 32 bits) and the format (the left channel separately, the right channel separately, the stereo pair of channels in the track).

If in any of the windows shown in Figs. 18.5 and 18.6 you press the **Device List** button, a dialog window (Fig. 18.7) opens. It contains a list with up to 16 devices of audio data input and output.

If there are several input/output devices in the system, it may become necessary to supply different values for the delays in the cells of the **Latency (ms)** column, taking into account the different operating speeds of these devices.

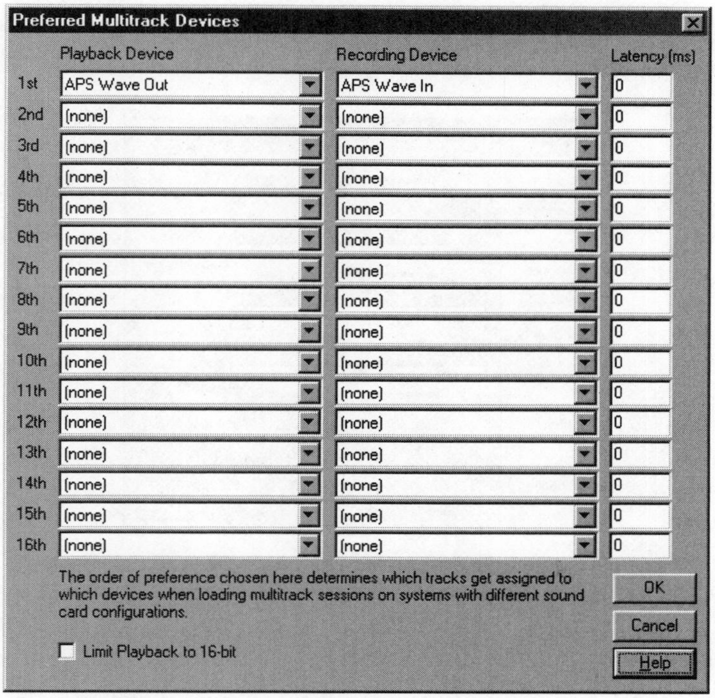

Preferred Multitrack Devices			✕
	Playback Device	Recording Device	Latency (ms)
1st	APS Wave Out ▼	APS Wave In ▼	0
2nd	(none) ▼	(none) ▼	0
3rd	(none) ▼	(none) ▼	0
4th	(none) ▼	(none) ▼	0
5th	(none) ▼	(none) ▼	0
6th	(none) ▼	(none) ▼	0
7th	(none) ▼	(none) ▼	0
8th	(none) ▼	(none) ▼	0
9th	(none) ▼	(none) ▼	0
10th	(none) ▼	(none) ▼	0
11th	(none) ▼	(none) ▼	0
12th	(none) ▼	(none) ▼	0
13th	(none) ▼	(none) ▼	0
14th	(none) ▼	(none) ▼	0
15th	(none) ▼	(none) ▼	0
16th	(none) ▼	(none) ▼	0

The order of preference chosen here determines which tracks get assigned to which devices when loading multitrack sessions on systems with different sound card configurations.

☐ Limit Playback to 16-bit

[OK]   [Cancel]   [Help]

Fig. 18.7. Dialog window for selecting the input/output devices

The three buttons in the main window placed one below another are used as follows:

🔲 (**Mute**)—mutes the track.

🔲 (**Solo**)—makes the track solo (mutes all the tracks besides the given track).

🔲 (**Record**)—prepares the mode of recording the audio data to the track.

By clicking the left mouse button on the unused field near the track number, you open the dialog box (Fig. 18.8) in which the functions of boxes shown in Figs. 18.3—18.7 are combined, as well as the 🔲, 🔲, and 🔲 buttons.

Now let's examine the waveform images in the tracks. Each waveform has the same name as the file in which it is contained. It allows you to understand the structure of the session without having to listen to the waveforms.

You can see two lines over the waveform images. The light green line is the signal level change graph (volume envelope) and the blue line is the panorama change graph (panorama envelope). To change the shape of any of these graphs, click on it. A control point is created. You can create as many control points as you need to give the graph the desired shape using the mouse.

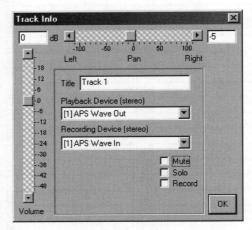

Fig. 18.8. Dialog window for selecting the track attributes

Thus the balance of the volume and the panorama are made by determining the initial parameter values in the corresponding dialog windows, and by dynamic adjustment using graphs.

After working in in the multitrack environment for a while, you will notice that after any change you make, the program uses the hard disk intensively. The reason is that in the multitrack environment of Cool Edit Pro, data exists as a number of files and a number of tracks, and in the output, a mix is created only in two channels (the right and the left). This mix is automatically recalculated by the program in the background mode. For example, if you have changed the graph shape or muted a track, the mix must be recalculated. While the program performs this operation, the indicator above the transport panel is gray. After recalculation completes, the indicator becomes green again. You can make changes not only statically, but also during playback. However, you should probably only do this on a powerful computer.

These are all the main features of the program's main window. Now we'll start describing the main window. The first menu is the **File** menu.

18.2. The *File* Menu—Working with Files

The **File** menu contains the commands used to work with files:

❑ **New Session...**—creates a new session

❏ **Open Session...**—opens (loads) an existing session

❏ **Append to Session...**—opens a session without closing the current session

❏ **Close Session**—closes a session

❏ **Close Session and Waveforms**—closes the session and waveforms

❏ **Close Only Non-Session Waveforms**—closes waveforms not belonging to the session

❏ **Open Waveform**—opens a waveform

❏ **Save Session**—saves a session with its previous name

❏ **Save Session As...**—saves a session with a new name

❏ **Save All**—saves all opened waveforms and the session

❏ **Free Hard Drive Space...**—opens the window with the information on free hard disk space

❏ **Exit**—exits the Cool Edit Pro application

18.3. The *Edit* Menu—Editing

The **Edit** menu contains the following commands and submenus:

❏ **Undo**—undoes the last editing action.

❏ **Wave Block Info...**—displays and edits the attributes of the selected waveform fragment.

❏ **Punch In**—enables the multiple recording mode of audio data that saves duplicate copies.

❏ **Crossfade**—enables the crossfade mode. The submenu is for selecting the crossfade law. Possible variants are: linear, sinusoidal, logarithmic increasing, and logarithmic decreasing. The most natural laws for changing the volume over time are logarithmic laws.

❏ **Take History**—returns to one of the previous versions of the audio composition.

❏ **Mix Down**—creates a mix. The following variants are possible: mixing all the non-muted tracks into a stereo mix; mixing all the selected and non-muted tracks into a stereo mix; mixing all the non-muted tracks into a mono mix; mixing all the selected and non-muted tracks into a mono mix.

❏ **Loop Duplicate...**—creates duplicate, looping copies of the selected waveforms.

❏ **Convert to Unique Copy**—creates interconnected copies of the selected fragments of audio data.

❏ **Mute Waveform**—mutes the selected fragment of audio data.

❏ **Lock In Time**—locks the beginning of the selected waveform fragment to a certain time.

❏ **Lock for Play Only**—the selected audio fragments become unavailable for recording.

❏ **Allow Multiple Takes**—enables the Take History function.

❏ **Splice**—cuts the waveform into two new waveforms at the marker position.

❏ **Merge/Rejoin Splice**—merges neighboring waveforms into a single waveform.

❏ **Insert/Delete Time**—inserts the waveform with the given duration and containing silence into a track, or deletes the selected waveform fragment.

❏ **Select All Waves**—selects all waveforms.

❏ **Adjust Boundaries**—adjusts the boundaries of the selected fragment.

❏ **Trim**—cuts all the waveforms besides the selected ones.

❏ **Cut**—cuts the selected fragment.

❏ **Full**—returns the selected waveform to its initial state.

❏ **Group Waves**—joins waveforms into a group. The grouped waveforms are highlighted in a colored frame.

❏ **Snapping**—selects the option of locking the boundaries of the selected waveform to the coordinate grid (submenu).

❏ **Refresh Now**—refreshes the image.

❏ **Remove Waves**—removes the selected waveforms from the multitrack session. Until audio files are closed, the removed waveforms are still available in the **Edit Waveform View**, and can be inserted into multitrack using the **Edit>Insert in Multitrack** command.

❏ **Destroy Waves**—closes and deletes the selected waveform.

18.3.1. *Wave Block Info*—Displaying and Editing the Attributes of the Selected Waveform

The **Wave Block Info...** command opens the dialog window (Fig. 18.9) in which the attributes of the selected waveform are displayed and available for editing.

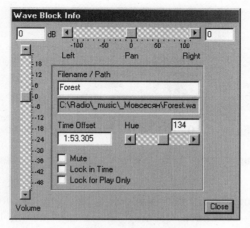

Fig. 18.9. The **Wave Block Info** window

Using the slider and the **Volume** input field, you can change the volume level of the selected waveform fragment.

The **Pan** slider is used to change the value of the waveform panorama.

In the **Filename/Path** fields, the filename of the file containing the waveform, along with the path to this file, are displayed.

In the **Time Offset** field, the starting time of the waveform playback is displayed. You can edit the value in this field.

The **Hue** slider allows you to change the color of the waveform selection.

If the **Mute** checkbox is checked, the selected waveform fragment is muted.

When the **Lock in Time** checkbox is checked, you cannot move the selected waveform to another time position.

When the **Lock for Play Only** checkbox is checked, the selected waveform becomes unavailable for recording, even if recording is allowed for the track in which it is placed.

18.3.2. *Loop Duplicate*—Creating Looped Copies of Selected Waveforms

The **Loop Duplicate** command opens a dialog box with the same name (Fig. 18.10).

The **Loop Duplicate** dialog box is used to create looped copies of selected waveforms.

Fig. 18.10. The **Loop Duplicate** dialog box

In the **Duplicate Waveform times** field, you should specify the number of times of duplication.

In the **Waveform Spacing** group, you should select the options for the waveform's duplication. If the **No gaps—continuous looping** option is selected, loops follow each other without any pause. When the **Evenly Spaced** option is selected, a field in which you can specify the duration of the pause between the loops becomes available.

18.3.3. *Insert/Delete Time*

The **Insert/Delete Time** command opens a dialog box with the same name (Fig. 18.11) that allows you to insert a waveform with the given duration and containing silence into a track, or to delete the selected waveform fragment.

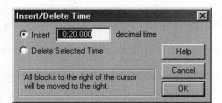

Fig. 18.11. The **Insert/Delete Time** dialog box

The **Insert** option is always available. If you have to move the audio data in all tracks at the same time, specify the time interval in the **Insert ... decimal time** field. After you apply the **Insert/Delete Time** function, the waveforms to the right of the marker position are moved to the right in all tracks.

The **Delete Selected Time** option is available only if there is a selected multitrack fragment. Just this fragment is deleted. Waveforms in all tracks are moved to the left (of the marker position).

18.4. The *View* Menu—Display Management

The **View** menu contains the commands and submenus you learned in *Chapter 11*. They do not require detailed description:

❑ **Edit Waveform View**—opens the waveform editor window

❑ **Show Pan Envelopes**—displays the panorama envelope

❑ **Show Volume Envelopes**—displays the volume envelope

❑ **Enable Envelope Editing**—enables the mode of editing the volume and the panorama envelopes

❑ **Show Level Meters**—shows the signal level meter

❑ **Show CD Player**—shows the CD player control panel

❑ **Viewing Range...**—selects the displayed multitrack range (time interval)

❑ **Display Time Format**—selects the time display format (submenu)

❑ **Vertical Scale Format**—selects the display format of values put along the Y-axis (submenu)

❑ **Status Bar**—selects the parameters displayed in the status bar

❑ **Info...**—opens the dialog box containing information on the composition processed in multitrack in the current session

❑ **Cue List**—shows the **Cue List/Ranges** dialog window

❑ **Time Window**—shows the window displaying the time corresponding to the current position indicator

18.5. The *Insert* Menu—Inserting Waveforms

Before a session or separate files are loaded into Cool Edit Pro, the **Insert** menu contains only two commands:

❑ **Wave from File...**—opens the dialog window used to insert the waveform from the file into the current position in multitrack

❑ **Waveforms List...**—opens the dialog window with the list of waveforms inserted into multitrack (see Fig. 17.1).

After loading even just one file into Cool Edit Pro, the command for inserting this file into the multitrack environment appears in the **Insert** menu. This command's name matches the filename. As soon as you select this command, the waveform is inserted into multitrack.

If a session is loaded into Cool Edit Pro, all the files contained in the session are listed in the **Insert** menu. They are inserted in multitrack automatically.

18.6. The *Transform* Menu—Transforming Waveforms

The **Transform** menu contains only two commands.

❑ **Envelope Follower...**—select the envelope follower options. The **Envelope Follower** function changes the amplitude envelope of the processed waveform according to the envelope of the model waveform.

❑ **Vocoder...**—select vocoder options.

You have probably heard many times that these options are not available. But that's not exactly the case. To make these options of the **Transform** menu available, the following conditions have to be true.

❑ In the multitrack environment, there must be at least two waveforms with overlapping times (two is best).

❑ Fragments of two processed waveforms matching in time must be selected.

The **Envelope Follower...** and **Vocoder...** commands are in the multitrack environment because they can be applied only to a pair of waveforms, and not to an individual waveform. We'll now describe these commands in detail.

18.6.1. *Envelope Follower*—Selecting Envelope Follower Options

The **Envelope Follower...** command opens a dialog window with the same name (Fig. 18.12).

The options of the **Envelope Follower** window allow you to change the envelope of the processed waveform's amplitude in accordance with the envelope of the model (analysis) waveform's amplitude.

You can apply this function, for example, if you want a bass guitar to sound only when a drum beats. To do so, you have to select the drum waveform as a model, and process the bass waveform.

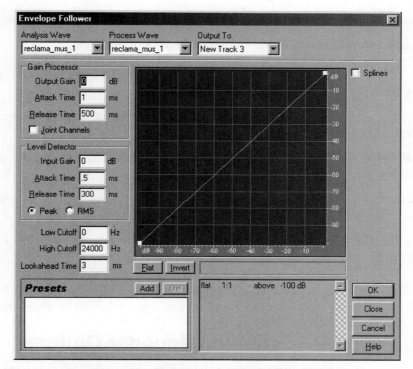

Fig. 18.12. The **Envelope Follower** dialog window

Besides the **Envelope Follower** function, you can change the dynamic processing parameters for the resulting waveform. We'll now describe the options of the **Envelope Follower** window.

The **Analysis Wave** drop-down list contains the name of the model waveform, and the **Process Wave** drop-down list contains the name of the processed waveform.

The **Output To** list indicates the track to which the resulting waveform is recorded after processing.

In the **Gain Processor** group, you can select the amplification parameters:

❑ **Output Gain**—amplification ratio at output

❑ **Attack Time (Out)**—attack time for the output signal

❑ **Release Time (Out)**—release time for the output signal

❑ **Joint Channels**—a checkbox; when checked, both channels are processed jointly

In the **Level Detector** group, the following detector parameters are selected:

❏ **Input Gain**—amplification ratio at the level detector input

❏ **Attack Time (In)**—attack time for the input signal

❏ **Release Time (In)**—release time for the input signal

Using the **Peak** and **RMS** switches, you can select the type of amplitude detector: peak or root-mean-square, respectively.

In the **Low Cutoff** field, you should input the lower cutoff frequency of the band filter, while the higher frequency is to be input in the **High Cutoff** field.

In the **Lookahead Time** field, you should input the time interval by which the dynamic processing device is enabled before the sharp change in the signal level.

By pressing the **Flat** button, the graph is reset to its default state.

The **Invert** button allows you to invert the graph relative to a diagonal between the points (10, 100); (0, 0).

If the **Splines** checkbox is checked, the graph spline approximation mode is enabled.

18.6.2. *Vocoder*—Selecting Vocoder Options

Vocoder is the special effect that in our case appears as a modulation of the processed waveform by another waveform—the control signal (usually, a singer's voice).

We'll now describe the options of the dialog window (Fig. 18.13) opened by the **Vocoder** command.

The **Control Wave** drop-down list contains the name of the waveform used as a control waveform; the **Process Wave** drop-down list contains the name of the processed waveform.

In the **Output To** drop-down list, indicate the track to which the resulting waveform will be written.

In the **FFT Size** drop-down list, you can select one of the standard size values for the Fast Fourier Transform algorithm, and in the **Overlays** field you can specify the over-sampling value (values 4 through 12 are recommended).

This window also contains options that improve the quality of effect processing.

❏ **Interval Size**—select the time interval for waveform processing according to the Fast Fourier Transform algorithm (values from 10 to 30 milliseconds are recommended).

❏ **Window Width**—select the window width, one of the Fast Fourier Transform parameters (a value of 90% is recommended).

❏ **Vocal Crossover**—the frequency of crossover frequency band separation.

❏ **Resynthesis Window**—select the width of the window used to resynthesize the signal with vocoder. When the value of this parameter is small, the consonants are reproduced more clearly. The value of the **Resynthesis Window** parameter should never be more than the value of the **Overlays** parameter.

❏ **Affect Level**—the mixing proportion for the source and the processed signals.

❏ **Amplification**

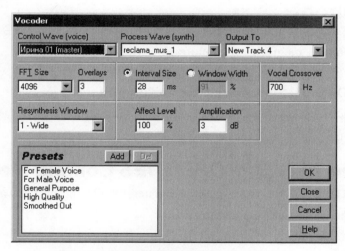

Fig. 18.13. The **Vocoder** dialog window

18.7. The *Options* Menu—Options of the Multitrack Editor

The **Options** menu contains the following commands and submenus:

❏ **Loop Mode**—looped playback of the selected waveform fragment (this command is disabled)

❏ **Monitor Record Level(s)**—enables the input signal level meter

❏ **Show Levels on Play and Record**—enables indication of the signal level in recording and playback modes

❏ **MIDI Trigger Enable**—enables editing control through the MIDI interface

❏ **SMPTE Slave Enable**—enables the mode for synchronizing with an external source through the SMPTE interface

❑ **SMPTE Start Offset**—editing the start offset time in SMPTE format

❑ **Pause Background Mixing**—pauses background mixing

❑ **Settings...**—sets the program's options

❑ **Device Preferences...**—selects device drivers for recording and playback for each of the tracks

❑ **Shortcuts (Keyboard & MIDI Triggers)...**—edits shortcut keys

❑ **Toolbars**—edits toolbars

18.8. The Context Menus of the Multitrack Environment

Besides the main menu, toolbars, and hot keys, Cool Edit Pro provides context menus. There are two context menus in the multitrack environment:

❑ **WAVE PROPERTIES**—commands for working with waveforms

❑ **TRACK PROPERTIES**—commands for working with tracks

You already know all the commands contained in the context menus, so we will only mention them briefly.

18.8.1. The *WAVE PROPERTIES* Context Menu

The **WAVE PROPERTIES** context menu is opened by clicking on the waveform.

This menu contains the following commands:

❑ **Edit Waveform...**—turns to the waveform editor window.

❑ **Wave Block Info...**—displays and edits the attributes of the selected waveform fragment.

❑ **Volume...**—adjusts the volume level.

❑ **Pan...**—adjusts the panorama.

❑ **Punch In**—enables the multiple recording mode for audio data, which saves duplicate copies.

❑ **Crossfade**—enables the crossfade mode. The submenu is for selecting the crossfade law. Possible variants are: linear, sinusoidal, logarithmic increasing, logarithmic decreasing. The most natural laws for changing the volume over time are logarithmic laws.

❑ **Take History**—returns to one of the previous versions of the audio composition.

❑ **Loop Duplicate...**—creates duplicate, looping copies of the selected waveforms.

❑ **Convert to Unique Copy**—creates interconnected copies of the selected fragments of audio data.

❑ **Mute Waveform**—mutes the selected fragment of audio data.

❑ **Lock In Time**—locks the beginning of the selected waveform fragment to a certain time.

❏ **Lock for Play Only**—makes the selected audio fragments unavailable for recording.

❏ **Allow Multiple Takes**—enables the Take History function.

❏ **Splice**—cuts the waveform into two new waveforms at the marker position.

❏ **Merge/Rejoin Splice**—merges neighboring waveforms into a single waveform.

❏ **Adjust Boundaries**—adjusts the boundaries of the selected fragment.

❏ **Trim**—cuts all the waveforms besides the selected ones.

❏ **Cut**—cuts the selected fragment.

❏ **Full**—returns the selected waveform to its initial state.

❏ **Clear Envelope**—returns the volume envelope or the panorama envelope to its initial state (submenu).

❏ **Remove Wave Block**—removes the selected waveforms from the multitrack session. Until audio files are closed, the removed waveforms are still available in the **Edit Waveform View**, and can be inserted into multitrack by the **Edit>Insert in Multitrack** command.

❏ **Destroy Wave**—closes and deletes the selected waveform.

18.8.2. The *TRACK PROPERTIES* Context Menu

The **TRACK PROPERTIES** context menu is opened by clicking on any unused part of any track. It contains commands similar to those in the the main menu:

❏ **Wave from File...**—opens the standard dialog window for inserting the waveform into the current multitrack position from a file

❏ **Mix Down to Track** (submenu)—creates a mix

❏ **Create Empty Waveform**

❏ **Mute**—mutes the current track

❏ **Solo**—enables the solo mode for the current track

❏ **Solo This Track Only**—enables solo only for the selected track

❏ **Record**—allows recording into the current track

❏ **Volume**—opens the dialog window for editing the volume

❏ **Pan**—opens the dialog window for editing the panorama

❏ **Track Info**—opens the window with information on the track

❏ **Recording Device**—selects the recording device (driver)

❏ **Playback Device**—selects the playback device (driver)

❏ **Select All Waves in Track**

And thus we finish describing the Cool Edit Pro editor—a program that will allow you to achieve fantastic audio processing results.

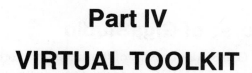

Part IV

VIRTUAL TOOLKIT

Chapter 19: Nemesys GigaStudio 160 (V.2)

**Chapter 20: Creating Your Own Sampler Libraries Using
GigaStudio Instrument Editor 2.0**

Chapter 21: Reason—a Virtual Audio Studio

Chapter 19: Nemesys GigaStudio 160 (V.2)

19.1. Introduction

In this chapter, we discuss the GigaStudio software sampler. We won't go into very much detail in describing its features, but we will share our opinion: it reminds us of an expensive studio hardware sampler. The only thing you will need to create a "cool" sound is a simple sequencer, since GigaStudio provides all the other features.

19.1.1. Features of GigaStudio

The virtual sampler GigaStudio consists of four modules: Port1, Port2, Port3, and Port4. Thus, you have $16 \times 4 = 64$ MIDI channels. Tools (patches) for each of the channels are selected using means built into GigaStudio. The parameters of the effects processor are also controlled from GigaStudio. All settings of GigaStudio are saved in GSP (GigaStudio Performance) files.

The waveforms for the sampler are stored in GIG files. This format is inherited by GigaStudio from the well-known GigaSampler software sampler. The GigaStudio Instrument Editor patches editor (from here on out called GSEdit) is included in the GigaStudio delivery set. Using this editor, you can edit existing GIG banks, or create your own. This editor also allows you to convert SoundFont 2.x banks and Downloadable Waveforms banks into GIG format.

Thanks to the **Distributed Wave** function, GigaStudio can reproduce normal WAV files. You can distribute the WAV files along the MIDI keyboard, and save and load the outline of WAV files along the MIDI keyboard in a special file. These distributed files represent a special instrument called *128 Track Wave Instrument*. This instrument can be assigned only to one of the MIDI channels.

Unfortunately, different hardware and software vendors call the same things by different names. What the vendors of the Akai samplers call "programs", the vendors of GigaStudio call "patches" or "instruments", and the vendors of SoundFont-compatible devices call "presets". Musicians call these things "timbres" or "instruments". In this book, sample banks of all of these vendors are described, so we will explain in each case what we mean by each term. However, the readers should also be able to grasp the meaning of these terms depending on the context.

GigaStudio also includes the QuickSound utility, which creates a database of all file formats supported by your PC during GigaStudio installation. This will allow you to quickly find the file you are interested in. The interaction between the user and this utility is implemented through a browser in the main window of the program: you select the required file in the directory tree, or input its full or partial name in the search field.

One of the main advantages of GigaStudio is its ability to read CD libraries of Akai S1000/S3000 samplers. Thanks to this feature, GigaStudio has been approved by professionals. With approximately twenty Akai CDs, you have almost completely solved the problem of your compositions' sound. Akai S1000/3000 CDs have a special format, and cannot be read without special programs such as SConverter, which is supplied with GigaStudio.

SConverter can read disks with Akai waveforms in a usual CD-ROM, and thus the waveforms are loaded much faster than if they were to be loaded through a SCSI interface. Akai waveforms are converted while loading from the CD-ROM, and are placed into temporary GIG files that are loaded into GigaStudio. SConverter also allows you to import WAV files included in sampler banks from Akai disks.

We have mentioned that instruments are "loaded" into GigaStudio. Actually, the waveforms remain on the disk and are played directly from it. This is done without any noticeable delay. However, when speaking about instruments, we will call this "loading" for convenience.

SConverter does not have any special interface. We can say that it is integrated into the QuickSound browser. When the Akai waveforms CD is inserted into a CD-ROM, the user gets access to the disk directory. The browser context menu (called by the mouse's right button) also changes: commands appear that allow the user to perform different actions on Akai waveforms. If you want, one of these commands can be assigned to the message from the mouse about double-clicking (*Section 19.2.5*). The SConverter utility simplifies working with Akai waveforms.

A composition created using GigaStudio can have the same quality as a composition created in an expensive hardware studio. It's not at all necessary to record it from the linear output of a sound card. Thanks to the **Capture** function supported by GigaStudio, the digital flow coming from the virtual sampler input can be recorded directly as a WAV file with 16-bit or 24-bit resolution. However, this is just theory. In practice, you have to have a sound card of at least SB Live! class to provide for monitoring.

But this limitation is not the only one. Cheap multimedia cards won't let you process the signals of separate channels with the GigaStudio effects processor. You can only add effects to a master signal. To implement the abilities of GigaStudio, you need a card supporting the GSIF technology developed by NemeSys. Such vendors as Aadvark, EgoSys, Echo, Midiman, Terratec, and others produce GSIF-compatible cards.

Since the total cost of an advanced software sampler can be compared with the cost of a hardware sampler, we recommend that you go for the software. GigaStudio is easy to use, is more effective, and you can load many more waveforms into it.

19.1.2. The Main Menu of the Program; Navigation Bar

The main menu of GigaStudio after the program is launched is shown in Fig. 19.1. Its upper part contains the following elements: the main menu (under the window name) and the toolbar. The window is divided into three parts by horizontal and vertical lines. You can move these lines using the mouse, and thus change the sizes of the areas. In the upper left part of the window, you see the navigation bar, which duplicates certain functions of the main menu. The contents of the right part of the window change depending on the currently selected item of the navigation bar. The name of the selected item is shown in bold font. The QuickSound browser is located in the lower part of the window. It allows you to quickly find, listen to, and load audio files.

The navigation bar is shown in Fig. 19.2.

Fig. 19.1. The GigaStudio main window

Fig. 19.2. The navigation bar

The navigation bar contains the following items:

❏ **Port1, Port2, Port3, Port4**—parameters of the sampler blocks (*Section 19.3*)

❏ **DSP Station**—effect processor (*Section 19.4*)

❏ **Settings**—general settings of the program (*Section 19.2*)

❏ **Diagnostics**—system diagnostics (*Section 19.2.6*)

❏ **Help**

19.2. Settings

We'll start learning the program beginning with its settings. Click on the **Settings** menu item. The region shown in Fig. 19.3 appears in the right part of the main window.

19.2.1. The *General* Tab

GigaStudio is just a sampler, and not a functionally complete audio editor. Thus, it can meet its maximum potential only when it is used together with a software sequencer (such as Cakewalk Pro Audio or Cubase VST), an audio editor (Cool Edit Pro), and a GS format sampler bank editor, all loaded into GigaStudio.

In the **General** tab (see Fig. 19.3), you can define the path to the **Sequencer**, **Patch Editor** (sampler banks editor), and **Wave Editor** (audio editor) using the **Browse** button.

Later, you can call these programs by pressing the corresponding buttons of the toolbar. You can use any sequencer and any audio editor, but you have almost no alternative to the patch editors of the GS format. Use the GS Edit program included in the delivery set of GigaStudio. By default, the editor is located in C:\Program Files\NemeSys\Gstudio.

After you define the paths, press the **Apply** button (equivalent to **OK**). If you want to cancel the settings, press **Cancel**.

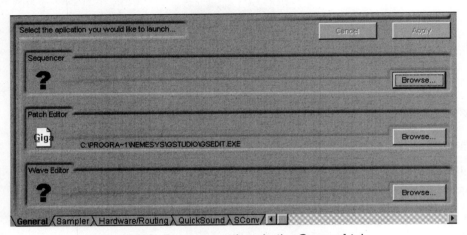

Fig. 19.3. Program settings in the **General** tab

19.2.2. The *Sampler* Tab

The **Sampler** tab (Fig. 19.4) defines the sampler parameters.

When several waveforms are played simultaneously, the volume of the summarizing signal increases. If a large number of waveforms (160 is the maximum) is played, clipping (signal level overflow) might occur, which results in nonlinear distortions. To avoid it, decrease the value of the **Master Attenuation** parameter (from 0 to −15 dB).

In the **Dither Type** group, dithering is enabled/disabled using the **Enabled** option. In the drop-down list, the dithering level is selected: 0 is high level, 1 is low level (preferred for multichannel sound cards).

The position of the **Alter Polyphony to change the number of simultaneous notes** slider defines the sampler polyphony—the maximum allowed number of simultaneous voices. One voice corresponds to a monophonic waveform, and two voices to a stereophonic waveform. For example, if a polyphony of 64 voices is defined, 64 monophonic or 32 stereophonic waveforms can play simultaneously. Usually, in a single composition, both mono and stereo waveforms are used, so the real polyphony is normally less than assigned.

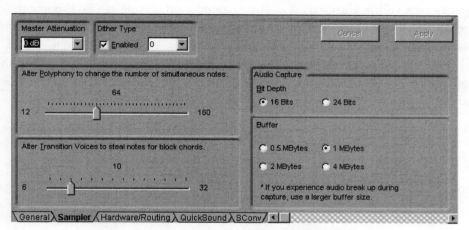

Fig. 19.4. Program settings in the **Sampler** tab

The **Alter Transition Voices to steal notes for block chords** slider defines the number of voices reserved for playing sounds in the fade phase. If you often use chords in your compositions, it makes sense to increase the value of this parameter.

In the **Audio Capture** group, the resolution of the captured WAV file (16 or 24 bits) and the buffer size (0.5, 1, 2, or 4 MB) are defined. If pops are heard in the captured WAV file, you should increase the buffer size.

19.2.3. The *Hardware/Routing* Tab

In the **Hardware/Routing** tab (Fig. 19.5), you specify the parameters of the MIDI input and output audio ports.

In the **Hardware** drop-down list, the available audio ports are selected. The audio signal generated by GigaStudio is output to these ports. Using the **Sample Rate** and **Bit Depth** lists, the sampling frequency and the resolution are defined for the selected audio port.

In the **Outputs Enabled** group, the audio channels available for the selected audio port are selected. They become available to GigaStudio as well. Audio channels are indicated by pairs of numbers: "1,2", "3,4", etc. The reason for this is that each audio channel corresponds to two stereo channels. For a typical (multimedia) card, only one stereo pair (one audio channel) is available. To use several audio channels, you have to buy a GSIF-compatible sound card developed by NemeSys. By the way, you'll see the words **GSIF Compatible:** above the **Hardware** list. If the sound card we use is GSIF-compatible, **Yes** will be displayed after these words; in our case, we see **No**. In the course of further operation, you will realize that GSIF-compatibility is a very important factor. Only a GSIF-compatible sound card allows you to implement all the abilities of GigaStudio. To compensate for the disadvantages of GSIF-non-compatibility, you'll need to use several sound cards.

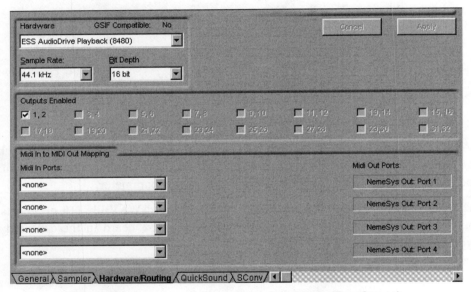

Fig. 19.5. Program settings in the **Hardware/Routing** tab

This is true for Nemesys GigaStuduio 160, version 2.0, which works only in Windows 95/98/ME. The most recent version, 2.5, will work in Windows 95/98/ME/2000/XP, but requires a GSIF-compatible sound card. At the moment this book was written, the following GSIF-compatible sound cards were on the market:

- ❏ Aardvark Aark 20/20
- ❏ Aardvark Aark 20/20+
- ❏ Aardvark Aark 24
- ❏ Aardvark Aark DirectPro 24/96
- ❏ Aardvark Aark DirectPro LX6
- ❏ Aardvark Aark TDIF
- ❏ Creamware Elektra
- ❏ Creamware Luna 2496

- ❏ Creamware PowerSampler
- ❏ Creamware Pulsar I
- ❏ Creamware Pulsar II
- ❏ Creamware SCOPE /SP
- ❏ Echo Darla
- ❏ Echo Darla 24
- ❏ Echo Gina
- ❏ Echo Gina 24
- ❏ Echo Layla
- ❏ Echo Layla 24
- ❏ Echo Mia
- ❏ Echo Mona
- ❏ EgoSys WaMi Rack 24-GSLE
- ❏ EgoSys WaMi Rack 24-GSLEch8
- ❏ EgoSys WaMi Rack 24
- ❏ EgoSys WaMi Box
- ❏ EgoSys Wave Terminal 2496
- ❏ Frontier Design Dakota
- ❏ Frontier Design WaveCenter PCI
- ❏ Hoontech Soundtrack Audio DSP 24
- ❏ Marian / SEK'D Marc 2
- ❏ Marian / SEK'D Marc 4 Digi
- ❏ Marian / SEK'D Marc 4 MIDI
- ❏ Marian / SEK'D Marc 2 Pro
- ❏ Marian / SEK'D Prodif Plus

- ❏ Marian / SEK'D Prodif A
- ❏ Marian / SEK'D Siena
- ❏ Midiman/MAudio Audiophile 24/96
- ❏ Midiman/MAudio Delta 1010
- ❏ Midiman/MAudio Delta 66
- ❏ Midiman/MAudio Delta 44
- ❏ Midiman/MAudio Delta DiO 24/96
- ❏ MOTU 308
- ❏ MOTU 24i
- ❏ MOTU 1224
- ❏ MOTU 1296
- ❏ MOTU 2408
- ❏ MOTU 2408mk II
- ❏ MOTU 828—Firewire
- ❏ RME Digi 96
- ❏ RME Digi 96/8
- ❏ RME Digi 96/8 PAD
- ❏ RME Digi 96/8 Pro
- ❏ RME Digi 96/8 PST
- ❏ RME Hammerfall 9636
- ❏ RME Hammerfall 9652
- ❏ RME Hammerfall DSP—digiface
- ❏ RME Hammerfall DSP—multiface
- ❏ Sonorus STUDI/O
- ❏ SoundScape Mixtreme

❏ TASCAM PCI 822   ❏ Terratec EWS88 MT

❏ Terratec EWS88 D   ❏ Terratec EWX 24/96

During installation, GigaStudio creates four MIDI ports in the system, intended for transferring MIDI information from the external software sequencer to GigaStudio. MIDI information arriving to these ports is reproduced by GigaStudio. However, in GigaStudio, in the **MIDI In to MIDI Out Mapping** group, you can select up to four MIDI ports, through which GigaStudio can accept MIDI commands from the external controller. Thanks to this feature, you can play in GigaStudio using a MIDI keyboard, a hardware sequencer, etc., without loading any additional programs. In the **Midi In Ports** lists, you select the ports into which the hardware MIDI controllers are plugged. Each of these input ports corresponds to an output port (**Midi Out Ports**). MIDI information arriving to these output ports from **Midi In Ports** is played by GigaStudio.

You can assign the same MIDI In port to several MIDI Out ports. For GigaStudio, none of the available MIDI ports is selected as an input port by default. If you use GigaStudio together with a software sequencer, you can leave the default settings of the **MIDI In to MIDI Out Mapping** group unchanged.

19.2.4. The *QuickSound* Tab

In the **QuickSound** tab (Fig. 19.6), the parameters for searching for audio files by keyword are defined.

In the **Search Mode** group, you select the search mode:

❏ **Recursive**—a search including all directories, starting from the assigned directory or disk

❏ **Local**—search within the assigned directory

In the **Results Display** group, you define the method of displaying the found files. One GIG file can contain several instruments. If the instrument found is in a GIG file that contains other instruments, these instruments are not displayed as search results if the **Show Only Instruments that match search** checkbox is chosen. If you have to output a detailed list of instruments contained in the GIG files found, choose the **Automatically Expand Gigs to show Instruments** checkbox.

In the **Hit Reporting** group, the output method for messages on the number of files found by keyword is defined:

❏ **Show Keyword Hit Report**—display the pop-up hint showing the number of files found (Hits)

❏ **Verbose Hit Report**—a more detailed pop-up hint

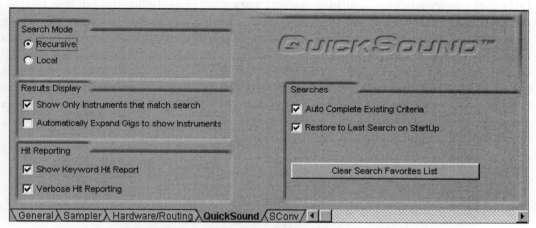

Fig. 19.6. Program settings in the **QuickSound** tab

If the **Auto Complete Existing Criteria** checkbox is selected, suggestions for automatic completion of the word will be made when you input the search object name: as the user inputs the keyword, the QuickSound program examines its internal list, searching for words starting with the characters you have already typed in. The words found are substituted automatically. The user can continue inputting the word. When the program outputs the desired word, he or she can press the <Tab> key to agree with the search result. If the **Restore to Last Search on Startup** option is enabled, the program remembers the search criteria and the results of the last search before it was closed.

The **Clear Search Favorites List** button removes the list of keywords used to automatically suggest search queries. Keywords input by the user that lead to a successful search are added to this list. If you find nothing using this word, or find certain files but don't load them, this keyword is not remembered. You should use the **Clear Search Favorites List** button only if you use a *huge* number of audio files with formats supported by QuickSound.

19.2.5. The *SConv* Tab, Import Parameters of Akai Sampler Banks

In the **SConv** tab (Fig. 19.7), the parameters of the SConverter utility are defined. This utility is used to load Akai sampler banks into GigaStudio.

Using the **Browse** button, you change the path to the directory for storing temporary GIG files converted from Akai files. As you work with GigaStudio, the number of temporary files increases. To avoid overfilling the hard disk, you have to periodically remove temporary files. If the **Empty Temp Directory When Disk is Ejected or Program Exits** option is enabled, temporary files are automatically deleted as soon as the CD with Akai waveforms is ejected from the CD-ROM, or as soon as the GigaStudio main menu is closed. If the **Empty Temp Directory Manually (using SConverter Context Menu)** option is enabled, temporary files are stored until the user decides to remove them with the **Clean Temp Dir** command of the SConverter context menu. This menu is called by right-clicking in the QuickSound browser while viewing the contents of the Akai format CD.

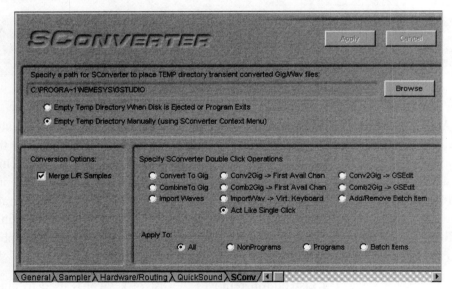

Fig. 19.7. The **SConv** tab

In the **Conversion Options** group, there is only one option—the **Merge L/R Samples** checkbox. Before we describe this option, we should give a short explanation.

GIG format sample banks can contain stereophonic waveforms. In these waveforms, the counts of the left and right channels are logically placed together (as in a stereo WAV file). However, many sampler bank formats (such as SoundFont and Akai S1000) do not support stereophonic waveforms. In such banks, waveforms for the right and left channels are stored separately. They are joined into a stereo pair on a higher level of the logical structure of the bank. Such joining may take place, for example, on the instrument level, when two mono waveforms made from one stereo WAV file are placed in one instrument and located in the extreme points of the panorama. Such an instrument sounds identical to the initial WAV file, even though it consists of two mono waveforms. If the **Merge L/R Waveforms** checkbox is chosen, the SConverter utility finds such instruments and joins the pairs of mono waveforms into single stereo waveforms. If the checkbox is not selected, the sample format is not changed during conversion.

The user sees the logical structure of Akai disks as a set of objects located on different logical levels. Objects of the lowest level are called *Programs*. In this case, this term means the same as "patches": the sound of the musical instrument that a MIDI channel "plays".

The *Volume* object is on a higher level. One volume can contain several programs. When the user performs any action on the volume, this action applies to all programs contained within a volume. The *Partition* object is on an even higher level. One partition can contain several volumes. The highest level is the Akai CD-ROM. One CD-ROM can contain several partitions. The user has the ability to combine different objects into the **Batch** list. If the disk contains hundreds of waveforms, and you are interested in only a few of them, you can place the waveforms, volumes, and partitions you need into the **Batch** list. The commands of the context menu of the **Batch** list apply to all the objects contained in it.

In the **Specify SConverter Double Click Operations**, you define the program's reaction to double-clicking on the objects of the Akai disks; their type is specified in the **Apply to:** group:

❑ **All**—all objects

❑ **NonPrograms**—all objects except programs (patches)

❑ **Programs**—only programs (patches)

❑ **Batch Items**—only objects of the **Batch** list

The program can react to double-clicking on objects of the Akai disks as follows:

❑ **Convert to Gig**—convert to a GIG file

❑ **Conv2Gig->First Avail Chan**—convert to a GIG file and then load into the first available MIDI channel

❑ **Conv2Gig->GSEdit**—convert to a GIG file and then load into GSEdit

❑ **Import Waves**—import WAV files and save them in the specified directory

❐ **Import Wav->Virt. Keyboard**—import WAV files and load them into GigaSampler

❐ **Add/Remove Batch Item**—place the object into the **Batch** list if it is not there, and remove the object from the **Batch** list if it is

❐ **Act Like Single Click**—react to a double-click as a single click (select the object)

Some options of the **Specify SConverter Double Click Operations** group are repeated twice. We think this is a bug. It seems, though, that even the vendors had to just let it go—even the Help section of the program contains illustrations of this group with duplicated options.

19.2.6. System Diagnostics

The navigation bar (see Fig. 19.2) in the main window contains the **Diagnostic** command. A similar command is contained in the program's main menu: **View>Diagnostic**. When you select it, the diagnostics information and the **Run Diagnostics** button are found in the right part of the main window. After you press this button, you get information on the state of the system. This information can be useful if you are familiar with MS Windows architecture.

19.3. *Port1, Port2, Port3, Port4*—Working with the Sampler

A simplified picture of digital audio streams inside a software sampler is shown in Fig. 19.8.

The names of functional blocks in the picture correspond to the terms accepted in the GigaStudio interface. Let's discuss the picture starting from the top. **Port1—Port4** are virtual MDI ports, each of them having 16 MIDI channels. All ports are joined into one general module—**MIDI Mixer**. The MIDI mixer module corresponds to the part of a MIDI synthesizer and/or sampler responsible for audio signal generation. Using a MIDI message, you can control such parameters as panorama, volume, etc. Signals coming from the **MIDI Mixer** are not processed by the effects processor. GigaStudio contains a software implementation of a real studio mixer. The mixer consists of a number of stereophonic lines. Line inputs are marked as **Inputs 1,2**, **Inputs 3,4**, etc.

Each of the outputs of the **MIDI Mixer** block can be connected to any of these inputs. The signal of each of the mixer lines can be processed by four different effects plugged into the insert mode (**Insert1—Insert4**). Besides which, each line has eight aux-sends. Four effects can be plugged into each of the **Aux1—Aux8** buses. Each of the mixer line outputs and aux returns can be connected to any of the stereo ports marked **Outputs 1,2**, **Outputs 3,4**, etc. All the above abilities apply only if your sound card is GSIF-compatible. The number of mixer lines and audio ports depends on the capabilities of the sound card. If the card is not GSIF-compatible, you will have the following limitations:

❑ **Mixer Inputs**—one line

❑ **Aux Buses**—two lines

❑ **Outputs**—one line

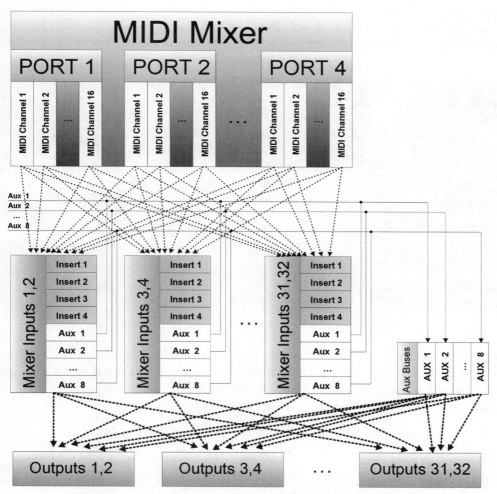

Fig. 19.8. Possible connections of GigaStudio blocks

Note that in GigaStudio there are two mixers—**MIDI Mixer** and a mixer without a name, whose inputs are marked as **Inputs 1,2**, **Inputs 3,4**, etc. To avoid confusion, we'll call the second mixer *audio mixer*.

Now you have an idea of the configuration of a virtual studio, and we can now start to study it in detail.

19.3.1. The *MIDI Mixer* Tab

To access one of the four blocks of the sampler, select the corresponding item of the navigation bar (see Fig. 19.2)—**Port1**, **Port2**, **Port3**, **Port4**—or use the command of the **View** menu in the program's main menu. The right part of the main window is shown in Fig. 19.9.

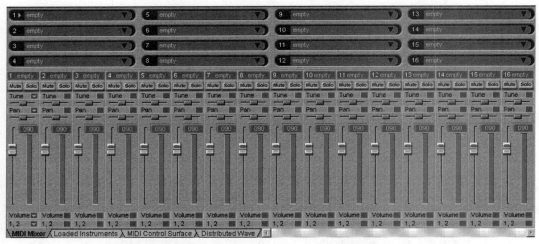

Fig. 19.9. Sampler parameters in the **MIDI Mixer** tab

The MIDI mixer panel is located in the **MIDI Mixer** tab. It consists of 16 lines corresponding to the MIDI channels. The controls of the current line are highlighted in green. Using the mixer, you can control any of the parameters of the sampler without using a software sequencer or a hardware MIDI controller.

By default, the following settings are available for each of the channels:

❑ **Volume**　　❑ **Pan**　　　❑ **Tune**　　　❑ **Mute**　　　❑ **Solo**

To reset any of these manipulators, click the ▼ button, or directly on the manipulator's name. The menu shown in Fig. 19.10 will appear.

This menu contains the list of all MIDI controllers supported by GigaStudio. Select the MIDI controller you need by double-clicking.

When the position of any of the controllers in any of the lines changes, its current position is displayed in the small window in the upper part of the **Volume** slider.

For each of the MIDI channels, you can specify a line of the audio mixer for it alone. In Fig. 19.8, this is shown as arrows directed from the **MIDI Channel** blocks to the **Inputs** blocks. Recall that the audio mixer channels are marked by pairs of numbers. For example, "1,2" indicates the first stereo channel, "3,4" indicates the second stereo channel, etc. To reset the audio channel, click on its number or on its ▼ button.

Select any of the available audio channels in the menu shown in Fig. 19.11. While writing this chapter, a PC with a typical multimedia card was used, and therefore only one stereo channel is available. If your sound card is GSIF-compatible, and the correct drivers are installed, the number of available audio channels significantly increases.

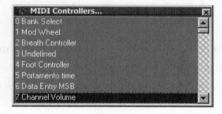

Fig. 19.10. Select MIDI controller

Fig. 19.11. Select audio mixer channel

In the upper part of the MIDI mixer, we see the instrument cells, numbered 1 through 16 (Fig. 19.12). Let's call this area the *MIDI channels bar*.

Fig. 19.12. MIDI channels bar

Each cell of the bar corresponds to a MIDI channel. By default, **empty** is displayed in each cell. The number of the current MIDI channel is marked with a small green triangle. To associate any instrument with a MIDI channel, double-click anywhere inside the corresponding cell (except for the small black triangle). The standard file load dialog box opens. Using this box, select the GIG file you want to load. Its name will be displayed in the cell. Usually a GIG file contains one instrument, but it may sometimes contain several instruments, or even several instrument banks. In such a case, all the instruments are loaded into GigaStudio, but the zero instrument of the zero bank is associated with the assigned MIDI channel. To select another instrument from the loaded bank, click on the small black triangle in the cell of a MIDI channel. The dialog box shown in Fig. 19.13 will appear.

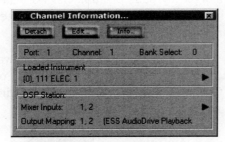

Fig. 19.13. MIDI channel information   **Fig. 19.14.** Select the instrument

To select another instrument, click on the small black triangle in the **Loaded Instrument** group. A dialog box appears, an example of which is shown in Fig. 19.14.

This list contains the instruments loaded into GigaStudio, and you should then select the instrument you need.

In the **Channel Information** dialog box shown in Fig. 19.13, the MIDI channel is dissociated from the assigned instrument using the **Detach** button. However, the instrument is not unloaded from GigaStudio. It remains in the **Loaded Instrument** list until it is "unloaded" with a special command (*Section 19.3.2*).

The GSEdit editor, described in *Chapter 20*, is displayed using the **Edit** button, and the instrument is loaded into it. Special files describing specific features of using GIG files can be attached to these files. You can view the contents of such a file by using the **Info** button. In the untitled group—between the **Detach**, **Edit**, and **Info** buttons—the information on the port number (**Port**), MIDI channel (**Channel**), and instrument bank (**Bank Select**) is displayed. The **DSP Station** group shows the mixer audio input (**Mixer Inputs**) corresponding to the current MIDI channel. You can change the input by clicking on the small black triangle. Besides this, the audio mixer input port is shown in the **DSP Station** group as well, but you cannot modify it in this window.

The main idea of this section was to describe how to associate instruments with MIDI channels. It is better to control such parameters as volume, panorama, etc., from the external sequencer.

19.3.2. The *Loaded Instruments* Tab—Instrument Loading/Unloading; Virtual Keyboard; Exporting the List of Instruments to a Text File

The main window with the open **Loaded Instruments** tab is shown in Fig. 19.15. In the upper part of the window, you can see the MIDI channels bar that was described in the previous section.

Under this bar, there is a list of loaded instruments. The instrument name is displayed in the **Instrument Name** column, the bank numbers are indicated in the **Bank #** column, the instrument numbers in the bank are indicated in the **Instruments #** column, and the lists of MIDI channels occupied by instruments (for each of the four MIDI ports) are indicated in the **Port 1—4: Channels** column.

By double-clicking on the elements of this list, you assign a particular instrument to the selected MIDI channel (the current MIDI channel is marked by a green triangle in one of the cells of the MIDI channels bar). By right-clicking above the list of the loaded instruments, you call the context menu shown in Fig. 19.16.

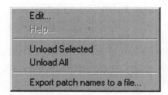

Fig. 19.16. Context menu of the loaded instruments list

Using this menu, you can:

❑ Call GSEdit to edit the current instrument (**Edit** command)

❑ View a special file containing information on the instrument (**Help** command), if this file exists

❑ Unload all the selected instruments (**Unload Selected** command)

❑ Unload all the instruments (**Unload All** command)

❑ Save the instruments' names in a text file (**Export patch names to a file** command)

To select several elements in the list, hold the <Shift> or <Ctrl> key down.

Even if only one instrument is selected, the names of all the instruments contained in the GIG file are still exported into a text file.

The virtual MIDI keyboard is located under the list of loaded instruments. You can play it using the mouse, but this is not its main purpose. The virtual keyboard in this case is a kind of indicator. Its appearance changes depending on the current instrument. In Fig. 19.15, the instrument **100 BPM 1** set for the 4th MIDI channel is current. A part of the keyboard is gray. This means that no samples are defined for the corresponding keys. Only the black-and-white part of the keyboard can produce sound. Active keys (ones currently making a sound) are colored in blue. Multilayer keys are marked with double gray lines (Fig. 19.17*a*). Compare them to the one-layer keys shown in Fig. 19.17*b*. Recall that *mulilayer* means that when a MIDI key is pressed, several samples are played.

a   b

Fig. 19.17. Multilayer keys (*a*) as opposed to one-layer keys (*b*) are marked with a double line

The key corresponding to *A* of the fourth MIDI octave (the conditional middle of the MIDI keyboard) is marked with a red dot. In GigaStudio, MIDI octave numbering starts from −1.

One of the MIDI keys is marked with a small green triangle. You can move it using the right mouse button. This triangle marks the key starting from which the loaded WAV files are placed. Loading normal WAV files is described in *Section 19.3.4*.

If a group of keys is colored in lilac, these keys are used to switch between the registers of the instrument. Depending on the selected register, different sets of waveforms, envelope parameters, filters, etc., can be set. Registers are described in detail in *Chapter 20*.

19.3.3. The *MIDI Control Surface* Tab

The main window, with the **MIDI Control Surface** tab open, is shown in Fig. 19.18.

In the upper part of the window, we have the MIDI channels bar (*Section 19.3.1*). The virtual MIDI keyboard is in the lower part of the window (*Section 19.3.2*), and its appearance depends on the current instrument. The remaining space is occupied by sliders of the MIDI controllers tab. Under each slider, the MIDI controller controlled by this slider is displayed. To reset the controller, click on the small green triangle ▼ and define the new controller in the list that appears. Above each slider, there is a small window in which the current slider position is displayed as a number from 0 to 127.

Note that under each slider there are turquoise lines on which to type notes. By default, they are marked as **empty**. The words **Type Here** tell you where to enter the text for a label for the current slider (highlighted in green).

LEDs might be placed next to some sliders. They are marked with the letters DIM (from *dimension*). These controllers are configured so that you can control switching the registers of the instrument.

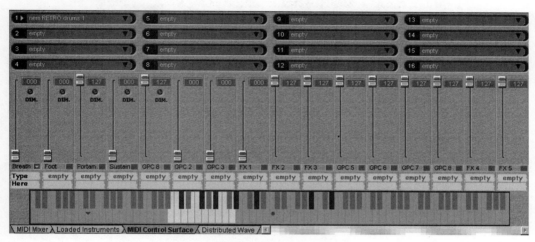

Fig. 19.18. MIDI controllers bar

The MIDI controllers bar contains a large number of controls, but not all of them control sound parameters. The purpose of most of these controls is determined by the person who creates the bank. Often, most of the controllers are not used, and so it makes sense to learn how to operate the GSEdit editor included with GigaStudio, and to make changes in settings of sampler banks.

19.3.4. The *Distributed Wave* Tab—Load WAV Files

The **Distributed Wave** tab (Fig. 19.19) allows you to create, store, and load layouts of WAV files along the MIDI keyboard.

You cannot load WAV files using the MIDI channels bar. We will describe how to load WAV files using the QuickSound browser located in the lower part of the main window (Fig. 19.20).

Before you load one or more WAV files, select the MIDI key starting from which the waveforms are placed using the right mouse button. This key is marked with a green triangle. Now look at the QuickSound browser (Fig. 19.20). In the left part of the window, select the directory containing the files; and in the right part, select the files you want to load. To select several files simultaneously, hold down the <Shift> or the <Ctrl > key. You can load the files using one of two methods:

❑ Right-click above the selected files and select the **Load** command in the context menu that appears

❑ Using the mouse, move the selected files to the **Loaded Waves** region (Fig. 19.19)

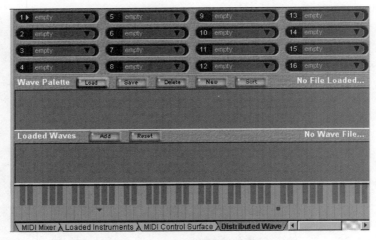

Fig. 19.19. The **Distributed Wave** tab

Fig. 19.20. Load WAV files using the QuickSound browser

Fig. 19.21. The names of loaded files are displayed in the **Loaded Waves** list

The loaded files are displayed in this region (Fig. 19.21), and under each file name the MIDI key to which this file is assigned is indicated. Note that on the virtual keyboard, several keys—starting from the key marked with the green triangle—are "lit up", and the current cell of the MIDI channels bar looks like ![1 ▶ 128 track Wave ▼]. Try to play the available keys.

To unload the loaded files, press the **Reset** button in the **Loaded Waves** region.

You can save the current layout of WAV files along the MIDI keyboard. Press the **Add** button in the **Loaded Waves** area. The list of loaded files is moved to the **Wave Palette** area. (Fig. 19.22). According to the terms used in GigaStudio, this list is called the *palette*.

Fig. 19.22. The WAV files palette

19.4. Audio Mixer; Using Effects

Before you start using the effects processor built into GigaStudio, look at Fig. 19.8 and recall the configuration of the virtual studio. You will now be operating with the audio mixer inputs, marked as **Inputs 1,2**, **Inputs 3,4**, etc. Select the **DSP Station** item from the navigation bar in the main window, or execute the **View>DSP Station** command in the program's main menu.

The virtual audio mixer consists of three components:

- ❏ **Inputs**—audio mixer lines
- ❏ **Aux Buses**
- ❏ **Master**—output channel faders

Each component is matched to a tab.

19.4.1. The *Inputs* Tab—Audio Mixer Input Lines, Automate the Audio Mixer Operation

The audio mixer input lines are located in the **Inputs** tab (Fig. 19.23). If the drivers of your sound card are not GSIF-compatible, only one line (the stereo pair of two channels) is available.

In the upper part of each line, there are four fields, by default marked as **empty**. Here, you specify the real-time effects plugged into the **Insertion** mode. Click on any green triangle opposite the word **empty**, and a list of available real-time effects appears.

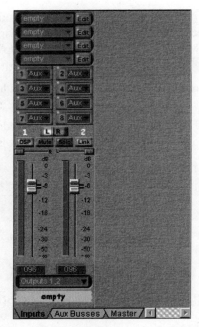

Fig. 19.23. Audio mixer input lines

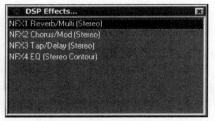

Fig. 19.24. Select real-time effect

Fig. 19.25. Adding real-time effects in the Insertion mode

Select the effect you need. You'll find it at the top of the cells of the plugged effects (Fig. 19.25*a*). The **Edit** button becomes available for the plugged-in effect. It allows you to call the window for editing the effect parameters. We describe specific features of real-time effects in *Section 19.5*.

If you click on the green triangle of any of the free cells and plug in another effect, it will appear in the next cell from the top (Fig. 19.25). The cells are filled only from the top. To unplug any of the effects, click on its green triangle, and from the list of available effects, select **Remove**.

Note that you can unplug or change only the most recently added effect. Another important note: each mixer line contains two stereo channels. When you plug effects in in the **Insertion** mode, you plug them not into the entire stereo pair, but rather into the channel selected as current by the ⬛ L | R button.

With the ⬛DSP button, you can temporarily unplug all the effects.

With the ⬛Mute button, you can temporarily mute both stereo channels. The ⬛Solo button mutes all channels of the mixer except for the current one.

The ⬛━━R L━━⬛ sliders control the panorama for each of the stereo channels. They allow you to narrow the stereo base or to exchange the stereo channels.

Using the faders shown in Fig. 19.26, the signal level for each of the stereo channels is set. If you unplug the ⬛Link button, you can move these faders independently.

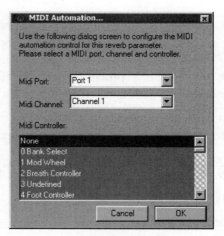

Fig. 19.26. Stereo channel level faders   **Fig. 19.27.** The **MIDI Automation** window

You can control any of the mixer parameters through the MIDI interface. Right-click on the control you are interested in. The dialog window shown in Fig. 19.27 will appear.

In this window, you have to select the **Midi Port**, the **Midi Channel**, and the **Midi Controller**. Then you can change the purpose of the selected parameter from a sequencer or directly from the MIDI keyboard (if it contains controllers—wheels, a lever, sliders, etc.).

You can use real time effects not only in the insertion mode. You can plug them into aux buses (*Section 19.4.2*) and send a signal from each of the mixer lines to any aux bus. In Fig. 19.28*a*, cells of sends to aux buses are shown.

To change the send level, click on the corresponding cell, and, holding the left mouse button, move the mouse up or down. The send level is displayed in the cell used (Fig. 19.28*b*).

  *a*   *b*

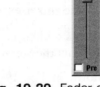

Fig. 19.28. Signal send to aux buses   **Fig. 19.29.** Fader of a signal send to an aux bus

There is another method of changing the send level. Click on the black triangle in any of the send cells. The fader shown in Fig. 19.19 appears. In the lower part of the fader, you'll find the **Pre** option. If you enable this option, the signal being sent is "taken" before the signal is processed by the effects plugged in while in the insertion mode. The level and panorama sliders also won't affect the signal being sent.

Note that the stereophonic signal, but not the signal of the current stereo channel (selected by the **Link** button), is sent to aux buses.

19.4.2. The *Aux Buses* Tab and the *Master* Section of the Audio Mixer

The lines of the audio mixer aux buses are located in the **Aux Buses** tab (Fig. 19.30).

For each bus, you can define the signal levels in the stereo channels. Th real time effects by which these signals are processed are plugged in as we described in *Section 19.4.2*. However, these effects apply not to separate channels, but to the entire stereo pair.

Each of the aux buses can be assigned its own audio port. Click on **Outputs 1,2**. The list of available ports will appear, and you should select the one you need. For a sound card not-compatible with GSIF techology, though, only one port is available.

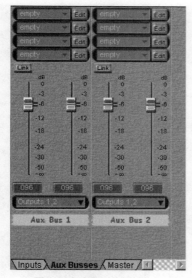

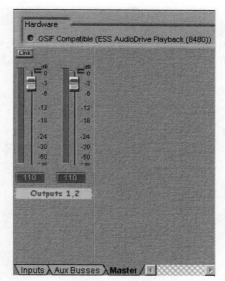

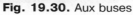

Fig. 19.30. Aux buses

Fig. 19.31. Master section of the audio mixer

The appearance of the main window in the **Master** tab is shown in Fig. 19.31.

This is the master section of the audio mixer. One or more mixer lines (depending on the abilities of the sound card) are located in this section. Each of them corresponds to an audio port marked as **Outputs 1,2**, **Outputs 3,4**, etc.

The only available parameters are the signal levels for each of the stereo channels.

We have talked much about real-time effects. Now we'll describe how to access them.

19.5. Description of Real Time Effects

We must mention that the effects for GigaStudio can be supplied separate from the program, and can be installed on their own. The effects we'll describe here are just the basic ones. It is possible that by the time you read this book there will be many more effects for GigaStudio.

19.5.1. Reverberation

Plug the reverberation effects (**NFX1 Reverb/Multi Stereo**) into the mixer line or to the aux bus and press the **Edit** button corresponding to the plugged effect. The effect parameters window shown in Fig. 19.32 appears.

Fig. 19.32. Reverberation parameters window

Fig. 19.33. Reverberation presets list

Fig. 19.34. Manipulator for selecting presets

In the upper part of the window, you'll find the **Program** field. If you click on it, a list of presets appears (Fig. 19.33).

This list contains presets that allow you to get many classical types of reverberation. Furthermore, you can add your own presets to this list. User-defined presets are saved using the **Save** button and loaded using the **Program** field or the **Load** button.

To select the effect presets, you can use the manipulator shown in Fig. 19.34.

With the horizontal arrows, you select the presets groups (for example, the **Hall** group of reverberation effects). The vertical arrows allow you to choose separate presets, regardless of the group they belong to.

In the upper part of the window (Fig. 19.32) are located the **A** and **B** buttons. They are used for comparing the changes made in the effect settings. As soon as you change the value of any parameter, its previous value is saved in the **B** buffer, and the new value is saved in the **A** buffer. Use these buttons to switch between the buffers.

In the left part of the window, we see a large empty field, called **DSP Effects—AUXES** or **DSP Effects—INPUTS**, depending on the effect plugging mode (Fig. 19.35). This field is called the *effects manager*. It displays the list of all plugged effects and indicates the channels into which they are plugged. When you navigate along the list, the parameters of the selected effect are displayed in the right part of the window.

The effect is unplugged using the **bypass** button (see Fig. 19.32).

The features described above apply to the parameters window of any of the effects.

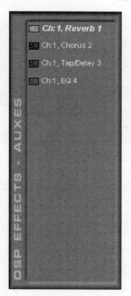

Fig. 19.35. Effects manager

Fig. 19.36. Basic reverberation parameters

The basic reverberation parameters (Fig. 19.36) are the following:

❑ **Room Size**

❑ **Pre Delay**—delay before the effect's implementation

❑ **Damping**—suppressing high-frequency components of the reflected sound

❑ **Decay**—fade time

❑ **Diffusion**—the effect is disseminated throughont the room

If you click on the small black triangle in any of the fields marked **NOT SELECTED** (by default) a menu containing two commands appears:

❏ **Choose Controller**—assign the MIDI controller with which you can control one of the effect parameters

❏ **Show Controller Selections**—call the list of controllers assigned to control the effect parameters

For some types of reverberation combined with the chorus effect, the additional **chorus** field shown in Fig. 19.37 becomes available.

Fig. 19.37. Chorus parameters

Fig. 19.38. Additional processing of the signal

Two parameters—**Speed** (modulation speed) and **Depth** (modulation depth) are available for chorus.

In the bottom of the reverberation parameters window, there is an area that is also common to some other effects (Fig. 19.38).

In this area, additional parameters of the signal processing are specified. We'll now describe them from left to right.

Input is the input signal level. It can be increased or decreased within a range from −12 to 12 dB (by increments of 6 dB). The **Clip** indicator is highlighted in case clipping occurs (digital overflow). The **L** and **R** buttons are used to temporarily unplug the stereo channels.

Effect is the effect depth. **Dry** is the level of the non-processed signal added to the processed signal.

L, M, and **H** are sliders of the graphic equalizer corresponding to low, middle, and high frequencies.

Contour is the graphic representation of the equalizer parameters. The whole range of frequencies of the audio signal is divided by three dashed lines into three regions that correspond to low, middle, and high frequencies. You can move the boundary between the low and middle frequencies using the mouse.

19.5.2. Chorus/Flanger

In the effects list, the chorus/flanger effect is called **NFX 2 Chorus/Flanger (stereo)**. The parameters window of this effect is shown in Fig. 19.39. Here, we do not show the effects manager window (see Fig. 19.35).

Fig. 19.39. The chorus/flanger parameters window

This window contains many elements in common with the reverberation parameters window. We only describe here the basic parameters of the chorus/flanger effect:

❑ **Speed**—modulation speed (more accurately, the modulation frequency)

❑ **Depth**—modulation depth

❑ **Feedback**—feedback level

❑ **Delay**—delay before the effect's implementation

19.5.3. Delay/Auto Panorama

In the effects list, the delay/auto panorama effect is called **NFX 3 Tap/Delay (stereo)**. The parameters window of this effect is shown in Fig. 19.40.

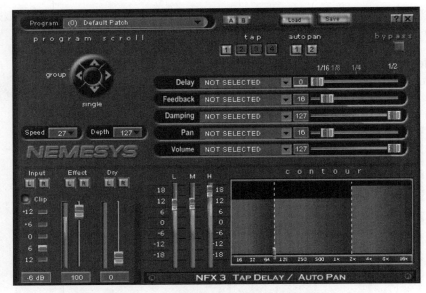

Fig. 19.40. The delay/auto panorama parameters window

The delay is implemented using four taps. Four delays are combined and each can be assigned its own parameters. The signal is delayed in each of the taps and specially processed. It is then returned to the effect input and passes through all the processing stages again. The result is an effect similar to a complex echo.

You select the tap using the **tap 1**, **2**, **3**, **4** buttons. Auto panorama functions are available for taps 1 and 2 (**auto pan 1**, **2**). The built-in generator of low-frequency signals controls the panorama of the processed signals. The **Speed** and **Depth** parameters correspond to low-frequency signal frequency and amplitude.

The processing parameters available for each of the four taps are the following:

❏ **Delay**—delay before the effect implementation

❏ **Feedback**—feedback level

❏ **Damping**—suppressing high-frequency components of the reflected sound

❑ **Pan**—panorama of the returned signal

❑ **Volume**—volume of the returned signal

19.5.4. Equalizer

In the effects list, the equalizer is called **NFX 4 EQ (Stereo Contour)**. The parameters window of this effect is shown in Fig. 19.41.

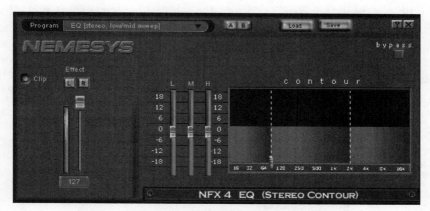

Fig. 19.41. The equalizer parameters window

This effect is actually a simplified version of the above effects, since each of them contained an equalizer, while here there is nothing but the equalizer itself.

19.6. The QuickSound Browser; Working with Akai CDs; Track Import from an Audio CD

We have already used the QuickSound browser to load WAV files (*Section 19.3.4*). However, this browser has some other abilities, which we'll describe here.

19.6.1. Search for Audio Files Stored on the Hard Disk

The QuickSound browser is shown in Fig. 19.42. In its left part, you see the directory tree from your PC. The root is called **Local Sampler**. This means that the developers of GigaStudio consider your PC only a sampler.

Fig. 19.42. The QuickSound browser

In the **Local Sampler** tree, only those directories with files whose formats are supported by GigaStudio are displayed. You can input the whole filename or just part of it in the **Search** field. The program searches for files in the QuickSound database. The search is performed not only by filename, but also using the additional information contained in these files, such as information on authors, comments, the list of keywords, etc. The names of the files found are displayed in the right part of the browser as a list of filenames (Fig. 19.43), and statistics (how many times the word is encountered) are displayed above the **Search**.

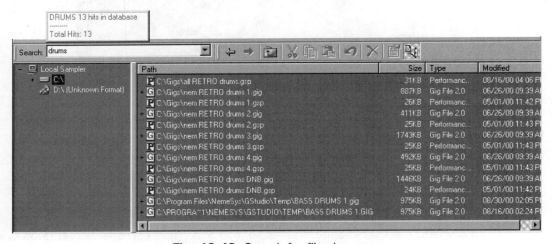

Fig. 19.43. Search for files by name

The list of the files found consists of four columns, where the following data is displayed:

❑ **Path**   ❑ **Type**

❑ **Size**   ❑ **Modified**—last modification date

The QuickSound browser understands the following file formats:

❑ **GIG** (GigaStudio Instrument files)—GigaStudio/GigaSampler instrument banks

❑ **GSP** (GigaStudio Performance files)—GigaStudio project files that contain information on loaded instruments, mixer configurations, etc.

❑ **PRF** (GigaSampler Performance files)—GigaSampler project files

❑ **ART**—articulation files that contain such instrument parameters as envelopes, low-frequency generator settings, etc.

❑ **WAV**

You can view the contents of instrument banks. To get a list of instruments stored in the bank, click on the "+" sign to the right of the filename.

In the **Search** line, you can input requests more complicated than fragments of filenames. The following keywords are allowed in these requests.

❑ **and**—logical AND

❑ **or**—logical OR

❑ **not**—logical NOT

❑ **contains**—the filename contains the given substring

Here are examples of requests:

❑ **.gig and .wav**—output list of all GIG and WAV files

❑ **contains bas**—output list of all files whose filenames contain the characters **bas**

If you do not use **contains** in the **Search** string, only those files in whose filenames the given fragment is separated from the rest of the filename by spaces are found. For example, you can find the nem RETRO drums 1.gig file with the **drums** fragment, but not with the **retr** fragment. If you type **contains retr**, the file is immediately found.

The database of audio files on your PC is created during the installation of GigaStudio. You can update it using the **Update** command of the context menu called by right clicking on the **Local Sampler** tree. This menu contains another command—**Convert all instruments to Gig 2.0**. Using this command, you can convert the files in the given directory from older versions of the GIG format into the GIG 2.0 format supported by GigaStudio.

If you right-click on the list of filenames, the context menu shown in Fig. 19.44 appears.

The commands contained in this menu are the following:

❑ **Load**

❑ **Copy Locally And Load**—copy the file locally and load (if the file is initially outside the PC—for example, on the Internet)

❏ **Copy To Palette**—load a WAV file into the **palette** area (*Section 19.3.4*)

❏ **Edit**—open a GIG file in the GSEdit editor

❏ **Properties**—open the window with information on the file (copyright, notes, the list of keywords for file search, etc.)

❏ **Display Instrument Details**—this item is not available

❏ **Sync Directory**—display the directory in the **Local Sampler** tree in which the file resides

❏ **Convert instruments to Gig 2.0**

Fig. 19.44. Context menu of the files list

There is a toolbar in the upper part of the QuickSound browser. The following buttons in this toolbar are available:

⬅—return to the previous search results

➡—forward

⬆—one level up the directory tree

▣—if this button is pressed after double-clicking on the filename, it is loaded to the current MIDI channel; if the button is released, the file is loaded to the free MIDI channel next to the current channel

The other buttons in the toolbar are not available

You cannot read a CD with sample banks in GIG format with the QuickSound browser. You'll see the words **Unknown Format** displayed in the directory tree. The user manual contains a special section in which you can learn all the steps for creating a new directory in Windows, for copying GIG files from a CD-ROM into this directory, and for loading instruments using QuickSound. QuickSound cannot keep a database of audio files.

For those who are not reading this book in order, we'd like to remind you that you can find information on the settings of the QuickSound utility in *Section 19.2.4*.

19.6.2. Working with Akai Disks

If you insert a disk in the Akai format into your CD-ROM, the QuickSound browser outputs the disk directory (Fig. 19.45). You cannot read the contents of this disk using just Windows.

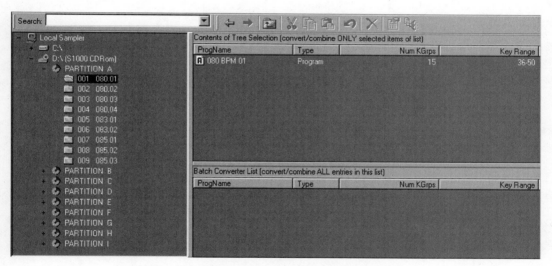

Fig. 19.45. Contents of a CD in Akai format

Recall the hierarchic structure of an Akai disk:

❑ The disk is divided into several *partitions*

❑ Each partition contains several *volumes*

❑ Each volume contains several *instruments*

The structure of the Akai disk is displayed in the left part of the QuickSound browser. In its upper left part, the contents of the selected object are displayed as a list. The list contains fields with the following information:

❑ **ProgName**—object name

❑ **Type**—object type

❏ **NumKGps**—the number of MIDI key groups, each of which has waveforms (applied to instruments)

❏ **Key Range**—the instrument range on the MIDI keyboard

Select any instrument and right-click on it. The context menu shown in Fig. 19.46 will appear.

Fig. 19.46. Context menu of the Akai disk objects list

The items of this menu are:

❏ **Import Waves**—import WAV files and save them in the specified directory (folder).

❏ **Convert to Gig**—convert Akai instruments into GIG files and save them in a specified directory.

❏ **Combine to Gig**—combine several Akai instruments into one GIG file.

❏ **Import->Piano**—import waveforms into WAV files, and then load them into GigaStudio.

❏ **Conv2Gig->1stAvailChan**—convert Akai instruments into GIG files, and then load them into the first available MIDI channel.

❏ **Conv2Gig->GSEdit**—convert Akai instruments into GIG files, and then load them into GSEdit.

❏ **Comb2Gig->GSEdit**—combine several Akai instruments into one GIG file, and then load them into GSEdit.

❏ **Add to Batch**—add instruments to the **Batch** list. If the **Set Prgm DblClickOperation** option is enabled, the operation defined in the settings is performed after double-clicking on the instrument name (*Section 19.2.5*). Otherwise, the program treats a double-click as a single click.

❑ **Merge Left/Right**—when converting Akai instruments, combine separate waveforms of the left and right channels into stereo waveforms.

❑ **Clean Temp Dir**—remove all temporary files, along with GIG files converted from Akai instruments.

Some commands of the above menu are not available, depending on the selected objects of the Akai disk. For example, if only one instrument is selected, the **Combine to Gig** command is unavailable.

To select several instruments, hold the <Shift> or the <Ctrl> key down.

Note that the commands of the above menu apply not only to instruments, but to volumes and partitions as well. For example, if you use the **Convert to Gig** command for any of the volumes, all the instruments contained in this volume are converted into GIG files.

We have already mentioned the **Batch** list in *Section 19.2.5*. Recall that with the **Add to Batch** command of the context menu of the Akai disk objects list, you can group the objects you are interested in into a special **Batch** list.

Fig. 19.47. Context menu of the **Batch** list

The context menu of the **Batch** list is shown in Fig. 19.47. This menu differs from the above menu (Fig. 19.46) in two new commands:

❑ **Remove from Batch**—remove the selected instruments from the **Batch** list

❑ **Clear Batch**—clear the **Batch** list

The remaining commands apply to all the instruments of the list. For example, the **Convert to Gig** command converts all the instruments from the **Batch** list into GIG files.

The QuickSound browser has the ability to work with Akai disks thanks to the built-in SConverter utility. We described the settings of this utility available to users in *Section 12.2.5.*

19.6.3. Audio CD Tracks Import

The AConverter utility is supplied with GigaStudio. It allows you to save Audio CD tracks in WAV format. This utility is integrated in the QuickSound browser, and is called automatically as soon as the CD is inserted into the CD-ROM.

In the right part of the QuickSound browser, a list of tracks is displayed (Fig. 19.48).

Fig. 19.48. The list of Audio CD tracks

Select the tracks you need and right-click on them. A context menu appears that contains only one command—**Convert track to Wave**. After you call this command, the dialog window shown in Fig. 19.49 appears.

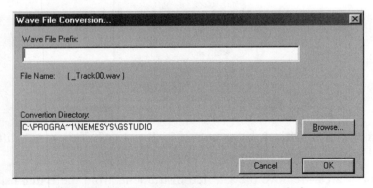

Fig. 19.49. Tracks import parameters window

In the **Conversion Directory** field, the path to the directory in which WAV files are to be saved is specified. These files are named as follows: the name begins with the characters you type in the **Wave File Prefix** field, followed by **TrackNN.wav,** where **NN** is the track number.

After you press **OK**, the process of capturing the Audio CD track into WAV files starts.

19.7. The Main Menu and Toolbar; Capture the Signal Generated by GigaStuio into a WAV File

In the upper part of the main window of GigaStudio, we find the main menu and the toolbar. Some of the main menu commands are duplicated by toolbar buttons.

You have to save any GigaStudio settings in special files. This allows you to continue working with any project at any time. The following are the buttons and the commands corresponding to them:

🔲 (**File>New**)—open new project; all settings are reset

🔲 (**File>Open**)—open project file

🔲 (**File>Save**)—save project

🔲 (**File>Save As**)—when pressed for the first time after creating the project, saves the project in the file with the given name

The following commands are not duplicated by buttons:

❏ **File>Save settings as default performance**—save current settings as default settings when a new project is created

❏ **File>Exit**—exit the program

❏ **View>Port1, View>Port2, View>Port3, View>Port4**—these commands are equivalent to commands of the navigation bar (*Section 19.1.2*)

❏ **View>DSP Station**—this command is equivalent to a command of the navigation bar (*Section 19.4*)

❏ **View>Settings**—equivalent to a command of the navigation bar (*Section 19.2*)

❏ **View>Diagnostic**—equivalent to a command of the navigation bar (*Section 19.2*)

❏ **View>Help**—opens the GigaStudio information resources window on the Internet

❏ **View>Navigation Bar**—shows or hides the navigation bar

❏ **View>Instrument Loader Pane**—shows or hides the QuickSound browser

❏ **View>Status Bar**—shows or hides the status bar in the lower part of the screen

Some of the buttons in the toolbar are unique. Their actions duplicate neither the commands of the main menu, nor the commands of the navigation bar.

After pressing the ⊙ button, all the settings are discarded. If you click on the arrow, a menu containing the following options opens:

❑ **Instruments**—discard only the loaded instruments

❑ **Hardware**—discard only the output ports settings

❑ **Mixer**—discard mixer settings

❑ **Load Default Performance Settings**—load default settings for a new project

❑ **All**—select all of the above options

The ▣ , ▣ , and ▣ buttons call, respectively, the GigaStudio instruments editor, the sequencer program, and the audio editor. For how to associate any of these buttons to any of the available programs, see *Section 19.2.1*.

The ⊙ button is special. It is associated with the **Audio Capture** function supported by GigaStudio. Thanks to this function, a signal generated by GigaStudio can be captured to a WAV file without any digital-analog or analog-digital conversions. From the user's point of view, the capture is performed as follows. The necessary preparations are made in GigaStudio, and then playback is started in the sequencer set to work with GigaStudio (using GigaStudio MIDI ports).

If the ⊙ button is pressed, the **GigaStudio Audio Capture** bar shown in Fig. 19.50 appears.

Fig. 19.50. The capture control bar

After pressing the ▣ button, the standard dialog box for saved file filename input appears. As soon as you press **OK**, the signal arriving to the output ports begins being recorded into the WAV file with the given name. After that, you should switch to the sequencer window and start the playback of your arrangement. When playback is over, switch to the GigaStudio window and press the capture stop button ▣ . The ▣ button may be useful if you decide to discard the recording. The captured WAV file is deleted, and the **GigaStudio Audio Capture** bar returns to its initial state.

It is not necessary to capture the entire arrangement into one WAV file. You can play the tracks of the arrangement continuously and save them in different files. You can then load them into a multichannel audio editor and combine the fragments. The ▣ button is used for just this purpose. If it is pressed, each time after the ▪ button is pressed, the program offers a new filename for the file containing the recording sequence number.

The ▨ button enables the option of synchronizing recording start and stop through MIDI. If this option is enabled, and the ▪ button is pressed, the recording starts only when the MIDI message for the sequencer start arrives. If the MIDI message for the sequencer to stop arrives, the recording stops.

The ▨ button switches the progress indicator display modes. It shows how many sound samples or bytes have been recorded, the duration of the recorded fragment, and the recording time remaining.

Additional parameters of the **Audio Capture** function are defined in the **Sampler Settings** tab (Section 19.2.2).

We'll now return to the control panel of the main window. The ▣ button calls the window with information on the program. The ▨ button allows you to obtain information on the bar of the main window you are interested in. Just press it and click on the object you need.

19.8. Practice

Some of our readers might criticize us because we describe the abilities of different programs, but do not give exact instructions. Composing music is creative, and therefore there cannot be any exact instructions. However, we can describe how to make GigaStudio and Cakewalk Pro Audio work together right off the bat.

Launch GigaStudio.

If your system has one input MIDI port to which the MIDI keyboard is attached, you have to decide which program to assign that port. Since you will spend most of your time working with Cakewalk Pro Audio, and use GigaStudio as a tone generator, it makes the most sense to give the port to Cakewalk Pro Audio: free all the input ports in GigaStudio (navigation bar>**Settings**>the **Hardware** tab>**MIDI In Ports** set to <**none**>).

Now you can start Cakewalk Pro Audio. In its settings, make GigaStudio MIDI ports available. To do this, use the main menu command **Tools>Midi Devices**, and call the **MIDI Ports** dialog box (Fig. 19.51). Select the GigaStudio ports (they are called **NemeSys Midi Out: Port1—NemeSys Midi Out: Port4**) and press **OK**. In our example, **NemeSys Midi Out: Port1** corresponds to the first virtual port of Cakewalk Pro Audio (the first of the selected ports), the second GigaStudio port corresponds to the second Cakewalk Pro Audio port, etc.

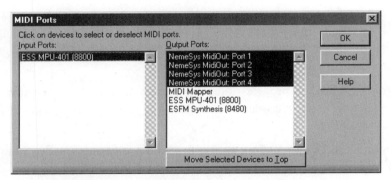

Fig. 19.51. Select GigaStudio ports in Cakewalk Pro Audio

Now we'll set one of the tracks of Cakewalk Pro Audio to work with GigaStudio (Fig. 19.52).

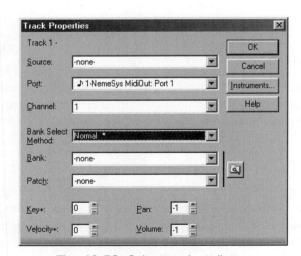

Fig. 19.52. Select track attributes

Assign one of the GigaStudio ports (say, the first port) to this track, and select the MIDI channel—**Channel 1**. Now Cakewalk Pro Audio is ready to work. The track you have selected is set to work with the first channel of the first port.

Switch to the GigaStudio window and load any of the GIG files so that it corresponds to the first channel of the first port. We described how to load instruments in *Section 19.3.1*. After you have loaded the instrument, return to Cakewalk Pro Audio and play this instrument.

In the navigation bar, we see the process indicator shown in Fig. 19.53.

Fig.19.53. The process indicator

This indicator displays in real time the number of waveforms played (**Voices**), the maximum number of waveforms that can be played (**Peak**), memory (**Memory**), and the processor load. It also contains information on the ports presently accepting MIDI data (the color of the numbers 1, 2, 3, and 4 changes from green to red). Numbered boxes are not only indicators but also buttons. By clicking on them, you can attach and detach MIDI ports. The corresponding changes in the MIDI ports settings (*Section 19.2.3*) remain.

The image of the MIDI keyboard in Fig. 19.53 is really a button used to switch the MIDI information routing modes. By default, all the commands arriving to the input MIDI ports of GigaStudio are translated to their respective output ports (*Section 19.2.3*)— this is the first mode. In the second mode (in which the keyboard image is blinking), the information from **Midi In Ports** is not transferred to **Midi Out Ports**.

Chapter 20: Creating Your Own Sampler Libraries Using GigaStudio Instrument Editor 2.0

There are, currently, a fair number of GIG files for sale and available on the Internet. However, most of them are "semi-finished products". Most of these files have appeared as a result of converting sampler banks of other formats. Modern programs for converting sampler banks convert the files themselves from any format to any other format without a problem. But information like envelope parameters, LFO generator parameters, and the purpose of MIDI controllers is often converted incorrectly, or is not converted at all. GigaStudio Instrument Editor 2.0 is included in the package that comes with the GigaStudio software sampler described in *Chapter 19*. This program is also known as GSEdit. It allows you to load banks of samples with GIG, SF2, and DLS formats, and to edit and save them in the GIG format.

It is best to learn what the editor can do by creating your own sampler bank. But in order to create a bank, you have to have the samples. You can easily find hundreds of gigabytes of WAV samples on CDs and on the Internet, but to make the experiment purer, we decided to start creating our own sample banks using waveforms we generated ourselves.

20.1. Creating Your Own Sample Using Cool Edit Pro

We will now try to create a type of "electronic" synthesizer timbre. Using Cool Edit Pro, we first generate a signal with a duration of 1 second with a triangular wave in the format 44 kHz:16 bits:stereo (Fig. 20.1). The *A* of the second MIDI octave (numbering starts from −1) corresponds to a frequency of 110 Hz. To make the tone life-like, we added the phaser effect (see the **Phasing** group) with a modulating frequency of 1 Hz. One second of its duration contains one oscillation period, modulating the tone by phase. Besides which, the waveform contains a whole number of periods of the triangular wave. In further processing, this will help us to find the starting and the ending points of the sampler loop. In our case, these points are the first and the last sound measurements.

Select the entire waveform in Cool Edit Pro (double-click on its image) and call the **View>Sampler Info** command of the main menu. In the **Sampler Information** dialog box (Fig. 20.2), set **Note** to **A2** (*A* of the second octave), and using the **New** button, create an infinite (**Sustain (infinite loop)**) loop with a starting point of 0 and an ending point of 44,099 (a total of 44,100 measurements in a sample with a duration of 1 second).

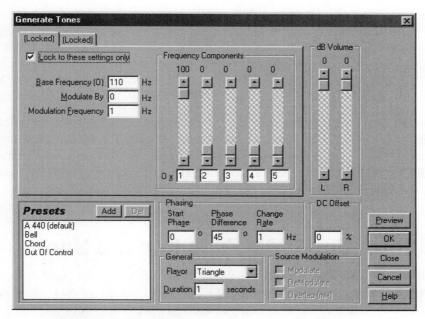

Fig. 20.1. Generating a waveform using Cool Edit Pro

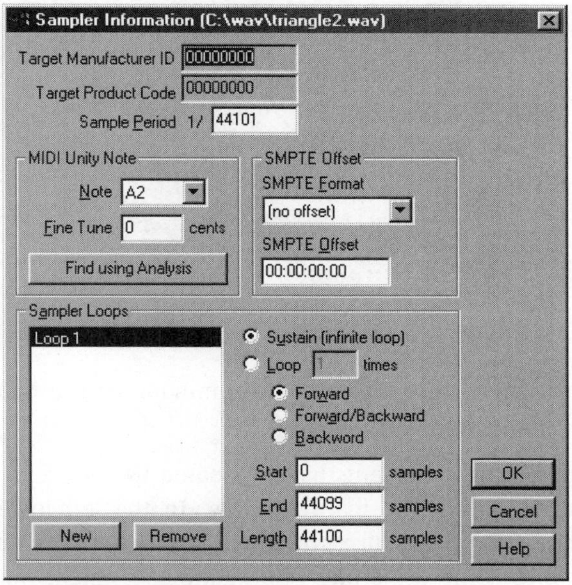

Fig. 20.2. Creating a sampler loop in Cool Edit Pro

The resulting sample is saved in the triangle2.wav file.

To demonstrate using the multisampling technique, we'll generate some similar samples, but the frequency of each subsequent sample will be double the previous one's (220 Hz for *A* of the third MIDI octave, 440 Hz for *A* of the fourth MIDI octave, etc.). The resulting samples are saved in triangle3.wav, triangle4.wav, etc.

Multisampling is the mapping of different zones of the MIDI keyboard to different samples. This method usually provides a higher sound quality for the sampled instruments. Ideally, each MIDI key must have its own sample mapped to it (or even several samples, to play different waveforms depending on the speed of pressing the MIDI key). In our example, one sample is mapped to an octave.

20.2. Importing WAV Files into the Bank

Now we'll start GSEdit and GigaStudio, which is used as a sampler (GSEdit itself cannot reproduce the sampler banks it contains). The main menu of SGEdit is shown in Fig. 20.3. It looks like this until any sampler bank project is opened.

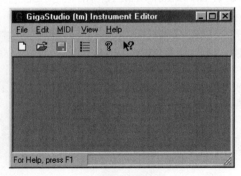

Fig. 20.3. GSEdit main menu

We'll create a new project using the **File>New** command of the main menu, or by using the ⬜ button of the main window's toolbar.

You can see that many control elements have appeared in the project window (Fig. 20.4), which in turn is opened within the main window. In the left lower part of the project window, there is a list of samples (currently empty). For the user's convenience, samples are grouped according to some principle. For example, it might make sense to group all samples related to the same instrument. By default, the only empty group of instruments is called **Default Sample Group**. Let's rename it **triangle**. To do this, select the group folder, and after some time, click on it. The folder name becomes available for editing.

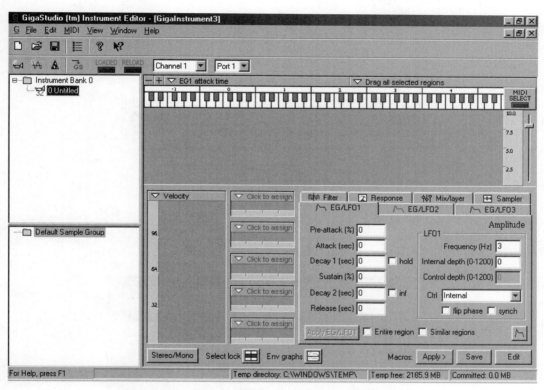

Fig. 20.4. GSEdit main menu (new project is open)

Now we'll place our samples into the folder. Right-click on the **triangle** folder. From the context menu that appears, select the **Import Samples** command. Select the samples using the standard dialog box (Fig. 20.5). To select several samples at once, hold the <Shift> or <Ctrl> keys down.

After we have finished importing, all our files are in the samples list (Fig. 20.6).

Right-click on any of the names. In the context menu, select the **Properties** command. The **Sample properties** window appears (see Fig. 20.7). You can also open it by double-clicking on the sample name. The window contains attributes of the sample, some of which you can edit.

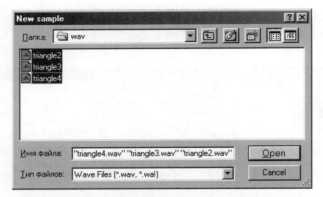

Fig. 20.5. Importing samples from WAV files

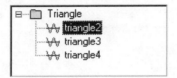

Fig. 20.6. List of samples

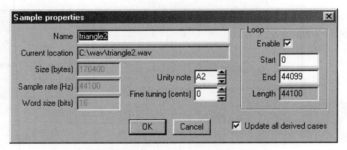

Fig. 20.7. Sample properties

Parameters such as **Current location**, **Size (bytes)**, **Sample rate (Hz)**, and **Word size (bits)** are just for your information. Other fields available for editing already contain the data for the sampler. (Recall the **View>Sampler info** command of Cool Edit Pro).

❑ **Unity note**—the base note corresponding to the sample playback with the normal sampling frequency (**Sample rate (Hz)**)

❑ **Fine tuning (cents)**—fine tuning to the cent

In the **Loop** group:

❑ **Enable**—using the loop (enabling the loop mode)

❏ **Start**—the loop starting point

❏ **End**—the loop ending point

❏ **Length**—the loop length (not changeable)

As you can see, there are no functions for loop "adjustment". For this, it is more convenient to apply external audio editors.

The **Update all derived cases** checkbox, if checked, indicates that the same sample properties are saved for all the registers that use it, and not only for the current register. We'll describe this option in the next section.

20.3. Creating an Instrument

Now we have our group of samples. The next step is to create an instrument based on this group. An instrument is an object of a higher logical level than samples. Instruments are the objects that you map to MIDI channels.

In the upper left part of the project window, you see a list of instruments. The list is structured like a tree: the higher level is made up of banks, and the lower level contains instruments. In our example, there is only one bank—**Instrument Bank 0**, and this bank contains only one instrument—**0 Untitled**. It is impossible to have an instrument without a bank to contain it. You cannot change the bank's name, or to be more precise, banks cannot have names. They are numbered, starting from zero. You can, however, change the instrument's name (the editing mode is called by double-clicking on the instrument). The number is the instrument's number within the bank.

By default, only one bank is created (with the number 0) containing one empty instrument—**Untitled** (Fig. 20.8). An empty instrument contains no samples.

Fig. 20.8. List of instruments

20.3.1. The Logical Structure of GIG Files, GSEdit Terms

Before we start filling in the instrument with samples, we have to look at the logical structure of GigaStudio sampler banks.

Fig. 20.9 shows the logical structure of GIG files. We constructed it based on the functionality of GSEdit. The number of banks is not limited by any factor but common sense; the number of instruments is limited to 128.

Each instrument consists of one or more regions. A *region* is a zone of a MIDI keyboard—one or several MIDI keys positioned next to one another. The maximum number of regions (128) is equal to the number of keys of a MIDI keyboard.

One or more registers correspond to each region. A *register* can be defined as a group of pipes in an organ, a group of strings on a harpsichord, and so on. We can also say that a register is a set of sample modulation parameters (in GigaStudio). In this case, we consider the register to be a set of parameters of various generators that provide for sample modulation. Any sample from any group can correspond to a register.

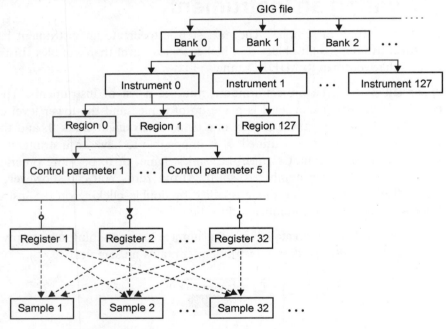

Fig. 20.9. Logical structure of GigaStudio sampler files

Registers permit one instrument to have different timbres, depending on the register. Switching between registers is done by user-defined control parameters (register switches). MIDI messages (Note On, Note Off, Channel Aftertouch, Controller) and even the numbers assigned to MIDI keys can be used as register switches. The maximum number of registers is 32. In each region, 5 bits are used to code the register's configuration; that is to say, if you have only one switch, it can have $2^5 = 32$ positions. If you have 5 switches, each of them has only two positions.

There are situations in which two (or more) registers can sound at the same time:

❑ When the region is stereophonic—one register is used for each stereo channel

❑ When the region is multilayer (several samples are played at the same time)—one register is used for each layer

In each of the above cases, the number of available switches decreases by 1.

Registers are most often used for changing the timbre of an instrument in real time using MIDI controllers or certain MIDI keys. You can create complex timbres using different samples at different sound generation phases (before and after pressing the keys). Such features as stereophonic sound, multilayer structure, and changing samples depending on the speed of pressing the keys are also implemented using the registers.

In GSEdit, the terms "register" and "register switch" correspond to "dimension" and "control source", which doesn't much help us in understanding the concepts. Dimension is an array of sample modulation parameters. Switch positions are called "splits".

The structure of a GIG file might seem a bit confusing to you. Most presently available banks do not use all the branches of this structure (one bank, one instrument, one or two registers). The most important thing is that you have an idea of the potential abilities of GIG-format files.

20.3.2. Creating an Instrument with a Wizard

The simplest way to fill in an instrument with samples is to use the instrument wizard. To call it, right-click on an empty instrument and select the **Instrument Wizard** command from the context menu. Another way is to select an empty instrument and press the ⚠ button in the toolbar of the project window.

20.3.4. Determining the Instrument's Parameters

In the first step, the wizard allows you to determine the parameters of the created instrument (Fig. 20.10).

The available instrument parameters are:

❑ **Name**

❑ **Bank number**

❑ **Patch number**—the instrument number in the bank

❑ **Drum**—indicates drums

❑ **Effects send**—reserved for future use

❑ **Attenuation (dB)**—lowering the total volume level

❑ **6 dB boost**—raising the total volume level by 6 dB

❑ **Tuning adjust (cents)**

❑ **Pitch bend (semitones)**—the range of pitch shifting by the pitch bend controller

❑ **Dimension key start**—the starting key of the MIDI keyboard region reserved for register switching

❑ **Dimension key end**—the final key of the MIDI keyboard region reserved for register switching

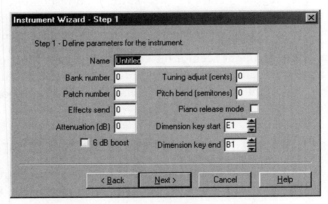

Fig. 20.10. Instrument parameters

Right now, we won't change any parameters; we'll just give our instrument the name **Triangle**. To move to the next step, press the **Next >** button.

20.3.5. Determining the Range Occupied by the Instrument on the MIDI Keyboard

The next step in the instrument wizard—determining the range occupied by the instrument on the MIDI keyboard—is shown in Fig. 20.11.

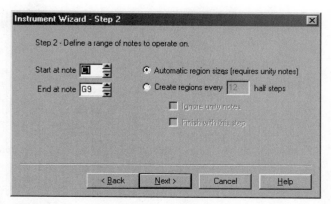

Fig. 20.11. Determine the range occupied by the instrument on MIDI keyboard

In the **Start at note** and **End at note** drop-down lists, you should specify the keys of the range beginning and the range end.

Usually, multiple samples on the MIDI keyboard are used in instruments (multisampling). Our instrument is created in the same way. Each sample occupies a region on the MIDI keyboard that can consist of one or more keys. If the **Automatic region sizes (requires unity notes)** option is enabled, samples are distributed along the keyboard automatically, optimized for the playback quality. To make this option work, you should specify unity notes for all samples. We will use this option, and not the alternate one— **Create Regions every ... half steps**. The latter option allows you to create regions with semitone steps. It has its own parameters:

❏ **Ignore unity notes**—ignore the information about sample unity notes

❏ **Finish with this step**—stop the wizard after completing the current step (create empty regions without samples).

Now we'll go on to the next step by pressing the **Next >** button.

20.3.6. Creating Registers

Creating registers is shown in Fig. 20.12.

This window contains the following fields:

Description—fields containing the description of registers.

Controller source—lists of objects that can be used to switch between the registers.

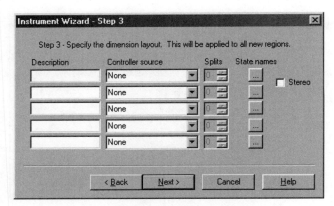

Fig. 20.12. Creating registers

In each of the **Splits** fields, you should specify the number of switch positions (2, 8, 16, or 32) according to the number of registers.

Call the register name editor using the **State names** button. We'll describe how to use it in *Section 20.4.5*.

The samples we create are stereophonic, and it makes sense to apply this feature to the instrument as well. To do this, check the **Stereo** checkbox. This feature uses two registers that need not be switched. We won't create any other registers, so we'll just press the **Next >** button.

20.3.7. Assigning Sample Groups; Loading the Instrument in GigaStudio

Now we have only one register ("stereo" doesn't count), and we now just have to map our only sample group, **Triangle**, to our only register, **No splits defined**. To do this, click on **0-127**, and **Triangle** appears in the **Assigned to** field (Fig. 20.13).

We press the **Next >** button and get the instrument: there are three regions on the MIDI keyboard (Fig. 20.14). The current region is in yellow and the rest are white. A sample is mapped to each region.

Using the **File>Save** command of the main menu, or the 🖫 button of the toolbar, save the bank with the instrument in a GIG file.

We can now listen to the created instrument. We should first load it into GigaStudio. This can be done in GSEdit. There are two drop-down lists on the toolbar (see Fig. 20.4, top). In the one list, you should specify the MIDI channel, and in the other, you should specify any one of the four GigaStudio MIDI ports.

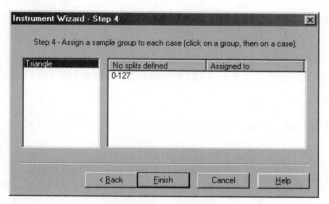

Fig. 20.13. Assign sample groups

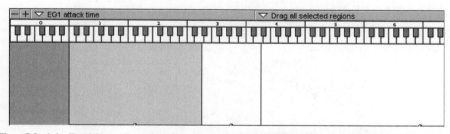

Fig. 20.14. Position of regions on the virtual MIDI keyboard GS Edit (region map)

If the **RELOAD** indicator on the toolbar is lit, you have to reload the instrument into GigaStudio to listen to the latest changes made to its settings. A lit **LOADED** indicator means that the edited instrument is loaded into GigaStudio, and should not be re-looded.

In our case, the **RELOAD** indicator should be lit. Press the ⬛ button, and the current instrument will be loaded into GigaStudio into the assigned MIDI channel of the assigned MIDI port.

20.4. Editing Modulation Parameters

In the right lower part of the project window (see Fig. 20.4), there is a field containing seven tabs (Fig. 20.15).

Here, the modulation parameters for the current instrument register are edited. All zones of our instrument are of the same type, so we can edit the modulation parameters for all zones at the same time. To do so, select all the zones: while holding the <Shift> key, click on them all on the GSEdit virtual MIDI keyboard.

20.4.1. The *EG/LFO1* Tab—Amplitude Modulation Parameters

Amplitude modulation parameters available on the **EG/LFO1** tab are shown in Fig. 20.15.

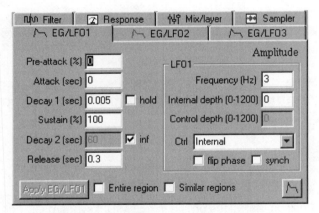

Fig. 20.15. Amplitude modulation parameters

EG is the abbreviation for Envelope Generator (in this case, the amplitude envelope), and *LFO* is the Low Frequency Oscillator.

Now we'll describe the parameters of the envelope generator. Creating sounds in Giga-Studio consists of several phases shown in Fig. 20.16.

Pre-attack is the initial volume, and **Attack** is the attack time. If the **hold** checkbox is selected, the **Decay1** phase starts at the beginning of the loop (sample looped playback). Before the loop, the volume is held at 100%. If the checkbox is not checked, the **Decay1** phase starts immediately after the attack. After the **Decay1** phase completes, the volume is lowered to the **Sustain** level.

After that, there are several options. If the **inf** checkbox is selected, the volume is held at the **Sustain** level until a MIDI key is pressed. Then the **Release** phase starts, in which the volume is lowered to 0%. If the checkbox is not checked, the **Decay2** phase starts after the **Decay1** phase, and the volume is lowered within the assigned period of time. If the MIDI key is released before the phase has completed, the volume is lowered to 0%, but within the period of time assigned by the **Release** parameter.

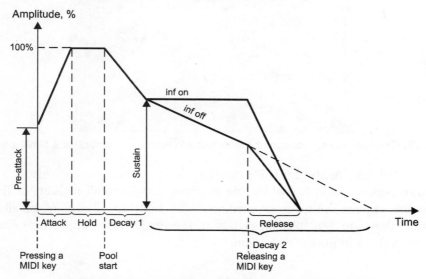

Fig. 20.16. Phases of the amplitude envelope's behavior

In the **LFO1** group, the parameters of the tremolo effect are set:

❏ **Frequency**—amplitude modulation frequency.

❏ **Internal depth**—modulation depth. If the modulation depth is to be controlled by MIDI, select the name of the corresponding MIDI controller in the **Ctrl** list in place of **Internal**. Then the **Control depth (0—1200)** field becomes available, and you should supply the modulation depth reached at the controller's maximum value.

❏ **flip phase**—phase inversion.

❏ **Synch**—using one LFO generator for all the notes that sound. If this option is enabled, tremolo is synchronous for all the notes that sound, regardless of whether they start simultaneously or not.

The ⊡ button switches to the mode in which you can graphically edit the amplitude envelope generator's basic parameters (Fig. 20.17).

Using the ⊕ and ⊖ buttons, you can change the image zoom. The ⊞ button returns you to the normal editing mode for the amplitude frequency parameters.

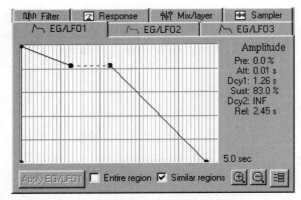

Fig. 20.17. Graphic representation of the amplitude envelope generator's basic parameters

After you press the **Apply EG/LFO** button, all the changes you made are saved. If the **Entire region** option is enabled, these changes apply to all registers of the region. If the **Similar regions** option is enabled, changes apply to all regions of all registers. The above options are available for all tabs of the modulation parameters editor, so we won't mention them in further discussion.

20.4.2. The *Filter* Tab—Filter Parameters

Each sample that plays can be processed by a filter. The filter type is defined in the **Type** field (Fig. 20.18):

❒ **Lowpass**   ❒ **Highpass**   ❒ **Bandpass**   ❒ **Bandreject**

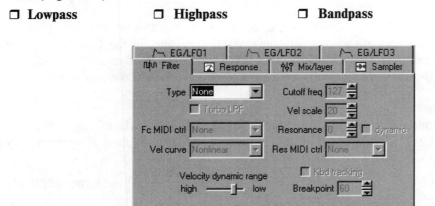

Fig. 20.18. Filter parameters

For the lowpass filter (sometimes called the *resonance cutting filter*), the **Turbo LPF** option is available, which increases the sharpness of the amplitude frequency response of the filter. This results in a more accented "wow-wow" effect.

In the **Fc MIDI ctrl** field, the controller that controls the filter cutoff frequency is defined. **Vel curve** indicates the dependence of the filter cutoff frequency on the key pressing speed (**Velocity** parameter):

❐ **Nonlinear**   ❐ **Linear**   ❐ **Special**

Velocity dynamic range is the sensitivity of the filter cutoff frequency to the key pressing speed. It can be **high** or **low**.

The **Cutoff freq** parameter, defining the filter cutoff frequency, is available only if the MIDI controller that controls this frequency (**Fc MIDI ctrl**) is not defined.

If the MIDI controller control is not defined (**Fc MIDI ctrl = None**) the **Vel scale** parameter—the dependence of the filter cutoff frequency on the MIDI key pressing speed—is available. When the **Vel scale** value is lower than 20, the sound becomes hollow, and if it is over 20, the sound is clearer.

If the MIDI controller control is defined, the **Min cutoff** parameter is available. It determines the minimal cutoff frequency that can be set using this controller. Limiting the range of changing the filter cutoff frequency allows you to avoid low-frequency resonance (when the cutoff frequency is near the base frequency of a note) as well as a sharp increase of the signal level caused by the resonance.

Resonance is the filter quality factor. **Res MIDI ctrl** is the controller that controls the filter (its quality factor).

Kbd tracking—changes the cutoff frequency, depending on the distance between the pressed MIDI key and the base MIDI key whose number is defined by the **Breakpoint** parameter.

20.4.3. The *EG/LFO2* Tab—Parameters of the Envelope Generator and the Low-Frequency Oscillator that Control the Filter Cutoff Frequency

The only difference between the second envelope generator used to control the filter cutoff frequency and the amplitude envelope generator (*Section 20.4.1*), is that it does not have the **Hold** phase (the generator waits for the beginning of the loop). The low-frequency oscillator used to create the "wow-wow" effect is no different from the one used to create the tremolo effect. You can see this by comparing the available parameters of both generators (Figs. 20.19 and 20.15).

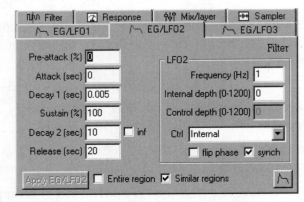

Fig. 20.19. Parameters of the envelope generator and the low-frequency oscillator that control filter cutoff frequency

20.4.4. The *EG/LFO3* Tab—Frequency Modulation Parameters

Frequency modulation parameters are shown in Fig. 20.20. The **EG3** envelope generator has only one phase (**Attack**). During this phase, the pitch is shifted by the number of cents set by the **Depth** parameter.

The **LFO2** generator is used to create the frequency vibrato effect.

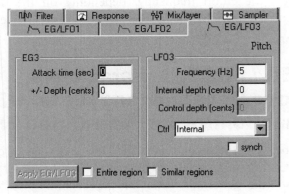

Fig. 20.20. Frequency modulation parameters

20.4.5. The *Response* Tab—Parameters that Define the Sampler's Reaction to the Key Pressing/Releasing Speed; Practice with Registers

In the **Response** tab, parameters are set that define the sampler's reaction to the key pressing and releasing speed.

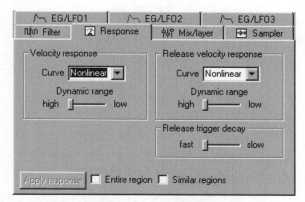

Fig. 20.21. Parameters that define the sampler's reaction to the key pressing and releasing speed

The **Velocity response** group contains parameters related to the key pressing speed.

Curve indicates the volume's dependence on the speed of pressing the key:

❏ **Nonlinear**   ❏ **Linear**   ❏ **Special**   ❏ **Dynamic range**

The **Release velocity response** group contains similar parameters, but they concern the key releasing speed.

There is an interesting feature possible in the GigaStudio sampler bank format: when a MIDI key is pressed, certain registers sound, and when the key is released, other registers sound. This can be accomplished by creating the **Release trigger** switch for two registers: one of them sounds while the key is being pressed, and the other sounds when the key is released. There can be more than two registers, but the principle is that same: certain registers sound while the key is pressed, and others sound once it is released.

Let's try to create such a switch.

It is easy to find a column of five unused switches (as shown in Fig. 20.22*a*). When you click on **Click to assign**, the dialog window shown in Fig. 20.23 appears.

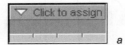 *a* 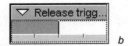 *b*  *c*

Fig. 20.22. Creating the release trigger switch: (*a*) the switch is not used; (*b*) release trigger switch is created, one of two splits is selected for editing; (*c*) both splits are selected for editing

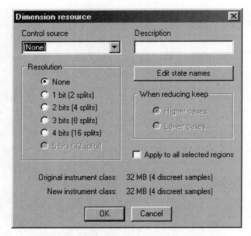

Fig. 20.23. Assigning the switch

In the **Control source** field, select **Release trigger**. In the **Resolution** field, select the number of bits used to code the switch positions: 2 bits allow for 4 positions of the switch, 3 bits allow for 8 spits, etc.

Release trigger, just like any trigger, can have two positions (before and after releasing the key). Two splits are coded by one bit; so select **1 bit (2 splits)**.

In the **Description** field, you may supply the register switch with a name.

To make things more convenient, you can give names to each of the splits, that is, you make comments on the switch positions. When you press the **Edit state names** button, the dialog window shown in Fig. 20.24 will appear.

Our switch can be in one of two positions, and therefore only two fields are available. We call one of them **before**, and the other **after** (before and after releasing the key).

We'll now close the **State names** box and return to the **Dimension source** window (see Fig. 20.23). Only one option—**Apply to all selected regions**—is available. However, in our situation, this option does not mean that much, since we're only experimenting. We then close all the windows by pressing **OK**. Then we see the **Release trigger** switch (see Fig. 20.22*b*).

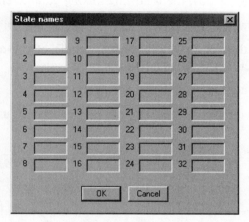

Fig. 20.24. Switch position name editor

We used stereophonic samples, so initially there were two registers in each region: one was used for the left channel and the other for the right channel. Now, the number of registers has doubled. Each of the tabs shown in Fig. 20.21 will only reflect the parameters of those registers selected by the **Release trigger** switch and the stereo channels switch, combined with the **Velocity** switch (see details in *Section 20.5*).

The current position of the switch is indicated by a green square on the switch itself, and by the note in the status bar of the main window. In our case, there are only two notes: **RTrg: before** and **RTgr: after**. If you need to edit the parameters of several registers at the same time, you can remove all the splits by holding down the <Ctrl> key (see Fig. 20.22*c*).

By default, the same sample is used in both new registers. Further on, you will learn to distribute samples along the keyboard and bind them to any of the registers without using the wizard (*Section 20.5*).

Now we'll return to the **Response** tab (see Fig. 20.21). The **Release trigger decay** parameter is relevant only once the **Release trigger** switch has been created. This parameter determines the speed of decreasing the volume of the register that sounds after the key is released. Note that the **inf** parameter (infinite support) in the **EG/LFO1** tab must be disabled. Otherwise, the note "freezes": after releasing the key, another register starts to sound, and the amplitude envelope generator never leaves the **Sustain** phase (because the next MIDI message about releasing the key never arrives).

20.4.6. The *Mix/layer* Tab—Mixing Parameters

In the **Mix/layer** tab (Fig. 20.25), the following mixing parameters are defined:

❑ **Attenuation (dB)**—lowering the volume level for the sample of the current register

❑ **6 dB boost**—raising the volume level for the sample of the current register by 6 dB (if this option is selected, the **Attenuation** option is canceled)

❑ **Attn control**—MIDI controller used to control attenuation

❑ **Dim bypass**—MIDI controller used to ignore the register parameters

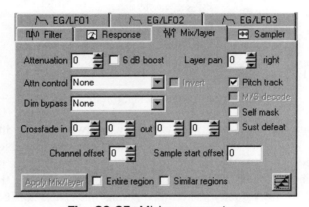

Fig. 20.25. Mixing parameters

We have already mentioned that regions can be multilayered. To implement multilayers, registers are used. To create a multilayered region, create the **Layer** registers switch, and define the number of splits you need. Each of these splits will correspond to one layer. Create the **Layer** switch just as we did the **Release trigger** switch (Fig. 20.26).

In truth, this switch switches nothing, since all the layers of the region can sound at the same time, and this is possible only when all the "contacts" of this switch are "fastened". By changing the split of the switch shown in Fig. 20.26, you select the register whose parameters you want to edit.

You can, of course, use different samples and different modulation parameters for them in different layers.

You can also make it so that samples of different layers are played not at the same time, but sequentially, softly coming into and leaving the mix. You can implement this using the **Fade in** (smooth volume increase) and **Fade out** (smooth volume decrease) effects.

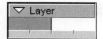

Fig. 20.26. The **Layer** switch

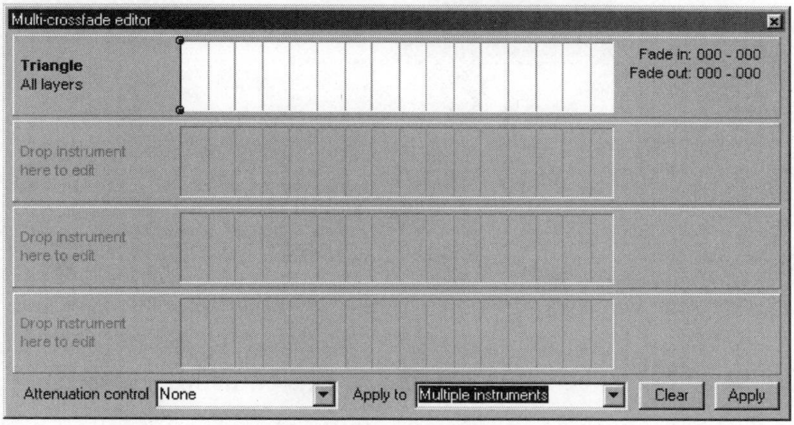

Fig. 20.27. Multi-crossfade editor

The starting and ending points of these effect's for the current register are specified in the **Crossfade in** and **Crossfade out** fields. However, it is more convenient to edit these parameters in a special editor, called by pressing the ![button] button.

The editor window is shown in Fig. 20.27.

By default, the editor is in the mode for editing the total amplitude envelope for the instruments. We have only one instrument; its envelope (or more accurately, its lack of one) is displayed in the topmost track called **Triangle** (the same as the instrument). If we had other instruments, we could drag them from the list directly to the given track of the editor. This window is not modal. That means that you may not close it in order to get access to objects of the main window. You can keep this window open and edit any parameters of any open project simultaneously.

In the **Apply to** field, you should select **Single inst, 2-layer regions**, since we intend to edit the amplitude envelopes of the layers of our only instrument.

The **Lock** option simplifies editing for a smooth crossing of two layers over time. When the **Lock** checkbox is checked, the points of fading out in one layer and fading in in another layer are matched up.

All that remains is to move the control points of the amplitude envelope. As a result, we should get something like what is shown in Fig. 20.28.

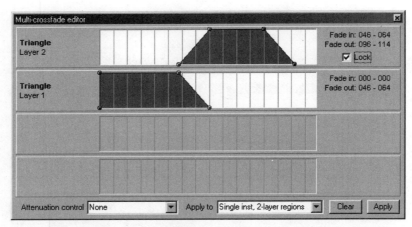

Fig. 20.28. Two layers of the instrument crossing smoothly over time

We return to Fig. 20.25 and continue with the options of the **Mix/layer** tab.

❐ **Channel offset**—play the sample through the audio channel following the current channel by the given number of audio channels (*Section 19.2.3*).

❐ **Sample start offset**—play the sample starting from the defined count.

❐ **Layer pan**—panorama of the current layer. This parameter often becomes useful when stereophonic sound is implemented using multilayers, when there are two monophonic channels instead of one stereophonic and each corresponds to its own stereo channel. Both registers in this case are moved to the extreme points of the panorama.

❐ **Pitch track**—support of the **Pitch** effect.

❐ **M/S decode**—the mode of decoding the samples created using *Mid-Side recording*. Mid-Side recording is implemented as follows: one microphone is located directly next to the sound source (recording is done to the left stereo channel) and the other microphone is placed at some distance (the right channel). Decoding a Mid-Side recording consists of putting the recorded sound source in the center of the panorama. The listener's impression of the quality of the sound improves.

❐ **Self mask**—the mode of saving system resources by terminating the playback of quiet sounds if they are masked by louder sounds. They usually cannot be heard, but take up resources anyway.

❐ **Sust defeat**—disable the support of the sustain pedal. This option may be useful if the sustain pedal is set only to switching between registers.

20.4.7. The *Sampler* Tab—Sample Properties

The following properties of the sample bound to the current register are available for editing in the **Sampler** tab (Fig. 20.29):

❏ **Sample**—sample name

❏ **Unity note**—the unity note corresponding to sample playback with normal sampling frequency (**Sample rate (Hz)**)

❏ **Tuning adjust (cents)**—exact tuning

In the **Loop** group:

❏ **Enable**—using the loop (enabling the loop mode)

❏ **Start**—loop starting point

❏ **End**—loop ending point

❏ **Length**—loop length (not changed)

When the **To all cases derived from same sample** checkbox is ticked, all the changes made apply not only to the current register, but to all registers using the given sample.

Changes are saved by pressing the **Apply** button (**Apply sampler info** in our case), but the changes in the **Loop** group will be heard only after the instrument is reloaded into GigaStudio. Whether or not this needs to be done is shown by the **RELOAD** indicator in the project toolbar.

The sample whose name is indicated in the **Sample** field corresponds to the current register of the current region of the current instrument. In our case, the **triangle3** sample was bound to the selected register using the wizard. How can we replace the sample?

20.5. Setting the Sample-Register Connection; Distributing Registers Along the Values of the *Velocity* Parameter

You cannot change the purpose of the **Velocity** switch (Fig. 20.30) in the project window (see Fig. 20.4).

To reset the sample of the current register, you have to drag it to the sample list and drop it in the field of the **Velocity** switch. If the sample is stereophonic and the region is monophonic, or vice versa, this cannot be done.

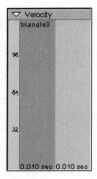

Fig. 20.30. The **Velocity** switch

By default, the **Velocity** switch has one position for monophonic samples, and two positions for stereophonic samples. Note that different registers correspond to the left and right channels. In most cases, you should define the same parameters for both channels. You may also need to set the same parameters for all registers of an instrument. The **Select lock** button may be useful in these cases. This button has three states:

▣—parameters of all registers are edited independently

▣—parameters of registers of the left and right channels are interconnected

▣—parameters of all registers are interconnected

Each region can contain only monophonic or only stereophonic samples. A case when one register of the region contains a stereo sample and another register contains a mono sample is impossible.

Properties of the **Stereo/Mono** region are changed using the window (Fig. 20.31) called by pressing the **Stereo/Mono** button.

In the **Resolution** group, you should select **Mono** or **Stereo**. When going from stereo to mono, one or more registers are lost. What modulation parameters of the registers of the left or the right channels should be saved? It's up to you: in the **When reducing keep** group, you can select the **Left articulation** from the left channel or the **Right articulation** from the right channel.

The **Apply to all selected regions** checkbox, if checked, indicates that the selection you make applies to all the selected regions.

By default, the **Velocity** switch has only one state: regardless of the speed of pressing the MIDI keys, the same registers are used. You can change the number of states of this switch (Fig. 20.32a).

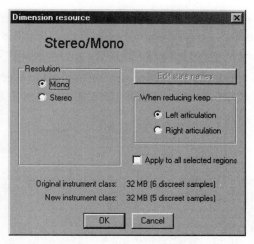

Fig. 20.31. Stereo/Mono region properties

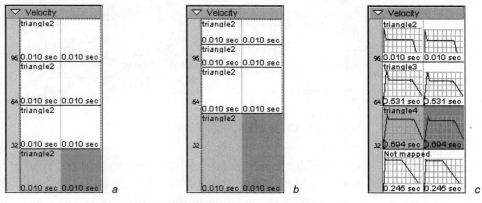

Fig. 20.32. Dividing the Velocity scale

By default, the vertical **Velocity** scale is divided into equal ranges. However, using the mouse, you can change the boundaries of the splits (Fig. 20.32*b*). With the **Env graphs** button, you can output the graphs of the amplitude envelopes directly to the switch splits (Fig. 20.32*c*).

20.6. Registers Revisited

The regions of GigaStudio are multidimensional. Each register switch corresponds to one dimension. The region space is discrete. A sample, along with certain modulation parameters, can be mapped to each element of this space. In our terms, these elements are called registers. By creating new switches or by increasing the number of splits of the existing switches, you divide the region into a greater number of registers.

GigaStudio instruments can have up to five dimensions. However, graphically, only one-dimensional, two-dimensional, and three-dimensional space can be represented.

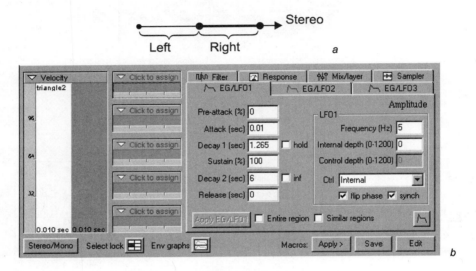

Fig. 20.33. A one-dimensional region

The simplest case is a one-dimensional region containing only two registers (the left and the right), which makes it stereophonic (Fig. 20.33a). You can set individual modulation parameters for each of the registers. The thick line in the picture corresponds to the currently selected register, whose parameters are currently available for editing. The corresponding state of the GigaStudio editor is shown in Fig. 20.33b.

We add another dimension—**Layer**. The multilayer stereophonic region is two-dimensional (Fig. 20.34a). It has two register switches, and each of them can be in one of two states. Each of the four registers can have its own modulation parameters. The register whose parameters are currently available for editing is indicated by a dark rectangle in the co-ordinate plane (Fig. 20.34a).

Now we'll add yet another dimension—**Velocity**. The region space along this axis is divided by two more splits (Fig. 20.35a). As a result, we have $2 \times 2 \times 2 = 8$ registers. The register selected for editing is indicated by the cube in Fig. 20.35a.

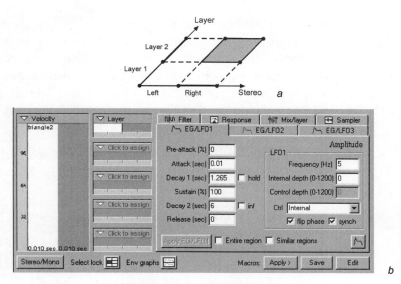

Fig. 20.34. A two-dimensional region

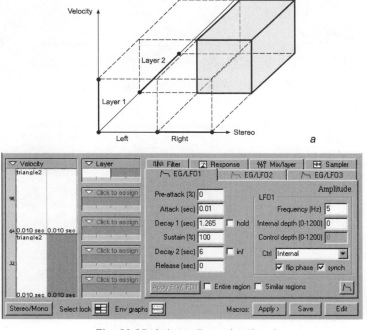

Fig. 20.35. A three-dimensional region

A bank containing stereo samples of drums and their reverberations can serve as an example of using three-dimensional regions. Reverberation samples are recorded using a high-quality, expensive studio effects processor. You can control the reverberation depth (the loudness of the corresponding samples) by changing the **Attenuation** parameter assigned to the usual controller, No. 91. For different values of the **Velocity** parameter, different samples are used. We can add another dimension to switch between reverberation types.

We return to our example and add another switch. You can, for example, select any of the available MIDI controllers. We have selected controller No. 80 (Fig. 20.36).

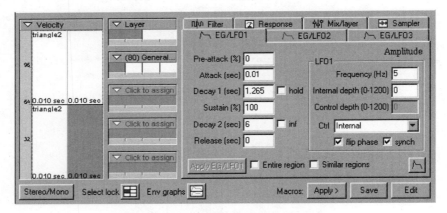

Fig. 20.36. A four-dimensional region

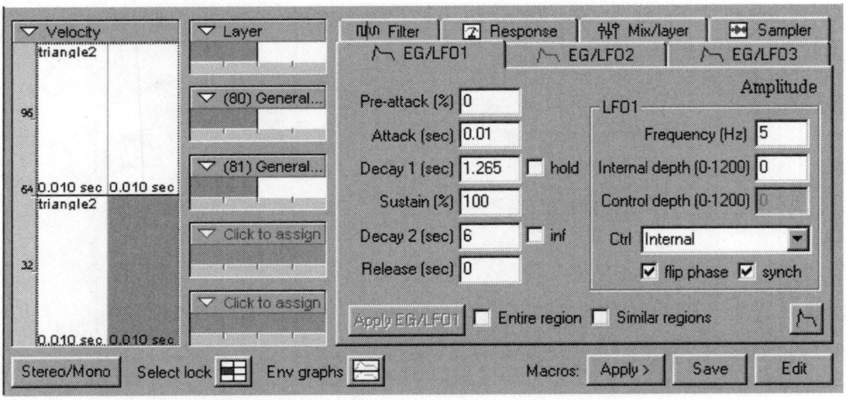

Fig. 20.37. A five-dimensional region

Let this switch be four-position. As a result, we get $2 \times 2 \times 2 \times 4 = 32$ registers (the maximum number allowed). To add another (fifth) dimension, we have to reduce the number of splits of the last switch to two (Fig. 20.37).

20.7. Creating Instruments without the Wizard; Working Effectively with the Regions Map

Until now, we have been working only with regions created by the instrument wizard. Now we'll try not using it.

Create a new instrument. To do so, right-click on the existing instrument. The context menu appears. Select the **New Instrument** command. The **Instrument Properties** dialog box will appear, similar to the one shown in Fig. 20.10. Input the instrument's name in the **Name** field (other parameters are not important now). We'll call it **My Instrument**, and press **OK**.

As you can see in Fig. 20.38, the new instrument is empty: it contains no regions, no registers, and thus, no samples.

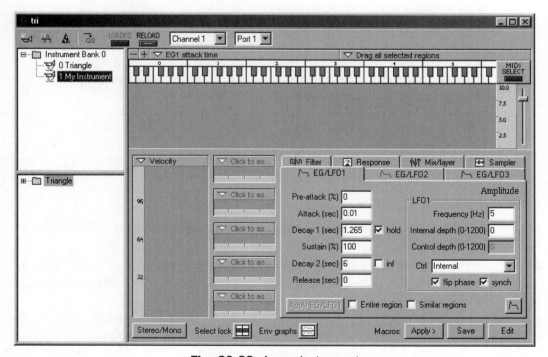

Fig. 20.38. A new instrument

The next step is creating one or more regions. Right-click on the empty region map (Fig. 20.39*a*). In the context menu that appears, select the **New region** command.

Below the place you have clicked, a new region appears (Fig. 20.39*b*). By default, it corresponds to one of the MIDI keys. Dragging the region's boundaries with the mouse, "expand" it along the virtual MIDI keyboard according to the position of future samples (Fig. 20.39*c*). Later you can change the position of the region if you like.

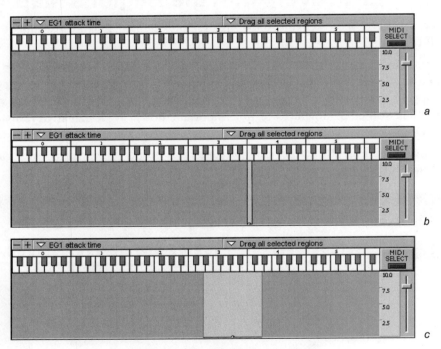

Fig. 20.39. Creating a region

Other regions can be created in a similar manner, if necessary.

Our samples are stereophonic, and so, using the **Stereo/Mono** button (Fig. 20.38), we should select **Stereo**.

Now select the name of the sample you need from the samples list, and move it to the **Velocity** switch with the mouse (Fig. 20.40*a*). The sample name is displayed on the switch (Fig. 20.40*b*).

Each of the regions, if necessary, is split into the required number of registers, and for each register its own modulation parameters are available. You can change the assigned parameters directly in the regions map, but not numerically.

In the upper part of the regions map, there is a long button that is by default called **EG1 attack time**. This is the parameter name (amplitude envelope generator attack time), which you can change using the regions map.

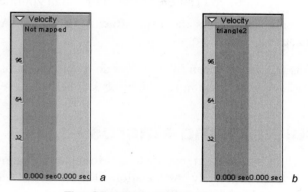

Fig. 20.40. Assigning a sample

This is done as follows. In the images for each of the regions, there is a horizontal line with a point in the center. By moving this line, you change the value of the parameter associated to it. The current value of the parameter is indicated by the numbers above the line (Fig. 20.41).

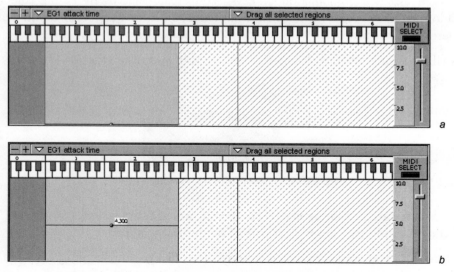

Fig. 20.41. Changing the selected parameter in the regions map

The regions map has two dimensions: the horizontal—MIDI keys, and the vertical—the value of the selected parameter. To the right of the regions map, there is a vertical slider that allows you to change the vertical zoom of the map. Using the ▬ and ➕ buttons above the virtual keyboard, you can change the horizontal zoom of the map.

To select any other parameter, press the **EG1 attack time** button. A list containing all available parameters appears. Make your choice.

If the ▦ button is pressed, you can select the regions for editing using the MIDI keyboard: press a MIDI key and the region to which this key belongs is selected.

20.8. Articulation and Macros

Articulation is the set of modulation parameters. Modulation parameters and samples in ART files can be stored separately. Articulation files are saved and loaded using the **File>Save articulation** and **File>Load articulation** commands.

You can copy the articulation from one register to another. To do so, right-click above one of the splits and call the context menu. In this menu, the **Copy articulation** and **Paste articulation** commands are available (articulation is pasted from the clipboard into the current register).

Macros are the set of articulations that you can save and then call using a special command or an assigned combination of keys. You create macros by editing the register modulation parameters and saving them as a macro. In further processing, you can apply this macro to any register.

Now we'll try a little practice. Right-click on the split you need (Fig. 20.42).

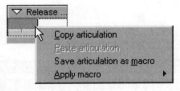

Fig. 20.42. Calling the split context menu

Select the **Save articulation as macro** command, which is equivalent to the **Save** button in the **Macros** group (the lower right part of the project window).

In the **Save articulation macro** dialog window (Fig. 20.43), you should specify the macro name (**Save as**) and the shortcut key. Set the input focus to the **Hot key** field, and press the key you want, or a combination of this key and the <Shift> key. In the **Include these pages** group, specify the tabs whose parameters are to be saved in the macro (*Section 20.4*).

The buttons are:

❏ **Set all**—selects all options

❏ **Clear all**—refuses all options

❏ **Save**—saves the parameters

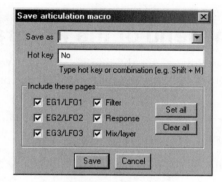

Fig. 20.43. Saving a macro

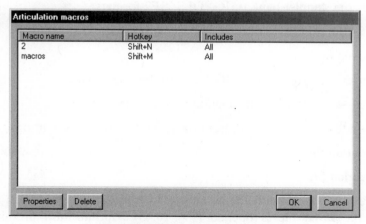

Fig. 20.44. The list of macros

Now you can select another register and apply the macro to it. Press the keys you have assigned, or use the context menu of the next split by selecting the **Apply macro>your**

macro name command. You can also press the **Apply** button in the lower right corner of the project window and select the macro from the list.

The **Edit** button is located near this button. When you press it, a window containing the list of macros appears (Fig. 20.44).

Using the **Delete** button, you can delete the selected macro. With the **Properties** button, you open another window in which you can change the macro name and edit the keys that call this macro.

20.9. The Main Menu of the Program

The information in this section is mostly reference-type. We have used many of the commands listed, and here we will briefly describe the other commands.

20.9.1. *File*—Working with Files

This menu contains the following commands:

- ❏ **New**—creates a new project
- ❏ **Open**—loads the sampler bank (GIG, DLS, SF2 formats)
- ❏ **Close**—closes the project
- ❏ **Save**—saves the project
- ❏ **Save As**—saves the project in a GIG file with the given name
- ❏ **Save Limited**—saves limited information in the project file
- ❏ **Merge file**—adds the information from the given file to the current project
- ❏ **Load articulation file**
- ❏ **Save articulation file**

After you select the **Save Limited** command, the dialog box in which you select the optimization of the saved file is opened (Fig. 20.45). Optimization in this case means throwing out a part of the information related to instruments that occupy more than 64 or 32 MB of memory (the **Instrument requiring more than 64 MB** and **Instrument requiring more than 32 MB** options), and samples not used in any instruments, but that are taking up memory (the **Unreferenced samples** option).

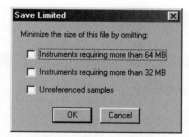

Fig. 20.45. The **Save Limited** window

This function may be useful when you want to load a big instrument (such as NemeSys_1GB_Grand.gig) and there is not enough RAM memory. If the 32 MB or 64 MB optimization is enabled, and you save this file under another name, some of the splits —the ones corresponding to the **Velocity** parameter—will be lost. Although the piano timbre that depends on the speed of pressing the MIDI keys will not be reproduced with the same quality, you can use that timbre anyway, even if there is not enough memory.

20.9.2. The *Edit* Menu

The **Edit** menu contains commands that allow you to edit objects related to different hierarchic levels:

❑ **Undo**—cancels the last action

❑ **Cut instrument**—cuts the instrument into the clipboard

❑ **Copy instrument**—copies the instrument into the clipboard

❑ **Paste**—pastes the instrument from the clipboard

❑ **Delete instrument**

❑ **Import samples**—imports samples from the assigned file

❑ **Import sample directory**—imports all files from the assigned directory

❑ **Edit macros**—opens the macro edit window (*Section 20.8*)

❑ **Instrument wizard**—starts the Instrument Wizard (*Section 20.3.2*)

❑ **Combine instruments**—combines several selected instruments into a single instrument using the registers (Fig. 20.46)

❑ **Crossfade editor**—calls the **Multi-crossfade** editor (*Section 20.4.5*)

❑ **File info**—calls the standard window for information on a multimedia file (Fig. 20.47)

❑ **Preferences**—calls the window shown in Fig. 20.48

After you call the **Combine instruments** command, the dialog box shown in Fig. 20.46 appears.

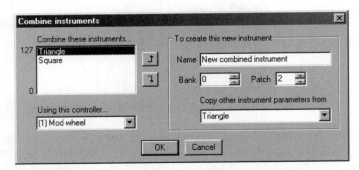

Fig. 20.46. Combining several instruments into one instrument

In the **Using this controller...** list, you select the controller used as a timbre switch for the combined instruments.

In the **Combine these instruments** list, the instruments you have selected are listed.

Using the arrow buttons, you can change the order of the instruments within the list and, accordingly, the order of the given switch's splits.

Name is the name of the newly created instrument; **Bank** is the bank in which this instrument is placed; **Patch** is the number of the instrument within the bank.

Some of the instruments' parameters cannot be combined by placing them in different registers. For example, the **Attenuation (dB)** parameter (*Section 20.3.1*) can only exist in an instrument by itself.

In the **Copy other instrument parameters from** list, you select the prototype instrument whose parameters are used as the basis for the new instrument.

The **File info** command opens a window giving standard information on the RIFF-format multimedia file to which the GIG files are associated (Fig. 20.47). The fields of this window are filled by whoever creates the GIG file, according to his or her preference.

The **Preferences** command calls the preferences window shown in Fig. 20.48.

In the **Middle C** group, you select the *C* note of one of three octaves. It is then considered the middle key of the MIDI keyboard.

In **Unity note for imported .wav files**, you assign the method for getting information on the unity note while samples are imported from WAV files:

❏ **Default to middle C**—select the middle key of the MIDI keyboard as the unity note

❏ **Guess from filename (e.g. *61.wav)**—take the information on the unity note from the filename in the **nn*.wav format, where nn is the note number

❏ **Guess from filename (e.g. *C#4.wav)**—take the information on the unity note from the filename in the **abc*.wav format, where abc is the note number (alpha-numeric definition of the note)

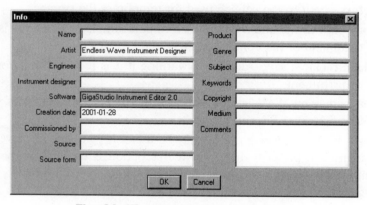

Fig. 20.47. Information on the project

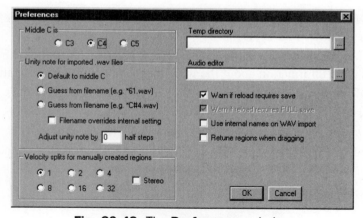

Fig. 20.48. The **Preferences** window

These options work only if the WAV file itself does not contain information on the unity note. Otherwise, regardless of the selected option, the unity note contained within the file is selected. To ignore this information, you should enable the **Filename override internal settings** option.

The remaining options of the preferences window are the following:

- ☐ **Adjust unity note by ... half steps**—offsets the unity note by the assigned number of semitones
- ☐ **Velocity splits for manually created regions**—the number of **Velocity** splits created by default when a region is created
- ☐ **Stereo**—creates stereophonic regions by default
- ☐ **Temp directory**—path to the catalog used for temporary file storage
- ☐ **Audio editor**—path to the audio editor used to edit samples; this editor is called by the **Edit Audio** command of the context menu of the samples list
- ☐ **Warn if reload requires save**—displays a warning if it is required that you save the file to reload the instrument
- ☐ **Use internal names on WAV import**—when importing WAV files, uses sample names stored in WAV files—not filenames

The **Retune regions when dragging** option may be useful if you have to move regions along the MIDI keyboard but preserve their key. If this option is enabled when you move the region, the unity notes of the region are moved accordingly. Otherwise, you'll have to manually change the sample settings in the **Sampler** tab (described in *Section 20.4.6*).

20.9.3. *MIDI>Channel Status*

The **MIDI** item of the main menu contains only one command, which displays the **Channel status** window (Fig. 20.49).

In the **Port** list, you should select one of the MIDI ports of GigaStudio. For each MIDI channel of this port, information about the instruments loaded into the channel is output.

The remaining commands of the main menu are typical for all Windows applications—**View**, **Window**, and **Help**.

Now you know not only how to use the GigaStudio virtual sampler, but how to create banks with unique sounds for this sampler as well.

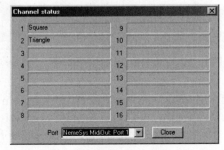

Fig. 20.49. The MIDI channel status window

Chapter 21: Reason—a Virtual Audio Studio

Just five years ago, no one could even imagine that there would be musical software like Reason. Software synthesizers were then in the beginning stages of their development, and were more often used as toys than for serious matters. The well-known software synthesizer Rebirth 338 had a unique but limited sound: it contained two one-voice synthesizers and two drum machines (version 2.0). When compared to modern virtual studios, these abilities are not even adequate today. Reason and Rebirth are products of Propellerhead Software. Reason seems to have the same kind of nostalgia for the sound of an analog synthesizer and hardware samplers as Rebirth. This all means that sooner or later, virtual studios will replace traditional studio equipment. Reason is a virtual studio oriented towards modern styles of electronic and dance music. If such a studio is what you need, then you've found your answer in Reason. Let's see what it consists of.

Virtual Devices

Reason includes the following virtual devices:

- Remix—mixer
- ReDrum—drum machine
- SubTractor—polyphonic analog synthesizer
- NN-19—digital sampler
- Dr. REX Loop Player—drum loop player
- Matrix Pattern Sequencer—sequencer for creating grooves

Various effect processors:

- RV-7—reverber
- DDL-1—delay line
- D-11—distortion
- ECF-42—filter controlled by the envelope
- CF-101—chorus/flanger
- PH-90—phaser
- COMP-01—compressor
- PEQ-2—two-band parametric equalizer

The number of these virtual hardware devices depends on your needs and the perform-ance of the real (not the virtual!) processor.

The Reason project window is a virtual rack stand (Fig. 21.1) that contains the above listed equipment. Depending on the currently selected device, different commands of the main menu are available.

Fig. 21.1. A Reason project is a virtual rack stand

You select devices by right-clicking on their panels. The selected device is marked by a special marker—a rectangle around the body of the device.

In the lower part of the rack stand, you see the transport panel, used to control recording and playback. We describe its functions in *Section 21.9.*

To add a new device to the stand, call the context menu with the right mouse button, select **Create**, and then select the name of the created device (Fig. 21.2). You can also select the **Create>***the device you need* command from the main menu.

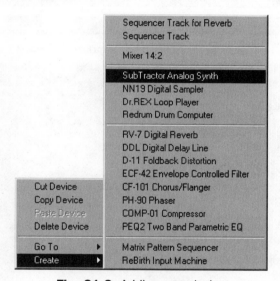

Fig. 21.2. Adding new device

Using this menu, you can also "cut" a device into the clipboard (**Cut Device**), copy it to the clipboard (**Copy Device**), paste it from the clipboard (**Paste Device**), and delete it (**Delete Device**). However, it's probably more convenient to delete a device using the **<Delete>** key.

When the project contains many devices, the **Go To** command may be useful.

Each device has a label with its name on the left. You can change this name. To do so, click on the label. The input field for the new name appears.

Each device can be displayed in two modes: full and minimized. Switching between the display modes is done by pressing the small triangular buttons in the left part of the control panel. In minimized view, the device panel contains the minimum number of controls used for loading preset settings (patches). Both view modes of the NN-19 sampler are shown in Fig. 21.3.

a

b

Fig. 21.3. NN-19 sampler in the full (*a*) and minimized (*b*) view modes

Fig. 21.4. A reason project —"rear view" of the stand

You can "turn" to the rear of the stand (by pressing the <Tab> key or using the **Options> Toggle Rack Front/Rear** command of the main menu) and connect the inputs and outputs of various devices with virtual cables (Fig. 21.4).

Connection is easy: drag the jack with the mouse cursor and move it to another jack, or click on the jack, and in the menu that appears, select the other jack to which you wish to connect (Fig. 21.5).

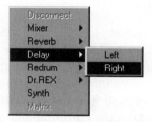

Fig. 21.5. Selecting a jack to connect to the virtual cable

Types of Signals: Audio and CV/Gate

In Reason, there are two types of signals transferred to virtual cables—Audio and CV/Gate.

The devices generating the sound (synthesizers, samplers) have only outputs (mono, stereo left/right). The devices processing the sound have inputs and outputs.

CV means control voltage. Before there was a MIDI standard, various electric musical devices communicated through this interface. Using the control voltage level, you can transfer the information on what key was pressed, or what position a particular control is in. There was no general CV standard, and synthesizers from different vendors could interpret the same CV level differently. But this is not a problem, since all Reason virtual devices are CV-compatible. CV signals in Reason are normally used to modulate one parameter of one device by another parameter of another device.

Near the CV-inputs, there are always sliders that allow you to change the device's sensitivity to control signals.

Signals of the Gate type are a type of CV. They allow you to transfer one of two states of something (for example, a pressed/released MIDI key), and the value of any parameter (for example, the voltage level corresponding to the number of the pressed key). To make things simpler, you can consider the Gate signal a rectangular impulse whose front side indicates an event's arrival (for example, pressing a MIDI key), and whose rear indicates the termination of this event. The height of the rectangle is proportional to the value of the transferred parameter. If the height is zero, there is no rectangle, and therefore no event.

The Gate inputs do not have sensitivity regulators, since the parameter transferred by these signals can be interpreted in only one way.

Automated Connection

So as not to be confused with virtual electric wires, certain connections in Reason are done automatically. For example, when you add a new device, its audio output is connected to the first unused line of the mixer. If you add an effect processor, and the mixer is currently selected, this effect is connected to the first unused aux bus of the mixer. When you add an effect processor, and a sound generation device is selected, this effect is connected in the insertion mode to the corresponding line of the mixer.

These are two useful commands in the main menu:

❏ **Disconnect Device**—disconnects the device from everything you can

❏ **Auto-route Device**—connects the device automatically

Main Sequencer, Automation

Besides different virtual equipment, Reason provides a real software sequencer that is implemented in a manner similar to the sequencers of such programs as Cakewalk/Sonar, Cubase, Logic, and others. In Reason, there are also virtual-hardware sequencers, and so we call this software sequencer the *main sequencer*. Just the presence of the complete sequencer allows us to consider Reason not as a set of software synthesizers and samplers, but rather as original software for creating music.

The main sequencer automates the control of virtual devices. One MIDI controller corresponds to each parameter of the virtual device. MIDI tables of correspondence are provided in the MIDI Implementation Charts document included with Reason. You won't need to work with MIDI controllers directly or remember their numbers. The only exception to this is when you are controlling Reason's virtual synthesizer from another program or from an external MIDI device.

From the user's point of view, automation is implemented as follows. You start recording in the main sequencer, and turn any virtual knobs. All the actions you perform are fixed in *subtracks* for storing automation data. When the composition is played, all the actions you have performed are repeated: the knobs turn themselves the way you turned them originally. If you want to change any of the parameters, open the subtrack you need, and redraw the graph to change the necessary parameter using the **Pencil** tool. Controls whose corresponding subtrack is not empty are displayed within a frame.

Each device has a corresponding track in the main sequencer. In this track, any information addressed to the virtual device can be stored. This information can be displayed in several subtracks for several elements of the virtual device interface. The number of subtracks corresponds to the number of knobs on the virtual device control panel.

File Formats

The main file formats used with Reason are WAV and AIF sample files, REX2 and RCY drum loop files, various patches for virtual devices, RNS and RPS project files (songs), and a special category of files—RFL (ReFill). This last format is for archives that can contain files of any of the above listed formats. Using Reason, you can open an RFL file as a simple directory, and select the necessary samples, patches, or songs. One of these RFL files (factory sound bank.rfl, about 500 MB) contains many useful features, and is included with Reason. You have to have this file on CD-ROM or on your hard disk for Reason to be able to operate.

In Reason, much attention is given to upholding copyrights. You can use samples from RFL files, but you cannot save them in your project. Later, to play the composition, you will need the RFL files whose contents were used in the given project. This is related to protecting the copyrights for Reason's audio banks. Users' copyrights are protected in Reason as follows: projects are stored either in RNS files (normal songs), or in RPS files (songs for publishing). After you have completed your composition, save it in RPS format, and publish the file on the Internet. No one can then make any changes to your composition, and most definitely, no one can declare it his or her own composition. Unless, of course, you run into a hacker.

21.1. Program Settings

In this section we describe:

❑ Basic settings of the program

❑ MIDI and AUDIO routing

❑ Remote control of virtual device parameters by MIDI

❑ Remote control of virtual device parameters from a PC keyboard

21.1.1. Basic Settings of the Program

All the basic settings of the program are kept in the dialog box (Fig. 21.6) called by the **Edit>Preferences** command of the main menu. This dialog box opens automatically when the program starts for the first time. The settings window contains four pages. The current tab is selected in the **Page** list.

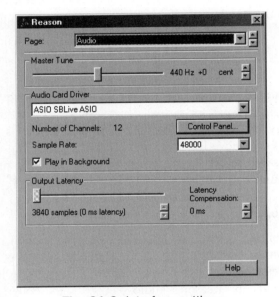

Fig. 21.6. Interface settings

In the **Audio** page, you can select the sound card driver from the **Audio Card Driver** list. The same driver can have different program interfaces, for example, MME drivers (a multimedia interface from the 16-bit Windows versions that is still alive and kicking), DirectX, and ASIO (the interface promoted by Steinberg).

In the **Number of Channels** field, the number of audio channels supported by the selected driver is displayed.

In the **Sample Rate** list, select the sampling frequency. When the **Play in Background** checkbox is ticked, Reason can play in the background. The Reason window is inactive, and you work with another program.

By pressing the **Control Panel** button, you call the window of the sound card parameters. Drivers of this sound card support ASIO. The contents of this window are determined by the particular sound card driver.

The **Master Tune** (general tuning) parameter allows you to adjust the tune within the range from −100 to 100 cents.

The **Output Latency** parameter indicates the maximum allowed delay between the event (pressing a MIDI key, changing any of the synthesis parameters, etc.) and the audible reaction to this event. The less this parameter value is the better. However, your PC's performance might not be good enough to implement very small values of the **Output Latency** parameter. You will hear clicks when you perform actions like scrolling, moving windows, etc. during playback. You then have no choice but to increase the value of **Output Latency**. To some extent, you can compensate for this delay by performing the commands written in the main sequencer ahead of time. The time by which it will be pre-empted is defined by the **Latency Compensation** parameter.

In the **MIDI** page (Fig. 21.7), you can select the MIDI port (**Port**) and the MIDI channel (**Channel**) used to input information into the main sequencer. In the **External Control** group, you select MIDI ports to control virtual devices without using the main sequencer (**Bus A—Bus D**). Routing MIDI information is described in more detail in the next section.

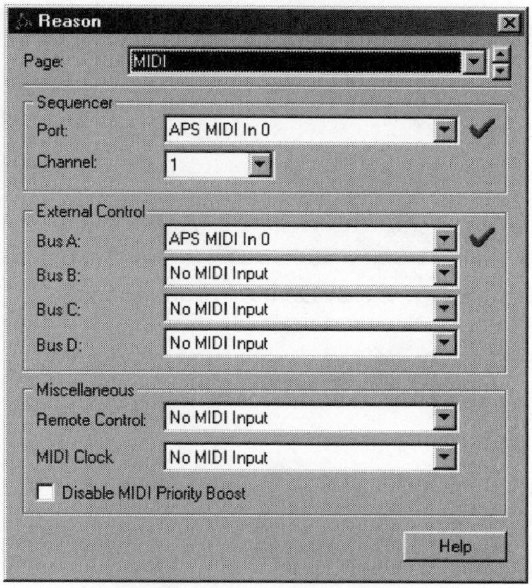

Fig. 21.7. MIDI interface settings

In the **Miscellaneous** group, you can specify the MIDI port (**Remote Control**) used for remotely controlling the selected parameters of virtual devices (*Section 21.1.3*) and the **MIDI Clock** source synchronization port (*Section 21.9*).

By default, the highest priority in Reason is given to MIDI information processing. This is so because the majority of resources are used to generate the audio. When you lack resources, it is important to accept the MIDI message in time and to react to it. However, the vendors do not guarantee that everything will operate normally when using this approach to MIDI information processing in a system with MIDI equipment. So, if you come across any problems, untick the **Disable MIDI Priority Boost** checkbox.

Reason's main options are located in the **General** page (Fig. 21.8).

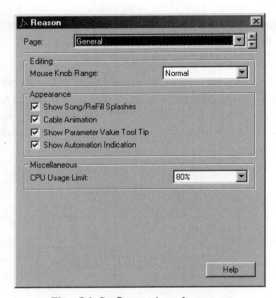

Fig. 21.8. General preferences

Mouse Knob Range—sensitivity of the regulators (when you capture a regulator and change its position using the mouse):

❑ **Normal**—normal sensitivity

❑ **Precise**—lowered sensitivity (you can define the position of the regulators precisely)

❑ **Very Precise**—very low sensitivity (to turn any switch 180°, you have to move the mouse cursor almost half a screen)

Projects and RFL files may contain information on authors and vendors, including a 256 × 256 pixel picture. If you disable the **Show Song/ReFill Splashes** option, these pictures are not displayed.

❑ **Cable Animation**—cables flail about like real cables

❑ **Show Parameter Value Tool Tip**—display a balloon tip with the current value of the changed parameter

❑ **Show Automation Indication**—select the elements of the virtual device's interface for which recording automation exists

In the **Sound Locations** tab (Fig. 21.9), you can specify the path to the main directories (maximum four directories) in which files associated with Reason (samples and patches—sets of synthesis parameters) are stored.

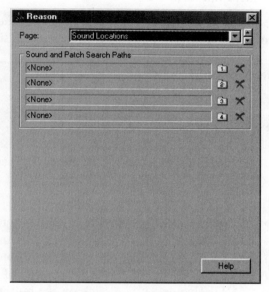

Fig. 21.9. Paths to samples and patches

When working with the patches browser (*Section 21.3.1*), you can open the contents of any of these directories just by pressing one button.

21.1.2. MIDI and AUDIO Routing

The term *routing* here means control of MIDI and Audio data and their distribution between different virtual devices and objects of these devices.

MIDI Routing

The commands received through MIDI can be routed using two methods.

The first method, *Via the Sequencer*, means that the MIDI data from the MIDI port and the MIDI channel you define arrive to the selected track of the main sequencer, and then are transferred to the device corresponding to that track. This method of MIDI command routing is widely used in practice.

The second routing method, *By using the MIDI "External Control" inputs*, means that each virtual device directly receives the MIDI commands from the assigned MIDI port and the MIDI channel. This method is usually used during joint operation of Reason and any external software or hardware sequencer.

The virtual rack device that implements the tuning of MIDI and audio ports is always on the top of the rack stand. It cannot be removed. Its front panel is shown in Fig. 21.10.

Fig. 21.10. The **Hardware Interface** virtual device, by means of which
Reason communicates with external devices

When using the external sequencer, you should associate the MIDI channels of the selected device to the virtual devices you need. Reason supports up to four MIDI-In ports, and thus $4 \times 16 = 64$ MIDI channels. You specify these ports in the **MIDI** tab of the basic settings window (*Section 21.1.1*). The buttons marked **A** through **D** each correspond to one port. Each **CHANNEL** *n* field, in which *n* is the number of a MIDI channel from 1 to 16, corresponds to a MIDI channel. If you click on the button with the small triangle near the particular MIDI channel number, a list appears containing all the devices existing in the current project, as well as the **Disconnect** item. After you select the device from the list, its name is displayed in the virtual display under the MIDI channel number. Each channel has a virtual LED, which flashes when data is admitted through its MIDI channel.

AUDIO Routing

Reason supports up to 64 audio channels. The number of available audio channels depends on the abilities and the settings of the sound card driver (*Section 21.1.1*). The minimum number of channels is 2 (the left and the right stereo channels). The corresponding **AUDIO IN** jacks are located on the rear panel of the **Hardware Interface** device (Fig. 21.11). Available audio channels are marked with LEDs on the front panel of **Hardware Interface** (see Fig. 21.10, **AUDIO OUT** channels).

Fig. 21.11. Rear panel of **Hardware Interface**

The **AUDIO IN** name in the rear panel of **Hardware Interface** is relevant only to the given virtual device. You have to consider these jacks input jacks: through them, the audio data flow from Reason to the sound card driver, and are then reproduced as real audio.

Virtual devices must somehow be connected to the **AUDIO IN** jacks of the **Hardware Interface**. Otherwise you won't hear the sound of these devices.

Even if you have only two stereo channels, this does not limit your ability to create music in practice. All the devices are connected to at least one mixer. The output of one of these mixers (to which other mixers are connected) is connected to the available stereo jacks of the **Hardware Interface** device. The number of mixers and the number of devices connected to them are determined only by the processor's performance. Certainly, additional audio channels provide some advantages, such as listening to certain devices without the mixer, and being able to process them separately using hardware-implemented effects (if your sound card supports them).

21.1.3. Remote Control of the Virtual Device Parameters by MIDI

Most parameters of virtual devices can be controlled in real time with MIDI or the PC keyboard. In some cases, this is more convenient than turning virtual regulators with the mouse. If you want to use a MIDI data input device as a remote control, it is good to have a separate device selected only for this purpose. You have to select a separate MIDI for this device, not the MIDI port used to input the data into the main sequencer.

Here is an example of an optimal configuration: the regular MIDI keyboard is used for track recording in the main sequencer, and a special device of the Phat-Boy type is used for remote control of the virtual device parameters. The Phat-Boy device is a remote control panel with a number of regulators, and certain MIDI controllers can be assigned to each of these regulators.

Assigning the MIDI port to accept remote control commands is done as follows. Select the **Edit>Preferences** command from the main menu. In the **MIDI** tab, in the **Miscellaneous** group, open the **Remote Control** list and select the MIDI port you need.

Then enable remote control support. To do so, select the **Options>MIDI Remote Mapping** command from the main menu, and then call the **Options>Edit MIDI Remote Mapping** command, enabling the mode for editing MIDI remote control commands. After this, any regulator in a virtual device that supports remote control will be marked with a green arrow. Click on any one of them. The dialog box shown in Fig. 21.12 appears.

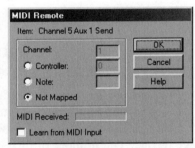

Fig. 21.12. The **MIDI Remote** dialog box

Here you can assign the MIDI channel (**Channel**), MIDI controller (**Controller**) or the MIDI key (**Note**) to be used to remotely control the selected parameter. It is simpler to select the **Learn MIDI Input** option and use a MIDI controller or a MIDI key. Just touch the pitch shifting wheel, or press one of the MIDI keys on the keyboard. The program understands the controller or the key number automatically. The accepted command is displayed in the **MIDI Received** field.

Not Mapped—disables remote control of the selected parameter.

To disable the mode of assigning remote control MIDI commands, call the **Options> Edit MIDI Remote Mapping** command of the main menu again.

21.1.4. Remote Control of Virtual Device Parameters from a PC Keyboard

The remote control from a PC keyboard mode is enabled by the **Options>Enable Keyboard Remote** command of the main menu, or by pressing the <Ctrl>+<G> keys.

The mode for assigning remote control keys is enabled by the **Options>Edit Keyboard** command of the main menu. After you enable this mode, each regulator on the virtual devices that supports remote control is marked with a yellow arrow. Clicking on one of them calls the dialog box shown in Fig. 21.13.

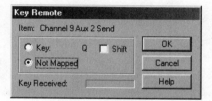

Fig. 21.13. The **Key Remote** dialog box

Select the **Key** option and press the key or the combination of keys on your PC keyboard. You can use any keys except the spacebar, <Tab>, <Enter>, and the additional numeric pad, which are reserved for controlling the transport panel (*Section 21.9*). The **Shift** option means that the selected parameter will react to a combination of the <Shift> key and the assigned key.

To disable the mode for assigning remote control, call the **Options>Edit Keyboard** command of the main menu once more.

21.1.5. Saving the Remote Control Parameters

The remote control parameters are saved, along with other information, in project files. If you actively use remote control, it makes sense to create a template project containing only the remote control settings. Later, instead of creating a new project (**File>New**), load this template file and save it under another name using the **File>Save As** command. This might not be that convenient, but it is the only allowable way to save the remote control parameters.

Now you have enough information to begin learning the abilities of the virtual hardware.

In any case, keep in mind the method that allows you to switch virtual regulators (of which there are so many in Reason) to their default position: click on them while holding the <Ctrl> key down.

21.2. Remix Mixer

The **Remix** mixer (Fig. 21.14) contains 14 stereophonic channels. You may think 14 channels is not that many. Well, 14 might not be a lot for one mixer, but remember that you can have any number of mixers. If you lack channels, create another mixer.

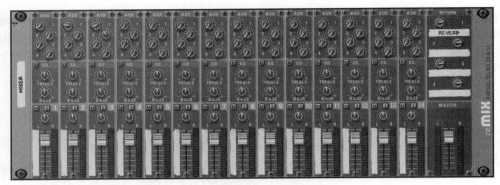

Fig. 21.14. Remix mixer

Each line of the mixer contains the following elements:

❏ Fader and the signal level indicator

❏ **Pan**—panorama

❏ **EQ**—two-band equalizer (+/-−24 dB, 12 kHz and +/−24 dB, 80 Hz)

❏ **Mute** and **Solo** buttons

❏ Four aux sends

Also, each line has a label with the name of the device connected to the given channel.

All aux sends operate according to the Post scheme. The signal travels according to the scheme shown in Fig. 21.15.

The master module of the mixer contains aux return regulators with labels that are the names of the plugged effects, and master fader that controls the total volume.

In the rear panel of the mixer (Fig. 21.16), you'll find the following jacks: **AUX Send Out** (four mono aux sends), **AUX Returns** (four stereo aux returns), **Master Out Left/Right** (master output). There is also a **CV Master Level** input used to control the total volume of other devices through CV.

The **Chaining Aux** and **Chaining Master** inputs are used to combine several mixers into a chain. For example, let's say that the 14 channels of one mixer is not enough for you, and you create another mixer. Reason automatically connects the **AUX Send Out** and **Master Out** outputs of the second mixer to the **Chaining Aux** and **Chaining Master** inputs of the first mixer. Now you have a 28-channel mixer that consists of two devices. This combined mixer still has four aux sends and one master output. If 28 channels is not enough, you add a third, and then a fourth mixer, and so on, until you have enough channels.

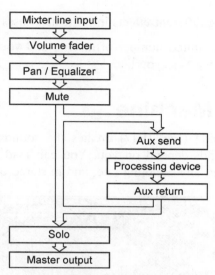

Fig. 21.15. Signal routing

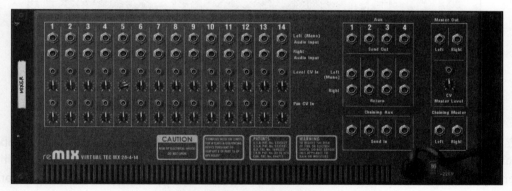

Fig. 21.16. Rear panel of the mixer

Of course, several mixers needn't be combined into a chain. They can be independent. Here are the basic ways of using several mixers:

❑ Outputs of each mixer are connected to different **AUDIO IN** inputs of the **Hardware Interface**. However, the sound card drivers may not support all of these independent audio ports of the **Hardware Interface** device.

❑ Outputs of several mixers are led to the channel inputs of one mixer (the main mixer in that case), and its output is connected to the **AUDIO IN** input of the **Hardware Interface** device.

In both cases, you can plug different effects into the aux buses of any of the mixers.

Generally, you have an unlimited number of mixers, and you can interconnect them or connect them to various devices as you like.

21.3. ReDrum Machine

The **ReDrum** drum machine (Fig. 21.17) creates the sounds of ten percussion instruments. The particular sounds depend on you. You can load samples in WAV or AIFF formats with any resolution, any sampling rate, and in stereo or mono formats.

Fig. 21.17. Front panel of **ReDrum**

Each drum has its own channel. The channels are numbered 1 through 10. In the upper part of each of the lines, you have the ▶ button. By pressing this button, you can listen to the drum's sound. The **M** (Mute) and **S** (Solo) buttons are found near this button.

For each of the samples, its own set of modulation parameters can be specified. The set of all these parameters for all drums is called a patch. Patches can be saved and loaded from DRP files.

21.3.1. Load ReDrum Patches Using the Browser; Control the Playback Quality

The browser in this case acts as a dialog box used to load projects, samples, and patches into Reason. You will encounter this dialog many times. In our book, we'll give you some initial information on the browser while you read about **ReDrum**.

In the left lower part of the **ReDrum** front panel, you'll see the field shown in Fig. 21.18.

Fig. 21.18. Patch load/save buttons, playback quality control parameters

Using the ▣ button located in this field, you can call the browser (Fig. 21.19*a*).

In the left part of the browser, there is a list of files and subdirectories of the current directory. In the upper part, there is a list containing the most recently used directories and a number of buttons:

⬆—one step up the directories tree

✏—selects desktop

① ② ③ ④—selects one of four previously assigned directories (*Section 21.1.1*)

▣—finds and displays all the ReFill files (see *"File Formats" above in this chapter*)

C—refreshes the information on the current directory

In the right part of the browser, the information on the selected file is displayed. If the file is selected from the ReFill archive, the information on this archive is also displayed. The appearance of the browser window may change, depending on the format of the file being loaded by the browser. The format is shown in the upper part of the browser window under the title. Fig. 21.19*b* shows the browser called to load a sample: in it you will now find the **Play/Stop** button (sample preview start/stop) and the **Autoplay** preview auto start button.

We turn again to patch loading and to Fig. 21.18.

A patch is a file containing the set of a sample's modulation parameters. You can load pre-prepared patches (using the browser), or create your own patches. Using the ▣ buttons, list all the patches within the current directory. Then save the current patch with the ▣ button.

In the field shown in Fig. 21.18, there are two other buttons that control the operation of ReDrum:

❑ **High Quality Interpolation**—enables the mode for high quality sound count interpolation. In this mode, the quality of drum sounds becomes normal. If this mode is disabled, the quality is lower, and the processor load is lessened.

❐ **Channel 8 & 9 Exclusive**—exclusive mode for the ReDrum channels 8 and 9 (it does not affect other channels). In this mode, only one of the channels can sound: channel 8's playback is interrupted when the sample in channel 9 is playing, and vice versa. The main application of this mode is interrupting a sample with the sound of an open hi-hat by the sound of a closed hi-hat.

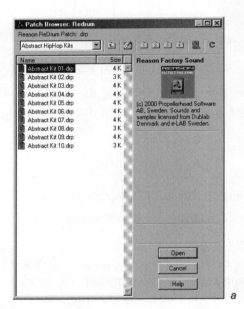

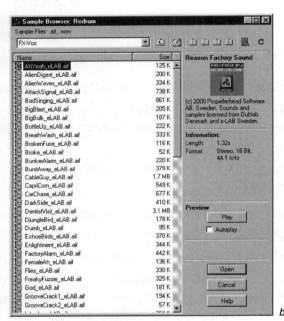

Fig. 21.19. Browser

21.3.2. Create Your Own Patches

If you want to create your own set of drums, or modify an existing one, you should perform some of the steps below for each of the ReDrum channels you are interested in.

Load the sample you need using the ▣ button (Fig. 21.18), which calls the browser (Fig. 21.19b).

Pay attention to the fact that different lines of ReDrum channels can take on various appearances (Figs. 21.20a—21.20c). The difference is in the sample modulation abilities. The parameters that vary have a darker background.

Now that you have loaded the sample, try to control the parameters below.

a   *b*   *c*

Fig. 21.20. Parameters of ReDrum channels

❏ **S1** and **S2**—sends to effects. By default, they are commuted to AUX1 and AUX2 of the mixer, respectively.

❏ **L-PAN-R**—panorama for mono samples, or stereo balance for stereo samples. If the sample is stereophonic, the indicator above this regulator is highlighted.

❏ **LEVEL**—volume.

❏ **VEL**—the ratio of the volume's dependence on the Velocity parameter (the key pressing speed). If the **VEL** value is positive, when Velocity increases, the volume also increases. For negative values of **VEL**, when the Velocity value increases, the volume decreases. The Velocity parameter is ignored in the 0 position.

To the right of the **LENGTH** regulator, we see the sample playback switch. In the lower position, the sample volume smoothly fades to zero (Fade Out) within the time specified by the **LENGTH** regulator. It does not matter how long the MIDI key is held, or what the length of the MIDI key imprint in the main sequencer is. If the switch is in the upper position, the sample is played with a constant volume for the time specified by the **LENGTH** parameter. However, if ReDrum is controlled by a MIDI keyboard or from the main sequencer, the sample plays while the MIDI key is being pressed, or for the length of the MIDI key imprint, or until the sample finishes. The sample may never end if a loop is defined for it. The loop parameters are saved in the sample file. You can edit these parameters using any audio editor (such as Cool Edit Pro).

Although there are not an infinite number of drum sounds, who ever said ReDrum can only reproduce drum samples?

We continue listing the parameters that you can change while working with the loaded sample.

❏ **PITCH**—pitch shifting within a range of one octave higher and one lower.

❏ **BEND** (this parameter is available for channels 6 and 7)—the depth of pitch shifting (Pitch bend). The pitch is increased if the parameter is positive, decreased if negative, and there is no effect if it is equal to 0

❏ **RATE**—pitch shifting speed.

❏ **VEL**—sensitivity of the **BEND** parameter to the MIDI key pressing speed. The **BEND** and **VEL** regulators have indicators that are highlighted when the values of these parameters are non-zero.

❏ **TONE**—this parameter (available for channels 1, 2, and 10) determines the timbre background of the sound. You can see similar regulators on cheap recorders. In most cases, this "equalizer" is adequate. If it is not, you can connect the corresponding channel of ReDrum to the PEQ-2 parametric equalizer.

❏ **VEL**—the ratio of the **TONE** parameter's dependence on the MIDI key pressing speed.

❏ **START** (this parameter is available for channels 3, 4, 5, 8, and 9)—the starting point of the sample playback (this means you don't have to play the sample from the very beginning).

❏ **VEL**—sensitivity of the **START** parameter to the MIDI key pressing speed. A negative **VEL** value when **START** = 0 does not affect the sample's sound.

After you have specified all the necessary parameters for all the ReDrum channels you need, you can save the current patch (the state of all controls) using the ▣ button (see Fig. 21.18).

Each of the ten lines of ReDrum has a **Select** (select the channel) button. This button relates to the built-in sequencer of ReDrum.

21.3.3. Built-in Sequencer

ReDrum contains a built-in sequencer (Fig. 21.21).

Fig. 21.21. ReDrum sequencer

The operating principle of this sequencer is the same as for analog sequencers: there are buttons numbered 1 through 16, and each button corresponds to one step (beat). Using the **Select** buttons (see Fig. 20) select the drum you need and press the buttons that correspond to the beats in which this drum is to be played. Then do the same with the other drums. The resulting sequence of programmed steps is called a *pattern*. Up to 32 patterns can be kept in the sequencer memory at once. You can select a pattern using the buttons numbered 1 to 8 (the pattern number within a bank) and A through D (the bank).

The **RUN** button starts the pattern playback. However, the pattern is played only when the **PATTERN** button is pressed. The action of this button is similar to the mute button, i.e., by disabling this button, you disable the playback of the programmed sequence of sounds. Playback is enabled and disabled not immediately, but starting from the next bar.

The playback tempo is common to all the devices included in the project. It is specified in the input field located on the transport panel (*Section 21.9*).

During playback, a button is highlighted for each step. The number of steps in the pattern specified in the **STEPS** field may go over 16. The maximum number of steps is 64. However, you can only use 16 buttons. To get access to the other steps, use the **EDIT STEPS** switch. For example, if you move this switch to the **17-32** position, you can edit steps 17 through 32 using the same 16 buttons. In the **RESOLUTION** field, set the musical resolution of the steps. You can define the Velocity parameter for each step. The loudness and the sound character depend on its value. To set this parameter, use the three-position **DYNAMICS** switch: **HARD**—maximum velocity, **MEDIUM**—middle velocity, and **SOFT**—minimum velocity.

With the **Shuffle** button, you enable the mode for changing the rhythm, which gives a swing-like sound to the piece. How much the rhythm is changed is defined by the **PATTERN SHUFFLE** parameter of the transport panel (*Section 21.9*). This parameter is common to all of Reason's pattern sequencers.

FLAM—is the mode for double playback of samples. Using the regulator, you define the delay before the repeated playback. This mode is enabled by the button to the right of the regulator. The **FLAM** mode applies only to those sounds that were programmed when the **FLAM** button was pressed.

If **ReDrum** is selected as a current device, the following commands become available in the main **Edit** menu or in the context menu of this device called by the right mouse button:

❑ **Copy Patch**—copies patch to clipboard

❑ **Paste Patch**—pastes patch from clipboard

❑ **Initialize Patch**—initializes the patch (when you apply this command, all the settings are reset)

❑ **Cut Pattern**—cuts sequencer pattern to clipboard

❑ **Paste Pattern**—pastes sequencer pattern from clipboard

❑ **Clear Pattern**—clears pattern (clear all the information on the events)

❑ **Shift Pattern Left/Right**—shifts all the programmed sounds one step left (**Left**) or right (**Right**)

❑ **Shift Drum Left/Right**—shifts all the programmed sounds of the drum currently selected left or right using the **SELECT** button

❑ **Randomize Pattern**—fills the pattern randomly

❑ **Randomize Drum**—places the sounds of the selected drum randomly (sounds of other drums are not affected)

❑ **Alter Pattern**—makes random changes in the pattern

❑ **Alter Drum**—makes random changes in the location of the sounds of the selected drum

❑ **Copy Pattern To Track**—converts the ReDrum sequencer pattern into a sequence of messages in the corresponding track of the main sequencer (*Section 21.10*)

21.3.4. ReDrum Control with MIDI

As most virtual devices do, Reason ReDrum understands MIDI messages. Using two groups of keys on the MIDI keyboard, you can enable and disable the mute and solo modes for each of 10 ReDrum channels. Pressing the keys from C of the second octave to E of the third octave (except for the black keys) mutes the corresponding ReDrum channels. The keys from C of the fourth octave to E of the fifth octave (except for the black keys) set the solo mode for the corresponding channels.

You can use ReDrum as a tone generator controlled by MIDI from an external MIDI device (program) or from the Reason main sequencer. To do so, disable the **Enable Pattern Section** mode, and playback for all ten ReDrum channels will be controlled by the MIDI keys of the first octave from C to A (including the black keys).

21.3.5. ReDrum Connection

On the rear panel of ReDrum (Fig. 21.22), there are ten identical groups of jacks to connect separate channels to devices external to ReDrum.

Fig. 21.22. Rear panel of ReDrum

The jacks are as follows (from top to bottom):

❑ **Left (mono) Audio Output**—audio output of the left stereo channel (mono channel if the right channel output is not connected).

❑ **Right Audio Output**—audio output of the right stereo channel.

❑ **Gate Out**—the signal on this output is present when samples are played. This output gives you the ability to use the ReDrum sequencer to send simple commands, such as enabled/disabled, to other devices.

❑ **Gate In**—the input for accepting similar commands from other devices.

❑ **Pitch CV In**—the input to control the pitch of the played sample with the control voltage (CV) level.

Besides the listed jacks, there are two **Send Out** send jacks (the levels of the signals sent to this bus are controlled by the **S1** and **S2** regulators). By default, these jacks are connected to AUX1 and AUX2 of the mixer.

Stereo Out—the main stereo audio output. The **MASTER LEVEL** regulator located on the front panel controls the total volume of ReDrum.

The **Sample Memory** indicator displays the number of loaded samples.

21.4. Dr. REX Loop Player—Specialized Drum Loop Player

To make things easier, we'll call the Dr. REX loop player simply REX (Fig. 21.23).

Fig. 21.23. Front panel of **REX**

You might have come across a situation where you had a good drum loop with a particular tempo, but your composition had another tempo altogether. So you thought you might adjust the tempo. But just by changing the playback speed, you change the key. And it's not guaranteed that this will improve the quality of the loop. Another way to get around this problem is to apply algorithms to change the sample duration without changing its tone (for example, the **Transform>Time/Pitch>Stretch** command of Cool Edit Pro (*Section 12.36*)). You can try this, but the result won't be satisfying: it is impossible to select a clear tone in noisy drum sounds, because there is none. The Stretch algorithm won't work the way you want it to. But, by using REX, you can change the tempo of drum loops easily. It is done as follows: in the drum loop, select the moments where the drum attacks. The loop is thus no longer considered a continuous waveform, but rather a sequence of several fragments of drum sounds called *slices*. When the tempo is changed using the input field on the transport panel (*Section 21.9*), the starting moments of playback for these samples are offset accordingly. As a result, the tempo is changed, and the quality of the loop preserved.

The drum loop is "sliced" into shorter samples, so it is a good idea to make their modulation parameters independent. This capability is also implemented in REX. For each of the drum sounds within a loop, you can assign its panorama, its tone, its volume, etc. Note that the settings of these parameters are saved not in special patch files, but are rather stored in the project file.

REX can load drum patches in RCY (ReCycle) and REX2 formats. The main advantage of the latter format (which is newer) is that it supports stereo samples.

21.4.1. Loading a Loop

In the left upper part of REX, you see the loop select field. Press the button, and load any file of drum loops supplied with Reason. The ▨ buttons list other loops stored in the selected directory. The name of the selected loop is displayed in the field to the left of these buttons.

To hear the sound of the loaded loop, use the **PREVIEW** button, or press the *D* key of the first MIDI octave on the MIDI keyboard. In the second case, messages from the MIDI keyboard (either through the main sequencer or directly) are routed to REX.

Using the **TO TRACK** button, the loop's information is converted into MIDI messages, and they are transferred to the correct track of the main sequencer. Each slice of the loop has a corresponding MIDI key, and its imprint size is proportional to this slice's duration. We'll describe this in detail in *Section 21.10.4.*

21.4.2. Playback Parameters of Separate Slices

First, select any of the loop slices. You can do these three ways:

❏ Click on the slice image (Fig. 21.24)

❏ Use the **SLICE** regulator

❏ Press the corresponding key on the MIDI keyboard

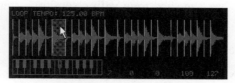

Fig. 21.24. Select a loop slice

For the third method, the **Select Slice Via MIDI** option must be enabled. The *C* of the first octave corresponds to the first slice. When you select a slice using the MIDI keyboard, this slice is played. The MIDI key corresponding to the selected slice is marked in the image of the MIDI keyboard fragment.

After you have selected the slice, you can specify the following parameters for it:

❏ **PITCH**—transposes the slice tone with a semitone step within a range of more than eight octaves

❏ **PAN**—panorama

❏ **LEVEL**—volume

❏ **DECAY**—volume decreasing speed

By decreasing the value of the **DECAY** parameter, you can decrease the duration of the slice.

Be careful! When loading a new loop, the settings of the above parameters are reset.

21.4.3. Synthesis Parameters

REX is also a synthesizer: drum loops are modulated by filters and various generators, and thanks to this, you can change the loop's sound in any way. The modulation is done during playback, and the samples themselves are not affected.

The modulation parameters can be classified into the groups described below.

OSC. PITCH—Controlling the Oscillator Tone

Samples of slices are used as an oscillator in REX. An individual pitch can be defined for each of them. In this group, the pitch is controlled for the entire loop:

❏ **OCT**—pitch shifting by intervals of one octave

❏ **TRANSPOSE**—transposes the slice tone with a semitone step (this regulator is an exception and is outside the group)

❏ **FINE**—pitch shifting by intervals of one cent

❏ **ENV AMOUNT**—how much the envelope generator for filter control (**FILTER ENVELOPE**) effects the total pitch

You can set the **TRANSPOSE** parameter by clicking on the image of the MIDI keyboard (Fig. 21.25).

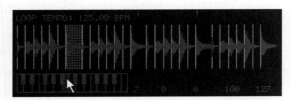

Fig. 21.25. Transposing (**TRANSPOSE**)

FILTER—Filter Parameters

Here, the filter is used to create various effects, rather than to correct the timbre.

The filter type is selected using the **MODE** button, or by clicking on the corresponding indicator (Fig. 21.26).

Fig. 21.26. Filter parameters

Control of the following filter types is possible:

❏ **NOTCH**—the rejecting filter

❏ **HP 12**—high-pass filter with a slope of 12 dB per octave

❏ **BP 12**—band-pass filter with a slope of 12 dB per octave

❏ **LP 12**—low-pass filter with a slope of 12 dB per octave

❏ **LP 24**—low-pass filter with a slope of 24 dB per octave

Depending on the selected type of filter, the **FREQ** parameter controls the central frequency or the cutoff frequency. All the filters except the rejecting filter are resonance filters: at the **FREQ** frequency there is a slope, and its height depends on the value of the **RES** parameter. If the filter is a rejecting filter, the **RES** parameter controls its quality.

Near the **FILTER** group name, you'll find a button that allows you to switch off the filter.

The filter cutoff frequency can be controlled by the **FILTER ENVELOPE** envelope generator.

FILTER ENVELOPE—the Envelope Generator for Filter Control

The envelope generator for filter control is shown in Fig. 21.27.

Its settings are as follows:

❏ **AMOUNT**—effect of the generator on the **FREQ** parameter

❏ **A**—duration of the attack phase

❏ **D**—duration of the decay phase

❏ **S**—duration of the sustain phase

❏ **R**—duration of the release phase

The envelope generator is started when the next slice-sample begins to play.

Fig. 21.27. Envelope generator for the filter control

AMP ENVELOPE—the Amplitude Envelope Generator

The generator (Fig. 21.28) is used to control the volume during the slice-sample play-back.

Fig. 21.28. Amplitude envelope generator

The **LEVEL** is the total volume level. The remaining parameters are similar to the parameters of the **FILTER ENVELOPE** (see Fig. 21.27).

LFO—the Low-Frequency Oscillations Generator

LFO is used to modulate the assigned parameter. The modulated parameter is selected using the **DEST** button, or by clicking on the corresponding LED (Fig. 21.29):

OSC—frequency modulation (vibrato)

FILTER—modulation of the filter cutoff frequency ("wow-wow")

PAN—panorama modulation

You select the oscillation form by pressing the **WAVEF.** Button (Fig. 21.29) or by clicking on the corresponding LED. Generation of the following shapes of signals is possible:

❐ Triangular

❐ Saw-tooth

❐ Reverse saw-tooth

❐ Meander

❐ Random stepped

❐ Random smoothed

Fig. 21.29. Low-frequency oscillations generator

The regulators are: **RATE**—oscillation frequency, and **AMOUNT**—oscillation depth.

VELOCITY—Sensitivity of the Modulation Parameters to the Key Pressing Speed

When you control REX from a MIDI keyboard or from the main sequencer of Reason, the Velocity parameter (the MIDI key pressing speed) can be used to control the character of the sound (Fig. 21.30).

Fig. 21.30. The ratio that determines the modulation wheel's reaction to the Velocity parameter

The controls are following:

❐ **F.ENV**—the dependence ratio of the **AMOUNT** parameter of the filter control envelope on the Velocity value

❏ **F.DECAY**—the dependence ratio of the **D** (Decay) parameter of the filter control envelope on the Velocity value

❏ **AMP**—the ratio of the total loop volume to the Velocity

Modulation Wheel (MOD.WHEEL) and Bend Wheel (BEND)

These wheels look like any other wheels built into a MIDI keyboard. We can say that the **MOD.WHEEL** is programmable: you can precisely define the ratios of dependence of different parameters on the position of this wheel (see Fig. 21.30):

❏ **F.FREQ**—the level of the effect of the MOD.WHEEL on the filter cutoff frequency

❏ **F.RES**—the level of the effect of the MOD.WHEEL on the filter quality (RES parameter)

❏ **F.DECAY**—the level of the effect of the MOD.WHEEL on the D (Decay) parameter of the filter control envelope

In the **RANGE** field, you can specify the range of pitch shifting for the **BEND** wheel. The number you input will be the number of semitones.

21.4.4. Polyphony; Control of the Sample Playback Quality

Polyphony is defined in the **POLYPHONY** field (Fig. 21.31). When the tempo is increased, the samples of the loop slices may overlap (one of the drums continues to sound while the other one starts). To provide for the normal sound of the loop with an increased tempo, and to limit the processor load at the same time, the developers recommend that polyphony consist of 3—4 voices.

Fig. 21.31. Polyphony and parameters that determine the quality of sound

The **High Quality Interpolation** option enables a more precise interpolation, which occupies more system resources.

The **LO BW** option (Low Bandwidth) decreases the internal frequency of the loop sampling and frees system resources. Enabling this options makes sense if you:

❏ Use the currently-fashionable Low-End loops, whose quality of sound is rather low. (This is an acceptable artistic decision.)

❏ You specially narrow the spectrum of a high-quality loop with a low-frequency filter (to achieve the Low-End sound).

21.4.5. REX Connection

The following signals are located on the "rear" panel of REX (Fig. 21.32.).

Fig. 21.32. "Rear" panel of REX

❏ **Slice Gate Output**—output of the control signal that transfers the loop slice playback moments and their numbers.

❏ **Modulation Input**—inputs to control different modulation parameters.

❏ **Modulation Output**—outputs of control signals:

- **Voice 1 Filter Env**—the signal from the envelope generator that controls the filter
- **LFO**—the signal from the generator of low frequency signals

❏ **Gate Input**—inputs to accept the following control signals:

- **Amp Env**—the signal to start the amplitude envelope generator
- **Filter Env**—the signal to start the envelope generator for controlling the filter

❏ **Audio Output**—stereo input

The **Sample Memory** indicator displays the number of loaded samples.

21.5. NN-19 Digital Sampler

You can consider both ReDrum and REX to be samplers. NN-19 is a traditional sampler. The abilities of **NN-19** (Fig. 21.33) are not as numerous as the abilities of GigaStudio (*Chapter 19*), however, all the main functions of a sampler are implemented in this virtual device:

❏ Using a multisample as an oscillator (the base sound generator)

❏ Oscillator modulation by low-frequency generators and the envelope generator; processing by filters

Many WAV files and patch files for NN-19 (SMP files) are included in the delivery set of Reason. SMP files contain descriptions of sample layouts along the MIDI keyboard and their modulation parameters. Note that samples and patches—the modulation settings of these samples—are stored separately. This is typical for Reason, but differs from working with SoundFont and GIG files.

Fig. 21.33. NN-19 sampler

At first, you might decide to simply load any of the ready-to-use patches supplied with Reason. Look at the field shown in Fig. 21.34.

Fig. 21.34. Patch load/save field

This field contains the usual buttons for loading patch files, listing patches within the selected directory, and saving the current patch. When you load a patch, the samples for which this patch was created are also loaded.

You can load your own samples in the AIFF and WAV formats, place them along the MIDI keyboard (thus creating multi-samples), edit their modulation parameters, and save your own patches in the SMP file format.

We will try to create our own patch based on samples we created after learning the material in the previous Chapter (*Section 20.1*).

21.5.1. Creating Multisamples

Using the 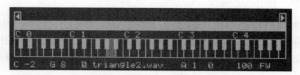 button located above the LCD screen of NN-19, load the triangle2.wav sample. When the sample is loaded in the "empty" NN-19, the zone of this sample occupies the entire MIDI keyboard. The current zone (in this case the entire MIDI keyboard) is displayed with a bright blue stripe above the image of the MIDI keyboard. One of the keys is selected. This is the key that corresponds to the unity note of the sample.

Fig. 21.35. The triangle2.wav sample is loaded

You can load several samples simultaneously. To do so, select several files in the browser window called by the ▣ button by holding the <Shift> or <Ctrl> key down. Only one of these samples, however, is associated directly with the current zone.

Under the indicator showing the MIDI keyboard, there are regulators that are related only to the current zone:

❏ **LOWKEY**—the key corresponding to the lower boundary of the zone

❏ **HIGHKEY**—the key corresponding to the upper boundary of the zone

❏ **SAMPLE**—selects a sample from simultaneously loaded samples

❏ **ROOTKEY**—the sample unity note (may be located outside the zone)

❏ **TUNE**—tunes the pitch

❏ **LOOP**—enables/disables and selects the loop mode

The current values of these parameters are displayed in the indicator just under these regulators.

We should comment on the above listed parameters. If there is only one zone, you cannot change its boundaries. If you want to limit the active zone of only one sample, you have to create "empty" zones (ones not related to any sample) in those places of the MIDI keyboard where this sample is not to be played.

You can indicate the sample unity note by clicking the mouse on the MIDI keyboard image.

A few words about the **LOOP** parameter: if the beginning and the end of the loop is not specified in the sample file, the beginning and the end of the entire sample are selected. Two loop modes are available: **FWD**—the loop's continuous playback from the beginning to the end, and **FWD-BW**—the loop's continuous playback from the beginning to the end, and then from the end to the beginning.

To create another zone, use the **Edit>Split Key Zone** command of the main menu, or the analogous command of the context menu called by the mouse's right button. As a result, the current zone is divided into two zones.

Now you have to make the new zone current. To do so, click on the correct place in the indicator (Fig. 21.36*a*) or press the MIDI key related to the zone you need. To implement the second method, the **SELECT KEYZONE VIA MIDI** option must be enabled.

The left zone contains the source sample (see Fig. 21.36*a*), and the right zone is still empty (Fig. 21.36*b*). You can move the boundary of the zones to any place on the MIDI keyboard (Fig. 21.36*c*).

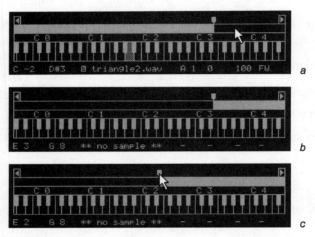

Fig. 21.36. Creating a zone and changing its boundaries

You can delete a newly created zone that is selected as current. To do so, use the **Edit> Delete Key Zone** command of the main menu. Well, we won't delete this zone, but will rather load another sample (trinagle3.wav), which occupies a new zone (Fig. 21.37*a*). We'll then divide this zone again into two zones and load another sample (triangle4.wav) (Fig. 21.37*b*).

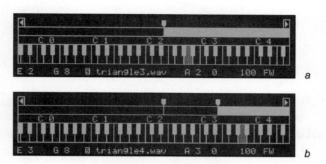

Fig. 21.37. Creating new zones

The keys corresponding to the unity notes may be outside the boundaries of the sample zone.

If you have to replace the sample in any of the zones, you can do it in one of two ways:

❐ Load the new sample over the old one

❐ Using the **SAMPLE** regulator, select any of the previously loaded samples instead of the current one

If you have to delete a sample, use the **Edit>Delete Sample** command from the main menu, or the a same command in the context menu.

If you have to "detach" a sample from a zone, but not delete it, select **no sample** using the **SAMPLE** regulator, or replace the sample with any of the previously loaded samples.

To remove from memory all the loaded samples that are not related to any zones, you should use the **Edit>Delete Unused Samples** command of the main menu.

We have chosen not the most convenient, but the most demonstrative method of creating our new sample. Actually, if you have a set of WAV or AIF files that are a single multi-sample, you can use the function to automatically distribute samples along the MIDI keyboard. But in order for this function to work correctly, information on the unity note must be stored in each file. In our example, this condition is true, so we could load all three files—triangle2.wav, triangle3.wav, and triangle4.wav—at the same time, and then use the **Edit>Automap Samples** command of the main menu or the analogous command from the context menu. The optimal sample distribution along the MIDI keyboard in this case is done automatically.

21.5.2. Synthesis Parameters

There are the following two types of synthesis parameters:

❑ **OSC**—oscillator parameters

❑ **FILTER**—filter parameters

OSC—Oscillator Parameters

The oscillator parameters are controlled from the panel shown in Fig. 21.38.

Fig. 21.38. Oscillator parameters

SAMPLE START—the sound count from which sample playback should start (the offset relative to the beginning of the sample).

HIGH QUALITY INTERPOLATION—enables high quality interpolation.

ENV AMT—the ratio of the pitch shifting's dependence upon the current value of the filter control envelope.

PITCH—pitch shifting regulators:

❑ **OCT**—octave intervals

❑ **SEMI**—semitone intervals

❑ **FINE**—cent intervals

If you disable the **KBD.TRACK** option, the pitch of the played sample will not depend on the number of the pressed MIDI key or on the level of the CV control signal.

FILTER—Filter Parameters

The options for filter parameter control are shown in Fig. 21.39.

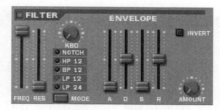

Fig. 21.39. Filter parameters

The filter of the NN-19 sampler is similar to the filter used in REX. It differs only in the additional **KBD** parameter. **KBD** is the ratio of the filter cutoff frequency's dependence on the pitch of the generated note. For example, you can make low notes sound quieter than higher notes, and vice versa.

The envelope generator that controls the cutoff frequency of the NN-19 filter is also similar to the generator used in REX, with the exception of the additional **INVERT** option. If this option is enabled, the direction of the envelope change alterate: when the attack takes place, the current envelope value is not increased but decreased, etc. Using this option, you can achieve an effect that is the "opposite" of "wow-wow".

The amplitude envelope generator (**AMP**) and the low frequency signal generator (**LFO**) are exactly the same as the ones used in REX.

21.5.3. User Parameters

All user parameters are located in the area of the **NN-19** panel shown in Fig. 21.40.

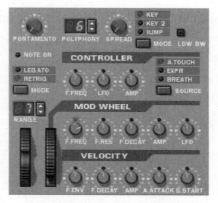

Fig. 21.40. User parameters

VELOCITY—Ratios of Various Parameters' Dependence on Velocity

❑ **F.ENV**—the dependence ratio of the filter envelope **AMOUNT** parameter on the Velocity parameter

❑ **F.DECAY**—the dependence ratio of the filter envelope **D** (Decay phase) parameter on the Velocity parameter

❑ **AMP**—the dependence ratio of the total volume on the Velocity parameter

❑ **A.ATTACK**—the dependence ratio of the **A** (Attack phase) parameter of the amplitude envelope generator on the Velocity parameter

❑ **S.START**—the dependence ratio of the sample playback's starting point on the Velocity parameter

Modulation Wheel (MOD.WHEEL) and Bend Wheel (BEND)

The wheels of the NN-19 sampler are similar to REX's wheels. There are two additional parameters programmed for the **MOD.WHEEL** wheel (built into the MIDI keyboard):

❑ **LFO**—the depth of modulation by the low frequency oscillations generator

❑ **AMP**—the ratio of the total volume's dependence on the position of the modulation wheel

MOD.WHEEL is programmed so that you can specify the ratios of different parameters' dependence upon the position of this wheel. More precisely:

❑ **F.FREQ**—the level of the effect of the **MOD.WHEEL** on the filter cutoff frequency

❑ **F.RES**—the level of the effect of the **MOD.WHEEL** on the filter quality (**RES** parameter)

❑ **F.DECAY**—the level of the effect of the **MOD.WHEEL** on the **D** (Decay) parameter of the filter control envelope

In the **RANGE** field, you can specify the range of pitch shifting for the **BEND** wheel. The number you input is the number of semitones.

POLYPHONY—the maximum allowed number of simultaneous voices. Some of the effects described below are most effective in the single voice mode (**POLYPHONY** = 1) of the NN-19 sampler. Select the sound mode using the **MODE** button or by clicking on the corresponding LED:

❑ **RETRIG**—the "normal" operation of the sampler, where for each voice the envelope generators start from the attack phase.

❏ **LEGATO**—it is recommended that you apply this in the single voice mode: press one MIDI key, and holding it down, press another one. For the second sound, the envelope generators are not restarted (at the very least there will be no attack phase).

In the polyphony mode, **LEGATO** works only when all the reserved voices sound. Let's say, for example, that **POLYPHONY** = 3. Press one key, then another (holding the first key), and then the third key. There is no effect. Only when the fourth sound starts to play does **LEGATO** work, and the envelope generators are not restarted for it.

CONTROLLER Group

In the **CONTROLLER** group, you select one of the three MIDI controllers—**A.TOUCH** (Aftertouch), **EXPR** (Expression), or **BREATH**—with the **SOURCE** button, or by clicking on the corresponding LED. You can specify the ratios of dependence for the selected controller for three synthesis parameters:

❏ **F.FREQ**—the **FREQ** parameter in the **FILTER** (filter cutoff frequency)

❏ **LFO**—the **AMOUNT** parameter (the depth of low frequency signals' modulation by the generator) in the **LFO** group

❏ **AMP**—the **LEVEL** parameter (total volume) in the **AMP** group

Other Parameters

There are three modes of voice panorama control that are switched either by using the **MODE** button (in the upper part of the panel shown in Fig. 21.40) or by clicking on the corresponding LED:

❏ **KEY**—each of the voices has its own panorama, depending on the MIDI key number

❏ **KEY 2**—the panorama changes from left to right for all halves of octaves

❏ **JUMP**—the panorama changes from left to right for each next voice (the MIDI key number is not taken into account)

The **SPREAD** regulator defines the panorama's "intensity": if **SPREAD** = 0, there is no automated panorama, if **SPREAD** = 127, the panorama changes by the maximum allowed interval.

PORTAMENTO is smooth pitch shifting when going from one note to another. The portamento time is controlled with the **PORTAMENTO** regulator (**PORTAMENTO** = 0—portamento is disabled). This effect is best applied in the single voice mode.

We have already mentioned the **LOW BW** button. Using this button narrows the frequency band of the sound and releases system resources.

21.5.4. Connection

The rear panel of **NN-19** is shown in Fig. 21.41.

Fig. 21.41. Rear panel of NN-19

Gate and **CV** inputs combined into the **Mono Sequencer Controls** group are used to connect the pattern sequencer to control the NN-19 sampler (*Section 21.7.2*).

The inputs combined into the **Modulation Input** group are used to control the modulation parameters whose names are noted near the corresponding inputs.

The **Modulation Outputs** group combines the inputs to which signals from the envelope generator for controlling the filter arrive (**Voice 1 Filter Env**) and the signal from the low frequency generator (**LFO**).

The **Gate Inputs** group includes the inputs intended to control the amplitude envelope generator's (**Amp Env**) start and the envelope generator for the filter control (**Filter Env**).

Audio Output—stereophonic output.

The **Sample Memory** indicator shows the number of loaded samples.

21.6. SubTractor Synthesizer

The **SubTractor** panel is shown in Fig. 21.42.

This device is a "pure" synthesizer: there are no samples, and signal values are calculated mathematically.

Fig. 21.42. SubTractor panel

21.6.1. Synthesis Parameters

Two oscillators—**Osc 1** and **Osc 2**—constitute the basis of SubTractor. They are comprised of two sound frequency signal generators and the **Noise** generator (Fig. 21.43).

Osc 1 and Osc 2—Oscillator Parameters

For subtractive synthesis, one generator is enough; but in **SubTractor**, several synthesis methods are implemented. These methods require at least two oscillators. Developers did not intend to make the pseudo-analogous synthesizer sound like traditional instruments. There are samples in Reason if you want the sound of a traditional instrument. To synthesize electronic sounds, two oscillators are adequate.

Thanks to the noise generator, you can create effects like "blowing wind", "sea surf", percussion sounds, etc.

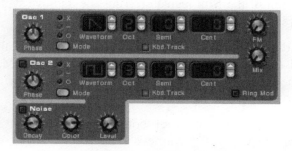

Fig. 21.43. Oscillator parameters

The following synthesis method is implemented within the **Osc1** and **Osc2** oscillators:

❏ A periodic signal with the defined waveform is created. (The form of the wave is determined by the **Waveform** parameter; there are 32 forms.)

❏ A copy of this signal delayed over time is created. (The phase difference is defined by the **Phase** parameter.)

❏ The delayed copy of the signal is subtracted from the source signal (subtractive synthesis method), or the source signal is multiplied by its delayed copy (multiplying synthesis method).

The synthesis method is selected using the **Mode** button: **x** is the multiplying method; - is the additive method; • means that no method is applied. (The generated signal of the given form arrives in the oscillator without any transformation.)

Using the **Oct**, **Semi**, and **Cent** parameters, you change the generator frequency relative to the note's base frequency, using intervals of octave, semitone, and cent, respectively.

We mentioned the **Kbd. Track** parameter while introducing NN-19. If you disable this parameter, the oscillator frequency does not depend on the number of the pressed key or the level of the CV signal.

The **Osc 2** and **Osc 1** oscillators are the same, except for the button (near **Osc 2**) with which you turn the oscillator on and off.

The signal of the noise generator—**Noise**—is mixed with the **Osc 2** signal. As with **Osc 2**, you can turn it on and off using the button next to the word **Noise**. The amplitude of the generated noise is changed first by immediate attack, and then by smoothly fading within the time that is set by the **Decay** parameter. **Color** is the timbre regulator. **Level** is the total signal level at the noise generator output.

You can mix the signals of two oscillators (**Osc 1** and **Osc 2 + Noise**) in proportions determined by the position of the **Mix** regulator. Thus the additive synthesis method is implemented (signals are added).

You can modulate the signal of the first oscillator (**Osc 1**) by frequency, using the signal of the second oscillator (**Osc 2 + Noise**). Two-operand FM synthesis is implemented in this manner. The modulation depth is determined by the position of the **FM** regulator.

Finally, you can multiply the signals of both oscillators. As a result, you'll get a sound similar to bells ringing. This synthesis method is enabled with the **Ring Mod** button.

Filter 1 and Filter 2—Filter Parameters

By applying the above listed synthesis methods, you can create signals of a rather compli-cated form and with a wide spectrum, and then process the resulting signals using the two filters, **Filter 1** and **Filter 2** (Fig. 21.44).

Fig. 21.44. Filter parameters

The first filter is almost exactly the same as the NN-19 filter, the only difference being that the filter type select button is called **Type**, not **MODE**. The second filter is a low-pass filter with a slope of 12 dB per octave. The presence of two filters instead of one allows you to make interesting effects.

To enable the second filter, press the button next to **Filter 2**. The **Link** option associates the **Freq** (cutoff frequency) parameters of both filters. The values of these parameters can be different. Changing one of the **Freq** parameters results in a change in the other **Freq** parameter by the same value.

Envelope Generator Parameters

SubTractor has three envelope generators (Fig. 21.45):

❏ **Amp Envelope**—controls the volume

❏ **Filter Envelope**—controls the filter cutoff frequency

❏ **Mod Envelope**—controls the modulation

Fig. 21.45. Envelope parameters

The first two generators are similar to those generators used in the devices described above. The **Mod Envelope** generator allows you to control one of the following parameters:

❑ **Osc 1**—frequency of the first oscillator

❑ **Osc 2**—frequency of the second oscillator

❑ **Mix**—mixing proportions of the signals of the first and the second oscillators

❑ **FM**—frequency modulation depth

❑ **Phase**—phase shift of source signals and their delayed copies when subtractive synthesis takes place (for both oscillators)

❑ **Freq 2**—cutoff frequency of the second filter

The necessary parameter is selected using the **Dest** button or by clicking on the corresponding LED.

Generators of Low Frequency Signals

SubTractor has two generators of low frequency signals—**LFO 1** and **LFO 2**.

LFO 1 (Fig. 21.46) modulates one of these parameters:

❑ **Osc 1,2**—frequencies of both oscillators (to create the vibrato effect)

❑ **Osc 2**—frequency of the second oscillator

❑ **F.Freq**—cutoff frequency of the first filter (to create the "wow-wow" effect)

❑ **FM**—frequency modulation depth

❑ **Mix**—mixing proportions of the signals of the first and the second oscillators

The necessary parameter is selected using the **Dest** button or by clicking on the corresponding LED.

Fig. 21.46. Parameters of the first generator of low frequency signals

The form of the low frequency signal is selected using the **Waveform** button or by clicking on the corresponding LED.

Rate is the frequency of the generated signal, and **Amount** is the modulation depth.

LFO 2 (Fig. 21.47) modulates one of these parameters:

❏ **Osc 1,2**—frequencies of both oscillators

❏ **Osc 2**—frequency of the second oscillator

❏ **F.Freq 2**—cutoff frequency of the second filter

❏ **Amp**—total volume (to create the tremolo effect)

Fig. 21.47. Parameters of the second generator of low frequency signals

Rate is the frequency of the generated signal, and **Amount** is the modulation depth.

The frequency of the generated signal may depend on the number of the MIDI key. The effect is defined by the **Kbd** parameter.

Delay is the delay before the generator starts. It is counted starting from the next note generation.

21.6.2. User Parameters

The panel used to control the user parameters is shown in Fig. 21.48.

Fig. 21.48. Parameters of the second generator of low frequency signals

❏ **Velocity**—effect of the key pressing speed upon the synthesis parameters.

❏ **Amp**—effect upon volume

❏ **FM**—effect upon frequency modulation depth

❑ **M.Env**—effect upon the depth of modulation by the **Mod Envelope** envelope generator

❑ **Phase**—effect upon the **Phase** parameters of both oscillators

❑ **Freq 2**—effect upon the cutoff frequency of the second filter

❑ **F.Env**—effect upon thr depth of modulation by the **Filter Envelope** generator

❑ **F.Dec**—effect upon the **D** (Decay) parameter of the **Filter Envelope** generator

❑ **Mix**—effect upon the mixing proportions of the oscillator signals

❑ **A.Atk**—effect upon the **A** (Attack) parameter of the **Amp Envelope** generator

Modulation Wheel (MOD.WHEEL) and Bend Wheel (BEND)

The wheels of SubTractor are shown in Fig. 21.49.

Fig. 21.49. Modulation wheels

In the **RANGE** field, specify the range of pitch shifting for the **BEND** wheel in semitones. The **Mod** modulation wheel can control any of the following parameters:

❑ **F.Freq**—cutoff frequency of the first filter

❑ **F.Res**—quality of the first filter

❑ **LFO1**—depth of modulation by the **LFO1** generator

❑ **Phase** —phase parameters of both oscillators

❑ **FM**—frequency modulation depth

Other Parameters

The control elements of other parameters are shown in Fig. 21.50.

There are **Polyphony** and **Portamento** controls.

Fig. 21.50. Other parameters

One of three MIDI controllers—**A.TOUCH** (Aftertouch), **EXPR** (Expression), or **BREATH**—is selected with the **Ext.Mod** button or by clicking on the corresponding LED. For the selected controller, you can define the dependence ratios of four synthesis parameters:

☐ **F.FREQ**—cutoff frequency of the first filter

☐ **LFO1**—depth of modulation by the first generator of low frequency signals

☐ **AMP**—volume

☐ **FM**—frequency modulation depth

You select the sound mode with the **MODE** button, or by clicking on the corresponding LED:

☐ **RETRIG**—the "normal" operation of the sampler, where for each voice the envelope generators start from the attack phase

☐ **LEGATO**—best applied in single voice mode

☐ **LOW BW**—narrowing the bandwidth

Many patches for SubTractor are included in the Reason delivery set. You can load them using the standard method for virtual devices of Reason: in the upper part of the panel shown in Fig. 21.50, you see buttons for loading, selecting, and saving patch files.

21.6.3. Connection

The rear panel of SubTractor is shown in Fig. 21.51. Subtractor has a set of inputs and outputs similar to the set in NN-19 (*Section 21.5.4*). The difference is that SubTractor has a mono audio output and more inputs to control the modulation parameters.

Fig. 21.51. Rear panel of SubTractor

21.7. Matrix Pattern Sequencer

Matrix is the pattern sequencer, and generally it is the same as the sequencer built in ReDrum.

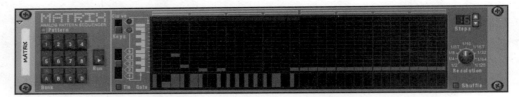

Fig. 21.52. The **Matrix** pattern sequencer

21.7.1. Program the Sequencer

Almost all devices of Reason (and Matrix) contain a patch by default. Several patterns are already loaded into its memory, which are selected using buttons **A** through **D** (the bank) and **1** through **8** (the preset number within a bank). You can start Matrix with the **Run** button, and the built-in groove will start to play. Matrix does not generate the sound itself, but by default it is connected to SubTractor, whose sound you should have heard already.

You can start or stop the playback from the beginning of the next beat with the **Pattern** button.

The display occupies the greater part of Matrix's front panel. You can not only view the contents of the current pattern, but also draw using the mouse cursor. The sequence of columns in the lower part of the display (**Gate**) corresponds to the moments the sounds are made, and the height of these columns is by default in proportion to the values of the Velocity parameter (the key pressing speed). Most commonly, the height of these columns is in proportion to the levels of the control voltage of Gate signals. In the Keys mode, this display is similar to the **Piano Roll** window—the window of key imprints. The height of the rectangles corresponds to the notes' pitches, and their horizontal position corresponds to the moments that these notes are played within the pattern (Fig. 21.53*a*).

To the left of the display, there is a five-position switch for the keyboard ranges. A note's duration can be arbitrary within 32 steps of the sequencer. You can "draw" a long note using the mouse holding the <Shift> key pressed, or when the **Tie** mode is on. You should draw the **Gate** columns, and not the key imprints.

The **Curve** mode displays (Fig. 21.53*b*) the envelope of the values of a certain parameter, not the key imprints. (By default, this parameter is the SubTractor filter cutoff frequency.)

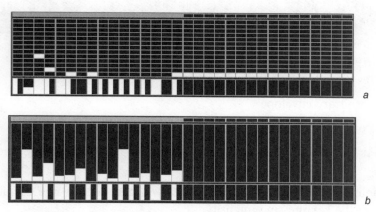

Fig. 21.53. Operating modes of the **Matrix** display

In the **Steps** field, you specify the number of steps in the pattern. In the **Resolution** field, you specify the duration of these steps.

The **Shuffle** button enables the mode for changing the rhythm, which allows you to produce a swing-like sound. In Fig. 21.54, two lines of the key imprints are shown: the upper line corresponds to the disabled **Shuffle** mode, and the lower line corresponds to the enabled mode. The extent of the rhythm's change is determined by the **PATTERN SHUFFLE** parameter in the transport panel (*Section 21.9*). This parameter is common for all pattern sequencers of Reason.

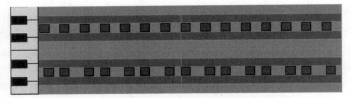

Fig. 21.54. Illustration of the **Shuffle** mode's operation

21.7.2. Connection

The rear panel of Matrix is shown in Fig. 21.55.

Fig. 21.55. Rear panel of Matrix

Matrix generates three types of control signals:

❑ **Curve CV**—arbitrary envelope

❑ **Note CV**—control voltage in proportion to the number of keys

❑ **Gate CV**—signals of the Gate type that transfer the notes' beginnings and their durations

Using the amplitude of signals of the last type, you can control one of the parameters that characterize the key pressing intensity.

By default, **Curve CV** controls the cutoff frequency of the Subtractor filter, **Note CV** controls the note pitch, and **Gate CV** controls the duration and the Velocity parameter.

What to use Matrix for is up to you. With this program, you can control not only the synthesizer or the sampler, but also the parameters of effect processors and mixers.

The **Bipolar/Unipolar** switch selects how **Curve CV** will be presented: in bipolar mode (Fig. 21.55*a*), in which the parameter can take negative values, or in unipolar mode (Fig. 21.55*b*) in which the value of the parameter is always positive. For example, the bipolar mode is more useful for representing information on the position of the **Bend** wheel, while the unipolar mode is more convenient for the modulation (**Mod**) wheel. The unipolar mode is selected by default.

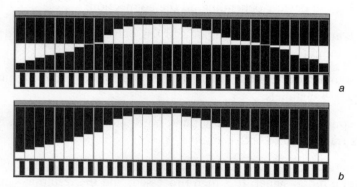

Fig. 21.56. Bipolar and unipolar modes of **Curve CV** display ·

Matrix has another specific feature: this sequencer is the source of the control information, but it itself does not have control inputs. No device other than the main sequencer can control it.

21.8. Effect Processors

All the effect processors of Reason have common interface elements. The three-position **Bypass/On/Off** switch is on the front panel (Fig. 21.57):

❏ **Bypass**—the signal is passed without processing

❏ **On**—effect is on (normal position)

❏ **Off**—effect is off; the signal is not passed

Fig. 21.57. Operating mode switch, input signal level indicator

Under this switch, we see the indicator of the input signal level.

All effects processors have stereophonic inputs and outputs. Most effect processors have CV control inputs on the rear panel. There are also two or three graphs describing the operation of the given device, depending on the connection:

⊡—cables are connected to the left input and left output. The processed signal is transferred to the left output.

⊡—cables are connected to both stereo inputs and both stereo outputs: independent processing for stereo channels.

⊞—cables are connected to the left input and both outputs. After processing, the monophonic signal is transferred to both outputs.

⊞—cables are connected to both stereo inputs and both stereo outputs. The input signal is converted into a mono signal. It is then processed, and the resulting signal (which usually has stereophonic features) is transferred to stereo outputs.

The last processing method is applied to reverberation and delay effects.

If we say that a cable is connected to an input or to an output, we assume that the other end of this cable is certainly connected to another device. In Reason, there are no cables connected only to one end.

21.8.1. RV-7 Digital Reverb

The front panel of the **RV-7** reverber is shown in Fig. 21.58.

Fig. 21.58. RV-7 reverber

On the left side of the panel, there are buttons for selecting the algorithm to implement the effect. **SIZE** is the room size. **DECAY** is the fade speed. **DAMP** is suppression at high frequencies. **DRY/WET** is the proportion of the source and processed signals in the resulting mix.

On the rear panel of RV-7 (Fig. 21.59), there is a CV input for controlling the **DECAY** parameter, the stereo input, and the stereo output.

Fig. 21.59. Rear panel of the **RV-7** reverber

21.8.2. DDL-1—Digital Delay Line

DDL-1 is the simplest monophonic delay with the ability to pan the processed signal. The front panel of **DDL-1** is shown in Fig. 21.60.

Fig. 60. Front panel of **DDL-1**

In the left part of the front panel, you see the delay select buttons. The delay's units of measure are selected using the **UNIT** button, or by clicking on the corresponding LED:

❑ **MS**—milliseconds

❑ **STEPS**—sequencer steps whose absolute duration depends on the tempo common for the entire project

STEP LENGTH—the step size: 1/16 or 1/8 triola. **FEEDBACK** is the feedback ratio; **PAN** is the panorama. **DRY/WET** is the proportion of the source and processed signals in the resulting mix.

On the rear panel of **DDL-1** (Fig. 21.61), we have the **Pan** and **Feedback** control inputs, the stereo input, and the stereo output.

Fig. 21.61. Rear panel of DDL-1

If you want to create any complex effects based on delay (rolling echo, etc.) you should consider the DDL-1 modules as building blocks. For example, to get a stereophonic delay, you should connect at least two DDL-1 devices and set the PAN value for each of them. You can make the effect more complex by using the Matrix sequencer to control the **PAN** and **FEEDBACK** parameters.

21.8.3. D-11 Foldback Distortion

On the front panel of **D-11 Foldback Distortion** (Fig. 21.62), there are only two parameters: **AMOUNT**—the depth of the effect, and **FOLDBACK**—the distortions.

Fig. 21.62. Front panel of **D-11**

On the rear panel (Fig. 21.63), there is a CV input to control the **AMOUNT** parameter, the stereo input, and the stereo output.

Fig. 21.63. Rear panel of **D-11**

The D-11 effect is best used in the insertion mode.

21.8.4. ECF-42 Envelope Controlled Filter

ECF-42 (Fig. 21.64) is basically meant to be used together with pattern sequencers.

Fig. 21.64. Front panel of **ECF-42**

EFC-42 has a built-in envelope generator that is started by a command from another device, or by a MIDI command from the corresponding ECF-42 track of the main sequencer, such as Note On. Almost all sound generating devices of Reason have a similar filter and envelope generator. However, in these devices, the envelope generator is started for each note. Here you can modulate sequences of notes using a single envelope. The ECF-42 generator can be started by one device modulating the signal of another device.

FREQ is the filter cutoff frequency, **RES** is the resonance level at the filter cutoff frequency, and **ENV.AMT** is the effect of the envelope generator upon the filter cutoff frequency.

VEL. is the effect of the Velocity parameter upon the **ENV.AMT** parameter. The value of the Velocity parameter is transferred along with the generator start command.

By clicking the **MODE** button or the appropriate LED, you can define the filter type:

❑ **BP 12**—band-pass filter with a slope of 12 dB per octave

❑ **LP 12**—low-pass filter with a slope of 12 dB per octave

❑ **LP 24**—low-pass filter with a slope of 24 dB per octave

The group of **ENVELOPE** regulators controls the phases of the envelope generator:

❑ **A**—attack

❑ **D**—decay

❑ **S**—sustain

❑ **R**—release

The **Gate** indicator is highlighted when the generator is started.

On the rear panel of ECF-42 (Fig. 21.65), there is a set of control inputs:

❑ **Freq CV**—control the frequency cutoff

❑ **Decay CV**—decay phase duration

❑ **Res CV**—resonance depth

❑ **Env.Gate**—here you should give the generator start command

Fig. 21.65. Rear panel of ECF-42

Of course, we also have the stereo input and output.

It is best to use ECF-42 in the insertion mode.

21.8.5. CF-101 Chorus/Flanger

The **CF-101** module (Fig. 21.66) implements the chorus and flanger effects. **DELAY** is the time by which the source signal is delayed. **FEEDBACK** is the feedback ratio, and **RATE** and **MOD AMOUNT** are, respectively, the modulation frequency and the depth of the delayed signal.

Fig. 21.66. Front panel of the **CF-101** module

If you want to use the effect in send mode, press the **SEND MODE** button. Only the processed signal will be at the output of the effect processor. In the insertion mode, this button must be released (to let the source signal pass).

On the rear panel of CF-101 (Fig. 21.67), there are inputs to control the **Delay** and **Rate** parameters, stereo inputs, and stereo outputs.

Fig. 21.67. Rear panel of CF-101

21.8.6. PH-90 Phaser

In Reason, the phaser effect is implemented as follows. The source signal comes through the filter whose amplitude-frequency response is equivalent to the amplitude-frequency responses of the four rejecting filters. The distance between the central frequencies of the rejecting filters is controlled by the **SPLIT** parameter (Fig. 21.68), and the width of hollows in the amplitude-frequency response is controlled by the **WIDTH** parameter. To create the phaser effect, the central frequencies of these filters are synchronously moved up and down the spectrum. The frequency around which these oscillations take place depends on the **FREQ** parameter. The oscillation frequency is **RATE**, and the amplitude is **FREQ.MOD**. The feedback, whose level is determined by the **FEEDBACK** parameter, creates the rises in the amplitude-frequency response before each of the hollows. Because of this, the effect is more emphasized.

Fig. 21.68. Front panel of PH-90

It is recommended that you apply phaser in the insertion mode.

On the rear panel (Fig. 21.69), we find the inputs for controlling the **FREQ** and **RATE** parameters, as well as the stereo input and output.

Fig. 21.69. Rear panel of PH-90

PH-90 is best used in the insertion mode.

21.8.7. COMP-01 Auto Make-up Gain Compressor

The only difference between the **COMP-01** compressor (Fig. 21.70) and a classic compressor is that the output increase (**GAIN**) is controlled automatically. Recall that by increasing the signal at the compressor output, you can compensate the decrease in signal amplitude by compressing the signal. After applying the compressor, the sound becomes louder and more aggressive.

Fig. 21.70. Front panel of COMP-01

RATIO is the compression ratio, **THRESH.** is the compressor threshold, **ATTACK** is the delay before the compressor starts, and **RELEASE** is the delay before the compressor is disabled.

The stereo input and output can be found on the rear panel of **COMP-1** (Fig. 21.71).

You should use COMP-01—like any other compressor—in the insertion mode.

Fig. 21.71. Rear panel of COMP-01

21.8.8. PEQ-2 Two-Band Parametric Equalizer

Fig. 21.72. Front panel of PEQ-2

PEQ-2 (Fig. 21.72) consists of two independent filters, **A** and **B**. **FREQ** is the central frequency of the filter, **Q** is quality, and **GAIN** is the signal increase or decrease at the **FREQ** frequency. The second filter is turned on by pressing the button to the right of the letter **B**.

On the rear panel of PEQ-2 (Fig. 21.73), there are outputs to control the central frequencies of both filters (**Freq 1** and **Freq 2**), the stereo input, and the stereo output.

Fig. 21.73. Rear panel of PEQ-2

21.9. Transport Panel

Before we start to describe the main sequencer, we should explain the transport panel. It is used to control the playback of information recorded in the main sequencer.

The transport panel (Fig. 21.74) is located in the lower part of the project window.

Fig. 21.74. Transport panel

On the transport panel, there are several groups of controls. We'll describe them not from left to right as usual, but in the order of their importance.

The main element of the transport panel is the deck (Fig. 21.75).

Fig. 21.75. The deck

We'll list the buttons of the deck from left to right, and mention their shortcut buttons:

■—<0> or <Enter>—stop playback or recording; pressing it twice results in moving the current song position to the beginning of the composition or to the nearest locator position (towards the beginning)

▶—<Enter>—playback

«—<7>—rewind

»—<8>—fast forward

●—<*>—recording

To start recording, you should first press **record**, and then **play**.

For convenient playback start and stop, use the <Space> bar.

In the **POS** fields, the current position is displayed in the Bar:Beat:1/16 Bar format. You can change the values of these fields by clicking on the ⬍ buttons. If you want to type in the exact position, double-click on any of these fields. The 1.3.2 field appears. Input the new position in this field.

In the Reason sequencer, there are two special markers, called the left and right locators. A part of a song is marked off by these locators. You can use it to play a part of the song in a loop. To move the current position of the song to the position of the left or right locator, you can use the <1> and <2> keys on the numeric pad of the PC keyboard.

The two-position **OVERDUB/REPLACE** switch is used to select the recording mode:

❑ **OVERDUB**—records the new information and preserve the old information

❑ **REPLACE**—records the new information, erasing the old information

In the group shown in Fig. 21.76, the positions of the left (**L**) and right (**R**) locators are displayed and defined. The **LOOP ON/OFF** button enables and disables the looped playback mode of the song placed between the locators.

In the group shown in Fig. 21.77, the tempo (**TEMPO**) and the musical signature (**SIGNATURE**) are specified.

Fig. 21.76. Locator positions, loop enabling/disabling

Fig. 21.77. Tempo and signature

In the group shown in Fig. 21.78, you can turn the metronome on with the **CLICK** option. Each of its ticks indicates the beginning of a beat. The loudest tick corresponds to a bear's beginning.

LEVEL—is the metronome's volume.

The **MIDI SYNC** and **FOCUS** (Fig. 21.79) groups contain options related to synchronization by MIDI.

Fig. 21.78. Metronome

Fig. 21.79. MIDI synchronizing options

The **ENABLE** button switches Reason to the synchronization by MIDI mode. In this mode, playback starts and stops upon the arrival of the appropriate MIDI commands. The playback tempo completely depends on the source device of MIDI synchronization.

The **SYNC INPUT** indicator is highlighted when MIDI synchronization commands arrive.

Because several projects can be opened in Reason, which project the MIDI commands should be addressed to becomes an issue. The **MIDI** and **PLAY** buttons, when enabled, mean that all "normal" MIDI commands (**MIDI**) and the MIDI synchronization commands (**PLAY**) will be addressed to the given project (if the given project has received the MIDI information input focus (**FOCUS**)). If the MIDI synchronization mode is not enabled, all the MIDI information is addressed to the currently active project: the **MIDI** and **PLAY** buttons are enabled automatically after the project window is selected as active, and are disabled when switching to another project window. This does not occur in the MIDI synchronization mode.

For example: say you have started recording, and in the process, you changed the position of a certain regulator. All your actions are saved in the corresponding track of the main sequencer. If you start playback, all your actions are repeated. This is called *automation*. Suppose that during playbck, you again change the position of the regulator for which an automation record already exists. As soon as you touch the regulator, Reason "forgets" about the automation record, and allows you to do as you like. Otherwise, you would not be able to control the regulators, which would move themselves. While Reason is ignoring the automation record for the regulator you have moved, the **PUNCHED IN** indicator is lit (Fig. 21.80). To restore the previous state, press the **RESET** button, and the automated controls will start moving according to the automation record again.

We have already mentioned the **PATTERN SHUFFLE** parameter (Fig. 21.81) several times while describing pattern sequencers. Recall that this parameter defines the depth of a "swing" sound effect.

Fig. 21.80. Blocking indicator and the automation unblocking button

Fig. 21.81. The PATTERN SHUFFLE parameter

In the left part of the deck, there are indicators (Fig. 21.82) for the processor load and clipping (exceeding the maximum allowed signal level at audio outputs).

Fig. 21.82. Processor load and clipping indicators

21.10. Main Sequencer

The main sequencer (Fig. 21.83) is located above transport panel in the project window. In other words, an instance of the main sequencer exists in each project.

You can change the area occupied by the main sequencer (even until it becomes invisible) by dragging its upper boundary.

We'll begin learning about the main sequencer using a real example. In the project loaded by default (after starting Reason), there are the following devices:

❏ Mixer

❏ Effects processors RV-7 (reverber) and DDL-1 (delay)

❏ ReDrum drum machine

❏ REX drum loops player

❏ SubTractor pseudo-analog synthesizer

❏ Matrix pattern sequencer

Everything is already connected, and when a song is played, we hear music.

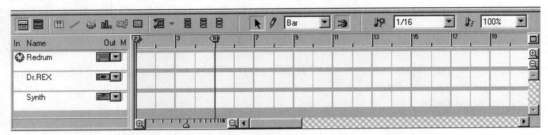

Fig. 21.83. Main sequencer

21.10.1. Track Parameters

The main sequencer is divided into two main sections. The track parameters section is on the left (Fig. 21.84).

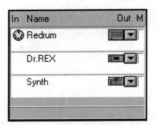

Fig. 21.84. Track parameters section

It is actually a table, and each line of the table corresponds to a track, while each column corresponds to a parameter.

❏ **In**—in this column, you select the track to receive the MIDI information. There can be only one such track.

❏ **Name**—the user-defined track name (to change the name, double-click on this field).

❏ **Out**—virtual device to which the information recorded in the track is addressed.

❏ **M**—in this field you should specify the tracks to be muted (Mute mode).

The right part of the sequencer represents the tracks themselves.

When selecting a track in the main sequencer, the project window is scrolled so that you can see the device for the selected track.

21.10.2. Record the Automation; Interaction Between the Main Sequencer and the Matrix Pattern Sequencer

By default, Matrix controls the SubTractor synthesizer. When a song's playback is started, Matrix starts automatically. By default, Matrix has no track in the main sequencer. Let's create one now. Right-click on the main sequencer. A context menu appears in which you should select the **Create Sequencer Track** command. The **New Track** track appears.

We assign the Matrix device to the new track by clicking on the appropriate button in the **Out** column. Select **Matrix** from the menu that appears (Fig. 21.86).

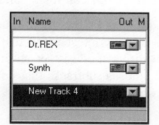

Fig. 21.85. A new track is created

Fig. 21.86. Assigning a device

To record any information to that track, you should give it a focus for receiving MIDI information (Fig. 21.87).

Matrix itself is a sequencer, so the only commands addressed to Matrix and stored in the main sequencer are commands for playback start/stop and for switching between patterns.

Let's record these commands. After the sequencer starts on the recording (using the transport panel), we turn on/off the **Pattern** button on the front panel of **Matrix** and select various patterns. Then we stop recording.

The controls you used during recording are marked with special markers if the **Show Automation Indication** option in the program settings is not disabled (*Section 21.1.1*). This means that automation recording is available (Fig. 21.88) for these controls.

Fig. 21.87. Give the track a focus to receive MIDI information

Fig. 21.88. Automation recording is available for selected controls

Two modes of operating with the sequencer are available. They are selected by the following buttons:

—arrangement mode (*Section 21.10.3*)

—editing mode (*Section 21.10.4*)

In the arrangement mode, you can operate with entire blocks of MIDI information. You can move them from one track position to another, from one track to another, etc.

In the editing mode, you can view and edit the values of the MIDI controller parameters.

Now we'll switch to the editing mode. It is easiest to do so as follows: right-click on the control for which the automation recording was done. In the context menu that appears, select the **Edit Automation** command. After this, the editing mode is set automatically, the track corresponding to the given device is selected, and its subtracks that contain the automation records are shown. In our case, there are two subtracks (Fig. 21.89).

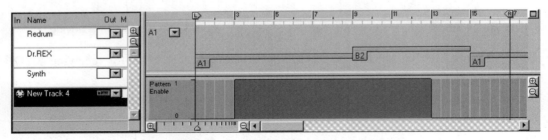

Fig. 21.89. Subtracks with automation records

Pattern switching commands are displayed in the upper subtrack. **A1** and **B2** are the pattern codes.

In the lower subtrack, the position of the controller (trigger) is displayed. It turns the Matrix playback on and off.

Note the slider in the lower part of the sequencer. Using this slider, you can change the horizontal display zoom of the MIDI information. Similar buttons exist for the vertical axis (for those subtracks in which it makes sense).

If you start playback, then SubTractor, controlled by the Matrix module (which in turn is controlled by the main sequencer) sounds exactly the way you recorded it.

This is one approach to using pattern sequencers together with the main sequencer. Another approach is transferring the MIDI information from a pattern sequencer to the track of the main sequencer. Let's try this.

To make things clearer, switch the main sequencer to the arrangement mode. Now right-click on **Matrix**, and from the context menu that appears, select the **Copy Pattern to Track** command.

The current pattern is copied from **Matrix** to the track of the sequencer to which the focus for receiving MIDI information is assigned. A pattern is like the MIDI version of a loop. It can be played in a loop infinitely. The duration of the song is limited by the **E** locator (Fig. 21.90), which you can move as you like. It wouldn't be good if the information you transfer from the pattern sequencer occupied the entire track. Therefore, the information should be transferred only to the area of the track set off by the **L** and **R** locators.

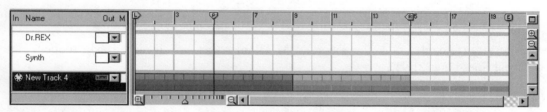

Fig. 21.90. Track of the main sequencer after transferring the information from the pattern sequencer

We should mention the **P** locator, which indicates the current position of the song. You can move all these locators using the mouse.

We have transferred the information from the pattern sequencer to the track that corresponds to it. But this is not exactly correct, however, since these commands are to be executed not by Matrix, but by the synthesizer that it controls. To correct this situation, you should select blocks of recorded MIDI information and move them to the corresponding track, which in our case is called **Synth**. However, before you do this, you had best disable Matrix and delete its automation data. Otherwise, **SubTractor** will be controlled by two sequencers at a time. It is easy to delete the automation data. Right-click on the automated controls (see Fig. 21.88), and select the **Clear Automation** command from the context menu.

You can transfer the information from the pattern sequencer directly to the **Synth** track. To do so, you should give it a focus for receiving MIDI information, select **Matrix**, and execute the **Copy Pattern to Track** command. A warning appears that informs you that the track to which you are going to transfer the information does not belong to the selected device. This is nothing to worry about; just click OK.

21.10.3. Arrangement Mode; Recording from a MIDI Keyboard; Quantization

Switching to the arrangement mode is done with the ⊞ button.

In the arrangement mode, the MIDI information is represented by rectangles. Each of the rectangles, in this case, corresponds to the entire pattern cycle. In Reason terms, these rectangles are called *groups* (groups of MIDI messages).

The **Synth** groups on the track are created automatically. We'll now try to write several messages using the MIDI keyboard and combine them into a group.

Start recording, play something on the MIDI keyboard, and stop recording.

In the arrangement mode, the recorded MIDI messages are displayed as a sequence of vertical lines (Fig. 21.91).

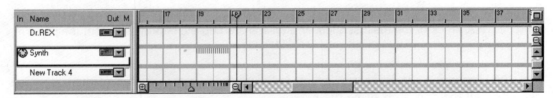

Fig. 21.91. Recording from the MIDI keyboard

In the toolbar, there are two buttons that allow you to select the editing mode:

▶ (**Arrow**)—in this mode, you can select and move blocks of MIDI messages

✎ (**Pencil**)—in this mode, you can create groups

We select the **Pencil** tool and combine the recorded messages into a group (Fig. 21.92).

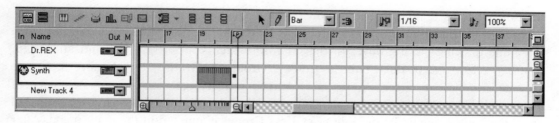

Fig. 21.92. Creating a group

To do this, move the pencil along the "lines" of MIDI messages. As a result, a new group appears. The black square to the right of the group means that this group is selected.

You can perform various actions on selected blocks of MIDI information with the clipboard. The **Edit** submenu of the main menu, as well as the context menu of the main sequencer, contains the **Cut**, **Copy**, **Paste**, and **Delete** commands. The **Select All** command (select all MIDI information in all tracks) may also be useful.

There are special commands for operating with groups:

❑ **Group**—combines the selected information into a group

❑ **Ungroup**—ungroups (the group disappears, and only the lines of MIDI messages remain)

❑ **Find Identical Groups**—finds a group identical to the currently selected group and select them

We'll now continue describing the main sequencer toolbar. The `Bar ▼` list and the `»⸬` button should be considered as one unit. Using this button, you enable the mode used for "snapping" all of your actions to the grid, and from the list, you should select the step: **Bar**, **1/2**, **1/4**, **1/8**, (a bar or its parts).

The `♪⸬` button (or the **Quantize Notes** command of the context menu, or the **Edit> Quantize Notes** command of the main menu) is used to enable quantization during recording. In the list, which is similar to the list described above, select the quantization step. The `♪⸬` button starts the quantization algorithm for the selected blocks of information. In the `100% ▼` list, define how strictly the quantization algorithm is implemented. For example, if the quantization step is equal to a beat, and the quantization strictness is set to 100%, the processed MIDI messages are placed to the closest bar beginnings. If you choose a value of 50%, the MIDI messages are also moved towards the closest bar beginnings, but they only make it halfway. The quantization command is more demonstrative if used in the editing mode (*Section 21.10.4*).

Reason supports template quantization (**Groove Quantize**). Unlike normal quantization, in groove quantization, the "attachment" is made not to the nodes of a grid, but to a rhythmic drawing—to a groove. In the list from which you select the quantization step, you can select one of three built-in grooves: **Groove 1**, **Groove 2**, or **Groove 3**, or one user-defined groove, **User**. As the user-defined groove, you can use any sequence of notes. Select it using the main sequencer, and then select the **Get User Groove** command from the context menu, or the **Edit>Get User Groove** command in the main menu. After you have done this, the user-defined groove is stored in the memory until you call this command again, or until you finish the Reason session.

Here are the remaining commands of the context menu and the **Edit** submenu of the main menu in the editing mode.

The **Insert Bars Between Locators** command inserts empty bars between the **L** and **R** locators (Figs. 12.93*a*, 12.93*b*).

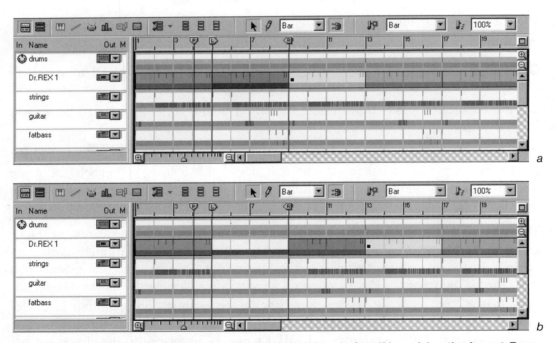

Fig. 21.93. Tracks of the main sequencer before (*a*) and after (*b*) applying the **Insert Bars Between Locators** command

The **Remove Bars Between Locators** command removes the bars between the locators.

21.10.4. Editing Mode

Now we turn to the editing mode and find out what information is contained on the **Synth** track, as well as what we can use it for.

Moving to the editing mode is done by pressing the ▤ button on the main sequencer toolbar.

In the editing mode, multiple buttons become available. They are for switching between modes of different MIDI information representation. All these modes can be enabled at the same time, and the buttons can be pressed simultaneously. If this is the case, the track is represented as several subtracks.

The ▥ button enables the mode in which notes are represented as key imprints (Fig. 21.94). Using the ▶ and ✐ tools, you can move the key imprints, change their duration, and draw new imprints.

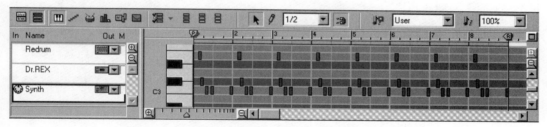

Fig. 21.94. Note representation as key imprints

Using the mouse, you can play the MIDI keyboard, which is also the vertical axis of the coordinate system in which the key imprints are displayed.

The ⟋ button enables a mode in which notes are represented as imprints of the drum loop slices (Fig. 21.95). This mode is more convenient for displaying information transferred from REX. This can be done by pressing the **To Track** button on the panel of this device (or with the **Copy REX Loop to Track** command of the context menu, or by using the **Edit>Copy REX Loop to Track** command of the main menu).

Each mark in the vertical scale corresponds to a slice of the drum loop. In our example, all slices are played continuously, and the corresponding imprints are located diagonally. However, you can change the location and the duration of the imprints as you like.

The ☺ button enables the note displaying mode optimized for representing the information transferred from the pattern sequencer of the ReDrum drum machine (Fig. 21.96).

We still see the imprints of the notes. The information from the ReDrum pattern sequencer is transferred the same way as it is with Matrix.

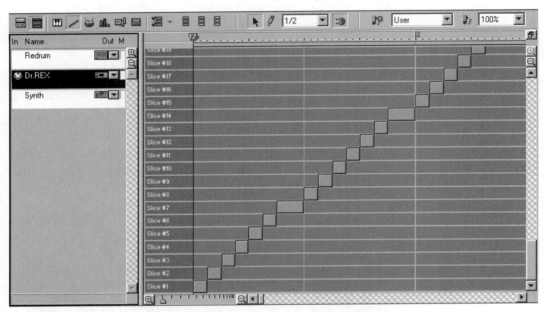

Fig. 21.95. Imprints of the drum loop slices

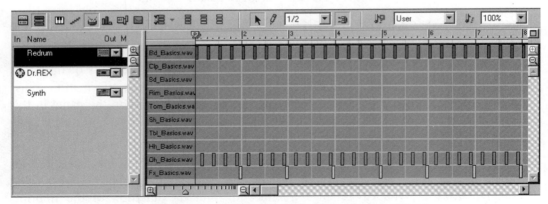

Fig. 21.96. Representation of ReDrum drum patterns

The vertical axis is divided into ten positions, corresponding to ten ReDrum channels. For each of the positions, the name of the corresponding sample is indicated.

The 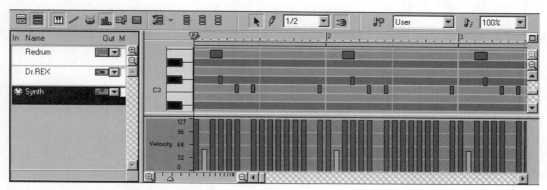 button enables the display of information on the MIDI key pressing speeds (Velocity) (Fig. 21.97).

Fig. 21.97. Representing information on MIDI key pressing speed

Obviously, you can change the height of the columns in proportion to the values of the Velocity parameter using the mouse. Selecting a **Velocity** column results in selecting the corresponding note. The shades of key imprints and the **Velocity** columns correspond to values of the Velocity parameter (Fig. 21.98).

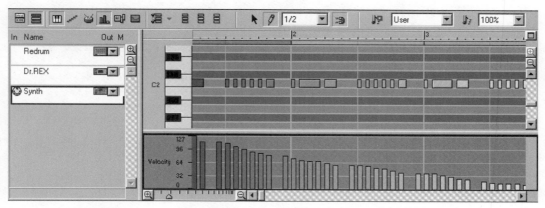

Fig. 21.98. Shades of key imprints and **Velocity** columns correspond to values of the Velocity parameter

The 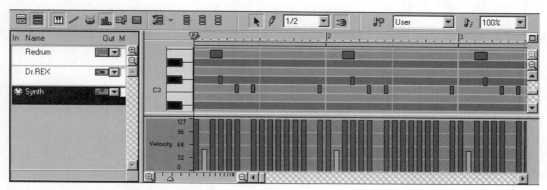 button enables the display of pattern change commands for pattern sequencers (Fig. 21.99).

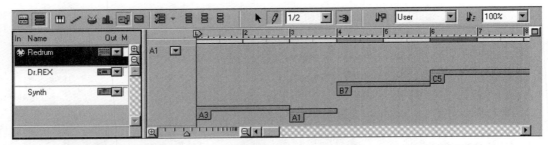

Fig. 21.99. Showing the pattern change commands for pattern sequencers

The button enables the display of the graphs for changing MIDI controllers' positions. The button opens the list of controllers available for the corresponding track of a virtual device. You have to tick the necessary controllers. The graphs for changing the ticked controllers are shown. Note that MIDI controllers take the names of parameters of a particular virtual device. There are no numbers and no standard names of MIDI controllers.

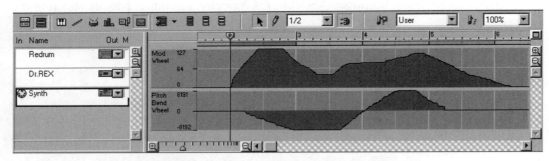

Fig. 21.100. Graphs for changing MIDI controller positions

The following three buttons represent a kind of filter, which limits or allows the display of several MIDI controllers:

—shows all subtracks of all MIDI controllers

—shows all subtracks of those MIDI controllers that contain information

—hides all subtracks of MIDI controllers

The state of all the buttons in the main sequencer toolbar is saved individually for each track.

21.10.5. Changing the Properties of MIDI Messages

The **Change Events** command of the main sequencer main menu (or the **Edit>Change Events** command of the main menu) calls the dialog window shown in Fig. 21.101.

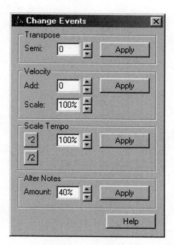

Fig. 21.101. Changing the properties of MIDI messages

Using the **Change Events** window, you can change the properties of the selected MIDI messages.

❏ **Transpose**—transposes the notes by the given number of semitones (**Semi**).

❏ **Velocity**—changes the Velocity parameter value (**Add**—by absolute value, **Scale**—as a percentage of the current value).

❏ **Scale Tempo**—changes the tempo. Actually, it is not the tempo of the entire project that is changed, but rather the duration and the location of the selected MIDI messages. The ***2** and **/2** buttons input values of 200% and 50% into the field in which the tempo changing scale is input.

❏ **Alter Notes**—changes the number (pitch), the duration, and the Velocity parameter of the selected notes.

❏ **Amount**—the extent of the given algorithm's effect upon the listed parameters of the notes.

Using the button in the upper right corner of the sequencer, you can maximize the sequencer to fill the entire available space, and minimize it to its initial state.

21.11. Commands of the Main Menu

The main menu contains the following menus:

- ❑ **File**—working with files
- ❑ **Edit**
- ❑ **Create**—creates a virtual device or a sequencer track
- ❑ **Options**

We briefly describe the purpose of each of them.

21.11.1. *File*—Working with Files

As usual, the **File** menu contains the commands for operating with files.

- ❑ **New**—creates new project
- ❑ **Open**—loads project from disk
- ❑ **Close**—closes project
- ❑ **Save**—saves project
- ❑ **Save As**—saves project with the given name
- ❑ **Song Information**—edits the project information
- ❑ **Publish Song**—saves project in a special format intended for publication. In this format, no one can make changes to your project
- ❑ **Import MIDI File**—imports project from a MIDI file
- ❑ **Export MIDI File**—exports project into a MIDI file
- ❑ **Export Patch**—saves the selected patch of the current device into a file
- ❑ **Export Song As Audio File**—exports project into a WAV or AIFF file for further mastering, recording on a CD, compression into MP3, etc.
- ❑ **Export Loop As Audio File**—similar to the previous command, except that only the area of the song between the **L** and **R** locators is exported
- ❑ **Export Rex As MIDI File**—exports information from the selected REX drum loop player into a MIDI file

Selecting the **Song Information** command calls the dialog window shown in Fig. 21.102. In this window, you can edit information on the project.

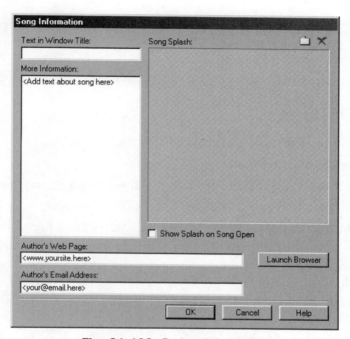

Fig. 21.102. Project information

Text in Window Title is the text in the header of the window containing the information on the project. **Author's Web Page** is the address of the author's web page on the Internet. The **Launch Browser** button launches the Internet browser and loads the given page. **Author's Email Address** is, well, the author's e-mail address. **More Information** contains any additional textual information. The button with the folder icon opens the standard dialog box for selecting the file, where you select the file that contains the picture that is to be displayed along with the information on the project. When the **Show Splash on Song Open** checkbox is selected, the **Song Information** window is automatically displayed when the project is opened.

21.11.2. *Edit*

Here we remind you of the two commands that provide for non-destructive editing:

❑ **Undo**—cancel the last action (an infinite number of undo steps is supported)

❑ **Redo**—cancel the last undo action

The contents of the remaining commands of the given **Edit** menu depends on the currently selected device or MIDI messages. We have described all these commands in the context of working with the program.

21.11.3. *Create*—Creating the Sequencer Track or a Virtual Device

The commands of the **Create** submenu correspond to the Reason virtual devices.

21.11.4. *Options*

The commands of the **Options** menu are the following:

☐ **Internal Sync**—internal synchronizing

☐ **MIDI Clock Sync**—synchronizing through MIDI from an external source

☐ **ReWire Sync**—synchronizing according to the ReWire protocol

☐ **Enable Keyboard Remote**—enables Reason remote control using the PC keyboard (*Section 21.1.4*)

☐ **Edit Keyboard Remote**—edits shortcut keys for the Reason remote control from the PC keyboard

☐ **Clear All MIDI Remote Mapping**—clears all settings for the Reason remote control from the PC keyboard

☐ **Enable MIDI Remote Mapping**—enables the mode of Reason remote control using MIDI (see *Section 21.1.3*)

☐ **Edit MIDI Remote Mapping**—edits MIDI commands for Reason remote control

☐ **Clear All MIDI Remote Mapping**—clears all settings for Reason remote control using MIDI

☐ **Toggle Rack Front/Rear**—shows front (rear) side of the virtual rack stand

☐ **Show Cables**

☐ **Follow Song**—scrolls the main sequencer during playback so that the current position can be seen

We specially skipped the description of one of the virtual devices (the Rebirth Input Machine), which is intended for using Reason and Rebirth together. Those who use Rebirth in their creative work can easily figure out how to plug this program into Reason with the Rebirth Input Machine.

We have just described the standard delivery set of Reason. In the future, there may of course be various service packs, or additions to the program, which include new virtual devices. To get the latest information, visit the Propellerhead Software site on the Internet (**http://www.propellerheads.se/**). And here is another useful resource dedicated to Reason and Rebirth—**http://www.peff.com/**.

Part V

DIGITAL MASTERING

Chapter 22: Theory

Chapter 23: Mastering with T-RackS 24

Chapter 24: DirectX Plug-Ins Useful for Mastering

Chapter 22: Theory

Mastering is the final stage of processing the recording before its distribution to CDs, audiotapes, TV, video, films, etc. The source material for mastering is the master copy, or the final stereo recording after mixing. The main task of mastering is to provide the maximum possible subjective quality of sound for the given type of media (usually, CD Digital Audio). When mastering of an album takes place, all the tracks of the album are driven toward some common sound; the differences between the tracks are smoothed both by spectrum and by volume.

We have come across the idea that in some cases, when mixing is done with a high level of quality, there is no need to master at all. Indeed, some mixing mistakes can be removed during mastering, but this is not nearly the main task of mastering. As we already mentioned, during mastering, the record is adapted for transfer to some type of media. In certain cases, the record on the initial media after mastering can sound worse than before mastering. We can assess the results of mastering only after the record is transferred to the final media. If mastering is done for distribution of the record on audio cassettes, the quality of the mastering can be assessed only after listening to an audio tape.

22.1. Main Mastering Tools

The main tools used for mastering are the equalizer, the compressor, and the limiter.

22.1.1. Equalizer

Using the *equalizer*, you can correct the spectrum of the recording. Spectral correction is done in two steps:

❏ Balancing the signal spectrum (there must be "enough" low, middle, and high frequencies to make the listener feel comfortable).

❏ Adjustment to spectrums of other recordings included in the album (to avoid the listener's having to change the equalizer settings while listening to the album).

Using the equalizer, you can affect the clarity of the sound. A clear sound contains many high frequency components; a dull sound thus lacks these components. Another quality of sound—transparence—is indirectly connected with the equalizer. Transparence indicates the listener's ability to select single instruments and listen to them with a certain clarity. Generally, transparence depends on many factors, such as the location of the source of sound along the panorama. (If they are located in the same place and are playing at the same time, it is hard to distinguish them). Transparence also depends on the timbres that are being played at the same time, on the applied effects, and on certain other factors.

22.1.2. Compressor

When you apply the *compressor*, the dynamic range is narrowed. The compressor can be used, for example, when you are going to distribute a recording on a media with a small dynamic range (i.e., an audio cassette). When the dynamic range is narrowed, sharp changes in the volume are smoothed, and quiet places in the recording sound louder so that the level of the signal level can overcome the noise level of the tape.

Compressor is a signal dynamic processing device. Recall that the classic compressor (*Section 4.2*) operates according to the following principle. The signal passes through the compressor without any changes as long as the signal level at the input does not exceed the assigned value (the threshold). As soon as the signal level at the input exceeds the threshold, the compressor begins to suppress the signal. This type of compression is called *hard compression*. The soft compressor does not have a determined threshold. Its transfer ratio changes smoothly as the signal level at the input increases. The sound of hard and soft compressors is different (hard and soft, respectively), but not everyone will notice this difference.

A recording with a narrow dynamic range can potentially sound louder. To realize this potential, you should normalize to a level of 0 dB after applying the compressor. Software and hardware compressors also usually have what is called the Gain (amplification) parameter. By increasing the value of this parameter, you can entirely compensate for the loss in loudness that results from compression without any normalization.

Even those recordings that are to be distributed on CD are usually processed by the compressor. The real dynamic range of records distributed on CD is narrower than the theoretically possible range of 96 dB; it does not exceed 50—60 dB. The reason for this is that, at lower levels of the signal, the distortions caused by its quantization become audible. A 16-bit sinusoid signal with a level of −80 dB is shown in Fig. 22.1 (there are 16 dB yet until the theoretical limit). A similar signal with a level of −60 dB is shown in Fig. 22.2, and you can see that it looks more like a sinusoid than the previous signal.

We should mention that the sinusoid signals shown in Figs. 22.1 and 22.2 have very small amplitudes (the signals are very quiet). The amplitude of the first signal is greater than the amplitude of the second signal by 20 dB. The amplitude of the second signal, in turn, is less than the maximum possible amplitude by 60 dB.

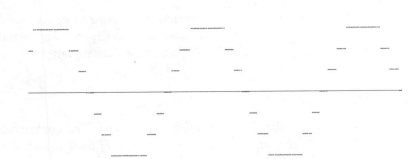

Fig. 22.1. A sinusoid signal with a frequency of 440 Hz and a level of −80 dB in 16-bit/44.1 kHz format

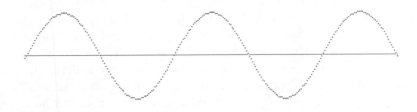

Fig. 22.2. A sinusoid signal with a frequency of 440 Hz and a level of −60 dB in 16-bit/44.1 kHz format

22.1.3. Is It Really That Horrible to Lose Sound Dynamics?

A symphonic orchestra has a wide dynamic range (over 100 dB), but there are not many sharp changes in level. Changes in the loudness just emphasize the composer's idea. We do not lose that much if we narrow the dynamic range of a symphonic orchestra to approximately 60 dB. This is due to the peculiarities of human hearing, developed over millions of years, that allow us to process audio information selectively. Basically, we pay more attention to louder sounds. From this the concept comes the idea of *masking* sounds. Suppose a powerful Diesel engine is running, or someone is using a jackhammer somewhere next to you. What do you hear? This sound, and it alone, even though your eardrum is at the same time perceiving sounds of birds chirping as well. These sounds, however, you cannot hear, because your brain completely switches to the louder sound, since it is potentially dangerous. If we didn't switch all of our attention to these louder sounds, we wouldn't be alive today. Some other form of life would be dominant on this planet, one better able to adapt. Switching your attention takes time in itself, and so the effect of the temporary masking appears, in which a short, loud impulse mutes other impulses for a certain time.

Let's continue with our imaginary experiment. Let's say that another engine or jackhammer starts up. You'll hear both of them because their loudness is almost the same, and they are both potentially dangerous. So we can draw the conclusion that we hear only sounds of approximately equal loudness. At night, we can hear how water drips from the faucet, crickets making noise outside the window, etc., because at the moment, these sounds are the loudest ones.

The motors and jackhammers were just an example. Actually, masking effects appear at lower changes in loudness.

There are natural limits—the minimum loudness that the human ear can perceive, and the maximum loudness (the pain threshold). These limits are different for different ranges of the sound spectrum. The human ear range is large (120 dB); however, the brain does not analyze all information in that entire area. Psycho-acoustics studies specific features of human hearing. Different algorithms of data compression—such as Mp3, Real Audio, and others—use some of these features. If we could apply all modern psycho-acoustic knowledge, we would have the ability to compress audio data hundreds of times without audible distortions.

Let's continue with our example of a symphonic orchestra. You're probably not going to be recording an orchestra, but the example is convenient when trying to explain the principles. If the dynamic range of the signal created by the orchestra is 120 dB, this does not mean that your brain will collect and analyze all the information it receives. If the volume of certain fragments of the composition increases and decreases smoothly, the listener cannot feel these dynamics. He or she gets used to the current loudness, even though it is changing. Smooth changes in volume are not usually noticed. When the volume changes sharply, you do, of course, notice it. The question is, by how much is the volume changing? If, for example, the signal jumps from −90 to 0 dB, then you'll likely jump along with it from the chair you're sitting in. A symphonic orchestra is best listened to in a concert hall. Only listening to one live will have the intended effect of truly moving you. But if you want to comfortably listen to symphonic music, there should be no sharp changes in volume. The composer's idea can be expressed well enough using a dynamic range of 60 dB.

For pop and rock music, you can make do with an even narrower dynamic range. Some loud and rhythmic sounds can mute the sounds of other instruments. To avoid this, there must not be a large difference in volume, and thus the dynamic range can be not too wide.

And so we see that there is also an artistic aspect to applying the compressor. Such features of the recording as density and loudness are associated with applying the compressor. A dense sound is a feature of such genres as rock music, pop music, and modern dance music, but, for example, the sound of a symphonic orchestra should not be dense. Two different volume envelopes are shown in Figs. 22.3a and 22.3b. The first one is from the song "Ayla" by "Kosmonova", and the other is from the "Intermezzo" from Rakhmaninov's opera "Aleko". The durations of both recordings are the same. It is clear that they are different: the first recording is dense (the signal almost all the time is at the maximum level), while the other is loose (sharp changes in the loudness are noticeable).

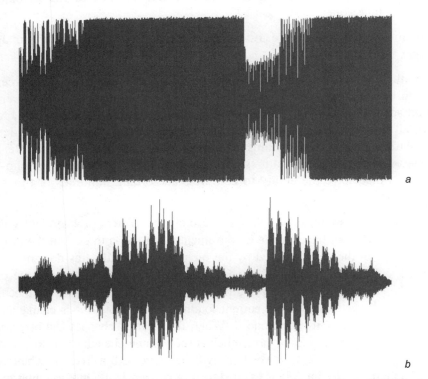

a

b

Fig. 22.3. Volume envelopes for recordings with the same duration but of different genres— (a) envelope typical for modern dance music; (b) envelope typical for classical music

22.1.4. Limiter

Using the limiter, you can give the sound more density and volume of the sound. However, after you apply the limiter, some audio information could be lost. When software processing is applied, the losses from applying the hard limiter are usually estimated as a percentage: after limiting, a certain percent of sample measurements are clipped. (We discuss clipping in the next section). Experienced sound engineers can estimate these losses by ear. Applying the limiter is reasonable when the losses are insignificant (not audible) and the result is significant (the volume can be increased by a number of decibels if required). A hard sound to a recording is associated with applying the limiter. The sound becomes hard due to clipping, the distortions resulting from limiting the signal by level.

Both compressors and limiters are in the same class of devices—dynamic processing devices that suppress or amplify the signal at the output, depending on its level at the input.

Most dynamic processing devices have such important parameters as *attack time* and *release time*. During these intervals of time, the device analyzes the change in the signal level and makes a decision to amplify it, attenuate it, or to leave it unchanged. For example, if you specify a very small value for the attack time, the compressor starts to react to short peaks in the signal. If, in conjunction with this, a large value is specified for the release time, then after short splashes of loudness, the signal "falls" for a long time (for example, a short loud sound of a drum and a sharp decrease in loudness just following it). The volume is restored during the release time, but as soon as the next peak comes, the unpleasant effects repeat. When you specify a large attack time, the compressor "thinks" too much before it reacts to continuous jumps in the signal level. As a result, you may get a clipped signal at the output.

Each of the described devices—the equalizer, the compressor, and the limiter—distorts the audio signal (the form of the signal and its spectrum change). However, a recording with such distortions could potentially sound better. But don't forget that by simply applying the above devices you do not necessarily improve the perception of the recording. Using the equalizer, the compressor, or the limiter, you can improve the sound or spoil it. We have already given you such examples.

22.1.5. Spectral Dynamic Processing Devices

The typical dynamic processing devices significantly distort the spectrum of the signal. If you have achieved a sound balanced by frequency, your work may be useless after applying the compressor and the limiter. To avoid these foolish mistakes, spectral dynamic processing devices are applied. These are a set of devices combined into one device: the crossover (the set of filters for splitting the signal spectrum into several frequency bands) and certain classical devices used for dynamic processing, one for each of the bands. You may affect the sound of the instruments in different ways when the main energy of these instruments is concentrated in different frequency ranges. But some devices may not provide this ability: the parameters of dynamic processors for different frequency ranges may be defined automatically.

22.1.6. How Can We Avoid Overcompressing?

If you squeeze the signal too much using the compressor and the limiter, the feeling of the sound dynamics disappears, the stereo image of the recording is distorted, the sound becomes opaque, and unpleasant distortions caused by the compressor appear. The above problems are all combined under the term *overcompressing*.

One of the ways to prevent overcompressing is to use high quality acoustic monitors. You must hear your mistakes. For this, you of course have to have a good sound engineer's ear, and be able to hear weak, non-linear distortions.

You are the only one who determines the dynamic processing parameters, so you are responsible for overcompressing, not a device or software. That is, in order to avoid overcompressing, you have to learn to avoid making silly mistakes. Various equipment that measures the volume and the signal level will help you prevent overcompressing.

Let's use as an example the quasi-peak indicator of the signal level in Cool Edit Pro. It is called quasi-peak because it displays not the instant values of sound measurements, but the average volume calculated during the last several milliseconds. It is convenient to use this indicator when the **Show Valleys** and **Dynamic Peaks** options (in the context menu called by right-clicking on the indicator) are enabled. In this mode, the minimum and the maximum signal levels are displayed by yellow dashes. These dashes are reset every 1.5 seconds. By estimating the distance between these dashes, you can estimate the current value of the signal's dynamic range.

After dynamic processing has been applied, it is best to select a fragment of the recording in which you suspect the presence of overcompressing. Use the **Analyze>Statistics** command of the Cool Edit Pro editor (*Section 14.2*). Subtract the value of the **Total RMS Power** parameter from the value of the **Peak Amplitude** parameter. You get the value of the peak factor as your result (the relation between the signal's maximum amplitude and its average level). The value of this parameter is considered normal if it is between 6 dB and 14 dB (depending on the recording).

22.2. Analog and Digital Mastering

In some studios, mastering is performed as follows: the recording is made on a tape with a raised level of recording, after which it is digitized into a WAV file, which is finally recorded on a CD. We have heard some people make recommendations to this effect: before the next analog-digital conversion, let the tape sit for a while. This does make sense, because an analog recording on a magnetic tape changes its features over time. After the recording is made on magnetic tape, its sound becomes warmer and denser. Sometimes, the recording is passed through different analog devices like electronic valve devices. This type of mastering is called *analog mastering*.

The main principle of digital audio recording is that the digitized signal should never be converted using analog-digital conversion. If you have mixed without using an analog mixer, but rather in a multichannel audio editor, the mastering should only be digital. Only then can you get the maximum sound quality. Of course, you need to have professional knowledge, as well as some specific knowledge related to the peculiarities of digital audio recording. It is this knowledge that we'd like to share with you.

You can achieve a warm and dense sound without using any analog devices. You have already learned what a "dense" sound is. When the recording level is heightened, the magnetic tape acts as a compressor. In this case, the signal level during playback is lower than during recording, and the dynamic range of the signal decreases. We'll now look at the "warmth" of a sound.

22.2.1. What is the Reason for the "Warmth" of an Analog Sound and the "Hardness" of Digital Sound?

The main advantage of analog recording, when compared to digital recording, is that analog devices have a reserve of signal level. This means that the level of the signal transferred between different studio devices can be over 0 dB. If the signal level slightly exceeds 0 dB, the changes in the sound quality are almost inaudible. But if you continually increase the signal level, non-linear distortions become clearly perceptible. A sound is considered "warm" when these distortions are insignificant.

In a digital recording, a signal with the maximum possible amplitude normally corresponds to a level of 0 dB. What happens if this level is exceeded? In the oldest equipment, there would be resolution overflow. For the sake of simplicity, let's assume that our monophonic signal is not 24-bit or 16-bit, but 4-bit. Assume that after amplifying this signal (with software) the amplitude of one of the sample measurements becomes equal to the maximum possible binary number, $1111_{(2)}$. If you increase this value, say, by $0010_{(2)}$, the result is $1111_{(2)} + 0010_{(2)} = 10001_{(2)}$. But we only have 4-bit resolution, and so the high-order bit disappears, and we are left with the four low-order bits: $0001_{(2)}$. Finally, if we amplify a value of $1111_{(2)}$ by $0010_{(2)}$, we get $0001_{(2)}$. If this does not explain anything to you and you cannot imagine how such non-linear distortions sound, just try it yourself. In Cool Edit Pro, generate a sinusoidal signal of any frequency (for example, 440 Hz) with a level of 0 dB. Load the resulting WAV file in Cakewalk Pro Audio (put it on any track). Then listen to that track and remember its sound. Using the **Options>Audio** command, call the **DirectShow Audio** dialog box, and in the **Advanced** tab, disable the **Clip Audio Mix Upon Overflow** option. Then increase the volume by 3 dB using the fader of the master module of the **Console** window, and start playback. Sounds terrible, right? The distortions you hear are caused by an overflow in the number of bits.

The source oscillation is shown in Fig. 22.4*a*, and its spectrum is shown in Fig. 22.4*b*.

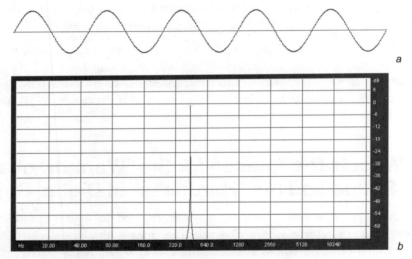

Fig. 22.4. Source oscillation (*a*) and its spectrum (*b*)

The signal distorted as a result of the resolution overflow is shown in Fig. 22.5*a*, and its spectrum is shown in Fig. 22.5*b*.

You can clearly see the difference between Figs. 22.4 and 22.5. In practice, this means that very slightly exceeding the level of 0 dB results in significant distortions that spoil the recording. As a result, we see the rise of many legends about "digital" distortions, and a fear of "digital" sound.

But now, the "problem of 0 dB" has been completely solved in modern devices.

Let's turn again to the above example. We will now introduce the following condition: if the number of bits of the sum exceeds the maximum allowed number of bits, then the sum is equal to the maximum value that can be encoded using the maximum allowed number of bits. So $1111_{(2)} + 0010_{(2)}$ is now equal not to $0001_{(2)}$, but to $1111_{(2)}$. In fact, the signal is strictly limited at a level of 0 dB, and it is this limiting that is called *clipping*. The implementation of this idea requires a few resources. For example, if the audio signal is encoded by 16-bit numbers at the input and output of some digital device or software, a higher resolution needs to be used for internal processing of the signal.

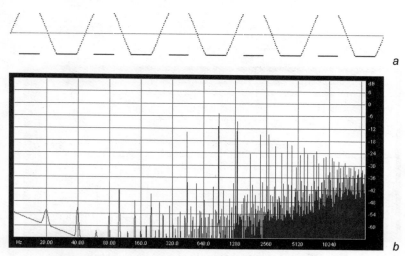

Fig. 22.5. The signal distorted as a result of the resolution overflow (*a*) and its spectrum (*b*)

A clipped signal is shown in Fig. 22.6*a*, and its spectrum is shown in Fig. 22.6*b*.

The **Clip Audio Mix Upon Overflow** option in the settings of Cakewalk Pro Audio enables the clipping algorithm. Enable this option and listen to the sinusoid signal whose level is too high. This sound can be characterized as "computerized". Of course, the distortions are audible, but they are not as unpleasant as the distortions caused by exceeding the bit capacity. If the level of 0 dB is somewhat exceeded in some places of the recording, this won't spoil the entire recording. Such distortions will not even be noticed. By the way, there are those who prefer the computer sound, just as there are fans of the analog sound. The distortions caused by clipping can be used in creative work. The hard computer sound may be useful in dance music, where clipping occurs at each beat of a rave drum.

Almost all modern devices and software for digital sound processing use 24, 32, 48, or even more bits for the internal representation of sound measurements. This significantly increases the accuracy of processing. There are now devices and software that have a reserve of level: the signal level can go significantly over 0 dB without any distortions. Near the maximum allowed level, special algorithms can be enabled that will limit the signal softly, as is done in analog devices. In Fig. 22.7*a*, our test signal is shown, processed by T-RackS, which emulates the operation of analog devices. The spectrum of this signal is shown in Fig. 22.7*b*.

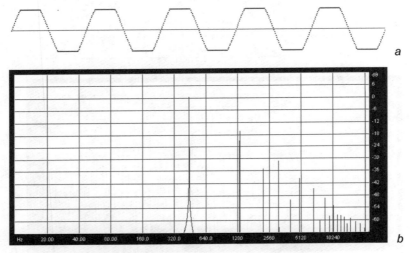

Fig. 22.6. A clipped signal (*a*) and its spectrum (*b*)

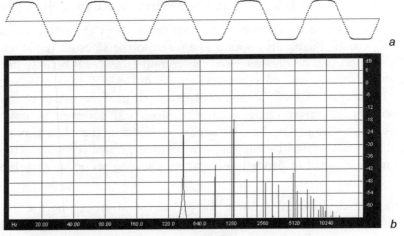

Fig. 22.7. A signal processed by T-RackS (*a*) and its spectrum (*b*)

Where is all this leading? One of the basic aims of mastering is to save the level of the signal, and thus clipping cannot be avoided during mastering. The only question is then: how will the recording sound? When you assess the sound of different multitrack editors, special software, or plug-in modules intended for mastering, you are in fact comparing different algorithms for limiting the signal to somewhere around a level of 0 dB. The algorithms may be quite different, from hard limiting at a level of 0 dB, to modeling the processes that take place in the electric circuits of valve amplifiers.

22.2.2. How to Avoid Quantization Noise

If 24-bit or 32-bit sound counts are used for audio representation, the quantization noise does not affect anything, since it is very low. However, the most popular audio format is the CD: 16 bit/44.1 kHz/stereo. Even in the case of 16-bit resolution, the quantization noise is very low, but it now causes a serious problem: it is correlated to the legitimate signal. It is because of this that the quantization noise makes the most significant contribution to creating a negative image among listeners towards the digital sound. This sound is often said to be flat, metallic, synthetic, and so on. All these qualifiers were applied to 16-bit sound too. This was true until certain methods of digital sound processing—*dithering* and *noise shaping*—appeared. Dithering means that before the number of bits is decreased, a very low, specific noise is added to the useful signal. As a result, the quantization noise is simply muted by this specific noise, which, due to its features, less affects the listener's state of mind. Of course, the resulting record becomes noisier, but this noise, as well as the quantization noise, is almost inaudible.

Another method of removing quantization noise is called noise shaping. This consists of applying special algorithms that round the values of sound measurements when the number of bits is decreased. After applying noise shaping, the greater part of the energy of the quantization noise is concentrated in the region of the high frequencies; thus the human ear, not as sensitive to these frequencies as to others, does not feel it as much. Normally, noise shaping and dithering are used together.

To illustrate dithering and noise shaping, we performed an experiment. In Cool Edit Pro, a sinusoidal signal with a frequency of 440 Hz and a level of −80 dB was generated, which resulted in a very quiet sound. A 32-bit representation of the signal was used. After that, using the **Edit>Convert Sample Type** command, the audio representation format was changed into 16-bit format. The **Enable Dithering** option was disabled. The source signal is shown in Fig. 22.8. The same signal with 16-bit resolution is shown in Fig. 22.9.

The curve in Fig. 22.9 looks more like a staircase than a sinusoid. (For a clearer picture, the display of the interpolation curve connecting discrete points was enabled). If we subtract this signal from the initial signal, the quantization noise is the result. The quantization noise itself is shown in Fig. 22.10*a*, and its spectrum is shown in Fig. 22.10*b*.

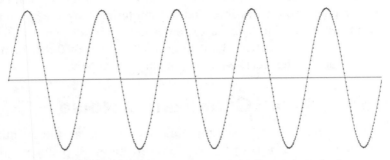

Fig. 22.8. The source signal (32-bit representation)

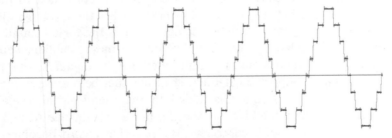

Fig. 22.9. The signal after converting to 16-bit representation

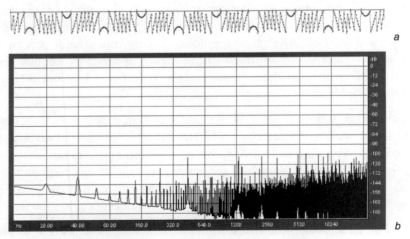

Fig. 22.10. Quantizing noise (*a*) and its spectrum (*b*)

We then converted back to the initial 32-bit signal, and decreased its number of bits to 16. But now, we apply dithering with a depth of 1 bit, and type C1 noise shaping (*Section 10.14*). The resulting signal is shown in Fig. 22.11.

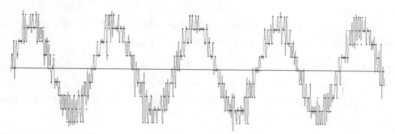

Fig. 22.11. The signal converted from 32-bit format to 16-bit format with dithering and noise shaping

The noise resulting from decreasing the number of bits of the signal, along with dithering and noise shaping, is shown in Fig. 22.12*a*, and its spectrum is shown in Fig. 22.12*b*.

Let's compare the "pure" quantizing noise (see Fig. 22.10*a*) to the noise resulting from applying dithering and noise shaping when the number of bits is decreased (Fig. 22.12*a*).

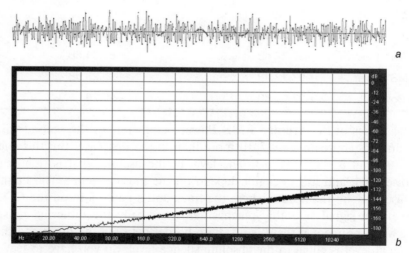

Fig. 22.12. The noise resulting from decreasing the number of bits of the signal along with dithering and noise shaping (*a*), and its spectrum (*b*)

It is clear that in the first case, the noise, as well as the legitimate signal, is periodical, because of the correlation with the legitimate signal (the quality most unpleasant to our ears).

The noise is also asymmetric relative to the zero level, which is not good. In the second case, the periodicity of the noise is not obvious. This noise looks rather like a random process.

Now we compare these signals in the frequency area (see Figs. 22.10*b*, 22.12*b*). In the first one, the energy of the noise is spread along the frequencies unevenly, and the large number of peaks shows this. In the second case, the energy of the noise smoothly increases as the frequency increases, and there are no peaks.

If we calculate the area under the curves, we find that in the second case, the noise level is higher than in the first case. This was just as we expected. For both cases, statistics were retrieved using the **Analyze>Statistics** command of Cool Edit Pro (*Section 14.2*). These data are presented in Table 22.1.

Table 22.1. Noise Statistics for Two Cases of Lowering the Number of Bits

Parameter	Value without applying dithering and noise shaping	Value after applying dithering and noise shaping
Min Sample Value	−1	−2.68
Max Sample Value	0	2.74
Peak Amplitude	−86.79 dB	−81.56 dB
DC Offset Minimum	−0.002	0
RMS Power	−97.72 dB	−90.77 dB
Maximum RMS Power	−97.72 dB	−89.84 dB
Average RMS Power	−97.72 dB	−90.28 dB
Total RMS Power	−97.72 dB	−90.28

Compare the values of the **Average RMS Power** parameter. In the second case, the energy of the noise is approximately 7 dB more than in the first case. But this energy is still very small—its level is only −90 dB. The level of the useful signal is significantly more than the noise level, and this does not depend on the musical genre. The human ear can hear this noise only on the border where the track and a pause join on the CD, when the level of the useful signal smoothly reaches zero, and only the dithering noise remains. The listener won't notice it if there is no sharp border between the noise and the pause in which the signal level is equal to the absolute silence level. So you have to leave the dithering noise in pauses, or apply the additional Fade in and Fade out processing in the beginning and in the end of the recording after lowering the number of bits to 16.

So the problem of digital overflow, as well as the problem of quantization noise, can be solved. The digital sound then will not appear to be so "synthetic".

Did you know that analog sound is not only analog but also digital? How can this be? You see, a finite number of molecules in the air knock on your eardrum per a certain unit of time, which causes the pressure to rise and fall, which, in turn, lengthens sound waves. And maybe you think that an analog tape recorder is analog? Wrong again. For a certain unit of time, the head of the tape recorder reads the information stored by a finite number of magnetic domains. However, these "digital" devices are not as straightforward as microprocessor devices. They contain neither digital code nor any algorithms for the signal processing implemented as programs. Everything the software developers aim to accomplish here comes naturally.

The above methods of signal processing—dithering and noise shaping—are applied only when the number of bit representation of the signal is decreased. This is all well and good when the initial format of the recording is 24-bit. But does it really make sense to apply dithering or noise shaping when the initial recording has a 16-bit format? Yes, it does. In certain cases, only this will allow you to make fine changes while mastering.

Now we'll turn to discussing the problems related to another term well known to sound engineers who work with digital sound.

22.2.3. Truncating

Truncating is what was before called lowering the resolution of the digital audio. When the signal is 24-bit and then becomes 16-bit, truncation takes place. On the one hand, lowering the resolution is not a big deal. Was it really worth thinking up a new term? However, the word "truncation" also includes the idea of a set of problems related to digital audio with a resolution higher than 16 bits. First of all, this implies the hidden lowering of the resolution. For example, let's say that the signal successively passes through three digital audio processing devices. The S/PDIF interface is used to connect these devices. However, the person responsible for the connection did not pay attention to the fact that the first and the third devices are 24-bit, and the second device is 16-bit. These devices can easily interact: each of the 24-bit devices, while setting the connection through S/PDIF, determines that it is connected to a 16-bit device and switches to the proper mode. As a result, the signal transferred from the first device to the second one is truncated. As you know, the quantizing noise of a 16-bit signal is bad for a recording. If multiple truncations occur during the record processing, the quality of the sound continuously decreases.

This problem related to truncation can appear not only in an expensive professional digital studio with lots of devices involved. You can also encounter it while operating in a one-PC recording studio. For example, say you are mixing your arrangement in Cakewalk Pro Audio. A 24-bit representation mode for audio measurements is set. You are also using a plug-in module supplied by other vendors. According to the DirectX standard, the exchange of audio information between plug-in modules is done with 32-bit resolution. However, not all the modules use a 32-bit resolution of the signal to process it. If you have processed your 24-bit WAV file with a 16-bit plug-in module, you will certainly run into truncation.

The only way to overcome uncontrolled truncation is to thoroughly study the manuals that are supplied with the equipment. As for the software, particularly the DirectX plug-in modules, there are special utilities for controlling them. One of these is called BitPolice (from AnalogX), which is a plug-in module itself. This module does not perform any type of processing; it simply passes the digital flow of audio data and indicates how often the bits 1 through 32 get a value of 1. These indicators are called *bitoscopes*. You can download this module free from **http://www.analogx.com**.

Here is another way to apply BitPolice to check all other modules:

❏ In Cakewalk Pro Audio, create a project with an audio data representation of 24 bits.

❏ Import a WAV file containing any test signal with 24-bit representation of sound measurements to one of the tracks.

❏ Plug in three real time effects to this track: BitPolice, the plug-in being tested, and BitPolice again.

❏ Open both BitPolice windows, start the playback, and watch what happens (Fig. 22.13).

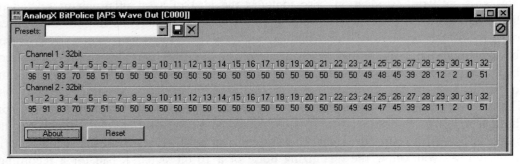

Fig. 22.13. BitPolice bitoscope

Channel 1 and **Channel 2** are the stereo channels. The bits are numbered 1 through 32. Under each of these values, the frequency at which the corresponding bit takes the value of 1 is indicated. The ideal case is one in which the bits get the number 50, i.e., the bits take values of 0 and 1 relatively evenly and at the same rate. This means that they are used to transfer data. If the bits have small numbers (0 is the worst) or numbers that are too large (100 is worst), the values of these bits change rarely, or do not change at all (are always 0 or 1). This means that the bits are not holding useful information. If you see a chain of 0's or 100's, there's a good chance that your problem is the plug-in module.

The second aspect of truncation is planning it within the interval between the beginning of mixing and the final stage of mastering. You have to decide where truncating should occur if it is inevitable. In most cases, special high-precision (and expensive) measuring devices are not worth using if they are combined with their less refined "colleagues".

The audio recording studio is also a measuring system. Instant values of sound oscillations are measured in this system. This information is saved, processed, and finally recorded to a CD or to a magnetic tape. It makes no sense to use an expensive electronic valve microphone if the vocal part is digitized using a cheap sound card. It also makes no sense to store the audio data recorded using this sound card in 24-bit format. No, it's not worth it, and in the end you're just wasting space on your hard disk. If your devices are hi-end, then it is reasonable to store all the tracks of your project in 24-bit format and to mix these into a 24-bit WAV file. If you are working with a 16-bit sound card, it'd probably be best to store all the tracks, including those containing the parts of MIDI instruments and recorded with the same sound card, in 16-bit format.

If your sound card is 16-bit, but you intend to process tracks with a great number of effects that will make minute changes to the character of the sound, it is better to store the tracks in 24-bit format. If that is not possible, you should apply the effects in "batches", in real time. This is done as follows: plug in as many real-time effects as possible to the tracks, set all the parameters, and then apply these effects all at once, saving the results directly in 16-bit audio tracks. This approach allows you to avoid multiple truncations during continuous processing when you process a 16-bit track with a 32-bit effect many times and then save the result on the same 16-bit track.

If it is possible, it is better to mix this project in a 24-bit WAV file, though sometimes mixing in a 16-bit WAV file is also OK. For example, if you are preparing the recording for publishing, especially on the radio or on the Internet in MP3 or Real Audio format with low quality, or for its later recording on an audio tape, it won't contain the minute features that can be heard thanks to 24-bit audio. In practice, the master copy of the recording transferred from the recording studio to the mastering studio is usually stored on a DAT tape, which are normally 16-bit. However, modern inventions provide us with the ability to record up to a 24-bit signal on a DAT tape, and the compatibility with typical 16-bit DAT format is preserved. These "16 bits" effect neither the popularity of artists nor the CD sales.

Things are easier for you however—you have a traditional recording studio and a mastering studio all included in your PC. You thus have the choice of which format to use to store sound data. It does not make sense to premaster a record in a 16-bit WAV file if the source tracks are in 24-bit format. If this is the case, you should avoid truncation until the final stage of mastering. Even though the source record is stored in 16-bit format, you should convert it to 24-bit or 32-bit format before you start mastering.

In practice, mastering almost always ends with truncation, due to the fact that the CD is the most popular audio medium, and it appeared in the '70s, when 16-bit audio was the answer to prayers.

Dithering and noise shaping are used to eliminate the results of truncation. As you have already learned, when these methods are applied, the loss of the signal's dynamic range is compensated for by adding some noise to the signal. You should apply noise shaping only once, during mastering. You may apply dithering even when there is no clear truncation. For example, if you are processing 16-bit tracks with 32-bit effects, using dithering to emphasize the details of effects makes sense. As a result, you get the same 16-bit track, but containing a dithering noise. When dithering is applied multiple times, the noise accumulates. You should consider this fact, but you should not fear it and allow that to affect your decisions.

22.2.4. Discretization Error, Multisampling Versus Aliasing

The *discretization error* is another legendary problem told to computer musicians by those who are used to analogous sound. You personally will never directly run into it. You needn't look for a checkbox that will start the magic algorithm to compensate for the problem either, because there isn't any. Therefore, the contents of this section are simply informative.

A digital audio signal is quantized by level, regardless of the resolution with which it was recorded. It is also discrete over time. In an ideal case, the sound counts represent instantaneous measurements of the audio signal at certain moments of time. These measurements come one after another over time. The frequency of their succession must be at least two times more than the upper limit of the spectrum of the signal that needs to be digitized.

It may seem to some people that digital recording lacks the high-frequency audio components (above 20 kHz) that are present in the real audio world. They say that, although these components are not audible, it is exactly these components that on a subconsciousness level make the sound natural. This statement is not true. Ultrasound cannot penetrate into the subconscious because the information on it does not reach the brain. This is the nature of the human ear. There is a different, more banal reason for the decrease in digital sound quality. Along with the useful signal, different noises arrive at the input of the analog-digital converter. These noises may be located not only within the audible frequency range, but also outside it. The inaudible infrasound noise (with a frequency below 20 Hz) penetrates into the recording band and takes up its resources. This signal, along with the legitimate signal, can cause an overload. Thus, the recording level must be decreased, and the dynamic range of the legitimate signal will be narrowed. To get rid of infrasound noise, high-pass filters are used. They are usually built into the microphone's pre-amplifiers, mixers, and even the microphones themselves.

Ultrasound noise penetrates into the recording band not through the microphones, but through parasite induction. If this inaudible noise is not filtered, it turns into audible noise during discretization, and the listener hears a "metallic", "synthetic", and "computerized" sound. The ultrasound noise's penetration into the audible region of frequencies after discretization is often called *aliasing*. This noise is not necessarily the noise itself. It can be any signal whose frequency components are above one half of the sampling frequency.

In Fig. 22.14, you see the source signal, discrete measurements after its "digitization", and the signal restored by the values of these measurements during the digital-analog conversion. In Fig. 22.14a, the frequency of the source signal is less than half of the sampling frequency; in Fig. 22.14b, it is greater than half of the sampling frequency.

Previously, only analogous low-pass filters were used to avoid aliasing. The main disadvantage of analogous filters is the phase distortion. Phase distortions can be decreased by giving the filter response less of a slope. The boundary between the filtered and unfiltered frequency ranges becomes less clear. However, in this case, you can "capture" the ultrasound area of the spectrum and suppress the high-pass components of the audible signal. In modern analog-digital converters used in audio recording, only low-pass analog filters with a response sloping gently are used. These filters do not touch the audible range of frequencies. The signal is then digitized with a very high sampling frequency, and passes through the digital filter that cuts all ultrasound components. The digital filter indeed allows practically no phase distortions. After digital filtering, the sampling frequency is typically lowered to values of 44.1 kHz, 48 kHz, or 96 kHz.

The above method of the signal processing is called *oversampling*. All these conversions take place within the analog-digital converter.

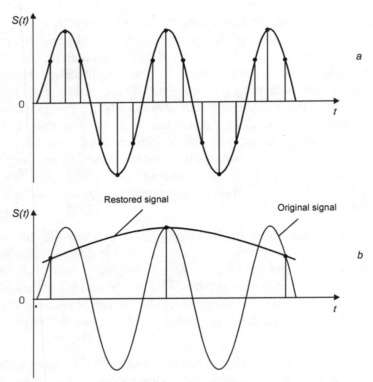

Fig. 22.14. Signal conversion at different discretion frequencies

22.2.5. Jitter the Terrible?

Another legendary problem of digital audio recording is jitter—small occasional changes in the location of the fronts of the rectangular signals used to transfer digital signals. As a result of jitter, sound counts come unevenly over time. Jitter is caused by the instability of clock generators and of phasal frequency auto-adjustment systems (when selecting the synchronization signal from the serial flow of digital data).

It is hard to explain how jitter is heard. In any case, it may affect the perception of the sound. In analog devices, there is also an event similar to jitter called *detonation* (uncontrolled changing of the magnetic tape's speed, which makes the sound "float").

If you use the external analog-digital converter linked to the sound card through the S/PDIF interface, you won't face any of the consequences of jitter. In practice, jitter's effects can be noticed only if several digital devices are connected one after another.

However, unlike analog detonation, they can be completely removed. This is done by introducing a synchronizing signal that is common to all studio devices. One of these devices can be the source of the synchronizing signal. This device is called the *master*. Other devices, called *slaves*, disable their own generator and use the synchronizing signal of the master device. Such a synchronization system is called *master-clock*.

Of course, even if master-clock synchronizing is applied, the phase of the synchronizing signal may tremble. However, this trembling is synchronous for all devices, and the order of digital data describing the sound does depend on this trembling. Finally, all zeros and ones are put in the correct order on a CD (even if they are not ideally uniform). The data read from a CD is first loaded into a buffer, and then transferred to the input of the digital-analog converter. High-stability generators are used for this purpose. The quality of the signal is completely the CD player manufacturer's responsibility.

In a PC-based virtual studio, the only place where jitter can appear is in the analog-digital converter of the sound card. But the problem of a high quality analog-digital converter has no relation to digital mastering performed using a PC. If the digital part of your studio consists of a PC, a modern sound card, and a CD-R(W) drive with the IDE or SCSI interface, you need not worry about jitter.

22.2.6. Digital and Analog Equalizers

An equalizer is basically a set of filters. From the sound engineer's point of view, the main disadvantage of filters is that they cause phase distortions. As we know from the theory of digital filter synthesis, they can be designed so as not to allow any phase distortions at all. But this is theory, and in practice the quality of software-implemented digital filters can differ. We cannot say that any digital equalizer is better than an analog equalizer, and the statement to the contrary is also wrong. We should compare the sound of particular models of analog equalizers with the sound of specific versions of software-implemented digital equalizers. The only thing we can add is that at the stage of designing analog and digital equalizers, different mathematical methods are used. That's why there is no need to programmatically model the processes that take place in the circuits of analog equalizers.

22.2.7. Digital and Analog Dynamic Processing Devices

The dependence of the output signal level on the input signal level is determined by the *transfer characteristic*. However, it does not completely determine the device's behavior.

The most important parameters are the *attack time* and the *release time*. During these periods of time, the device examines the level of the signal. Indeed, the average signal level is continuously calculated within the time intervals $[t-t_a, t]$ and $[t-t_r, t]$, where t_a is the attack time, and t_r is the release time. The most interesting fact is that digital devices do not need time to examine the signal level. The value of each sound measurement can be calculated according to the formula $b = f(a)$, where a is the count value at input, b is the calculated count value at the digital compressor output, and f is the transfer function of the digital compressor. Nevertheless, there are no digital devices or audio dynamic processing software without the attack time and release time parameters.

Thus, in digital dynamic processing devices, the average values of the signal level at the assigned intervals of time are calculated. These devices operate not with separate sound measurements but with the average level of the output signal. We can say that the attack time and the release time parameters have artistic value. Attack and release are the most important features in forming our perception of musical timbres. Dynamic processing devices affect these parameters. However, during mastering, you cannot influence the sound of separate timbres, since that will affect the features of the entire recording. For example, if a short attack is set for the compressor, it will react too fast—the attack phases of the instruments will be smoothed out, and the recording will be a bit amorhpous.

If the compressor attack lasts for a long time, it cannot react to sharp changes of the signal level when sounds appear. The recording will contain sharp peaks and valleys in the signal level. Everything would be a lot easier if the recording didn't contain drum sounds, since their short attacks are also very loud. You'll just have to experiment.

As for the technology used for audio dynamic processing, there is no principal difference between digital and analog methods. However, if your recording is already digitized, there should be no digital-analog-digital conversion. One more DA-AD conversion means at least truncation and jitter at the same time.

Programs and devices that work in real time can work only with information on the current and previous values of the signal. Although dynamic processing programs cannot operate in real time, they have many advantages. They keep the information on the entire recording being processed, since the sound file is completely in their hands. However, not all programs know how to work with this information. However, the dynamic processing processor of the Cool Edit Pro editor has the **Lookahead Time** parameter, which determines the period of time that you should "look ahead" when analyzing the signal level in the current position of the recording. By selecting the parameters accurately, you can, for example, make the compressor decrease its transfer ratio before the signal level sharply increases. In this way, you can avoid clipping completely. Real-time programs and devices do not have this ability. Of course, all analog compressors operate only in real time.

22.3. Compatibility of the Recording with Playback Equipment

22.3.1. Mono Compatibility

Mono compatibility is the compatibility of the stereophonic recording with monophonic equipment. Incompatibility arises when the signals in the left and right channels have a phase opposite from one another. When the recording is played on equipment incompatible with it, the signals of the left and right channels are added, and the audio waves with opposite phases annul each other. Thus some sounds become inaudible. If you cannot catch the mono incompatibility by ear, you can use special measuring devices. One such device is implemented as a DirectX plug-in module, and is described in *Section 24.2.4*.

It is too late to avoid mono incompatibility if you are already at the mastering stage. All you can do is note the problem, or possibly cause it by incorrectly using devices or software that widen the stereo image of the recording. We will describe these problems too.

You should aim towards mono compatibility during all the stages of creating music that come before mastering. In a PC-based studio, there are two main sources of mono-incompatibility: samples and effects that widen the stereo base.

22.3.2. Compatibility of the Recording with Playing Equipment of Different Classes; the Spectral Balance of the Recording

One problem that is more complicated than mono compatibility is the problem of compatibility with equipment of different quality. Situations may arise where a recording sounds great in the studio, but terrible when played in the usual devices. Besides which, television sets and FM tuners have their own specific features of translating sound. Some experts recommend that you make several variants of the mastered piece, each for its type of reproduction. Our opinion is that there should be only one copy of the recording, and it should sound adequate in different environments—at home, on the radio, on TV, etc.

The problem of the incompatibility of the recording with cheap devices usually appears when talking about the region of low frequencies. Most of the energy of the signal is concentrated in the region of 20—80 Hz. In studio monitors, the bass sounds dense and springy, but this is not heard in cheap, low-end devices. In the recording, there is thus no space left for the middle and high frequencies that can be reproduced in cheap devices, since the information on the bass is physically present in the recording, and it takes up real resources. As a result, the sound is not very clear at all.

The main method used to provide compatibility with low-end devices is to balance the spectrum of the recording. In this case, it means even distribution of the energy between the frequencies. On the spectrum indicator of a stereo system, a balanced recording looks as follows: the peaks of all columns are near one line parallel to the horizon. If you do not have a stereo system but do have a SB Live! sound card, you can use the Surround Mixer spectrum indicator supplied with the SB Live! software.

The human ear has non-linear properties, and the concept of "loudness" is subjective: the human ear perceives signals with the same amplitude but with different frequency as signals having a different loudness. And, signals with the same loudness but with different amplitude may be heard as signals with equal loudness. The curves of signals of equal loudness, obtained through experimenting, are shown in Fig. 22.15. Each of these curves correspond to a certain level of sound pressure of a standard sound at a frequency of 1 kHz.

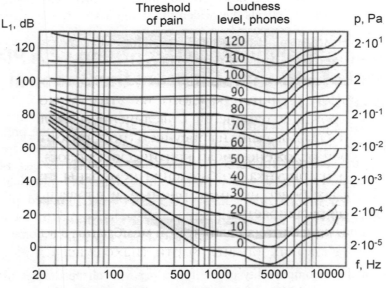

Fig. 22.15. Curves of signals of equal loudness

Look at the graphs. To make a signal with a frequency of 100 Hz sound as loud as a signal with a frequency of 1 kHz, its level must be higher by a certain amount of decibels. In some spectrum analyzers, such as Surround Mixer supplied with the SB Live! software, this feature of the human ear is considered, while in others (the spectrum analyzer of Cool Edit Pro) it is not.

Fig. 22.16 shows one possible spectral shape of a recording balanced by frequency. Fig. 22.17 shows one possible spectral shape of a recording not balanced by frequency. The non-balanced recording does not mean that it is a "bad" recording. Its sound is great when its played in expensive devices, but in cheap devices it lacks the high frequencies.

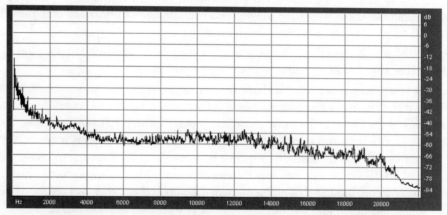

Fig. 22.16. Possible spectral shape of a recording balanced by frequency

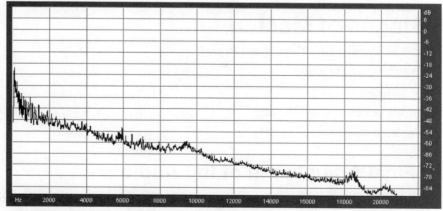

Fig. 22.17. Possible spectral shape of a recording not balanced by frequency

Ideally, the problem of the compatibility of the recording with cheap home devices must be solved at the mixing stage by selecting the timbres. If it is too late though, the first thing you can do is to adjust the controls of the equalizer. However, the equalizer only allows you to suppress or amplify the components of the signal within a certain range of frequencies; you cannot "move" them to another range of frequencies. Then there is the phenomenon of psycho-acoustics. When you listen to the sound of a bass guitar from a small speaker that cannot reproduce low frequencies, you cannot hear the main frequency corresponding to the played note, but your brain, by analyzing the higher harmonics it hears, restores this frequency. The played note is restored, even though you don't hear it! Thus, to make the low frequencies that aren't reproduced on certain cheap equipment heard, you can generate the corresponding high-frequency harmonics. The form of the signal (and its spectrum) will be distorted, but the listener does not care how the source signal sounds. Those who have the high-end equipment can hear not only these harmonics, but also the source signal as well.

The problem of the sound of low frequencies is solved using the well-known plug-in module Waves MaxxBass (*Section 24.1*), so far without serious competition.

Sometimes it really does make sense to have different mastered versions. For example, for home use, you can make the recording longer, and if it is intended for the radio or TV, shorter (standard duration is 4 minutes). If the same recording is played with a different loudness, the listener notes that the louder version sounds better. This secret is well-known. As a result, many recordings for the radio and TV are loud and expressive. However, after listening to music with a dynamic range of 10 dB for 30 minutes, the listener gets tired. Making the dynamic range wider is not the best way to get around this problem—when compared to other recordings, your recording would sound too quiet, and the listener will not pay enough attention to it. Maybe the only way to make your music notable is to compose outstanding music?

22.4. Stages of Mastering

Mastering can be divided into three main stages:

- Final adjustment of the audio
- Assembly editing
- Audio output in the required format

Now we'll describe these stages in detail.

22.4.1. Final Adjustment of the Audio

At the stage of the audio's final adjustment, two main actions—frequency correction and dynamic processing—are performed. The characteristics of the sound greatly depend on the order in which the processing is performed—first by the compressor and then by the equalizer, or vice versa. You can do some experimenting and listen to the results when you process in both orders. It is convenient to perform these experiments using the T-RackS software by IK Multimedia Production, which we will describe in detail in *Chapter 23*. In this program, there is a special button that allows you to change the processing order. The processing is done in real time, so you can feel the difference at once.

If instead of the traditional compressor (even if it is implemented as software) you use psycho-acoustic processing programs to increase the subjective loudness, such as **LoudnessMaximizer** by Steinberg (see *Section 24.2.2*), they should be applied last, and there should be no more processing done after that.

Equalization and compression are the basic types of processing, but they are not the only ones. We must mention such types of processing as changing the stereo image, or creating an effect of 3D sound. (This just means *widening the stereo base*.) There are many algorithms for widening the stereo base, and while the vendors try to keep them secret, they all come down to working with the signal phase. One gets the impression that 99% of modern music played over the radio is processed this way. So, whether you like it or not, you have to widen the stereo base. Otherwise, in the stream of music that flows from an FM radio, your composition will sound one-dimensional. But widening the stereo base during mastering is not the best solution. You should use this type of processing in the mixing stage: make the sound of some instruments dimensional, while others remain flat, but in the end they should all be correctly panned. So you see, application of this effect, too, is creative work.

22.4.2. Assembly Editing

During assembly editing, musical compositions are ordered with the assigned intervals between them (or without them). If it becomes necessary, the beginnings and/or ends of the compositions fade to silence (the fade in and fade out operations).

22.4.3. Output in the Required Format

Normally, CD Digital Audio (CD-DA) is the required format. In this case, everything is clear: you put the blank disk into a CD Recorder, drag the WAV files (future tracks) into the image of the disk in the special program, and press the record button.

CD-DA can be recorded by one of two methods.

❏ Track-at-Once—laser is turned on and off to record each of the tracks. Tracks may be separated by pauses of 2 or 3 seconds, or can follow one another without pauses. In practice, we encountered clicks during the playback of disks recorded in the Track-at-Once mode without pauses between the tracks. The advantage of this method is the ability to record additional tracks when it becomes necessary (if the disk is not closed). This recording method is supported by all CD-R(W) drives. The disadvantage of this method is the inability to program the duration of pauses for most CD-R(W) drives.

❏ Disc-at-Once—all the tracks are recorded to a clean disk without turning off the laser; the disk must be closed. Not all CD-R(W) drives support this mode. The advantage of this method is the ability to program pauses (if this ability is supported by the software). Its disadvantage is the inability to add tracks.

The quality of CD-DA recording is determined by a number of parameters. One of these parameters is the Block Error Rate—BLER—when reading blocks of information from the disk. The errors are found and corrected by the applied Reid-Solomon method of data storage on CD-DA. Some errors cannot be found and corrected. A small number of errors found generally means that there are not many errors. The "Red Book" standard developed by Philips and Sony for CD-DA states that the value of the BLER parameter can not exceed 220. For the worst models of modern CD-R(W) drives and clean disks, the value of the BLER parameter is about 100 in the central part, and about 200 on the periphery. You cannot determine this value without special equipment. However, if you are seriously interested in the recording quality of your disks, you can find various publications and test results for many popular models of CD-R(W) drives on the Internet.

When the recording is manufactured professionally, additional requirements to the quality and the format of the master disk arise. The requirements might be as follows:

❏ The disk must be recorded only according to the Disk-at-Once method

❏ A BLER parameter whose value is significantly less than the "Red Book" standard requires should be specified

However, nowadays you can usually find a company that will accept your information for further distribution in any format—it is only a question of how much you're willing to pay.

As you have seen, the CD-DA format is not so perfect. This format was developed rather long ago, when the technologies available were not that advanced. Though an audio CD's nature is digital, it does not mean that the information you read from this disk bit by bit is the same as the information recorded onto it. More reliable encoding could be applied, but this would require that you significantly increase the size of the disk or reduce the duration of the recording. At that time, there was no way to increase the density of the recording.

If you want to ensure that your music is read in the same way as you have recorded it, you should use CD-ROM, and not the CD-DA format, since the CD-ROM format is specifically intended for computer data storage. This format uses reliable encoding with a high surplus. In CD-ROM, you cannot fit as much material in WAV files as you can in CD-DA (the duration is less), but this is not the end of the world.

Chapter 23: Mastering with T-RackS 24

There are a great many applications for sound processing, and even more plug-in modules. But there are not very many programs optimized exclusively for mastering. We managed to find only one—T-RackS (**http://www.t-racks.com**), from IK Multimedia Production. Here we'll describe version 2.0 of this program, also known as T-RackS 24.

T-RackS is a real-time software sound processor used for mastering. The following components are included in this program:

❏ Six-band parametric equalizer

❏ Soft compressor (emulation of a tube compressor, plus a stereo base widening device)

❏ Three-band spectral limiter

T-RackS is based on the principles of mathematically modeling the schematics of real analog sound processing devices. Mathematical models of the processes that take place in electric circuits are converted into digital signal processing algorithms.

We must mention that using this program does not guarantee the best sound quality. T-RackS simply provides the classical set of devices for mastering, implemented as software. Which device to use and with which parameters is up to the individual. If you don't know how to correctly use these devices, you might very well ruin the sound.

After mixing, you have a WAV file. Processing this file with T-RackS should be the last stage in adjusting the sound.

If you want to apply such effects as reverberation, various spectral enhancers, exciters, and so on to your recording, you should do it before using T-RackS. Any dynamic processing (including programs that increase the relative loudness) or dithering and noise shaping algorithms should be applied neither before nor after processing your recording in T-RackS. Before you load a WAV file into T-RackS, it is recommended that you perform only one operation—normalization at a level of −0.1 dB, and only if the initial peak level of the signal is less than −6 dB.

The general view of the **T-RackS 2.0** window is shown in Fig. 23.1. Find the **?** button in the lower part of the window and press it. A tip on the devices and their controls appear in the right upper corner of the window. To see a tip for another device, place the mouse cursor above any of the controls. This makes learning how to work with the program much easier.

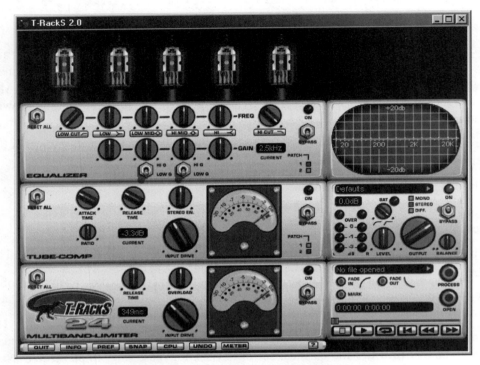

Fig. 23.1. General view of the T-RackS window

The T-RackS window recalls a device that consists of several modules. Let's describe them, from top to bottom.

In the upper part, we see flashing radio lamps. Their flashing depends on the program settings and the load on virtual devices.

EQUALIZER is the equalizer module. To the right of this device is the **SCOPE** device. Its function is to display the amplitude-frequency response of the equalizer. Values along its horizontal axis are in Hz, and the values along its vertical axis are in dB.

Under the equalizer we see the **TUBE COMP** (tube compressor). To the right of it, there is the output signal module (**OUTPUT STAGE**).

The multiband limiter (**MULTIBAND-LIMITER**) is located under the compressor. There are no controls for any parameters for different frequency bands. This device is semi-automatic. You can control only the value of three main parameters. All the remaining settings are assigned by the program so that the frequency balance is preserved in the signal processed by the limiter.

To the right of the limiter, we have the **CONTROL PANEL** module.

The lower module is called the **CONSOLE**, which is basically a button menu.

We'll start learning the program from the control panel.

23.1. Control Panel

The control panel is shown in Fig. 23.2. The two main buttons that start and stop the operation of the program are located in the control panel. Use the **Open** button to open the audio file you get after mixing.

Fig. 23.2. Control panel

The open file window is shown in Fig. 23.3.

Fig. 23.3. Window for opening a file

This panel differs from the standard open file panel in the presence some additional options. If the **Preview** checkbox is checked, the files that have been selected but not yet loaded are played. You can stop playback with the **Stop** button.

In the **Use Preset** list, you can select a preset—a number of preliminary settings that are used for previewing. You can add your own presets to this list. If the **As mono** checkbox is ticked, the preview is monophonic.

Two types of audio files are supported: WAV and AIF (or AIFF). Note that, unlike previous versions, T-RackS 2.0 supports 24-bit files. The format of the selected file is displayed above the **Use Preset** list.

If the source audio file has a 16-bit format, it makes no sense to convert it into 24-bit format before processing it in T-RackS. All T-RackS effects work in real time using 32-bit representation of signals, and there are no intermediate results. Thus it is guaranteed that there will be no truncating during the processing.

We have to make one important note about opening a file. There is no "loading" of a file, and a copy of the file is not created in the working directory. The file remains in its initial location. After the file is opened, T-RackS does not make changes to it. The file is read-only, and T-RackS won't allow you to make any changes to a file it opens. The mastering results are saved in a separate file that you specify. By default, its name is created as follows: the source filename, plus "master".

Open any WAV file and work with control panel shown in Fig. 23.2. In the lower part of the panel, you'll see the deck—a set of buttons for controlling the playback:

■—**Stop** button

▶—**Play** button

⟳—looped playback button

◀◀|—button for moving to the beginning of the file

◀◀—"rewind" button, with stops at marked spots (if they are present)

▶▶—"fast forward" button, with stops at marked spots

To add marks during playback, the **Mark** button is used.

On the `0:00:18 0:03:32 M6 0:02:50` indicator, the following data are displayed in the Hour:Minute:Second format: the current position, the duration of the file's playback, and then the number of the current mark (**M6** means "mark No. 6") and its position. If the looped playback mode is enabled, and the beginning and the end of the loop have been selected with the mouse, the beginning and the ending positions of the looped part are displayed instead of the position of the current mark. The loop's beginning is indicated as **SL** (Start Loop), and the loop's end is indicated as **EL** (End Loop). By default, the beginning and the end of the loop are the same as the beginning and the end of file.

The ▬▬▬▬▬ slider is convenient for changing the current position in the file. Marks are indicated as triangles above the line along which it moves. Using the mouse, you can select the current mark and move it to another place. To delete a mark, select it, and then press the <Delete> key.

During the looped playback, the appearance of the slider changes: the beginning and the end of the loop are displayed on it: ▬▬▬▬▬. Using the mouse, you can move the boundaries of the loop.

The **Fade In** and **Fade Out** buttons call the panels shown in Fig. 23.4.

Fig. 23.4. The **Fade In** (*a*) and **Fade Out** (*b*) panels

Using these panels, you control the volume's smooth increase (**Fade In**) at the beginning of the recording, and its smooth decrease (**Fade Out**) at the end of the recording. In the **FADE OUT TIME** and **FADE IN TIME** fields, the effect's time is specified. You can change the values of these parameters in two ways. You can move the numeric field horizontally using the mouse. The field itself remains in its position, but its value changes. Another way is to double-click on the field and to input the value from the keyboard.

Next are the buttons for selecting the effect type (linear and non-linear increase/decrease in volume). When the volume is changed non-linearly, the sound is more natural. The effect is not enabled until one of these buttons is pushed. When the effect is on, the corresponding button on the control panel is lit up. You can also move the **Fade In** and **Fade Out** panels. They are closed by pressing the **CLOSE** button.

In the `Track01` field, the name of the opened audio file is displayed. If you click on the arrow located in the right part of this field, a menu containing three items—**Load**, **Save**, and **Auto On** or **Auto Off**—will open. Using the **Save** and **Load** commands, you can save and load the settings of the control panel in special files. You cannot change the filenames of these files. They have the same names as the audio file you have opened. But their extension is not WAV or AIF, but TRS (T-RackS Session). These files are located in the same directory as the opened audio file. If the **Auto** option is **On**, the corresponding file of the control panel settings is loaded automatically when the audio file is opened.

23.2. Equalizer

The equalizer module is shown in Fig. 23.5.

Fig. 23.5. Equalizer module

The equalizer consists of six filters:

LOW CUT—high-frequency filter (suppresses low frequencies)

LOW—band/rejecting filter of low frequencies

LOW MID—band/rejecting filter of low frequencies

HI MID—band/rejecting filter of high frequencies

HI—band/rejecting filter of high frequencies

HI CUT—low-frequency filter (suppresses high frequencies)

Each of the six filters has its own regulator of either the cutoff frequency or central frequency of the band (**FREQ**). Under each of these regulators, you'll see shutdown button (with the name of the corresponding filter). The **GAIN** regulators allow you to change the extent of amplification/suppression of the signal by band/rejecting filters.

Notice the **CURRENT** field. In this field, the value of the parameter you change is displayed. To turn the T-RackS regulator to its default state, right-click on it.

The quality level of the **LOW MID** and **HI MID** filters can be changed using the **HI Q/LOW Q** tumbler. The **HI Q** position corresponds to high quality, and the **LOW Q** position means low quality.

The **PATCH** switch changes the order of the virtual devices: position **1**—first equalizer processing, then compressor processing; position **2**—the reverse order. The order affects the sound.

The **RESET ALL** tumbler resets all the settings made. The **BYPASS** switch turns the equalizer on. By default it is off, so the signal bypasses the equalizer.

To the right of the equalizer, we see the virtual screen (**SCOPE**), shown in Fig. 23.6. This is the device that displays the amplitude-frequency response of the equalizer.

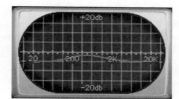

Fig. 23.6. The **SCOPE** module

23.3. Compressor

The compressor module is shown in Fig. 23.7.

Fig. 23.7. Compressor module

The classical soft tube compressor allows you to control the following parameters:

❏ **ATTACK TIME**

❏ **RELEASE TIME**

❏ **RATIO**—compression ratio

❏ **INPUT DRIVE**—signal amplification at the compressor input

❏ **STEREO EN.**—widening the stereo base

Note that there is no Threshold parameter (the level of the input signal at which the compressor starts). The reason for this is that the compressor will operate at any level of the signal; the compression, however, is not constant, but dependent on this level. The T-RackS compressor operates the same way as would a soft compressor (Fig. 23.8). By changing the **RATIO** parameter, you change the slope of the transfer characteristic.

We must specially mention the ability to widen the stereo base. This effect is easily heard. Even after applying this effect, the mono compatibility of the recording is retained. After you have applied this effect, the instruments sound like they have been moved in different directions from the center. The sound seems to surround you.

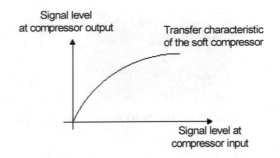

Fig. 23.8. General view of the transfer characteristic of the T-RackS compressor

The arrow indicator displays the actual compression level in decibels (how much the signal level is lowered by the compressor). When the level of the actual compression is increased, the arrow moves from the right to the left. The arrow in the rightmost position indicates the minimum effect of the compressor upon the signal (the compression is too low and/or the level of the input signal is too low). When the arrow is in the leftmost position, it indicates the maximum effect of the compressor upon the signal (the compression is too high and/or the level of the input signal is too high). As usual, you should find the best variant in between the two extremes.

❏ **PATCH**—the order in which the compressor and the equalizer are used

❏ **BYPASS**—turning the compressor off (it is off by default)

❏ **RESET ALL**—reset all the settings

23.4. Multiband Limiter

The module of the multiband limiter is shown in Fig. 23.9.

Fig. 23.9. Multiband limiter module

The main parameters of the limiter module are: **RELEASE TIME** and **INPUT DRIVE** (amplification of the input signal).

OVERLOAD is the parameter that defines the level of the signal at which the limiter starts. The lower the value of this parameter, the more often the limiter starts, and the lower is the possibility of clipping. The higher the value of this parameter, the more clipping is possible. Constant limitation of the signal at a small level is bad, as well as is too much clipping. In most cases, a value of 0 dB for **OVERLOAD** is adequate.

BYPASS means tuning the limiter off (it is off by default). **RESET ALL** resets all the settings.

The arrow indicator displays the decrease in the signal level caused by the limiter.

23.5. Input Signal Module

After processing by the equalizer, the compressor (or, vice versa, by the compressor and then the equalizer), and the limiter, the signal arrives at the input of the output signal module (**OUTPUT STAGE**) shown in Fig. 23.10. Here the signal is finally processed, since it is in this module that the algorithm of analog clipping is implemented.

Fig. 23.10. Input signal module

The clipping algorithm operates as follows. In the region of 0 dB, the signal is smoothly limited. The "smoothness" of the limiting depends on the position of the **SAT** regulator. If it is in the rightmost position, then the algorithm operates like the algorithm of a hard limiter; in the leftmost position the algorithm operates like the algorithm of a soft compressor.

LEVEL is the signal amplification at the module input. The higher the signal level at the input, the more the chance of clipping. The big red light is lit when the clipping algorithm starts.

If the level of the input signal is so high that it cannot be limited smoothly, the **OVER** indicators on the four-segment indicators of the output signal level are lit. If this is the case, actual digital clipping takes place.

OUTPUT is the output signal level. By increasing the value of this parameter, you can simply add the digital clipping.

Using the **MONO**, **STEREO**, and **DIFF.** options, you switch between playback modes: monophonic, stereophonic (default), and the monophonic mode as the difference between the signals of the stereo channels. Using this switch, you can easily check your recording for mono compatibility (**MONO** mode), as well as hear which components of the sound disappear when the recording is played on mono devices (**DIFF.** mode).

The **BYPASS** tumbler turns off all the functions of T-RackS, and you can compare the sound of the recording before and after mastering. If you are still not satisfied with the quality of the sound, you need to do some more work. If it is OK, you can save your work using the **PROCESS** button on the control panel (*Section 22.2.1*) and create the material for your CD. But this is done using other programs.

There are many built-in settings for mastering in different styles.

In the upper part of the module we see the ▭Defaults▭ ▶ field. After clicking on it, a large list of presets for different modules is opened. You can tell to which device a preset belongs by its name. If the name starts with COMP, the preset is used for the compressor; EQ means a preset used for the equalizer; LIM indicates that the preset belongs to the limiter; OUTPUT designates a preset of the output signal module; and SUITE means a preset for all modules. For example, the SUITE—FM Broadcast preset contains settings for the program that masters an FM radio recording. Of course, these settings can be effectively applied only if the source recording has not been dynamically processed, if it has adequate volume, and if its spectrum is already balanced.

In the right part of the preset select field there is a small triangle. If you click on it, a menu appears containing the following commands:

❑ **Load**—load program settings from file

❑ **Save**—save settings

❑ **Save As...**—load in the file with the assigned name

❑ **Delete**—delete the current preset file

23.6. Console

The console (Fig. 23.11) contains a number of buttons.

Fig. 23.11. Console

The first two buttons are **QUIT** (quit the program) and **INFO** (information on the program). We also see the **PREF** button, which calls the system settings panel (Fig. 23.12).

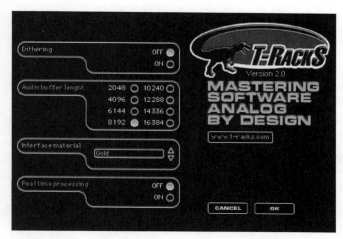

Fig. 23.12. Panel of the program's system settings

The options below are available.

Dithering—dithering enabling (ON) and disabling (OFF).

Audio buffer length—specify the audio data buffer size (the less the size the better, if there are no clicks during playback).

Interface material—interface appearance (the so-called *skin*). There are a large number of skins available, including even "used".

Real time processing—when this option is enabled, the recording is saved to the disk while it is being played and processed in real-time mode using the **PROCESS** command. This means that you can correct the processing parameters directly when the master audio file is being recorded.

The **SNAP** button (Fig. 23.13) located on the panel calls a tool that allows you to save (using the **TAKE** button) all the current processing parameters in temporary memory (up to eight presets), and then to call them quickly when necessary. Each shot of the processing parameters corresponds to one of the LEDs numbered 1 through 8. The **RESET** button deletes all shots from memory. To delete a certain shot, drag its LED outside the instrument using the mouse. The **CLOSE** button closes the SNAP tool.

The **CPU** button on the console calls the CPU load indicator (Fig. 23.14).

Using the **UNDO** button, you cancel any of your previous actions related to changing the processing parameters. If you press this button twice, the previous state is restored.

Fig. 23.13. The **SNAP** tool

Fig. 23.14. Processor load indicator   **Fig. 23.15.** Peak indicator of the signal level

Of course, such a serious mastering program as T-RackS has a level indicator. It is called by the **METER** button on the console (Fig. 23.15).

The limits within which you can change the signal level by the peak indicator are from −72 dB to 0 dB. The **x10** option changes the measurement limits: from −7.2 dB to 0 dB. Using this option, you can see in detail what happens to the level of the signal near 0 dB.

HOLD—don't lose the marks for the peak values of the signal level.

This is basically all the general information about the T-RackS program, a tool that is simple to work with, yet very powerful. We have not provided any recommendations as to which controls to use, or when and how to use them. Mastering is creative work, and it does not have any exact algorithms.

We must mention that the final signal processing should be performed in T-RackS. This means that after T-RackS, you cannot perform frequency processing, dynamic processing, or other types of processing. All you can do with the files you get as a result of operating with this program is write them to a CD.

Chapter 24: DirectX Plug-Ins Useful for Mastering

There are many various DirectX plug-ins. New modules appear very often, and we don't have enough room to describe them all. In this chapter, we'll look at some of these plug-ins that are used for mastering. They are not the latest ones, but they work adequately.

24.1. Using Waves MaxxBass to Provide Compatibility of the Recording with Low Quality Equipment

If you have not read this book from the very beginning, and skipped *Section 22.1.3*, it is high time to turn to it. This section will explain exactly what the Waves MaxxBass plug-in is for.

This module is used to generate harmonics of low frequency audio components in order to provide for the compatibility of the recording with low-quality audio reproducing equipment. Such equipment cannot reproduce low frequency components. The Waves MaxxBass module also allows you to achieve frequency balance in the lower part of the spectrum. We recommend that you use this plug-in in the beginning stages of mastering. If you decide to process the recording using MaxxBass, it is better to do it just after mixing.

The Waves MaxxBass version 2.3.5 plug-in window called from the Cool Edit Pro editor is shown in Fig. 24.1.

Even if you thoroughly learn the plug-in window, it is not so easy to understand its operating principles. However, after analyzing the functional abilities of Waves MaxxBass, we can create the substitution scheme shown in Fig. 24.2.

The level of the input signal is set by the **Input** regulator. During processing, the signal level can increase significantly. We recommend that you set the **Input** regulator to −6 dB.

The signal given to the module input arrives to the crossover, where the signal spectrum is split into high-frequency and low-frequency bands. The splitting frequency of the crossover bands depends on the position of the **Freq** regulator . It can vary, and be anywhere from 32 Hz to 256 Hz. The high-frequency components of the source signal arrive at the module output unchanged.

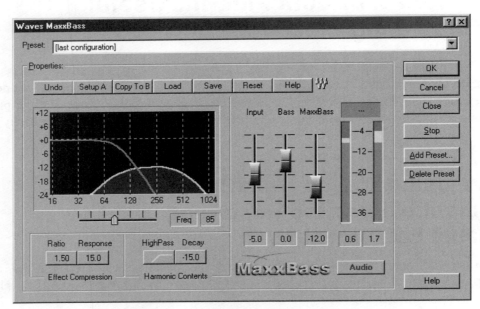

Fig. 24.1. Waves MaxxBass plug-in window

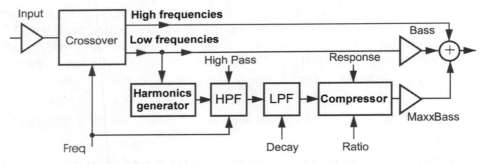

Fig. 24.2. Signal processing using Waves MaxxBass

The level of the low-frequency components transferred to the total mix depends on the position of the **Bass** regulator. The same low-frequency signal is sent to the harmonics generator, and after that, having been enriched with harmonics, it passes through the high-pass filter. The cutoff frequency of this filter is controlled by the same **Freq** regulator that is used to control the splitting frequency of the crossover bands. This is how the harmonics are separated from the low-frequency source signal. The slope of the amplitude-frequency response of the filter is set by pressing the **High Pass** button in the **Harmonic Contents** group multiple times. The signal then passes through the low-pass filter, where the unnecessary high-frequency harmonics are cut off. The decay slope of the amplitude frequency response of the filter is set in the **Decay** field.

As a result of these transformations, a signal with a limited spectrum is formed. The spectrum consists of the harmonics of the low-frequency source signal. The specific feature of the signal is that its energy is concentrated above the **Freq** frequency. If you set the **Freq** frequency equal to the lower boundary of the acoustic system range, you can make non-audible low-frequency harmonics components audible. To emphasize this effect, the signal processed by the above method is compressed. The parameters of the compressor are set in the **Effect Compression** group: **Ratio** is the compression ratio, and **Response** is the compressor attack time and the release time in milliseconds.

In the general mix, the level of the processed signal is determined by the position of the **MaxxBass** regulator.

The main controls are **Freq** and **MaxxBass**. The normal position of the **MaxxBass** regulator is from −18 to −8 dB, depending on the recording. The crossover splitting frequency (**Freq**) is usually within a range from 50 Hz to 90 Hz. When selecting the value of this parameter, the developers recommend that you consider the following values:

❐ 110 Hz for multimedia acoustic systems with 3-inch speakers

❐ 90 Hz for TV sound

❐ 80 Hz for radio sound

After experimenting with these two regulators, you can start fine-tuning the effect: selecting the parameters of the filter and the compressor.

In the module, we have an indicator of the peak signal level. In case of overload (clipping), the rectangular field above this indicator becomes red. To make it green again (normal level), click on it.

There is a useful switch that looks like a button under the level indicator. By default, it is in the **Audio** state, and you hear the normal sound of the recording processed by MaxxBass. When this switch is in the **MaxxBass** state, you hear only the signal generated by the plug-in (the MaxxBass effect itself). If it is in the **OrigBass** state, you hear only the signal from the low-frequency output of the crossover (original bass). By comparing the sound of all these modes, you can better understand how each plug-in works. It helps in more precise tuning.

You also have the ability to visually control the module settings (Fig. 24.3). The amplitude-frequency response of the crossover low-pass filter is blue in the coordinate plane. The amplitude-frequency response of both filters used for low-frequency signal harmonics processing is yellow.

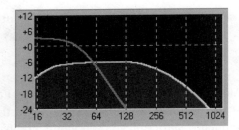

Fig. 24.3. Amplitude-frequency response of filters

If you don't yet understand how the plug-in operates, but still want to apply it, don't try experimenting—use the built-in presets. You can call the list of presets by pressing the **Load** button. In the future, you'll save your own plug-in settings using the **Save** button.

Reset resets all settings to the initial state. **Undo** cancels the last change made to the settings.

You can work with two variants of the plug-in settings at the same time. One variant is stored in the A bank, the other in the B bank. You select the current bank using the **Setup A/B** button. Using the **Copy to A/B** button, move the parameters from one bank to another.

24.2. Plug-Ins from the Steinberg Mastering Edition Package

In this section, we won't describe all plug-ins of the Steinberg Mastering Edition package, just those that, according to our experience, affect the quality of the processed materials.

24.2.1. Adjusting the Spectrum of Your Recording to the Spectrum of the Model Recording Using FreeFilter

FreeFilter is an intelligent 30-band equalizer that corresponds to the DirectX standard. Its "intellect" comes from the fact that it can analyze the spectrum of a model recording and provide for the frequency correction of your recording. After this processing, your recording begins to sound like a model recording.

Select a musical composition from an original CD as a model that you feel is close to your music in style and fashion. Grab the recording from the CD and make it into a WAV file. To do this, you should use a special program like AudioGrabber.

Load both recordings—your recording and the model one—into Cool Edit Pro. First, let the FreeFilter module "listen to" the model recording. Open the page with the model recording, and open the FreeFilter window. Turn on the **Learn** and **Source** buttons. Press the **Preview** button. In the preview mode, FreeFilter will remember the spectrum of the model recording (Fig. 42.4).

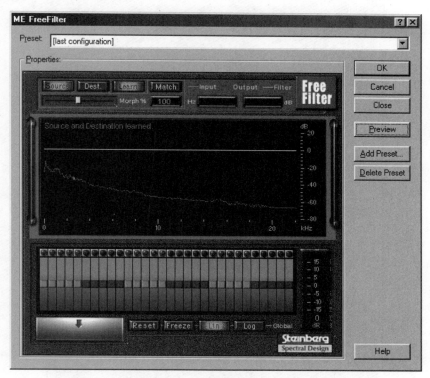

Fig. 24.4. Spectrum analysis of the model recording

When you feel it's enough, stop the preview and close the plug-in window with the **Close** button (not the **OK** or **Cancel** buttons).

Now the FreeFilter module has to "listen to" your recording. Switch to the corresponding page of Cool Edit Pro and open FreeFilter again.

Press the **Dest** and **Learn** buttons in the **FreeFilter** window. Start the playback of your recording using the **Preview** button. FreeFilter remembers its spectrum.

After that, press the **Match** button. FreeFilter calculates the frequency response of the equalizer so that your recording sounds like the model recording (Fig. 24.6).

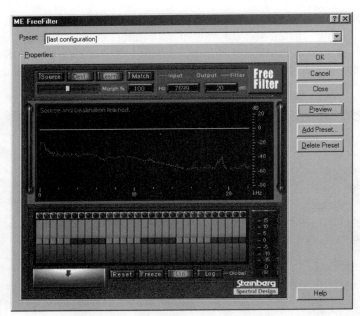

Fig. 24.5. Spectrum analysis of the corrected recording

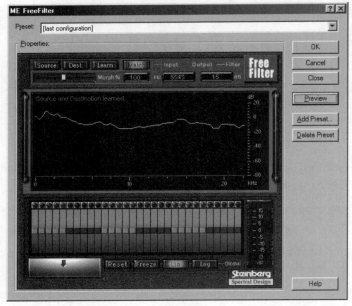

Fig. 24.6. Frequency correction of the recording by the spectrum of the model signal

The graph of the calculated frequency response of the filter is displayed in yellow.

Start the **Preview** again and listen to the recording corrected by the FreeFilter plug-in. If you feel it's OK, press the **OK** button to apply the effect. However, you are able to change the calculated frequency response of the filter if you want.

To do so, move the faders of the 30-band equalizer. If you need to change the response within a wide range of frequencies, it is more convenient to use special tools. Open the "metal lid" located in the lower left corner of the **FreeFilter** window. Under it, you'll see the buttons for three special tools.

The leftmost tool allows you to combine several faders into one group and to move them all at once.

To combine several faders into one group, select the area of the frequency response you want to change using the mouse (Fig. 24.7).

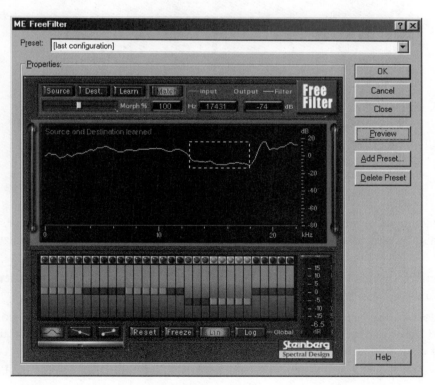

Fig. 24.7. Combining several faders of the equalizer into one group

Now try to move any of the faders located in the assigned area. All of the faders of this area will change their position.

The next tool—the ruler—allows you to change the slope of the amplitude-frequency response within the entire range of frequencies (Fig. 24.8).

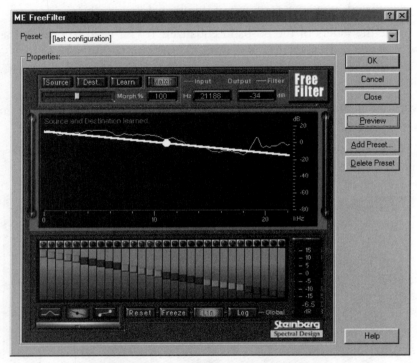

Fig. 24.8. Aligning the equalizer faders with the ruler

The "attachment" point of the ruler is marked by a thick dot. Using the mouse, you can move this dot and rotate the ruler around this attachment point. The equalizer faders trace all the movements of the ruler.

The rightmost tool is also a ruler, but one attached in two points. The attachment points are the ends of the ruler. Working with this tool is shown in Fig. 24.9.

If you do not trust the program, and want to implement manual frequency correction, press the **Reset** button. The frequency response of the equalizer turns into a straight line. You can change it as you like.

The **Lin** and **Log** buttons enable, respectively, the linear and logarithmic modes of the frequency response display.

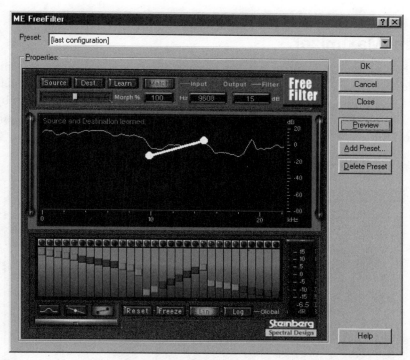

Fig. 24.9. Aligning the group of equalizer faders by the ruler in the assigned section

The **Freeze** button allows you to "freeze" the frequency response remembered by the filter that we got from the **Learn** mode before playing back the entire recording.

After you have selected all the parameter values for the equalizer, press **OK**.

You can also use the FreeFilter plug-in module to smooth out the differences in the sound of the compositions for a future album. Select the composition that you feel has the best sound as the model recording.

Do not overuse the FreeFilter module. In the model recording, other instruments are used, so it is not necessarily the best idea to simply adjust the spectrum of your recording to the spectrum of the model. However, using the FreeFilter module, you can catch bugs in the spectrum of your recording, and correct them using not only FreeFilter, but also any other equalizer. Also, FreeFilter implements a particularly useful function called Morph, whose regulator is located in the FreeFilter window. Using this regulator, you can define how stictly the spectrum of your recording is to be adjusted to the spectrum of the model recording. If you set a low value for the **Morph** parameter, the effect of FreeFilter is moderate.

24.2.2. Increasing the Apparent Loudness Using LoudnessMaximizer

Applying the LoudnessMaximizer plug-in module allows you to significantly increase the apparent loudness of the processed sound (which was preliminarily normalized). No audible distortions are made in the sound timbre. LoudnessMaximizer works by applying a compressor and the limiter that continuously analyze the input signal according to the special algorithm.

Open LoudnessMaximizer (Fig. 24.10) for your recording in Cool Edit Pro.

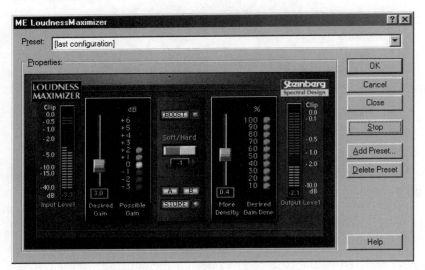

Fig. 24.10. The parameters window of the LoudnessMaximizer plug-in module

Start playback of your recording with the **Preview** button, and start setting up LoudnessMaximizer.

In the left part of the window, you'll see an indicator for the input signal level (**Input Level**). Using the **Desired Gain** regulator, set the desired loudness. While increasing the loudness, look at the **Possible Gain** indicator. The lit column of the indicator must not go below 0 (into the red area).

When the **Boost** option is enabled, the signal is additionally amplified by 2 dB. It is recommended that you use this option only for modern dance music, and only when it is really needed. Using the **Soft/Hard** double button, you can make the sound soft (parameter values from −9 through 0) or hard (0 through 9). It is better to use low values of this parameter when you process classical music. High values are best for jungle or dance music.

The **More/Density** parameter affects the density of the sound. Try to gradually increase the value of this parameter from 0 to 0.4. The higher the value, the more you can increase the loudness (**Desired Gain**). However while increasing the loudness, make sure to keep the sound quality in mind.

The **Desired Gain Done** indicator conditionally displays how much of the desired loudness has been reached. When the values of the **More/Density** parameter are low, the lit column of this indicator must not be over the 50% mark for long. If the values are high, the lit column should be at a level anywhere from 70% to 90%.

The **Output Level** indicator displays the level of the processed signal. It is important not to exceed the 0 dB mark. If this happens, the **Clip** indicator will be lit. Notice that the scale of the **Output Level** indicator starts from −10 dB. The level of the processed signal practically never goes below this mark.

LoudnessMaximizer must be the last effect in the number of processing effects you apply to your recording during mastering.

You could use the multiband equalizer supplied with the Steinberg Mastering Edition software instead of LoudnessMaximizer.

24.2.3. Multiband Compressor

The Compressor plug-in is a multiband compressor. (The maximum number of bands is five.) Its window is shown in Fig. 24.11.

In the left part of the Compressor window, we have a graphic editor. Using this editor, you can change the width of the frequency bands and set the amplification for them. By default, there are three bands. If you need more bands, drag the leftmost or the rightmost node, which indicates the lower or upper boundary of the band, and move it to the center of the graphic image of the frequency bands.

The current band is brighter than other ones. You can select the current band using the mouse. Using the **On/off Solo** button, you can enable **Solo** mode for the current band, and only this band will play. On the right, we see the graphic editor for the transfer ratio of the compressor for the selected frequency band. By default, this characteristic is linear, and the plug-in operates only as a graphic equalizer. Using the mouse, you can draw any transfer characteristic you please (Fig. 24.12).

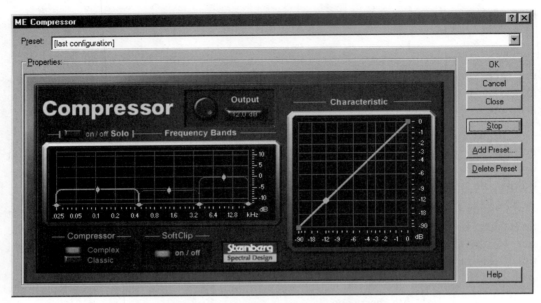

Fig. 24.11. Compressor plug-in window

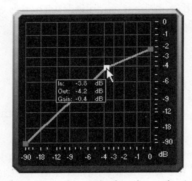

Fig. 24.12. Editor of the transfer ratio for the selected compressor band

The **Output** regulator controls the level of the output signal. The **on/off** button located in the **SoftClip** field enables the soft clipping mode (similar to analog devices).

There are no settings for the attack time and the release time, like there are in classical compressors. The plug-in controls these parameters itself. All you can work with are two buttons that switch the compressor mode. By pressing the **Classic** button, you get the sound of a classic compressor. If you press the **Complex** button, the compressor reacts to the changes of the signal level according to a complex algorithm. As a result, you can get a louder sound with minimal distortions.

24.2.4. Mono Compatibility Control Using PhaseScope

The PhaseScope plug-in (Fig. 24.13) is a software implementation of the control display of the stereo sound. The greater part of its window is occupied by an oscillograph, which displays the phase and the amplitude of a stereo signal in real time. If components with opposite phases are contained in the signal, the picture is stretched.

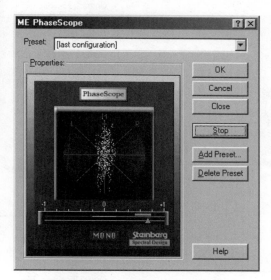

Fig. 24.13. PhaseScope plug-in window

In the lower part of the PhaseScope window, you see the correlation between the left and right stereo channels measured. A value of +1 on its scale corresponds to a monophonic signal. If the arrow of this virtual device is in the green part of the scale, everything is OK. If the arrow is in the red part of the scale, then the recording is not compatible with monophonic equipment.

With this, we yet finish another chapter and the entire book as well.

Index

A

Absolute acoustic level, 11
Acoustic:
    guitar, 94
    level, 17
    power, 8
    signals, 8
Active electronic crossovers, 68
ADSR, 60
Akai disk, 451, 452, 453
Aliasing, 597
Amplification ratio, 254, 255, 268, 269, 312
Amplitude, 8, 245, 246, 253–255, 261, 264–266, 269, 270,
    273–275, 277, 278, 281, 295, 303–309,
    311–314, 317
Amplitude-frequency characteristic, 295, 303–309,
    311–314, 317–320, 322, 323, 331, 336
Analog-to-digital conversion, 44
Anti-formant, 10
Articulation, 492
Attack time, 89, 269, 583, 600
Audibility threshold, 11, 20
Audible sound frequencies, 10
Automatic level stabilizer, 84, 85
Automation, 504, 509, 561, 563–565
Aux buses, 440, 441

B

Band-pass filters, 62
Band-stop filters, 62
Band-pass variation, 64
Bandwidth, 64
Bank:
    samples bank, 460
Bass drums, 93
Bass guitar, 93, 94
Beats, 14, 203, 213, 214, 217, 223, 224
Bessel filter, 78, 322, 323
Binaural effect, 14
Binaural time, 14
Butterworth filter, 78, 322, 323

C

Cakewalk Pro Audio, 290
Capacitors, 72
CD-DA, 54, 605, 606
CD-R(W), 599, 606
Cent, 10
Center channel, 281, 282, 283, 284
Channel mixer, 257, 258, 259, 260, 284
Chebyshev filter, 78, 322, 323

Chorus, 245, 284, 285, 286, 287
Chunks, 354, 356
Clipboard, 203, 204, 205, 206, 207, 208
Clipping, 246, 277, 278, 279, 324, 327, 329, 330
Compound noise suppressors, 84
Compression, 88
Compressor, 23, 85, 578, 579, 582–585, 600, 605, 607, 608,
    612–616
Console, 616–618
Control panel, 609–611, 616
Convolution, 30, 246
Cool Edit Pro, 19, 30, 38, 49, 67, 80, 92, 98
Crossfade, 207, 404, 413
Crossover, 61, 65, 68
Cue list, 210, 217
Current, 8
    spectrum, 31
Cutoff frequency, 60, 64, 295, 311, 312, 527, 528, 530, 537–
    539, 543–547, 549, 550, 555
CV/Gate signals, 503
Cymbals, 95

D

De-esser, 92
Delay, 245, 270, 284, 286, 288, 292, 296, 297
DFT, 47
Digital filters, 72
Digital IIR filters, 72
Digit-to-analog conversion, 43
Discrete Fourier transform, 47
Distortion, 246
Distribution laws, 18
Dithering, 589, 596
DLS, 2, 58
Dynamic level of the acoustic signal, 17
Dynamic processing, 81, 260, 262, 267–272
Dynamic range, 81, 262, 268, 270–272, 579–581, 584, 585,
    596, 597, 604
    compressors, 84
    expanders, 84
    of an acoustic signal, 22
    of the processing channel, 22

E

Echo, 288–290, 296, 298, 346, 356
    chamber, 245, 284, 290
Effects manager, 443, 445
Electric guitar, 94
    power, 8
Envelope, 245, 264–267, 273–277, 333
    generators, 60

Equalizer, 61, 65, 578, 583, 599, 604–608, 612, 614–616
Expander, 85
Exponential weight function, 17

F

Fast Fourier Transform, 48, 62, 326, 330, 334, 339
Favorites, 377–382
Fechner's law of psychophysics, 11
FFT, 48, 62
filter, 246, 301, 302, 308
Filter, 60
    band filter, 527, 555
    finite memory filter, 72
    low frequency filter, 527, 555
    rejecting filter, 527
    order, 77
Filtering, 61
Finite impulse response filters, 72
FIR filters, 72
Flanger, 245, 284, 291, 292
FM synthesis, 55
Formant, 10
Fourier expansion, 24
    integral, 28
    method, 24
    series, 10
    transform, 30, 31
Frequency, 8
Frequency-Modulation synthesis, 55
Fundamental:
    frequency, 28
    tone, 10, 13

G

Gate, 85
Gaussian law, 18
GigaStudio, 55, 416–421, 424, 426, 428, 430–432, 434, 435, 437, 441, 447–449, 452, 454–459
Graphic equalizer, 65
Gyrators, 61

H

Half-tone, 10
Harmonic oscillations, 8
Hearing:
    adaptation, 12
    time constant, 14
High-pass filters, 62
Higher harmonics, 10
Hiss reduction, 246, 324, 330, 331, 333, 334
Histogram, 372, 374, 376

I

IIR filters, 72
Impulse, 342, 344–347
Inductors, 72
Infinite impulse response filters, 72
Instantaneous spectrum, 35
Instrument wizard, 467, 468
Inversion, 245, 247, 248, 260, 292

J

Jitter, 598, 599, 600

L

LFO generators, 60
Limiter, 23, 84, 578, 582–584
    multiband, 614
Loudness, 9
    level, 12
Low-pass filters, 62

M

Macros, 384, 492
Main sequencer, 504, 505, 507, 510, 511, 519, 522, 525, 529, 551, 554, 558, 561–563, 565, 567, 568, 569, 572, 573, 576
Masking, 580, 581
Master-clock synchronizing, 599
Mastering, 23, 578, 584, 585, 589, 593, 595, 596, 599, 600, 601, 604, 605
Microphone, 96
MIDI:
    channel, 427, 431, 432, 433, 434, 450, 452, 459
    controller, 430, 431, 434, 444
    keyboard, 55, 416, 424, 434, 435, 437, 440, 452, 457, 459
    messages, 522, 525, 566, 567, 573, 575
Monaural sound, 9
Mono compatibility, 601
Multilayering, 57
Multisampling, 55
Multitrack View, 396, 397
Musical acoustics, 10

N

NN-19 sampler, 58
Noise, 358, 361–365
    reduction, 246, 324, 330, 331, 333–339
    shaping, 589, 591–593, 596
    suppression, 96
Non-linear hearing properties, 13
Non-recursive digital filter, 73
Non-recursive filters, 72
Normalization, 255, 279, 329
Notch filter, 246, 301, 314–316
Nyquist theorem, 44, 45, 56

O

Octave, 10
Overcompressing, 584
Oversampling, 597
Overtones, 10

P

Parametric equalizer, 67, 246, 301, 317
Partition, 427
Passive crossovers, 68
Patches, 416, 427, 501, 505, 509, 516, 517, 524, 532, 547
Pattern, 521, 522, 540, 548, 549, 554, 561, 562, 564–566, 569–572

Peak factor, 22
Percussion instruments, 95
Period, 8
Periodic function, 24
Phaser, 299, 301
Pitch, 9
    bend, 520
    bender, 246
Plug-in:
    compressor, 629
    freeFilter, 623
    LoudnessMaximizer, 628
    PhaseScope, 631
    Waves MaxxBass, 619
Polynomials, 77
Presence filter, 61, 65
Preset, 320, 323, 326, 348
Probability:
    density, 18
    theory, 18
Program, 418, 420–422, 425–427, 442

Q

Quality factor, 60, 64, 67
Quantization noise, 50, 95, 589, 590, 591, 592, 593
Quasi-maximum:
    level limiters, 84
    value, 20
Quasi-stationary process, 18
QuickSound, 416–418, 424–426, 435, 436, 447, 448, 450,
    451, 454, 455

R

Random:
    functions, 14
    process, 14
RC-circuit, 77
Reason, 58
Recursive filters, 72
Redrum, 499, 516–523, 531, 548, 562, 569, 570
Register, 465–470, 474, 477–480, 482–484, 486, 489, 490,
    495, 496
Release time, 91, 269, 583, 600
Remote control, 507, 511–513, 576
Resolution, 221
Reverberation, 245, 284, 292, 294–299, 345
Rhythm guitar, 94
RLC-circuit, 77
RMS, 16
Root mean square, 16
Routing, 505, 509, 510, 515

S

S/PDIF interface, 54
Sampler, 55, 250
    polyphony, 58
Sampling, 55
SConverter, 417, 426–428, 454
Script, 384, 385
SES file, 398
Session, 397, 398, 402–405, 408, 409, 414

Shortcut, 387, 389, 390, 391
Silence, 203, 210, 217, 358
Sine curve, 8
Slice, 525, 526, 528, 569
Snapping, 203, 218
Sony/Philips Digital Interface Format, 54
Sound:
    bank, 55
    cards, 49
    intensity, 8, 10
    pressure, 8
    vibrations, 8
    waves, 8
SoundFont 2, 58
Spectral:
    analysis, 370, 371
    density, 30
    view, 225–227, 233
Spectrum:
    canonic definition, 31
Spectrum Analyzer Professional, 36
Spline:
    approximation, 264, 275, 304
    interpolation, 59
Statistics, 369, 372, 374, 375
Stereo:
    mode, 95
    panorama, 340
Stereophonic:
    samples, 57
    sound, 9
Stretch, 246
Subwoofers, 14
Suppression band, 75
Sustain time, 97

T

Telegrapher's equation, 24
Theoretical definition, 20
Threshold noise suppressor, 85
Timbre, 10, 61
    regulators, 64
Time:
    display format, 225, 231, 232
    shift, 240, 242, 243
Tone, 9
    color, 10
T-RackS, 607, 608, 610–614, 616, 618
Transfer characteristic, 599
Transport panel, 501, 513, 521, 524, 549, 558, 559, 561, 563
Tremolo, 60
Trigonometric functions, 24
Truncate, 593

V

Vibrato, 60
Voltage, 8
Volume, 427, 431, 447

W

Waveform View, 396, 397, 405, 408, 414
Weight function, 41